D1278409

MANAGEMENT

Management

INDIVIDUAL AND ORGANIZATIONAL EFFECTIVENESS

MICHAEL H. MESCON

Georgia State University

MICHAEL ALBERT

San Francisco State University

FRANKLIN KHEDOURI

President, Kay Industries, Inc.

1817

HARPER & ROW, PUBLISHERS, New York

Cambridge, Hagerstown, Philadelphia, San Francisco,
London, Mexico City, São Paulo, Sydney

Permissions:
Feature 13-4 reprinted by permission of the Harvard Business Review. Copyright © 1977 by the President and Fellows of Harvard College; all rights reserved.
Table 14-1 reprinted from *Leadership and Decision-Making* by Victor H. Vroom and Philip H. Yetton by permission of the University of Pittsburgh Press. © 1973.
Table 14-2 and Figure 14-6 © 1973 by AMACON, a division of American Management Associations. All rights reserved.

Sponsoring Editors: John Woods / Art Sotak
Special Projects Editor: Peggy Waldman
Project Editors: Carol Pritchard-Martinez / Jon Dash
Designer: Al Burkhardt
Designer: Nancy Benedict
Production Managers: Marion Hartsough / Marion Palen
Compositor: Computer Typesetting Services, Inc.
Printer and Binder: R.R. Donnelley & Sons Company
Artist: John Foster

To our motivators, Enid, Martha and Larry, and Amy

Library of Congress Cataloging in Publication Data

Mescon, Michael H
Management: individual and organizational effectiveness.

Includes index.
1. Management. 2. Organizational effectiveness.
I. Albert, Michael, 1950– joint author.
II. Khedouri, Franklin, joint author. III. Title.
HD31.M3984 658 80-28202
ISBN 0-06-166401-4

Contents

Preface

Management: Individual and Organizational Effectiveness is a textbook for introduction to management courses. We assume the reader has never taken such a course and has had only the usual exposure to behavioral sciences and mathematics.

The overall objective of *Management* is to communicate a fundamental understanding of formal organizations—profit and nonprofit, small and large—and their management. By *effective* management, a term we use often, we mean managing in a way that best enables the organization as a whole to formulate and attain objectives. We believe this requires managers to make efficient use of all available resources, to make the organization responsive to its environment, and to enable individuals to perceive a positive relationship between the organization's objectives and their own. The effective manager takes situational differences into account and recognizes that even the most desirable course of action usually has some negative consequences. He or she is proactive—anticipates the future and prepares for it—rather than reactive.

The field of management has grown to the point where it is impossible to cover comprehensively even the major conceptual approaches in a single volume. An author, in management jargon, must limit a text's specific content objectives to material that can reasonably be covered within an academic quarter or semester. The most common way of doing so is by concentrating on a single conceptual approach, such as management processes or systems. Unfortunately, no single approach to date is fully accepted by all in the field. Each of the major schools and approaches has made important, lasting contributions to understanding organizations and their management. Each has flaws. We therefore feel that basing an introductory text on a single approach is a disservice to students.

Although we do stress a contingency or situational view of management because it seems most consistent with reality and best able to cope with the complexities of contemporary organizations, our approach would best be described as eclectic. We have tried to select and integrate the most useful, influential, and widely accepted contributions of all major approaches.

Instead of using a particular school of thought to unify the discussion, we do so through what may be thought of as a strategic choice. That is, we stress more strongly than other texts the need to consider the organization *as a whole* when making management decisions. In many places and ways we point out that the manager should always consider interrelationships between parts of an organization (internal variables), the organization and its environment (external variables), and that any decision affects all aspects of the organization in some way. This should not be interpreted as a purely top management perspective. Our aim, rather, is to make the reader a more effective manager irrespective of position in the organization by helping him or her understand the factors involved in making a decision that is genuinely effective.

Virtually all contemporary texts state something to this effect. However, none that we knew of consistently and deliberately presented material in a way that *actively* supported and reinforced the need to consider the whole, not just the parts, when making management decisions. The pattern, rather, has been to discuss each major concept within a single block of chapters, i.e., all topics related to motivating in one part, all topics related to organizing in another.

There is a definite logic and simplicity to such an approach. However, in our opinion there are serious disadvantages that outweigh the gains of doing so. Because the variables and functions *are* interrelated it clearly is not really possible to treat any one aspect comprehensively until the reader has at least *some* understanding of *all* critical functions and variables. The traditional sequence of topics forces an author to either treat some topics in an oversimplified manner or to raise issues the reader is not prepared to grasp. Equally important, when a topic is discussed in one long block and never returned to, it becomes all too easy for the student to forget some of what he or she has learned and very difficult for him or her to perceive the relationship between earlier and later topics. Thus, even though the author may clearly *state* that interrelationships should be considered, the traditional sequence of presentation tends to encourage a fragemented perspective, concentration on the trees rather than the forest.

This text covers essentially the same topics most popular texts do, but presents them in a different, unique order. What we have done, in basic terms, is to apply Alfred Chandler's wise saying, "Structure follows strategy," to the organization of our material. That is, we organized topics in a way that most effectively supports our primary objective of communicating the need to view the organization as a whole and take into account interrelationships and interdependencies when making and implementing decisions. Our structure also actively supports the important concept that management theory and practice are *evolutionary* and that even currently accepted explanations may later prove erroneous.

Part I gives the reader an overview of the book and field and a rudimentary understanding of the primary internal and external variables affecting organizational success. Our discussion of what managers actually do begins with what are called the linking functions of communication and decision making in Part II. Thus, from the very beginning the reader is encouraged to view management from an overall perspective and be aware of interrelationships, situational factors, and the lack of absolutes. This is reinforced by examples and the way in which specific topics are presented. For example, the concluding section of the communicating chapter both synthesizes the discussion of that function and reviews the management process.

Part III describes in some detail the primary functions of the management process, which we have chosen to identify as planning, organizing, motivating, and controlling. The organizing function is covered in two chapters simply because the number of topics was too great to fit within one chapter conveniently. Relationships between the function specifically addressed and others are noted within each chapter. Management by Objectives, for example, is covered at the end of the control process discussion because it is a technique that illustrates the need to integrate planning and control.

Part IV, which treats groups and leadership, is effectively a discreet learning unit. The three chapters within it are a cohesive block, a sort of mini-text on understanding informal relationships and coping effectively with them.

Part V presents several significant contributions of the quantitative or management science approach. The treatment is largely descriptive. The intent is to show what management science techniques and other quantitative techniques can do to facilitate effective decision making, rather than enable the reader to actually apply such techniques. Our coverage fully meets AACSB requirements.

Part VI extends the reader's knowledge with a description of important issues not previously covered, or only mentioned briefly: human resource management, contingencies in organization design, change and conflict. Because a sufficient base of knowledge has been acquired, we are able not only to treat these topics in a relatively sophisticated way, but also to point out and stress interrelationships between these issues and others. We also return to certain important topics and examine them from a different perspective. For example, Woodward's research on technology and structure, first presented in Chapter 3, is covered again in Chapter 19.

We believe this is an extremely efficient order of presentation, since we were able to cover more topics in more depth than the typical text of this length. However, we recognize that some instructors may disagree with our choice and prefer to cover certain material in a different sequence. We therefore presented and organized material in a way that permits considerable flexibility.

There should be no difficulty whatsoever in covering Parts II, IV, and V whenever prefered. Similarly, Chapter 8, Organizing Authority Relationships, and Chapter 12, Group Dynamics, can readily be covered earlier. The three chapters dealing with management science and quantitative approaches are wholly independent of one another to permit elimination of one or variations in order, such as covering control techniques in conjunction with the control function. Moreover, whenever possible we made material *within* the chapter a set of cohesive knowledge blocks. This permits subsections to be assigned in a different order or even eliminated without causing serious problems. For example, budgeting can be covered without covering financial analysis techniques, operations management can be covered separately from MIS.

We tried to write prose that is clear, concise, and reasonably interesting. Particularly complex or important concepts are presented in a somewhat painstaking manner and amplified with commonplace examples. Jargon and managerial concepts are always defined the first time they are used, if a precise understanding is essential to the discussion. With respect to research citations, we do not feel an introductory text is a suitable forum for exploring the state of the art. We therefore have largely confined our research citations to studies that enjoy widespread acceptance or have been especially influential.

Learning Aids, Special Features, and Ancilliaries

Because *Management* is primarily intended for classroom use, we have amplified the text with several learning aids and ancilliaries. Learning aids include chapter and part introductions, a list of key terms for each chapter, review and thought questions, case incidents, and comprehensive cases. (All incidents and cases are based on *true* situations.)

Also within the text are two special features substantially different in nature than those of other management texts:

> *Interviews* with successful managers appear at the beginning of each part. These are not "fluff" pieces or simple descriptions of the person's job and achievements. The questions were deliberately designed to elicit comments about concepts covered in the text.
>
> *Features,* primarily exerpts from periodicals and books, are incorporated within every chapter. Like the interviews, each makes a *substantive* contribution to understanding a management concept covered in the text.

Instructors who wish to supplement the text are urged to consider Michael Albert's *Effective Management: Readings, Cases, and Exercises.*

We believe the instructor's package, which includes an extremely comprehensive manual, transparency masters, and extensive computerized test bank is among the finest available. Your Harper & Row representative will be pleased to provide an examination copy.

Acknowledgments

A text of this size and scope is very much a team effort. Without the assistance and contributions of the Harper & Row editorial staff and the instructors who reviewed the manuscript, we never could have won our struggle to convert our ideas into the book you are holding. We therefore would like to take this opportunity to acknowledge our debt to these people and express our graditude for their help.

The following reviewers each made a genuine, meaningful contribution to this book. Their criticisms and suggestions enabled us to refine our ideas and our execution. Their sharp eyes helped us catch and correct countless errors of fact and ommission. Thanks are due to Carl Anderson, University of Maryland; Henry Beam, Western Michigan University; Allen Bluedorn, Pennsylvania State University; William Brown, Towson State University; Thomas Calero, Illinois Institute of Technology; Dan Dudley, Tarleton State University; W. Bruce Erickson, University of Minnesota; Claude Graeff, Illinois State University; David Gray, University of Texas, Arlington; James Greene, Georgia State University; Mark Hammer, Washington State University; John Hartley, Rochester Institute of Technology; James Higgins, Auburn University; Lawrence Hill, California State University, Los Angeles; Marvin Karlins, University of South Florida; James Logan, University of Arizona; Beaufort Longest, Northwestern University; Aprile McFarland, Georgia State University; Ralph Mengel, Central State University; Roy Moore, University of Southern Mississippi; William Moore, California State University, Hayward; Eugene Owens, Western Washington State University; John Pharr, Cedar Valley College; William Reif, Arizona State University; Tim Singleton, University of Houston at Clearlake; Roger Stanton, California State University, Long Beach; Dennis Strouble, Texas Tech University; Jeffrey Susbauer, Cleveland State University; John Ward, Loyola University; and Phillip Van Auken, Baylor University.

Michael H. Mescon
Michael Albert
Franklin Khedouri

PART ONE

The Elements of Organizations and Management

We are embarking together on a journey. Much territory will be new, or what is often more confusing, will not conform to what you *think* you know. Complicating our expedition are the limitations of time and pages. Despite these difficulties, our destination makes the trip well worth undertaking. We are headed toward a basic understanding of management and organizations, a topic of practical value and critical importance to almost every member of our contemporary society.

Most journeys are smoother and more likely to be successful if one has a general idea of what lies ahead. Ours is no exception. Therefore, just as one might study a map of the entire country before driving across it, we begin in Chapter 1 with a general description of organizations, their importance, and the nature of management. Similarly, Chapter 2 briefly outlines the evolution of management thought and practice, concentrating on those approaches to management upon which this book is based.

Before driving across country you probably would want to make sure *all* the important parts of your car are in good working order. You realize, of course, that new spark plugs won't help if the brakes give out at the top of Pike's Peak. You also probably would want to check certain aspects of the trip beyond your car, such as whether gas is available and what road conditions are like. Similarly, the manager needs to understand and consider *both* the critical factors, or parts, of the organization itself *and* the forces in the environment that affect the organization. The parts of the organization, referred to as *internal variables,* are described in Chapter 3. The forces in the environment, the *external variables,* are described in Chapter 4.

An Interview with James W. McLamore

Managers seldom get much coverage in the media. Very often their companies and products are familiar to all, their names familiar to none. A case in point is James W. McLamore. In 1954 Jim McLamore and David R. Edgerton opened a small restaurant in Miami. Its first year sales were $40,000, and for several more years the brink of bankruptcy remained too close for comfort. But Jim's belief that Americans wanted low-priced food and fast service remained steadfast. It didn't take long for that struggling little company to live up to its royal name—Burger King Corporation. Under Jim McLamore's 21-year-tenure as president or chairman of the board, Burger King grew into a worldwide organization of over 2400 restaurants with sales of 1.7 *billion* per year. Today Burger King is a subsidiary of The Pillsbury Company, and Jim McLamore is no longer active in its operating management. Jim McLamore, however, has not let his managerial talent and expertise go to waste. He is a director of Burger King Corporation, The Pillsbury Company, Southeast First National Bank of Miami, Storer Broadcasting, and the Ryder System. Always an active community citizen, he also is a trustee of the University of Miami and the United Way of Miami, chairman of Miami's community television station, and a director of the Miami Heart Institute and several other community organizations, educational organizations, and hospitals.

Author: You've been both an entrepreneur who started a small business and a top manager of a billion-dollar subsidiary of a major conglomerate. Could you comment on the differences between these roles?

McLamore: I guess an entrepreneur uses instinct more than a professional trained manager. I don't judge myself to be a particularly good manager. I think I was good at inspiring people, at sensing opportunity, at selling the financial community what I needed to sell to attract the funds to fuel our growth. But I think that as an administrator I was a poor one.

Author: Why?

McLamore: Well, I didn't have the patience and the discipline that I think is necessary to become a good manager. I wasn't very good at respecting organization charts. I wasn't even good at conceiving how they should be produced and built.

Author: Well, you obviously built one. What happened?

McLamore: I suppose I was smart enough to get people who knew how to do all those things, and I knew the fundamental part of the business: how a restaurant should be run.

Author: Change is a factor that affects all organizations. How has change affected Burger King and how has Burger King responded?

McLamore: Burger King is a corporation that has constantly been changing with changing times. The reason that it is as big as it is today is a measure of our ability to recognize change and to react to it.

Author: Can you give me some examples?

McLamore: Well, to begin, there was no such thing as fast food in 1954 when Burger King was started. So the first change, you might say, is that we recognized there might be a market for fast service, limited menu restaurants. The consumer was changing, and we thought the kind of eating experience that the consumer of the mid-fifties wanted was our kind of restaurant service. As time passed and our customers changed, we changed our menus to include such things as the Whopper and, more recently, upgraded the decor of our restaurants.

Author: Planning is often cited as one of the essential functions of management. Have you always engaged in formal planning and had goals?

McLamore: Not formal planning, but goals. I don't think anybody can do anything unless they have precise goals, and we had them. They were unwritten, not formalized.

Author: How about when Burger King grew larger, particularly after you became part of The Pillsbury Company?

McLamore: When I was in the position of being president and major owner of the company, I could make plans in a much more informal fashion, and they could easily be implemented. But as the company grew and more people came on board, it was required that they be formally apprised of our goals and objectives. Now the process of forward planning extends to a five-year strategic plan; plus an annual business plan is a formal procedure in the company. This was brought in after we became part of The Pillsbury Company who had that kind of understanding and expertise, and really by that time the company was getting so big it was required.

Author: Do you allow lower-level managers at Burger King to participate in the planning process?

McLamore: The plans come up from the grass roots of the organization, and they are formalized through a procedure that includes an awful lot of involvement by all of the people in the company.

Author: Burger King and McDonald's are noted for introducing automation in the food industry. How has this affected productivity? Any negative reactions from your workers?

McLamore: We recognized right from the beginning that high efficiency in production was important to our ability to deliver a low-priced product. Our business was built on the elements of price and speed, so we've always been automated. But I've never known our employees to object to being a part of a mechanized system. In fact, because the restaurants are usually so busy, they are grateful to the system for its ability to deliver a product at the level the consumers want.

Author: What is Burger King's stance on decentralization, the diffusion of authority and responsibility to lower levels of management?

McLamore: The new president has just implemented a decentralization plan. The regional manager now has enormous power over decisions heretofore ultimately reserved for headquarters. It seems to be working. Of course, it's traumatic because mistakes can be made by executives learning the process. But I think the new responsibility and authority given the regions has made for more enthusiastic people out in the field.

Author: How about when you were starting Burger King? Did you delegate authority right from the beginning?

McLamore: I think that if I look back on my career I tended to reserve too many of the decisions of running the business to myself. But you have to realize that during the first three or four years this company was insolvent. Survival was the critical issue, so a lot of the decisions that had to be made were for survival. I suppose that kind of an experience prompted my management style of giving out less operating authority than maybe another manager might have done under different circumstances.

Author: A top manager also has to be an effective leader. There are many ways a person can lead and influence others. Which do you use?

McLamore: Well, I was always very close to my colleagues, my executives. I think I probably used a technique of inspiring them to recognize the good of the company and the opportunity it offered them. I think we had a strong esprit de corps in the company. It seems to me that in our case this worked very, very well. We had a strong cadre of officers and department heads that developed this company from nothing up to something very sizable.

Author: In closing do you have any words of advice for people planning a management career?

McLamore: I'd say dream a lot. And you've got to have precise goals about what you want to be. Of course, I don't think there is much of a substitute for hard work. I don't know how any business can succeed unless there is a strong application of time and energy put into the job. So if somebody has lofty ambitions, they've got to recognize that they've got to make a very strong commitment of time and energy to whatever they set out to accomplish.

CHAPTER 1

Managers, Management, and Organizations

With this chapter we begin what we hope will be an interesting and useful learning experience: the study of organizations and their management. The subject is a complex one. The true role of management and organizations is widely misunderstood, even by some people who are practicing managers. Therefore we shall begin by separating myth from reality and by showing why management and organizations are not only important but essential. Your objective in reading this chapter and much of the rest of this book should be to acquire a fundamental understanding of the concepts, as opposed to merely memorizing definitions and details.

After reading this chapter, you should understand the following important terms and concepts:

organization
formal organization
necessity of management
levels of management
supervisor
middle manager
top manager
roles of the manager
entrepreneur
proactionary management

Management: Myth and Reality

Managers: quasi-mythical beings, frequently male, who live out their lives in boxlike spaces called offices. It usually is easy to differentiate managers from the other beings who also inhabit the office ecosystem. The managers are the ones with the most padding on their chairs and the largest desks. Also, managers tend to wear too much clothing and the males usually have peculiar, nonfunctional pieces of cloth around their neck. Managers frequently assemble in groups about the size of a primitive hunting band, which they call conferences or committees. The exact purpose of these gatherings remains a mystery. One theory, based on the pile of dirty cups always left behind, holds the gatherings are ritualistic coffee tastings. But the best explanation is that these gatherings are primarily a means of wasting time so that managers can justify staying late at the office and thereby create the impression that they work harder than anybody else. (Only the managers' mates actually fall for this ruse.) Aside from these meager facts, the only things known for certain about managers are that they make more money than they deserve, are prone to ulcers, and never answer their own phones.

Management: managers (see preceding) in the collective; also, an entity composed of nameless, faceless individuals often referred to as *them* or *they. They* are to blame for just about everything that goes wrong at work and most of the world's major problems as well. It is relatively easy to distinguish them from us. When things do turn out right despite them, we were the ones who did all the work and deserve all the credit.

These definitions of this book's subject, of course, are not meant to be taken seriously. But perhaps they should be, for they come surprisingly close to reflecting the views of many people. Although almost everyone has heard of managers, few people have an accurate understanding of what management is really all about and what managers really do.

This ignorance is somewhat surprising. Managers and management are among the most popular topics in the media today. Hundreds of books have been written about them in just the last few years. Dozens of periodicals are devoted to them. Every issue of every major newspaper contains articles related to management. Managers have loomed large on the screen ever since Orson Wells directed *Citizen Kane,* the famous film glorifying newspaper magnate Randolph Hearst. Managers have even scored high ratings on prime-time television in such productions as *Dallas* and *Wheels,* both adaptations of best-selling novels portraying vice and corruption in the executive suite.

On the other hand, it is not at all surprising that people are confused by what they have read or seen about managers and management. There are few topics on which opinions of writers differ more widely. According to Upton Sinclair, who roused the public's anger against managers with his novel *The Jungle,* they are heartless villains who trample the flesh and spirit of workers just to make a buck. Karl Marx would agree, along with numerous advocates of Marx's socialist vision. The late George Meany, longtime head of the AFL-CIO would probably have agreed. At the opposite pole are people like Malcolm Forbes, owner and publisher of the magazine bearing his family name, and like famous management consultant and writer Peter Drucker. According to Forbes and Drucker, managers are the heroes and heroines of our age.

Which of the widely differing views of management are correct? Are managers essentially good or basically evil? Do we need managers to get work done, or could more get done without their interference? Are you almost certain to have more money and power than most people if you become a manager? If you concluded that it all depends, that things could be one way or the other, you are off to a good start. As Henri Fayol, one of the first management writers, observed: ". . . there is nothing rigid or absolute in management affairs, it is all a question of proportion."

In management, as we shall stress throughout this book, everything depends on context, on the situation. What is "right" in one situation could easily be the worst possible action in another. One might think, to give a simple example, that it would always be desirable to hire the most talented, brightest person available for a job. Yet, experience has shown time and again that if a person is too highly trained for a task, he or she will find it boring and may perform less well than a person whose skills are lesser, but adequate. Imagine how you would feel and perform if you as a college graduate were compelled to work at what you considered to be an easy, dull assembly line or office job. Who do you think would do the job better over the long run—you, or a high-school dropout who really enjoys the job?

This need to always consider the situational context is one reason why we did not begin this chapter with a nice, pat definition of management. Rather, in Table 1-1 we have simply listed some well-known managers and nonmanagers. This list should give you a feel for the scope of managerial work. Also, because many people have misguided ideas on the subject, in Table 1-2 we listed a few common misconceptions about management and tried to show why they are false. Note that although we call these notions "misconceptions," in certain circumstances they may be a correct interpretation of a particular situation. For instance, in the past some managers have shown concern for society only because the government forced them to; the famous robber barons of the nineteenth century—John D. Rockefeller, J. Pierpont Morgan, and Cornelius Vanderbilt—are examples. Sometimes (although not very often) it is necessary to be tough with people to be an effective manager; a Marine Corps sergeant during a battle would be an example.

There is, however, one thing we can say about management that is definitely true all the time. Management has an enormous impact on your life. Today the decisions of managers affect virtually everything you do to some degree. Yes, *everything.* How can we make such a broad statement about a

Table 1-1 Managers and Nonmanagers

Manager	Nonmanager
Jimmy Carter: President, United States of America	Richard M. Nixon: private citizen
Francis Ford Coppola: film director *(The Godfather, Apocalypse Now)*	Faye Dunaway: actress
Don Kirshner: record and concert producer	Dolly Parton: singer
Jesse Jackson: preacher and civil rights leader	Jesus Christ: teacher and prophet
Katherine Graham: president and publisher, *Washington Post*	Carl Bernstein: formerly a reporter for *Washington Post*
Don Shula: Coach, Miami Dolphins football team	O. J. Simpson: football player
Mao Tse Tung: former chairman, Communist Party and premier of People's Republic of China	Karl Marx: political and economic writer and philosopher

field that universities did not even acknowledge existed until this century was well underway? Because today we live in a society of *organizations.*

Organizations are the basic context, the core situation, in which managers operate. Before one can begin to understand management or define it meaningfully, one must first learn what organizations are and how important they are in the modern world.

Organizations

Organizations are an integral part of your life. All businesses—from a tiny snack bar with only two workers to American Telephone and Telegraph Corporation (AT&T) which has over 900,000 employees—are organizations, as are not-for-profit and political entities ranging from a scout troop to The People's Republic of China. In modern societies virtually everything necessary for our survival, pleasure, and growth is either directly provided by an organization or at least indirectly furthered by one. It is almost impossible to understate the importance and pervasiveness of organizations in today's world.

The Importance of Organizations

Impact on Individuals. According to the 1970 census, over 93 percent of all working Americans are employees. Thus the average person spends around 40 hours a week, 50 weeks a year, for 40 to 50 years as part of some work organization. How much an organization rewards special talents and expertise determines one's economic status. Barring inherited wealth, which is a

Table 1-2 Common Misconceptions About Management

If you believe:

1. All that really matters to managers is that their companies earn bigger profits.
2. Management is never having to say you're sorry—because you can fire anyone who disagrees with you.
3. Managers always earn more than the people who work for them.
4. Experience acquired while running a business isn't very useful in running a nonprofit organization or in government, and vice versa.
5. Managers do not really work very hard.
6. The only time managers and companies show concern for society is when government forces them to.
7. You have to be a conservative thinker and a "yes person" to climb to the top in management.
8. To be effective in management, you have to be tough with people. Otherwise, they will not follow orders.

Try to explain away:

1. A very substantial percentage of managers work in government and the nonprofit sector of the economy and therefore are not the least bit concerned with profits. Also, when management invests a substantial sum in new equipment or research, profits almost always decrease for that year.
2. It is considerably easier to get a divorce than to get rid of bumbling incompetents with AFL-CIO union memberships or civil service cards in their wallets.
3. Marlon Brando earned over $3 million for less than three weeks' work on the film *Superman,* several times the annual salary of the president of Warner Communications Company who made it.
4. Frank Borman, former military officer and astronaut, is widely acknowledged to be responsible for the improved fortunes of Eastern Airlines, the company he now heads. The late Nelson Rockefeller, Jimmy Carter, and John Connally were all very successful businessmen before they became successful in government.
5. According to Mintzberg's research, the typical high-level manager works between 60 and 80 hours a week on the average. A standard nonmanagerial work week today averages less than 40 hours.
6. Colleges, public television, many museums and symphony orchestras, and charities are heavily endowed by corporate grants and gifts from individual top managers.
7. Almost without exception, the people who run large companies today are the people who took big risks during the course of their careers—and won. McDonald's is so concerned with fostering creativity in its managers that it had a special "think tank," a room filled with one enormous waterbed, constructed at its headquarters. Also, just because a manager holds conservative political and economic views, one cannot assume that person has a conservative nature. Malcolm Forbes's hobbies, for instance, are piloting hot-air balloons and riding large motorcycles at high speed.
8. Almost every contemporary book on management and every successful manager stresses that one key to effective management is positive human relations. The manager depends on people and cannot afford to alienate them with harsh talk or punishment.

FEATURE 1-1

The 25 Best-Paid Corporate Executives in 1978

Note that in most cases these chief executives earned more from stock appreciation and contingent remuneration than they received in salary. These forms of extra earnings are based solely on the performance of the organization as a whole and are intended to compensate the chief executive for doing an excellent job for the stockholders.

Rank	Company	Chief Executive Officer	Salary, Bonus, Directors' Fees	Payment on Stock Appreciation Rights	Personal and Vested Benefits, Etc.	Contingent and Other Forms of Remuneration	Total
1.	Louisiana-Pacific	Harry A. Merlo	$ 353,500	$2,546,540	$ 31,300	$ 491,880	$ 3,423,220
2.	Warner Communications	Steven J. Ross	1,036,913	—	31,390	1,392,105	2,460,408
3.	Boeing	Thornton A. Wilson	516,744	709,875	73,241	817,648	2,117,508
4.	Norton Simon	David J. Mahoney	916,667	1,120,388	—	27,203	2,064,258
5.	American Standard	William A. Marquard	550,000	—	10,092	1,493,750	2,053,842
6.	Braniff International	Harding L. Lawrence	470,127	1,448,715	—	21,794	1,940,636
7.	Intl Harvester	Archie R. McCardell	1,906,658	—	—	—	1,906,658
8.	Harris Corporation	Joseph A. Boyd	374,658	1,092,000	—	223,961	1,690,646
9.	20th Century-Fox	Dennis C. Stanfill	581,255	—	8,189	728,000	1,317,444
10.	Cabot	Robert A. Charpie	558,611	452,700	—	280,011	1,291,322
11.	Mobil	Rawleigh Warner Jr.	792,000	—	25,393	401,112	1,218,505
12.	Continental Oil	Howard W. Blauvelt	549,867	—	20,449	646,631	1,216,947
13.	NCR	William S. Anderson	523,215	—	—	676,636	1,199,851
14.	SmithKline	Robert F. Dee	453,131	—	10,706	699,062	1,162,899
15.	Atlantic Richfield	Robert O. Anderson	700,000	—	27,091	387,219	1,114,310
16.	City Investing	George T. Scharffenberger	682,700	—	5,415	394,676	1,082,791
17.	Ford Motor	Henry Ford II	705,000	—	1,132	350,938	1,057,070
18.	Gulf United	E. Grant Fitts	450,000	—	34,496	562,245	1,046,741
19.	Colt Industries	George A. Strichman	540,850	—	158,429	316,500	1,015,779
20.	American Broadcasting	Leonard H. Goldenson	750,000	—	—	248,115	998,115
21.	Exxon	Clifton C. Garvin Jr.	767,500	—	55,256	174,561	997,317
22.	General Motors	Thomas A. Murphy	475,000	—	21,000	500,000	996,000
23.	Allis-Chalmers	David C. Scott	517,059	—	21,755	453,309	992,123
24.	Dun & Bradstreet	Harrington Drake	450,000	—	—	534,082	984,082
25.	Northrop	Thomas V. Jones	350,000	—	180	625,309	975,489

SOURCE: *Forbes*, June 11, 1979, p. 118.

FEATURE 1-2

A Society of Organizations

Society in this century has become a society of organizations. Social tasks, from providing goods and services to education and care of the sick and the elderly, which only a century ago were done by the family, in the home, in the shop or on the farm, are increasingly performed in and through large organizations. These organizations—whether business enterprises, hospitals, schools and universities—are designed for continuity and are run by professional managers. Managers have thus become the leadership groups in our society. The leadership groups of old—whether landed aristocracy, business tycoons or priests—have disappeared or become less significant.

SOURCE: Peter F. Drucker, "We Have Become a Society of Organizations," *The Wall Street Journal*, January 9, 1978, p. 12. Reprinted by permission of Peter Drucker.

by-product of organizations, the people who live best in a material sense are generally those who perform best in an organizational setting.

Even the self-employed individual usually works at least indirectly for an organization. A freelance writer, for example, may seem to work entirely alone, but it is an organization—the publishing company—that gets manuscripts into the hands of interested people and pays the writer for them. Similarly, even physicians with independent practices often work in conjunction with organizations such as hospitals and clinical laboratories and derive part of their income from other organizations such as Medicare and insurance companies.

Everyone in our society, including people who do not work at all, is highly dependent on organizations. For example, educational organizations taught the writer to use the language. Manufacturing organizations provided the paper, pen, typewriter, and desk that are the tools of the trade. Organizations build the houses we live in, provide us with food and clothing, and entertain us with television, films, and sporting events. Governmental organizations preserve law and order, care for the disadvantaged, and defend us from foreign aggression, among other essential services. For thousands of years millions of people have depended on religious organizations for spiritual guidance and solace.

Impact on Society. The United States today is characterized by large, powerful organizations. Sales of several companies on *Fortune* magazine's list of the 500 largest industrial firms exceed the entire Gross National Product (GNP) of most small countries. Many of these organizations or companies are *interdependent.* When even a single large organization fails to operate effectively, many other organizations are affected. The ramifications may be felt by millions of people, perhaps even the whole world.

If General Motors, Ford, and Chrysler stop making cars, for example, the steel industry loses the biggest customers for its products, and the rubber industry cannot sell tires. This causes unemployment in these industries, which hire millions of people. Because of the unemployment, people have less money to spend and save. This means that retailers will not sell as much clothing or as many appliances. Also, savings banks will not have as much money to lend, making it difficult for people to buy homes and for businesses to expand. Thus, more and more people are forced out of work by business slowdowns: not just Detroit but the whole country is affected. Actually, the whole world would be affected because Americans would not be able to afford as many foreign vacations or foreign-made products or be able to provide as much aid to underdeveloped countries.

There are many other examples of this interdependence. If the price of steel goes up, the price of everything made of steel increases. Unions ask for wage increases to cover the rising cost of these products, which is passed on to consumers, causing other prices to further increase. If the Teamsters union strikes, most of the trucks that carry products all over America stop moving. When Consolidated Edison, the New York electric utility, failed for only 12 hours in 1977, there were billions of dollars in direct losses. The actions of governmental organizations have an even more powerful and widespread effect on both individuals and organizations. Think about the impact of tax laws, equal rights laws, and consumer protection laws. Or consider the influence of governmental spending on scientific research and the ramifications of the decision to commit U.S. troops in Vietnam.

Contribution to Quality of Life. It is popular to yearn for the good old days, when life was simple and people lived close to the land. The plain truth, however, is that the quality of life for most people has improved considerably during this century. This, by no coincidence, is the same period during which we became a society of organizations.

Of course, many individuals and factors have contributed to our present well-being, the most obvious being technology. It was organizations that applied technology, even when they did not create it themselves. What good would it have done the world if Edison's lightbulb, phonograph, and motion picture inventions had never been produced inexpensively in large quantities by companies like General Electric and RCA? Would Bell's telephone be more than an amusing toy if millions of them had not been produced and linked together by the companies of the Bell system?

This is not to imply that organizations only have positive benefits for individuals and society. War on a massive scale is possible because of organizations. Organizations sometimes are created to spy, to torture, to enslave. Sometimes they cheat the public and pollute the environment deliberately to increase profits, giving no thought to the long-term consequences. Organizations also bill us by computer for charges already paid and create a host of other aggravations.

Despite these negative features, our lives literally depend on a vast web of organizations functioning successfully. Thus when we speak of organizations and their management, we are talking about one of the most important subjects on earth. We are talking about something that touches *you* every single day. It, therefore, clearly behooves us to learn how organizations operate. Let us proceed and learn what an organization is and what management's role is within it.

What an Organization Is

As you may have surmised from the wide variety of preceding examples, an entity needs to meet only a few requirements to be considered an organization. These are:

1. At least *two people* who consider themselves part of a group
2. At least one *objective* (desired end state or result) shared in common by these group members
3. Group members who *deliberately* work together to attain their shared objective

By combining these essential requirements we arrive at the following important definition:

> *An organization is a group of people whose activities are consciously coordinated toward a common objective or objectives.*[1]

Formal Versus Informal Organizations. Actually, what we just defined is not simply an organization but a **formal organization**. There are also *informal* organizations, groups that emerge spontaneously whenever people gather together with sufficient opportunity to communicate. Informal organizations are very significant in management and will be discussed at length later. However, although informal organizations do have leaders, they do not have managers in the sense that we use the term. Therefore, in keeping with common usage, when we speak of informal organizations we specifically identify them as such. When we use the term *organization,* we are always referring to a *formal* organization.

Subunits. It is important to realize that many organizations are composed of several interrelated units. These subunits are also considered organizations. They, too, consist of a group of people whose activities are consciously coordinated toward a common objective or objectives. An organization's subunits are actually a set of smaller organizations that comprise the whole. A man-

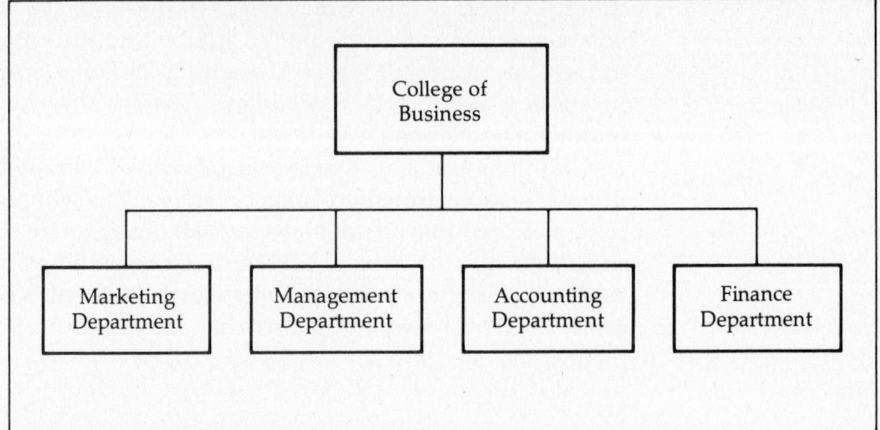

Figure 1-1 Subunits of the College of Business
If the management department, an organization itself, does not meet its objectives, the college cannot attain all of its objectives.

agement class, for example, is an organization within the Department of Management, which is a subunit of the College of Business, which is a subunit of the university as a whole. Similarly, a sales department is a subunit of the marketing department, which is one of many subunits of the overall large business organization.

Organizational Objectives. As our definition stated, an organization always has at least one objective shared in common by its members. The management profession, however, does not concern itself with organizations so small that they have only one objective. This book is primarily about the management of *complex* organizations. Such organizations have a *set of interrelated objectives.* If one counts the objectives of its subunits separately, a very large organization such as Exxon, Gulf and Western, or the United States could have several thousand objectives. It is not uncommon for the management of large organizations to formulate a dozen or more broad objectives for the organization as a whole. These objectives are as varied as organizations themselves. A business, for example, tries to make a profit by providing the public with certain goods or services. For General Motors, these are products related to the internal combustion engine. IBM earns its profit by providing products and services in the area of information processing. Some objectives of a university are to disseminate knowledge and to extend the boundaries of knowledge by conducting research. The choice of objectives, understandably, is one of management's most important decisions because objectives define what the organization is trying to do. However, many other factors determine whether an organization will be successful.

Success for an Organization. Organizations and organisms have much in common. The primary need of every biological organism is to survive. Just as a species is considered unsuccessful if it becomes extinct, *an organization is successful only if it survives for a selected period of time and accomplishes its objectives.* As will be explained in later discussions of the external environment and planning, in order to survive and succeed an organization must respond quickly to external opportunities and threats.

Sometimes an organization is deliberately designed to be disbanded after it accomplishes its objectives. Examples of this are a government commission created to study a unique situation, such as the Warren Commission which investigated the assassination of President Kennedy, and a high-school prom committee. But most formal organizations try to survive as long as possible. That is very long, indeed; for unlike living organisms, organizations have the *potential* to exist indefinitely. While the average life span of organizations is less than that of a human being, some businesses, like the great wineries of France, have existed well over a century and remain strong. Because the Roman Catholic church has survived and grown continuously for almost two thousand years, it is often considered one of the most successful organizations in history. To remain successful, most organizations periodically select new objectives.

An organization can succeed only if management ensures that it is both *effective* and *efficient*. According to popular management writer Peter Drucker, effectiveness results from "doing the right things," whereas efficiency results from "doing things right." The former is often more important, a fact many people fail to recognize. For example, Chrysler engineers were as able as their General Motors counterparts when it came to developing efficient procedures for assembling cars. The costs of labor, materials, and equipment are doubtless about the same for all the large auto makers. However, General Motors management has consistently been far more effective at predicting what sort of cars the public would desire. Thus, in 1979 Chrysler was "doing things right" from the standpoint of efficiency, but narrowly avoided bankruptcy because it was "doing the wrong thing" by not producing enough models of the highly fuel-efficient cars demanded by the public due to rising oil prices. Of course, in the typical business situation there is considerable competition. Several firms, for example, did the "right thing" by deciding to build microcomputers because the demand for them was clearly great. However, many of these firms quickly collapsed because they were not able to produce and market their products as efficiently as did Tandy Corporation, Apple Computers, and Wang Laboratories.

Organizations and the Environment. During the 1960s, the words *ecology* and *environment* entered the average American's vocabulary. Most of us are now painfully aware that to survive humanity must consider the impact its actions have upon the environment. There is no way that even Homo sapiens, the most intelligent being on the planet, can survive a break in the fragile chain of life of which we are only one link. Interestingly, it was also during the 1960s that management came to recognize that organizations, too, must actively consider their environment. Moreover, this concern must extend far beyond the important issues of social responsibility, such as preventing pollution.

The environment of an organization affects every aspect of its success and consequently every decision managers make. The external environment is referred to often throughout this book. In later chapters we will learn what managers can do to help make their organizations more responsive to changes in the environment.

Division of Labor

With even a little thought, it becomes apparent that *division of labor* is an inherent characteristic of organizations. If at least two people work toward the same objective together, they obviously divide the work between themselves. Visualize, for example, an organization of two people whose objective is to sail a boat to a point ten miles away. They might divide the work involved by having one person handle the sails while the other handles the tiller.

Far less obvious even in simple instances of organized endeavor is that for the group to be successful another job must be performed; namely, somebody must *coordinate* the group's work. To continue our example, unless one of the sailors acts as captain and ensures that the sails are coordinated with the tiller and that the boat heads in the right direction relative to its destination, the group will be unlikely to attain its objective. Instead they will wind up wherever the wind and current (their environment) pushes them.

Horizontal and Vertical Division of Labor. Thus, there are two forms of division of labor in an organization. Division of work into component tasks, such as steering and sail handling or marketing and production, is referred to as *horizontal* division of labor. Separation of the work of coordination from the performance of these tasks is called *vertical* division of labor. How work is divided horizontally and vertically within an organization is a strong determinant of how successful it will be. We will discuss the subject at length in later chapters.

The Need for Management

Putting aside the complexities of division of labor and the nature of organizations, an important point remains clear—that the work of organizational members must be *coordinated* for the organization to attain its objectives. There must be some vertical division of labor, if only transitory. Managers are the ones specifically responsible for doing this work of coordination. In other words, performance of managerial activities is essential for a formal organization to attain its objectives.

Small Organizations. Very small organizations can get by without clearly delineating who is to perform these necessary managerial activities. Management work is not clearly separated from nonmanagerial work. Consider the example of a small store owned and operated by two partners. One person might make purchasing decisions—a managerial activity—one week, the other the next. Both coordinate the work schedules of their few employees to make sure the store is always open during business hours. But both partners also perform nonmanagerial tasks such as waiting on customers and stocking shelves. Neither partner considers the other his boss or manager. Nevertheless, managerial activities are essential and are being performed.

Larger Organizations. Even in a very large organization like General Electric or American Telephone and Telegraph most managers frequently perform some nonmanagerial tasks. Sales managers, for example, usually do some actual selling in addition to their managerial work of supervising sales representatives. However, when an organization grows to a certain size or if its work is complex, coordination of effort becomes too time-consuming. The job of managing becomes so large that for the organization to attain its objectives, managing must be clearly *distinguished from nonmanagerial tasks.* In fact, most scholars would agree that the large organizations of today only become possible when the need to separate management from technical and commercial activities became widely appreciated.

Although management can be applied to any objective-oriented group endeavor, this book is primarily concerned with organizations that have a clearly defined body of managers. The work of managing, as the following sections begin to illustrate, is not only a job in itself but an exceptionally diverse one.

Managerial Work: Commonalities and Variations

As we just learned, all organizations share several common characteristics, including the need for management. They also differ in important ways. Organizations have different objectives, are of different sizes, are made up of different people, and face different environments, among others. The specific variations are countless and extend to subunits within an organization. Managerial work, a direct outgrowth of the organization and its needs, by necessity reflects these commonalities and differences; that is, a manager is a manager. The work of the president of the United States has much in common with that of an assembly line foreman at Volkswagen's new plant in Pennsylvania. Yet, the requirements for being a successful marketing manager at Procter & Gamble are in many respects very different from being one for Tandy Corporation's Radio Shack stores.

Commonalities in Managerial Work

The commonalities of managing, the aspects of management common to all managers in all organizations, are generally far less obvious than the differences.

The Nature of Managerial Work. A good example of a hard-to-perceive commonality is the nature of managerial work, what the work of managing is like on a day-to-day basis. Most people, practicing managers included, assume that the work routine of a plant foreman is not very different from that of the operatives he supervises. This seems reasonable since the supervisor and operatives interact continuously and earn about the same amount of money. But research studies show that managerial work is radically different in nature from nonmanagerial work. In fact, the work of a plant foreman has much more in common with that of a company president than it does with the work of the people the foreman supervises. Commenting on this, Mintzberg, who synthesized previous research and completed in-depth, original studies of five chief executives in his book *The Nature of Managerial Work*, states:

> Most work in society involves specialization and concentration. Machine operators may learn to make one part and then spend weeks doing so; engineers and programmers often spend months designing a single bridge or a computer program; salesmen often spend their working lives selling one line of products. The manager can expect no such concentration of efforts. Rather, his activities are characterized by brevity, variety, and fragmentation. Guest, whose foremen averaged 583 incidents each day, comments:
>
>> Interestingly enough, the characteristics of a foreman's job—interruption, variety, discontinuity—are diametrically opposed to those of most hourly operator jobs, which are highly rationalized, repetitive, uninterrupted, and subject to the steady, unvarying rhythm of the moving conveyor.[2]

Roles of the Manager. Tackling the question of what managers do, Mintzberg describes another area of commonality in managerial work, the roles of the manager. A **role**, as he defines it, "is an organized set of behaviors belonging to an identifiable office or position." Just as characters in a play have specific parts that call for them to behave in certain ways, managers have an identifiable position as designated head of an organizational subunit that sets parameters on their work behavior. "Individual personality may affect *how* a role is performed, but not *that* it is performed. Thus, actors, managers, and others play roles that are predetermined, although individuals may interpret them in different ways."[3]

Through his studies Mintzberg identified ten roles that he believes all managers play at various times to varying degrees. He classified them within three broad categories: interpersonal roles, informational roles, and decisional roles. Table 1-3 summarizes the ten roles by category and gives an example of each.

Table 1-3 The Ten Managerial Roles As Identified by Mintzberg

Role	Description	Identifiable Activities from Study of Chief Executives
Interpersonal		
Figurehead	Symbolic head; obliged to perform a number of routine duties of a legal or social nature	Ceremony, status requests, solicitations
Leader	Responsible for the motivation and activation of subordinates; responsible for staffing, training, and associated duties	Virtually all managerial activities involving subordinates
Liaison	Maintains self-developed network of outside contacts and informers who provide favors and information	Acknowledgements of mail; external board work; other activities involving outsiders
Informational		
Monitor	Seeks and receives wide variety of special information (much of it current) to develop thorough understanding of organization and environment; emerges as nerve center of internal and external information of the organization	Handling all mail and contacts categorized as concerned primarily with receiving information (e.g., periodical news, observational tours)
Disseminator	Transmits information received from outsiders or from other subordinates to members of the organization; some information factual, some involving interpretation and integration of diverse value positions of organizational influencers	Forwarding mail into organization for informational purposes, verbal contacts involving information flow to subordinates (e.g., review sessions, instant communication flows)
Spokesman	Transmits information to outsiders on organization's plans, policies, actions, results, etc.; serves as expert on organization's industry	Board meetings; handling mail and contacts involving transmission of information to outsiders
Decisional		
Entrepreneur	Searches organization and its environment for opportunities and initiates "improvement projects" to bring about change; supervises design of certain projects as well	Strategy and review sessions involving initiation or design of improvement projects
Disturbance Handler	Responsible for corrective action when organization faces important, unexpected disturbances	Strategy and review sessions involving disturbances and crises
Resource Allocator	Responsible for the allocation of organizational resources of all kinds—in effect the making or approval of all significant organizational decisions	Scheduling; requests for authorization; any activity involving budgeting and the programming of subordinates' work
Negotiator	Responsible for representing the organization at major negotiations	Negotiation

SOURCE: Henry Mintzberg, *The Nature of Managerial Work* (New York: Harper & Row, 1973), pp. 93–94.

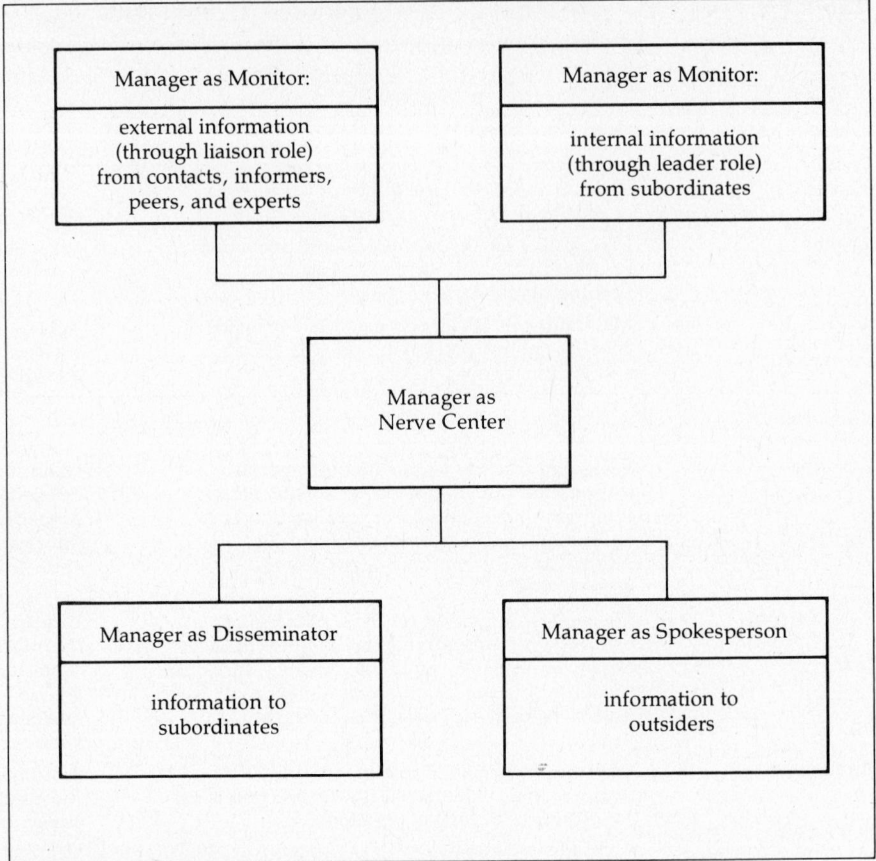

Figure 1-2 The Manager as Information-Processing System

SOURCE: From Henry Mintzberg, *The Nature of Managerial Work* (New York: Harper & Row, 1973) p. 72. Copyright © 1973 and reprinted by permission.

As Mintzberg points out, these roles are not independent of one another. Instead, they are interdependent and interact to form an integrated whole. The interpersonal roles arise out of the manager's authority and status in the organizational unit and involve interactions with people. These interpersonal roles may make the manager a focal point of information, enabling and compelling the manager to play the informational roles, and in effect to act as an information processing center. By playing interpersonal and informational roles, the manager is able to play the decisional roles: allocating resources, resolving conflict, seeking out opportunities for the organization, and negotiating on behalf of the organization. Taken together, the ten roles comprise and define the work of the manager, whatever the organization.

For example, a supervisor of production operations interacts with production workers on a daily basis. The workers come to the supervisor for specific instructions, with work problems, and often simply to socialize. Through this interaction the supervisor receives a great deal of information on how well work is proceeding. Much of this information would not be obtained through other sources, such as output reports. Based on this information, the supervisor can identify existing or potential problems and may take action to resolve them.

Managerial Functions: Management Defined. Mintzberg's analysis of managerial work is a useful explanation of what managers do. It has been well received and is often quoted. However, not all writers agree with Mintzberg's definitions and categories. This does not mean they are invalid. There is, in fact, no description of the manager's job, roles, and functions that is universally accepted. Even in the seemingly simple matter of defining what management is, there are no pat answers in management.

However, it is widely accepted that there is a process of management applicable to *any* organization consisting of functions that *every* manager should perform. The current trend in management literature is to define management in terms of these functions. As we will explain more fully in Chapter 2, there is not uniform agreement on exactly what these functions are, but much of the disagreement is semantic. The following definition is acceptable in principle to most management experts:

> *Management is the process of planning, organizing, motivating, and controlling in order to formulate and attain organizational objectives.*

We will briefly define the functions of planning, organizing, motivating, and controlling when we describe the process approach to management in the next chapter, and we will elaborate on them in Part IV. It is important that you understand these functions and how they interact to comprise a process, an unending series of interrelated activities.

Variation in Management Work. Because of differences in people, objectives, work, and other factors within the organization and its environment, the specific techniques managers must use to perform their functions and roles and make their particular organization or subunit successful vary widely. The national sales manager of *Encyclopedia Britannica* and a Marine Corps officer both need to motivate people to work effectively for their organization. But the sales manager usually uses the technique of monetary reward as an incentive for outstanding performance, whereas the military officer usually depends primarily on instilled discipline and loyalty.

Furthermore, in a large organization there are many managers. Obviously, although all managers may perform certain general roles and functions, they do not all do the same work for the organization. The job of the president of a company clearly differs in important ways from those of its marketing and personnel managers. Thus an organization of any size needs to differentiate managerial work within itself. One way it differentiates is by dividing itself into subunits—such as production, finance, and marketing departments—and by placing a manager in charge of each activity. Another, more elemental, form of differentiating managerial work is the creation of levels of management.

Levels of Management: Differentiating Managerial Work

Organizations large enough to clearly distinguish managers from non-managers generally have so much managerial work that it, too, must be divided and coordinated. In large organizations some managers must spend time coordinating the work of other managers, who in turn coordinate the work of yet more managers, until one reaches the manager who coordinates the tasks of nonmanagers who actually produce goods or provide services. This extension of vertical division of labor results in **levels of management**.

Organizations traditionally make it easy to determine what level a manager is on relative to other managers by giving each a title. However, titles are not a very reliable guide to a manager's true level. This is especially true when comparing managers in different types of organizations. A simple example is that a captain is a junior officer in the army but a senior officer in the navy. Some companies call all their salespeople "territorial sales managers," although they supervise nobody but themselves.

The number of actual levels varies widely from organization to organization. The number is partially but *not necessarily* a function of size. For reasons explained later, there is a point in size where an additional level is needed. However, many factors determine how many levels the organization ought to have in order to attain its objectives most effectively. There are examples of organizations that have far fewer levels than others of comparable or even smaller size, especially if their basic objectives are very different. The enormous Roman Catholic church has only three levels between the pope and the parish priest. Sears, the world's largest retailer, is famous for having just a few managerial levels. An army battalion of a thousand people, on the other hand, has around twenty levels between general and private.

No matter how many actual levels there are, managers are traditionally classified within three categories. Talcott Parsons, a sociologist, described these levels in terms of the functions they fulfilled for the organization. According to Parsons, people on the *technical level* are primarily concerned with day-to-day operations and activities required for efficient, smoothly flowing production or services. Those on the *managerial level* are primarily concerned with internal administration and coordination of diverse organizational activities and subunits. *Institutional level* managers concern themselves primarily with making long-range plans, formulating objectives, adapting the organization to change, and monitoring the relationship between the organization and the community and society in which it operates.[4]

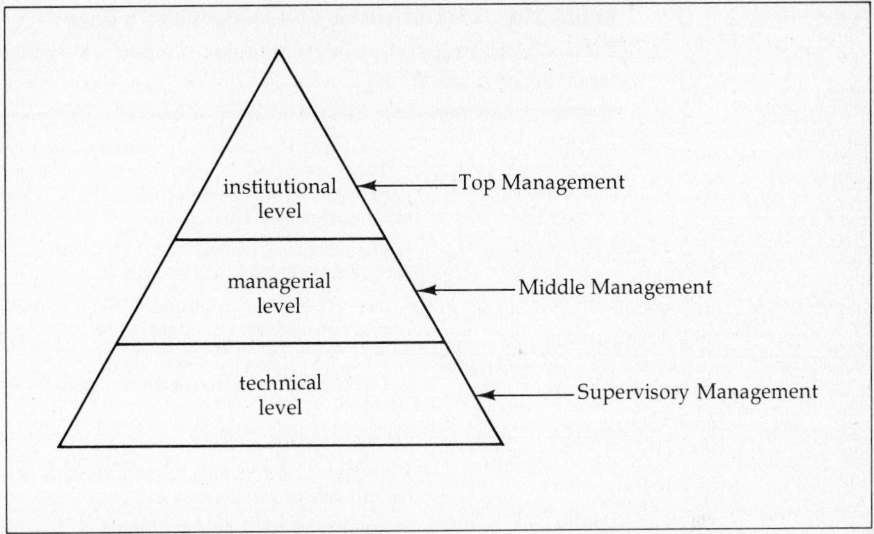

Figure 1-3 Two Ways of Describing Levels of Management

A pyramid shape is used here to indicate that there are fewer people on each level as one ascends in the organization.

A more common way of describing the levels of management is to call them *supervisory* or *operating management, middle management,* and *top management.* Figure 1-3 shows how these designations correspond to Parsons's.

Supervisors. **Supervisory management**, also referred to as *first-line* or *operating management,* is the organizational level immediately above nonmanagerial workers. Supervisors primarily oversee performance of tasks to ensure on a first-hand, continuing basis that they are done correctly. Supervisors are often responsible for directly managing resources, such as supplies and machinery. Some typical titles associated with supervisory positions are foreman, shift boss, sergeant, section head, ward nurse, and chairperson of the department of management. The numerical majority of managers are supervisors. Naturally, most people entering management for the first time begin at the supervisory level.

Studies show that the supervisor's job is busy and action packed. It is characterized by frequent interruptions and shifts between tasks. These tasks tend to be brief: one study showed that a foreman's activities took an average of only 48 seconds to complete.[5] The time perspective of the supervisor's decisions is similarly brief: they are almost always implemented in less than two weeks. Foremen were found to spend about half their time on communication.[6] Supervisors communicate most often with their subordinates, spend some time with peers, and spend very little time with superiors.

Table 1-4 11½ Minutes of a Supervisor's Day

Pat is a typical supervisor in an automobile plant. Her activities were observed by a researcher.

Time	Description
2:15 p.m.	Pat checks with scheduler S. Looks at hourly report of number of cars coming through body shop.
2:16	Walks over to R (repair man) on pickup line and checks to see if earlier repair trouble was corrected.
2:17	Calls over inspection foreman to show him a hole missing in a piece. Inspection foreman acknowledges he will notify the trim department.
2:19	Pat tells repair man to locate the hole by eye until it comes through all right.
2:19½	Pat has a drink.
2:20	Pat walks over to station 5 and asks his utility man how many men he still has to relieve.
2:20½	Moves along the line—stations 5, 6, 7—checking visually on the quality of work.
2:21	Checks a loose nut on a fixture at station 7. Speaks with operator.
2:22	Man at station 3 calls for materials.
2:22¼	Pat tells man at subassembly bench E to make up more material.
2:23	Walks over to MH (stock man). Tells stock man the line is getting low on hinges. They discuss the number short and agree there is enough for tomorrow.
2:25	Pat walks from MH to station 1 and makes visual inspection of the car body to check on the hole discussed earlier at the pickup line.
2:26	Pat sees foreman from preceding section and tells him about the missing hole.
2:26½	A hand signal from welder W.

SOURCE: Robert Guest & Frank Jasinski, "Foremen Relationships Outside the Work Group," *Personnel*, vol. 36, 1959, pp. 25–31.

Middle Managers. The work of supervisors is coordinated and overseen by **middle managers**. The middle-management level has grown considerably in size and importance in recent decades. A very large organization may have so many middle managers that it becomes necessary to subdivide the group. When this happens the higher level is referred to as upper-middle management, and there are four basic levels. Some typical titles of middle managers are department head (in a business), dean (in a college), regional or national sales manager, and branch manager. Army officers from lieutenant to colonel and church bishops would be considered middle managers.

It is difficult to generalize about the middle manager's job because it varies considerably between organizations and even within the same organization. Some organizations give their middle managers a great deal of responsibility, making their jobs more like those of top managers. A study of 190 managers in 8 companies found that middle managers were an integral part of the decision-making process. They identified problems, initiated deliberations, recommended action, and developed innovative, creative proposals.[7]

The middle manager is often in charge of a large subunit or department of the organization. The type of work this subunit performs, rather than the work of the organization as a whole, helps determine the nature of the middle manager's work. For example, the activities of a production manager in a manufacturing firm primarily involve coordinating and monitoring the work of various supervisors, analyzing data on productivity, and working with engineers to determine the feasibility of making a new product. Meanwhile, the public relations manager of the same firm would spend much time on paperwork, reading, conversation, and committee meetings.

Basically, however, middle managers are buffers between top and supervisory management. They prepare information for top management decisions and communicate those decisions, usually after translating them to specifics, to supervisors. Although there are variations, most middle-management communication is oral: conversations with other middle managers and supervisors. One study of middle managers in a manufacturing company found that they spent 89 percent of their time on verbal interaction.[8] Another study, which found that middle managers only spent an average of 34 percent of their time alone, indicated that most time was spent on oral communication.[9]

Top Managers. The highest organizational level, *top management*, is by far the smallest in size. Even the largest organizations have only a few top managers. Typical top management titles in a business are chairperson of the board, corporate director, president, corporate vice-president, and corporate treasurer. Army generals, the secretary of state, and college chancellors are top managers.

The **top manager** is responsible for the organization as a whole or for a large segment of it. They are the ones who make major decisions, such as what the organization's objectives are and what strategies it should use to attain them. The success or failure of the organization rides on these decisions. If the top management of RCA decides (as it once did) to commit the company to computers before it is capable of competing with IBM, there is little middle managers or supervisors can do to prevent a large loss. Strong top managers stamp their personality on the whole organization. For example, the ambiance of the federal government and even the whole country usually changes considerably under a new president. Think of the contrast between the administrations of Kennedy, Johnson, Nixon, Ford, and Carter.

Successful top managers of large organizations are highly valued and therefore usually highly paid. But the burdens are great, and the job is often a lonely one. Mintzberg, after making a detailed study of five chief executives, concluded:

> Thus the work of managing an organization may be described as taxing. The quantity of work to be done, or that the manager chooses to do, during the day is substantial and the pace is unrelenting. After hours, the chief executive (and probably many other managers as well) appears to be able to escape neither from an environment that recognizes the power and status of his position nor from his own mind, which has been trained to search continually for new information.[10]

The primary reason for this high pace and workload is that the top manager's job is open-ended. Unlike the salesperson who has made the required ten calls or the production worker who met quota, there is no point, short of complete failure of the enterprise, where the work ends. Nor can the top manager ever be assured that he or she has succeeded. As long as the organization continues to operate and the environment continues to change, the potential for failure always exists. Whereas the surgeon can finish an operation and consider the task complete, the top manager always feels that there is something more to be done. Hence, he or she imposes pressure on himself to keep on working: a 60–80 hour week is not unusual. Figure 1-4 shows how these many hours are spent.

The Manager Versus the Entrepreneur

The term *entrepreneur* was introduced by the early eighteenth century French economist Richard Cantillon. Since that time **entrepreneur** has been used to describe one who takes the risk of starting a new organization or introducing a new idea, product, or service to society.

Entrepreneurs. The foundations of American industry were laid by a handful of bold entrepreneurs during the late nineteenth and early twentieth centuries. Their names—John D. Rockefeller (oil), J. P. Morgan (steel and banking), Andrew Mellon (aluminum), Andrew Carnegie (steel), Henry Ford (automobiles)—are still household words. Some great entrepreneurs of recent decades are Jean Paul Getty (oil), H. L. Hunt (foods), Aristotle Onassis (shipping), Edwin H. Land (Polaroid Corporation), and John D. McArthur (insurance). Although their names may never appear in history books, the hundreds of thousands of people who start new businesses each year are also entrepreneurs.

One writer states that "today about 9.4 million of the 10 million American business enterprises are entrepreneurial or small businesses run by their owners. The Small Business Administration reports that these firms employ 59 percent of all private sector employees and that self-employed persons account for 8 percent of the private sector."[11]

Entrepreneurs As Managers. Since all entrepreneurs actively select the objectives of an organization and run it at the beginning, all can be considered

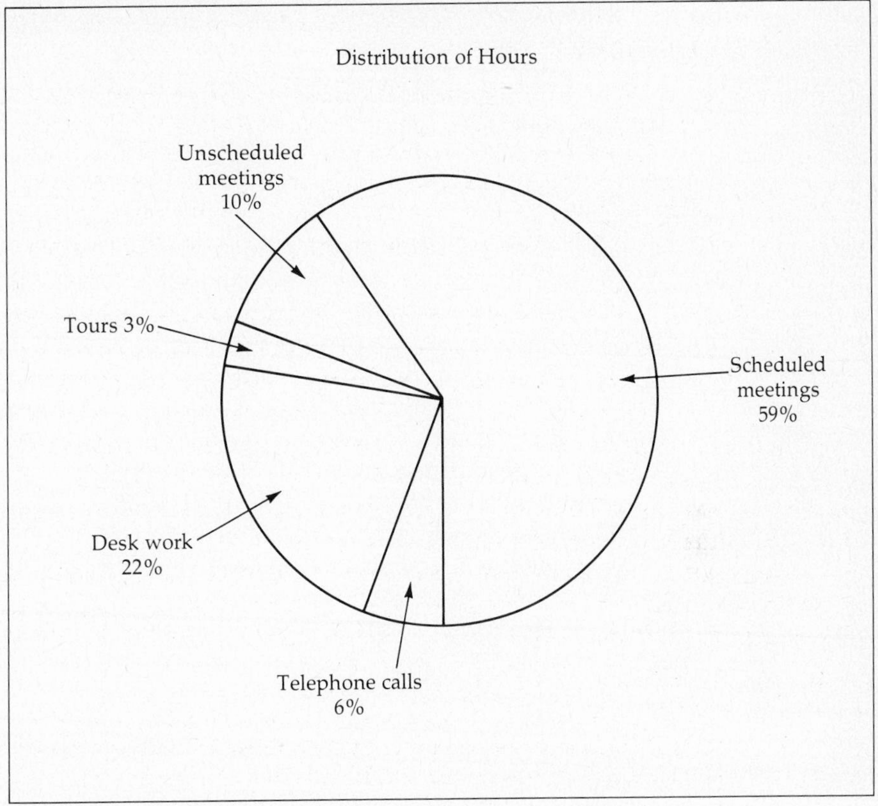

Figure 1-4 How Chief Executives Spend Their Time

SOURCE: Henry Mintzberg, *The Nature of Managerial Work* (New York: Harper & Row, 1973) p. 39. Copyright © 1973 and reprinted by permission of the publisher.

managers in the broad sense. Some entrepreneurs are outstanding managers. Mao Tse Tung founded The People's Republic of China, managed (literally) not only to hold it together but also to build it into a major world power. When you learn about the complexities size alone creates, you will better appreciate how monumental a management feat this was.

Under the continued stewardship of Edwin H. Land, who invented instant photography, Polaroid grew rapidly and is considered one of America's best-managed companies.

Although Ray Kroc did not found McDonald's (there were two restaurants when he bought the "firm" and name from the McDonald brothers), he "industrialized" the hamburger. Kroc's entrepreneurial act revolutionized the fast-food business and is considered one of the most innovative management feats of recent decades. Today McDonald's is famous for its thorough, systematic management. James McLamore, whose comments appear in this

FEATURE 1-3

Can Entrepreneurship Be Taught?

Most recruiters doubt that B-schools are the best places to tap entrepreneurial talent. They feel entrepreneurs are born, not taught. "An entrepreneur is a person who can put . . . skills together creatively," says Robert N. Mills, General Electric Co.'s manager of professional recruiting. "You don't teach those things."

Curiously, most instructors of entrepreneurial studies agree, noting that their courses are designed to develop qualities that are innate. "You can't teach someone to be an entrepreneur, but you can help him or her formulate a very aggressive strategy for success," insists Columbia's MacMillan. Adds Robert E. Coffey, director of USC's program: "While we can't give students the personal qualities to make things happen, we can provide them with technical knowledge."

Those personal qualities can be drawbacks in both corporate and campus bureaucracies. Max McCreery, Exxon's coordinator of professional recruiting, admits that as welcome as entrepreneurial MBAs are at Exxon Enterprises, they may be too "independent-minded" for other Exxon departments.

SOURCE: "How the Classroom Turns Out Entrepreneurs," *Business Week*, June 18, 1979, p. 90. Reprinted by permission.

book, is so adept at management that Burger King, the company he founded, gives giant McDonald's serious competition.

Often, however, such characteristics as taking personal risks, responding to financial opportunities, and willingness to put in long, hard hours at work that make a person a great entrepreneur do not necessarily enable that same person to effectively *manage* the organization as it grows larger. Some entrepreneurs simply may not have the ability or inclination to perform the managerial functions of planning, organizing, motivating, and controlling effectively.[12]

One study that compared successful entrepreneurs to successful managers found that "the successful business hierarchs [managers] were able to organize unstructured situations and to see the implications of their organizations. They were able to make decisions. The entrepreneurs, however, did not show this pattern. . . . [In addition] the successful business executives had a positive attitude toward authority. The entrepreneurial personality, in short, is characterized by an unwillingness to submit to authority, an inability to work with it, and a consequent need to escape from it."[13]

Consequently, it is not unusual for an outstanding entrepreneur to be a rather ineffective manager. The organization the entrepreneur created may fail as a result. Government studies indicate, in fact, that most new businesses fail, and the main reason for failure is poor management, not bad ideas.

If the organization is fortunate, an effective manager will take the helm before it fails. Sears for example, did not become a giant of retailing under the founders for whom it is named. Julius Rosenwald, who bought Sears on the edge of failure, and General Robert E. Wood were the ones who made Sears an industry leader through innovative management and marketing. Similarly, Avis Rent-A-Car was losing money consistently before Robert Townsend took over as president.

The Organization As Entrepreneur. There is still ample opportunity for an individual entrepreneur with good ideas to start a business venture. However, in today's complex organizational society, the entrepreneurial role is by necessity also played by large, established organizations. Critics of big business often complain that this severely restricts the opportunities open to individuals with little capital. But as long as society wants incredible missions accomplished, such as transporting oil from the North Sea by pipe across a thousand miles of frozen wilderness, it will have to rely on big organizations taking the risks and initiative of the entrepreneur.

A good example of the organization as entrepreneur is the pioneering support of NASA, a joint venture of business and government, in the development of aerospace technology. No individual could possibly have assembled the resources needed to place a man on the moon, a phenomenally complex project whose only immediate "profit" was abstract knowledge and technological achievement. Other examples of organizations as entrepreneurs are companies like IBM and AT&T that allocate hundreds of millions of dollars a year for research and development they hope will result in a successful new product or service. In fact, many of the discoveries in electronics that have revolutionized communication, including the transistor and microprocessor, originated in the laboratories of these firms.

Proactionary Versus Reactionary Management. That large, powerful organizations are increasingly assuming the entrepreneurial role does not mean that opportunities for individual initiative are being wiped out. It should always be kept in mind that it is individual people, not "management" or the "organization," who perform all work and make all decisions. Thus, for the organization to play the role of entrepreneur, its managers should think and operate as entrepreneurs. The effective manager of today cannot simply await change and react to it. The effective manager is also **proactionary**. He

FEATURE 1-4

Entrepreneurship in the Organization

Some organizations are making an effort to encourage entrepreneurial thinking on all levels of the organization. A vivid example of the potential results occurred at an aircraft manufacturing plant. For years the plant had made the wing skins for fighter aircraft by cutting a ¾-inch aluminum plate in the pattern illustrated in Figure (a). Area C was considered waste and sold back to the supplier who converted the scrap into sheets which were sold back to the aircraft firm. A creative worker realized that by doubling the size of the sheet, two wing skins could be made with one cut and no waste, as shown in Figure (b). The savings from this one simple idea amounted to $4 million the first year, with an additional saving of $1.7 million for several years thereafter.

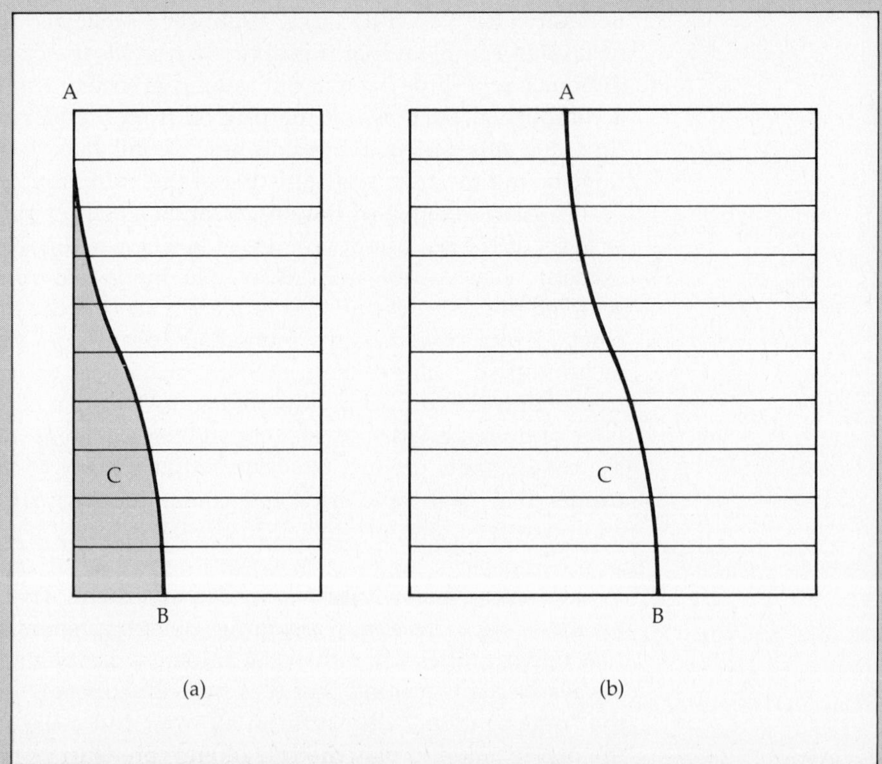

(a) (b)

SOURCE: Adapted from J. H. McPherson, "Structural Approaches to Creativity," report no. 348 (Menlo Park, CA: Stanford Research Institute, 1969) p. 11.

or she, as Mintzberg found, actively seeks out opportunities and deliberately risks introducing change and improvements.

Major entrepreneurial acts, those that involve substantial risk for the organization, are decided upon by top management. But these decisions are usually based on information and ideas supplied by middle managers. If middle management is unable or unwilling to risk introducing new ideas, the entrepreneurial capacity of the organization is seriously diminished. Managers on all levels, even supervisors, need to seek opportunities for improving the organization's effectiveness. The foreman who discovers and implements a more efficient way of getting a job done is as entrepreneurial in spirit as the chief executive who invests ten million company dollars in starting a new product line.

Being an entrepreneur is not easy, whether one operates as an individual or within an established organization. Both organizations and society tend to resist change, however beneficial it may be. In later chapters we will learn some of the techniques management uses to facilitate its capacity to respond to society's changing needs and to make it easier for individual managers to make entrepreneurial decisions.

SUMMARY

Almost everyone in a modern society works either directly or indirectly for an organization. A vast web of interrelated organizations provides the materials and resources on which our lives, pleasure, and growth depend. If even a single powerful organization like General Motors malfunctions seriously, everyone feels the effects. Without organizations, our quality of life would be seriously diminished.

An entity need meet only three criteria to be considered a formal organization: at least two people, at least one objective, and people who deliberately work together to attain their common objectives. Because labor is always divided in an organization, it must be coordinated for the group to attain its objectives. Hence, all organizations must be *managed*. Small organizations can get by without a clearly defined set of managers. Large organizations, however, have so much managerial work they must clearly establish who the managers are and often must coordinate the work of managers as well as nonmanagers.

Management is the process of planning, organizing, motivating, and controlling in order to formulate and attain organizational objectives through other people. All managers perform these universal functions. But every manager's job is diverse and unique. The differences are most apparent between levels of management.

Although the actual number may be much greater, managers are traditionally divided into three levels: supervisory management, middle management, and top management. Supervisors oversee the performance of nonmanagerial workers or deal directly with material resources. Middle managers are buffers between supervisors and top management. Top managers are responsible for the organization as a whole or a very large segment of it.

One of the manager's most important roles is that of entrepreneur. An entrepreneur is a person who takes the risk of introducing a new product or idea to society. Because our society is characterized by large, powerful organizations and its needs are so complex, the entrepreneurial role is increasingly played by organizations rather than by individuals. This means that managers on all levels have to be proactionary rather than reactionary.

Other roles of the manager include those of creator, figurehead, leader, liaison, and resolver of conflict. All these roles are interrelated. When thinking of management, one cannot fall into the trap of pigeonholing and fitting everything into a neat category. One always must look at the whole and be aware of interactions.

REVIEW QUESTIONS

1. Briefly define management.
2. What impact do organizations have on individuals and society?
3. What requirements must an entity possess to be considered an organization?
4. What are organizational objectives?
5. What must an organization do to survive?
6. Describe the three levels managers are traditionally classified in.
7. What is an entrepreneur?
8. Why is management necessary?
9. What are some commonalities in management work?
10. Define formal organization.

DISCUSSION QUESTIONS

11. Distinguish between the role of a manager in a large and a small organization.
12. Distinguish between entrepreneurs as managers and the organization as an entrepreneur.
13. What roles do a supervisor, middle manager, and top manager play in a large organization?
14. As an organization increases in size, division of labor becomes more specialized. Explain this phenomena.

CASE INCIDENT

North Chain Company

Howard Gregg was a staff member of Developmental Enterprises, Inc., a consulting firm specializing in packaged training programs for business and industry. Developmental Enterprises had just secured a sizable contract with North Chain to formulate and implement a major training program that would encompass all levels of management. According to Scott Warnock, North Chain's chief executive officer, it was getting almost impossible to recruit top quality management personnel so North Chain would simply have to "grow its own."

Scott Warnock was the classical entrepreneur turned manager. A college dropout (he supported his mother and two younger sisters), he started North Chain as a one-person operation and literally ran the entire show. However, Warnock was smart enough to recognize that there are distinct differences between being a manager and being an entrepreneur. He realized that if North Chain were to grow and develop, he would have to reassess his role and look within North Chain for persons with management potential. It was during this period of reassessment and reevaluation that Warnock decided to contact Developmental Enterprises. Actually, Warnock was at a trade association meeting and heard a Developmental representative make a presentation about management during the next decade. Warnock was so impressed that he immediately asked Developmental to "work something up" for North Chain. Howard Gregg from Developmental was assigned the North Chain project. He approached it with particular relish since this was to be the first project where he would be in charge.

Gregg was a strong advocate of first-level management training. "Build a sound foundation, and the house will stand forever," was a phrase he often repeated. For this reason, he recommended to Warnock that the initial training effort begin with first-level supervisors who are, according to Gregg, "the folks who really make things happen."

The first of a ten-session program was held on Monday, November 5, 1979, in the company cafeteria. After being introduced by Scott Warnock, who then excused himself because of other commitments, Gregg talked about the management process with special emphasis upon the critical role of first-level supervision. With fifteen minutes of a scheduled one-hour meeting remaining, Gregg asked if there were any questions. Without the slightest hesitation, one first-level manager asked, "If my job is so important, why do I make less money than most of the people I supervise?" There was loud applause from the others.

Questions

1. If you were Howard Gregg, how would you reply to this question?
2. Comment on Gregg's approach to develop organizations from the bottom up.
3. Can management skills be developed, or is it simply a matter of common sense, experience, and intuition?

NOTES

1. This definition is an adaptation of one provided by Chester Barnard, a leading earlier writer on management. Barnard defined a formal organization as a "system of consciously coordinated activities of two or more persons." See Chester Barnard, *Functions of the Executive* (Cambridge, MA: Harvard University Press, 1938), p. 71.
2. Henry Mintzberg, *The Nature of Managerial Work* (New York: Harper & Row, 1973), p. 31. The comments come from Robert H. Guest, "Of Time and the Foreman," *Personnel*, vol. 32, 1955–1956, pp. 478–486.
3. Mintzberg, op. cit., p. 54.

4. Talcott Parsons, *Structure and Process in Modern Society* (New York: The Free Press, 1960).
5. Guest, op. cit.
6. Ibid.
7. L. V. Blankenship and R. V. Miles, "Organizational Structure and Managerial Decision Making," *Administrative Science Quarterly*, vol. 13 (1968), pp. 106–170.
8. E. E. Lawler, L. W. Porter, and A. Tannenbaum, "Managers' Attitudes Toward Interaction Episodes," *Journal of Applied Psychology*, vol. 52 (1968), pp. 432–439.
9. Rosemary Stewart, *Managers and Their Jobs* (New York: Macmillan Inc., 1961).
10. Mintzberg, op. cit., p. 30.
11. William F. Glueck, *Management* (New York: The Dryden Press, 1977), p. 61.
12. Eleanor D. Schwartz, "Entrepreneurship: A New Female Frontier," *Journal of Contemporary Business*, Winter 1976, pp. 47–76.
13. O. Collins and D. Moore, *The Enterprising Man* (Michigan State University: Bureau of Business and Economic Research, 1964), pp. 239–240.

CHAPTER 2

Perspectives on Managing

Chapter 1 illustrated the importance of managing. This chapter outlines the evolution of management thought, showing how management has progressed toward becoming a systematic, scientific discipline and profession. There are, as we shall learn, no universally applicable techniques or firm principles for managing effectively. There are, however, approaches, or perspectives, that help managers increase the probability of attaining organizational objectives as effectively as possible. Each of the following approaches has made a lasting contribution to our understanding of management and organizations. Thus this chapter may be considered a preview of what we will later cover in depth, as well as an overview of approaches to management.

After reading this chapter, you should understand the following important terms and concepts:

- schools approach
- scientific management school
- classical management school
- behavioral science school
- quantitative school
- management process
- management functions
- system
- open versus closed system
- equifinality
- contingency approach

An Ancient Practice, a New Discipline

We established that performance of the managerial function is necessary for an organization to succeed. The *practice* of management is as old as organizations, which makes it very old indeed. Clay tablets dating back to 3000 B.C. record business transactions and laws in ancient Sumeria, clear evidence of organizational practices. The use of organizations can be traced back even further through archeological evidence indicating that prehistoric peoples often lived in organized groups.

However, both management and organizations of antiquity were quite different from the way we describe them in this book. Although management is old, the idea of management as a discipline, profession, and field of scholarship is relatively new. Management did not become a recognized field until the twentieth century. We will partially explain why later in this section. First, let us briefly trace the history of organizations and their management to show what they were like in times past.

Management and Organizations Before 1900

Ancient Organizations. The accomplishments of larger organizations clearly indicate that they were managed formally and had levels of management. The Hanging Gardens of Babylon, the Inca city of Machu Picchu, and the pyramids of Egypt could only have been built through coordinated organized endeavor. There also were large political organizations long before the birth of Christ. Those of the Macedonians under Alexander the Great, the Persians, and later the Romans stretched from Asia to Europe. Kings and generals are managers, of course. So are the lieutenants, keepers of graineries, slave drivers, territorial governors, and keepers of the treasury whom we know helped keep these early organizations operating.

As the years passed management in some organizations became even more distinct and sophisticated, and the organizations themselves grew more powerful and enduring. The Roman Empire, which lasted hundreds of years, is a good example. The legions of Rome, with their well-defined structure of generals and officers, troop divisions, discipline, and planning, marched roughshod over the poorly organized peoples of Europe and the Middle East. Conquered lands were administered by governors responsible to Rome, and roads were built to speed communication with the hub of the empire. Communication, as we shall learn, is a requisite for organizational success. The famous roads, some of which are still in use, helped get taxes and tribute to the emperor. Perhaps more important, the roads enabled home legions to reach outlying provinces quickly, if either the natives or local administrator rebelled against Roman rule.

Rudimentary forms of almost every basic activity of contemporary management practice can be found in these large, successful organizations of antiquity. But, in general, the pattern of management then was very different from that of today. For example, the ratio of managers to nonmanagers was

Table 2-1 Comparison of Old and Contemporary Organizations

Old Organizations	Contemporary Organizations
Few large organizations, no giant businesses	Many extremely large, powerful organizations, both business and nonprofit
Relatively few managers, almost no middle managers	Many managers, large middle-management group
Managerial work often not clearly distinguished and separated from nonmanagerial activities	Well-defined managerial group, managerial work clearly recognized and separated from nonmanagerial activities
Succession to top management based primarily on birth or violence	Succession to top management based primarily on competence, orderly transition period
Few people able to make important organizational decisions	Many people able to make important organizational decisions
Emphasis on command and intuition	Emphasis on teamwork and rationality

much smaller, and there were very few middle managers. Primitive organizations tended to have a very small core of top managers who made almost every significant decision themselves. Frequently management was practically a one-man show. If the top man—and it almost always was a man—was an effective leader and administrator like Julius Caesar or Hadrian, things went fairly smoothly. When an ineffective leader like Nero took the throne, life could become rather unpleasant.

There were exceptions to this pattern, instances of organizations being managed very much as they are today. A notable example is the Roman Catholic church. The simple structure—pope, cardinal, archbishop, bishop, parish priest—chosen by the church's founders and still used today is more "modern" than structures of many organizations begun this year. This may be one reason why the Catholic church has prospered for centuries, while nations and businesses have come and gone. Contemporary military organizations, too, are strikingly similar in many respects to those of ancient Rome. But in general, as Table 2-1 illustrates, management and organizations of antiquity differed considerably from the contemporary pattern.

Lack of Interest in Management. The fact is that although organizations may be as old as humanity, before the twentieth century hardly anyone thought *systematically* about how to operate them. People were interested in *using* organizations to acquire money or political power, but not in managing them.

Even pragmatic evidence of the benefits of effective management barely drew a glimmer of genuine interest. During the early nineteenth century, Robert Owen gave a great deal of thought to attaining organizational objectives through other people. He provided workers with adequate housing and safer conditions, developed a system for fairly and openly evaluating employees, and paid incentives for better performance. These reforms, phenomenally innovative for the times, showed startling insight into human nature and the manager's role. Owen's work became widely known. People came to his mill in New Lanark, Scotland, from far and wide to observe this "magnificent social experiment." But, even though the mill was exceptionally profitable, other businessmen of that time saw little practical value in Owen's reforms. Not a single one is known to have followed his lead.[1]

The Emergence of Systematic Management

The first genuine burst of interest in management came in 1911. This, the year in which Frederick W. Taylor published *Principles of Scientific Management*, is traditionally considered the starting point of management as a recognized field of scholarly inquiry. But, of course, the notion that organizations can be systematically managed to attain objectives more effectively did not really emerge at any specific moment in time. The concept evolved sporadically and gradually over an extended period ranging from the mid-nineteenth century to the 1920s. The major force that first spurred serious interest in management was the Industrial Revolution, which began in England. But the idea that *management* could in itself make a major contribution to organizations first arose in America.

Factors at Work. Several factors help account for why America was the birthplace of modern management. Even as late as the early twentieth century, the United States was practically the only place where a person could readily overcome the circumstances of birth through personal competence. Millions of Europeans, anxious to improve their lot in life, immigrated to America during the nineteenth century, creating an enormous pool of hardworking laborers. The United States, almost from its inception, strongly supported education for everyone who wanted it. Education created an increasingly large body of people intellectually capable of filling various business roles, including management.

The transcontinental railroad, completed in the later nineteenth century, made America the largest unified market in the world. Not insignificantly, there was almost no governmental regulation of business at the time. Nonregulation allowed the early successful entrepreneurs to create monopolies. These factors and others made it possible to form big businesses—businesses so large they *had* to be managed formally.

Management's emergence as a discipline, a field of scholarly inquiry and research, was partly a response to big business's needs, partly an effort to reap more of the benefits of technology created during the Industrial Revolution, and partly the achievement of a handful of curious individuals with a burning interest in finding the most efficient way of accomplishing a job.

Management's Evolution As a Discipline

Management's development as a discipline has not been a series of distinct steps. Rather, the pattern has been one of varying approaches which have often overlapped chronologically in development. One reason for this is that management is extremely eclectic because the manager deals with both technology and people. Consequently advances in management theory have always been dependent on advances in many supporting disciplines, such as mathematics, engineering, psychology, sociology, and anthropology. As these fields advanced, management researchers, theorists, and practitioners became more knowledgeable about the factors affecting organizational success. This knowledge helped the experts to perceive why certain earlier theories sometimes did not hold up and to develop new approaches to management.

At the same time, rapid changes were occurring in the world. Technological innovations became more frequent and significant, for example, and government began to make itself felt more strongly. These and other factors caused management thinkers to become more aware of forces outside the organization. New approaches were developed for this purpose.

Approaches to Management. To date, there have been four major approaches that have contributed significantly to management thought and practice:

- The *schools approach* (actually four approaches) views management from four distinct perspectives. These schools are scientific management, administrative management, human relations and behavioral, and management science or quantitative.
- The *process approach* views management as an ongoing series of interrelated management functions.
- The *systems approach* stresses that managers should view an organization as a number of interrelated parts, such as people, structure, tasks, and technology, that tries to attain diverse objectives in a changing environment.
- The *contingency approach* stresses that the appropriateness of various management techniques is determined by the situation. Because there are so many factors in both the organization and the environment, there is no single "best" way to manage. The most effective technique in a particular case is the one most appropriate for that situation.

Now, let us briefly describe the schools of management which are the foundation of modern management thought and practice.

The Schools of Management

Four distinct schools of management thought evolved during the first half of the century. In chronological order they are the scientific management school, the administrative school, the human relations and behavioral school, and the management science (quantitative) school. The strongest adherents of each at one time believed that they had found *the* key to attaining organizational objectives in the most effective way possible. Later studies and breakdowns in application proved that many of their answers to management problems were at best partially correct in certain limited situations. Yet, each of these schools has made a lasting contribution to the field. Even the most progressive contemporary organization still uses some concepts and techniques originated by these schools. Our goal is to help you appreciate the evolutionary nature of management thought and recognize that techniques that worked in one time and place do not always work in another.

Scientific Management (1885–1920)

Scientific management is most closely associated with the work of Frederick W. Taylor, Frank and Lillian Gilbreth, and Henry L. Gannt. These writers of the **scientific management school** believed that by using observation, measurement, logic, and analysis, one could redesign many manual tasks to make them far more efficient. The first phase of the scientific management approach was to analyze a job and determine its basic components. Taylor, for example, painstakingly measured the amount of iron ore and coal a man could lift with shovels of varying size. The Gilbreths invented a device called a microchronometer which they used in combination with a motion picture camera to determine exactly what motions were made in performing a task and how much time each took. Based on this information, the job was redesigned, usually made simpler, to eliminate wasted motion and employ standardized procedures and equipment to the greatest degree possible. Taylor discovered, for example, that the maximum amount of iron ore and coal could be moved if every worker used a shovel with a 21-pound capacity. In comparison to the earlier system in which each worker provided his own shovel, the gain in output was phenomenal.[2]

Scientific management did not ignore the human element. An important contribution of the school was the systematic use of financial incentives to motivate people to produce as much as possible. They also allowed for rest and unavoidable delays, so that the amount of time allowed for a job was fair and realistic. This enabled management to set standards of performance that were attainable and give pay to those who exceeded the minimum. A key element in this school was that people who produced more actually were rewarded more. Scientific management writers also recognized the importance of selecting people physically and mentally suited to their work, and they emphasized training.

Scientific management also advocated the separation of thinking and planning—managerial work—from the actual performance of tasks. Taylor and his contemporaries recognized, in effect, that the work of managing is a distinct speciality and the organization as a whole would benefit if each group concentrated on what they did best. This approach contrasted sharply from the old system in which workers had to plan their work themselves.

Table 2-2 Contributions of Scientific Management School

1. Application of scientific analysis to determine the best way of performing a task
2. Selection of workers best suited to the task and provision for training them
3. Providing workers with the resources required to perform their tasks efficiently
4. Systematic, fair use of pay incentives to improve productivity
5. Separation of planning and thinking from the actual work

Scientific management, in sum, was a major conceptual breakthrough. Largely because of it, management became widely recognized as a distinct field of scholarly inquiry. For the first time managers and scholars recognized that the methods and approaches of science and engineering could be applied with equal effectiveness to facilitate attaining organizational objectives.

However, scientific management writers focused on what is called shop management. They concentrated on improving efficiency *below* the managerial level. It was not until the rise of the administrative school that writers systematically approached making the management of the overall organization more effective.

Classical or Administrative Management (1920–1950)

Like most workers in the late 1800s, Taylor and Gilbreth began as common laborers, which doubtless influenced their thinking about managing organizations. In contrast, the major contributors to administrative management, more popularly known as the **classical management school**, had more direct experience with upper-level management in big business. Henri Fayol, credited with originating the school and sometimes known as "the father of management," managed a large French coal mining firm.[3] Lyndall Urwick was a management consultant in England.[4] James D. Mooney, who wrote with A. C. Reiley, worked under Alfred P. Sloan at General Motors.[5] Consequently, their primary concern was the broader problem of efficiently administering the overall organization.

Like scientific management, the classical school did not show strong concern for the social aspects of managing. Furthermore, their contributions relied heavily on personal observation rather than scientific methodology. The classicists tried to look at organizations from a broad perspective to determine what all had in common. The classical school's objective was to identify *universal principles* of management applicable to all organizations. The underlying idea was that following these principles would invariably lead to organizational success.

These principles covered two major areas. One was the design of a rational system for administering an overall organization.[6] By identifying the major *functions* of a business, the classical theorists believed they could determine the best way to divide the organization into work units or depart-

FEATURE 2-1

Gilbreths and Therbligs

As an apprentice bricklayer, Frank Gilbreth noticed that the men teaching him to lay bricks used three different sets of motions. He wondered which of these was most efficient, so he methodically studied them and the tools used. The result was an improved method that reduced the number of motions needed to lay a brick from 18 to 4½, increasing productivity by 250 percent.

In the early 1900s Frank and his wife, Lillian, began to study motions using a motion picture camera in combination with a microchronometer. This was a clock Frank invented that could record time intervals as small as 1/2000 of a second. With stop-motion photography, the Gilbreths were able to identify 17 different operations in hand motions. They called these therbligs, which is Gilbreth spelled backward with the *th* transposed.

ments. Traditionally, these business functions are finance, production, and marketing. Closely related to this was the identification of the basic functions of management. Fayol made a major contribution to management by viewing management as a universal process consisting of several related functions such as planning and organizing. We will discuss the management functions at greater length in the next section of this chapter.

The second category of classical principles was concerned with *structuring* organizations and *managing* employees. An example is the principle of unity of command, which holds that a person should receive orders from only one superior and answer only to that superior. Feature 2-2 is an abridged list of Henri Fayol's 14 principles of administration. Many of these still provide useful guidance, despite the many changes that have taken place since Fayol formulated them.

Human Relations (1930–1950) and Behavioral Science (1950–Present)

The scientific management and classical schools developed when the science of psychology was in its infancy. Many people of the early twentieth century seriously questioned Freud's then new concept of the unconscious mind. Moreover, since persons interested in psychology were rarely interested in management, the little existing knowledge of the human mind was not related to the problems of work. Consequently, although scientific and classical writers recognized the importance of people, they limited themselves to such things as fair pay, economic incentives, and establishing formal relationships. The human relations movement evolved partly in reaction to this

FEATURE 2-2

Fayol's Principles of Management

1. *Division of Work.* Specialization belongs to the natural order of things. The object of division of work is to produce more and better work with the same effort. It is accomplished through reduction in the number of objects to which attention and effort must be directed.
2. *Authority and Responsibility.* Authority is the right to give orders and responsibility is its essential counterpart. Wherever authority is exercised responsibility arises.
3. *Discipline.* Discipline implies obedience and respect for the agreements between the firm and its employees. The establishing of these agreements binding a firm and its employees from which disciplinary formalities emanate, should remain one of the chief preoccupations of industrial heads. Discipline also involves sanctions judiciously applied.
4. *Unity of Command.* An employee should receive orders from one superior only.
5. *Unity of Direction.* Each group of activities having one objective should be unified by having one plan and one head.
6. *Subordination of Individual Interest to General Interest.* The interest of one employee or group of employees should not prevail over that of the company or broader organization.
7. *Remuneration of Personnel.* To maintain the loyalty and support of workers, they must receive a fair wage for services rendered.
8. *Centralization.* Like division of work, centralization belongs to the natural order of things. However, the appropriate degree of centralization will vary with a particular concern, so it becomes a question of the proper proportion. It is a problem of finding the measure that will give the best overall yield.
9. *Scalar Chain.* The scalar chain is the chain of superiors ranging from the ultimate authority to the lowest ranks. It is an error to depart needlessly from the line of authority, but it is an even greater one to keep it when detriment to the business ensues.
10. *Order.* A place for everything and everything in its place.
11. *Equity.* Equity is a combination of kindliness and justice.
12. *Stability of Tenure of Personnel.* High turnover increases inefficiency. A

continues on page 44

FEATURE 2-2 continued

mediocre manager who stays is infinitely preferable to an outstanding manager who comes and goes.

13. *Initiative.* Initiative involves thinking out a plan and ensuring its success. This gives zeal and energy to an organization.
14. *Esprit de Corps.* Union is strength, and it comes from the harmony of the personnel.

SOURCE: Abridged from Henri Fayol, *General and Industrial Management* (London: Sir Isaac Pitman & Sons, Ltd., 1949), pp. 20–41.

failure to fully appreciate the human element as a major factor in organizational effectiveness. Being a reaction to shortcomings of the classical approach, the human relations school is sometimes known as the *neoclassical school.*

Human Relations Movement. Two particularly influential contributors to the human relations movement were Mary Parker Follett and Elton Mayo. It was Miss Follett who originally defined management as "getting work done through others."[7] Elton Mayo's famous experiments, particularly those conducted at Western Electric's Hawthorne plant (described later in this text), opened a new dimension of management thought. Mayo found that an efficiently designed job and adequate pay would not always lead to improved productivity, as the scientific management school believed. Forces arising from interaction between people could and often did override managerial efforts. People sometimes responded more strongly to pressure from others in the work group than to management's desires and incentives.[8] Later research conducted by Abraham Maslow and other behavioral scientists (also described later) helped explain why. Human beings, Maslow learned, are motivated not by economic forces, as the scientific management writers believed, but by various needs that money only partially and indirectly fulfills.

Based on these findings, writers of the human relations school believed that if management showed more concern for their employees, employee satisfaction should increase, which would lead to an increase in productivity. They recommended the use of human relation techniques such as more effective supervision, employee counseling, and giving workers more opportunities to communicate on the job.

Behavioral Science Movement. Advances in the supporting disciplines of psychology and sociology and the development of more sophisticated re-

Table 2-3 Contributions of Classical Management School

1. Development of principles of management
2. Description of the functions of management
3. Systematic approach to management of overall organization

Table 2-4 Contributions of Human Relations and Behavioral Schools

Human Relations	Behavioral Science
Application of human relations techniques to increase satisfaction and productivity	Application of behavioral science to management and the design of organizations so that each employee is used to full potential

search techniques after World War II made the study of behavior in the workplace more of a true science. Some of the major figures in this more recent behavioral phase are Chris Argyris, Rensis Likert, Douglas McGregor, and Frederick Herzberg. These and other researchers studied various aspects of social interaction, motivation, patterns of power and authority, organizational design, communication, leadership, job redesign, and quality of work life. We will describe their work in conjunction with these topics in later chapters.

The behavioral science school departed significantly from the human relations movement's emphasis on human relations techniques. The new approach was more concerned with helping employees to realize their full potential by applying behavioral science concepts to the design and management of organizations. In basic terms, the aim of the **behavioral science school** was to increase organizational effectiveness by increasing the effectiveness of its human resources. This could be accomplished by using scientific analysis to describe, explain, and predict human behavior in the workplace. Table 2-4 lists the major contributions of both the behavioral and human relations schools.

The behavioral approach became so popular that it almost took over the field of management during the 1960s. However, like earlier approaches, it advocated a "one best way" approach. Its contention was that the correct application of behavioral science would *always* improve individual and organizational effectiveness. However, as we shall learn in the last part of this book, techniques such as job redesign and participation are only appropriate for certain individuals and situations. Thus, despite its many important contributions, the behavioral approach was sometimes found wanting in situations different from those studied by its researchers.

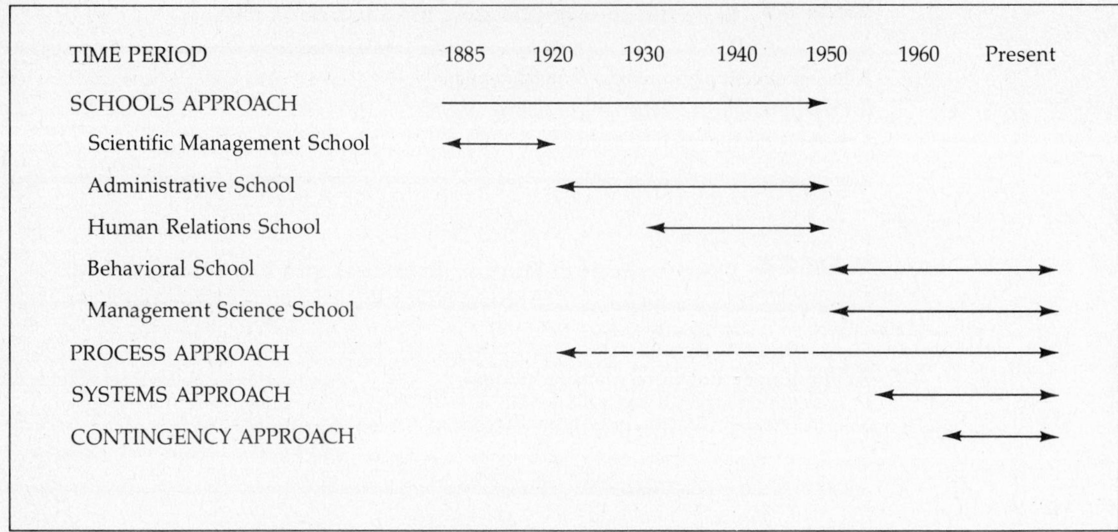

Figure 2-1 The Evolution of Management as a Discipline

Quantitative or Management Science Approach (1950–Present)

Mathematics, statistics, engineering, and related fields have also contributed significantly to management thought. Their influence can be traced to Frederick W. Taylor's application of the scientific method of work analysis. But management did not draw upon quantitative tools heavily until World War II. The British were forced to find a way to use their very limited fighter airplanes and antiaircraft defenses at peak efficiency to avoid being destroyed by massive German air strikes. Later, a way had to be found to maximize the effectiveness of military supply lines fueling the invasion of Europe. Quantitative techniques, grouped under the term *operations research,* were used to solve these problems and others such as those encountered in submarine warfare and the mining of Japanese harbors.

Operations Research and Models. Basically, operations research is the application of scientific *research* methods to *operational* problems of organizations. After the problem is identified, the operations research group develops a model of the situation. A **model** is a representation of reality. Usually, the model simplifies reality or represents it abstractly. Models make it easier to comprehend the complexities of reality. A road map, for example, makes it easier to visualize the relationships among places. Without such a model, it would be far more difficult to reach a destination: one would have to rely on trial and error. Similarly, the models developed in operations research simplify a complex problem by reducing the number of variables to be considered to a manageable number.

After the model is created, the variables are *quantified.* This enables each variable and the relationships between them to be compared and defined

Table 2-5 Contributions of Management Science School

1. Improved understanding of complex management problems through development and application of models
2. Development of quantitative techniques to help managers make decisions in complex situations

objectively. A key characteristic of the management science approach is this substitution of models, symbols, and quantification for verbal and descriptive analysis of a problem. Perhaps the biggest boost of all to the application of quantitative techniques to management was the development of the computer. The computer enabled operations researchers to contruct mathematical models of increasingly greater complexity that more closely approximated reality and were therefore more accurate.

Influence of Quantitative Approach. The influence of the management science or quantitative approach has not been as wide as that of the behavioral approach.[9] This gap is partly because many more managers deal with human relations problems on a daily basis than the sort of problems operations research treats. Also, until the 1960s few managers had the educational background needed to use or even understand sophisticated quantitative techniques. However, this pattern is rapidly changing as more business schools make courses in quantitative techniques and computers a requirement for graduation.

The Process Approach

A major conceptual breakthrough widely accepted today, the process approach was first suggested by writers of the administrative management school. It was they who first attempted to describe the functions of the manager. However, administrative writers tended to consider these functions to be independent from one another. The process approach, in contrast, considers management functions to be *interdependent.*

Management is considered a *process* because the work of attaining objectives through others is not a one-time act but an *ongoing series of interrelated activities.* These activities, all of which are essential to organizational success, are referred to as the **management functions**. The managerial functions are also referred to as processes because they consist of a series of activities. The **management process** is the sum total of these functions.

Henri Fayol, who is credited with originating the concept, believed that there are five primary functions. In his words: "To manage is to forecast and

FEATURE 2-3

Management: A Science or an Art?

The emphasis of twentieth-century management thought has been on making management a science. At every step toward this goal there has been a continuing debate over whether this is, in fact, possible.

Management scholar Luther Gulick states that management is becoming a science because it has systematically studied phenomena that have been organized into various theories and it "seeks to systematically understand why and how men work together systematically to accomplish objectives and to make these cooperative systems more useful to mankind."[10]

On the other hand, many experts contend that management is really an *art,* something that can only be learned by experience and performed well by those with a talent for it. Some practicing managers, including a number who are very successful, feel that scientific theories of management belong in the ivory towers of academia, not the real, everyday world of organizations.

The basis of science is the ability to measure objectively the phenomena being studied. The difficulty of doing this has haunted management since it first became a discipline. Some aspects of organization can be quantified, measured, and analyzed precisely. For example, it is not too

plan, to organize, to command, to coordinate, and to control."[11] Other writers have come up with different lists. A search of current literature would include the following: planning, organizing, supervising (command), motivating, leading, coordinating, controlling, communicating, investigating, evaluating, decision making, staffing, representing, and bargaining or negotiating. In fact, almost every management text employs a slightly different framework of functions.

This book takes the approach of combining essential managerial activities into a relatively small number of categories, all of which are currently widely accepted as applicable to all organizations. We consider the management process per se to consist of the functions of *planning, organizing, motivating, and controlling.* In keeping with modern practice, *communication* and *decision making* are considered *intervening* processes, essential activities that overlap the four primary functions. *Leadership* is treated not as directly part of the primary management process, but as an independent activity involving influencing individuals and groups to work harder toward attaining

difficult to determine the most efficient procedure for performing a mechanical task. The scientific management writers analyzed mechanical tasks with great success; this led some to believe management could become a true science.

The optimism was shortlived. Practicing managers discovered that while you could design a job for maximum efficiency, you could not always get somebody to *perform it* that way. People, it was discovered, are not as simple as machines. One cannot stick a meter in a person's mind to objectively measure his or her response to a proposed method of work. Moreover, managers deal not just with individuals but with groups. There are so many possible social factors operating in a large group that it is difficult even to identify them, let alone to measure precisely their strength and importance.

The same is true of the myriad factors in the external environment that affect an organization and compound potential interactions to the point where it is often impossible to identify clear-cut relationships. Therefore, in our opinion, management is still at least partially an art. Management should learn from experience and accordingly modify practices suggested by theory. This does not mean, however, that management theory is useless. Rather, the manager must recognize the limitations of theory and research and use them appropriately.

Management theories and research findings should not be considered as absolute truths but as tools to help us understand the incredibly complicated world of the organization. Used correctly, theories and research help the manager predict what *probably* will happen, thereby helping the manager make decisions more effectively and avoid needless errors.

objectives, which is extremely important to organizational success. All of these concepts are elaborated on in separate chapters of this text. The following brief explanation of each should give you a general overview of the ground we will cover.

Functions of the Management Process

The management process as a whole consists of four interrelated functions: *planning, organizing, motivating, and controlling.*

Planning. In Chapter 1 we defined an organization as a group of people whose activities are consciously coordinated toward a common *objective* or *objectives.* The *planning function* is the process of deciding what the organization's objectives should be and what members should do to attain them.

Most basically, the planning function addresses three fundamental questions:

1. *Where are we now?* This involves assessing the organization's strengths and weaknesses in important areas such as finance, marketing, produc-

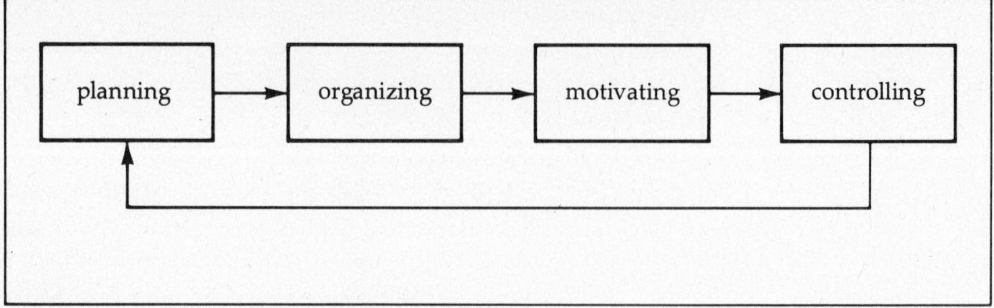

Figure 2-2 **The Management Functions**

tion, research and development, and human resources. The underlying idea is to determine what the organization can realistically accomplish.

2. *Where do we want to go?* This involves assessing the opportunities and threats in the organization's environment, such as competitors, customers, laws, political factors, economic conditions, technology, suppliers, and social and cultural changes. By doing so management decides what the organization's objectives should be and what could hinder the organization in attaining objectives.
3. *How are we going to get there?* This involves deciding both generally and specifically what the organization's members must do to attain objectives.

Through planning management attempts to establish guidelines for channeling effort and decision making that will create unity of purpose within the organization's membership. In other words, planning is one of the ways in which management gets all of its people pulling in the same direction—toward the organization's objectives.

Organizational planning is a process, not a one-time event, for two primary reasons. First, although some organizations disband after attaining the objectives for which they were originally created, most want to survive as long as possible. They therefore redefine or change their objectives if complete attainment is imminent. An example of this is the March of Dimes, originally created to fight polio. When Salk vaccine virtually eliminated new cases of polio in children, the March of Dimes avoided obsolescence by redefining its primary objective as aid to crippled children in general.

The second reason why planning must be a continous process is that the *future is always uncertain.* Due to changes in the environment or mistakes in judgment, events may not turn out as management intended when it formulated its plans. Consequently, plans must be revised as necessary to make them consistent with reality. For example, a firm may have planned to build a new headquarters in five years, using revenues from projected profit increases to pay for it. If profits do not actually increase as projected, or if a more urgent need for the funds arises, the firm will have to revise its future

FEATURE 2-4

Fotomat in a Changing Environment

Recent changes in the environment of Fotomat Corporation, whose familiar film-processing kiosks dot shopping-center parking lots across America, illustrate why planning must be a continuous process.

The bulwark of Fotomat's business traditionally has been the sale and processing of 110-format print film, the type used in the inexpensive snapshot camera made popular by Kodak. However, several changes in the camera industry in recent years have forced Fotomat to rethink its plans and seek new markets.

To begin, sales of 35-mm cameras doubled between 1977 and 1978. People who invest several hundred dollars in photo equipment typically do not want what they fear may be less than adequate film processing. This is a problem for Fotomat, whose deliberately created image is that of an inexpensive processor. There have also been technological changes affecting the film-processing business. Kodak introduced a new instant photography system. And Polaroid introduced its sonar-focusing cameras. These developments increased the percentage of cameras being sold that require no film processing, hence no business for Fotomat.

Fotomat management recognized that unless the company could adapt to these changes, it would be unable to maintain growth and profitability in coming years. Consequently, its management launched an ambitious new marketing program. By spending an additional $6 million (up from $7 million) on advertising, primarily television spots, Fotomat hopes to convince consumers that it can do a good job with 35-mm processing. In addition Fotomat has begun selling video tapes, in the hope it will be able to expand by reaching the new, rapidly growing market created by the sales of video recorders.

SOURCE: Based on James O'Hanlon, "Bedlam in Fotoland," *Forbes*, February 5, 1979, pp. 35–36.

building and operating plans. Feature 2-4, which describes the experience of Fotomat Corporation, is an example of environmental changes forcing a revision of plans.

Organizing. **Organizing**, the function whose name is derived from the word organization, is the creation of structure. There are many elements that must be structured for the organization to carry out plans and thereby attain its objectives. One element is work, the specific tasks of the organization, such as building houses, assembling radios, or providing life insurance. The Industrial Revolution was touched off by the realization that organizing work in certain ways enables a group of people to accomplish much more than it otherwise could. Organizing work was also the primary concern of the scientific management movement.

Since it is ultimately people who perform the work of the organization, another essential aspect of the organizing function is deciding *who* is to accomplish each of the many tasks of the organization, including the work of managing. The manager matches people with work by delegating tasks and the authority, or right, to use the organization's resources to individuals. These recipients of delegation assume responsibility for the successful completion of their duties. In doing so, they agree to hold themselves accountable to the manager. As we shall see, delegation is the vehicle by which management gets work done through others. The concept of organizing work and people systematically can be extended (as will be discussed at a later time) to create a structure for the entire organization. In that discussion we will learn how modern organizations are able to grow without becoming too confusing and chaotic to function effectively.

Motivating. The manager must always keep in mind that the best-formulated plans and finest organizational structures have no value whatsoever unless somebody actually performs the work of the organization. The role of the *motivating function* is to get members of the organization to perform their delegated duties according to plan.

Managers have always motivated, whether they were aware of it or not. In ancient times they did so primarily with whips, threats, and for a select few, with valuable rewards. Then, for a period ranging from the late eighteenth century well into the twentieth, it was widely believed that people would *always* work harder if given an opportunity to earn more. Motivation therefore was thought to be a simple matter of offering suitable monetary rewards in exchange for effort. This was the motivational approach of the scientific management school.

Research in the behavioral sciences demonstrated the inadequacy of a purely economic approach. Management learned that *motivation,* energizing of an inward drive to act, is the result of an extremely complex set of needs that are in continuous flux. We now realize that to motivate effectively a manager must determine what the needs of workers actually are and provide a way for workers to satisfy them through performance.

Controlling. An important point to keep in mind about managing is that almost everything the manager does involves something that takes place in the future. The manager plans to accomplish a goal at some point a week, a month, a year, or even further in the future. During this span many things could go wrong. People could refuse to perform their assigned duties according to plan. New laws could be passed prohibiting the approach chosen by management. A new, strong competitor could enter the field, making it more difficult for the organization to meet its goals than originally anticipated. Or, people could simply make mistakes in carrying out their duties.

In essence such unforeseen events cause the organization to stray off the course management planned for it. Unless management is able to detect and correct these deviations from plans before serious damage is done, the attainment of objectives—perhaps even the very survival of the organization—could be in jeopardy.

Controlling is the process of insuring that the organization is actually attaining its objectives. This is why Figure 2-2 shows an arrow going from control to planning. There are three aspects to managerial control. One is determining precisely what should be accomplished within a set period of time. This is called *setting standards* and is based on plans created during the planning process. Another aspect is *measuring* what has actually been accomplished and *comparing* this to what was anticipated. If these two phases are done correctly, management should not only know that a problem exists but also its source. Knowing the source is required for successfully performing the third phase: taking action, if necessary, to correct serious deviations from plans. One possible action may be to revise objectives to make them more realistic or more appropriate for changes that have occurred in the environment. Your instructor, for example, may discover through testing—a control technique for measuring your class's and individual performance against his or her standards—that your class is able to handle more than originally planned. As a result your instructor may revise instructional plans to cover more material.

The Linking Processes

The four management functions of planning, organizing, motivating, and controlling have two things in common: all require decisions to be made; all require communication both to obtain information for making a good decision and to get that decision understood by others in the organization. Because of this bond and because they connect and interrelate the four functions, communication and decision making are often referred to as the *linking processes.*

Decision Making. Managerial work is largely mental. It is something like trying to put together the pieces of an enormously complicated jigsaw puzzle after somebody added the pieces of ten other puzzles to the box. To complete its picture management continuously has to sift through numerous potential actions to find the one just right for its organization at that given time and place. In essence, for the organization to operate smoothly, the manager must make a continuous series of good choices from among several alternatives. A choice between alternatives is a decision. Hence, decision making—choosing *how* and *what* to plan, organize, motivate, and control—is the manager's primary activity in a general sense.

An essential requirement for making an effective, objective decision or even understanding the true dimensions of a problem is adequate, accurate information. The only means of obtaining information is communication.

Communication. The ability to communicate abstract ideas is one of humanity's most important attributes. *Communication* is the process of exchanging information and meaning between two or more people. It is essential to all social relationships. The strength and quality of relations between people—whether with friends, family, or business associates—is largely a function of how clear and honest their interpersonal relationships are. Since an organization is a deliberately structured pattern of relationships among people, it depends heavily on good communication to function effectively.

Obviously, unless people communicate effectively, they cannot select a common objective, a requisite for being an organization. The information transmitted by communication is necessary not only to make sound decisions on each management function but also to implement them. Plans cannot be carried out, for example, unless they are communicated to people who must carry them out. Usually, if management can communicate the "why" of its decisions to subordinates, it will considerably improve the chances of getting them carried out successfully. Unless people understand what rewards the organization offers, they may not be motivated to work for it. Communicating is also very important in the control function. Managers need information about what has been accomplished to determine whether objectives are being attained.

The Systems Approach

The structure of an organization is sometimes depicted with a flat, two-dimensional organizational chart such as those appearing in Chapter 9. These charts are convenient models that help us visualize the complicated relationships among the units and people of a large organization. But if it were possible to do so, it would be more accurate to portray structure with a mobile instead of a chart. As you probably know from experience, when you touch one piece of a mobile it is not the only one that moves. All other pieces also move to a greater or lesser degree, depending on which piece you touched and how hard you touched it. Moreover, the changes of position are not instantaneous but continue over time, again depending on where and how hard you touched the mobile. Similarly, when management changes one element or part of the organization, all other parts are affected to some degree and the ripples of change can affect the organization's future effectiveness.

This ripple effect is true for physical changes, such as hiring a new person or changing technology by buying a new machine, and also for changes in one of the management functions. For instance, if top management decides to give a subordinate manager more freedom of action, this will affect that manager's motivation, the way the manager deals with subordinates, and the way subordinates respond to the manager. In addition, perhaps the motivation of other managers in similar positions who were not given added authority will be reduced or they will become resentful, and on and on through many aspects of the organization related to that manager's job. In addition, all of these changes will occur at various points in time. Consequently, in the future the organization will be a somewhat different entity and at some different position on the road to its objectives than it would have been without the change.

To visualize these interactions and multiple consequences, managers—especially those on upper levels—need an overall perspective on the organization and its relationship to the environment. The managers need to know not just their own jobs but also how their jobs and all others fit into what the organization is trying to achieve. Managers need to be aware of the immediate ramifications of a decision and its indirect impact on various aspects of the organization. They should take into account the environment's impact on the organization and the organization's effect on the environment. In today's complex organizational world, however large or small one's own organization, it is extremely difficult to see the "forest" since there are many "trees" to distract attention from or block off one's view of the broad picture. The inherent flaw of the various schools approaches to management is that they focused on only one important element, rather than seeing management effectiveness as contingent on many diverse factors.

The application of systems theory to management has made it easier for managers to conceptualize the organization as an entity of interrelated parts that is inexorably intertwined with the outside world. It also has helped to integrate the contributions of the schools that dominated early management thought.

Systems Concepts

Systems theory was first applied in the sciences and in engineering. The application of systems theory to management in the late 1950s was one of the important contributions of the management science school. The systems approach is not a set of guidelines or principles for managing, but a *way of thinking* about organizations and management.[12] To understand how the systems approach helps managers better understand the organization and attain objectives more effectively, let us first define what a system is:

> *A system is an entity composed of interdependent parts each of which contributes to the unique characteristics of the whole.*

Cars, computers, and television sets are all examples of systems. They are made up of many parts, each of which works in combination with all the others to form an entity with specific properties. These parts are *interdependent.* If one is omitted or malfunctions, the entire system will not operate properly. For example, a television will not operate if the tuner is not installed correctly. All biological organisms are systems. Your life depends on the proper functioning of the many interdependent parts that together constitute the unique being that is you.

All organizations are systems. The parts of an organization, in a general sense, are people (the social component) and the technology it uses to get work done. Hence, to be specific, organizations are *sociotechnical* systems. As with biological organisms, the parts of an organization are interdependent. It does not matter how hard the national sales manager of RCA works at generating customers for videotape recorders if the engineering department's designs are faulty, or if people on RCA assembly lines refuse to make the machines, or if the company cannot pay for the parts.

In the next chapter we describe an organization as consisting of five basic parts: structure, tasks, technology, people, and objectives. These parts, as just mentioned, are interrelated. Just as a physician would gather information on your respiration, metabolism, pulse, eating habits, and other vital functions before making a diagnosis and prescribing medication, an effective manager should gather information on all relevant parts of the organization in order to accurately diagnose a problem and take corrective action.

Open and Closed Systems. There are two major types of systems: closed and open. A **closed system** has firm, fixed boundaries; its operation is relatively independent of the environment outside the system. A watch is a familiar example of a closed system. The interdependent parts of a watch move continuously and precisely once the watch is wound or a battery is inserted. As long as the watch has sufficient energy stored within it, its system is independent of the external environment.

An **open system** is characterized by interaction with the external environment. Energy, information, and material are exchanged with the environment through the system's permeable boundaries. The system is not self-sufficient but dependent on energy, information, and materials from outside. In addition the open system has the *capacity to adapt* to changes in the external environment and must do so to continue operating.

Managers are concerned primarily with open systems because *all organizations are open systems.* All organizations are dependent on the world outside themselves for survival. Even a monastery needs to bring in people and supplies and to maintain contact with its parent church in order to operate over the long term.

Another reason why the early schools approaches to management failed to hold up in all situations is that they assumed, at least implicitly, that organizations are closed systems. They did not actively consider the environment as an important variable in management.

Subsystems. The major parts of a sophisticated system like an organization, a human being, or an automobile are often systems themselves. These parts are called *subsystems.* The concept of subsystems is an important one in managing. Through the device of departmentation, described in a later chapter, management deliberately creates subsystems within the organization. Subsystems, such as departments or divisions, and different levels of management, each play a crucial role in the overall organization, just as your body's subsystems of circulation, digestion, nerves, and skeleton do within you. The social and technical parts of an organization are considered subsystems.

Subsystems can, in turn, be composed of still smaller subsystems. Since all are linked interdependently, a malfunction in even the smallest subsystem can affect the overall system. A corroded battery cable, for example, prevents the electrical system of a car from working and thereby halts the whole car. Similarly, the work of every department and every individual in an organization is important to the success of the organization as a whole. This is yet another reason why managers must pay close attention to the needs of people.

The realization that organizations are complex, open systems composed of several interdependent subsystems helps explain why each of the various schools proved to have only a limited capacity for application. The school approaches each tended to focus primarily on a single subsystem of the organization. The behavioral schools concentrated on the social subsystem. Scientific management and management science concentrated primarily on technical subsystems. Therefore they often failed to correctly identify all of the major components of the organization. None of the schools, moreover, gave serious, scientific thought to the impact of the environment. Later research showed it was necessary to do so. It is now widely accepted that forces external to the organization are sometimes primary determinants of what management techniques are appropriate and most likely to be successful.

Open System Model of an Organization. Figure 2-3 is a simplified model of the organization as an open system. The organization imports information, capital, human resources, and materials from its environment. These imports are referred to as *inputs.* In the *throughput* stage the organization processes these inputs, transforming them into products or services. These products or services are the organization's *output,* which it exports to the environment. If the organization is managed effectively, the throughput process will add value to the inputs. The result is many possible additional outputs such as profit, increased market share, increased sales (in the case of businesses), achievement of social responsibilities, employee satisfaction, growth, and so forth.

Equifinality. The concept of equifinality is an important characteristic of open systems and is of practical significance to managers. **Equifinality**

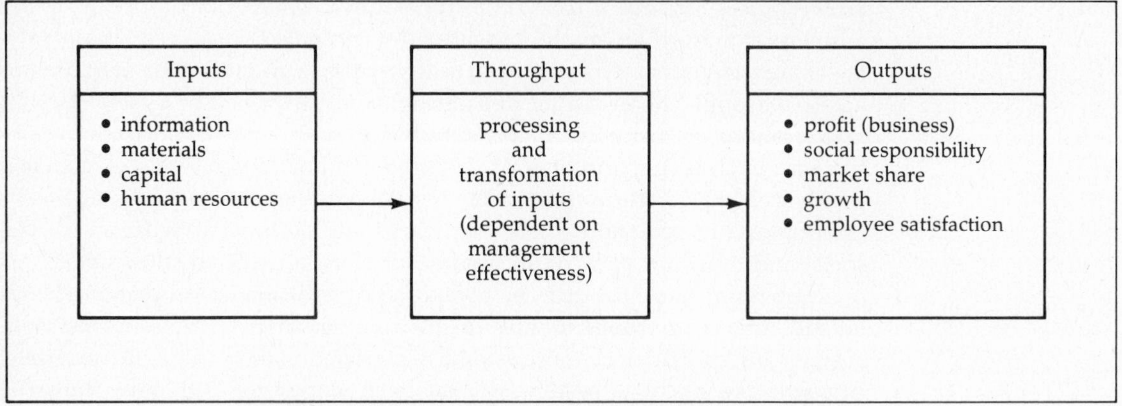

Figure 2-3 The Organization as an Open System

means that the same end result can be reached from different starting conditions and in different ways. Because of this there may be several acceptable solutions to some organizational problems. For example, management can achieve a given level of profits by increasing sales, reducing costs, or a combination of both. It may possibly increase sales by producing a new product or by selling more of an existing one, to give another example.

Equifinality implies that there is no single "best way" to attain organizational objectives, as some early management theorists believed. What works for one organization in a particular time and place may not work for another. What failed in one situation may work in another. The most effective solution is dependent on the specific attributes of the organization and its relationship to the environment.

Variables and the Systems Approach

Because it is so new, the true impact of the systems approach to management cannot be fully evaluated. Nevertheless, it seems to be a major contribution that will have a continuing influence. According to Professors Rosenzweig and Kast, systems theory has provided the management discipline with a framework for integrating the concepts of the earlier schools approaches.[13] Many of these earlier ideas, though not wholly correct, continue to have considerable value. The systems framework probably will help synthesize new knowledge and theories that will be developed in the future.

However, systems theory per se does not tell managers exactly what the significant elements of the organization as a system are. It tells only that the organization consists of many interdependent subsystems and is an open system that interacts with its environment. Not established are the crucial matters of what specifically are the major variables affecting management functions. Nor does systems theory specifically identify what in the environment affects management and how the environment influences the performance of organizations. Clearly, managers need to know what the variables of the organization as a system are to apply systems theory to the process of managing. This identification of variables and their impact on organizational effectiveness is the major contribution of the contingency approach, which can be thought of as a logical extension of systems theory.

The Contingency Approach

The traditional schools of management tried to identify principles related to the functions of management. This theoretical body of knowledge on how management should work was traditionally considered the *scientific* component of management. *Applying* the principles in practice has traditionally been considered an *art*, something to be learned only by experience and trial and error. The contingency approach made a major contribution to management theory by extending science to direct application in particular situations. By using the contingency approach, managers can better understand exactly which techniques will best contribute to the attainment of organizational objectives in a particular situation.

The contingency approach, developed in the late 1960s, does not imply that the concepts of traditional management theory, the behavioral school, and the management science school are wrong. Like the systems approach to which the contingency approach is so closely allied, it attempts to *integrate* the various segmented approaches.[14] It also stresses the interrelationships among the management functions, rather than considering them independently. The focal point of the contingency approach is the *situation*, the specific set of circumstances that influences the organization most at a particular time. Because of this focus, the contingency approach stresses the importance of "situational thinking."

Considering the situation to be important is not new in management thought. Well ahead of her time, Mary Parker Follett, spoke of the "law of the situation" in the 1920s. She observed that "different situations require different kinds of knowledge, and the man possessing the knowledge demanded by a certain situation tends in the best managed businesses, other things being equal, to become the leader of the moment."[15] Two decades later, in 1948, Ralph Stogdill of Ohio State University made an exhaustive study of leadership traits and also concluded that the situation largely determines which traits and skills a leader requires.[16] However, it was not until the late 1960s that management and related social-science disciplines developed to the point where it became possible to cope with the variables influencing organizations and managerial effectiveness in different situations.

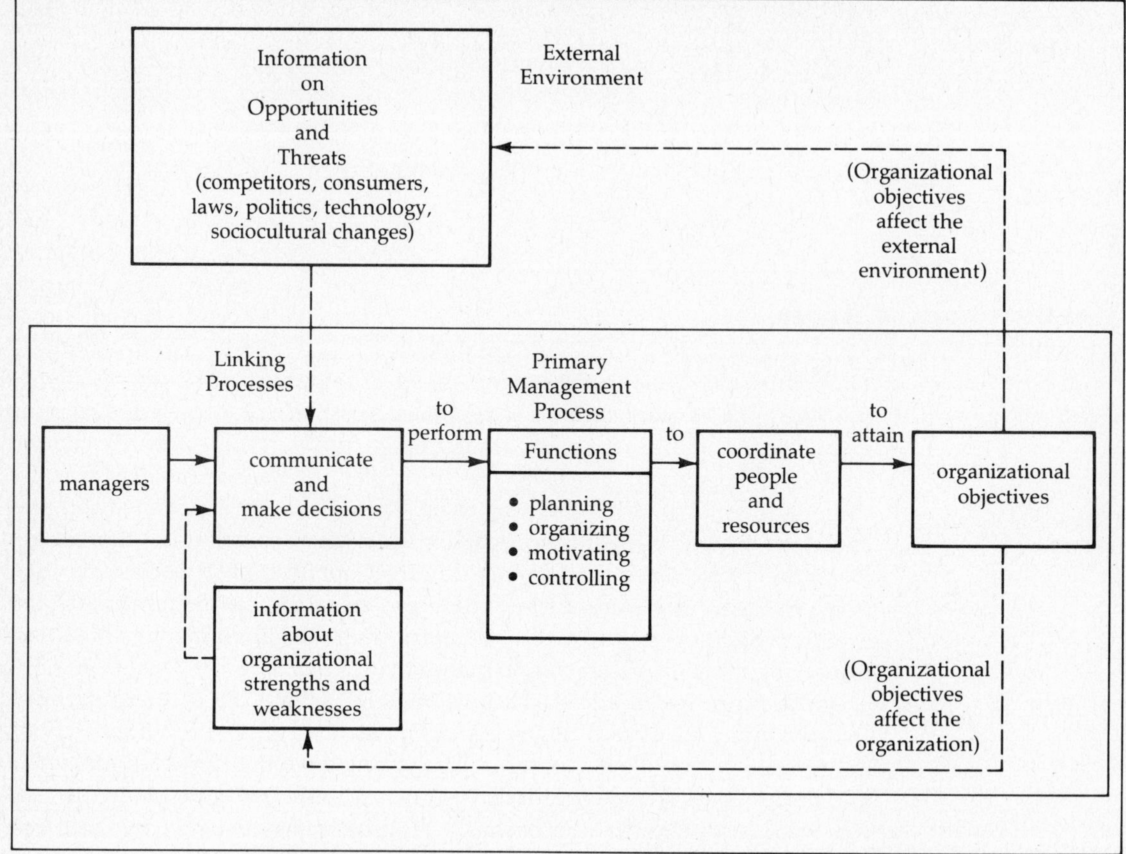

Figure 2-4 The Management Process from an Open-System Perspective

Contingency Approach and the Management Process

Like the systems approach, the contingency view is not a set of prescriptive guidelines but a *way of thinking* about organizational problems and their solutions. It, too, does not set aside the concept of a management process applicable to all organizations. But the contingency approach recognizes that although the general process is the same, the *specific techniques* managers must use to attain organizational objectives effectively may vary widely.

For example, all organizations must create a structure in order to attain their objectives. However, there are many possible ways to structure an organization. There can be many levels of management or just a few. Middle managers and supervisors could be given a great deal of latitude in decision making, or top management could reserve the right to make most important decisions. A particular activity could logically fit in two or more subdivisions, and management must decide which. For example, research and development people could report to the firm's marketing manager or its production manager, or be treated as a major activity reporting directly to the company's president. Management has to decide which structural and other techniques are most appropriate to its unique situation. Moreover, since the situation may change, management may have to change the organization's structure accordingly to remain effective.

> *The* **contingency approach** *tries to match specific techniques or concepts of managing to the specific situation at hand in order to attain organizational objectives most effectively.*

The contingency approach focuses on *situational* differences both between and within organizations. It tries to determine what the significant variables of the situation are and how they influence organizational effectiveness. The methodology of the contingency approach can be expressed as a four-step process:

1. The manager must become familiar with the tools of the management profession that have proven themselves effective. These include an understanding of the management process, a basic understanding of individual and group behavior, systems analysis, techniques for planning and control, and quantitative decision-making techniques.
2. Every management concept and technique has both advantages and disadvantages, or *trade-offs* when applied to a specific situation. The manager must be able to predict the probable consequences, both good and bad, of applying a given technique or concept. To give a simple example, offering to double the salary of all employees in exchange for added work would probably increase their motivation considerably, at least temporarily. Traded off against this are the added costs, which may cause the organization to go broke.
3. The manager needs to be able to properly interpret the situation. It must be determined correctly which factors are most important in a given situation and what effect changing one or more of these variables would probably have.
4. In the final step of the contingency methodology, the manager matches the specific techniques with the fewest potential drawbacks to the specific situation, thereby attaining organizational objectives in the most effective way under the existing circumstances.

Situational Variables. The success or failure of the contingency approach rests heavily on Step 3 above, identifying the situational variables and their influence. Unless this is done correctly, one cannot fully evaluate the trade-offs or match the technique to the situation. If one can analyze the situation, on the other hand, there is no need to resort to guesswork or trial and error for finding an appropriate solution to organizational problems. Fortunately for management, although the contingency approach has not been fully corroborated by research in all areas as yet, current findings indicate that situational variables can, in fact, be identified, at least in some areas. Establishing what these major variables are, particularly in the areas of leadership and behavioral applications, organizational design, and quantitative applications has been the contingency approach's greatest contribution to management. This book relies heavily on the contingency approach because it is the most comprehensive and most satisfactory system yet developed for making management effective.

It is not really possible, however, to identify *all* variables influencing an organization. Literally every facet of human nature, every previous managerial decision, and everything taking place in the outside environment affects every organizational decision to some degree. For practical purposes one can only consider those factors of greatest significance, the ones most likely to strongly affect an organization's success. By eliminating the thousands of less significant differences among organizations and situations, the number of variables is reduced to comprehensible dimensions without appreciably diminishing accuracy.

The specific choice of variables, as with the management functions, differs somewhat among writers but most agree that there are less than a dozen major factors. In the next two chapters, we shall describe these variables, which are grouped in two major classifications: internal variables and external variables.

SUMMARY

The practice of management is as old as organizations. However, prior to 1900, most organizations and the way in which they were managed bore little resemblance to modern practice. Until management became a discipline, around 1910, there was little interest in it.

Early efforts to systematize management tended to approach it from a single perspective. Scientific management concentrated on redesigning work to improve efficiency at the nonmanagerial task level. The classical school tried to identify broad, universal principles or laws for administering an organization. The behavioral school felt that the key to effectiveness was understanding human needs and social interaction. The management science school, whose influence is growing, uses quantitative tools such as models and operations research to make decisions more objective and to maximize efficiency of work flows. Each of the schools made an important, lasting contribution to management; but, because they tended to advocate a "one best way" approach, examined only part of the organization, or ignored the external environment, none proved itself wholly successful in all situations.

The approaches or conceptual frameworks most widely accepted today are the process approach, the systems approach, and the contingency approach.

The concept of a management process applicable to all organizations originated with the classical school. This book considers the core functions all managers must perform to be planning, organizing, motivating, and controlling. Communicating and decision making are considered intervening functions needed to perform these four basic processes.

Systems theory helped integrate the various schools approaches. The systems approach helps managers grasp the interrelationships among parts of an organization and between the organization and its environment. All organizations are open systems consisting of interdependent subsystems. The organization imports resources from its environment, processes them, and exports goods and services to the environment. An important characteristic of open systems is equifinality, the concept that the same result can be attained from different starting conditions and in different ways. Thus, there are usually many acceptable solutions to an organizational problem.

The contingency approach extended the practical application of systems theory by identifying the major variables that affect the organization. The contingency approach is often called situational thinking because it holds that techniques or concepts must be matched to the specific situation at hand in order to attain organizational objectives in the most effective way. Because of differences both between and within organizations, there is no "best" way to manage.

REVIEW QUESTIONS

1. Describe some differences between ancient and modern organizations.
2. Briefly describe three approaches to management covered in the text.
3. Briefly describe the three schools of management thought developed during the first half of the twentieth century.
4. What are the four functions of the management process?
5. What three fundamental questions does the planning function address?
6. What are some of the essential aspects of the organizing function?
7. What are sociotechnical systems?
8. Differentiate between an open and a closed system.
9. Discuss the methodology of the contingency approach.
10. Is management an art or science?

DISCUSSION QUESTIONS

11. What role does communication play in the structuring of organizations?
12. Compare and contrast the systems school of thought and the contingency school of thought.
13. Integrate an organizational experience you have had within the management process model.
14. Briefly describe the commonality present in the approaches to management presented in this chapter.

CASE INCIDENT 1

Rags to Riches to Rags . . . But Not Always

According to an article that appeared in *The Atlanta Journal,* Joe Profit's company, Gourmet Profit, Inc., had sales of more than $2 million in 1978. Unless you are a professional football afficionado, it is unlikely that you've heard about Joe Profit who was a 1971 first-round draft pick for the Atlanta Falcons. An alumnus of Northeast Louisiana U., Profit went to Atlanta, then New Orleans, and finally to Birmingham of the now defunct World Football League. If Profit's professional athletic career had flourished, it's unlikely that he would be a successful business person today.

In examining how he did what he did, it is evident that the secret is that there is no secret. Of course, what makes the Profit story so exceptional is that many professional athletes have made tremendous sums of money, and almost as many have seen this wealth vanish because of poor management and lack of proper business judgment.

Joe Profit's rags to riches story is filled with elements that are well worth considering. For example, he spends up to 17 hours a day on his business. Before he actually ventured out on his own, he held a public relations position for a profit-making organization and also worked with the U.S. Department of Commerce. In addition Profit demonstrated his selling ability by securing private-sector employment for almost 1500 students. One statement made by Profit appears to have a special message for students of management; namely, not only is it important to understand how to start a business, but it's essential that you learn how to maintain one.

Questions

1. In regard to the Joe Profit story, would you agree that good management theory leads to sound management practice?
2. How would you relate the concept of equifinality to this vignette?
3. How can scientific analysis be employed in starting and maintaining a successful organization? Can you cite some examples?
4. How might you apply elements of Mr. Profit's strategy to your own academic career?

CASE INCIDENT 2

Cleve Johnson

Cleve Johnson found it hard to believe. In less than a year, his automobile business had almost literally moved from the peak to the valley. It was small comfort that the entire industry was distressed, that the prime rate had "dropped" to 17%, and that the housing industry was all but completely shut down. Even the most optimistic concurred that the recession of 1980 had arrived.

Johnson had been in the automobile business for 11 years. At 41, he had a major interest in three dealerships, and was now in the process of opening a fourth which would sell only a well-known Japanese import. The other dealerships carried U.S.-made automobiles.

While automobile sales were significantly down, Johnson's service business was flourishing. According to Johnson, this was the one bright spot. However, no matter how bright the spot, it could not obliterate the fact that there were bills and banks to pay, and the service operation, no matter how good, could not carry the entire burden.

Cleve Johnson had graduated from college with a B.B.A. in 1960. Upon graduation, he received an army commission and served in Viet Nam for eighteen months. Upon separation from the service, Johnson was hired by a bank and spent a few years in the consumer loan area and it was during this period that he developed an interest in the automobile business, and was particularly hopeful of having his own organization.

For the most part, Johnson had led a charmed life. A student of management who believed in putting theory to work, his dealerships won several national sales and service awards. Three years ago, he was inducted into the Young Presidents Organization, a body made up of highly successful business people from all over the world. According to Johnson, this was one of the highlights of his business career.

At the present time, however, Johnson was more concerned with survival than recognition. Last January, a sales quota of 11 new cars a month was established for each of the 23 salespeople at this Sandy Creek dealership. Only six had met quota and five left the organization for a variety of reasons. Johnson wasn't sure he would or could replace those who left.

At the weekly staff meeting, Johnson described the present situation and indicated that the recession required that they all get back to basics.

Questions

1. In view of the chapter you've just completed, what do you think Johnson meant when he talked about getting back to basics?
2. How can management cope with conditions that are essentially external to the firm?
3. If you were Cleve Johnson, what would you do about the present sales quota and would you replace those who left?

NOTES

1. Peter F. Drucker, *People and Performance: The Best of Peter Drucker on Management* (New York: Harper & Row, 1977), p. 19.
2. Frederick W. Taylor, *Principles of Scientific Management* (New York: Harper & Row, 1911). For contributions of Gilbreth, see Frank B. Gilbreth, *Primer of Scientific Management* (New York: D. Van Nostrand Company, 1912).

   Two management historians recently claimed that F. W. Taylor may have used material from an unpublished book, *Industrial Management* by Morris L. Cooke, a person with whom Taylor is known to have corresponded, to prepare the text of *Principles of Scientific Management*. However, even if this is true, it was still Taylor personally who had the profound effect on management thought and practice. See Charles D. Wrenge and A. M. Stotka, "Cooke Creates a Classic: The Story Behind F. W. Taylor's *Principles of Scientific Management*," *Academy of Management Review*, vol. 3 (1978), p. 736.

3. Henri Fayol, *Industrial and General Administration*, trans. J. A. Coubrough (Geneva: International Management Institute, 1930).
4. Lyndall F. Urwick, *The Elements of Administration* (New York: Harper & Row, 1943).
5. James D. Mooney and Alan C. Reiley, *Onward Industry* (New York: Harper & Row, 1931).
6. Although he was not really a member of the classical management school, many of the concepts of rational administration were outlined by sociologist Max Weber, whose model of a bureaucracy appears in Chapter 9.
7. For more information on Mary Parker Follett's contributions see her collected papers in H. C. Metcalf and L. Urwick, eds., *Dynamic Administration* (New York: Harper & Row, 1941).
8. See Elton Mayo, *The Human Problems of an Industrial Civilization* (New York: Macmillan, Inc., 1933) and F. J. Roethlisberger and W. J. Dickson, *Management and the Worker* (Cambridge, MA: Harvard University Press, 1939).
9. We have classified management science as a distinct school of management thought. However, it is very common to consider quantitative approaches as an *aid* to management, especially in the area of decision making, rather than as a complete conceptual framework. This latter view seems to represent the current pattern of thought and application.
10. Luther Gulick, "Management Is a Science," *Academy of Management Journal*, vol. 8, no. 1, pp. 7–13.
11. Henri Fayol, *General and Industrial Management* (New York: Pitman Publishing Corp., 1949), pp. 5–6. Note how similar Fayol's list is to functions listed by contemporary writers—a strong indication of the magnitude and insight of his contributions to management thought.
12. For additional information on the systems approach see Kenneth Boulding, "General Systems Theory—The Skeleton of Science," *Management Science*, April 1956, pp. 197–208; F. E. Emery, ed., *Systems Thinking* (Baltimore: Penguin Books, Inc., 1969).
13. F. E. Kast and J. E. Rosenzweig, "General Systems Theory: Applications for Organization and Management," *Academy of Management Journal*, vol. 15 (December 1972): no. 4, pp. 447–465.
14. Fred Luthans, "The Contingency Theory of Management: A Path Out of the Jungle," *Business Horizons*, June 1973, pp. 62–72.
15. Metcalf and Urwick, op. cit., p. 277.
16. Ralph M. Stogdill, "Personal Factors Associated with Leadership, A Survey of Literature," *Journal of Psychology*, January 1948, p. 63.

CHAPTER 3

The Internal Variables

In Chapters 1 and 2 we stressed that an organization is an open system, an entity composed of many interdependent parts that is inexorably intertwined with the outside world. In this chapter we will briefly define and describe the most important internal variables of an organization, parts of the system within the organization as opposed to the environment. We also will introduce the concept of interrelatedness among variables. Your objective in studying this chapter should be to understand the essential characteristics of these key variables in organizational effectiveness and perceive that they must be considered as parts of a whole, not independent areas as they were thought to be in the early schools of management.

After reading this chapter, you should understand the following important terms and concepts:

internal variables
objectives
structure
functional area
specialized division of labor
span of management
need for coordination
short structure
tall structure
task
technology
standardization
mechanization
moving assembly line
Woodward's classifications of technology
Thompson's classifications of technology
interrelatedness of internal variables
sociotechnical system

The Internal Variables

Internal variables are situational factors within the organization itself. Since organizations are contrived, human-made systems, the internal variables are largely the result of decisions related to the management process. This does not mean, however, that all internal variables are actually under the control of management. In many instances an internal factor must be considered a "given" that management has to work around. For example, there are problems, such as boredom and fatigue, associated with assembly-line production; yet, General Motors cannot abandon assembly lines because doing so probably would threaten the company's very survival.

The major variables within the organization that management must consider are *objectives, structure, tasks, technology,* and *people.* In this chapter we will describe their essential characteristics; later we will discuss the interrelationships among them.

Objectives

An organization is by definition a group of people with a conscious, common objective or objectives. **Objectives** are the specific end states, or desired results, the group wishes to attain by working together.[1] Management's development of objectives through the planning process and communication of them to members of the organization is a powerful mechanism of coordination because it lets members of the organization know what they should be trying to accomplish.

Diversity of Objectives. There is great diversity of objectives among organizations, especially those of a radically different type. Business organizations are primarily concerned with providing a particular good or service within specific cost and profit constraints. This concern is reflected in objectives for such areas as profitability and productivity. Other organizations, such as governmental agencies, educational institutions, and nonprofit hospitals, are not primarily concerned with profits. They are, however, concerned with costs. This concern is reflected in a set of objectives revolving around providing a specific service within specific budget limits.

This diversity of concerns extends further, since large organizations have many objectives. In order to earn a profit, for example, a business should set objectives in areas such as market share, new product development, quality of service, management training and selection, and even social responsibility. The nonprofit organization requires a similar set of multiple objectives in diverse areas but will probably want to place higher relative stress on social responsibility. The net result is a vast difference in mental orientation of management among organizations corresponding to the differences in their objectives. The orientation provided by objectives permeates all subsequent decisions of management.

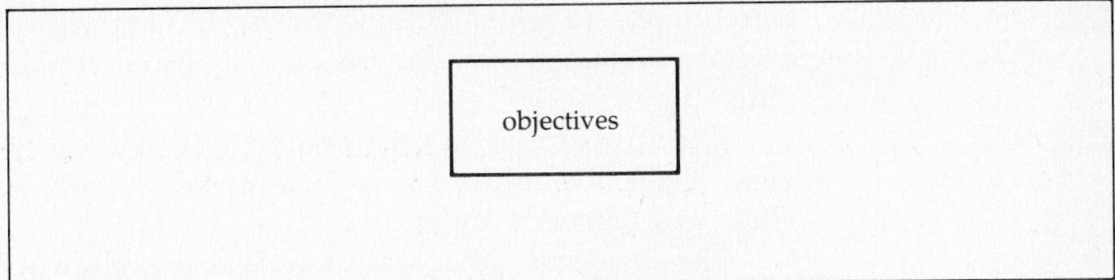

Figure 3-1 Objectives as End States of the Organization

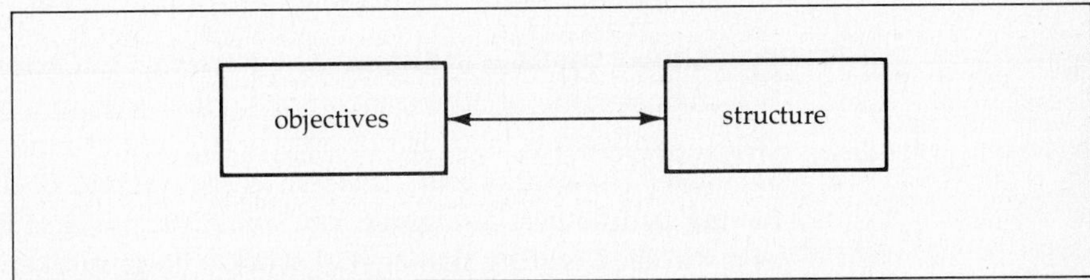

Figure 3-2 How Structure Helps the Organization Attain Its Objectives

Subunit Objectives. The subunits of an organization, being organizations themselves, also require objectives. This further increases diversity. For example, a subunit in finance might have an objective of decreasing credit losses to 1 percent of sales. The marketing subunit of the same organization might have an objective of decreasing customer complaints by 20 percent over the next year.

In general the objectives of subunits engaged in similar activities in different organizations will be more alike than those subunits performing different activities within an organization; that is, the objectives of the marketing department of Sony Corporation will be more like those of marketing at Procter & Gamble in nature than those of the production area in Sony. Because of these differences in subunit objectives, management must make a conscious effort to coordinate the objectives of subunits with one another. The basic guideline for doing so is the overall objectives of the organization. The objectives of a subunit should make a specific contribution to the objectives of the organization as a whole and not conflict with those of other subunits.

One of the most important points for a manager to keep in mind is that every managerial decision and work activity should make a contribution to attainment of the *overall objectives of the organization as a whole.*

Structure

We learned in Chapter 1 that formal organizations are comprised of several levels of management and several subunits. Another term for these subunits is *functional areas,* not to be confused with the functions of management.

Functional area refers to the work the unit performs for the organization as a whole, such as marketing, producing, personnel training, or financial planning.

The **structure** of an organization is the logical relationship of management levels and functional areas arranged in such a way as to permit the effective attainment of objectives.[2]

The structural variable is one we will explore at length in conjunction with our discussion of the organizing process. At this point we will focus only on two fundamental concepts related to structure: specialized division of labor and the span of management.

Specialized Division of Labor. As we learned in Chapter 1, division of labor is a characteristic of all organizations. However, in a majority of contemporary organizations labor is not merely divided at random among the people available. The characteristic pattern is **specialized division of labor**, that is, having people best at a given job, *specialists*, perform it for the organization as a whole. Dividing managerial work among marketing, finance, and production experts is an example. Dividing the work of manufacturing an automobile into many small jobs, such as installing headlights, would be considered *extreme* specialization of labor.

The advantages of even rudimentary division of labor among specialists are so apparent that even primitive tribes assigned some people to hunt, others to make tools, to cook, and so on. Management historian Claude George has traced specialization in China as far back as 5000 B.C.[3] In Plato's ideal city-state, all work was to be divided among those who did it best under the guidance of a philosopher-king. The European guilds of the Middle Ages carried the application of specialization still further by strongly encouraging lifetime devotion to a single type of work. However, it was not until the Industrial Revolution that the type of extreme specialization prevalent in manufacturing today emerged. The reasons for this late blossoming will become clear when we discuss the variables of tasks and technology and how they interrelate with structure.

For now, let us simply note that in all but the smallest organizations, labor is *horizontally divided along specialized lines.* If the organization is of sufficient size, specialists are usually grouped together within functional areas. Exactly how labor is to be divided is one of management's most crucial decisions. The selection of functional areas determines the organization's basic structure and to a large degree its potential for success. The efficiency and effectiveness of the ways in which work is divided among people—down to the lowest levels of the organization—in many situations determines how productive the organization can be relative to competitors. Equally important is how labor is divided *vertically.*

Span of Management. Vertical division of labor, that is, separation of the work of coordination from the performance of tasks, is needed for group

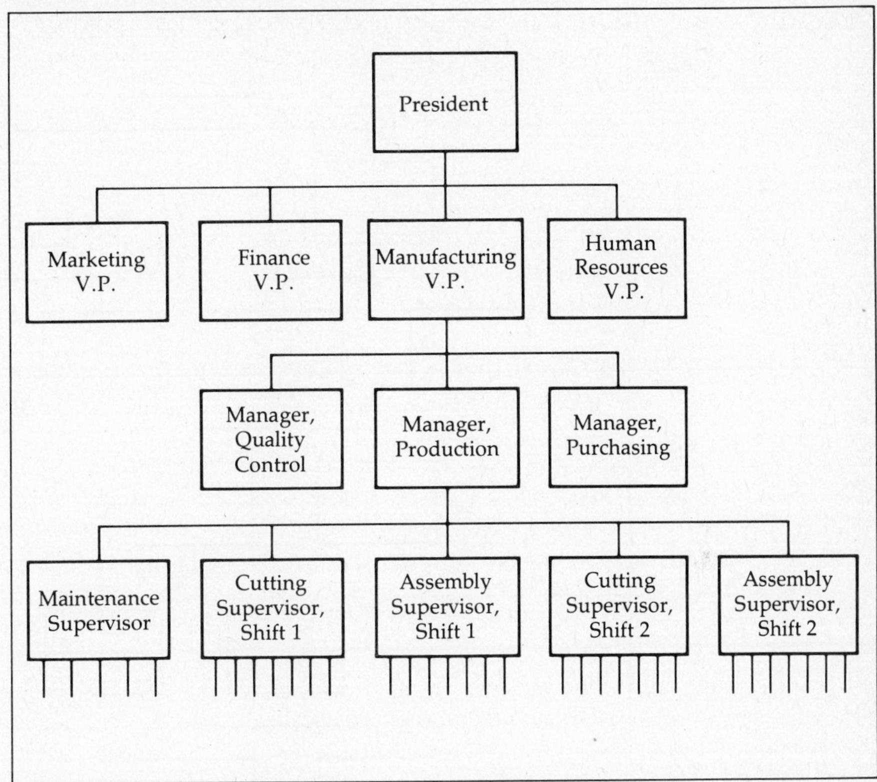

Figure 3-3 Span of Management for Three Levels of Management

endeavor to succeed. *Deliberate* vertical division of labor within the organization results in the hierarchy of management levels described in Chapter 1. A central characteristic of this hierarchy is a formal reporting relationship among people on each level; that is, the person on the highest level of management may have several middle-level managers from various functional areas reporting to him or her. These middle-level managers, in turn, each have a number of subordinates from the supervisory level reporting to them. For example, the production manager might have ten supervisors from various shifts or activities reporting to him or her. This hierarchy continues through the organization until finally nonmanagerial workers report to the supervisor on the lowest level of management. Figure 3-3 illustrates this vertical hierarchy.

The number of people who report *directly* to a manager is referred to as the **span of management**. The span of management is a major aspect of the organizational structure. If a relatively large number of people report to each manager, the span is wide, and the result is a **short structure**. If the span of management is narrow—relatively few people report to each manager—the result is a **tall structure**. Generally a large organization with a short structure

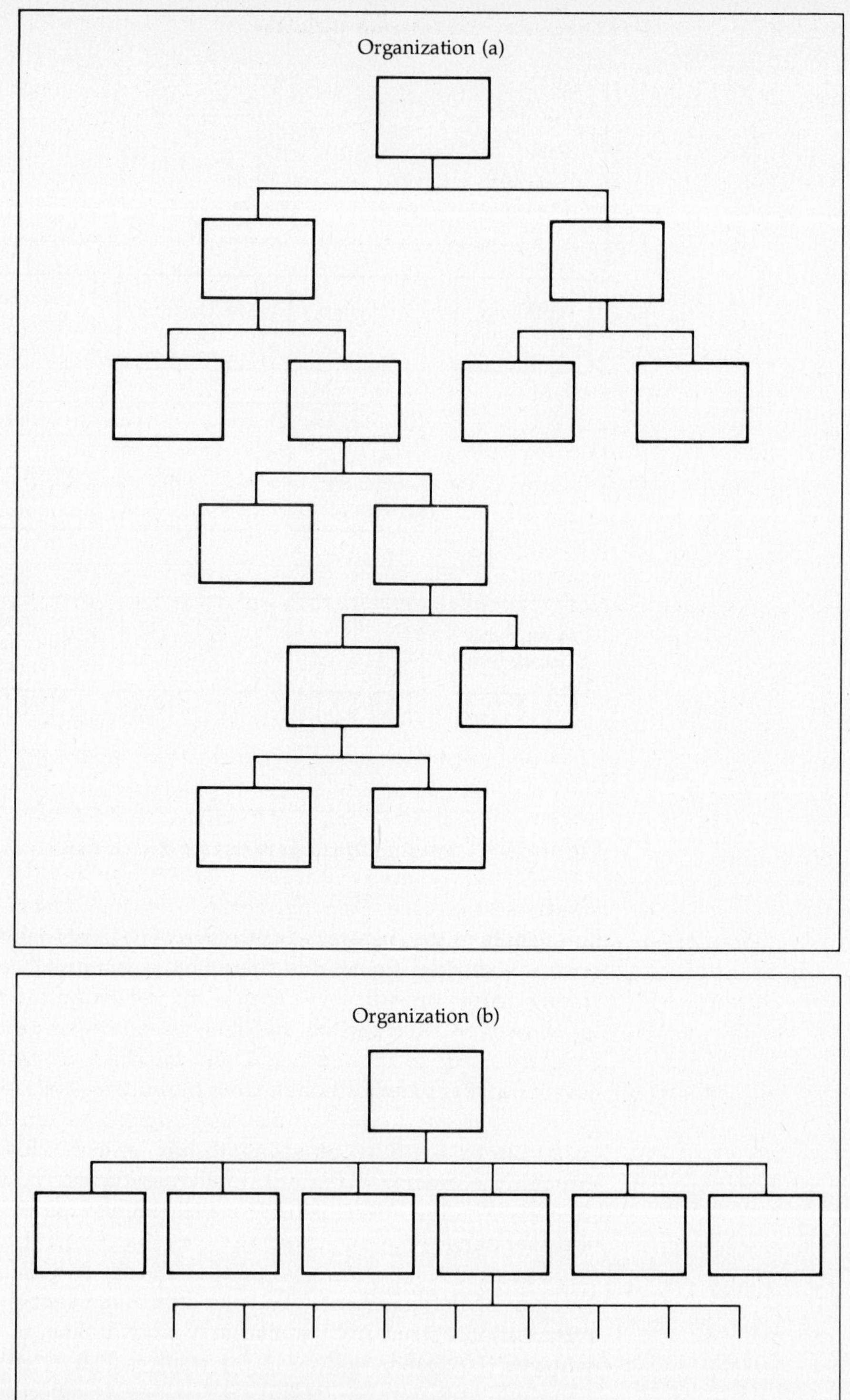

Figure 3-4 Flat and Tall Organizations

has fewer levels of management than one of comparable size with a tall structure. This relationship between span of management and organizational structure is illustrated in Figure 3-4.

Organization (a) in Figure 3-4 has 31 managers, each of whom has a span of 2. The result is 5 managerial levels. In Organization (b), where the span of management is 6, there are only 3 levels, despite the greater total number of managers. It is important to note that these numbers were chosen to illustrate the concept. In practice, the spans of management within an organization often vary widely between both levels and functional areas.

Please keep in mind that there is no "ideal" span of management. Many variables within the organization and its environment can determine which size span is most appropriate in a given situation. Moreover, neither the span nor the structure's relative height are wholly a function of size. For example, the Roman Catholic church and Sears, despite the vast differences in their objectives and activities, are famous for having very wide spans of management and few levels. The church, an organization with millions of members around the world, has only three levels. A typical army company of 100 people, in contrast, has over a dozen levels. Several successful retail firms far smaller than Sears also have many levels.

Need for Coordination. While always required, the need for coordination becomes intense when labor is extensively divided both horizontally and vertically, as it is in the modern large organization. Division of labor literally divides the organization. Unless management creates formal coordinating mechanisms, people will be unable to work *together.* Without appropriate formal coordination, different levels, functional areas, and individuals might easily focus on their own interests, rather than those of the organization as a whole.

The formulation and communication of objectives for the organization and each subunit is but one such mechanism. Every function of management plays a role in effectively coordinating specialized division of labor. Managers continuously need to ask themselves what their coordinational requirements are and what they are doing to meet them. Therefore, coordination is a topic we will return to often throughout this book.

Tasks

An outgrowth of division of labor is the creation of tasks. A **task** is an assigned job, series of jobs, or piece of work that is to be completed in a specified manner within a specified period of time. Technically, tasks are assigned not to people but to positions. Based on management's decisions about structure, each position is assigned a set of tasks intended to make a necessary contribution to the attainment of the organization's objectives. Presumably, if every task is performed as and when it should be, the organization will succeed.

Characteristics. Organizational tasks are traditionally classified within three categories. These are working with *people,* working with *things* (ma-

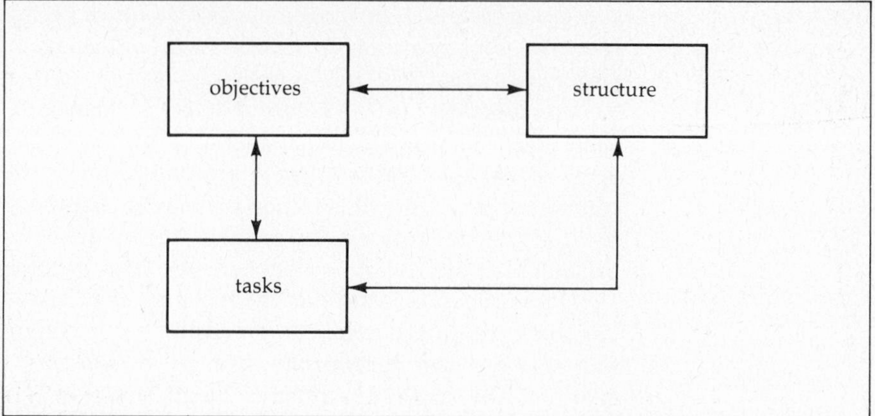

Figure 3-5 How Tasks Are Designed Within the Structure to Attain Objectives

chines, raw materials, or tools), or working with *information.* For example, in a typical factory assembly line employees' tasks involve working with things. The first-level, or supervisory manager's, tasks primarily involve working with people. The corporate treasurer's tasks involve information.

Two other important variables are how repetitive the task is and how long it takes to perform. A machine operator, for example, may repeat the task of drilling a hole thousands of times a day. It takes only a few seconds to perform this task. A research scientist performs a wide variety of complicated tasks and may not repeat some of them in the course of a day or even longer. Certain of the scientist's tasks take several hours or even days to perform. In general, the repetitiveness of managerial tasks decreases and the time span increases as one progresses from the supervisory level to top management.

Tasks and Specialization. Historically, changes in the prevailing design of tasks have been closely related to the evolution of specialization. As Adam Smith pointed out in his famous pin manufacturing example, illustrated in Feature 3-1, when a job is divided among specialists instead of being performed from beginning to end by one person, the potential gain in productivity is enormous. This graphic example and others in *The Wealth of Nations,* published in 1776, is sometimes credited with launching the Industrial Revolution. In any event entrepreneurs of the era quickly grasped the concept that task specialization increased profits because the increased productivity lowered costs. Task specialization was quickly applied to many simple manufacturing jobs. From that time until very recently, the basic trend has been to make tasks increasingly specialized and therefore an increasingly smaller segment of the overall work. During this century innovations in technology

FEATURE 3-1

The Pins That Made The World Jump

The following description of the advantages of specialization in pin manufacturing, from Adam Smith's *The Wealth of Nations,* helped launch the Industrial Revolution, a momentous event in history.

(Without division of labor) . . . a workman . . . could scarce . . . make one pin a day, and certainly could not make twenty. But in the way in which this business is now carried on, not only the whole work is a peculiar trade, but it is divided into a number of branches, of which the greater part are likewise peculiar trades.

One man draws out the wire, another straights it, a third cuts it, a fourth points it, a fifth grinds it at the top for receiving a head; to make the head requires two or three distinct operations! to put it on, is a peculiar business, to whiten the pins is another; it is even a trade by itself to put them into the paper; and the important business of making a pin is in this manner divided into about eighteen distinct operations, which in some manufactories are all performed by distinct hands, though in others the same man will sometimes perform two or three of them. . . . ten persons, therefore, could make among them upward of forty-eight thousand pins in a day. Each person, therefore . . . might be considered as making four thousand eight hundred pins in a day. *But if they had all wrought separately and independently, . . . they certainly could not each of them have made twenty; perhaps not one pin in a day; that is . . . perhaps not the four thousand eight hundredth part of what they are at present capable of performing, in consequence of a proper division and combination of their different operations.* [Emphasis added.]

SOURCE: Adam Smith, *The Wealth of Nations* (London: J. M. Dent & Sons, 1910), vol. 1, p. 5.

and the systematic combination of technology and specialization have made task specialization both more extreme and more sophisticated than Smith could possibly have imagined.

Technology

Technology, the fourth important internal variable, has a much broader meaning than commonly believed. Most people think of it as associated exclusively with inventions and machines such as semiconductors and computers. However, sociologist Charles Perrow, who has written extensively on

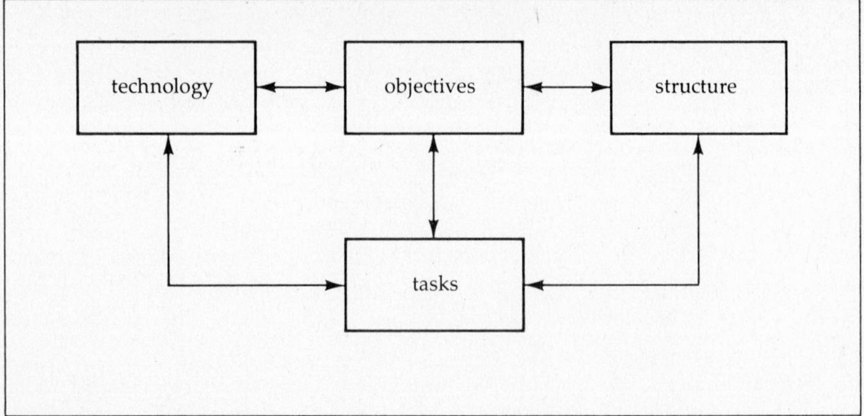

Figure 3-6 How Technology Is Used Within a Structure to Attain Objectives

its effects on organizations and society, describes technology as a means of transforming raw materials—people, information, or physical materials—into desirable goods and services.[4] Lou Davis, who has researched and written on the design of jobs, offers a similarly broad description: "Technology includes the combination of skills, equipment, facilities, tools, and relevant technical knowledge needed to bring about desired transformations in materials, information, or people."[5]

Tasks and technology are closely related. Performing a task by necessity involves using a particular technology, a particular means of transforming materials inputs into desired outputs. Thus, in the words of Wieland and Ullrich, "Machines, equipment, and supplies, of course, can all be viewed as components of technology, but the most important component by far is the process whereby raw materials are transformed into the desired outputs. Technology basically is a technique which enables this transformation."[6]

The impact of these variables on management was strongly affected by two major technological breakthroughs of the Industrial Revolution: standardization and the moving assembly line.

Standardization. The first application of **standardization**, that is, the use of uniform, interchangeable components in manufacturing, is attributed to Eli Whitney, inventor of the cotton gin. He came up with the idea of standardization while working on a contract to produce army muskets, which until then had been individually handcrafted. Using standardized parts drastically reduced both the initial cost and the cost of repair. Because the parts of a Whitney musket were interchangeable with others of the same type, one could easily be repaired in the field by simply replacing the defective part.

The concept of standardization stimulated the use of a high degree of specialization by opening up new avenues for the use of unskilled or minimally skilled labor. On it is based the mass production of goods and services characteristic of our society. Very few products today are not standardized to some degree. Even custom-built automobiles use many standardized components. Standardization and **mechanization**, the use of machines in place of people, are now widely used even outside of manufacturing. Low-cost fast food, for example, is based on Ray Kroc's (of McDonald's) application of such practices to making hamburgers.

The Moving Assembly Line of Henry Ford. Standardization and mechanization were already in widespread use when the automobile industry was started at the turn of this century. In its first years, workers followed each auto through production, changing work stations whenever it was time to add a major new component. Then, in August, 1913, Henry Ford introduced the idea of moving the cars by a conveyor belt and having the workers remain stationary. Because workers no longer lost time changing work stations, the time required to build a Model T car was greatly reduced. To comprehend what this meant, you should know that before Ford used the conveyor belt the average auto wholesaled for $2100. Ford's Model T retailed for $290 in 1918.

Today the moving assembly line is used almost universally in the manufacturing of complex products of all kinds. To take full advantage of it, tasks performed by workers have become increasingly more narrow. Some assembly-line jobs are now so specialized that a worker might do nothing more than tighten a few screws on the same component day in and day out.

Standardization, mechanization, and the moving assembly line had a profound effect not only on the design of tasks but on all of management. As a result of these and later innovations, technology and tasks can strongly affect organizational effectiveness. The classification of technologies by Joan Woodward and James Thompson described in the following section reflects the interrelationship between tasks and technology.

Woodward's Technology Categories. One of the best-known systems of classifying general types of technologies is that of English management researcher Joan Woodward.[7] She found, through a study of manufacturing firms, that the technologies of production firms all fit within one of three types of technology:

1. *Unit, small-batch, or custom processing* is a type of technology in which only one unit or a small quantity of items is produced at one time. Often the item is custom-made to the buyer's specifications or is a prototype. Large IBM computers, Boeing commercial and military jet aircraft, state-of-the-art medical equipment, and space vehicles are produced by a unit-processing technology. So, too, are all custom-made products, such as custom surfboards, boats, furniture, and clothing.

2. *Mass or large-batch production* is used to make very large quantities of items that are identical or very similar. This production makes heavy use of mechanization, standardized parts, and assembly-line techniques. Almost all consumer goods are built with mass-production technology.
3. *Process production* uses automated equipment, usually around the clock, to continuously produce very large quantities of an identical product. Examples of process production operations are gasoline refining, steel and copper smelting, and operating of electric utilities.

Although Woodward's categories specifically describe technologies of manufacturing, they can be applied to other activities as well. The printing of books, for example, is accomplished through mass-production technology. However, writing and editing books would fall into unit or small-batch processing. Most managerial work also would be considered unit work. Surgeons and other professionals also employ a unit technology.

Thompson's Technology Categories. James Thompson, a sociologist and organizational theorist, developed a different, but not contradictory, system of classifying technologies by type.[8] According to him, technologies can be described within the following three categories:

1. *Long-linked technology* is characterized by a series of interdependent tasks that must be performed in sequence. A mass-production assembly line is a typical example of long-linked technology. Each task in the assembly of an automobile, for example, must be performed in a specific order. The engine, for instance, cannot be mounted before the frame is built.
2. *Mediating technology* is characterized by a process involving the meeting of groups, such as clients or customers, who are or wish to be interdependent. For example, banking is a mediating technology that links together depositors and borrowers. The telephone company, similarly, mediates between people who wish to make calls and those who wish to receive them. Employment agencies link suppliers of labor with buyers of labor.
3. *Intensive technology* is characterized by a process involving the application of specific techniques, skills, or services to make a specific change in a specific input. Editing a film would be an example of intensive technology.

The categories proposed by Thompson are not inconsistent with those of Woodward. Long-linked technology is essentially equivalent to mass production and some forms of process production. Intensive technology is equivalent to custom technology. Its intent is to maximize flexibility. As Thompson states, "At any moment an emergency admission may require some combination of dietary, X-ray, laboratory, and housekeeping or hotel services, occupational therapies, social work services, and spiritual or religious services. Which of these, and when, can only be determined from evidence about the state of the patient.

"The intensive technology is a custom technology. Its successful employment rests in part on the availability of all the capacities potentially needed, but equally on the appropriate combination of selected capacities as required by the individual case or project."[9]

Mediating technologies fall between custom and mass-production technologies in many respects. They are used primarily when some standardization is possible and efficient, but output cannot be wholly uniform. A mediating technology enables the organization to deal with variations in the needs of the parties linked to some degree. For example, some depositors want immediate access to their funds at any time, whereas others desire a greater return on their deposits and are able to leave the funds untouched for an extended time. Banks cope with this variation by offering a wide range of accounts, each of which has special characteristics. The same is true of loans, which can be very short-term, as with credit-card purchases, or very long-term, as with commercial mortgages.

The difference in terminology stems from the orientation of each writer. Woodward was primarily concerned with technology in industrial organizations. Thompson sought a scheme that would encompass almost every organization. As a result, manufacturing firms are probably best described through Woodward's categories. Thompson's categories seem better suited for describing the technologies of the broad range of organizations in other fields.

In closing this discussion, let us note that no type of technology is "best." Each has unique advantages and is most suitable for performing certain tasks or attaining certain objectives. To give an obvious example, a custom-built Ferrari racing car is mechanically superior in every respect to a mass-produced car. However, while the custom technology used to build a Ferrari is extremely appropriate for attaining the objective of winning the Le Mans Grand Prix, the mass-produced car also has advantages. It costs much less to make and is perfectly adequate for an average driver limited to 55 mph. Thus, mass-production technology is superior to custom technology when the objective is to produce an affordable car that meets the transportation needs of many people.

People determine the ultimate appropriateness of a given technology in their role as consumers of the organization's output. People are also an important determinant of the relative appropriateness of specific task designs and technologies within the organization. No technology is useful and no task can be performed without the cooperation of people, the fifth internal variable.

People

Throughout this book we often speak of organizations doing this, management doing that. But it is important to recognize that "management," the "organization," and "subordinates" are simply descriptive terms for groups

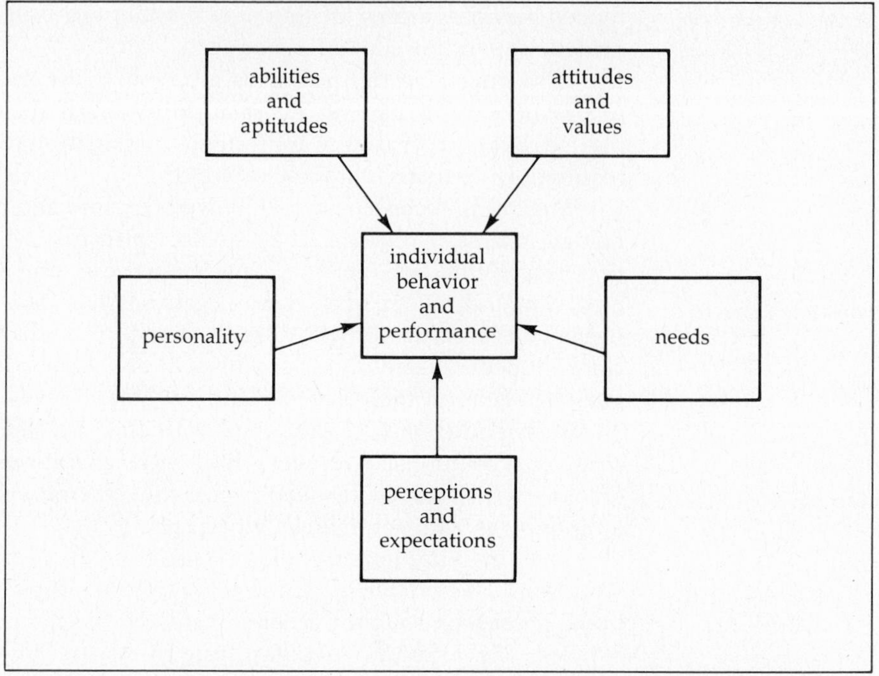

Figure 3-7 Individual Factors Affecting Behavior and Performance

of *people.* When a plant closes, some individual, not an abstract management made the decision. When output is of low quality, it is not "workers" but several individuals who have not been motivated or taught to do the work correctly. If management—individual managers—fails to recognize that employees are all unique individuals with unique feelings and needs, the organization's ability to attain objectives will be seriously impaired. Management, after all, attains objectives through *other people.* People, therefore, are a central factor in any model of management, the contingency approach included.

There are three major aspects of the people variable in the contingency view of management: the behavior of individuals, the behavior of people in groups, and the behavior pattern of the manager, that is, how the manager functions as a leader to influence individuals and groups to attain objectives. Understanding and coping with the human variable is so complex and critical to management that a substantial portion of this book deals with people.

The ways in which a person behaves in general and at work result from a complex combination of several individual and environmental characteristics. The most important of these are briefly described in the following section. In no two people do these characteristics take the identical form. Consequently, the number of potential specific combinations is virtually infinite, and therefore the probability of any two people behaving in an absolutely identical manner in all situations is nil.

FEATURE 3-2

Industrializing Service Businesses

Cyrus McCormick was able to almost triple the output of a wheat farmer, and Henry Ford was able to slash the cost of a car in half. But how do you boost the output of a school teacher, government bureaucrat, TV repairman or journalist?

Well, Harvard Business School Professor Theodore Levitt thinks he has an answer—what might be called the "Big Mac" theory of economic development. If today's executives were to apply the same kind of imaginative thinking to services that men like Eli Whitney and Cyrus McCormick brought to bear on the industrial sector, contends Levitt, then major productivity gains would ensue.

"What's required is to apply the analysis and organization that are commonplace in manufacturing to service," says Levitt. "The service sector must now be industrialized."

McDonald's, Levitt maintains, is the "supreme example" of how service can be industrialized. Each variety of McDonald's hamburger is in a color-coded wrapper. Parking lots are sprinkled with brightly painted, omnivorous trash cans that even the most chronic litterer finds difficult to ignore. A special scoop has been devised for French fries so that each customer will believe he is getting an overflowing portion, while actually receiving a uniform ration. Employee discretion is eliminated; everything is organized so that nothing can go wrong.

"There is not even a sandwich knife or a place to put it," says Levitt admiringly. "McDonald's has built 4,000 factories in the field. [Chairman] Ray Kroc is the service sector's equivalent of Henry Ford and belongs right there in the history books with him."

Look around, says Levitt, and you can see many another service industry that has become more productive in the last decade: the charge card that substitutes for periodic credit clearances; surgical facilities that specialize in low-risk operations at low cost (Northwest Surgicare outside Chicago provides a tonsillectomy for $200, *vs.* $560 at neighboring Michael Reese Hospital); the electrocardiogram done by the technician instead of a lavishly paid M.D.; specialized shops like Midas that provide fast, low-cost, guaranteed auto service. "People say they can't get reliable repair service," says Levitt. "But when General Electric's radio-dispatched repair truck rolls into my driveway, I know that I am going to get better service than in the so-called good old days."

continues on page 82

FEATURE 3-2 continued

Why, then, do so many businessmen view the prospects for productivity gains so pessimistically? Because, says Levitt, too few comprehend the impact management can have on the service sector. Even during the Industrial Revolution, maintains Levitt, management, not technology, played the predominant role. For example, when Eli Whitney in 1798 established the first mass-production line (to manufacture muskets), he was mostly employing technical knowledge that had been widely circulated since the 1300s. "The technology required for the Industrial Revolution was available for over four centuries," says Levitt. "Whitney's contribution was less technological than managerial."

The supermarket was a pioneering example of how management alone can revolutionize a service industry. It was in 1930 that Michael "King" Kullen, building on the self-service grocery idea of Piggly Wiggly founder Clarence Saunders, first proposed the supermarket to his bosses at the Kroger chain. When Kroger management turned him down, Kullen resigned and set up the nation's first supermarket in Jamaica, Long Island.

SOURCE: *Forbes* staff, "The 'Big Mac' Theory of Economic Progress," *Forbes*, April 15, 1977, p. 137.

Abilities. Perhaps the most obvious way in which people differ is in *ability*, the capability to perform a specific activity. Some people have more ability than others, for example, to perform such tasks as typing, computer programming, conducting meetings, preparing written reports, supervising others, planning, and just about every other type of work the organization needs performed to attain its objectives. These differences in ability are partly the result of inherited characteristics such as intelligence and physical stature. But usually, especially at work, ability is primarily learned. For example, by reading this book you should be increasing your ability to be an effective manager.

Organizations almost always attempt to take advantage of differences in ability when deciding who is to perform a task. Selecting the person best able to perform a job is a logical means of increasing the potential gains of specialization. One would assume that the person with the greatest ability should perform a given task most effectively. However, in practice it is common for other factors influencing behavior to cause a person not to perform in accordance with his or her true ability. This is one reason why many organizations prefer to increase a person's ability to perform a specific task through training whenever possible, if that person's other characteristics seem well suited to the new work. Ability is perhaps the easiest individual characteristic to change.

Aptitude. A factor closely related to ability is aptitude. *Aptitude* is a person's *potential* capacity to do something. The result of either or both inborn qualities and learned experience, aptitude can be thought of as one's latent talent in a specific area. The influence of aptitude is often most apparent in areas such as music and sports. For example, outstanding athletes often can play a new sport well almost immediately. An aptitude in a specific area usually facilitates aquiring an ability to perform effectively in that area. This characteristic becomes important to management when selecting people for training. Unless the manager can correctly assess a person's aptitude for the work, there is a strong possibility the time and expense of training will be wasted.

Needs. A *need* is an internal state of psychological or physiological deficiency. As we will explain in detail when we discuss motivation, the most basic needs are physiological ones for food, water, and shelter, and the psychological need for affiliation, the companionship of other people. Many people also seem to have needs for power and achievement, but these may not surface until more basic ones are met. When an active need is *not* satisfied, a person will behave in a way that will lead to satisfaction, even though the individual may not even be consciously aware of the need.

A familiar example of need-motivated behavior is the class clown, a person whose antics are a clear plea for social approval and acceptance. Although the class clown's behavior is counter productive in relation to the school organization's objective of learning, it satisfies the clown's personal needs. A similar example in a work organization is the secretary or manager who leaks confidential information about impending decisions in order to win stature among friends.

The managerial implication of needs is that the organization must strive to create a situation in which satisfaction of personal needs can be attained through behavior conducive to attainment of organizational objectives.

Expectations. Based on past experience and an assessment of the present situation, people form *expectations* about the probable outcome of a given behavior. Consciously or unconsciously, they decide how likely or unlikely it is that something will occur. These expectations exert a strong effect on present behavior. For example, if a salesperson expects that making ten more sales calls a week will increase sales by 15% and thereby lead to a bonus, he or she will probably make those calls. However, if the salesperson believes that the product is so good or bad that a sales call will not change the outcome, or if there is no reward associated with higher sales, this expectation may lead to the behavior of taking the afternoon off. As you can probably see from even this simple example, if people do not expect that the behavior the organization desires will, in fact, lead to either desired objectives or satisfaction of personal needs, they probably will not perform effectively.

Perceptions. Perception is a factor that strongly affects expectations and virtually every other aspect of behavior. For practical purposes we can define *perception* as the mental awareness of a stimulus received by the senses. Perception is critical because it determines "reality" for the individual. People respond not to what *actually* is occurring in their environment, but what they *perceive* to be occurring. No two people perceive anything in exactly the same way. Differences in perception of the same stimulus are sometimes astounding. A vivid example of this and of how perception distorts interpretation of events is a phobia. There is nothing inherently harmful about a common spider, a garden snake, or being at the top of a ladder, but some people become extremely fearful over them.

Perception determines whether a person senses a need and what his or her expectations are in a given situation. What is "really" happening only affects behavior to the degree it is perceived. Thus, if management wants people to behave in ways that will lead to attainment of objectives, it cannot just create an environment encouraging this. Management must also *communicate* effectively to people that this environment exists and that desired behavior will in fact lead to satisfaction of individual needs. Unless workers believe in the "reality" management creates and perceive it, they will not behave accordingly. A negative perception of management is one reason why organizations with a long history of distrust between workers and management often experience great difficulty introducing changes that objectively are clearly positive for the workers.

Attitudes. Another way in which people differ from one another is in their attitudes. Prominent social psychologist Daryl Bem defines *attitudes* as "likes and dislikes ... our aversions toward and affinities to objects, persons, groups, or any other identifiable aspect of our environment."[10] Attitudes bias our perception of the environment and thereby influence our behavior. An example is racial or sexual prejudice. People who hold the attitude that blacks or women are incompetent, inferior workers will tend to exaggerate any mistakes they make and fail to perceive evidence that they are, on the average, as competent as anyone else. Attitudes are learned, mainly from the people with whom we interact most often.

Attitudes toward work are important determinants of how people will respond to such things as changes in work conditions, long hours, and pay incentives. The English coal-mining study at the end of this chapter describes a situation in which workers developed negative attitudes toward a particular technology.

Values. Values are often confused with attitudes. Whereas attitudes are specific beliefs or feelings about aspects of the environment, *values* are general beliefs about what is good, bad, or neutral in life. "I hate manual labor" is an attitude. "Working with your hands is the most noble form of work" is a value. A value always involves a subjective ranking of importance, quality,

FEATURE 3-3

Boredom on the Job—A Matter of Perception

Interviews conducted by *U.S. News and World Report* indicate that jobs which many people consider extremely boring are not always seen that way by the people who do them.

Mr. Sorrentino, the toll collector, remarks: "It's just the type of job that you have to accept for what it is, and enjoy it. I'm always moving in and out of the booth, meeting people and just keeping busy."

When traffic slows up at the Lincoln Tunnel gate, he and other toll collectors converse over their intercom phones. Some bring small radios to work. Mr. Sorrentino sings to himself, and might even whip a harmonica from his pocket at idle moments.

Incidents, big and little, break the monotony. There's a bus driver who gives candy to the collector each time he passes through. Police ask that they be on the lookout for a particular car. Motorists ask directions, or voice complaints. Jacqueline Onassis occasionally goes by on the way to her New Jersey horse farm, and sports figures are often recognized—and are asked for their autographs.

No such distractions visit the workplace of Mr. Clay, who assembles pieces of electrical regulators for Ford automobiles, beginning at 5:30 each weekday morning.

"It's not really a boring job," insists Mr. Clay. "The bad thing is that you have to sit in one spot for so long. I guess you could say it's boring from that standpoint."

To occupy his mind, Mr. Clay converses with other assemblers working nearby. Often, he practices singing the compositions that his country-music band, "North Country Grass," performs on week-ends around the Detroit area.

"It gives me a chance to learn my new songs," says Mr. Clay. "I tape the words onto that cable that they use to stop the assembly line in cases of emergency, and sing to myself. Sometimes my co-workers join in."

He once turned down a foreman's job because it would have meant staying at the plant until the next shift began.

"That's what I'd call boring," he says.

Away from work, he mentally notes the makes of stalled autos, and wonders, when it's a Ford car, "Is that my regulator in there?"

continues on page 86

FEATURE 3-3 continued

Pushing elevator buttons hour after hour is hardly a challenging chore, but 65-year-old Mrs. Cobb insists it is neither dull nor demeaning. She sees herself performing a personal service. "I feel useful here," she says. "I go out of my way to be courteous and helpful. Without this work, I would be on relief. There aren't many jobs I could handle with my leg troubles."

The public image of a file clerk is a stodgy one—days spent pulling pieces of paper out of cabinets, and putting others back inside. But that's not how Dorothy Watson sees herself.

"We do a lot of detective work—looking for reports or research," says the Houston oil-company employee. "I get a certain amount of satisfaction in being able to remember things that someone who is newer to the job wouldn't even know about."

Almost nine years of sorting correspondence and reports have kindled in Mrs. Watson a growing fascination with the oil industry.

"All the reports and research done in the production department come through here," she explains. "I've got a good setup here."

Not everyone in circumstances similar to those of these . . . Americans can claim to be free of boredom. One Atlanta woman who teaches keypunch skills calls it "dullsville from the word go." A Chicago woman in a supervisory job she dislikes blames her shopping sprees on the boredom of her work.

SOURCE: "Those 'Boring' Jobs—Not All That Dull," *U.S News and World Report*, December 1, 1975, pp. 64–65.

or goodness. Other examples of values are: hard work is good; democracy is preferable to dictatorship; ownership of property should rest with the state, not the individual; and being rich beats being poor.

Values, like so many other individual characteristics, are learned. In many cases they are deliberately taught in schools and religious institutions and strongly reinforced by parents and even entertainment media. That honesty is better than dishonesty, for example, is learned in school, on mother's knee, and reinforced again and again whenever the good guys win on television.

Organizations and managers, as might be expected, have values that tend to parallel those of their culture. The predominance of private-enterprise firms in the West and the reluctance of Japanese managers to fire a worker under any circumstances are behaviors that reflect widely held societal values. The specific values of managers, particularly top-level managers, often are felt throughout the organization and are reflected in its objectives and policies. Most top managers, believing in the desirability of high ethical standards, express ethical values in writing and strictly enforce rules and policies governing ethics.

Impact of Environment on Personality and Behavior. The characteristics described in the preceding sections define our individuality. However, although an individual may behave somewhat differently in different situations, we all have a consistent behavior pattern or cluster of characteristics that is relatively constant. This composite of stable characteristics defines our personality. *Personality* is specifically defined as "an individual's characteristics and ways of behaving which are organized in such a way that they reflect the unique adjustments he makes to his environment."[11]

Traditionally, psychologists have described an individual's behavior in terms of personality traits such as aggressive, honest, self-assured, extroverted, introverted, decisive, and indecisive. Prior to the 1970s, most psychologists believed that these traits were constant in all situations; that is, a confident person would exhibit confident behaviors in all relevant situations, a shy person would always act shy. Many psychologists today, such as Walter Mischel, criticize a rigid-trait approach, contending that an individual's behavior varies with the situation. Mischel's research found that even such fundamental traits as honesty and trustworthiness are dependent on the situation. Almost everyone is honest in some situations and dishonest in some.[12] Follow-up studies by other behavioral scientists indicated that whereas both personality traits and the environment do act jointly in causing behavior, the situation seems to have a greater influence than the traits.[13]

These recent findings are significant because they indicate it is very important to create a work environment that supports the type of behavior the organization desires. However, the studies should not be interpreted as implying that personality traits are unimportant. A series of studies by Thomas Harrell of Stanford demonstrates that personality traits are a strong factor in work success. Harrell compared the earnings of Stanford MBA students 5, 10, and 15 years after graduation. He found that the high earners, the more successful group, were characterized by traits such as a lot of energy, self-confidence, social boldness, and little apprehension about making decisions.[14]

Thus management will increase its ability to channel behavior in ways leading to attainment of organizational objectives by *both* using people with personality traits desirable for a given task *and* creating a work environment that supports these traits. A sales organization, for example, should use psychological tests, interviews, and evaluations of prior work experience to select for sales jobs individuals with the most aptitude and ability in sales and assertive personalities. If an organization wants its salespeople to be extremely assertive and competitive but to deal honestly with customers, it should reward assertive, competitive behavior and penalize dishonesty. An individual characterized by high ambition, self-assurance, and decisiveness probably would be relatively ineffective in a nonsupportive, constraining work environment.

The work environment is composed of the aggregate of all the internal variables, as modified and applied for the organization's specific needs through the management process. The number of factors involved, the countless potential variations within each variable, and the fact that all of these factors are interrelated and change over time, make the work environment *extremely* complex. Management and behavioral science researchers are still far from able to fully explain and predict the impact of the work environment on individual behavior. Because of this complexity and because we have not yet discussed many factors related to it, we will hold off discussing work environment and its effect on work behavior for later chapters. Two aspects of the work environment, however, influence individual behavior so strongly that they must be mentioned, even though an entire part of this text is devoted to them. These aspects are groups and managerial leadership.

Groups. Anyone who has taken part in a social demonstration or attended a rock concert knows that groups can powerfully influence individual behavior. Recognition of the effect of groups on behavior in the workplace, attributed to Harvard's Elton Mayo, is often considered the starting point of the behavioral school of management. Groups form spontaneously in every formal organization because of the many opportunities for social interaction. And, of course, an organization and its subunits are themselves groups by definition.

The members of a group develop shared attitudes, values, and expectations about what is appropriate behavior. These are called *norms.* To the degree that a person values membership in the group, he or she will exhibit behavior that conforms to its norms.

The norms of groups may facilitate or detract from attainment of the formal organization's objectives. An example of a norm that facilitates objectives is a high value on team spirit within the group, which can encourage unity of action and purpose provided it is channeled toward organizational objectives. Another norm that facilitates objectives is support of openness in communication. A group norm that would detract from attainment of organizational objectives is considering anyone who produces more than a set amount a "rate buster." The study of English coal mining at the end of this chapter, primarily intended to illustrate the interrelationship between technology and people, also demonstrates the impact of groups on individual behavior.

Leadership. To be effective as a manager, one usually has to be an effective leader as well. Leadership is the means by which the manager influences people to behave in a certain way. There are several possible approaches to leadership in an organizational setting. The one the manager uses is his or her style of leadership.

Style of leadership reflects such things as the manager's values, attitudes toward subordinates, self-concept, and personality. The effectiveness of a given style is dependent on the situation, which includes the nature of work being performed and the individual characteristics of the subordinates. The degree to which the manager's chosen leadership style is effective strongly determines how well managers will be able to channel effort toward attaining objectives, resolving conflict, building teamwork, and managing stress.

Interrelatedness of Internal Variables

When we described the major internal variables, we discussed each separately to simplify explaining their basic characteristics. However, it is crucial to realize that in management practice these critical variables can *never* be considered independently. We explicitly pointed out, for example, the close relationship between tasks and technology. In later chapters, we will point out further interrelationships. Eventually we hope to convey that a significant change in *any* variable will affect every other variable to some degree. The impact of these consequential changes, as we will very soon learn, may overwhelm that of the initiating change.

A Systems Model of the Internal Variables

While the schools approaches each made a major contribution to understanding various internal variables, it was the development of systems theory that helped management readily conceptualize an organization as an entity composed of interrelated parts. Figure 3-8 is a model showing the interrelationship among the internal variables of objectives, structure, tasks, technology, and people. (In later chapters we will expand this model to include groups, leadership, and other factors in the work environment.)

Sociotechnical Subsystem. It is important to keep in mind that organizations are *open* systems. Therefore Figure 3-8 cannot be considered a comprehensive model of variables affecting organizational success. It only depicts internal variables. External variables, as described in the following chapter also strongly affect the organization. Thus Figure 3-8 would be properly considered a model of the organization's internal sociotechnical subsystem. The internal variables are commonly described as a **sociotechnical subsystem** because they have a social component—people—and a technical component—the other internal variables.

The following example of British coal mining comes from a landmark study that helped give rise to the concept of sociotechnical subsystems. We present it here primarily to illustrate that management needs to consider interrelationships among critical factors before taking action.

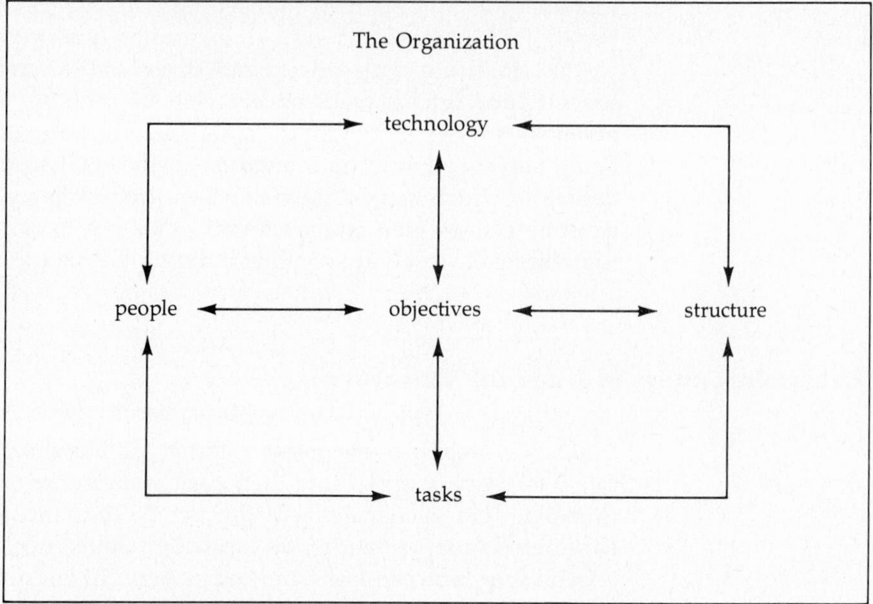

Figure 3-8 Interrelatedness of the Internal Variables

An Example of Interrelatedness

The English coal-mining industry underwent massive technological change after World War II. Prior to this change coal mining was performed with a mass-production technology referred to as the "longwall method."[15] This method involved three major work operations: removing the coal from the coal face, loading and then transporting the coal to the surface, and constructing roof supports and then moving mining equipment deeper into the coal face. Work was performed by groups of six men, two for each of the three operations. The miners worked in shifts. A given shift would perform whatever tasks were necessary to the best of their ability. The following shifts would simply begin where the earlier shift had stopped.

Due to the nature of the longwall method, the men were able to form close personal relationships with fellow miners. They found this satisfying, and one result was highly cohesive work teams. Furthering the sense of unity was that all six men received identical wages, the exact amount being a function of the quantity of coal the group as a whole mined. Also, hiring was based on self-selection; the group selected who would join it. Thus under the longwall technology, the social and task structure created "a dynamically interrelated system that permitted enduring social balance."[16]

Management, desirous of making use of improved technology, implemented what was called the "new longwall method." Although the name was almost the same, the way in which work was done changed completely. Under the new technology, mining was highly mechanized. Shifts were enlarged, with 40 to 50 men in each. Moreover, under the new technology each shift performed only one of the three basic operations, whereas before each performed all aspects at various times. Furthermore, each worker within a shift was assigned a highly specialized task. This was necessary, as the work was divided into a standardized series of component tasks that had to be performed in strict succession over all three shifts.

The new technology was adopted because it seemed logical to management that the efficiencies obtained through increased standardization, mechanization, and task specialization would greatly increase productivity. Unfortunately, management proved shortsighted. It considered technology as the only important variable in successfully attaining the objective of mining coal. Management failed to consider people and tasks as equally important determinants of success when deciding to implement the new longwall method. The result was several unforeseen negative consequences.

To begin with, because under the new method tasks were highly specialized and involved only a small part of the total operation, the workers' sense of accomplishment diminished. Because the narrower jobs took less skill, they were found less satisfying. Also, because the men were no longer working as a team, the opportunity for friendly social interaction diminished. This tendency away from friendly interpersonal relations was exaggerated by a new pay system in which people performing different tasks were paid at different rates, whereas before all men on a shift were paid the same.

Another factor contributed to a breakdown in social relationships among the miners. Under the old system, the groups enjoyed a great deal of freedom and independence in their work. Under the new, workers were dependent not only on others on their own shift but also on workers on other shifts. If the first shift did not mine enough coal, the second would not have enough to load on the conveyer, and the third would be unable to move the conveyer to a new position. Since the shifts were dependent on each other for productivity, they tended to blame each other for slowdowns and substandard output. Conflict among the groups was also fueled by the lack of opportunity to communicate with one another.

Thus, contrary to management's expectations, under the new longwall method absenteeism and costs were higher and productivity was lower. In other words, management failed to attain its objectives.

Fortunately, management realized its error in time. Aided by outside consultants, it recognized the need to consider variables other than technology and changed the design of work accordingly.

The changed method was called the "composite longwall method." Groups of 41 miners were divided into three shifts of about 14 men each. Instead of performing only a few specialized tasks, each shift performed all mining operations. This enabled workers to regain the sense of challenge and satisfaction of the original method. Management also permitted the groups to reassign members among the three shifts if the need arose. This required contact among the shifts and induced more cooperation. Furthermore, the groups were once again paid according to the productivity of the shift as a whole and were again allowed to select new workers. The result of the composite longwall method was lower absenteeism and absentee costs and higher productivity than at any time in the past.

This study of coal mining brought to light the concept of the organization as a sociotechnical system, one comprised of an interrelated social and technical system. As we saw, when management considered only technology, it failed to attain objectives. When it redesigned work to take individual and group behavior into account, negative outcomes subsided, and the organization attained its objectives.

SUMMARY

The internal variables are situational factors within the organization: structure, objectives, tasks, technology, and people.

In contemporary organizations of even moderate size, labor is divided horizontally along specialized lines into functional areas. It also is divided vertically, which creates levels of management. Structure is the logical relationship of management levels and functional areas so as to permit effective attainment of objectives. An aspect of structure is span of management, the number of people who report directly to a manager. When the span is wide and there are few levels, the resulting structure appears short. When the span is narrow, there are many levels, and the structure appears tall.

Objectives are specific end states or desired results the group wishes to attain by working together. Establishing and communicating objectives is a powerful means of coordinating the work of specialized work groups provided that the many diverse objectives of the organization and its subunits are themselves coordinated.

A task is an assigned job or piece of work to be completed in a specified manner within a specific period of time. Tasks may be classified as working with things, with people, or with information. Ever since Adam Smith wrote *The Wealth of Nations,* there has been a consistent trend toward making tasks increasingly more specialized. This trend is partly a result of the very close link between tasks and technology.

Technology is virtually any means by which inputs can be converted to outputs, including machinery, skills, knowledge, and tools. Standardization and the moving assembly line were major technological innovations that greatly increased the potential productivity gains of extreme specialization of labor.

In Woodward's classification system, small-batch or unit technology is custom production. In mass-production technology, a large quantity of essentially identical products is made. Process production involves the use of automated equipment to produce very large quantities of an identical output.

According to Thompson's classification system, a technology characterized by a series of interdependent tasks that must be performed in sequence is termed long-linked. Mediating technology involves a process in which groups who wish to be interdependent are brought together. An intensive technology is one involving the application of specific skills, techniques, or services to make a specific change in a specific input.

People are a central variable because all work is done by them. The manager is concerned with the behavior of people as individuals, group behavior, and how the manager behaves as a leader. The key aspects of individual behavior are abilities, aptitudes, needs, attitudes, values, expectations, and perception. The environment often has a determining affect on personality and behavior. Management therefore should attempt to create an environment that encourages people to behave in ways conducive to the attainment of objectives.

All of the internal variables are interrelated. In aggregate they are considered a sociotechnical subsystem. A change in one variable invariably affects the others to some degree. Thus, what appears to be an improvement in one variable, such as technology, may not have an overall positive affect on attaining objectives if the change has a negative effect on another variable, such as people.

REVIEW QUESTIONS

1. What major variables within an organization must management consider?
2. Briefly define the major concepts relevant to organizational structure.
3. Describe the general types of technology employed by contemporary organizations.
4. Why are tasks designed and assigned in conjunction with the horizontal and vertical division of labor in an organization?
5. Why is management's development of objectives a powerful mechanism of coordination?
6. How do Davis and Perrow define technology?
7. Briefly describe Woodward's and Thompson's technology categories.
8. Why must management understand that internal variables are interrelated?
9. What are the components of the sociotechnical subsystem?
10. Define values, attitudes, abilities, aptitudes, and perception.

DISCUSSION QUESTIONS

11. What are the interrelationships between tasks and technology?
12. Discuss this quote in light of the chapter: "No type of technology is best."
13. Is technology the most important internal variable? Discuss.
14. What is the relationship among objectives, tasks, and people?
15. Give an example showing how perception and expectations affect behavior at work.

CASE INCIDENT

Philip Bowdoin

Make no mistake about it. Philip Bowdoin was the person in charge, the chief executive officer of one of the largest corporations in the world.

Lately, he was more and more concerned with issues of inflation, productivity, and labor. Bowdoin was convinced there must be a better and more effective way of doing things. This feeling was heightened by an article he read dealing with organizational effectiveness. In the article the authors stated, "It is critical that the reader understand the values we hold relative to the use of human resources in organizations, and thus the framework from which we developed choices concerning the direction of organizational change in the corporation described here. In the most fundamental terms, these are our beliefs: An individual is born with a unique set of inherited characteristics and aptitudes, which in turn determine the kind and extent of learning that can occur for that individual. Within these limitations, individuals are capable of acquiring a tremendous range and variety of behaviors. We believe that individuals are not born with a predisposition to behave in any specific fashion. The individual who behaves in nonconstructive ways has learned this mode of behavior. Consequently, we believe the individual, within the appropriate environment, is capable of significant and permanent changes in behavior.

With respect to the organization, we believe that an organization is an open system comprised of several interdependent subsystems. For an organization to achieve its objectives effectively it must design its system to optimize the use of resources within and between these interdependent subsystems. We feel that, traditionally, organizations have emphasized the optimization of the technical subsystems and have neglected the social and human systems.

SOURCE: From Carl A. Bramlette, Jr., Donald O. Jewell, and Michael H. Mescon, "Designing for Organizational Effectiveness," *Atlanta Economic Review*, Vol. 27 (September–October 1977): no. 5.

Questions

1. Discuss some of the relationships that might exist between the way organizations are managed and individual need satisfaction.
2. Do you agree that the technical aspects of organization have been emphasized while the human dimension has been neglected? Explain your answer.
3. Do you agree that, "the individual, within the appropriate environment, is capable of significant and permanent changes in behavior"? What is the relevance of this for you as a practicing manager?

NOTES

1. Note that in this book we use the terms *objective* and *goal* interchangeably. Some writers distinguish between them, considering goals to be more specific desired results or refinements of objectives. For example, in their view "to earn a profit"

would be considered an objective, whereas "to earn one million dollars in 1984" would be a goal. We agree with Steiner and Miner, respected authorities on organizational planning, that this distinction is primarily semantic and causes confusion. George A. Steiner and John B. Miner, *Management Policy and Strategy* (New York: Macmillan, 1977), pp. 19–20.

2. William G. Scott, "Organizational Theory: An Overview and Appraisal," *Academy of Management Journal*, vol. 4 (1961), pp. 7–26.
3. Claude S. George, *The History of Management Thought*, 2d. ed., (Englewood Cliffs, NJ: Prentice-Hall, 1972).
4. Charles Perrow, *Organizational Analysis: A Sociological View* (Belmont, CA: Wadsworth, 1970).
5. Lewis E. Davis, "Job Satisfaction Research: The Post Industrial View," *Industrial Relations*, vol. 10 (1971), pp. 176–193.
6. George F. Wieland and Robert A. Ullrich, *Organizations: Behavior Design, and Change* (Homewood, IL: Irwin, 1976), p. 78.
7. Joan Woodward, *Industrial Organization: Theory and Practice* (New York: Oxford University Press, Inc., 1965).
8. James E. Thompson, *Organizations in Action* (New York: McGraw-Hill, 1967).
9. Ibid., pp. 17–18.
10. Daryl J. Bem, *Beliefs, Attitudes, and Human Affairs* (Monterey, CA: Brooks/Cole, 1970), p. 14.
11. Stanley K. Fich, *Insights into Human Behavior* (Boston: Holbrook Press, 1970), p. 158.
12. Walter Mischel, "Toward a Cognitive Social Learning Reconceptualization of Personality," *Psychological Review*, vol. 80 (1973), pp. 252–283.
13. I. G. Sarason, R. E. Smith, and E. Diener, "Personality Research: Components of Variance Attributable to the Person and the Situation," *Journal of Personality and Social Psychology*, vol. 32 (1975), pp. 199–204.
14. Thomas W. Harrell and M. S. Harrell, "A Fifteen Year Longitudinal Study of MBAs," *Western Psychological Association*, April 22, 1978.
15. Eric L. Trist and K. W. Bramforth, "Some Social Psychological Consequences of the Long Wall Method of Coal Getting," *Human Relations*, vol. 4 (1951), pp. 3–38.
16. Ibid., p. 8.

CHAPTER 4

The External Environment

Thus far our discussion of the major variables affecting organizational success has centered on factors *within* the organization. It seems obvious and logical that the primary concern of management should be its own organization. However, it is now widely recognized that forces outside of the organization, in the external environment, often have a determining effect on the success or failure of the organization. Understanding these issues is essential in performing the management functions effectively in today's complex world. Therefore, in this chapter we will outline the characteristics of the external environment, describe the factors in it of major importance to management, and also point out a few techniques for coping with the environment.

After reading this chapter, you should understand the following important terms and concepts:

importance of the environment
environmental complexity
environmental volatility
environmental uncertainty
turbulent environment
direct-action environment
social responsibility
indirect environment
organizational darwinism
buffering
leveling
anticipation
rationing
dominating
changing

The Organization and Its Environment

Earlier we briefly described basic characteristics of the internal variables. These internal factors on which the success of an organization is dependent were the focal point of the schools of management. Each school directed its attention primarily to those aspects it felt management had to affect for success to occur. The scientific management school, for example, concentrated primarily on tasks and technology. Administrative management focused on creating a structure that would facilitate attaining organizational objectives. The human relations school, of course, concentrated on people.

Writers of these early schools of management paid little attention to factors outside of the organization itself. While viewed as a major shortcoming today, it was not seen as one at the time. Each school's contributions, in fact, proved effective in increasing an organization's ability to attain objectives. Thus these schools were, in a sense, correct in concentrating on internal issues because they were of a much higher *relative* importance to an organization's effectiveness and survival.

The Importance of the Environment

The **importance of the environment** and the need to consider forces external to the organization were first incorporated in management thought during the late 1950s. It was one of the major contributions of the systems approach to management, which stressed the need for managers to view their organization as an entity of interrelated parts that is inexorably intertwined with the outside world. The contingency approach extended systems theory by developing the concept that the most appropriate technique in a particular situation is determined by the specific internal and external factors that characterize and affect the organization.

The systems and contingency views arose in response to changes which we will soon discuss that were affecting organizational success to an ever greater degree. Today these changes in the outside world have made the need to consider the environment more important than ever. As Alvar Elbing states, "The external environment of an organization is a subject of increasing challenge for today's managers. In fact, the managers of societies' major organizations—business, education, government—have been forced by recent events to place an increasing focus on a rapidly changing environment and its effect on the internal organization."[1]

Even if change were not so significant, management still would have to consider the environment because, being an open system, an organization is dependent on the outside world for supplies, energy, labor, and customers for its output.

Defining the Environment

The first problem facing the manager wishing to adopt an open-systems perspective is defining the environment. The world, after all, is large, and it would be hopelessly confusing to attempt to consider every factor in it. Man-

FEATURE 4-1

Internal and External Factors Affecting Productivity

As we learned, the combination of specialization and technology led to dramatic increases in productivity during this century. In the past several years, however, productivity has actually declined in American industry. This is a matter of deep concern to both government and industry, and many people are attempting to determine its causes.

Productivity expert John Kendrick of George Washington University has identified five factors that affect productivity in a particular industry. One is the rate at which sales are increasing. Productivity tends to increase more rapidly when sales increase rapidly. This is partly due to greater economies of scale, and partly because to meet increased demand firms must add to their production capacity, which gives them an opportunity to introduce innovations. A second factor is spending on research and development. The more spent on R & D, the greater the long-term productivity gains. A third factor is the average educational level of the workforce. A fourth is the degree to which the industry is affected by business cycles. An industry strongly affected by recessions, such as construction, finds it difficult to make long-term improvements. Kendrick also feels that labor

agement clearly must limit its consideration of the environment to those aspects of the outside world of major importance to the success of an organization. According to Gerald Bell, for example, "An organization's external environment consists of those things outside an organization such as customers, competitors, government units, suppliers, financial firms, and labor pools that are relevant to an organization's operations."[2]

Direct-Action Versus Indirect Environment. One way of defining the environment and making its influence on the organization easier to comprehend is to divide environmental forces into two major categories. In this chapter, we will consider forces external to the organization as either *direct-action* or *indirect*.

According to Elbing, the **direct-action environment** consists of those factors that directly affect and are affected by the organization's operations.[3] These factors would include suppliers, labor unions, laws and governmental regulatory agencies, customers, and competitors. The **indirect environment**

unions tend to restrict productivity gains by forcing management to accept rigid work rules.

A study conducted by *Fortune* magazine suggested two additional factors of major importance. The first, governmental regulation, is most apparent. The cost of meeting governmental requirements has increased enormously. This diverts capital from activities, such as R & D and investing in new plants, that tend to increase productivity. Governmental regulations also now prohibit certain production processes that are highly efficient. The second factor is the degree to which an industry converts electromechanical production processes to electronic technology. Since the 1950s, the relative cost per function of electronic technology has decreased 100,000 times. Thus, it is not surprising that the industries that have been most successful in adopting such technology have also shown the highest productivity gains, or are about to. (Many of the industries that are cornerstones of the American economy, such as automobile manufacturing, steel, and construction, have made relatively little use of electronic technology for production operations.)

Fortune also observes that higher energy costs have adversely affected productivity in some industries. When fuel was cheaper, certain industries deliberately substituted machinery for human labor. Now, rising fuel costs have made some of these older plants so uneconomical they must be shut down or remodeled.

SOURCE: Based on Edward Meadows, "A Close-Up Look at the Productivity Lag," *Fortune*, December 4, 1978, pp.83–84.

is those factors that may not have an immediate, direct effect on operations but nevertheless influence them. These would include such factors as general economic conditions, technology, sociocultural and political developments, interest groups, and the influence of events in foreign countries.

Texas Instruments, for example, is directly affected by suppliers of materials used to manufacture semiconductors, laws regulating pricing and hiring, customer preferences, and the actions of its major competitors such as Hewlett Packard. Texas Instruments must directly respond to these factors to stay in business. However, factors such as new technological developments in the semiconductor field, inflation, recession, and a story by columnist Jack Anderson alleging unethical business practices, while not immediately affecting the daily operations of Texas Instruments, also must be considered for the company to be successful in the long run.

We will describe the major factors in the direct-action and indirect environments in more detail later in the chapter. Before we do, let us focus on some general characteristics of the environment.

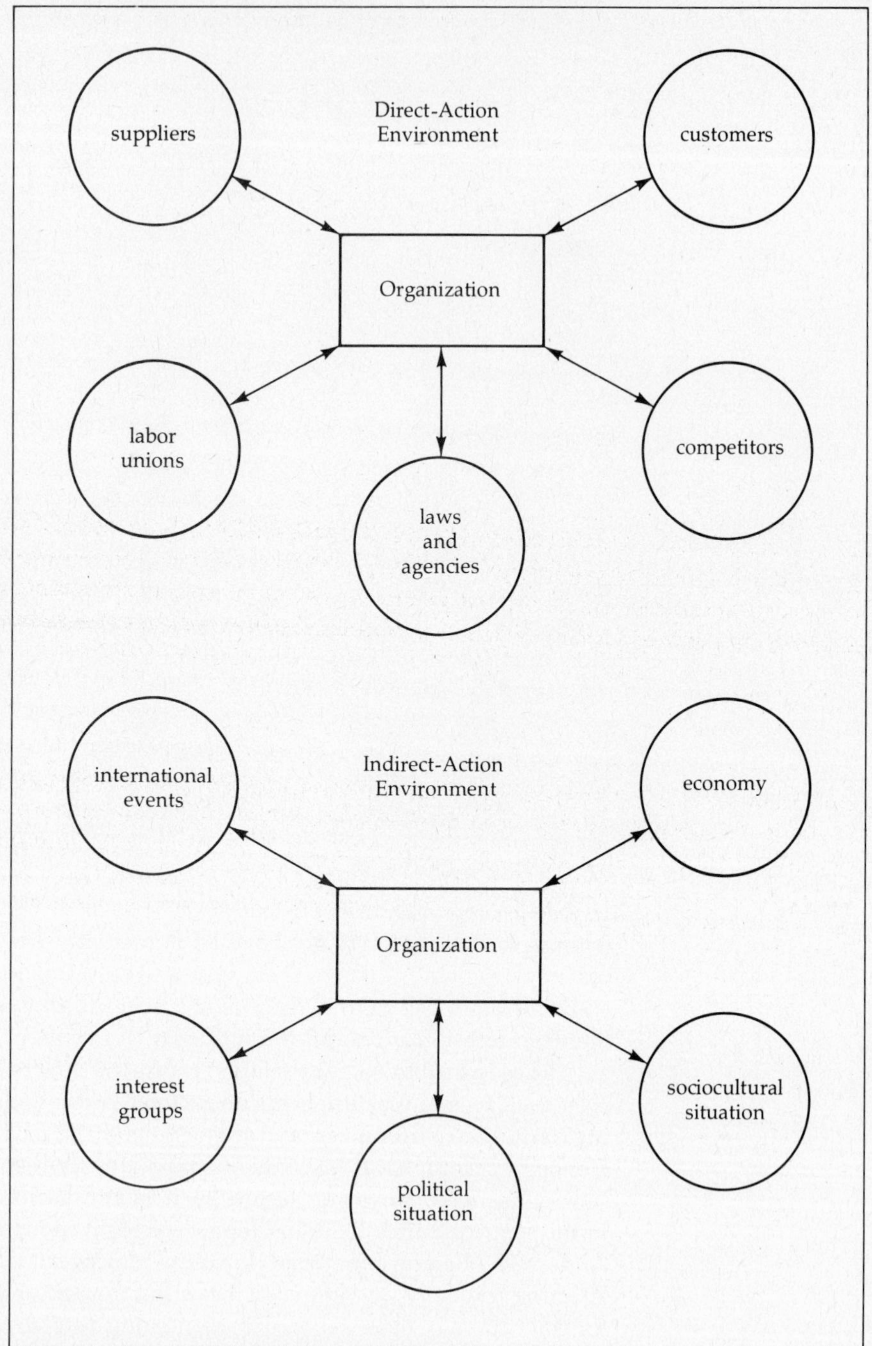

Figure 4-1 The External Environment

Characteristics of the Environment

From even the brief description just given, it should be apparent that many diverse environmental factors can affect an organization. Stressing this environmental diversity, Steiner and Miner state, "In the past, managers concentrated attention on their economic and technical environments. In recent years, however, changes in human attitudes, social values, political forces, and legal liabilities have forced managers to broaden the scope of the environmental forces they consider."[4]

Interrelatedness of Factors

The environmental factors are interrelated. Just as a change in one of the internal variables may affect the others, a change in one external factor can cause changes in others. For example, decreased supplies of oil, primarily due to changes in the political structure and aims of foreign countries, most notably Iran, had a strong affect on general economic conditions in the United States. Higher prices for petroleum products caused a general increase in prices of almost all products. They also catalyzed a wave of governmental action, such as attempts to regulate temperatures in public places, fuel allocation, windfall-profits taxes on oil companies, and the initiation of a massive federal project to overcome dependence on foreign energy.

The direct environment of many organizations was also affected because unions demanded more pay to compensate for inflated prices. Certain firms, such as those manufacturing recreational vehicles and large automobiles, and automobile-dependent tourism suffered a loss of customers. In some cases the effect was beneficial. Business improved for firms supplying insulation, developing synthetic fuels, and producing solar energy devices and electric cars. However, competition in these fields increased as more firms sought a share of this increased business.

Increasing Turbulence. The effect of the interrelatedness of the various environmental factors, according to Emery and Trist, has been to create a **turbulent environment** for contemporary organizations.[5] It no longer is feasible for managers to consider environmental factors independently, as they once could. Managers must realize that the factors are interrelated and changing. Emery and Trist cite the example of an unsuccessful firm in the British food canning industry that "failed entirely to appreciate that a number of outside events were becoming connected with each other in a way that was leading to irreversable general change."[6] As they go on to state, "survival becomes critically linked to what an organization knows of its environment."[7]

Contemporary managers, according to Emery and Trist, need to consider four basic relationships both within and between an organization and its environment. These are illustrated in Figure 4-2.

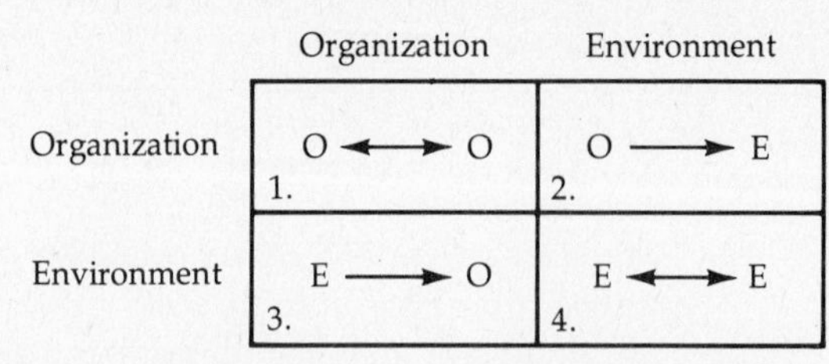

1. O ↔ O refers to the interrelatedness among the internal variables within the organization (discussed in Chapter 3).

2. O → E refers to the organization's transactions with its environment, such as selling its products and services, improving the society it operates in, excessive pollution, etc.

3. E → O refers to the environment's transactions with an organization, such as the acquisition of labor, materials, equipment, etc.

4. E ↔ E refers to the interrelatedness among the factors in the environment, such as the affect of decreased oil suppliers on economic, legal, political and technological factors, all of which affect each other.

Figure 4-2 The Basic Relationships Within and Between an Organization and Its Environment

Complexity

Environmental complexity refers to the number of external factors to which the organization must respond and also to the degree of variety within each factor.[8]

With respect to the *number* of environmental factors to which an organization must respond, an organization that is subject to much government regulation, frequent negotiations with unions, several interest groups, many competitors, and rapid technological development would be considered more complex than an organization only concerned primarily with a few suppliers, a few competitors, no unions, and a field in which technological development is slow. Similarly, with respect to *variety*, an organization that uses only a few raw materials, employs only a few specialists, and deals with only a few firms would have a less complex supply environment than one in which the reverse were true. An organization that uses many different technologies that are undergoing rapid development would also be considered more complex with respect to variety than one that does not.

One researcher summarizes the managerial implication of complexity as follows, "Organizations dealing with non-complex environments have one advantage: there are fewer critically important information categories necessary for decision making."[9]

Rate of Change or Volatility

Volatility refers to the rate at which an organization's environment is changing. Many writers have stated that the environment of contemporary organizations is changing at an increasing rate.[10] Perhaps the best-known work on the subject is Alvin Toffler's best seller *Future Shock*.

However, although the overall rate of change is increasing, environmental volatility is greater for some organizations than for others. For example, two researchers found that the rate of change in the technological and competitive environments was greater in the drug, chemicals, and electronics industries than in the machinery, auto parts, and confectionary industries.[11]

Furthermore, environmental volatility can be greater for some subunits of an organization than others. In many firms, for example, the research and development department, because it must keep track of newly developing technological applications, faces high volatility. The production department, on the other hand, may deal with a relatively slow-changing environment characterized by a steady flow of raw materials and labor. As with complexity, organizations or subunits facing a highly volatile environment must obtain more diverse information in order to make effective decisions concerning its internal variables. This makes decision making more difficult.

Uncertainty

Environmental uncertainty is a function of the amount of information one has about a given factor and one's confidence in that information. Although other writers define uncertainty in different ways, we use this definition because there is general agreement about the relevance of the amount of information and one's confidence in it.[12] If very little information is available, or one has little confidence in its accuracy, the environmental factor is more uncertain than in a situation where adequate information is available and there is good reason to consider it highly accurate. The more uncertain the environment, the more difficult it is to make effective decisions.

The Direct-Action Environment

When considering the effect of the environment on an organization it is important to understand that the *characteristics* of the environment are distinct from but related to the *factors* in the environment. The characteristics of complexity, volatility, and uncertainty are, as we have already implied, descriptive of the nature of both the indirect and direct-action factors.

This relationship will become more apparent as we discuss the major factors in the direct-action environment. These, in turn, are suppliers, laws and governmental agencies, customers, and competitors.

Suppliers

From a systems perspective, an organization is a vehicle for transforming inputs into outputs. The major types of inputs are materials, equipment, en-

Table 4-1 Characteristics of the Environment

1. Interrelatedness: the degree to which changes in one factor affect other factors
2. Complexity: the number of factors that significantly affect the organization and the variety within each
3. Volatility: the relative rate of change
4. Uncertainty: the relative amount of information available about the environment and one's confidence in its accuracy

ergy, capital, or labor. The relationship between the organization and the network of suppliers from which these inputs are obtained is one of the clearest examples of forces in the environment directly influencing the operation and success of an organization. Clearly, if the organization is unable to obtain essential inputs of the quality, quantity, and price that are required to attain its objectives, it cannot possibly succeed in doing so.

In some cases virtually all organizations in a given area deal with the same supplier or at least a comparable one. Therefore, they all are affected equally by the supplier's actions. Energy is a good example. All organizations obtain electricity at rates that are determined by governmental agencies (an example of interrelated external variables) and rarely can they choose an alternative supplier, even if they feel their service is inadequate or too expensive. Changes, such as price increases, introduced by the supplier will affect each organization to the degree it uses that energy source. For example, the drastic increase in gasoline prices in 1979 had some impact on every organization in the world but a much greater relative impact on firms highly dependent on gas, such as trucking and taxi companies.

Materials. Certain organizations are highly dependent on a continuous inflow of materials. Examples would be any manufacturing firm, distributor, or retail store. Failure to obtain supplies as needed can cause severe problems for such organizations. Think about what it would cost General Motors to run out of a part that has to be installed at a particular point on the assembly line. Similarly, if a retail store runs out of stock on a popular item, its customers are likely to go to a competitor.

Firms attempt to avoid materials shortages by negotiating delivery with a network of dependable suppliers and, when possible, arranging for an alternative supplier. They also maintain an inventory of critical supplies that is large enough to meet immediate needs and provides a cushion of safety. Major beer producers, for example, contract with several paper companies to make the cardboard cartons for six packs, and they keep a large supply on hand at all times. In this way they ensure that a strike or production problems at one paper company will not force them to stop offering six packs. However, inventory ties up money for both the material and its storage that might be used for other purposes. This relationship between money and supplies is an obvious example of the interrelatedness of variables.

Capital. Just as there are suppliers of materials, there are suppliers of capital, which the firm needs to grow and flourish. There are several potential suppliers of capital: banks, federal agency loan programs, stockholders, and individual investors who accept notes of the company or buy its bonds. In general, the more successful an organization, the better able it is to negotiate attractive terms with these suppliers and obtain the amount of capital it desires. Small businesses, and in particular new ventures, are experiencing great difficulty in obtaining capital today. Some fear that because of this the very survival of small business in America is in jeopardy.

Labor. An adequate supply of people with the ability and skills required to perform the tasks involved in attaining objectives is vital to an organization's effectiveness. Without people able to use them effectively, sophisticated technology, capital, and materials are of little value. The growth of several industries today is hampered by labor supply shortages. An example is almost every aspect of the computer business, especially firms requiring highly trained technicians and expert programmers and systems designers. Similarly, in 1979 California aerospace firms experienced difficulty obtaining enough qualified engineers and assembly personnel to meet their contract obligations.

In many cases, maintaining a labor supply is a matter of one-on-one negotiations with potential employees and offering competitive salaries and benefits. Most organizations also attempt to cope with labor supply problems through training and development of current personnel. A study by George Steiner asked 259 executives in 202 companies to rate 71 factors of importance to their firm over the next five years. These factors included general management, finance, marketing, materials, production, and products. The two factors rated most important, however, were getting high quality top managers and training future domestic managers.[13] That training managers was rated as more important than profits, customer service, and providing a competitive return to stockholders, is a clear indication of how vital this labor supply is to organizations.

When a firm signs a contract with a labor union it is, in effect, negotiating with a supplier of labor. The proliferation of unions is yet another example of change affecting the need for managers to take external factors into account when making internal decisions. A few decades ago there were few unions, and these were often weak. However, with the passage of the National Labor Relations Act of 1935, employers were required to recognize and negotiate with a union chosen by a majority of its employees. Now, unions represent about 23 percent of the American labor force. Whereas initially only blue-collar workers belonged to unions, they currently represent white-collar workers such as retail clerks, government employees, teachers, and in a few cases even college professors. Thus, a very large organization such as General Motors or AT&T may have to negotiate with many different unions, and therefore labor would be considered a complex variable.

The National Labor Relations Act, the Taft-Hartley Act of 1947, which required unions to bargain in good faith with employers, other legislation, and the countless contracts negotiated between specific unions and employers all directly affect several aspects of internal operations. They determine such things as who can and will perform certain tasks, which people can be promoted, who can be terminated or demoted or transferred, which productivity standards to set, what sort of training is provided, and what sort of incentives management can offer, among others.

Laws and Government Agencies

We already noted how labor legislation has affected management. There are many others as well. Pure capitalism, as Adam Smith recognized in the 1700s, does not exist. Even in basically private enterprise economies such as ours, the interaction between buyers and sellers of every input and output is subject to many legal restrictions. Every organization has a specific legal status, such as sole proprietorship, partnership, corporation, or nonprofit corporation that establishes how it can conduct business and how it will be taxed. The number and complexity of laws specifically directed at business have increased steadily and dramatically during the twentieth century. Whatever management thinks of these laws, it must heed them or face the consequences, which may range from a fine to being forced to go out of business.

The legal environment is one that often is characterized not only by complexity but by rapid change and sometimes even uncertainty. One writer, discussing the rapidly changing legal environment, states that as recently as ten years ago the major legal concern of large companies revolved around matters related to antitrust laws. Her survey of businesses found legal concerns have expanded to include: antitrust, securities and stockholder matters, consumerism, environmental legislation, fair employment practices, safety, government contract requirements, and wage-price controls.[14] These added concerns stem from the passage of laws regulating advertising practices, restraint of trade, price discrimination, acquisition of large blocks of stocks in a competing firm, pollution, and job discrimination on the basis of race, religion, or sex.

Agencies. Organizations are subject not only to federal and state laws but also to demands of governmental regulatory agencies. These agencies enforce laws in their respective field and also introduce requirements of their own that often have the power of law. The Interstate Commerce Commission (ICC) regulates trade practices of businesses operating in more than one state. The Federal Communications Commission (FCC) regulates interstate telephone, telegraph, television, and radio. Its ability to issue and cancel broadcasting licenses gives it enormous power over organizations in these industries. The Securities and Exchange Commission (SEC), among other things, establishes how public companies must conduct financial and accounting practices. The Food and Drug Administration (FDA) regulates both sales and product development in those industries. The Occupational Safety and Health Administration (OSHA) sets standards for working conditions. The Environmental Protection Agency (EPA) regulates activities having an ecological impact. The uncertainty of today's legal environment stems from the fact that some of the requirements of these agencies conflict with one another, yet each has the full weight of the federal government behind it to enforce compliance.

State and Local Legal Requirements. Further complicating the legal environment today is that state and local governmental regulation has also proliferated. All states and most communities require every business to be licensed; limit business to certain locations; impose taxes; and in the case of power, intrastate telephone, and insurance set prices. In some cases, state and local laws modify or amplify federal standards. For example, California's auto emission requirements are more stringent than those set by the EPA. Thus, although an effort was made through the Uniform Commercial Code to create consistency among states with respect to business laws, there remain significant differences. It is easy to imagine what the complexity of these regulations does to an organization conducting business in all 50 states and perhaps several dozen foreign countries.

Customers

There are many who would agree with popular management writer Peter F. Drucker's view that the only valid business purpose is to create a customer. By this Mr. Drucker means that an organization's survival and reason for existence are directly dependent on its ability to identify a customer for its output and meet its needs. The importance of customers to a business is obvious. However, nonprofit and governmental organizations also have "customers" in the broad sense Drucker uses the term. The government of the United States and its management exist solely to serve the needs of United States citizens. That citizens are customers and deserve to be treated as such is, unfortunately, sometimes not apparent in daily interactions with governmental bureaucracies. However, at election time the use of advertising and personal appearances by candidates is a clear indication that prospective office holders view voters as customers who need to be "sold."

An organization's customers determine virtually everything related to its output by deciding which goods and services are desirable and at what price. The need to meet customer requirements thereby affects interactions with suppliers of both material and labor. The impact of customers on the internal variable of structure is very significant. We will learn later that many organizations revolve their structure around the major customer groups on which they most heavily depend.

FEATURE 4-2

Pros and Cons of Government Intervention

Government helps organizations in many ways. Government protects and enforces property rights, a function critical for the smooth operation of business. Governmental agencies also help businesses by providing information about population trends, economic conditions, distribution of labor, and even effective management. Government also directly supports many businesses by being a customer for goods and services, by supporting research and development, by negotiating tariff agreements with foreign countries, and by protecting small business from predatory competitive practices. Sometimes the government even makes direct loans to small business through the Small Business Administration and occasionally to large businesses, as occurred when Lockheed Corporation faced bankruptcy.

On the other hand, the complaints of conflicting regulation and excessive reporting requirements are often justified. In certain industries the number of forms that must be filed is astronomical. For example, largely because of FDA requirements, it takes about seven years to get a new drug on the market. As long ago as 1966, Eli Lilly and Company, a major pharmaceutical firm, had to fill out more than 27,000 forms a year at an estimated direct cost of over $15 million. There are many other examples. Fortunately, spurred by President Carter and Senator Kennedy, in 1979 the federal government began a program to decrease reporting requirements.

Thus there are both costs and benefits of governmental intervention. Often the question of whether a particular requirement is good depends on one's values and on what side of the fence one stands.

SOURCES: "Paper Weight: Companies Often Find They Must Put Forms Ahead of Substance," *Wall Street Journal*, July 16, 1976, p. 1; "Red Tape Blues," *Newsweek*, August 30, 1976, p. 77.

Competitors

The final factor in the direct-action environment, competitors, is an external factor whose effect is never disputed. The management of every business is acutely aware that unless it meets the needs of customers as effectively as its competitors, the firm cannot long survive. In many cases it is not customers but competitors who determine what sort of output can be sold and what price can be charged. This is why the government goes to great length to keep business as competitive as possible. Whereas at one time a powerful business could cope with competitors by using unfair, predatory practices to eliminate them, today's managers usually have to meet innovation by making their organization more innovative and efficient than others in the same field.

It is important to realize that customers are not the only area of competition among organizations. Organizations also often compete for labor, materials, capital, and the right to use certain technical innovations. Thus responses to competition affect such internal factors as working conditions, pay, and how management deals with subordinates, as well as creating a structure that enables the organization to be proactionary. In today's complex organizational society the relationship with competitors sometimes takes peculiar twists. In 1979, for example, General Motors agreed to loan several hundred million dollars to its traditional rival Chrysler Corporation. GM probably wanted to help Chrysler to prevent foreign auto manufacturers from making further gains in the American market. If Chrysler collapsed, a large foreign firm might have been able to pick up its large dealer network and thereby expand quickly.

The Indirect Environment

Factors in the indirect environment usually do not have as marked an effect on the organization's operations as those in the direct-action environment. However, management must also take them into account. For example, the breakdown of the Three Mile Island nuclear power plant in Pennsylvania in 1979 did not just affect Babcock and Wilson, the firm that designed it. Wide news coverage of the event, coupled with the coincidentally simultaneous release of the popular film, *The China Syndrome,* had a strong impact on people's attitudes toward the use of nuclear energy. This indirectly, but noticeably, influenced every organization in the energy field and caused a flurry of activity in many governmental agencies, environmental groups, and consumer protection groups.

The indirect environment is usually more complex and uncertain than the direct. Management is often compelled to make assumptions about it based on incomplete information in order to predict what the impact on the organization will be. We will elaborate on this during our discussion of the planning function, and later in this chapter we will mention some general ways in which organizations attempt to cope with indirect external forces. First, however, let us briefly describe the major factors of the indirect environment. These are technology, economic conditions, sociocultural factors, and political factors.

Technology

Technology is both an internal variable and an external factor of major importance. New technological developments affect the efficiency with which products can be manufactured and sold; when a product will become obsolete; how information can be gathered, stored, and distributed by an organization; and what customers expect of organizations in the way of services and new products, among others.

Several writers have described the very rapid rate at which technology has changed in recent decades and contend this trend will continue.[15] One reason for this rapid change is that more scientists are living today than ever lived before.[16] Some major technological developments that have profoundly affected organizations and society are the computer, laser, xerography, integrated circuits, semiconductors, television, satellite communication, nuclear power, synthetic fuels and foods, and birth control pills. Daniel Bell, a renowned sociologist, believes that the capability to miniaturize is the technological development future generations will consider most remarkable.[17] Today innovations such as microdots and magnetic bubble memories make it possible to store in a small container what once would have required buildings full of file cabinets. Semiconductors and microprocessors have made calculators, small computers, and a host of new games widely affordable. They also have changed the nature of wristwatches from mechanical to electronic.

Clearly, an organization that deals directly with high technology must be able to respond quickly to new developments and create innovations of its own. However, today all organizations need to keep abreast of at least those developments affecting the efficiency of operations in order to remain competitive.

Economic Conditions

Management also must assess the effect changes in general economic conditions will have on the organization's operations. Economic conditions affect the cost of all inputs and the ability of customers to buy certain goods and services, particularly those that are nonessential. If inflation is predicted, for example, management may find it desirable to increase inventories of supplies and negotiate fixed-cost labor contracts to hold down costs in the future. It may also find it desirable to borrow because when repayment is due the money will be worth less, offsetting the cost of interest. Similarly, if a recession is predicted, the organization may find it necessary to reduce its inventory of products because they may not be saleable, or it may be forced to reduce the size of its labor force, or at least postpone plans for expansion.

Economic conditions can strongly affect an organization's ability to obtain capital. This is largely because the federal government often attempts to minimize shifts in broad economic conditions through adjustments in taxation, the money supply, and the interest rate charged by the Federal Reserve Bank. If the Federal Reserve Bank increases its requirements for loans and raises interest rates, commercial banks must follow suit. This makes loans harder to obtain and more expensive for business. Similarly, a tax cut increases the amount people can spend for nonessentials and tends to stimulate business.

Variations Among Organizations. It is important to understand that a given change of economic conditions may have a positive effect on some organizations and a negative one on others. For example, historically the film business has prospered when economic conditions are worst. There are also local variations. Whereas a recession might badly hurt most retail stores, for example, those in very affluent neighborhoods might scarcely feel the effects. Organizations operating multinationally often find dealing with economic conditions a particularly complex, important concern. Fluctuations in the price of the dollar relative to other currencies in recent years have caused some large firms to gain or lose millions of dollars overnight.

Sociocultural Factors

All organizations operate within at least one culture. Therefore, sociocultural factors, including the prevailing attitudes, values, and customs of that culture, influence the organization. For example, the American public has certain expectations and values about what constitutes ethical business practice. Such practices as paying bribes to obtain contracts or political favors, promotion on the basis of favoritism instead of competence, and spreading unfavorable rumors about a competitor are considered unethical and immoral here, even when not actually illegal. In other nations, however, such practices are seen as normal and accepted business practice because of differing sociocultural conditions.

Another example of sociocultural influence on business practice is the traditional and unfortunate stereotype that women are poor risks or incompetent as managers. This attitude is reflected in discriminatory hiring and promotion practices which, although illegal, are difficult to eliminate.[18] Studies also document that attitudes of workers are changing. Generally, younger workers seem to dislike traditional authoritarian relationships and desire more autonomy and social interaction in work.[19] Other studies indicate that many (but not all) blue- and white-collar workers want jobs that offer more challenge, freedom, and self-esteem.[20] These changing attitudes directly affect what employees consider fair organizational practices. They become particularly important to managers in the essential function of motivating people to actually work toward organizational objectives.

Sociocultural factors also affect the products or services an organization provides. A good example of this is the clothing business. People are often willing to pay much more for an item bearing the name of a high-status designer such as Pierre Cardin or Gloria Vanderbilt because they believe it adds to their personal prestige. Another example is the current sentiment against nuclear power plants, which has had a drastic effect on firms in that business. Another is the demand by certain groups that breakfast cereals should contain less sugar and that advertising aimed at children should be highly regulated. The new awareness of the importance of exercise and good nutrition has led to a proliferation of products such as jogging shoes and vitamin supplements.

Sociocultural factors affect the ways in which organizations can do business. For example, several companies have been forced by social pressure to stop doing business with South Africa because of that country's racial apartheid policies. More apparent and widespread is the impact of the way a person expects to be treated as a customer on the daily business practices of retail stores and restaurants. A major sociocultural influence on organizations has been an increased emphasis on the concept of social responsibility, a subject we will discuss later.

Stressing the need for management to consider sociocultural influences, Reginald Jones, chairman of the board of General Electric, states that organizations must be able to "anticipate the changing expectations of society, and serve them more effectively than competing institutions. This means that the corporation itself must change, consciously evolving into an institution adapted to the new environment."[21]

Managing in a Multinational Environment. The effect of sociocultural forces on organizational operations is particularly noticeable when management must cope with a multinational environment. In fact, in this context culture may be a direct, rather than indirect, factor. Each country has its own values, attitudes, and customs. Inadequate knowledge of these cultural factors can cause serious problems in business negotiations and transactions.[22] Studies have shown that special training in the cultural characteristics of the country can decrease problems for managers posted abroad.[23]

Behaviors that are valued and preferences in leadership style also can vary markedly among countries. Studies have shown that being supervised in a coersive manner was strongly preferred in Switzerland but not in Norway. Managers in Greece and India have a favorable view toward passive and disinterested subordinates, whereas British managers do not.[24] The Japanese are famous for their reliance on group decision making and heavy stress on personal honor.

In today's world, even organizations that are not actively conducting business in other countries are frequently involved with foreign firms. There is a vast international trade in supplies, with American firms attempting to sell goods abroad and foreign firms attempting to sell goods here. Thus it is not unusual for a business to have foreign competitors and be affected by foreign economic conditions.

Political Environment

Two aspects of the political environment are of particular concern to managers. One is the relative pro vs. antibusiness sentiment of the administration, legislature, and courts. Strongly related to sociocultural trends in a democratic nation, this influences governmental action on such matters as corporate income taxes, preferential tax treatment or trade tariffs, minority hiring and promotion requirements, consumer protection legislation, safety standards, pollution standards, wage and price controls, and the relative power of labor and management. In recent years there has been a trend toward

FEATURE 4-3

Social Awareness Becomes a Standard for Promotion

More and more companies are making it clear that those who aspire to the top levels of management must be aware of changing social needs and demands, and be capable of directing the company's activities to meet them in an acceptable fashion. For example, A. W. Clausen, president and chief executive officer of Bank of America National Trust & Savings Assn., set forth several criteria which are to be used in selecting senior management people at the bank. One of them is *sociopolitical sensitivity*. Clausen says, " . . . it is imperative that the senior corporate manager understand . . . sociopolitical forces. While there are many of these forces, if I were asked today to rank them in terms of their importance . . . I would suggest this order: consumerism, demands of minorities, demands of women and the crisis of the environment. We do not feel that anyone can aspire to a senior management position in Bank of America . . . without an acute awareness of the impact these forces may have on our operations."

SOURCE: George A. Steiner, "Institutionalizing Corporate Social Decisions," *Business Horizons*, December 1975.

antibusiness sentiment in the political environment. This has led to more stringent consumer protection laws and the windfall profits tax President Carter proposed for oil companies in 1979 which was recently signed into law.

The other factor of importance is the political stability and policies of a country. This most strongly affects multinational firms. A positive political relationship between a foreign country and the United States government enables American firms to trade and set up operations in that country. For example, when The People's Republic of China was recognized, one of the world's largest potential markets was opened up to American business for the first time. However, political instability in a foreign country may make business difficult or impossible, whatever the formal relationship the current government has with the United States. For example, many months before the hostage incident in Iran, most American firms were forced to close down their operations after the Shah was deposed in 1979 because the political climate had gone from very stable to very unstable.

Local Community. For the majority of organizations, the prevailing climate in the local community in which they operate is the most significant aspect of the political environment after federal influence. Almost every community has specific laws and attitudes toward business that determine where one can operate certain types of businesses. Some towns, for example, go out of their way to provide incentives for industrial concerns to start operations within their borders. Others will fight in court for years to keep out a proposed manufacturing facility. In some communities the political climate favors making business the mainstay of the tax base. In others property holders prefer to absorb a greater share of the costs of government in order either to lure new businesses to their community, or to be able to do without the pollution and other problems a business may bring along with the jobs it provides.

Therefore, many organizations make a concerted effort to maintain good relations with the communities in which they operate. This may take the form of contributing to local schools and charities, or providing managerial talent in lieu of cash gifts. For example, I. Magnin, a department store chain, sponsored the King Tut exhibit when it came to San Francisco in 1979. McDonald's sometimes has helped charity drives by donating a quarter for each milkshake purchased within a specific time. Pizza Hut, a subsidiary of Pepsico Company, agreed to provide financing and grant more concessions to minorities after meeting with Governor Jerry Brown of California.

Figure 4-3 illustrates the interaction between the internal and external environments, completing our contingency model of organization.

Coping with the Environment

We have described a number of environmental factors that directly and indirectly influence organizational operations and the organization's ability to succeed. Obviously, since these factors affect the organization's very survival, management must be able not only to identify the factors in its environment but also to cope with them.

In this respect organizations are similar to biological organisms. According to Charles Darwin's theory of evolution, the species that have survived have done so because they were able to evolve and adapt to changes in their environment. Organizations, too, must adapt to changes in their environment in order to survive and be effective. Thus management must follow a policy of **organizational darwinism** to ensure that in a world of rapid change where only the fit survive, their organization will not be among those that become extinct.

Let us therefore briefly describe some techniques organizations can use to adapt to change and respond to environmental factors.

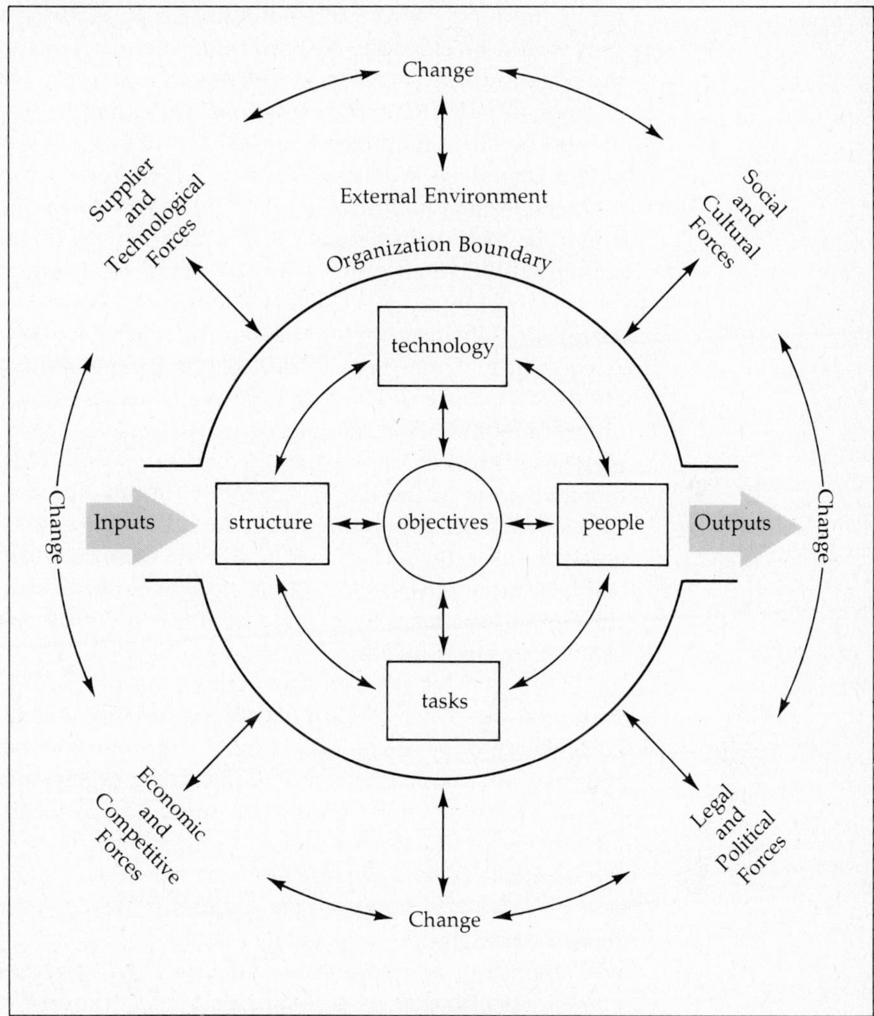

Figure 4-3 Contingency Model of Organization

SOURCE: Adapted from Howard M. Carlisle, *Situational Management* (New York: American Management Association, 1973) p. 29.

Coping Techniques

There are a variety of techniques that organizations can use successfully to cope with their environment. James Thompson, a management researcher and theorist, describes a number of these as follows:[25]

Buffering. **Buffering** techniques are used to soften the impact an environmental factor will have on the organization. Stockpiling of materials and supplies, repairing equipment on a regular schedule of preventative maintenance, training personnel, and maintaining an adequate inventory of outputs would be examples of buffering. These precautionary measures enable the organization to avoid the effects of environmental change to varying degrees, depending on the situation. For example, by maintaining a supply of steel equal to its projected needs for 120 days, General Motors would be able to operate at full capacity, even if there were a protracted strike by steel workers. Formal planning, which will be discussed later, is also considered a buffering technique because it is a mechanism for predicting change and coping with it in an orderly way to attain organizational objectives.

Leveling. **Leveling** techniques are similar to buffering in many respects. According to Thompson, "whereas buffering absorbs environmental fluctuations, smoothing or leveling involves attempts to reduce fluctuations in the environment."[26] An example of leveling is the practice of telephone and electric utilities to offer price incentives to those who use services at low demand times of the day or charge premiums for use during peak periods. This spreads the demand for their services more evenly through the day and week. Retail firms and others faced with seasonal fluctuations use the leveling technique of price incentives, too, in order to spread sales more evenly throughout the year. Special air fares for midweek and night flights are another example of leveling.[27]

Anticipation. **Anticipation** involves acquiring information about occurring or probable environmental changes and taking action on the basis of this information. For example, a manufacturing organization usually tries to anticipate demand for its product in order to take actions such as effectively scheduling production and supply orders, hiring personnel, and maintaining adequate inventories. Other areas in which organizations frequently assess changes are competition, customer needs, technology, and human resource availability. Long-range planning, predicting what the organization will attempt to do two or more years in the future, and research and development are also examples of anticipation techniques.[28]

Rationing. **Rationing** is allocating organizational resources according to a system of priorities. Organizations resort to rationing when they are not able to serve all of their customers or demands for a product or service. Rationing also occurs when organizations must assign different priorities to their products and services. For example, Thompson states, "The Post Office may assign priority to first-class mail, attending to lesser classes only when the priority task is completed. Manufacturers of suddenly popular items may ration allotments to wholesalers or dealers, and if inputs are scarce, may assign priorities to alternative use of those resources."[29] Although rationing is a solution, organizations would rather not have to resort to it. As Thompson states, "Some system of priorities to the allocation of capacity under adverse conditions is essential if a technology is to be instrumentally effective—if action is to be other than random."[30]

Dominating. In all the techniques described above, the organization attempts to assess change and adapt its practices to it. In some situations, however, the organization may have the power to change the environmental factor, as opposed to changing itself. Through **dominating** techniques the organization makes an effort "to control events in its environment and reduce its dependency on it."[31] There are a number of ways in which organizations can attempt to dominate successfully. By developing relationships with many suppliers and customers, organizations become less dependent and will not be as strongly affected by difficulties with any one of these. Organizations also can gain more control over their environment by developing cooperative exchanges and making formal contracts between labor and management, with suppliers, and with customers. This is because a contract is a promise enforceable by law, which means the organization is not dependent on the good will of outside people or organizations to get exactly what it agreed to. Advertising, public relations, and lobbying are also examples of dominating techniques.

Changing. If an organization is not as successful as it would like to be in coping with a specific factor in its environment, it can respond by **changing** itself, its operations, or its output. For example, if management perceives that sales are not as high as possible, it can change its product line to one better suited to customer needs or the competitive situation. As new technological developments occur, the organization may find it desirable to change its operations to make use of them. Many organizations, for example, created data processing departments in order to use computers effectively. If an organization is having difficulty with key suppliers, it may be able to buy one of its existing suppliers or build a plant to manufacture the needed material itself. Changing is often the most difficult response to environmental factors to implement and is the essence of organizational darwinism. In general the most successful organizations of today are those that have proven themselves most adept in evolving in response to a rapidly changing environment. In Part 6, we will describe many techniques for accomplishing change.

When taking action in response to its environment, management must take into account both the interrelationships among the environmental factors and the ways in which they interact with the internal variables. These many potential interrelationships are shown in Figure 4-3, which amplifies our model of the organization's sociotechnical subsystem with the external factors.

The Proper Role of Business in Society

As we have noted, all organizations exist within a culture, and the attitudes and values of people within that culture often change. Due to changing attitudes and values within the United States, the role of business within society has become a major issue. The number of answers to the question, "What responsibility does business have, if any, to the society in which it operates?" are almost as varied in specifics as organizations and managers. However, most of these opinions fit within one of two broad categories.

Two Views of Social Responsibility

Profit and Efficiency. One view, closely associated with its strong advocate, Nobel Prize-winning economist Milton Friedman, is that the proper role of business is "to use its resources and energies in activities designed to increase its profits so long as it stays within the rules of the game. . . . (and) engages in open competition, without deception and fraud."[32] Thus, according to Friedman, the socially responsible business is one that is concerned primarily with efficiency and providing its owners with the best possible return on investment, within the parameters established by law and ethical conduct. Solving social problems, such as eliminating racial inequity and poverty, is the task of government. If business directly deals with social problems, the costs of doing so will be reflected in the prices of goods and services and therefore be unfairly borne to a high degree by the customers and owners of businesses, rather than by the taxpayers as a whole.

Direct Social Activism. Other writers contend, in contrast, that because businesses have a responsibility to society, they should channel some of their resources and efforts toward social ends. Profits and stockholder interests should not be management's only concern. The organization should, if necessary, sacrifice a little for the welfare and improvement of society. In support of this view, Keith Davis states that business must be actively socially responsible because of "an iron law of responsibility," contending that "in the long run those who do not use power in a manner that society considers responsible, will tend to lose it."[33] For example, organizations may lose power through increased government regulation, loss of customers to a competitor viewed as more responsible, and poor social conditions in the community that diminish purchasing by customers.

Arguments for and Against Direct Social Responsibility

Arguments for and against each of the views just presented are illustrated in Table 4-2.

Although one's views on the "correct" role of business in society is a reflection of one's own values and, thus, there is no one right or wrong answer, it is our contention that organizations should channel some of their resources and efforts toward their society. Discussing this issue, John Miner states that "organizations must adapt to the cultural environments in which they operate or change the environment; otherwise there is a high probability that they will not survive. In the case of social responsibility pressures the major response has been to change the organization and adapt to the environment."[34] It is our position that by being socially responsible, the costs of the related activities will be justified by various improvements in different sectors of society as well as more favorable attitudes by the public.

Table 4-2 Arguments for and Against Social Responsibility

A. Major Arguments *For* Social Responsibility:

1. It is in the *long-run self-interest* of the firm to promote and improve the communities where it does business.
2. It improves the *public image* of the firm.
3. It increases the *viability of the business system.* Business exists because it gives society benefits. Society can amend or take away its charter. This is the "iron law of responsibility."
4. It is necessary to *avoid government regulation.*
5. *Sociocultural norms require it.*
6. Laws cannot be passed for all circumstances. Thus, business must assume responsibility to maintain an *orderly legal society.*
7. It is in the *stockholder's best interest.* It will improve the price of stock in the long run (as John Narver argues in the March 1971 *Academy of Management Journal*) because the stock market will view the company as less risky and open to public attack and, therefore, award it a higher price-earnings ratio.
8. Society should *give business a chance* to solve social problems that government has failed to solve.
9. *Business,* by some groups, *is* considered to be *the institution with the financial and human resources* to solve social problems.
10. *Problems can become profitable* if firms become involved.
11. *Prevention of problems is better than cures*—so let business solve problems before they become too great.

B. Major Arguments *Against* Social Responsibility:

1. *Violates profit maximization.*
2. *Cost* of social responsibility too great and would increase prices too much.
3. *Business lacks social skills* to solve societal problems.
4. *It would dilute business's primary purposes.*
5. *It would weaken U.S. balance of payments* because price of goods will have to go up to pay for social programs.
6. *Business already has too much power.* Such involvement would make business too powerful.
7. *Business lacks accountability to the public.* Thus the public would have no control over its social involvement.
8. *Such business involvement lacks broad public support.*

SOURCE: McGuire, *Contemporary Management: Issues and Viewpoints,* © 1974, p. 616. Reprinted by permission of Prentice-Hall, Inc., Englewood Cliffs, New Jersey.

This could result in greater customer loyalty and less government regulation.

We believe that organizations do not have to set up a food collection service for the natives of Pago Pago to be socially responsible. Rather, organizations should analyze their direct and indirect-action environments and choose those social responsibility programs which will help them most. One should not consider social responsibility something that only large organiza-

FEATURE 4-4

Managers Speak Out on Business Ethics

A number of groups, committees and individuals have made attempts to draw up a code of ethics.

Businessmen and corporations have offered rules of thumb:

- Quaker Oats: "A reasonable and practical standard of ethical behavior in business decisions and actions is that which would not be embarrassing to you, your family, or our company if it were revealed publicly and, more fundamentally, that behavior which would seem right to those who live by the best standards and moralities."
- Fletcher Byrom, chairman of Koppers Corp.: "Possibly the best test—for a person with a family—might be to think whether you would be happy to tell your spouse and children the details of the action you are contemplating, or whether you would be willing to appear on television and explain your actions in detail."

Chase Manhattan Bank drew up its own code of ethics and chairman David Rockefeller expounded its principles in a speech.

tions can do. The neighborhood cleaner or pizza place are fulfilling a socially responsible role by sponsoring a neighborhood baseball or bowling team. The small manufacturing company that allows grade schools to visit their operations is being socially responsible. So is the hospital that sends a representative to a high school to discuss careers in the health industry.

Research investigating executive perceptions of corporate social responsibility indicates that there is a clear shift toward greater social responsibility by business. These executives felt that social responsibility pressures were real, important, and will continue.[35] Other studies have shown that top executives have become involved in community work as volunteers.[36] However, the biggest constraint executives mentioned in developing social responsibility programs is the pressure by owners and managers for increased earnings per share on a quarterly basis. Pressure for short-run profits and earnings directs managers away from allocating some of their resources to social responsibility programs.[37] As we discuss in conjunction with planning and control, this problem can be alleviated if an organization sets specific objectives in social responsibility areas and measures performance in these various areas.

"In developing such a code, I think we are reaffirming our own belief that ethics are an essential ingredient of business behavior; that honesty, integrity and fair dealings are indeed sound business practices as well as vital parts of our moral underpinning.

"Unfortunately, cynicism has reached the point in many parts of our society where such reaffirmation is necessary and where dishonesty and unfairness need to be restigmatized in the minds of many."

As an example of ethics in action, Rockefeller cited Chase's policy to make no loans to South Africa that tend to support that government's apartheid policies or reinforce discriminatory business practices.

Harold M. Williams, chairman of the Securities and Exchange Commission, said: "In my judgment there is no such thing as corporate morality or corporate ethic. There is only a corporate environment that is conducive and supportive of individual morality and ethics.

"My own conviction is that ethics begin with the individual and end with the individual and, in essence, they do not change once the individual dons a corporate hat."

Williams looked to corporate leadership, which he accused of being invisible, to set the tone. A declared high-level commitment to ethical behavior, he said, would make it "harder for lower levels of an organization to countermand that commitment."

SOURCE: John F. Sims, "Business Grapples with Complex Ethics Issue," *Atlanta Constitution* (UPI), December 25, 1977, p. 2E.

Still, when all is said and done, there is no escaping the fact that profit is essential to the survival of a business organization. Profit is to a business what food, water, and air are to an individual. Just as a drowning person cannot afford to spend energy worrying about starvation in India, the unsuccessful enterprise must ensure its own survival before tackling major problems of society. Unless a business is able to make a profit, the question of coping with social responsibilities voluntarily is largely academic.

SUMMARY

Management must consider factors external to its organization because an organization is an open system continuously dependent on an interchange of inputs and outputs with its environment.

Factors in the environment can be described as direct action or indirect, depending on whether they have an immediate effect on the organization's operations. All of these factors are interrelated and interactive. Different factors vary in importance among organizations and subunits of the same organization. Similarly, the environment may have different characteristics with respect to volatility, complexity, and uncertainty for different organizations.

Volatility refers to the rate at which the environment changes. Many writers feel the environment is moving toward turbulent change. Complexity refers to the number of external factors to which the organization must respond and also to the variety within each factor. Uncertainty is a function of the amount of information available on an environmental factor and one's confidence in its validity.

The major factors in the direct-action environment are suppliers of materials, labor, and capital, laws and governmental agencies, customers, and competitors.

The major factors in the indirect environment are technology, economic conditions, sociocultural factors, and the political environment.

In order to survive and attain their objectives, organizations must be able to respond effectively to environmental change and adapt in accordance with the concept of organizational darwinism.

There are several techniques for coping with the environment. One is buffering, which is an attempt to lessen the impact of environmental change. Leveling refers to efforts to reduce fluctuations in the environment. Anticipation involves acquiring information about occurring or probable environmental changes and acting on it. Rationing is allocating resources according to a system of priorities. Through dominating techniques the organization may be able to control events in the environment or reduce its dependence on certain factors. Last, but not least, if the organization wishes to be more successful in a given area, it can respond by changing its outputs, operations, or structure.

The question of what the proper role of business is in society is of great concern today. One basic view on this subject is that of Milton Friedman. He holds that the proper role of business is to be as efficient as possible and earn the greatest profit it can for shareholders, within the bounds of law and ethics. The other viewpoint contends that business ought to use some of its resources to directly aid society and solve social problems. There are strong arguments in favor of each view, none being "right," since the issue is one of values, not absolutes. However, in the contemporary world it probably is necessary for business to look beyond profits and do what it can to be a good citizen of the society in which it operates.

REVIEW QUESTIONS

1. Distinguish between the direct-action environment and the indirect environment.
2. What is environmental uncertainty a function of?
3. Discuss the major factors in the direct-action environment.
4. Discuss the major factors in the indirect environment.
5. Why is it important to understand variations among organizations?
6. Why must management assess the effect changes in general economic conditions have on organizational operations?
7. In what situation should management follow a policy of organizational darwinism?
8. Describe these techniques an organization can use to successfully cope with its environment: buffering, leveling, anticipating, rationing, dominating, and changing.

9. What are some arguments for direct social responsibility and some arguments against direct social responsibility?
10. Discuss the two aspects of the political environment of particular concern to managers.

DISCUSSION QUESTIONS

11. Briefly describe the basic relationship within and between an organization and its environment.
12. From your own experience discuss an example of sociocultural influence.
13. How does social responsibility differ in these three organizations: steel mill, hospital, university?
14. Discuss this statement: "Let the free market system determine the outcome of society."
15. Compare and contrast the different types of environmental states discussed in the chapter and give an example of each.

CASE INCIDENT

Campus Services, Inc.

It had been a long, difficult, but exciting time since John Clark entered college to earn a business degree. A Vietnam veteran, Clark went to school on the G.I. bill. To help support his wife and daughter, Clark started a sandwich delivery service. Operating out of his trailer with the assistance of his wife, Clark made and delivered sandwiches to downtown students who wanted good late-night snacks. As the natural food movement took hold, Clark added yogurt, nuts, fruit, and other health foods. By his senior year, Clark's entrepreneurial venture had become a full-time, growing business which employed seven full-time employees and ten part-time workers. Fifteen years after John Clark's graduation, Clark's Campus Services, Inc. had sales of $18 million dollars and was about to become a fifty-state franchise operation.

Along with his business activities, Clark stayed productively busy in social and community work. One of his favorite activities was being education director of the local chapter of the Young President's Organization, an association of business people who had attained chief executive status before age forty. His major project was a "You and the American Economy" program, an annual event. Top seniors from the area's eight universities were invited to take part in a weekend retreat where meaningful and open dialogues were established between students and business people. The format was relatively simple. Four presidents would describe to the fifty students how they had attained their present positions and what their basic business philosophy was. This, according to the program brochure, would be followed by a "no holds barred" question-and-answer session.

Clark's first assignment was to return to his alma mater, and he anticipated this engagement with much pleasure. After being introduced by one of his former professors, Clark told the students all about Campus Services, Inc. and himself. Clark believed he had a story that would have special meaning to each student. After all, it wasn't too long ago that Clark had been in their position. Right after his presentation, Clark said he was ready for questions. Almost immediately, one of the students commented, "Mr. Clark, you've explained how you built your business and how profitable it has become, but isn't it true that making a profit ultimately leads to the destruction of our human and natural resources? It seems to me that you've wasted your education."

Questions

1. If you were Clark, how would you reply to the student's comment?
2. Realistically, what is the primary social responsibility of business?
3. How can a business sell itself to its various publics, for example, customer, employees, stockholders, and the many others that are less directly affected by its activities?

NOTES

1. Alvar O. Elbing, "On the Applicability of Environmental Models," in J. W. McGuire, ed. *Contemporary Management* (Englewood Cliffs, NJ: Prentice-Hall, 1974) p. 283.
2. Gerald D. Bell, "Organizations and the External Environment," in McGuire, op. cit., p. 260.
3. Elbing, op. cit., p. 282.
4. George A. Steiner and John B. Miner, *Management Policy and Strategy: Text, Readings, and Cases* (New York: Macmillan, 1977), pp. 41–42.
5. F. W. Emery and E. L. Trist, "The Causal Texture of Organizational Environments," *Human Relations*, vol. 18 (1963), pp. 20–26.
6. Ibid., p. 23.
7. Ibid., p. 24.
8. John Child, "Organizational Structure, Environment, and Performance: The Role of Strategic Choice," *Sociology*, vol. 6 (1972), p. 2–21.
9. Ray Jurkovich, "A Core Typology of Organizational Environments," *Administrative Science Quarterly*, vol. 19 (1974): no. 3, pp. 380–394.
10. Emery and Trist, op. cit.; Tom Burns and G. M. Stalker, *The Management of Innovation* (London: Tavistock Publications, 1961).
11. Raymond Aldag and Ronald Storey, "Environmental Uncertainty," *Proceedings*, Academy of Management, 1975.
12. Paul R. Lawrence and Jay W. Lorsch, *Organization and Environment* (Homewood, IL: Irwin, 1967); Henry Tosi, Raymond Aldag, and Ronald Storey, "On the Measurement of the Environment: An Assessment of the Lawrence and Lorsch Environmental Subscales," *Administrative Science Quarterly*, vol. 18 (1973): no. 1, pp. 27–36; H. Kirk Downey, Don Hellriegel, and John W. Slocum, Jr., "Environmental Uncertainty: The Construct and Its Application," *Administrative Science Quarterly*, vol. 20 (1975): no. 4, p. 613–629.
13. George A. Steiner, *Strategic Factors in Business Success* (New York: Financial Executives Research Foundation, 1969).

14. Eleanor Carruth, "The 'Legal Explosion' Has Left Business Shell-Shocked," *Fortune*, April 1973.
15. Emanuel G. Mesthene, *Technological Change: Its Impact on Man and Society* (New York: Mentor Books, 1970); Alvin Toffler, *Future Shock* (New York: Bantam Books, Inc., 1970).
16. Charles R. Walker, *Technology, Industry, and Man: The Age of Acceleration* (New York: McGraw-Hill, 1968).
17. Daniel Bell, *The Coming of Post-Industrial Society* (New York: Basic Books, 1973).
18. Ben Rosen and Tom H. Jerdee, "Sex Stereotyping in the Executive Suite," *Harvard Business Review*, vol. 52 (1974), pp. 45–48.
19. John B. Miner, *The Human Constraint: The Coming Shortage of Managerial Talent* (Washington, D.C.: BNA Books, 1974).
20. *Work in America*, Report of a Special Task Force to the Secretary of Health, Education, and Welfare (Cambridge, MA: MIT Press, 1973).
21. Reginald H. Jones, "What Is the Future of the Corporation?" (Address to the Detroit Economic Club, Detroit, Michigan, November 25, 1974).
22. Ion Amariuta, D. T. Rutenberg, and R. Staelin, "How American Executives Disagree About the Risks of Investing in Eastern Europe," *Academy of Management Journal*, vol. 22 (1979): no. 1, pp. 138–151.
23. Fred Friedler, T. Mitchell, and H. C. Triandis, "The Culture Assimilator: An Approach to Cross-Cultural Training," *Journal of Applied Psychology*, vol. 55 (1971), pp. 95–102.
24. E. C. Ryterband and G. V. Barrett, "Manager's Values and Their Relationship to the Management of Tasks: A Cross-Cultural Comparison," in B. M. Bass, R. Cooper and J. A. Haas, eds., *Managing for Accomplishment* (Lexington, MA: D. C. Heath & Company, 1970), pp. 226–260.
25. James D. Thompson, *Organizations in Action* (New York: McGraw-Hill Book Company, 1967).
26. Ibid., p. 21.
27. Ibid., p. 21.
28. Bell, op. cit., p. 282.
29. Thompson, op. cit., p. 23.
30. Ibid., p. 23.
31. Bell, op. cit., p. 281.
32. Milton Friedman, *Capitalism and Freedom* (Chicago: University of Chicago Press, 1963).
33. Keith Davis, "The Meaning and Scope of Social Responsibility," in McGuire *Contemporary Management*, pp. 630–631.
34. John B. Miner, *The Management Process*, 2d. ed. (New York: Macmillan, Inc., 1978), p. 571.
35. S. L. Holmes, "Executive Perceptions of Corporate Social Responsibility," *Business Horizons*, vol. 19 (1976): no. 3, pp. 34–40.
36. D. H. Fenn, "Executives As Community Volunteers," *Harvard Business Review*, vol. 49 (1971), pp. 4–16, 156–157.
37. L. L. Byars and M. H. Mescon, *The Other Side of Profit* (Philadelphia: W. B. Saunders Company, 1975).

PART ONE CASE STUDY 1

Henry Ford Versus Alfred P. Sloan, Jr.

"At Ford Motor Company there was only *one* person who made decisions of any consequence."

Henry Ford and Alfred P. Sloan, Jr. were two of the greatest managers in history. They confronted one another head on during the 1920s, the period in which the concept of management as a profession and as a scholarly discipline first arose.

Henry Ford was an archetype of the early dictatorial entrepreneur: a true loner, highly opinionated, insistent on always having his own way, scornful of theories and "useless" book learning. Ford considered his executives "helpers." If a "helper" dared to contradict Ford or to make an important decision on his own, that person usually became unemployed. At Ford Motor Company there was only *one* person who made decisions of any consequence. Ford described Alfred P. Sloan's proposal for reorganizing General Motors as "a great big chart with nice round berries . . . The buck is passed to and fro and all the responsibility is dodged by individuals, following the lazy notion that two heads are better than one." Ford's own general attitudes were summed up by the famous philosophy: "Any customer can have a car painted any color he wants, as long as it is black."

Ford had ample reason to sneer at Sloan's new-fangled ideas for GM. Ford made those black Model Ts so inexpensively almost any working person could afford one.

In the space of about a dozen years Ford built a tiny company into a giant industry that changed American society. Moreover, he did it by figuring out how to build a car that sold for as low as $290 while paying his workers one of the highest wages going—the then magnificent sum of $5 a week. So many people bought Model Ts that in 1921 Ford Motor Company held 56 percent of the American passenger car market and most of the worldwide market, too. General Motors, which at the time was several semi-independent small companies chicken wired into a confused hodgepodge, had but 13 percent of the market and was teetering toward bankruptcy.

Fortunately, to save its enormous investment in General Motors stock, the Du Pont family took the company over before it went broke. Pierre S. Du Pont, himself an important pioneer of modern management, installed Alfred P. Sloan, Jr. as president. Sloan quickly converted the plans Ford had laughed at into reality, thereby putting into effect what remains the primary form of large company management. The reorganized GM had a large, strong management team, with many people authorized to make important decisions on their own.

Sloan's personality contrasted sharply with that of Ford. Whereas the latter was notoriously rigid, opinionated, and intuitive, Sloan's favorite words were "concept," "methodology," and "rationality." The buck was not passed to and fro, as Ford predicted. Rather, each manager was given definite responsibilities and the freedom to do what was necessary to meet them. Equally important, Sloan devised an elaborate control system to ensure that he and other top managers always knew what was going on in their giant organization.

While Ford stuck to the black Model T and the tradition that the boss commands and all others follow, Sloan's new management team swiftly implemented new concepts in keeping with the changing needs of Americans. GM introduced practices such as frequent model changes, offering customers a wide range of styles and colors, and easy credit. Ford's market share slipped radically, and his executives defected by the score. In 1927 Ford was forced to shut down his assembly line to retool for the long overdue Model A. This procedure allowed GM to capture 43.5 percent of the auto market to Ford's less than 10 percent.

Despite this stunning setback, Ford failed to see the light. Instead of learning from GM's successes, he continued his old ways. For 20 consecutive years Ford Motor Company barely held on to third place in the auto industry and lost money almost every year. It escaped bankruptcy only because it was able to draw on a cash reserve of a billion dollars that Ford had accumulated during the successful years.

Questions

1. Who was a better manager, Ford or Sloan? Why?
2. What internal and external factors contributed to the successes of Ford and General Motors? What factors contributed to the decline of Ford?
3. Although General Motors is still much larger than Ford, today these companies are organized and managed in similar ways. Why is this so?
4. What was the essential cause of Ford's failure?

PART ONE CASE STUDY 2

Nutri-Way Health Foods, Inc.

SHEILA A. ADAMS

Department of Management, Arizona State University

Anti-Trust Division begins investigation of price-fixing in the health food industry.

"Yes, it's true! Better Foods Company has signed a lease on the old Edmonds Building. They expect to open within two months." Stephen Flanagan's tone was firm although his worried face betrayed the concern all present felt at his message.

Seven people sat around Mr. Flanagan's old oak dining-room table discussing this threat to Nutri-Way Health Foods, Inc.

"That chain's fluorescent-and-plastic interiors leave me cold," exclaimed Ray Robinson, current manager of Nutri-Way's original store. "Our customers will never be attracted by such artificial surroundings!"

Barbara Parkman, manager of Nutri-Way's downtown store, wasn't so sure.

"I don't like BFC stores either, Ray," she commented doubtfully, "but they're a big national chain. Those chains are only concerned with price. With inflation getting worse every day consumers are becoming more and more price conscious. If BFC can undersell us by a substantial amount I'm afraid we'll lose at least *some* customers."

"BFC can, indeed, undersell us, and substantially so!" Michelle Porter, Mr. Flanagan's wife and co-owner of Nutri-Way Health Foods confirmed angrily. "Take vitamins for example. You all know how important vitamins are to our volume. We normally have a 40% markup on vitamins, we need nearly 30% just to break even. But BF sells vitamins for nearly 20% less than we do. That will really hurt our business!"

"I hate to add to the gloom of this group," Tom Bierne, the firm's accountant, spoke reluctantly. "But last night at the Accounting Association meeting Fred Baxter told us that he had heard from his brother-in-law in Washington, D.C. The Anti-trust Division, he says, is about to bring charges of price fixing against some smaller retailers in the health food industry. Here, in Florida, is where they expect to begin the investigation."

A chorus of groans and "Oh, no!" greeted Bierne's announcement.

Michelle Porter, after earning an MBA from the University of Washington in 1963, went to work in the marketing department of the Kellogg Company's Battle Creek, Michigan office. She worked with a product development team for two years, moved into cereal promotion, and eventually became a regional promotional director. Although she enjoyed her work for Kellogg, Ms. Porter could not forget a years-old dream to own her own business.

During her stint with the product development team, Ms. Porter decided to buy a condominium. While seeking financing, she met and married Stephen Flanagan, a loan officer at a large Battle Creek bank. Mr. Flanagan, a former collegiate All-American swimmer, had spent three years with the U.S. Navy before joining the Michigan bank. He was selected for management training and moved steadily to his position as loan officer where he met Ms. Porter.

Flanagan, like Porter, had long dreamed of going into business for himself. His training in the bank and experience in the loan department had, he felt, given him a good understanding of the financial and managerial requirements for a successful business. His savings were substantial, and he was willing to work hard. Although Porter also wanted to strike out on her own, neither of them had a clear idea of the kind of business to enter.

The couple observed a growing interest in health foods and dietary supplements on the part of many of their acquaintances. Flanagan, a swimmer, and Porter, a water skier and tennis buff, had a life-long preference for light nutritious diets. This preference, combined with the observed growing public interest in health foods and the difficulty of finding desired products, led the two to invest their considerable savings into opening a health food store. Because of the presence of close relatives, a large retirement community, and very little competition they selected Sarasota, Florida for their new venture. Through hard work and sound management practices, business revenues grew by nearly 25% annually until, by 1979, four Nutri-Way stores produced combined annual sales of more than $1 million. A fifth store was in the planning stage.

When business at the first store became too much for Porter and Flanagan to handle alone, they hired Ray Robinson, an old Navy buddy of Flanagan's who had become bored with selling industrial cleaners and tired of the constant travel required. In a short time a second store was opened on the north edge of town and soon a third in the downtown area. Barbara Parkman, originally hired as a clerk in the first store shortly after she moved to Florida, performed so well during Nutri-Way's period of rapid growth that she eventually was asked to manage the downtown store. As each store opened, Porter assumed initial management responsibilities while Flanagan moved from store to store assuring coordination of effort. Porter had primary responsibility for the promotional and advertising activities for the firm while Flanagan, together with their accountant Tom Bierne, supervised the financial aspects of Nutri-Way. Personnel matters were usually shared, with Porter doing most of the interviewing and selection of new employees and Flanagan handling insurance, scheduling and training of new employees with the assistance of a clerk. Several employees assisted Flanagan in the purchasing, payroll, and personnel functions.

Employees of Nutri-Way seemed to develop great loyalty to the firm and its owners. Salaries were slightly above average for the area and Flanagan and Porter encouraged personnel to learn and grow with the business. Positions, whenever possible, were filled by promotion. All current store managers had originally been hired as sales clerks. Monthly meetings were held for all store managers with Porter and Flanagan to discuss plans for the coming month, any current or anticipated problems, and reports on the performance of each store during the past month.

Today's discussion, a regular monthly planning meeting of the owners and store managers, included the firm's accountant and attorney. All were concerned about the threat posed by Better Foods Company to their growing firm.

"How can they accuse us of price fixing?" demanded Ms. Porter. "Sure we cooperate to some extent with the other health food retailers in the area. We all want to protect our market shares, and we simply can't afford to get into price wars. That would destroy us all. But BFC can come in with their drastic discounts and flamboyant advertising and ruin every small retailer in the state."

Up to this point Scott Milner, the newest and youngest Nutri-Way store manager had maintained silence. Now he spoke slowly and thoughtfully. "Well, maybe it's not as bad as it seems right now. Let's not forget we all are pretty well informed about the foods and supplements we sell. Our customers depend on nutritional advice and information from us. Those big chains employ clerks with no expertise in nutrition. As long as BFC isn't too close to our stores perhaps we can still survive."

"But, Scott, didn't you realize," asked Helen Dobson, the firm's attorney, "the new store is planned for that vacancy where the shoe shop used to be—three doors down from the Edmonds building that BFC has leased! Besides that," Ms. Dobson looked intently at Mr. Flanagan and Ms. Porter, "my news tonight was that the deal on that property is ready to close. We have an appointment for Wednesday to sign the papers!"

Questions

1. What external environmental variables are affecting Nutri-Way Health Foods?
2. What steps can Nutri-Way take to respond to environmental threats?
3. Do you believe Nutri-Way is involved in price fixing? Defend your response.
4. Should Nutri-Way sign the papers for the new store? Why or why not?
5. How would you characterize the climate at Nutri-Way? What factors determined your answer?

PART TWO

The Linking Processes

Now that we have a basic understanding of the elements that influence an organization's success, we are prepared to examine the functions management must perform effectively to formulate and attain objectives. We will begin with communicating and decision making. As mentioned in our overview of the management process, communicating and decision making are referred to as *linking* processes because they bridge the functions of planning, organizing, motivating, and controlling. In a sense, what the manager does in the management process is make planning *decisions*, motivating *decisions*, and so on. We will discuss these processes in combination because decision making and communicating are highly interdependent. Communication is the means by which the manager obtains the information necessary for effective decision making and conveys these decisions to the organization's people. If communication is poor, people may misunderstand what management wishes of them, or interpersonal relationships may deteriorate. Therefore, the effectiveness of communication often determines how well decisions are actually implemented.

An Interview with Malcolm Forbes

Malcolm Forbes, Jr. is, to put it mildly, a most unusual person. Most top managers of large companies must answer to stockholders and are largely unknown outside of their own industry. The name Forbes is seen every day on every newsstand in the country. Malcolm Forbes is not only chairman, president, publisher, and editor of *Forbes* magazine, whose annual profits may exceed $10 million. He is the sole owner of it—and Forbes, Inc. a multihundred-million dollar financial empire. As might be expected of one of the wealthiest men in the world, Forbes is a staunch and vociferous supporter of capitalism and minimal government interference in business. Yet, he could scarcely be called a stick-in-the-mud conservative. His hobbies are flying hot air balloons and riding very large motorcycles fast and far. On business and most other topics, Malcolm Forbes is *very* outspoken. More important, he is *listened* to by many of the world's most influential business people. When it comes to communicating, especially about business matters, there are few who can surpass Forbes in wit, expressiveness, and sheer output. Therefore, although our own interview with Mr. Forbes certainly left us with no shortage of material, we decided to include also a few excerpts from his well-known interview in *Playboy* and his book *The Sayings of Chairman Malcolm* to give you a broader feel for his range and style.

Author: One of the most unusual things about *Forbes* is that it is wholly owned by one person—you. What are the advantages of this?

Forbes: Instant final decisions. The president of the United States, for example, has to sell his ideas to the cabinet and then congress. . . . This often isn't very easy. Our system is based on advise and consent, but there tends to be a lot of advice and very little consent. Here somebody with a problem can just present it. We have a few meetings to get everybody's input, just a few. Then there's instant final decision. (Also, most managers) need to worry about immediate profitability because they have to answer to stockholders. We can do things without being concerned about the immediate return.

Author: You obviously are the boss at *Forbes*, but how free are you to do as you please? What constraints are there on you as a manager?

Forbes: In a sense, they're fairly complete. You can't retain good editors if you constantly override their decisions. You have to let them express their opinions.

You know, a lot of people exercise power to prove they have it. Well, I don't have to establish that I'm the boss, so I don't exercise it very often. Sometimes my suggestions don't get taken up, but I very seldom impose my views.

Author: Do you engage in formal planning at *Forbes*?

Forbes: Yes, in the sense of budgeting, but not too much else. A plan is a point from which you take off, a projection of hopes and expectations. It shouldn't be a straight jacket. You need leeway. It's important to have the ability to deviate from a plan.

Author: How do you get people to perform for *Forbes*?

Forbes: One way is the motivation of paying well. Equally important is that no matter how junior an editor, his point of view is the tone the story takes. Being able to express his own views is a point of great satisfaction to a writer.

Author: What qualities do you look for when hiring a manager?

Forbes: Brains, track record, how they interview. The interview is very important, especially how well they express why they want to join us and why they want to do what they want to do . . . and how they express themselves in writing.

Forbes on the importance of management: My father used to say that he never bought the stock of a company based on its balance sheet. He always bought management, based on his personal impression of the top man, the guy at the steering wheel. That's the reason I make it a point to know all these guys. If they're capable and have the qualities that fit the company and the era and the industry's needs at the moment, that's of far greater value to a potential investor than whatever reserves a company may have or how long it's been in business. It's easy to forget that the benefit or harm of decisions made today in corporations, particularly large corporations, may not be reaped for four or five years, so what you'd better know is the caliber of the man making those decisions now. Those are enormous chips they're playing with, and if they don't have the ability to make the right decisions now, the company is going to eventually get into trouble. You've seen that happen time and time again.[1]

Forbes on the role of profit: In any case, profits shouldn't be the sole measure of success. It's also making sure that not too many people are getting screwed by the system, and that people understand that the system as a whole is working for the benefit of the most people. I'm not suggesting they do that just to be nice to everybody but to be damned sure the system survives, and it doesn't help if everybody thinks he's getting the short end of the stick.[2]

Forbes on taking risks in business: Enjoying life is the only solvency, and in business as in life, the biggest risk is too *much* caution. That's always the danger in business: when you stop charging. When you stop moving.

As soon as a business decides, this is how we used to do it and it worked so we'll keep on without changing, that's when it loses its momentum.

Safety doesn't lie in that. Just ask the Pennsylvania Railroad and the people who owned the Erie Canal bonds. Sure, I consider staying solvent important, but I believe it comes from keeping money moving. You know, planting money doesn't do you any good. It doesn't grow. So stashing it is not safety. Keeping it is not safety. Moving it, putting it to work, is safety.[3]

Some "Sayings of Chairman Malcolm":[4]

The top people of the biggest companies are, surprisingly, often the nicest ones in their company. I'm not sure, though, if they got there because they were good guys or that they're now good guys because they can afford to be.

To be agreeable while disagreeing—that's an art.

It's so much easier to suggest solutions when you don't know too much about the problem.

Writing enigmatically is often easier than coming to clear conclusions.

It's easier to tear up what you write than to take back what you say.

Boss Thoughts

You can't know if no one tells you.

You can't answer the question if no one asks it.

You can't solve the problem if no one poses it.

Never hire someone who knows less than you do about what he's (or she's) hired to do.

---

1. "Playboy Interview: Malcolm Forbes," *Playboy*, April 1979, p. 80.
2. Ibid.
3. Ibid., p. 106.
4. Malcolm S. Forbes, *The Sayings of Chairman Malcolm: The Capitalist's Handbook* (New York: Harper & Row, 1978).

CHAPTER 5

Communication

This chapter is about communicating—something everyone does daily, but few people really do well consistently. It is almost impossible to understate the importance of communication in management. Almost everything managers do to facilitate attaining organizational objectives requires effective communication. Clearly, unless people can communicate, they cannot work together to formulate and attain objectives. However, as we shall learn, communication is a complex process of interrelated steps. Each of these steps is critical to getting our ideas understood by another person. Each is a point where, if we are not careful and conscious of what we are doing, meaning can easily be lost. The purpose of this chapter is to acquaint you with the nature and complexities of communicating, the potential pitfalls in the road to understanding, and what you can do to communicate more effectively both in and out of management.

After reading this chapter, you should understand the following important terms and concepts:

communication process
steps in communication
feedback
noise
symbol
channel
nonverbal channel

The Communication Process

Describing managerial work in Chapter 1, we cited research studies that indicate managers spend between 50 and 90 percent of their time communicating.[1] This sounds incredible, but it becomes understandable when one realizes that managers must communicate in order to perform all their interpersonal, informational, and decisional roles as well as the management functions of planning, organizing, motivating, and controlling. It is because communication is integral to all primary managerial activities that we refer to communicating as a *linking process.*

Because managers perform their three roles and the four basic functions in order to formulate and attain organizational objectives, the quality of communication can directly affect the degree to which objectives are attained. This means that *effective* communication is necessary for individual and organizational success.

However, although it is widely accepted that communication is critical to organizational success, surveys have found that 73 percent of United States managers, 63 percent of British managers, and 85 percent of Japanese managers believed communication to be a key barrier to their organization's effectiveness.[2] These surveys would indicate that ineffective communication is a major problem area. But, hopefully, by gaining a better understanding of both interpersonal and organizational communication, we should be able to decrease the incidence of ineffective communication. As a result, we should become better, more effective managers.

Let us begin by examining the nature and purpose of communication.

The Nature and Purpose of Communication

There is a tendency to presume that communication occurs whenever a message is sent and apparently physically received. Suppose, for example, that you are screaming angry words at a friend across the room. Or, picture a famous scholar delivering a lecture on high-energy physics to a group of college freshman. Or, imagine a manager who posts a memo describing a complex technical discovery made by the research and development department on the bulletin board in the company cafeteria. Is there communication? Maybe. More important, is there *effective* communication? Is all of the information the sender wants known being understood by the other party? Or, from a managerial perspective, is the message an aid to performing tasks? Probably not.

To communicate effectively, a person must fully grasp that communication is an *exchange*. Merely transmitting information does not necessarily ensure communication will take place. Most communication takes place through an indirect process. We will examine the factors involved in turn.

Communication Is an Exchange. The physical presence of a second party in no way ensures that communication is even possible, let alone effective.

In fact, we truly communicate far less often than we think we do. This fact is illustrated by a study of foremen and their subordinates at a public utility as reported by Rensis Likert. Whereas 85 percent of the foremen thought their subordinates felt very free to discuss important job matters, only 51 percent of the workers actually felt they could do so.[3] In another study, a department manager recorded having given instructions or communicated decisions to subordinates on 165 separate occasions. Records maintained by the subordinates showed that they were aware of only 84 of these.[4]

Also, on many occasions the message gets across but is misunderstood. Hence communication is ineffective. John Miner, a prominent management researcher, states that typically only about 50 percent of attempted communication between people results in mutual agreement.[5] The cause of such breakdowns, more often than not, is failure to take into account that communication is an *exchange*.

In an exchange, *both* parties play an active and equal role. For example, your offering a friend five dollars for a used textbook only initiates an exchange. For it to take place, your friend must accept the money and give you the book. Similarly, communication takes place only after one party "offers" information *and* the other party understands it. For this to happen, the information must reach the intended recipient's conscious mind, not just the ears or brain, and it must be meaningful.

Thus, our definition of the communication process is:

> *Communication is the exchange of information and meaning between two or more people.*

To fully understand this definition, one must grasp the often subtle difference between exchanging meaning and merely transmitting information.

Information and Meaning. For the present, we can think of *information* as data or facts. It is possible, as we know from both personal experience and research, to exchange or transfer information without communicating a commensurate level of meaning. This is because the human brain, like a computer, can process and store information without understanding it. Just as a parrot repeats words, we can repeat information, a skill that often comes in handy when cramming for exams.

However, you probably have noticed that just memorizing facts may not be very useful if the instructor asks essay questions that require interpretation. Although you have memorized the information, you do not know its significance and how to apply it effectively in a specific situation. In essence, you do not have the underlying idea. Without the idea, you cannot answer the essay question in a way that successfully communicates to the teacher that you *understand*, that is, know the meaning of, the information.

As we progress through our discussion, it will become apparent that many requests managers make of subordinates require considerable interpretation. An effective manager, like an effective teacher, therefore tries to make certain that people understand the "why" or underlying meaning of organizational communication. To convey such understanding in an organizational setting can be quite difficult because most communication takes place through a complex, *indirect* process of several *interrelated steps.*

Direct and Indirect Communication

Certain information, in certain situations, can be communicated directly. The best example of this is a shared experience.

Shared Experience. One of the most effective ways to exchange meaning with other people is to share experiences with them. For example, your parents communicated to you the very complicated idea that they loved you long before you learned to speak. They did so by feeding you and making noises that you liked: experiences that felt pleasurable to you as a baby. They also communicated other information to you by having you actually go through an experience; how to hold a spoon, for instance. An experience impresses an idea directly on the mind. You understand the meaning of the information without having to first learn the words it would take to explain it.

However, sharing an experience is usually an awkward and time-consuming means of communicating information. Consider how long it would have taken you to learn your way around campus by trial and error or by being led around without words. If human beings had to depend solely on shared experience to communicate, we would still be a very primitive society. Almost all information we have acquired and understood was communicated to us through an *indirect* process. It is this indirect means of communication to which we refer when we speak of the communication process.

Elements of the Communication Process

There are four basic elements in the communication process. These are:

1. *A sender,* who is the person that originates an idea or selects information and transmits it
2. *A message,* which is the information itself encoded into symbols
3. *A channel,* which is the means by which information is transmitted.
4. *A receiver,* the person or persons for whom the information is intended, who interprets it

To communicate, both sender and receiver go through several interrelated steps. Their objective is to construct a message and use the channel to transmit it in such a way that both parties will share and understand the original idea on completion of the process. This is difficult because each step is a point where meaning may be distorted or wholly lost.

These interrelated steps are *idea origination, encoding and channel selection, transmission,* and *decoding*. We will describe them in the following section; they also are illustrated in Figure 5-1, a simple model of the communication process.

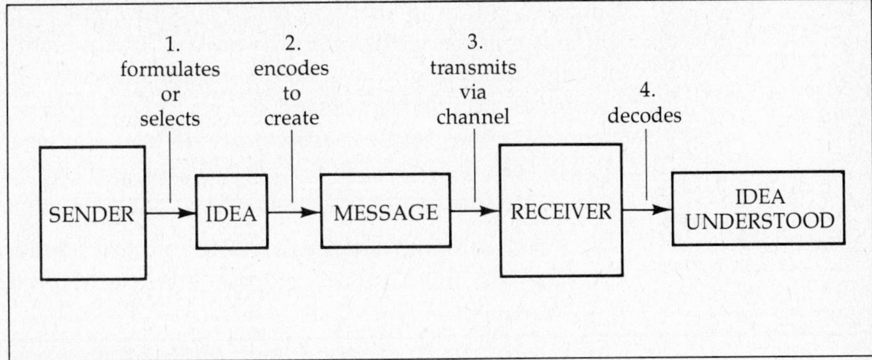

Figure 5-1 A Simplified Model of the Communication Process

Steps in the Communication Process

Although the entire communication process is often completed within a few seconds, making it difficult to discern the steps, we will analyze the steps to show how problems can occur at various points. This analysis is like examining each of the individual frames of a brief movie scene.

1. Idea Origination. Communication begins with the formulation of an idea or the selection of information. The sender decides what essential message or idea is to be communicated. Unfortunately, many communication attempts break down at this preliminary stage because the sender does not spend enough time really thinking through the idea. Keith Davis, an important writer and researcher whose insights into communication are the basis of much of this chapter, stresses the importance of this stage by stating: "A poor message will not be improved by glossy paper or a bigger loudspeaker. The motto for this step is 'Don't start talking until you begin thinking.' "[6]

It is important to remember that the idea has not yet been put into words or other forms. The sender has only decided what concept he or she really wants to communicate. To do so effectively, the sender may have to take many factors into account. For example, managers wishing to communicate performance appraisals must firmly understand that the idea is to give the subordinates specific information about their strengths and weaknesses and how their performance could be improved. The idea is not to give vague, general praise or to criticize the subordinate's behavior.

This example also shows the relationship between perception and communication. If managers perceive subordinates to be capable of development and improvement, thereby needing information on their performance, they are likely to have positive, constructive underlying ideas when communicating about performance. If managers perceive subordinates as children who need to be told what they did wrong and "put in line," they are likely to communicate the negative criticism this thinking implies.

Another example of potential problems in the ideation stage would be a plant manager who just received a message from top management that the company needs to increase the number of radios produced by 6 percent without increasing the overtime payroll. If the plant manager fails to think through what might be best communicated to his or her subordinates and just sends them this message exactly as received, a number of misunderstandings could result because workers would at best understand only *what* changes are necessary. If the plant manager really thinks about what ideas need to be communicated, he or she might conclude the following:

a. It is important for the work force to understand *what* changes are necessary. (In this case a 6 percent increase in production without added overtime.)

b. It is important for workers to understand *why* these changes are necessary. (Otherwise they might conclude that the company was trying to bleed more work out of them for less pay, and they might rebel.)

c. It is important for the workers to understand that quality and wastage should not be adversely affected by the necessary increased output. (Otherwise, true productivity will decrease, not increase as top management intended with its original message.)

Managers who only communicate ideas (a) might be doing so because this is how higher level managers communicate to them. This is because managers often serve as models for their subordinates. They affect behavior in much the same way, though not so strongly, as our parents. If our managers are coercive or not explicit in their communications with us, we may well behave similarly when trying to communicate to our subordinates. But, you are in a different situation than your manager. It therefore is not necessarily desirable to manage or communicate in the same style. What is necessary is to be aware of what ideas you want to communicate *before* you send a message.

2. Encoding and Channel Selection. The idea exists only as pure thought. Before a thought can be transmitted, the sender must encode it into symbols such as words, pictures, or gestures. This encoding converts the idea into a message.

The sender also must select a channel at this point that is compatible with the type of symbols used for encoding. Some common channels are speaking, writing, and electronic media. If the channel is not suited to the physical form of the symbol, transmission is impossible. A picture may sometimes be worth a thousand words, but not if the message will be sent by radio!

If the channel is not the most appropriate for the idea conceived in the first step, communication will be less effective. For example, a manager could warn a subordinate about a severe violation of safety procedures during an informal chat over coffee or with an informal memo. But these channels probably would not get the idea of severity across as effectively as either a formal meeting or letter. Similarly, simply sending a subordinate a memo about her exceptional performance would not communicate the idea of how important a contribution she made and would not be as effective as telling the person directly, followed up with a formal letter of commendation and a bonus.

You might understand this second step better if you would visualize it as packaging. Many perfectly good products do not sell unless they are packaged in a way that the consumer both understands and finds attractive. Similarly, many people with excellent ideas fail to package or wrap them in symbols and channels meaningful and attractive to the receiver. When this occurs the idea, no matter how sound, often is not "sold."

3. Transmission. Next, the sender uses the channel to get the message (an encoded idea or group of ideas) to the receiver. It is this physical transfer of a message that many people mistakenly consider to be the entire communication process. However, as we have seen, transmission is only one of several critical steps we must go through to get an idea across to another person. It is, thanks to modern technology, often the easiest phase of the process to complete without loss of meaning because it is usually the only step that requires no interpretation by either sender or recipient. An example of communication breaking down due to transmission failure would be the postal service losing a letter or delivering it to the wrong person.

4. Decoding. Then, assuming transmission were successful, the recipient *decodes* the message. *Decoding* is the translation of the sender's symbols into thoughts by the recipient. If the symbols chosen by the sender have exactly the same meaning for the receiver, the recipient will now know what the sender had in mind when the idea was formulated. This would complete the communication process if the idea does not call for a response.

However, for a number of reasons that we will soon explore, the recipient may attach a somewhat different meaning to the message than the sender intended during decoding. From a managerial perspective, communication would be considered effective if the receiver indicated understanding of the idea by performing the required action intended by the sender.

We will expand on idea origination, encoding, decoding, and transmission later in the chapter. Before we do, there are two other communication concepts you should understand: feedback and noise.

Feedback and Noise

Feedback. When providing feedback, the sender and receiver reverse communication roles. The original receiver becomes a sender and goes through every step of the communication process to convey his or her response to the original sender, who is now the receiver. Professor of Business Communication Phillip Lewis, discussing feedback in *Organizational Communication: The Essence of Effective Management*, states:

> *Feedback* is a basic response made to what is heard, read, or seen; information (either verbal or nonverbal) is fed back to the sender, indicating to what degree a message has been understood, believed, assimilated, and accepted.
>
> Effective communication must be two-way; feedback is necessary to determine the degree to which a message has been received and understood. . . . Managers cannot assume that everything they say or write will be understood exactly as intended. The manager who does rely on this false assumption is isolating himself from reality. The manager who does not allow for the receiving of feedback will find his managerial effectiveness severely limited. Likewise, if feedback from employees is discouraged, the manager will eventually be isolated or bypassed.[7]

Feedback can make a major contribution to the effectiveness of managerial communication. Several studies have been made contrasting one-way communication (no feedback) with two-way communication (an opportunity for feedback). Results indicate that although two-way communication is not as fast, it is less frustrating, much more accurate, and leads to greater confidence in the correctness of interpretations.[8] This holds true across widely different cultures.[9]

Noise. Feedback greatly improves the chances of communicating effectively because it enables both parties to overcome noise. In the jargon of communication theory, **noise** is anything that distorts meaning. The sources of noise range from language, either verbal or nonverbal; perceptual differences, which may alter meaning during encoding and decoding; to physical interference such as wide physical separation of the parties or loud background sounds in a room, which can distort transmission.

There is always some noise, both psychological and physical, and therefore there is some distortion of meaning at every step in the communication process. Usually, we manage to overcome it and get our message across. However, a high level of noise will surely result in significant loss of meaning and may completely block an attempted communication exchange. This, from a managerial perspective, would decrease the degree to which objectives dependent on the communication will be attained. We will describe some ways in which noise can be minimized later in the chapter.

Encoding Ideas

Keeping in mind that all steps in the communication process are interrelated, let us explore them in detail, beginning with encoding. In encoding, the sender converts the idea into symbols.

Symbols A symbol is something that represents something else. If this definition seems rather broad, it is because virtually anything can be a symbol or be

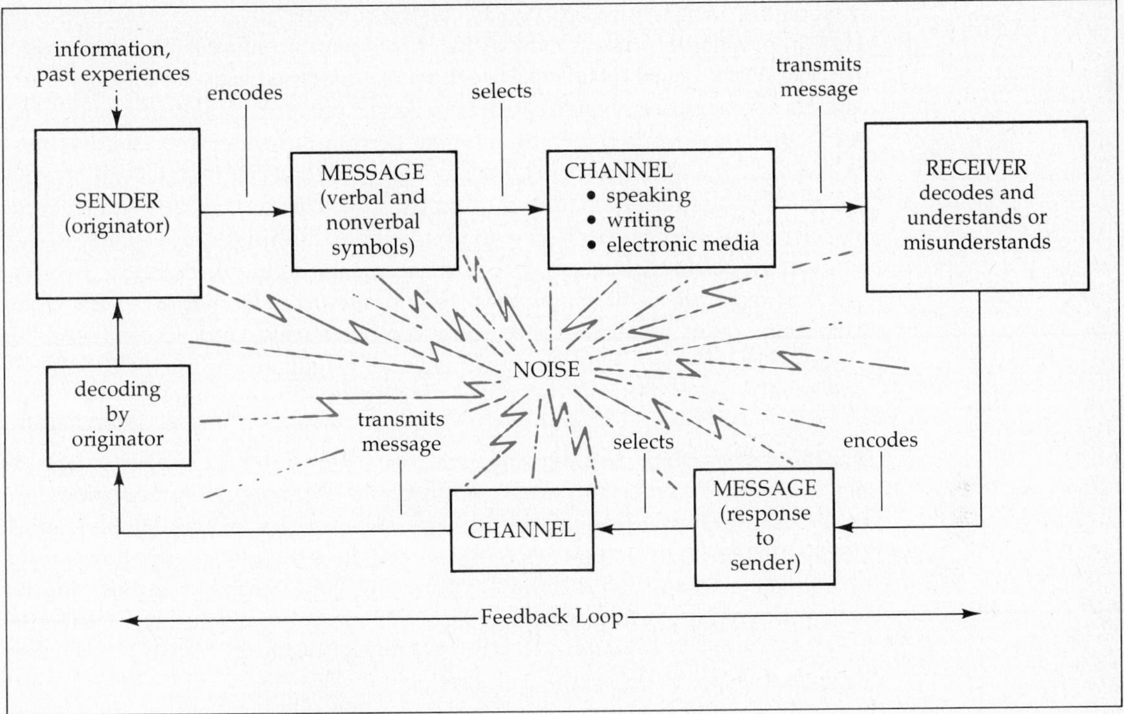

Figure 5-2 The Communication Process as a System with Feedback and Noise

represented by one. Confusing a symbol with the thing it represents is a frequent cause of misunderstanding. An organization chart, a symbol, is not the thing it represents—a formal organization. In fact, as we shall see when we discuss the organizing function, the chart can vary considerably from the true structure of the organization it supposedly represents.

The most familiar type of symbol is a word. Pictures, numbers, and gestures also are widely used as symbols. Frequently, a single thing may be represented by all of these types. For example, to represent the command "come to a halt," we could use:

- The spoken word *stop*.
- The letters "s-t-o-p."
- The gesture of a hand outstretched with the palm facing upward.
- A picture, such as an eight-sided red or yellow sign.
- The number "0" (in computer language).

Semantics. A given symbol often represents several different things. These are termed semantic variations, *semantics* being the study of the meaning of symbols. An unabridged dictionary of the English language contains about 14,000 possible definitions for the 500 most common words; 79 meanings for just the simple word *round*. The word *tip*, for instance, may be interpreted in several very different ways. A waitress might see a tip as part of her income. A gambler might interpret a tip to mean private information on a horse race. In publishing, the word tip is used to describe a special insert. And there is the more conventional meaning of an extremity, as in the tip of an iceberg.

Semantic variations often lead to misunderstanding, for in many cases it is not at all obvious precisely which meaning the sender ascribes to the symbol. For example, a manager who tells a subordinate that a report seems "adequate" may mean that it is very comprehensive and accomplishes its purpose. But the subordinate might decode "adequate" to mean that the report is only mediocre and could use considerable improvement.

Symbols, Meaning, and Communication. The need for a science of semantics highlights a very important point about symbols. A symbol does not have an inherent, fixed meaning. The meaning of a symbol is learned through experience and varies with *context*, the situation in which it is used. Since everyone has had different experiences, and every communication act is to some degree a new situation, one can never be absolutely certain that another person will assign the same meaning we do to a symbol. This is of profound importance in communication.

The symbol is the fundamental unit of communication. Except in the case of direct communication through shared experience, we communicate only by encoding our ideas into symbols meaningful to the recipient. Therefore people seldom can communicate effectively unless they first agree on the meaning of symbols. This is another reason why feedback is so often vital to effective communication.

Transmission: Selection and Use of Channels

Transmission is the physical transfer of the message, which has been encoded in symbols, to the receiver via a **channel**, often referred to as a *medium*. There are three primary channels or media that may be used to transmit a message: speaking, writing, and electronic media.

In many communication situations, the sender is able to choose any of these channels to transmit the message. Each has its advantages and disadvantages, no channel is best for all messages. The sender's objective is to select the most effective channel for the *situation at hand*. This usually will be the one with the least noise, and therefore greatest potential for accuracy. However, since speed and cost are also often important determinants of effectiveness when communication takes place in an organizational setting, managers must take them into account as well.

Choosing a medium does not imply that only one channel should be selected and used. It often is desirable to use two or more media in combination. This introduces complexity, for the sender must determine in which sequence the media should be used and how much time should elapse between transmissions. However, research indicates that using both spoken and written media is usually more effective than just written media.[10] As Professor Terrence Mitchell states in discussing this research: "A summary of all this work would suggest that the oral-combined-with-written message is likely to lead to the most effective communication in most settings."[11]

In the following section we will describe speaking, nonverbal communication, writing, electronic media, and their relative advantages and disadvantages.

Speaking

Speaking is by far the most frequently used channel for transmitting messages between people. Henry Mintzberg's studies indicated that managers spend between 50 and 90 percent of their time speaking.[12] Oral communication is popular for several very good reasons. To begin, almost everybody in the world has the physical ability to speak and hear. Because they use it more often, most people have a far better grasp of spoken language than written language. Another advantage of speaking is that no apparatus such as pencil or paper is required, which usually makes it the least expensive channel to use. In addition, when the receiver can see as well as hear the sender, word symbols are enhanced and amplified by nonverbal symbols, as will be described later in this chapter.

Advantages and Disadvantages of Speaking. The biggest advantage of speaking is that it offers an opportunity for immediate feedback. In a face-to-face situation, the receiver instantly responds nonverbally and often also verbally to the message. By using their perceptual skills to interpret these cues, the sender and receiver can use this feedback to determine whether understanding occurred and immediately correct any deficiencies. Thus, if both parties are genuinely open to two-way communication, speaking can be an exceptionally accurate way to transmit a message.

The advantages of speaking cited above are only *potential* gains. In some situations, speaking may be a highly undesirable channel. This is because speaking is especially susceptible to noise. There is the obvious potential problem of physical noise in the environment. Another potential disadvantage of speaking is lack of retention. This is an important consideration in management because much organizational communication is used over an extended period of time. As a lower-level manager, you probably will often be requested to perform tasks that may take weeks or months to complete and are much too detailed to remember from a conversation.

Another common situation in organizations is that a message is often communicated over several levels. The message you get from your supervisor, for example, may have originated with a top manager several levels above your boss in the organization. If speaking is used for transmission, almost the entire communication process must be repeated each time the message passes from person to person. This so greatly increases the chances of distortion that it is almost impossible to use speech to transmit information of any complexity without serious loss of meaning.

Thus, despite its many advantages, speaking is an unsatisfactory channel for transmitting a message when information is complicated, will be needed in the future, or when the channel has several levels. Another tradeoff of speaking is the cost of managerial and subordinate time. Spending excessive time transmitting a message personally could cause the manager to slight or not have enough time for other tasks that may be of higher priority in attaining objectives.

Nonverbal Communication

Although verbal symbols (words) are our primary means of encoding ideas for transmission, we also transmit messages through the use of body language, a nonverbal medium. A **nonverbal channel** is any communication medium that does not involve words. Often, nonverbal transmission takes place simultaneously with verbal during speaking, amplifying or changing the meaning of words. Eye contact, facial expressions such as smiles, frowns, raised eyebrows, moving versus steady eyes, a tense versus a relaxed face, and a look of approval or disapproval are examples of nonverbal communication. Finger pointing, covering the mouth with the hand, touching, and slouching also are nonverbal ways of transmitting meaning.

Another form of nonverbal communication is *how* we say words. This includes voice intonation, inflections, smoothness of speech, and so on. How we say words, as we know from experience, can greatly alter their meaning. The question, "Do you have any ideas?" is, on paper, a clear request for suggestions. Delivered with a scowl in a harsh, authoritarian tone, it may mean instead, "Don't offer any ideas that contradict mine if you know what's good for you."

Research indicates that a very high percentage of communication during speaking is perceived through body language and voice quality. In his book *Non-Verbal Communication*, Mehrabian states that 55 percent of the message is perceived from facial expression and physical posture and 38 percent is perceived from vocal intonation and inflection. This means that the words themselves only account for 7 percent of what is perceived by the receiver when we speak![13] In other words, in most cases, *how* we say something is more important than the words we use.

For example, try to imagine the following scene, which illustrates how nonverbal symbols can create noise during communication. You are going in to your manager's office to get some information about a project you are working on. As you enter, she continues to pay attention to the papers on her desk for a few seconds. Then, she glances at her watch, and in a distant, unresponsive tone says, "What can I do for you?"

Although her words, on their own, are helpful, her body language clearly states that you are an unwelcome distraction from her work. How are you going to feel about asking your questions? What thoughts are likely to occur to you the next time you have a question for your manager? Probably, your feelings would not be positive in either case. Contrast this with how you would feel if, as you entered, your manager had looked up at once, smiled brightly, and said in a cheerful tone of voice, "Hi, how's that project going? What can I do for you?"

The manager whose body language was negative could, in fact, be as willing to help subordinates as the one whose nonverbal symbols radiated warmth. The words were basically the same. However, in this instance, as in so many conversations, the nonverbal symbols completely overwhelm the verbal ones. The lesson is that it is essential to make sure that the nonverbal symbols you transmit are congruent with, support, the idea you are trying to communicate. Otherwise, the nonverbal symbols will create so much noise that the recipient will almost certainly misperceive the message.

Writing

Writing is the second most popular transmission medium. A typical white-collar worker spends 25 percent (9 percent writing, 16 percent reading) of the work day on written communication.[14]

Advantages and Disadvantages of Writing. A written message can be retained for thousands of years and passed through any number of people with little distortion. We can still read and understand laws, stories, and trade accounts written by Egyptians 5000 years ago. Another advantage is that the message can be reviewed by the receiver until it is understood. These advantages make writing a highly desirable channel for complicated messages and when one needs to send an identical message to several receivers.

A disadvantage of writing is that it usually takes more time than speaking and requires technology such as pen and paper. Because time is so important to them, many managers prefer the telephone to memos and letters, and often dictate their written correspondence. Dictation is a means of delegating to a subordinate the time-consuming physical aspect of writing. Another potential disadvantage is that storing written communication, to gain the advantage of retention, can be very costly. The federal government, for example, probably spends hundreds of millions of dollars a year just to store old messages.

The major disadvantage of written transmission is that it offers no opportunity for immediate feedback. Thus, misunderstandings in written messages sometimes go undetected until they become really serious. Managers who rely on a memo to transmit instructions, for example, sometimes do not find out that subordinates misunderstood them until the task is performed incorrectly. Businesses sometimes discover only after losing the account that a letter written with good intentions actually alienated a customer.

FEATURE 5-1

Nonverbal Communication: Hints for Female Executives

If a woman wants to succeed, she ought to look as if she meant business. Here are some success techniques for the ambitious woman.

Keep your hands still.

In moments of stress, men have a way of placing their hands palm down on their thighs, with the thumbs sticking up toward the waist, as if they were bracing themselves. This is usually a sign that a man means serious business, just as the appearance of his hands anywhere near his face indicates thought or hesitation.

Women should avoid all these hand signals, whenever possible.

The best thing a woman can do with her hands is to keep them folded neatly in her lap.

Avoid large, low chairs.

They are difficult to get in and out of gracefully, and if you're not careful they tend to push your knees up in the air, exposing most of your thigh.

If you're in a position to choose what kind of desk you have, insist on having one that is closed, rather than an open table-desk.

Avoid any hint of a prissy, nagging, schoolmarmish tone in your voice. For many men the voice of a woman is emotionally disturbing. The more you can develop a low, strong, firm voice, the better, since it is the relatively higher pitch of a woman's voice that triggers off this reaction in men.

Index of forbidden objects: glasses dangling from your neck on a chain; hats; high boots in the office; white gloves (they make you look like a temporary secretary from the 1940s); harlequin glasses; sequins on anything; blue jeans; turbans; T-shirts with comic or pornographic messages printed on them; and heavy dangling earrings.

Never play with your hair or your earrings if you're negotiating a serious piece of business. It gives the wrong impression, since men regard it as a sign of sexual interest, rightly or wrongly.

Dress as if you were already an executive. It costs a little more and takes some effort, but it is well worth the extra time and trouble. The important thing is to look as if you will fit in with those above you, not those at your level.

SOURCE: Michael Korda, *Success!* (New York: Random House, Inc., 1977), as reprinted in *New York Times*, September 4, 1977, pp. F-10–11.

Electronic Media

The major electronic communication media are the telephone, radio, television, and the computer. Also important are film, xerographic reproduction, and word processing. Electronic transmission channels often are used in combination. Computer terminals, for example, are frequently linked to a central processing unit by telephone lines. All electronic media must be used in conjunction with another medium such as speech or paper because human beings obviously cannot directly receive electronic impulses.

Electronic channels have made possible a major breakthrough in communication. We can now transmit an identical message to any number of people at virtually instantaneous speed. When the president of the United States goes on television his words and nonverbal gestures are relayed exactly as he delivers them to every person in the United States who turns on a television set. Relayed by satellite, still unchanged, they reach nearly every country on earth. Stored on videotape, those words and pictures will be the historical references of future generations.

The power of electronic media is staggering. A prime-time television show is seen by over 60 million Americans at the same time. As a result, electronic media have had a major influence on the environment affecting all organizations, especially political and governmental. They may come to have high impact within organizations as well, for a number of companies are now experimenting with television as a medium for keeping employees informed on company matters.

Advantages and Disadvantages of Electronic Media. The primary advantages of almost all electronic media are extremely high speed and almost total accuracy. Also, when the volume of communication is very high, the cost of electronic media is low in relative terms. The computer has several special advantages. Its magnetic medium can store an enormous amount of information in very little space. These advantages of electronic media have restructured our society and helped make possible the giant organization.

One disadvantage of many electronic media is that the initial cost of equipment is so high that only users with considerable resources and very high information volume are able to employ them. However, in some areas the cost of introducing electronic media is diminishing. New technology has resulted in inexpensive microprocessers that are as powerful as the early computer models that filled whole buildings. Another important disadvantage of mass communication media is that they cannot cope economically with individual differences. When the same message is transmitted to many thousands of people with no opportunity for feedback, a substantial percentage are likely to misinterpret it. This is one reason why television advertisers, who try to communicate to millions of people, repeat commercials, change commercials frequently, and also use other media such as periodicals to get across even a very simple message about a product.

FEATURE 5-2

The Power of Communication Technology

In Iran, the revolution of Ayatollah Ruhollah Khomeini was the first cassette revolution. It was the arrival of thousands of cassettes containing the ayatollah's speeches that first propagated his revolutionary ideas: there were already plenty of cassette players—many of them imported cheaply from Kuwait—and they could be used in mosques, away from the ears of the secret police.

While the shah imagined that he had effective control through tightly controlled TV, radio and newspapers, these thin little objects were secretly frustrating all his ambitions. They could produce two hours of inflammatory rhetoric out of an ordinary envelope.

At the same time, the Xerox machine was performing its own seditious role. When revolutionary "night letters" and pamphlets arrived mysteriously at offices in Tehran, sympathetic secretaries quickly produced piles of copies and the powerful propaganda suddenly began circulating.

Perhaps the cassette and the copier will prove as significant in the audio-visual age as Gutenberg's invention of book printing, which likewise enabled ideas to be spread over the world, away from governmental or religious controls.

SOURCE: Anthony Sampson, "How Copying Machines and Cassettes Can Topple a Government," UPI, *San Francisco Chronicle*, May 23, 1979, p. B-3.

Decoding: Perception and Meaning

After the sender's message has been transmitted successfully, the receiver must decode its symbols to understand the idea being communicated. It is here that the sender either interprets the message accurately or misunderstands it to some degree. It is here that most breakdowns in communication occur, because the receiver interprets the message from his own point of view, which may be very different from that of the sender.

At one time or another, everybody has had the experience of saying something to another person, knowing that they must have heard every word clearly, and suddenly realizing that the other person completely misunderstood what was said. This sort of experience, unfortunately all too common, drives home just how great a distance separates two minds in the same room. What happened was that the message was *re*ceived but not *per*ceived. Perceptual differences, as organizational theorist Mary Parker Follett recognized over forty years ago, are the primary cause of disagreements between people.

The Effect of Perception on Decoding

Individuals perceive information *selectively*, depending on their interests, needs, emotional state, and environmental conditions. This characteristic of people is extremely important in communications. It means that, in many cases, people only perceive part of a message they have received physically. As a result, ideas encoded by the sender may become distorted and not fully understood.

Selective perception is a factor managers must actively consider if they want to communicate effectively to all of the many different types of people within and without the organization whose understanding is necessary to attain objectives. One way of coping with decoding problems is by providing sufficient opportunity and encouragement for feedback. Another is to take perceptual differences into account in encoding and transmitting information by trying to empathize with the receiver.

Empathy. *Empathy* is feeling what other persons feel, putting yourself in their shoes. It is asking yourself, "Who is this person I want to reach? What are her needs and interests? What kind of mood is he in today?" Actively using empathy in communication implies that we try to accommodate the receiver and match the way we encode and transmit to the individual or group and the situation. Successfully using empathy can greatly reduce the potential for misunderstanding during decoding.

For example, some people prefer a lot of structure, detail, and repetition. We probably would reach such people more effectively with a letter or detailed memorandum. Others respond better to less structure and detail. An informal conversation might be the most appropriate way to communicate to them. Some people are anxious or insecure in certain situations, or respond badly to criticism. They may selectively weed out or misunderstand suggestions for improvement if they are not presented in a supportive, diplomatic fashion.

Situation. But, of course, nobody responds the same in all situations. Different situations may require different styles of communication. Formal, important situations call for formal words and media. For example, even though a foreign head of state may recognize that President Jimmy Carter is an informal person, he would not be likely to communicate a vital position effectively to Mr. Carter by using slang while sipping a cocktail. Similarly, it is reasonable to assume that a subordinate will feel at least mildly apprehensive and anxious during a performance appraisal. Therefore, a manager would show empathy and probably communicate suggestions for improvement more effectively by creating a relaxed, supportive climate. Conversely, it may be desirable for a manager to be more explicit, or even harsh in tone, in a situation where the employee's behavior or performance has become so bad that he or she may have to be terminated soon.

Emotional State of the Sender. To communicate effectively and minimize potential problems in decoding, it is also important for the sender to be aware of his or her own feelings and emotions. If we do not, in effect, actively empathize with ourselves before and during communication, there is a strong chance that we will unconsciously transmit nonverbal symbols that contradict the message we consciously want to get across. A person out of touch with his or her feelings, therefore, cannot hope to control the communication process to make it more effective. We cannot expect a recipient to decode a message into the idea we would have liked to have sent.

Managing the Communication Process

There are many similarities between the communication process and the general process of accomplishing any group activity. Communication, after all, is a true group endeavor. The sender and receiver must actively work together to successfully transfer understanding. Like members of an organization, the sender and receiver should have a common goal. The goal of a communication effort is to exchange relevant information and meaning. Communication and managing both involve using resources in the most effective way to attain an objective. When we communicate we use the resources of our personal skills in combination with media to attain the objective of getting an idea across to another person.

Another commonality between managing and communicating is that in both activities the most effective way of doing things usually is dependent or contingent upon the situation. There is no "best" way to communicate or to manage. The most effective means of communicating a given idea is affected by many different factors or variables. The manager must consider such variables as the nature of the task, the available resources, his or her own abilities and those of workers, and the environment, to cite just a few. The communicator must consider the nature of the idea, the available media, both his and the receiver's communication skills, and the climate of the exchange.

These many similarities between communication and organized endeavor make it possible for us to approach communication from a managerial perspective. We can view it as an unending process with several interdependent steps. Rather than relying upon fixed rules or principles, we can make our communication more effective by adopting a systems approach—considering the total communication situation. This is what we shall do in the following sections, beginning with a description of the basic steps in managing communication for effectiveness.

Steps in Managing Communication

Sometimes communicating an idea is so complicated an objective that it actually requires an organization. Examples of this are running for public office, making a motion picture, and convincing thousands or millions of people to buy a product. In these situations, one would apply the management process fully, as discussed in the rest of this book. Here, however, we are dealing only with relatively simple interpersonal communication—getting across a few ideas to one person or a small group. We therefore will present a simplified model for managing the exchange of relevant information and meaning, substituting the following steps for some of the functions of management. For an illustration, we will use something of interest to most people: getting a job.

1. Planning. Your chances of getting an idea across are much improved by planning communication just as you would plan a vacation. You would begin by setting your overall objective: determining exactly what idea you are trying to get across. Eventual success in job seeking is dependent upon your ability to conceptualize exactly what it is you want to accomplish. In job hunting, the overall idea you want to communicate is that you are very qualified for the position. But this type of idea is very broad. To get it across you will have to refine your plan by coming up with the ideas that are part of it. For example, you might want to communicate the ideas that you have a good education and relevant experience.

Naturally, you have to be realistic when you select an idea for communication. If you will soon be a college graduate, for example, your chances of communicating the idea that you are able to run IBM are nil. Geraldine, one of comedian Flip Wilson's characters, provided the most succinct definition of realism in communication we know: "Don't let your mouth write a check your body can't cash."

2. Organizing. We organize ideas by encoding or packaging them into symbols. Usually, we further structure them by putting those symbols into the accepted framework of language. If the idea is sufficiently complicated, we would extend our structure into paragraphs, chapters, or even books, just as a big business forms divisions. But, as with organizations, the best structure for communicating an idea is usually the simplest one that will attain the objectives.

There are many considerations in selecting a structure for an idea. The complexity of the information, the media of transmission, the frame of reference of the recipient, and the communication skills of both sender and receiver must all be taken into account. These are part of the communication situation, which we will discuss in the following pages. However, despite the large number of variables, the aim of structure is always the same: to provide a framework that will guide the recipient toward decoding the message in the way intended by the sender. A well-structured message is like a sturdy house. It contains the idea and insulates it from damage by noise.

You could structure the ideas related to your getting hired in several different ways. One would be a résumé that allows the employer to quickly determine your qualifications, but is favorable to you. Another might be a letter that elaborates how you can do the job you seek. You probably will also have to prepare speech communication for an interview, which in many cases is a deliberate test of how well you can orally communicate ideas about yourself and your objectives.

3. Using Resources to Implement Plans. Having an idea and a sound structure for expressing it are obviously of little value unless they actually reach the recipient. Transmission can be thought of as the implementation of the communication plan and structure. To transmit a message you use the resources of your communication skills, media, and the skills of the receiver. (Of course, you already used some of these resources to get the idea into a form suitable for transmission.) The objective of the transmission step is to get the message to the receiver intact and as efficiently as possible. You should have planned at least approximately how you would do this even before you structured the idea into a message.

You might implement the ideas related to getting a job by using media such as a résumé or letter, the telephone, and face-to-face speaking. The more media you can use, the greater your chances of transmitting the information successfully. How well you do so will depend on your communication skills, a topic we will discuss later in this chapter.

4. Using Feedback and Correction. People who try to get a job by mailing out a few hundred résumés and then waiting passively for an offer seldom are very successful. Those who actively encourage feedback by following up their inquiries to determine whether the idea got across usually do a lot better. A response from the receiver enormously increases the chances of eventually communicating an idea. At the very least, you will learn whether or not you actually communicated. For example, getting an offer is feedback that tells you that an employer definitely understood the idea that you should work for them. If this happens, you attained your objective!

But often in life we do not succeed in getting an idea across on the first try. This is when we really need effective feedback. By carefully analyzing the response of the recipient, you can determine where you went wrong. This allows you to take action that will correct whatever caused loss of meaning. The necessary action could range from going back and selecting a different transmission medium to going all the way back to step one and coming up with another idea.

In our example, we could get feedback by calling the person to whom we directed a résumé. Or, if there were an interview, we would get immediate response. We might learn from this feedback that the qualifications listed on our résumé did not seem quite right for the position. If we felt that they were sound, but did not come across, we would rephrase the message and

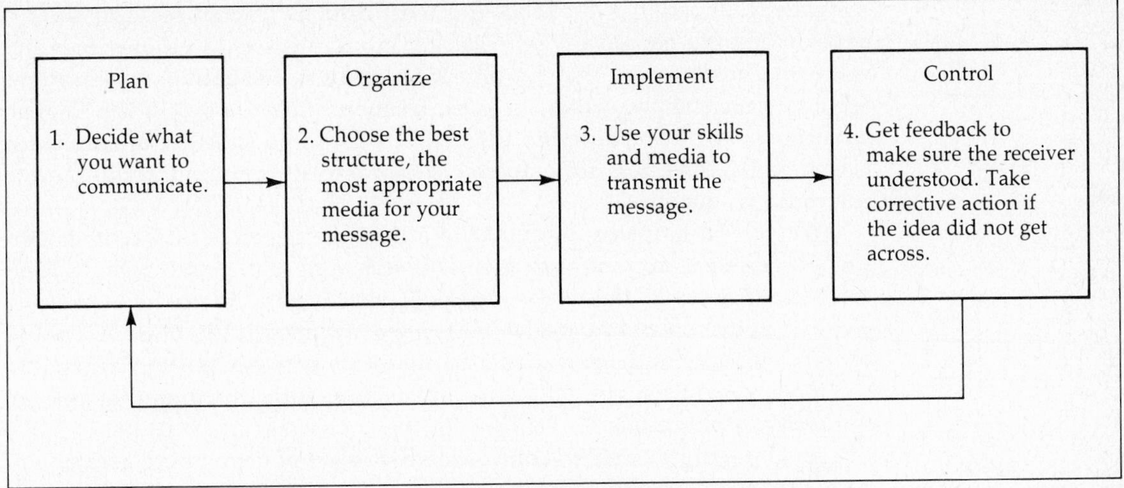

Figure 5-3 Steps in Managing Communication

try to transmit it again, preferably in person. If, however, there is obviously no reasonable chance of successfully communicating the idea that we should be hired, we must try for another job. This would involve repeating all of the steps in the process of managing communication. The effort is most worthwhile, for careful attention to both positive *and negative* feedback is an excellent way to improve one's overall ability to communicate well.

Communication Skills

In truth, one need not consciously think of communication as a process or to weigh its variables to be an effective communicator. These concepts were presented to help you exchange meaning in difficult situations, times where the message is complex or the perceptions of the sender are unusually incongruous with those of the receiver. Such situations arise in the management of large organizations far more often than they do in everyday life. No one, however, can communicate well on a consistent basis without making a deliberate effort to develop personal communication skills.

We will now describe seven basic communication skills needed by managers and most other people in a postindustrial society such as ours.

Thinking. It seems unnecessary to state that one must have something to say before one can say it. But, for some peculiar reason, we tend to be far more concerned with transmission of the message than the message itself. Thinking is probably the most overlooked aspect of communication. Failing to think through an idea before trying to express it is often the true cause of poor verbal communication. An unclear sentence is usually the reflection of an unclear thought. You cannot purposefully communicate an idea to another person unless you can first communicate it to yourself.

Empathy. Empathy is probably the most difficult communication skill to develop because people are generally far more interested in themselves and what they have to say than in others. A study of telephone conversations reputedly once showed that the most frequently used word in the English language is "I." But taking the trouble to increase your ability to empathize is well worth the effort, for empathy is crucial to all communication—and to success in management.

We exhibit empathy by phrasing a message in terms of the other person's experience, appealing to their interests, and taking into account their likes and dislikes. If the recipient senses our concern, he or she is likely to make an active effort to perceive our viewpoint. Be careful, however, not to confuse empathy with sympathy. The difference between putting yourself in the other person's shoes, empathy, and feeling sorry for the other person, sympathy, is enormous.

Encouraging feedback is one of the best ways of developing greater empathy. By really thinking about a person's response, we can determine how our message was perceived, which tells us a great deal about the other person's feelings and existing knowledge. A tried and true way of increasing the feedback you need to empathize better and simultaneously demonstrating empathy is to make frequent use of the word "you," a most powerful word for getting attention.

Speaking. Because they do it so often, many people presume they know how to speak reasonably well. Yet, relatively few people become effective speakers without formal training or a good deal of effort and self-analysis. If you think otherwise, have yourself videotaped while you talk. The first time you see and hear yourself from another's viewpoint is usually a shocking experience.

Fortunately, most people rapidly improve their speaking skills with just a little instruction in the techniques of effective delivery. Such instruction is readily available in most colleges. Since the way you say something communicates as much, if not more, than the words you use, it is an extremely worthwhile subject to study, especially for a prospective manager.

Writing. Many people feel that writing well is a mysterious talent reserved for a select few. This is far from true. While genuine mastery possibly does require a special genius, investigation usually reveals that so-called born writers became expert only after ten or twenty years of diligent effort. Also, the words you see printed seldom resemble the first draft. Ernest Hemingway reputedly revised every page an average of fifteen times before it satisfied him. Managers seldom need go through such painstaking effort. However, it is vital for managers to be able to express themselves lucidly in letters, formal proposals, customer presentations, and performance appraisals. The organization also needs to have its plans and policies written in

FEATURE 5-3

Negotiating Signals

Here are the important nonverbal signals you should be aware of to avoid communications impasses that can stall negotiations, interviews, sales situations, and the like.

- *Unbuttoning jacket.* Indicates friendliness, openness, readiness to reach agreement. Buttoning the jacket (or *leaving* it buttoned) could indicate that a settlement is a long way off.
- *Gestures with glasses.* Slowly cleaning them or chewing on the earpiece means the wearer is stalling for time.
- *Smokers.* Pipe smokers are more likely to play "cat and mouse" and will go through an elaborate series of filling, tapping, cleaning, etc.—all stalling steps. Cigarette smokers are generally more impatient. Cigar smokers rarely light up until their objectives have been reached, and if they blow the smoke upward and deliberately space the puffs, they're feeling confident and smug. (Similarly, cigarette smokers smoke only when relaxed. When they're tense, they either let the cigarettes burn in the ashtray or else put them out.)
- *Nose gestures.* Pinching the bridge (sometimes with eyes closed) indicates either deep thought about the impending decision or self-conflict (with the head lowered). Slight rubbing or touching the nose is a negative sign, no matter what the other person is telling you. (Don't confuse this gesture with genuine scratching to ease an itch, which is generally more vigorous.)
- *Steepling.* Hands placed fingertip-to-fingertip show self-confidence. May be open or covert. (Women usually hide the gesture in their laps when sitting or at waist level when standing.)
- *Interrupt gestures.* Variations on grade-school hand-raising may include tugging at the ear, raising the index finger to the lips, briefly flicking the hand upward a few inches. The extreme is placing the hand on the speaker's arm. If you find you can yield the floor without destroying your narrative, that is a good indication that you are effectively getting your message across.
- *Uncrossed legs.* Indicates a lessening of competitiveness and a diminishing need for attention. It indicates that you're about to close your sale, draw up the contract, etc.

continues on page 158

FEATURE 5-3 continued

Verbal Cues Frequently Ignored or Misinterpreted

- *"Incidentally."* When used at the beginning of a sentence, it probably means that what follows is *extremely* important to the speaker. He disguises this because he's either unsure or knows you won't like what he's going to say.
- *"We."* The speaker is *really* talking for himself, not a group, but he wants to be sure to keep you at arm's length.
- *"As you well know."* The speaker is aware that you really *don't* know, and is actually indicating his superiority.
- *"Needless to say."* Beware of this one. It may signal ambivalent feelings, superiority or self-righteousness, or an imposition of the speaker's feelings on the listener.
- *"Believe me. . . ."* What follows will be, at best, a half-truth.
- *"The matter is closed."* The speaker who uses abrupt and hostile terminations is letting you know that he feels his position is weak, or that he has lost the argument.
- *"Do you mind if I ask you. . . ."* May preface a curt or penetrating statement or question; conceals aggression.
- *"I'll try."* Whether included in a statement of promise or a report of work done, be prepared for underachievement.
- *"On the whole. . . ."* When used by a subordinate, all he is asking for is reassurance. But when the comment is made by a superior, he's gently putting you down.

Caution: Use these signals as *guides* to what's behind a speaker's words. Don't regard them as absolutes. Be sure to consider the person who's speaking, yourself as a listener, and the circumstances, before drawing hasty conclusions.

SOURCE: Gerald I. Nierenberg, "Negotiating Signals," *Boardroom's Business Secrets*, 1977, p. 22. Reprinted from Boardroom Reports, Inc. Management's Source of Useful Information, 500 Fifth Avenue, New York, N. Y. 10036.

language that everyone can understand so people know what its objectives are and what must be done to attain them.

The fact is almost anyone can learn to write clearly, with a little instruction and a lot of practice. If you are interested in a managerial career, you would be well advised to polish your writing skills, because your ability to express yourself in writing will be a major concern of almost any prospective employer. In addition, people on higher levels of management may well read your reports and recommendations. By writing clearly, you will probably be perceived as more effective by them.

Using Electronic Media. While the ability to use electronic media other than the telephone is not yet a skill needed for everyday interpersonal communication, it is of increasing importance in organizational communication. Almost every manager of a large organization now needs to at least know how to read information generated by computers. Most middle managers also are required to know basically how a computer can be used to supply data for decision making. They also need to learn enough computer terminology to communicate adequately with technical personnel such as programmers, systems analysts, and operators. Since experts predict an explosion in computer-related communications technology during the 1980s, a basic skill in using electronic media may soon become almost as fundamental for managers as reading and writing.

Reading. Like speaking, reading is a skill often taken for granted. Many people presume that because they passed English they read reasonably well. However, many people could use considerable improvement in this area. The average high-school graduate today reads at an eighth-grade vocabulary level, at a speed of 100 words per minute, and with only 40 percent comprehension. Special training in reading techniques can raise the average person's speed to over 500 words a minute with almost total comprehension.

The importance of reading faster becomes apparent when you realize how many periodicals and books managers should read just to keep up with new developments in their field that directly affect their unit's performance. This would include information on new decision-making techniques, ways to improve communication, ways to improve motivation, and specific technological advances. The manager also has to be aware of change in the environment, as reported in newspapers and business magazines. Even putting aside the need for outside information, just glancing at the stack of papers in the typical manager's "in-basket" justifies the need for rapid, accurate reading. If a manager can save just 18 minutes a day through improved reading, he or she will gain two weeks of productivity per year.

Listening. Relatively few people listen as well as they speak. This problem is partly physiological. The human mind can process words far faster than the typical speaking rate of 100–200 words per minute. Most people use the spare time to think of matters unrelated to the message. Particularly common is the tendency to think about what we will say next, rather than concentrating on what is being said. Such thoughts overlap part of the incoming message and block its perception. Thus, unless we develop our listening skills, we may frequently filter out important parts of other people's messages. As a result, tasks may not be performed correctly or at all, and objectives may not be attained.

FEATURE 5-4

Guides for Listening Effectively

Professor Keith Davis provides the following ten guides for effective listening. After reading each of these, pause for a minute, picture yourself communicating with a specific person, and then picture yourself using each technique.

1. *Stop talking!* You cannot listen if you are talking.
   Polonius (*Hamlet*): "Give every man thine ear, but few thy voice."
2. *Put the talker at ease.*
   Help a person feel free to talk.
   This is often called a permissive environment.
3. *Show a talker that you want to listen.*
   Look and act interested. Do not read your mail while someone talks.
   Listen to understand rather than to oppose.
4. *Remove distractions.*
   Don't doodle, tap, or shuffle papers.
   Will it be quieter if you shut the door?
5. *Empathize with talkers.*
   Try to help yourself see the other person's point of view.
6. *Be patient.*
   Allow plenty of time. Do not interrupt a talker.
   Don't start for the door or walk away.

SUMMARY

Communication is the exchange of information and meaning between two or more people. In management, communication is referred to as a linking process because all of the managerial roles and functions involve communication. Without effective communication, people cannot work together effectively to attain organizational objectives.

The basic elements of a communication exchange are a sender, a message, a channel or medium, and a receiver.

With the exception of a shared experience, most communication takes place through an indirect process with four interrelated steps. The process begins with the formulation of an idea or the selection of information by the sender. The sender next encodes the idea in symbols, creating a message. Third, the message is transmitted to the receiver via a channel or medium. Fourth, the receiver decodes the message. If the

7. *Hold your temper.*
   An angry person takes the wrong meaning from words.
8. *Go easy on argument and criticism.*
   This puts people on the defensive, and they may "clam up" or become angry.
   Do not argue: Even if you win, you lose.
9. *Ask questions.*
   This encourages a talker and shows that you are listening.
   It helps to develop points further.
10. *Stop talking!*
   This is first and last, because all other guides depend on it.
   You cannot do an effective listening job while you are talking.
   - Nature gave people two ears but only one tongue, which is a gentle hint that they should listen more than they talk.
   - Listening requires two ears, one for meaning and one for feeling.
   - Decision makers who do not listen have less information for making sound decisions."

To develop your listening skills, evaluate your communication with another person after the discussion ends. Ask yourself, what did I do effectively in terms of these ten techniques? Then ask, what do I need to improve on?

SOURCE: Keith Davis, *Human Behavior at Work*, 5th. ed. (New York: McGraw-Hill, 1977), p. 387.

process has been successful, the receiver will understand the idea as the sender intended.

Unfortunately, both physical and perceptual noise is always present at every stage of the process and may distort meaning if allowed to do so. Fortunately, noise and many other problems often can be overcome through effective feedback, a response from the receiver that enables misunderstandings to be made known and clarified. Thus, two-way communication that allows feedback is almost always more effective than one-way communication.

Each step has its inherent potential problems that must be overcome to communicate effectively. In encoding, the primary difficulty usually stems from the nature of symbols and the semantic variations in their meanings. The sender also must be aware of nonverbal symbols, which tend to be perceived more often than words in a conversation. Encoding will be more effective if the sender develops empathy for the receiver and is aware of his own feelings and emotions. Mistakes in encoding usually only surface when the message is decoded, a process with problems similar to those of encoding.

The key to effectiveness in transmission is choosing the best channel or combination of media for the situation. Each of the three primary channels—speaking, writing, and electronic media—has advantages and disadvantages. Speaking, for example, is usually the most accurate medium because it offers an opportunity for immediate feedback, but it is not suited to situations where information is complicated or must be retained for a long time. A combination of writing and speaking is usually the most effective in most situations, with electronic media becoming advantageous when many people must receive the information quickly and accurately.

We can all learn to communicate more effectively by developing the essential communication skills: thinking, empathizing, speaking, listening, writing, reading, and using electronic media. It is vital to our individual success in today's organizational society that we do so.

REVIEW QUESTIONS

1. What is the difference between direct and indirect communication?
2. Explain briefly the four basic elements in the communication process.
3. What role does feedback and noise play in the communication process?
4. Explain each of the steps of the simplified model of the communication process given in the chapter.
5. Compare and contrast the different media discussed in the chapter.
6. What is the relationship between perception and communication?
7. Discuss the ten guides for effective listening proposed by Keith Davis.
8. Describe some methods a manager may use to cope with decoding problems.
9. Show how each of the following affects the quality of communication: thinking, empathizing, speaking, writing, using electronic media, reading, and listening.
10. How can one learn to communicate more effectively?

DISCUSSION QUESTIONS

11. Discuss the similarities between managing and communicating.
12. How would you explain to a friend how she could use the steps in managing communication to secure a position?
13. Why must a manager be able to communicate effectively to his superiors, peers, and subordinates?
14. How can an organization determine the effectiveness of its communications?
15. Identify and discuss individual, group, and organizational factors that affect the communication process in a (a) hospital, (b) steel mill, (c) university.

CASE INCIDENT

Feeding Hours

Built to store cotton over a hundred years ago, the building was now used as a furniture and appliance warehouse by Goodsons department store. The majority of the workers pulled furniture orders. They located an order and then, usually by forklift, brought it to the shipping dock for delivery. Because of the warehouse layout, close supervision was not provided and occasionally a worker would "disappear," that is, simply take too much time when filling an order. Actually, a new facility was under construction, but the completion date was still eight months away. The new warehouse was to be a single-level structure with wide aisles and excellent accesses. It would be a significant change from the present five-story building, which was less than suitable for its present role.

For over 75 years, Goodsons was a major retailer with an enviable reputation for quality merchandise and outstanding customer service. Great emphasis was placed on the belief that the customer is always right, and customer service would provide Goodsons with its primary competitive edge. While these ideas were enthusiastically supported, many employees felt that some customers abused this philosophy. Nevertheless, at Goodsons, the customer ruled, and Goodsons was a tremendously profitable operation.

If the customer was either king or queen at Goodsons, the buyers and those in merchandising had all the internal clout. As a divisional vice-president observed, the name of the game is sales and if you're not in sales, you're not where the action is. Needless to say, those in areas other than sales took a rather dim view of this, and relationships among the various departments left much to be desired. Actually, it was almost a "them and us" situation with the "them" made up of staff and operating personnel, including delivery, workrooms, warehouse, accounting, to cite just a few.

The warehouse was a real enigma. Located seven miles from Goodsons' downtown location, its employees had developed an almost adversary relationship with personnel from the main store. Conversely, the main store merchants were often less than cordial to warehouse personnel. It was one of those classical line-staff feuds which did little to contribute to company goals and objectives.

At the warehouse, several attempts had been made to unionize the workers. Each attempt had been thwarted, but the margin of victory became less decisive with each successive drive. Many even viewed the construction of the new warehouse as a way to let warehouse employees know that they were not forgotten.

Andy Bennett was a "numbers man." An industrial engineer, he prided himself, although still in his thirties, as being a member of the old school. In some ways he was. Although he was 38 years old, he had worked for Goodsons 22 years including the six years it took him to get through college as a co-op student. Each day, like clockwork, Bennett would make an inspection of the warehouse to make certain everything was in order and to insure that no one was goofing off. Just as he was getting ready for his daily inspection, he was stopped by Will Garland, an employee who had actively pushed for unionization.

"This is the last straw," said Garland. "We're mad enough to walk out right now."

Andy Bennett was taken by surprise and wondered what this "troublemaker" was up to now. "What is it?" Bennett asked. "Aren't you people ever satisfied?"

Garland replied it wasn't a matter of satisfaction but of personal dignity. "Come along with me," said Garland, "and I'll show you why we've had enough."

Bennett followed Garland to the warehouse cafeteria where Garland pointed to a newly painted sign which read, "Feeding Hours—11 to 2."

Garland said, "This is not the zoo. We're walking out."

Questions

1. How do you think Bennett should respond to Garland? Why?
2. What might be done to improve internal communications at Goodsons?
3. What role does perception play in this incident?

NOTES

1. Henry Mintzberg, "The Manager's Job: Folklore and Fact," *Harvard Business Review*, vol. 53 (July-August 1975), no. 4, p. 52.
2. Tom Burns, "The Directions of Activity and Communications in a Departmental Executive Group," *Human Relations*, vol. 7 (1954), pp. 73–97.
3. Rensis Likert, *New Patterns of Management* (New York: McGraw-Hill, 1961), p. 53.
4. Robert R. Blake and Jane S. Mouton, *Grid Organizational Development* (Houston: Gulf Publishing Company, 1968).
5. John B. Miner, *The Management Process*, 2d. ed. (New York: Macmillan, 1978), p. 134.
6. Keith Davis, *Human Behavior at Work*, 5th. ed. (New York: McGraw-Hill, 1977), p. 372.
7. Phillip V. Lewis, *Organizational Communications: The Essence of Effective Management* (Columbus, OH: Grid Publishing Company, 1975), p. 95.
8. Ibid.
9. G. V. Barrett and R. H. Franke, "Communication Preference and Performance," *Proceedings, 77th Annual Convention, American Psychological Convention*, 1969, pp. 597–598.
10. D. A. Level, "Communication Effectiveness: Method and Situation," *Journal of Business Communication*, Fall 1972, pp. 19–25.
11. Terrence Mitchell, *People in Organizations: Understanding Their Behavior* (New York: McGraw-Hill, 1978), p. 214.
12. Henry Mintzberg, *The Nature of Managerial Work* (New York: Harper & Row, 1973).
13. A. Mehrabian, *Non-Verbal Communication* (Chicago: Aldine Publishing Company, 1972).
14. Ralph G. Nichols, "Listening Is Good Business," *Management of Personnel Quarterly*, Winter 1962, p. 2.

CHAPTER 6

Decision Making

Sitting behind a large desk does not make a person a manager. One operates as a manager only when either making organizational decisions or implementing them through other people. Decision making, the second linking process, is integral to every managerial function. It pervades virtually everything a manager does to formulate and attain objectives in an organization. Hence understanding the nature of decision making in organizations is critical to anyone who wishes to succeed in management. To help you gain this understanding, we will now describe the types of decisions managers make, the ways in which people make decisions, how the scientific method can be used to improve the effectiveness of decision making, and the major considerations in managerial decision making.

After reading this chapter, you should understand the following key terms and concepts:

decision
organizational vs. personal decisions
programmed vs. nonprogrammed decisions
rational problem solving
decision criteria
relevant information vs. data
conditions of certainty
probability
conditions of uncertainty

The Nature of Decision Making

No person can grow beyond early childhood and remain a stranger to decision making. Like the ability to communicate, the ability to make decisions is a skill sharpened by constant experience. We each make hundreds of decisions a day, an astronomical number during the course of our lives.

A decision is a choice between alternatives.

Decisions range from the minor choices of what to wear to work or to have for lunch to the major choices of what career to pursue and whether to marry. Even though the possible alternatives often are many—a menu might offer 50 food options, a university over 100 majors—we make the great majority of our everyday decisions with little conscious thought. With other decisions we deliberate for days, months, or years. Sometimes, due to unconscious psychological factors, we give disproportionate stress to certain decisions. For instance, some people agonize for weeks over buying a pair of shoes yet buy a $7000 automobile on pure impulse.

Decision making in management is essentially the same as in everyday life. The stakes, however, often are much larger. An individual's personal choices affect primarily his or her own life and those of a few others. Managers choose courses of action not only for themselves but also for their organization and other people. Those on the upper levels of a large organization may make decisions involving millions of dollars. Even more important, managerial decisions may strongly affect the lives of many people, at least everyone who works for the manager, perhaps everyone in the entire organization. If the organization is large and influential, decisions of its top managers may radically affect its local environment. Towns in New England that once bustled, for example, have nearly died out because the textile and shoe factories that sustained them were moved to the South or to foreign countries. A few managerial decisions literally change the course of history. Important governmental choices, such as President Truman's decision to use the atomic bomb, fall in this category.

Responsibility for major organizational decisions is a grave moral burden, as is apparent at high levels of government. But all managers deal with property that belongs to others, and all affect the lives of other people. If a supervisor decides to fire a subordinate, that person may suffer considerably. If the poor performer is not terminated, on the other hand, the performance of the organization may be impaired, injuring its owners and all its workers. Consequently, the manager cannot often afford to make decisions casually. Before learning how a manager can approach a complicated decision rationally and systematically, let us learn a bit more about the pervasiveness of decision making, its relevance to the management process, and the similarities and differences between organizational and personal decisions.

Table 6-1 Decisions of the Management Functions

Planning
1. What is our basic mission or the nature of our business?
2. What should our objectives be?
3. What changes are occuring in our external environment and how will they affect us now and in the future?
4. What strategies and tactics should we use to attain our objectives?
Organizing
1. How should the work of the organization be divided? How should we group work into larger units?
2. How can we coordinate these units so they work in harmony, not against one another?
3. What decisions should people, especially managers, at each level of the organization be allowed to make?
4. Do we need to change our structure because of changes in the external environment?
Motivating
1. What needs do my subordinates have?
2. To what degree are these needs being satisfied through working toward the organization's objectives?
3. If my subordinates' satisfaction and productivity have decreased, why?
4. What can we do to increase the satisfaction and productivity of subordinates?
Controlling
1. How should we measure performance?
2. How often should we measure performance?
3. How well have we succeeded in attaining our objectives?
4. If we have not made sufficient progress toward our objectives, why, and what corrective action should we take?

Pervasiveness of Decision Making

In Chapter 2 we referred to both communicating and decision making as linking processes. Like communicating, decision making affects every aspect of management.

Decision Making and Management Functions. A decision, as defined earlier, is a choice between alternatives. It is, in essence, answering questions. In today's complex, rapidly changing organizational world, there are a great many alternatives open to management, many questions that must be answered for a group of people to formulate and attain objectives. Each of the management functions has several broad, vital decisions associated with it. Some of the most important are listed in Table 6-1.

Organizational Decisions

Organizational decisions are choices managers make to fulfill the obligations of their position. The purpose of an organizational decision is to facilitate attainment of the organization's objectives. Therefore, the most effective organizational decision is the choice that, when *actually implemented*, makes the greatest overall contribution to goal attainment.

Organizational decisions can be classified as either *programmable* or *nonprogrammable.*

Programmed Decisions. Nobel Prize winner Herbert Simon, borrowing from the language of computer technology, used the term programmed to describe decisions that are highly structured. A **programmed decision** is reached by going through a specific sequence of steps or actions, similar to what one does in solving an equation. Usually, the possible alternatives are limited in number, and the choice must fall within guidelines established by the organization.

A hospital supervisor, for example, might base nurse and orderly work schedules on a formula that calls for a certain ratio of staff to patients. If hospital regulations call for 1 nurse for every 5 patients on the floor, the supervisor should automatically decide to assign 10 nurses to a floor with 50 patients. Similarly, if a financial manager is instructed by top management to invest surplus cash in either certificates of deposit, municipal bonds, or common stocks, whichever gives the highest return at the time, the choice is made by calculating the yield of each and simply selecting the most profitable.

Programming is an important aid to effective organizational decision making. By specifying how a decision is to be made, management reduces the chances of error. It also saves time because subordinates do not have to develop a new, correct procedure each time the applicable situation arises. Not surprisingly management most often programs decisions for situations that tend to recur frequently.

It is important for management to make certain that the decision procedure is actually correct and desirable. Obviously, if the programmed procedure becomes incorrect or undesirable, decisions made with it will be ineffective, and management will lose the respect of its people and those outside of the organization whom the decision affects. Moreover, it usually is highly desirable to communicate the rationale behind the programmed methodology to those who use it, rather than simply laying out the procedure. Failure to communicate the "why" of the decision-making procedure often is frustrating and insulting to people who must implement it. In extreme situations, this may result in hostility or outright refusal to follow the program.

Nonprogrammed Decisions. **Nonprogrammed decisions** are unique and nonrecurring. The decision maker must develop the procedure for making the decision. Nonprogrammed decisions are required for situations that are somewhat novel, inherently unstructured, or involve unknown factors. Examples of nonprogrammed decisions would be what the organization's objectives should be, how to improve a product, how to improve the structure of a management unit, and how to increase the motivation of subordinates. In each of these situations, as with most nonprogrammed decisions, the true cause of the problem could be any of a large number of factors. Also, many different options are open to the manager.

In practice, few managerial decisions are either purely programmed or nonprogrammed. These categories, rather, are the extremes of a continuum, as is the case with routine and basic decisions. Most decisions fall somewhere between these poles: they are mainly one or the other. Few programmed decisions are so structured that individual initiative is wholly eliminated. Even the most complex choice can be assisted by a programmed methodology. However, when we discuss rational problem solving later in this chapter, we are actually describing the procedure for making a sound, highly nonprogrammed, organizational decision.

Moreover, throughout our discussion of organizational decision making, you should keep firmly in mind that decision making is so closely related to the management process as a whole that it cannot be considered separately with any degree of realism. As stated, all the functions of planning, organizing, motivating, and controlling require the manager to make decisions. This chapter, in fact, should be considered only the preliminary groundwork for an extended discussion of organizational decision making. The primary objective of this text is to provide you with a framework for making these decisions more effectively. An essential, critical element of this framework is the personal decisions of both managers and the people they manage.

Personal Decisions

Personal decisions are the many choices people make to further their own goals as individuals. The manager does not necessarily have to take the organization or fellow workers into account when making a personal decision. In practice, however, it seldom is possible to fully separate personal and organizational decisions because work plays a major role in the lives of most people. What happens at work strongly determines the course of one's private life. Conversely, people are the major ingredient in an organization's success. Therefore, important decisions that people make about their personal priorities by necessity will influence the organization's effort to attain its objectives.

Interaction Between Personal and Organizational Decisions. To visualize this interplay between organizational and personal decisions, let us examine a few situations that could arise during a short period in a middle manager's life:

Monday: One of the manager's subordinates, a person with a five-year history of good performance, has had severe personal problems lately and allowed them to interfere with his work. Our manager's superior

FEATURE 6-1

Catastrophe Demands Rapid Decision Making

Unforeseen events have a way of cropping up and undoing the best-laid plans of management. An example is the May 25, 1979 crash of an American Airlines DC10. Diagnosing the cause to be cracks in the engine pylons, the Federal Aviation Administration (FAA) ordered all 137 of the nation's DC10s grounded.

A look at Continental gives a glimpse of the problems that have had to be considered by all the airlines with DC10 fleets. Among the topics demanding urgent decisions: how to reroute aircraft to fill the service gaps left by the idled jumbos; how to help stranded ticket holders; what advertisements to kill; what employees to lay off; and who, if anyone, could be sued to recover the huge damages resulting from the lost business.

There were no precedents to follow; never before had the government taken such sweeping action. The grounding came without warning. And its possible duration is frustratingly unpredictable; the carriers are braced for a long grounding, but they also must be prepared for any sudden lifting of restrictions on the DC10.

has begun to notice the man's mistakes. Today, he makes it clear that unless our manager fires this subordinate or changes his performance very soon, she personally will bear the consequences. This particular subordinate happens to be an old friend of our manager, not just a work acquaintance.

- *Tuesday:* Our manager takes part in a planning session to decide whether the company should relocate to a city in the Southwest. Everything indicates that the organization will benefit from the move, and, if it is made, the manager will also receive a nice promotion and raise. However, our manager's husband also has a blossoming career, one that he may not be able to transfer to the new city.
- *Wednesday:* Our manager is offered an important assignment that involves a week's travel to New York, leaving Monday. Her son's birthday, unfortunately, is the same week—and she missed it last year for the same reason.

Continental President Alexander Damm summoned his top executives to a 5 a.m. meeting; Chairman Robert Six was abroad. In shirt sleeves (at that early hour the air conditioning hadn't kicked on), the executives considered Continental's plight.

The grounding put Continental in special jeopardy. Over the years it has reduced its fleet to two planes, 15 DC10s and 55 Boeing 727s. Due to their larger size, the DC10s have some 41% of Continental's seats.

Until the crisis, the Continental fleet had been considered a model of streamlining; suddenly the asset of greater efficiency turned into a liability. United Airlines, for instance, still has jumbo Boeing 747s in its fleet, and Western Air Lines has Boeing 707s operating.

So, although both these competitors had lost their DC10s, they still could run long-range flights. The Continental executives immediately had to acknowledge the obvious: Service from the West Coast to Hawaii and the South Pacific had to be halted. The 727s don't have the range for such flights.

Contributing to the drain are painful personnel problems. The shutdown has idled almost 400 pilots of the airline's wide-body jets. These tend to be senior men, earning up to $80,000 and more a year, and they can't be laid off.

So, while maintaining them at almost full pay, the airline has begun a retraining program to let DC10 pilots qualify for the 727. When that is complete, perhaps in a couple of months, the airline could begin giving furloughs to some of its junior pilots.

SOURCE: Roy J. Harriss, Jr., "Winging It," *Wall Street Journal*, June 15, 1979, p. 1. Reprinted by permission of *The Wall Street Journal*,

- *Thursday:* The vice-president to whom our manager reports mentions that he has been considering transferring another work group to her department because she has been doing such a great job. With this added responsibility will come a healthy raise. It also means more hours on the job and less free time for our manager's personal life. Like many managers, ours has a strong desire to succeed in her career and move up the ladder as quickly as possible. But, like many people of her generation, she also wants enough free time to enjoy life and is determined not to become an all-work-and-no-play sort of person. Not unrealistically, she fears that if she refuses the added responsibility, the vice-president will brand her as competent but uneager for promotion.

Each of the preceding situations involves both a personal and an organizational decision. On Monday, our manager has to weigh friendship against both her responsibility to the organization and a risk to her own job. On Tuesday and Wednesday, she has to balance her career needs and job obligations against her family responsibilities. And Thursday's decision involves a long, hard look at personal priorities, what she really wants from life.

Any decision she makes will have a clear, definite impact on her private life and also will affect the organization. If she fires the subordinate, she probably will lose a friend. If she decides to give him a chance but proves unable to improve his performance, a job important to the organization may go undone. Should she decide to speak out in favor of the organization's move because it appears sound, she will place a strain on her marital relations and may even force herself to leave the organization. Should she choose to leave the organization, it will lose her valuable talents and suffer as a result. These interrelationships can be carried on and on in every instance.

Some of the stress associated with managing and working for organizations results from occasions where a necessary organizational decision is radically at odds with a choice that is highly desirable from a personal standpoint. Inconsistency between personal aims and organizational objectives leads to conflict and is highly dysfunctional. An important part of the human side of management, as we shall see when we discuss conflict and change, is creating a climate where conflict can be managed effectively before individual or organizational problems get out of hand.

Trade-offs. It is very important to note that in all of the situations described earlier it would be very difficult, if not impossible, for the manager to make a decision with no negative consequences. This is typical. As writer and management researcher Robert Katz states: each decision must "strike a balance among so many conflicting values, objectives, and criteria that it will be suboptimal from any single standpoint. Every decision or choice affecting the whole enterprise has negative consequences for some of the parts."[1] This is why it is necessary to view the organization from a systems perspective and consider the potential impact of a managerial decision on all parts of the organization.

The effective decision maker recognizes and accepts that the chosen alternative may have drawbacks, perhaps serious ones. He or she makes a given decision because, all factors considered, it appears to be the most desirable in terms of the net effect. This concept of trade-offs is a theme to which we will return often. In managing organizations, there are few situations so clear cut that only good can result from the best possible decision.

Effective managers and the people who are most successful in everyday life are individuals who do not allow these possible drawbacks to paralyze their decision making. They are people who realize that not making a decision at all, drifting with the tide, usually is as bad or worse than making a poor one. However, there are situations in which *deliberately* not making a choice is a good decision. For example, if additional information would soon be available and time is not critical, it might be best not to make a decision immediately.

FEATURE 6-2

Problems of Dual Career Professional Families Affect Organizations

Six months after he joined the major Chicago bank, the 31-year-old banker was offered the kind of job that could make his career: the chance to start up and head the brand-new European branch of his department.

Regretfully, he turned it down.

He explains that his wife has a top professional post with a "Big Eight" accounting firm, a job that would be hard, if not impossible, to duplicate in London. "It came down to my wife and her job. I would have gone if it wasn't for that," he says.

He admits to having second thoughts, especially since he hopes to head the department someday. While his superiors "talked a good story and said, 'we'll think of you again,' I do wonder, if anything else comes up, would they offer it to me?" he says.

The young man's concern about his difficulty accepting transfers is being matched by employers across the country. While it has been acknowledged that professional women have had such problems because of their husbands' jobs, companies are beginning to realize that professional men in so-called "dual-career" marriages are facing similar conflicts.

And the number of professional workers in such marriages is multiplying so fast that what's happening today could be just the tip of the iceberg of a major issue for business itself in the 1980s.

"Right now, it is an irritation. Within five years it will be a significant problem," says an affirmative action officer of the Chicago bank. Or as James Kennedy, a vice-president of United Air Lines Inc., puts it: "It is a down-the-line problem. But to solve it, we've got to start today."

Indeed, while women made up less than 5% of graduate business and professional school classes a decade ago, they comprise at least 20% and up to 50% of those classes today. That means that five or ten years from now, when these women and the men they marry come up for promotions, companies will be four times to ten times as likely to see such problems.

SOURCE: Liz Roman Gallese, "Manager's Journal," *Wall Street Journal*, July 23, 1979, p. 16. Reprinted by permission of *The Wall Street Journal*,

This brings us to the question of how people make decisions, the mental process people use to make a choice when faced with several alternatives.

Decision-Making Approaches

When considering the processes by which people make decisions, two things should be kept in mind. The first is that making a decision usually is relatively easy. All a person does is choose a course of action. The difficult part is making a *good* decision. The second is that decision making is a psychological process. As we all know from experience, human behavior is not always logical. We sometimes are moved by reason, sometimes by emotion. Therefore, it should come as no surprise that the ways in which managers make decisions range from spontaneous to highly reasoned.

Although a given decision rarely fits squarely within any one category, we can describe the decision-making process as being intuitive, judgmental, or rational.

Intuitive Decisions. A purely intuitive decision is a choice made solely on the basis of what the person *feels* is correct. The decision maker does not weigh the pros and cons of each alternative and need not even understand the situation. He or she simply makes a choice. What we refer to as hunches or gut reaction are intuitive decisions. Management writer Peter Schoderbek states that "while increasing amounts of information can considerably aid middle management in making decisions, the top echelon must still rely on intuitive judgment. [Furthermore,] electronic computers do enable top management to focus more attention on data, but they have not rendered obsolete the time-honored managerial intuitive know how."[2] The heavy reliance of top managers on intuition is corroborated by Professor Mintzberg's studies.[3]

Research into parapsychology has caused many people to acknowledge that certain people do seem to have a remarkable aptitude for making a correct choice by intuition. There have even been studies that indicate a correlation between business success and possessing a high degree of extrasensory perception (ESP).[4] However, there is a major difference between making an organizational decision and deciding whether a coin will turn up heads or tails or what card lies on top of a deck, which is the sort of situation used to measure ESP in these studies. Namely, there are many more options to choose from. In calling the toss of a coin, one always has a 50–50 chance of being right.

In a complicated organizational situation there may be thousands of possible choices. A business with enough money, for example, could make any product in the world. However, it could make and sell *profitably* only a relative few of these. Moreover, in some situations, as we will discuss later, the manager does not even know at the outset what the possible choices are. Thus a manager who relies exclusively on intuition faces monumental odds. Statistically, the chances of making a correct choice without any application of logic are very low. Most managerial decisions that seem to be intuitive really are primarily judgmental.

Judgmental Decisions. Judgmental decisions sometimes appear to be intuitive because their logic is not readily apparent. A *judgmental decision* is a choice made on the basis of past experience or knowledge. The person uses knowledge of what happened in similar previous situations to predict the outcome of the alternatives open in the situation at hand. Using common sense, he or she chooses the alternative that proved successful in the past. When, for instance, you choose between taking extra courses in management or in accounting, you probably will make a judgmental decision based on the experiences you had in the introductory courses in each subject. If you get an "A" in a few management courses and a "C" in a few accounting courses, many of you probably would choose further study in management.

Judgment is very useful in organizational decision making because many organizational situations tend to recur frequently. If the situation is the same, the chances are that what worked well once will work again. (This is the underlying premise of programmed decisions.) A simple example is the hiring of management trainees, which a large organization does hundreds of times a year. Despite advances in psychological testing, none has been devised that will predict management success 100 percent of the time. Therefore many organizations make a judgmental decision to hire only M.B.A. holders who earned good grades for management-training programs because, in the past, such persons proved more successful than trainees with just a B.B.A. or B.A. Another typical judgmental decision would be to allow a competent secretary to answer all routine correspondence without supervision. Many other examples could be given, for judgment is the basis for the vast majority of day-to-day managerial decisions. This is why employers tend to place a high premium on experience when evaluating job candidates.

Because a judgmental decision is made within the manager's mind, it has the big advantage of being fast and inexpensive to make. However, judgment also has its drawbacks. It is based on common sense, and there are few things so uncommon as common sense. This is especially true when, as it often is in dealing with people, the situation is distorted by needs and other factors. More significant, perhaps, is that judgment alone is an inadequate means of reaching a decision when the situation is unique or very complicated.

Judgment cannot cope with a situation that is really new because the manager has no experience on which to base a logical choice. This includes any situation that is novel to the organization such as launching a new line of products, development of new technology, or trying out a radically different system of compensation. In a complicated situation, judgment may fail because there are too many factors that must be considered for the unassisted human mind to grasp and compare.

Because judgment almost always is based on experience, relying heavily upon it biases decisions toward courses of action familiar to the decision makers. This bias may cause them to overlook a new alternative that would be more effective than familiar ones. More subtly, if managers are too firmly wedded to judgment and past experience, they may deliberately or unconsciously avoid opportunities for growth into new areas. If carried to extremes, shunning new areas can be disastrous. As semanticist Stuart Chase observed, many of us are often tyrannized by straight thinking. How often we hear the words, "we've always done it this way."

Coping with the new and complex obviously can never be easy. The danger of failure through making a bad decision cannot be eliminated. However, in many situations the manager can significantly improve the probability of making the right choice by approaching the decision rationally.

Rational Decision Making. The major difference between a rational decision and a judgmental one is that it is not dependent on past experience. A **rational decision** is reasoned out through an objective, analytical process, such as the one described in the following section.

Rational Problem Solving

Problem solving, like management, is a process because it involves an unending series of interrelated steps. The manager is concerned with not just the decision itself, but everything related to it and flowing from it. Problem solving involves not one decision but a series of choices, ending only when and if the problem is resolved. Thus, although we describe problem solving as consisting of five steps plus implementation and feedback, the actual number of stages is determined by the problem itself.

Steps in Rational Problem Solving

1. Diagnose Problem. The first step in problem solving is to define or diagnose the problem fully and correctly. In doing so, it is important to realize that there are two ways of viewing a "problem." One way is to only consider as problems situations in which objectives are not being attained. For example, a supervisor may find that his unit's output is below quota. This is reactive management and clearly is necessary. However, too often managers *only* view as problems those situations in which something should have happened but did not. It also is possible to view an *opportunity* as a "problem," that is, actively seek ways in which the effectiveness of one's unit can be improved, even though everything is going well. This is proactionary management.

Defining problems completely is often difficult because all parts of an organization are interrelated. The job of the marketing manager, for example, affects that of the sales manager, production supervisors, research and development, and everyone else in the business. So, too, does the work of laboratory technicians affect that of physicians in a hospital. If the lab makes a mistake, the physician is likely to compound it because he or she makes decisions on the basis of the lab's analysis. In a very large organization, there may be hundreds of such interrelated jobs. Therefore, the old saw that a properly defined problem already is half-solved still cuts sharply when applied to organizational decisions. Diagnosis, as a result, is itself often a procedure involving several steps and intermediate decisions.

The first phase in diagnosing a complex problem is to recognize and identify the symptoms of difficulty or opportunity. The term *symptom* is used here as it is in medicine. Some common symptoms of organizational malaise are low profits, low sales, low productivity, excessive costs, poor quality, much conflict within the organizations, and frequent staff turnover. Usually, there will be several of these symptoms: excessive costs and low profits, for example, often go hand in hand.

Identifying symptoms helps identify the problem in a general way. It also helps narrow down the number of factors to be considered to a manageable size. However, just as a headache could be symptomatic of any illness from mild tension to a brain tumor, a general symptom such as low profitability has many possible causes. It therefore is usually advisable to avoid the tendency some managers have of taking immediate action to correct a symptom. Just as a pathologist probes and studies to uncover the true causes of illness, so the manager must delve deeply to uncover the causes of organizational ineffectiveness.

To find the causes of a problem, one must collect and analyze information pertinent to it, considering factors both within and outside of the organization. This information may be gathered formally, using techniques such as market research to probe outside the organization and using computer analysis of financial statements, interviews, management consultants, or attitude surveys to delve within the enterprise. Or, as very often happens the information is gathered informally, by talking over the situation and by personal observation. A supervisor, for example, might discuss a productivity problem with subordinates, his immediate superior, and other supervisors to obtain ideas and information.

It is important to recognize that more data does not necessarily result in a more informed decision. As Russell Ackoff states, managers suffer from too much irrelevant information.[5] Thus, during observation it is important to be sensitive to and differentiate between relevant information and data. **Relevant information** is data that has been screened for a particular problem, person, goal, and time.

Naturally, since relevant information will become the basis for the decision, care must be taken to ensure that it is as accurate and relevant as possible. Obtaining complete, accurate information on an organizational problem can be extremely difficult. As described in our study of communication, both gathering and interpreting information is always somewhat distorted by

Figure 6-1 Screening Data
For data to be useful in decision making it must be screened to eliminate irrelevant facts, leaving only relevant information.

psychological factors. The very existence of a problem can cause stress and anxiety, which may aggravate considerably such distortion.

If people believe, for example, that superiors will consider *them* the cause of a problem, they will deliberately or unconsciously present information to improve their position. Or, unless their manager encourages honesty, people may simply say what they think the manager would like to hear. This, of course, is about as helpful in decision making as a patient's asking the doctor to touch up an x-ray because he cannot afford the operation, and it serves to highlight the need to foster good human relations.

2. Identify Constraints and Decision Criteria. When a manager diagnoses a problem for the purpose of making a decision, he or she must consider what can be done about it. Many possible solutions to organizational problems are not *realistic* solutions because either the manager or the organization lacks

FEATURE 6-3

The Managerial Woman: Succeeding in an Organization of Men Requires Tough Decisions

If you want a career, how do you help yourself achieve it in organizations made up predominantly of men?

There are techniques for managing one's emotions and women should learn them.

The technique of identifying patterns in the situations which have caused you trouble in the past, sitting down with pad and pencil and listing all the specifics you can recall, is an extremely useful one. From a clearer picture of the past you can much more clearly predict the future. You can anticipate your own reactions and those of others and think through ahead of time how you will deal with them.

Women describe themselves as waiting to be chosen—discovered, invited, persuaded, asked to accept a promotion.

Women describe themselves as hesitant, as waiting to be told what to do. What would it take to stop being reactive and to start initiating? To start asking questions about promotions and job opportunities? To start asking to learn new skills, to be given extra assignments, to take on new projects?

Women describe themselves as reluctant to take risk. If you're afraid of risk, ask yourself why. Do you think of risk as an uncontrollable gamble rather than as an accessible and manageable act? Have you ever thought of risk-taking as something over which you might have a certain degree of *control?*

Think about a career-related risk you might take. Make two lists on paper. The first should list the positives that might result, the second the things that could go wrong. Does one list or the other seem stronger? Put some odds on your entries. How possible, probable, likely, certain do they seem? Why? What might you do to increase the degree of certainty or decrease it where you don't want it?

Women often say that the only way they can deal with their feelings of guilt over having a career is to try to be a perfect woman/wife/mother simultaneously. How hard have you tried to keep your career life and your personal life totally separate? List the hours, the tasks, the responsibilities, the concerns you are trying to manage and then see whether it is humanly possible to continue to maintain the separation you have striven for.

SOURCE: Margaret Henning and Anne Jardim, "Office Tests Women Face—Social and Sexual," *New York Times,* May 1, 1977, p. 4-F, reprinted from *The Managerial Woman.* (Anchor Books, 1977).

the resources to implement them. Also, some elements causing a problem may be forces outside of the organization, such as laws, that the manager is unable to change. These limitations on corrective action impose constraints on the decision maker. Managers must objectively determine what these constraints are before taking the next step, identification of alternatives. If they do not, at the very least a lot of time will be wasted. At worst, failure to identify constraints may lead to choosing an unrealistic course of action. This, of course, would aggravate rather than resolve the problem at hand.

What will be a constraint on action varies widely among organizations, situations, and particular managers. Some common ones are: inadequate funds to carry out the decision; an insufficient number of people in the organization with the requisite skills and experience; inability to acquire resources at reasonable cost; a need for technology that is undeveloped or impractical from a cost standpoint; an extremely powerful competitive situation; laws; and ethical considerations. In most cases, a large, successful organization faces fewer constraints than one that is small or having serious difficulties.

A very significant constraint on all managerial decisions, but one that sometimes can be removed, is the limitation top management places on the authority of all organizational members, a subject discussed as part of the organizing process. Briefly, managers can only make a decision or implement one if top management gives them the right to do so.

In addition to identifying constraints, managers also need to identify standards against which alternative choices can be measured. These standards are referred to as **decision criteria.** The criteria are guidelines on how the decision will be evaluated. For example, in making the decision to buy a new car, you might establish criteria such as the car must cost less than $5500, must get at least 23 miles per gallon, must seat 5 adults, and must have a good maintenance record and be attractive. We will continue this example after describing the next step, identifying alternatives.

3. Identify Alternatives. The next step is to develop a set of alternative solutions to the problem. Ideally, one would identify all possible actions that could remove the causal factors and thereby enable the organization to attain its objectives. However, in practice managers rarely have enough time or knowledge to formulate and evaluate literally *every* alternative. Moreover, considering an extremely large number of alternatives, even if all are valid, tends to cause confusion. Managers therefore usually limit the number of choices that will be considered seriously to the several that seem most desirable.

Care must be taken, however, to consider a reasonably wide range of solutions. Developing several genuinely different alternatives, including the possibility of no action, helps to assure in-depth analysis of difficult problems. If, in some instances, management fails to evaluate what will happen if it does nothing, there is a danger of succumbing to pressure to take immedi-

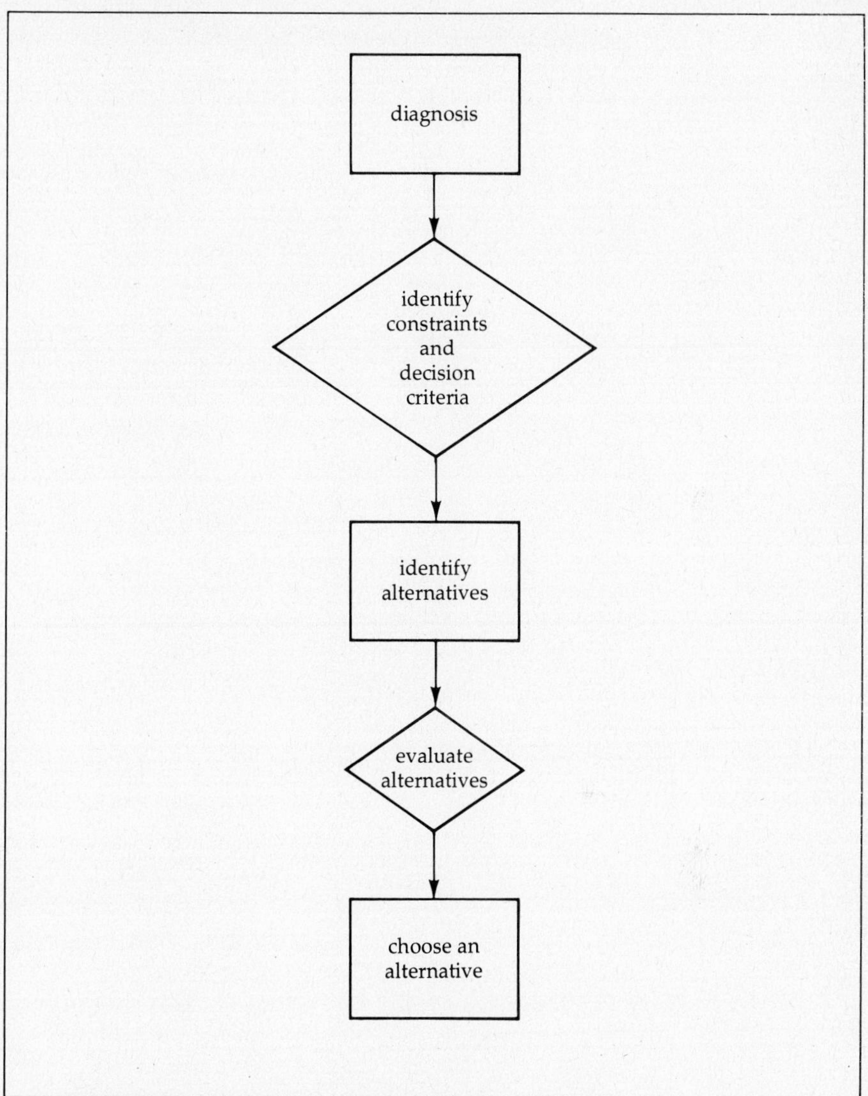

Figure 6-2 Steps in Rational Problem Solving

ate action. This reduces the possibility of reacting to a surface symptom, rather than a primary factor. Returning to our car example, you would now choose a number of cars that you feel meet the criteria you established. Having selected the alternatives, you must evaluate them.

4. Evaluate Alternatives. The next phase of the process is evaluation of the possible alternative courses of action under active consideration. (Some preliminary evaluation probably was necessary to determine which alternatives

FEATURE 6-4

Pillsbury's New Vice-President Stresses Communication in Decision Making

A top-management job is always difficult, but the problems are even more severe when the person is an outsider brought in to correct long-standing problems. This was exactly the situation of Raymond F. Good, when he left the presidency of Heinz U.S.A. to become an executive vice-president at Pillsbury Co.

Good . . . knew he needed to learn about the personalities and sensitive issues that govern etiquette there, and he needed to find out exactly what was expected of him. Rather than wait for things to gel spontaneously, he plunged into the new assignment with a series of marathon management conferences, using as a starting point information gleaned from in-depth interviews of both insiders and informed outsiders, who revealed anonymously what they believed was right and wrong with the group's management and its products.

Recognizing the difficulty of accomplishing this quickly, Good hired John D. Arnold, a consultant who specializes in communication and helping executives take over a job at a new firm.

"I had to make some immediate decisions," says Good, "and I didn't want to take three years to get into the job."

During the early days of an executive's tenure, Arnold gathers candid perspectives of the company by conducting intensive confidential interviews with top management as well as outside observers. For example, he asks: What is the image of your division in the market? What are its principal weaknesses? What customer needs are not being satisfied? What is your business strategy and how should it be improved? In short, what are the problems and how should they be solved?

SOURCE: "A New Face Jolts Pillsbury," *Business Week*, May 2, 1977, p. 92.

are to be evaluated in depth. However, research has shown that both the quantity and quality of alternative ideas increase when there is separation between idea generation [identifying alternatives] and idea evaluation.[6]) To evaluate solutions, the manager determines the advantages and disadvantages of each and weighs the possible overall consequences of each. That there will be negative aspects to every alternative is virtually certain. As mentioned earlier, most important managerial decisions involve a trade-off.

In order to compare solutions, one needs a standard against which the predicted results of each possible alternative can be measured. These standards are the decision criteria established in step 2. Returning to our car example, if any of the cars selected failed to meet one or more of the criteria you established, it would no longer be considered a realistic alternative.

Notice, however, that some of the criteria for selecting a car were expressed in quantitative terms, such as less than $5500. Others such as a good maintenance record and attractiveness require qualitative information. In order to assess and compare maintenance records, you might look up the ratings each received from *Consumer Reports.* To assess and compare attractiveness, you could rate each, in your opinion, as being very attractive, moderately attractive, average, below average, or not attractive. You could also rate each on a 1–5 scale, 5 being very attractive, or having an excellent maintenance record, 1 being the opposite.

Difficulty can arise at this stage because it is impossible to compare things unless they are alike—apples cannot be compared directly to oranges. All solutions must be expressed in a similar form. Preferably, this should be the same form in which the objective is expressed. In business, profit is a continuing need and governing priority, so solutions can be assigned a dollar value and their impact on profit weighed to make comparisons between them. In nonprofit organizations, the primary objective usually is to deliver the greatest total benefit at the lowest cost. Therefore, dollars often can also be used to compare the consequences of alternatives open to the managers of such organizations.

Returning again to our car example, you could express all the criteria in similar form by using a 1–5 scale for both the qualitative and quantitative factors. The least expensive car would be given a value of 5, the most expensive a value of 1, and so forth for mileage and the other standards you set. Probably some of these criteria are more important than others to you. For example, you might consider attractiveness to be twice as important as cost. If so, you would weigh the choice by multiplying the ranking of attractiveness by two. Similarly, if you consider maintenance only two-thirds as important as cost, you would multiply maintenance ratings by two-thirds. After going through this procedure for every criteria, the ratings for each would be added for each car. The car with the highest total rating would be the obvious rational choice, and the decision would be made.

Note that in evaluating potential solutions, the manager is attempting to predict something that will occur in the future. The future is always uncertain. Any number of factors, including changes in the environment and inability to implement the decision, could prevent the solution from coming to pass as anticipated. Thus an important consideration in evaluation is the probability each solution has of working out as intended. If a given solution has more favorable consequences than another but a much lower chance of being carried out, it probably will be a less desirable choice. The manager incorporates probability into the evaluation by taking into account the degree of certainty or risk, a topic discussed later in this chapter.

5. Choose an Alternative. If the problem has been properly defined and the alternative solutions thoroughly weighed and evaluated, making a choice—the decision itself—should be relatively easy. The manager would simply select the alternative with the most positive overall consequences, as illustrated by our car example. However, when the problem is complex and many trade-offs must be considered, or when much of the information and analysis is subjective, no alternative may stand out clearly as the best choice. This is where good judgment and experience play their most important role.

Although it would be ideal for managers to strive for a decision that is optimal, managers generally do not do so in practice. Herbert Simon's research indicates that when making decisions managers engage in what he terms "satisficing," instead of "maximizing" behavior. The optimal decision does not generally occur because of time limitations and the limited ability of people to consider all pertinent information and alternatives. Because of these constraints, managers generally select a course of action that, while clearly acceptable, is not necessarily the best possible. We will elaborate on Simon's views later in this chapter.

Implementation. The problem-solving process does not end when an alternative is chosen. Merely selecting a course of action is of little value to an organization. To resolve a problem or take advantage of an opportunity, the decision must be *implemented*. The degree to which decisions are effectively implemented can be increased if they are accepted by the people affected.[7] Acceptance, however, is seldom automatic, even when the decision is clearly a good one.

Sometimes a manager is able to force acceptance of decisions on those who must implement them. Usually, though, the decision maker must *sell* his or her point of view to others in the organization: persuade people that the choice is good for both the organization and them as individuals. Some managers regard having to sell decisions as being a waste of time, but taking the attitude that, "I'm the boss, right or wrong," is generally not effective in today's world of educated workers. As we will learn when we study motivation and leadership, the chances of effective implementation are greatly increased when the people involved have had a say in the decision and genuinely believe in what they are doing. Therefore, a good way to win acceptance of a decision is to include others in the decision-making process.

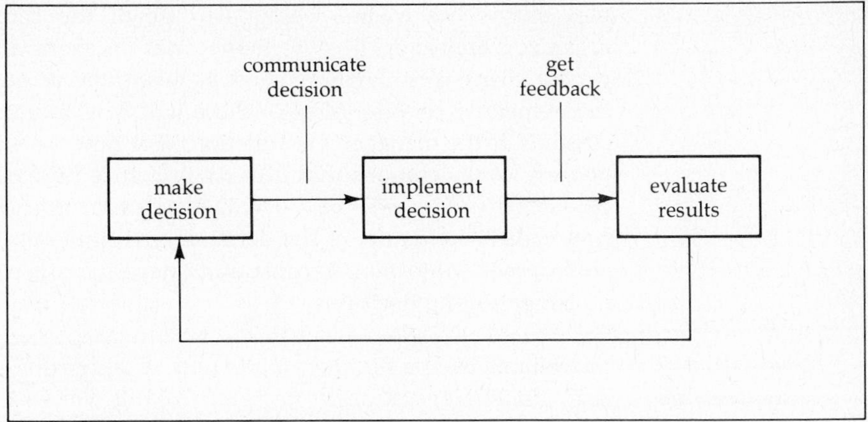

Figure 6-3 Decision-Making Process Subsequent to Problem Solving

However, as we will soon see, there are situations in which a manager should make decisions without consulting others. Participation in decision making, like every other management technique, is not a panacea effective in every situation.

Furthermore, winning support does not in itself ensure proper execution of the decision. Getting decisions implemented requires bringing the entire management process into play, especially the organizing and motivating functions.

Feedback. Another phase of managerial decision making takes place *after* the decision has actually been acted upon. This phase is measurement and evaluation of the decision's consequences: what actually happened. By obtaining feedback, which is historical data on what took place during and after implementation, managers can compare actual results with what they expected to accomplish with the decisions. This enables managers to evaluate the effectiveness of decisions and, if necessary, change them before serious harm is done to the organization. The evaluation of decisions in management is accomplished primarily through the control function, which is discussed in later chapters.

Considerations in Managerial Decision Making

Our discussion of the steps in rational problem solving are meant to serve as a guideline to help you make more effective decisions in complex situations. However, like all management techniques, they cannot be used in a vacuum. Organizations are complex entities that are extensions of an even more complex entity, the human being. Because of the complexities inherent in organized endeavor, because managerial decisions are made by and affect people, many considerations must be taken into account throughout the decision-making process. Most of these will be elaborated on in our later discussions of the management functions. For now we will describe only a few primary considerations that directly influence how decisions are made and how effective they will be. We will cover in turn the orientation of the decision maker, the nature of the decision environment, time and the changing environment, information constraints, negative consequences, and interrelationships among decisions.

Orientation of the Decision Maker

There have been a number of attempts at understanding and explaining an individual's orientation in decision making. We will describe two popular models of decision-making behavior, the *economic man* model and the *administrative man* model.

Economic Man. The *economic man* model of human decision making is often attributed to the famous Scottish economist Adam Smith, whose description of the benefits of specialization in *The Wealth of Nations* helped launch the Industrial Revolution. The economic man model makes several important assumptions. One of these is that people are completely *rational* when making work-related decisions. That is, people order their preferences in a hierarchy according to their values. When making a decision, they chose the alternative that *maximizes* the outcome according to the values established. For example, earning more money might be viewed as better than earning less. Thus, according to the economic man model, a person offered an opportunity to make more money should always take it, rather than select a course of action that allows him or her more leisure time. The economic man model also assumes that people have complete information about the situation, have identified all possible alternatives, and are aware of the potential results of each alternative.

Administrative Man. An alternative model of how people make decisions was set forth by Professor Herbert Simon.[8] He states that the economic person model is normative. It only describes how a person *should* make a decision. In real situations, according to Simon, people do not behave this way.

Simon disagrees with several assumptions implicit in the economic man model. First, people do not have complete information about anything and, therefore, cannot be fully aware of all aspects of a decision. This prevents them from identifying all possible solutions and correctly anticipating all potential outcomes. Furthermore, Simon does not feel that human beings are completely rational:

> When limits to rationality are viewed from the individual's standpoint, they fall into three categories: he is limited by his unconscious skills, habits, and reflexes;

> he is limited by his values and conceptions of purpose, which may diverge from the organization's goals; he is limited by the extent of his knowledge and information. The individual can be rational in terms of the organization's goals only to the extent that he is *able* to pursue a particular course of action, he has a correct conception of the *goal* of the action, and he is correctly informed about the conditions surrounding his action. Within the boundaries laid down by these factors his choices are rational-goal oriented.[9]

In lieu of the economic man assumption of objective rationality, Simon sets forth the notion of *subjective* rationality. People make choices depending on such factors as their personal values and the ways they have learned to perceive and think about situations. Thus, according to Simon's administrative man model, during decision making "choice is always exercised with respect to a limited, approximate, successful model of the real situation."[10]

Simon also disagrees with the assumption that people try to optimize, seek the best possible solution, when making a decision. He states, in contrast, that people "satisfice": they only continue to search for alternatives until they find one that meets some acceptable minimal standard, as opposed to searching until an optimal solution is found. Thus, in practice, there is no attempt to find all the alternatives and order them in a hierarchy of values, as the economic man model holds.

Additional Research Findings. Simon's administrative man model of decision making has enjoyed widespread acceptance and is consistent with modern theories of human behavior. Early research testing it totally supported the administrative man model.[11] However, more recent research indicates that some people do strive for optimal decisions, as the economic man model suggests.[12] Summarizing these findings, Professor John Miner states:

> The sum of the evidence seems to indicate that truly effective managers do study alternatives and try to maximize rather than satisfice or merely rationalize an early choice. In all probability they learn to do so as a consequence of experience. When a problem is very complex and there are a great many possible choices of action, however, real maximizing may prove very difficult.[13]

The reason why it is so often very difficult to identify an optimal alternative becomes clearer when one understands that decisions are made in widely differing environments.

Nature of the Decision Environment

Risk is always a major consideration in managerial decision making. Risk is not used here in the conventional sense of danger. **Risk** refers, rather, to the degree of certainty with which an outcome can be predicted. When evaluating alternatives and making decisions, the manager must assess the possible outcomes under different conditions or states of nature. Decisions, in effect, are made in different environments with respect to risk. These environments are traditionally classified as conditions of *certainty*, *risk*, or *uncertainty*.

Certainty. A decision is made under **conditions of certainty** when the managers know exactly what the outcome of each alternative will be. An example of a certain decision would be to invest excess cash in an 11 percent certificate of deposit. The manager knows that, excepting the extremely unlikely contingency of the federal government defaulting on its obligations, the organization will earn exactly 11 percent interest on its investment. Similarly, a manager can, at least in the short run, determine exactly what it will cost to produce a product because the cost of rent, materials, and labor is known or can be computed with high precision.

Relatively few organizational or personal decisions are made in an environment of certainty. However, some are, and often an element of a larger decision may be considered certain. Writers and researchers of the management science school refer to situations with certainty as *deterministic*. In Chapter 15, "Management Science Models and Methods," we will describe some deterministic decision-making models.

Risk. The decision-making environment is one of *risk* if the outcomes are not certain, but the *probabilities* of various outcomes are known. **Probability** refers to the degree of likelihood that a given event will occur, and can range from 0 to 1. The sum of the probabilities for all alternatives must be 1. In certainty, there is only one alternative.

The most desirable way to determine probability is objectively. Probability is *objective* when it can be determined by mathematical odds or by statistically analyzing past experience. An example of objective probability is that a coin will turn up heads 50 percent of the time. Another is the prediction of the death rate by life insurance companies. Since the entire population is used as a base of experience, insurance actuaries can predict with considerable accuracy what percentage of people of a certain age will die each year. They determine from this how much they must collect in premiums to pay claims and still earn a profit.

There are several ways in which an organization can obtain the relevant information it needs to compute risk objectively. Census, labor, and economic reports of the federal government contain monumental amounts of data on population patterns, price increases, income distribution, inflation, wages, and so forth. Large trade organizations produce information of specific interest to a particular industry, such as how many females between the ages of 19 and 25 read *Cosmopolitan* magazine, as opposed to *Time* each month. When outside information is unavailable, the organization can obtain its own by conducting research. Market research is so widely used to project acceptance of new products, television shows, movies, and politicians that it has become an important industry of its own and an integral activity of almost every large organization that deals with the public.

For a probability to be truly objective, there must be enough information for the projection to be statistically valid. One could not, for instance, predict whether millions of Americans will buy home computers by testing the idea out on only a few dozen families. The responses of several hundred would be needed. Moreover, probabilities are valid only as an average and in the long run. A coin conceivably could turn up heads 10, 20, or even more times in a row. Thus, while an insurance firm that covers 50,000 automobiles might be able to predict casualty losses accurately based on statistical averages for the entire population, the manager of a small company could not. One of the firm's 15 cars might wind up in a freak accident with a multimillion dollar property loss.

An interesting example demonstrating that even objective probabilities are uncertain is the decision to inoculate the American population against swine flu in 1976. The epidemic predicted by the Center for Disease Control failed to materialize. Moreover, the incidence of negative side effects was much higher than predicted from tests of the vaccine. Thus, instead of preventing illness, the vaccination program caused some people to get sick who might otherwise not have—at a cost of many millions to the taxpayers. (Not surprisingly, the head of the center was replaced shortly thereafter. Managers "live or die" by their decisions.)

In many situations, the organization will not have enough information to estimate probability objectively, but management's experience will give it a good feel for what is likely to happen. In these instances, the manager can use judgment to assign alternatives a *subjective* or *inferred probability*. The odds posted on horses prior to the beginning of a race are an example of an inferred probability. One has some information and experience—knowledge of how well the horse did in other races—but not enough for an objective probability.

Deciding whether to self-insure an automobile fleet is a good example of a decision made under conditions of risk. The manager responsible for this decision is not certain that an accident will occur or how much one would cost. But he knows from insurance industry statistics that one out of 10 drivers has an accident each year and the average loss is $2000. Thus, if the organization has 500 autos, there *probably* will be 50 accidents at a cost of $100,000. There may actually be fewer accidents, there may be greater losses. In contrast, if the manager decides to buy an insurance policy for the fleet, the cost might be exactly $110,000, no matter how many accidents there are, and the decision would be based on certainty.

Uncertainty. A decision is made under **conditions of uncertainty** when one cannot determine the probability of potential outcomes. This would occur in a situation in which the factors to be considered are so novel and complex that it is not possible to obtain sufficient relevant information about them. As a result, the likelihood that a certain outcome will occur cannot be predicted with reasonable confidence. Uncertainty is characteristic of some decisions that must be made in a rapidly changing environment. The greatest potential for uncertainty exists in socio-cultural, political, and high technology environments. Defense Department decisions to develop extremely sophisticated new weapons systems are often genuinely uncertain. Because one does not know how or whether the weapon will be used or what counter weapons the enemy may develop, the Defense Department cannot always determine whether the proposed new system will actually be effective by the time it is put into service, which may be five years in the future. However, in practice, very few managerial decisions have to be made in conditions of complete uncertainty.

When faced with uncertainty, two basic options are open to the manager. One is to try to obtain additional relevant information and analyze the problem further. This often reduces the novelty and complexity of the problem. Hopefully, by combining this added information and analysis with past experiences, judgment, or intuition, the manager will be able to assign subjective or inferred probabilities to the various outcomes. Our discussion of the Delphi Technique later in this book will describe an interesting, recent method for obtaining further information in partially uncertain situations.

The second option is to proceed directly with using past experience, judgment, and intuition, and assign inferred probabilities to the different outcomes. This is necessary when time is too limited to enable additional information to be gathered or when the cost of obtaining information is too high. Time and information constraints are critical considerations in managerial decision making.

Time and the Changing Environment

As pointed out in our discussion of the external environment, the passage of time usually changes the situation. If there is much change, the situation will have altered sufficiently to make the criteria for the decision invalid. Thus decisions must be made and implemented while the information and assumptions on which they are based is still relevant and accurate. This is often difficult, for the lead time in executing some decisions is very great. For example, it took Du Pont 25 years to develop nylon as a product. Also, as common sense dictates, a decision must be made quickly enough for the desired action to remain valid. It does little good to systematically analyze the best way of obtaining funds for future months, if you need the money in a week. Therefore, time considerations sometimes force managers to use judgment or even intuition when they normally would prefer rational analysis.

Similarly, the possibility of a decision being ahead of its time must also be considered. Many companies have poured millions of dollars into a project in an effort to beat competitors to the market only to find the latecomers faring better for having waited. Minnesota Mining and Manufacturing, for example, developed a color-copying process in 1961; Xerox introduced the first successful one in 1975. Berkey Photo and several other companies plunged into production of pocket calculators and suffered enormous losses when improved technology enabled newcomers to the field to make calculators at far lower costs less than a year later.

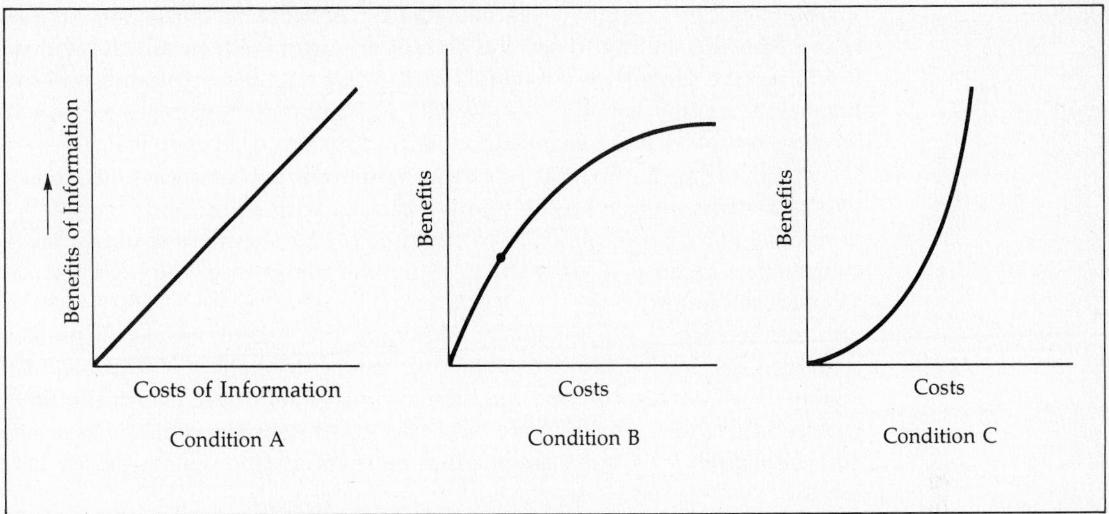

Figure 6-4 Costs versus Benefits of Additional Information

Information Constraints

Early in the chapter we distinguished between data and information, stating that information is data that has been screened for specific people, problems, goals, and a time horizon. Information is necessary for rational problem solving. However, it is important for managers to realize that sometimes the information needed to make a good decision is not available or may cost too much to obtain. The cost of information would include managerial time, subordinate time, and actual costs such as those for market research, computer time, outside consultants, and so forth. Thus, the manager has to decide whether the benefits of the added information, in terms of increased quality and quantity of alternatives and capacity to evaluate them, are significantly greater than cost of this information. An aspect of this is how important the decision itself is: whether it involves a substantial percentage of the organization's resources or an insignificant sum of money.

If the information is not immediately available at reasonable cost, but soon will be, the manager's best course of action may be to put off the decision. The assumptions here are that time is not critical and the cost of delay will be more than offset by the benefits of an improved decision made with the added information. These benefits and costs, in most cases, are subjectively estimated by the manager, especially with respect to how much the manager's own time is worth and what the expected improvement will be.

Figure 6-4 illustrates three different conditions a manager may encounter when assessing the benefits and costs of information.

In condition A, the benefits of each additional unit of information exactly equal the cost. (This is similar to the concept of marginal revenue and marginal cost you may have learned about in economics courses.) As long as management is willing to pay the costs of acquiring additional information, it will receive proportional benefits. However, both time constraints and the manager's limited mental capacity for absorbing and using information would eventually make acquiring more information uneconomical.

In condition B, the costs of obtaining more information are only offset by the benefits up to a certain point, indicated with a dot on the curve. Beyond this point, it would not be worthwhile for management to obtain more information because, even if the decision were improved, the organization would lose money.

In condition C, the benefits of additional information are clearly greater than its costs. In this situation obtaining more information is obviously desirable. However, again, time and mental constraints would eventually limit the usefulness of acquiring more information. As Russell Ackoff pointed out, managers often incorrectly assume that more information is necessarily better.

Negative Consequences

Management decision making, like life in general, is in many respects an exercise in the art of effective compromise. A gain in one area is almost always obtained at the cost of a sacrifice in another. Opting for a higher quality product will increase its costs: some customers will be pleased, others will turn to a less expensive alternate. Installing automated production machinery may lower overall costs: it may also force the layoff of many loyal employees. Simplifying a procedure may enable the firm to use unskilled labor. However, the simpler job may prove so boring that workers become dissatisfied, with the unanticipated result of increased absenteeism and turnover, and possibly decreased productivity.

These negative consequences must be taken into account when making a decision. In Chapter 3 we stressed the need to consider interrelationships among internal variables and gave several examples of the potential negative consequences of not taking a systems approach. The problem in decision making is one of comparing the negative disadvantages with the positive advantages in order to attain the greatest overall gain with respect to attaining organizational and personal objectives. Often the manager must judge subjectively which negative side effects are indeed acceptable in exchange for a desired end result. However, certain negative consequences are wholly unacceptable to managers of responsible organizations. Violating laws or ethical standards would be an example. In such instances, the negative consequences would be treated as constraints when establishing criteria.

Interrelationships among Decisions

In organizations all decisions are in some way related to other ones. Making a major decision for an organization is analogous to throwing a rock into the middle of a pond. It creates ripples that run through the organization from edge to edge. A single *important* decision could easily necessitate a sequence of hundreds of smaller ones. If, for example, an organization decides to move its headquarters to another state, it will also have to decide how to compensate employees for the move, who to take, whether to buy new furniture or move the old, who to hire for new positions and vacancies created by the move, whether different tax laws in the new state will mean a change in accounting procedures, and so forth.

Moreover, major decisions have ramifications for the entire organization, not just the segment directly affected. If a manufacturing firm, for example, decides to purchase new and more productive plant machinery, it will also have to find a way to sell its increased output. Thus, the new equipment purchase would affect not only the production department but also sales and marketing in a major way.

The ability to perceive just how decisions mesh and interact becomes increasingly important as one moves up the ladder to top management. Those on lower levels of management who demonstrate a facility for considering the interrelationships among decisions—seeing the "big picture"—are often the ones selected for promotion.

SUMMARY

A decision is a choice between alternatives. Decision making is considered a linking process because the performance of every management function is dependent on effective decision making. Organizational decisions, those pertaining to the attainment of organizational, as opposed to personal, objectives can be classified as either programmable or nonprogrammable.

A programmed decision is reached by going through a specific sequence of steps and is used most often for repetitive situations. A nonprogrammed decision, used in novel or complex situations, is one in which the decision maker develops the procedure for making a choice.

Decisions may be reached by intuition, judgment, or rational problem solving. In rational problem solving, the scientific method is used to increase the probability of making an effective decision in a new or complex situation.

The steps in rational problem solving are: diagnosis, identification of constraints and decision criteria, identification of alternatives, evaluation of alternatives, and choice of an alternative. However, the process cannot be considered complete until the decision is implemented and feedback indicates it has successfully solved the problem.

The orientation of the decision maker is a major consideration in decision making. One model of decision-making behavior is the economic man, which presumes that people are rational when making decisions and strive to make the optimal choice. Another example is the administrative man model proposed by Herbert Simon. This holds that there are limits to rationality and that most people satisfice, opt for the first acceptable solution, rather than seek the optimal decision.

The nature of the decision environment with respect to risk is also critical. A condition of certainty is one in which the manager knows exactly what the outcome of each alternative will be. A condition of risk is one in which the probability of various outcomes can be determined with confidence. A condition of uncertainty exists when there is too little information to confidently predict the probability of outcomes. In the latter environment, the manager must use judgment to assign an inferred probability to each possible outcome.

Time is a consideration in that decisions must be made quickly enough to be used but not so soon that the decision is ahead of its time.

Information is a constraint because obtaining more information costs money. The manager must decide whether the benefits of an improved decision offset the costs of added information. More information does not always lead to better decisions because people have a limited capacity to absorb and use it.

Every important decision involves trade-offs, negative consequences and side effects, that the manager must weigh against the decision's anticipated benefits. To do so the manager must understand the interrelationships among decisions. A really important decision will give rise to many additional decisions and will affect every aspect of the organization. To be an effective decision maker, the manager must choose those alternatives that make the greatest overall contribution to attainment of the organization's objectives.

REVIEW QUESTIONS

1. What is the difference between decision making in management and decision making in everyday life?
2. How do organizational decisions differ from personal decisions?
3. Briefly explain the difference between programmable and nonprogrammable decisions.
4. What is the difference between a rational decision and a judgmental one?
5. Describe the steps in rational problem solving.
6. In light of Simon's work what are the major weaknesses of the economic man model of human decision making?
7. Distinguish among the decision environments of certainty, risk, and uncertainty.
8. When faced with uncertainty, what two basic options are open to the manager?
9. What effect does time have on the decision-making environment?
10. Distinguish between data and information.

DISCUSSION QUESTIONS

11. In today's postindustrial society, explain why the administrative man theory is more appropriate than the economic man.
12. Use your current knowledge of management to develop a plan that will enable your firm to make effective decisions.
13. How would you apply the systematic methodology of scientific reasoning to personal and organizational decisions?
14. Why is it important for a manager to realize the difference between problem solving and decision making?
15. "Making a major decision for an organization is analogous to throwing a rock into the middle of a pond." From a management standpoint, what is the ramification of this statement?

CASE INCIDENT

The Air-Conditioned Cafeteria

Employee relations at Vickstone, Inc. had been particularly strained during the past several months. Grievances hit a new high and there was a short-lived, spontaneous walkout by eight maintenance workers.

Founded 10 years ago by Harold Edwards, Vickstone was now a well-respected company in the home lighting industry. Edwards grew up on the wrong side of the tracks, never completed high school, but was a self-educated engineering and financial genius. In addition to his regular work duties, Edwards was once a shop steward for the union and vowed that if he ever had his own company, he'd be far more sensitive to staff needs. One of Edwards's favorite expressions was "it's management's mistakes that keep the union going and growing." Edwards was absolutely convinced that he could do better than those he worked for, not only in the technological end of the business but in dealing with people.

With money borrowed from family and friends, Harold Edwards started Vickstone in his garage. The present location, while not a new facility, was a significant improvement over anything that Vickstone had before.

Edwards was a driver. He pushed others as hard as he pushed himself. This characteristic, said Vickstone's labor lawyer, probably led to last year's successful unionization drive. Actually, when Vickstone employees voted to join the union, it was interpreted as a personal insult and defeat by Edwards. Although a former union member, Edwards did not want to deal with a unionized work force and felt he had done everything possible to keep his employees happy.

In the process of upgrading the plant, Edwards decided to have the cafeteria air-conditioned. In discussing this with his personnel director, Edwards was told he was throwing his money away and that an air-conditioned cafeteria was not an important employee-relations priority. Edwards told the personnel director that his position was irrational and that common sense and logic clearly indicated that employees would respond favorably to having the air cooled.

As usual, Edwards did it his way and the cafeteria was air-conditioned. After this was done, the personnel director decided to talk with several of the employees about it. When he asked, "How do you like the air-conditioned cafeteria?" he received the following responses:

1. "I thought it was always air-conditioned."
2. "It doesn't matter to me one way or another since I never eat there."
3. "If the company could afford to air-condition the cafeteria, how come they couldn't afford to give me a raise?"

When the personnel director told Edwards about the reactions to the air-conditioning, Edwards said that the employees didn't know what was best for them and that the personnel director should stop asking questions.

Questions

1. How would you describe Edwards's decision-making process?
2. What elements in managerial decision making were apparently neglected by Edwards?
3. Why was this a nonprogrammed decision?

NOTES

1. Robert L. Katz, *Management of the Total Enterprise* (Englewood Cliffs, NJ: Prentice-Hall, 1970), p. 13.
2. Peter P. Schoderbek, *Management Systems*, 2d ed. (New York: John Wiley & Sons, 1971), p. 124.
3. Henry Mintzberg, *The Nature of Managerial Work* (New York: Harper & Row, 1973).
4. J. Mihalasky and H. C. Sherwood, "Dollars May Flow from the Sixth Sense," *Nation's Business*, vol. 59 (1971), pp. 64–66.
5. Russell E. Ackoff, "Management Information Systems," *Management Science*, December 1967, pp. 147–156.
6. Morris J. Stein, *Stimulating Creativity*, Volume 2 (New York: Academic Press, 1975).
7. Norman R. F. Maier, "Assets and Liabilities in Group Problem Solving: The Need for an Integrative Function," *Psychological Review*, vol. 74 (1967), pp. 239–249.
8. Herbert A. Simon, *Administrative Behavior* (New York: The Free Press, 1957).
9. Ibid, p. 241.
10. J. G. March and H. A. Simon, *Organizations* (New York: Wiley, 1971), p. 139.
11. G. P. Clarkson, "A Model of Trust Investment Behavior," in R. M. Cyert and J. C. March, eds., *A Behavioral Theory of the Firm* (Englewood Cliffs, NJ: Prentice-Hall, 1963), pp. 253–277.
12. D. L. Rados, "Selection and Evaluation of Alternatives in Repetitive Decision Making," *Administrative Science Quarterly*, vol. 17 (1972), pp. 196–206.
13. John B. Miner, *The Management Process*, 2d ed. (New York: Macmillan, 1978), p. 102.

PART TWO CASE STUDY

Davenport University

"Barfield had developed a reputation as a "tough" football coach."

"We want Barfield! We want Barfield!" The crowd of 50,000 screaming fans were calling for the reinstatement of Coach David Barfield, ex-head football coach at Davenport University.

The past few weeks had been tumultuous for Barfield, as well as the administration at Davenport University. The firing of Barfield, head coach at Davenport for 15 years, had created such an uproar among students, faculty, and alumni, that the national wire services had distributed throughout the United States daily reports on the problem at Davenport.

Davenport is a large (30,000 students) state-supported institution situated in the midwest. As a member of the powerful Central States Athletic Association, Davenport's athletic events are frequently televised on regional and national television. Barfield came to Davenport in 1965. Previously, as head coach at the perennial small-college powerhouse, Baxter College, Barfield's teams had won three consecutive national championships. Barfield's talents interested a number of larger universities.

Davenport enticed Barfield with an initial salary of $17,500 in 1965. His original appointment included the duties of head football coach, as well as an Assistant Professor of Health, Physical Education, and Recreation.

Since arriving at Davenport, Barfield coached teams, had accumulated a 115–35 won-lost record and had attended 10 postseason bowl games. During this period, Barfield had firmly endeared himself to local fans and had become a fixture on the Davenport campus.

Over the years, Barfield had also entrenched himself with the local business community. His 1979 salary of $52,500 was supplemented with $15,000 from his weekly television show that aired Sunday evenings after a Davenport game. Additionally, Barfield received well over $75,000 a year from commercials, speaking engagements, and personal appearance contracts. Through his contacts with the Davenport booster club, Barfield had invested heavily in a number of local projects. He was part owner of the Davenport Inn, a 100-unit motel across from the campus. He also was part owner of an automobile dealership in town and a local fast-food franchise. Recently, he had purchased (along with three other investors) large tracts of land in Davenport with plans to develop apartment complexes. This cozy relationship had recently been abruptly interrupted by a series of puzzling events.

Barfield had developed a reputation as a "tough" football coach. His preseason training sessions were particularly grueling and demanding on his players. Preseason practices were held in Butterworth, a town situated about 100 miles from Davenport. For three weeks the players were subjected to three-a-day practice sessions. Up at 5:30 a.m., the day began with a 6:00 practice. Following breakfast, the players saw one-and-a-half hours of boring films. After lunch, the players suited up again for a taxing two-and-a-half hours afternoon session. The evening practice was devoted to coordinating exercises and running. Despite all of this, student-athletes literally begged for the opportunity to play on a Barfield-coached team.

In 1977 Davenport had recruited a highly respected running back, Alfred Robinson, from a large high school in Warren, Ohio. To the delight of the entire university, Robinson elected to attend Davenport. Robinson's freshman year had been disappointing to many because the young running back simply did not live up to his press reports. Additionally, Robinson was not receptive to coaching at Davenport and walked out of three practice sessions. In high school he was allowed to "do his own thing," but this was not the case under Barfield's tutelage. Also, Robinson's grades were marginal and just equaled minimum conference grade-point requirements.

One month into the 1979 season, Robinson filed a suit that alleged Barfield struck him during a game. The university ostensibly stated that it stood firmly behind the coach and would finance all court costs incurred in the case. Robinson had a reputation as a troublemaker, and most of the players on the team made little mention of the suit during practice. Robinson was not popular with his teammates and was considered an outcast by many. Two weeks after the suit had been filed, Barfield, driving home from practice, heard a report on the radio that he had just been fired.

The report surprised Barfield because, earlier in the day, he had heard the president of the university deliver a press statement indicating the university was in full support of the coach and was quite certain that Coach Barfield would be absolved of all blame.

Thinking that the radio report was one big mistake, Barfield decided to contact athletic director Bobby White.

"Bobby, this is David. I just heard a report on the radio that said you fired me. I just wanted to confirm that it was a mistake so we can get them to cut the story."

"David," Bobby replied, "I didn't mean for you to hear the announcement over the radio, but I guess you know how the press operates. I received three anonymous tips from players that confirmed you had punched Robinson. I was left with no alternative but to fire you."

Questions

1. What is the primary problem evident in this case?
2. As athletic director, how would you have handled this situation?
3. What actions should Barfield now take?
4. To prevent similar events, what changes would you make?

PART THREE

The Management Functions

Approaching management as a process of interrelated functions helped synthesize the various schools approaches into a cohesive model of what management must do in order to formulate and attain objectives in an organization. As refined by the application of systems and contingency theory, the process approach is perhaps the most widely accepted approach in use today. Therefore, we shall now discuss the primary functions of planning, organizing, motivating, and controlling in more detail.

We begin with planning, the function by which management formulates objectives and decides how the organization should attain them. Our discussion of organizing, the process of creating structure, requires two chapters. Chapter 8 covers organizing authority relationships, with particular emphasis on the concepts of delegation, authority, and responsibility. Chapter 9 focuses on organizing the organization as a whole, designing a structure that is appropriate for the organization's plans and environment.

Planning and organizing are no more than interesting intellectual exercises unless management can get its people to *actually perform* the tasks required to attain objectives. This is the role of the motivating process, discussed in Chapter 10. Controlling, discussed in Chapter 11, is the process by which management determines whether the organization is in fact attaining its objectives. Effective performance of the control function enables management to identify problems and take corrective action before serious harm results. Controlling also enables management to know whether its plans need to be revised because they are unattainable or because they have been attained. This link between planning and controlling is what makes management a process. As we will stress often, these functions are interrelated. A change in one will affect all others to some degree.

An Interview with Jay Van Andel

Jay Van Andel is the founder and chairman of the board of Amway Corporation, an international firm headquartered in Ada, Michigan, that makes about 150 common household and personal products. Most large manufacturers of consumer products sell at wholesale to retailers and distributors. Amway, much like Fuller Brush and Avon Corporation, sells its output to a network of around 5000 independent contractors. These people, in turn, either sell them personally at retail or, as they become more successful, at wholesale to other Amway distributors. Thus, Amway is based on and dedicated to the traditional values of the American private enterprise system. The name stands for "American Way," and the company has built a museum of private enterprise near its headquarters. As Mr. Van Andel states: "Amway Corporation offers a business opportunity of extreme flexibility without investment to anyone who wishes to earn money. Much of the success of Amway Corporation is merely a reflection of the individual achievement of hundreds of thousands of these independent distributors."

The use of the masculine gender in the interview with Mr. Van Andel was entirely for convenience and applies equally to both males and females.

Author: Peter F. Drucker has written that organizations must act as entrepreneurs. How does Amway Corporation do this?

Van Andel: Peter Drucker was right. Amway remains entrepreneurial because of a commitment to do so. Within the corporate structure, particular groups of people are charged with the specific responsibility of discharging those creative activities which are the hallmark of the entrepreneur. Explicit effort is expended to avoid bogging these groups down in administrative detail, responsibility for implementation, and similar activities. To do so would be to stultify creativity and innovation.

Author: Is Amway's business purpose expressed formally and communicated to its people?

Van Andel: Yes, and reinforced constantly through monthly meetings which all employees are required to attend.

Author: How does Amway differ today from the Amway of ten years ago? What changes do you foresee in the next ten years?

Van Andel: Although Amway is more sophisticated today than ten years ago, it is not in any essential respect different. Nor do we foresee either market or legal forces which will require fundamental changes. There will, of course, be changes to the product line for both regulatory and marketing reasons. There may also be some changes to the marketing system per se, but they will be refinements rather than fundamental changes.

Author: Do you believe business organizations have responsibilities to society? If so, what are they?

Van Andel: The responsibilities of a business to society include delivering safe, effective products profitably, while conducting itself as a good neighbor within the immediate community in which it is physically located. If these responsibilities are met, everything else follows.

Author: Is Amway's management centralized (most important decisions made by top management) or decentralized (managers lower in the hierarchy allowed to make important decisions)? Why?

Van Andel: Amway's management is centralized in most respects. The dynamics of the business require it. This is true of every direct selling company of which I am aware.

Author: Do you rely more on gut reaction and judgment or methodical analysis in making decisions?

Van Andel: "Gut reaction" and individual judgment are far more important than technical analysis of information. There is no such thing as perfect information, and there is an economic point at which the search for more information must be ended because of the marginal cost involved. One uses technical analysis as part of the information base from which individual judgmental decisions flow. Much has been made of modeling and econometric projections in the past few years. One who relies entirely or even mostly on such techniques runs much higher risks, as proven by several multimillion dollar errors in the business world.

Author: What do you think of management theory? Do you think a person can learn anything useful about management from textbooks and college courses?

Van Andel: To answer the first question, I would have to ask *what* management theory do you refer to? Some management theories are sound, some are speculative and marginally effective in practice. People can learn useful management information from textbooks and college courses, as all of our executives have and continue to do. However, change is probably the single most constant factor in business management. The student who believes he "knows it all" upon graduation will have a harder time adjusting to the real world than one who believes he has learned certain fundamentals and precepts which he must now learn to apply and to test while retaining a readiness to change and learn.

Author: What characteristics do you look for in a prospective manager?

Van Andel: Ambition, creativity, flexibility and as broad a base of background as possible commensurate with the intended assignment. Effective verbal and written communicators are in special demand.

Author: Do you have any words of advice for people considering a career in management?

Van Andel: My advice to students thinking of a career in management is for them to carefully evaluate their goals in life. If they are looking for a 40-hour week, comfortable earnings and plenty of leisure time to pursue hobbies, they are not suited for management. A manager's fulfillment comes from managing, from the job itself. Managers are builders, innovators and practical dreamers. Successful managers are seldom completely satisfied with their own work, striving constantly for a higher degree of perfection. Although they know that absolute perfection is an unattainable goal, they do strive to get as close to that goal as it is possible for them to do. It follows from that that there is a fairly high level of frustration, because the effective manager must depend on others for performance to help him achieve those goals. Therefore, he must be effective at getting performance from others. Managers lead by explicit and implicit example. It is therefore quite evident that not everyone is cut out for a career in management.

CHAPTER 7

Planning

Now that we have gained a general understanding of what management is and the major variables affecting organizations, we are ready to examine the functions of management in more detail. This chapter discusses planning, the process of selecting objectives for an organization and deciding what should be done to attain them. We will learn what the components of organizational planning are, the benefits of formal planning, how organizations attempt to predict the future, and what the steps of the planning process are. This knowledge is fundamental to effective management. Planning, as we shall learn, forms the foundation for the other functions. All managerial decisions and the functions of organizing, motivating, and controlling are oriented around attainment of plans.

After reading this chapter, you should understand the following important terms and concepts:

planning process	policies	rule
mission	strategies	forecasting
objectives	tactics	premise
multiple objectives	procedure	budget

The Nature, Functions, and Benefits of Planning

Organizations, as we define them, are groups of people whose work is consciously coordinated toward a common objective or objectives. Both coordination and having objectives imply that some deliberate planning is an integral part of formally organized endeavor. Thus it is not surprising that virtually all writers include planning as one of the essential managerial functions. As a management function:

> *Planning is the process of selecting objectives and deciding what should be done to attain them.*

However, although some planning must have been done to bring an organization into existence, not all organizations engage in systematic, formal planning of the type described in this chapter. As evidenced by the fact that neither all organizations nor all individuals consistently practice deliberate planning, one assumes some people question whether planning is genuinely valuable. In this chapter we will address this question, along with a description of the functions performed by effective planning.

Planning and Individual Achievement

An individual obviously can attain many of the material hallmarks of success through luck alone. However, individuals who deliberately plan their lives, on average, seem to accomplish far more than others. Undirected people, the many of us with no set objectives, tend to diffuse enormous effort exploring dead ends. Time and again they discover only after long, hard experience that a particular career or activity will not prove fulfilling or attainable, and so they drift into another. The highly goal-oriented person, on the other hand, typically channels almost all of his or her talent, energy, and resources toward the chosen goal. Consequently, the undirected person is likely to make a small amount of progress in many areas, whereas the goal-directed one is more likely to make considerable progress in a single field or aspect of life.

A good example of the effectiveness of setting personal goals is the story of Curt Carlson, president of Carlson Company, as reported in the *Wall Street Journal*. "When he started working more than 40 years ago, he would write his next goal on a piece of paper and put it in his wallet. Once he had reached the goal, he would replace the slip of paper with another." Mr. Carlson started at $85 a month. He now heads a business empire including restaurants, hotels, catalogue showrooms, candy and tobacco wholesalers, and importers of optical and tennis equipment with sales of $1 billion a year and employs over 10,000 people.[1]

Some other people who strongly believed in the advantages of clearly defining and expressing one's personal goals are Charles Schwab (a founder of U.S. Steel), Andrew Carnegie, John D. Rockefeller, Thomas Edison, Henry

Ford, George Eastman (founder of Kodak), Julius Rosenwald (the man who built Sears), and W. Clement Stone (insurance billionaire).[2]

Research on Planning and Individual Achievement. Success stories, of course, cannot be considered scientific evidence that planning in the form of goal setting favorably affects individual performance. However, many management research studies confirm the positive effect that goal setting has on performance. One study found that the performance of individuals with specific goals was superior to that of those who merely tried to do their best. This study also found that by formulating specific goals, individuals with low motivation for a job were able to match the performance of those with much higher motivation.[3] Another study found that supervisors who set production goals achieved higher productivity than those who did not.[4] In a later study, these researchers found that training in the process of goal setting can enable supervisors to increase productivity and decrease absenteeism in the work group.[5]

Planning and Organizational Success

Like individuals, small organizations can succeed to *some degree* without doing much formal planning. Nor does planning, in itself, guarantee success. Just as a car with an excellent engine may fail to perform well because of low-quality gas, an organization that plans may fail because of faulty performance of the functions of organizing, motivating, or controlling. However, formal planning makes several important, often essential contributions to an organization:

1. Planning, in the form of formally expressed objectives, helps create unity of purpose within the organization.
2. Planning provides a framework for decision making. Knowing what the organization wants to accomplish and basically how it is to be accomplished considerably clarifies what course of action is most appropriate.
3. Formal planning helps decrease risk in decision making. By being thorough and systematic when making planning decisions, management reduces the chances of making an incorrect decision due to inadequate or faulty information about the organization's capabilities or the environment.
4. Planning helps the organization cope with a changing environment.

We will elaborate on these and other contributions of formal planning later in this chapter. Following is a brief description of what researchers have discovered about the effect of planning on organizational success.

Research on Planning and Organizational Success. Several research studies indicate a strong positive correlation between planning and organizational success. One study analyzed questionnaire responses from 217 vice-

FEATURE 7-1

"Invent Your Own Future"

LOS ANGELES (AP)—They say that if you don't know where you're going, any road will take you there. But a management expert says people who want to "invent their own future" can benefit greatly from business planning techniques.

George Steiner, professor of management and public policy at the Graduate School of Management at the University of California here, recommends six steps for effective life planning.

- Identify and maximize self-satisfactions. Each person must identify what makes them happy, with such things as health, money, love, power and job satisfaction among possible choices.
- Set tentative long-range goals. Steiner emphasizes that individuals should not attempt to look too far into the future and recommends setting two-year goals.

presidents in 109 of the largest American corporations. It found that executives who planned were the most successful, as measured by profit as a percent of sales and return on capital investment.[6] Other researchers surveyed 105 of America's largest companies and 105 middle- and smaller-size firms. They found that firms engaging in formal planning had the fastest growth rates.[7]

Yet another, more sophisticated study examined 36 firms in the drug, food, chemical, steel, oil, and machinery industries. To minimize the effects of other variables, the firms were matched in pairs according to size, industry, and other factors. When the study began, neither firm of the 18 pairs engaged in formal planning. Subsequently, one firm in each pair started using formal planning. The performance of all 18 pairs was observed for seven years. It was found that on such measures as return on investment, return on equity, and growth in earnings per share, the performance of companies that planned was superior to that of those that did not.[8] A follow-up study examined the drug and chemical companies for four additional years. It found that the firms with a formal planning process continued to outperform companies without formal planning and even increased the margin of success.[9]

The preceding studies dealt largely with top-management planning. There have also been studies indicating a correlation between planning and increased effectiveness at lower levels in the organization. A study of railroad foremen, for example, found that the foremen with superior perfor-

- Make a situation audit. Personal goals must be appraised against an audit of the individual's strong points and shortcomings. Such factors as temperament, background, financial standing and physical abilities might be considered.
- Firm up long-range goals. The person may modify his earlier goals in light of his situation audit. Some goals may have to be dropped, while others can be more definite. For example, a person who wants "to be rich" might decide how much money he needs to fit his definition.
- Formulate strategies. Once goals are determined, strategies to achieve them should be developed. If an individual wants "better health," for example, this is the time to decide how to get there. Sample strategies might be "reduce weight by dieting," "stop smoking" or "begin a regular exercise program."
- Set action plans. The final step is determine specific plans to accomplish the longer-range strategies. Examples might be "have a physical checkup" or "ask the boss for a raise."

SOURCE: "Invent Your Own Future," AP in *Atlanta Constitution*, May 15, 1977, p. 5E © Associated Press.

mance devoted more time to planning than foremen with poor production records.[10] Other studies, summarized by Filley, House, and Kerr, found that planning tended to be associated with increased productivity and satisfaction.[11]

Components of Formal Planning

Formal planning is deliberate, systematic preparation for the future. Management almost always expresses formal plans in writing. While all managers should engage in formal planning to some degree, formulating formal plans for the overall organization is primarily a duty of top management. Middle and supervisory management assist by providing relevant information and feedback.

In a large organization that engages in sophisticated formal planning, there might be thousands of written documents related to planning. Thus the specifics of planning and its many variations are beyond the scope of this text. Our focus will be on the key components of organizational planning. In order, we will discuss:

1. Objectives
2. Guides to action and decision making including strategies, policies, procedures, rules, and budgets
3. Predicting the future through forecasting
4. The basic steps of the planning process

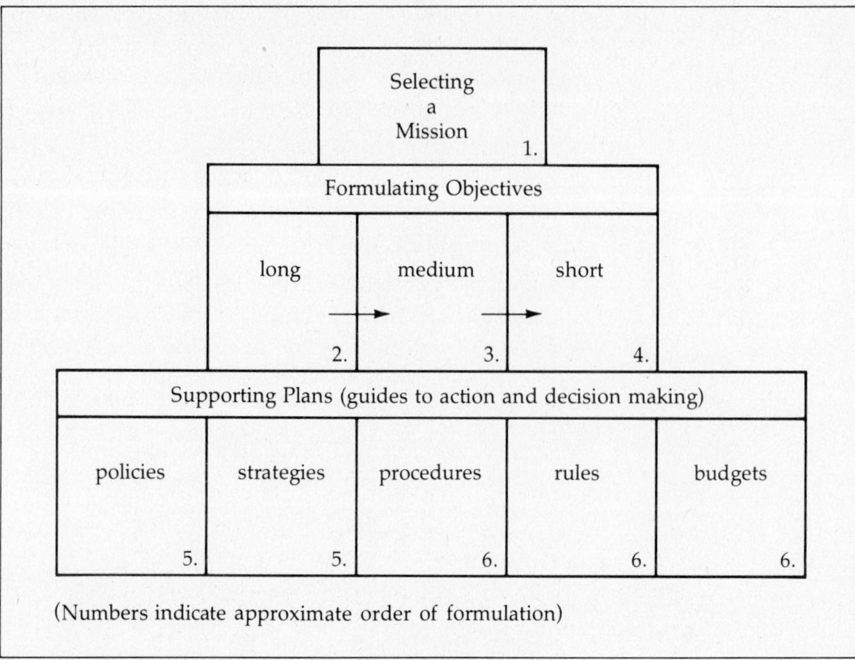

Figure 7-1 Components of Formal Planning

Organizational Objectives

The first, and perhaps most critical, planning decision is selecting an objective for the organization. As we have already noted and will stress below, organizations large enough to require distinct management levels also usually need several broad objectives and many others related to attaining these.

The Organization's Mission

The primary, overall objective of an organization—its expressed reason for existence—is referred to as its **mission.**

Importance of Mission. The importance of having a *suitable* mission that is formally expressed and effectively communicated to the organization's people cannot be overstated. The mission and the objectives derived from it serve as a criteria for all subsequent managerial decision making. If managers did not know what their organization's basic purpose was, they would have no logical reference point for deciding which alternative is best. To give an example, if Burger King's managers did not know that the firm's overall objective is to provide the public with inexpensive fast food, they could not logically decide whether to add a $10 steak dinner to the menu or add a new specialty sandwich retailing for $1.50. Indeed, powerful arguments could be made for the steak on the rationale that total sales would be greater if the company could get $10 for a meal.

Without a mission to serve as a guiding light, individual managers would have nothing but their own values on which to base a decision. The result would be enormous diffusion of effort, rather than the unity of purpose so critical to organizational success. Thus it is not surprising that virtually all enormously successful organizations, such as IBM, General Motors, the government of the United States of America, and Harvard University, have a formally expressed, well-communicated statement of purpose.

Selecting a Mission. Of course, many managers never bother to systematically select and formally state their organization's mission. One reason is that the mission often seems obvious. For example, if one asked a typical small businessperson what his mission was, the reply probably would be, "To make a profit, of course." But if one thinks through the matter, the inadequacy of profit as the overall mission becomes apparent, even though it is, indeed, an essential objective.

Profit is wholly *internal* to the enterprise. Because an organization is an *open* system, it can only survive in the long run by meeting some need *outside of itself*. To earn the profit it needs to survive, the firm clearly must look to the environment in which it operates for a customer. The environment therefore is where management seeks the overall objective of the organization. Management, in order to select a suitable mission, has to successfully answer the questions, "Who are our customers?" and "What needs of these customers are we able to fulfill?" A customer, in this context, is whoever uses the output of the organization. The "customers" of a nonprofit organization are those who use its services and provide it with resources.

The need for a mission was recognized by exceptional managers long before the development of systems theory. Henry Ford, a *very* profit-conscious manager, defined Ford's mission as providing the public with low-cost transportation. He correctly observed that "If one does this, one can hardly get away from profits."

In identifying the customers on whose needs the mission will be based, management must recognize that there often may be many customer groups that must be satisfied. Thomas Watson, Jr., realized almost from the start, for example, that middle managers, accountants, and technicians often have a strong voice in selecting a computer system. So he instructed IBM's sales force to approach all of these specialists, not just the top managers who made the final decision. Theodore Vail showed an even more insightful grasp of the need to satisfy several customer groups. When Vail became president of AT&T around 1900, the telephone company was already one of the country's most successful firms. Foreseeing that the public would pressure Congress for tight regulation if they felt abused by AT&T's monopoly of the telephone system, he publicly suggested providing service even when it was not imme-

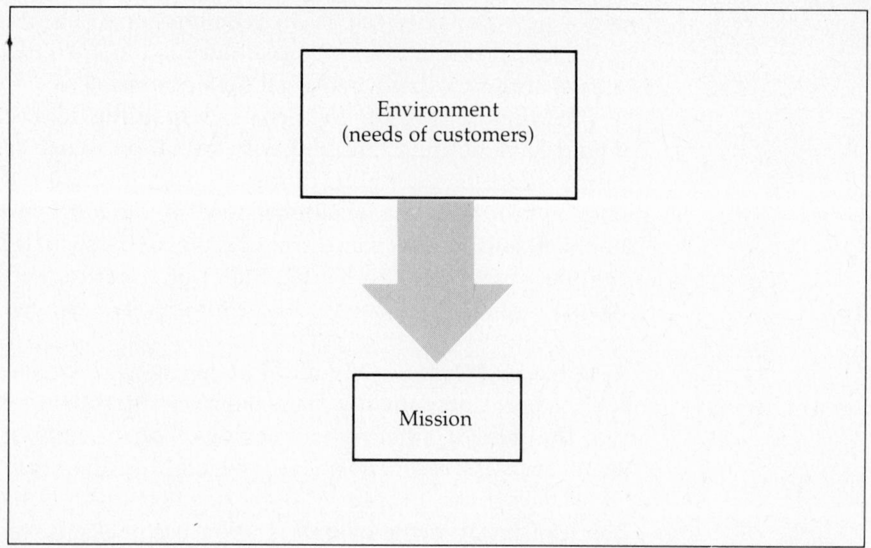

Figure 7-2 The Organization Seeking Its Mission in the Environment

diately profitable. He also suggested that limited government regulation might actually be desirable. These views got Vail fired.

By 1909 the public was screaming for nationalization of Bell. The board of directors asked Vail to return as president. On doing so, Vail formulated a new statement of the company's overall objective: "Our business is service."[12] This new mission acknowledged a subtle, but critical, fact. The telephone company has *two* major customers. One is the people who pay the bills. The other is the government agencies able to regulate Bell. By defining the firm's mission as service, not profits, he met the needs of both groups.

By defining its mission in terms of fundamental needs of customers and meeting them effectively, management in effect creates customers who will support the organization in the future. This is why Peter F. Drucker, a noted authority on managerial objectives, states: "There is only one valid definition of business purpose: *to create a customer.*"[13] If a business makes its mission creation of customers, barring mismanagement in execution, it will also make the profit it needs to survive. Similarly, if a nonprofit or public organization purposefully works at meeting the needs of its "customers" and does so successfully, it should gain the support it needs to continue operating.

Selecting an organizational mission, such as profit, that is overly narrow is a perceptual constraint that impedes management's ability to explore all feasible alternatives in decision making. As a result, some factors are not considered and the decisions may not result in a high level of effectiveness for the organization. For example, Theodore Leavitt suggests that the railroads failed to remain highly competitive and profitable because they defined their mission as the railroad business instead of the transportation business. This caused them to not see and take into account changes in technology and competition, such as trucking, air transport, and containerized sea transport.[14] Although other factors were also involved, a major reason why the giant Penn Central Railroad went into receivership was because it concentrated too heavily on just railroading.

The Mission of Nonprofit Organizations. One of the biggest problems facing many nonprofit organizations is that they have so many different "customers" it is difficult to come up with a workable statement of purpose. The agencies of our federal government are a good example of this. The Department of Commerce, for instance, is supposed to facilitate trade. But, in addition to the needs of American business, the Commerce Department must also satisfy Congress, the president, and the American public. Similarly, a hospital must answer to its patients, doctors, nurses, technicians, and the community in which it operates. Despite these difficulties, it is necessary for the nonprofit organization to formulate a suitable, customer-oriented mission for itself.

Mission of Small Organizations. The preceding examples, as many in this book, focus on large organizations. However, it is equally important for smaller organizations to have a suitable, expressed mission. Indeed, having one was one reason why firms like Ford, McDonald's, and IBM grew to their present magnitude. The danger, for the small organization, is selecting a mission that is *too* broad. While giant IBM can and should define its mission as meeting information needs, a newcomer to the computer field may have to limit its purpose at first to providing IBM compatible software, or word processing, or microcomputers for homes and small business. Exxon, for example, could have poured hundreds of millions of dollars into its subsidiary, Vydec Corporation, in an attempt to tackle IBM head on. Instead, Vydec began modestly in the word-processing market, a field with no dominant competitor.

Multiple Objectives

Selecting a mission based on the fundamental needs of customers makes a major contribution toward channeling effort within the organization. However, according to systems and contingency theory, many other factors may have a determining influence on organizational effectiveness and success. The actions of competitors must be considered because customers may come to find their output (product or service) appealing. For example, General Motors would not allow Ford to crank out black Model T cars forever, even though they were, indeed, providing the public with cheap transportation. The organization, as discussed earlier, also must be able to respond appropriately to other forces in its external environment, such as government and technology. Moreover, to accomplish its mission, the organization must be efficient and motivate and develop its work force.

FEATURE 7-2

The National Bank of Georgia Corporate Purpose

The continuing purpose of The National Bank of Georgia is to serve our customers, stockholders, staff members and communities by fulfilling these commitments:

- To be a strong, aggressive and growing regional bank, serving consumer and commercial banking needs by providing highest quality services at competitive and fair prices.
- To produce a fair and reasonable return for stockholders through effective planning, operation and management.
- To provide a working environment and career development opportunities that will enable all staff members to achieve their fullest potential and be recognized and compensated for their dedication, integrity, accomplishments and contributions.
- To fulfill our corporate citizenship responsibilities by being responsive to the economic, civic, social, cultural and educational needs of the people and communities we serve.

Note the integration of these corporate purposes with National Bank of Georgia's long-range corporate objectives in Feature 7-3.

SOURCE: Courtesy of National Bank of Georgia.

Because management cannot ignore any critical internal or external variable with impunity, it should formulate objectives in *every* area essential to the organization's success. In addition, because subunits of the organization also require objectives, most organizations need **multiple, interrelated objectives** that contribute to attainment of their mission.

Where Objectives Are Needed. It is difficult to pinpoint precisely the areas in which management should specify objectives. Almost every writer has a different list. For example, Professor Anthony Raia based the list in Table 7-1 on an intensive search of related literature. He also describes how these broad objectives for the overall organization might be expressed.

Although the examples given are for businesses, nonprofit organizations need objectives in all these areas except profitability. Also, the list is not

Table 7-1 Descriptions of Organizational Objectives

1. *Profitability* can be expressed in terms of profits, return on investment, earnings per share, or profit-to-sales ratios, among others. Objectives in this area may be expressed in such concrete and specific terms as "to increase return on investment to 15 percent after taxes within five years" or "to increase profits to six million dollars next year."

2. *Markets* may also be described in a number of different ways, including share of the market, dollar or unit volume of sales, and niche in the industry. To illustrate, marketing objectives might be "to increase share of market to 28 percent within three years," "to sell 200,000 units next year," or "to increase commercial sales to 85 percent and reduce military sales to 15 percent over the next two years."

3. *Productivity* objectives may be expressed in terms of ratio of input to output (e.g., "To increase number of units to *x* amount per worker per eight-hour day"). The objectives may also be expressed in terms of cost per unit of production.

4. *Product* objectives, aside from sales and profitability by product or product line, may be stated as, for example, "to introduce a product in the middle range of our product line within two years" or "to phase out the rubber products by the end of next year."

5. *Financial resource* objectives may be expressed in many different ways, depending upon the company, such as capital structure, new issues of common stock, cash flow, working capital, dividend payments, and collection periods. Some illustrations include "to decrease the collection period to 26 days by the end of the year," "to increase working capital to five million dollars within three years," and "to reduce long-term debt to eight million dollars within five years."

6. *Physical facilities* may be described in terms of square feet, fixed cost, units of production, and many other measurements. Objectives might be "to increase production capacity to 8 million units per month within two years" or "to increase storage capacity to 15 million barrels next year."

7. *Research and innovation* objectives may be expressed in dollars as well as in other terms: "to develop an engine in the *(specify)* price range, with an emission rate of less than 10 percent, within two years at a cost not to exceed $150,000."

8. *Organization*—changes in structure or activities are also included and may be expressed in any number of ways, such as "to design and implement a matrix organizational structure within two years" or "to establish a regional office in the South by the end of next year."

9. *Human resource* objectives may be quantitatively expressed in terms of absenteeism, tardiness, number of grievances, and training, such as "to reduce absenteeism to less than 4 percent by the end of next year" or "to conduct a twenty-hour in-house management training program for 120 front-line supervisors by the end of 1975 at a cost not to exceed $200 per participant."

10. *Social responsibility* objectives may be expressed in terms of types of activities, number of days of service, or financial contributions. An example might be "to hire 120 hard-core unemployables within the next two years."

SOURCE: Anthony Raia, *Management by Objectives* (Glenview, IL: Scott, Foresman, 1974) p. 158.

intended to be comprehensive: a given organization may need to express overall objectives in other areas as well. Prominent researchers and writers Steiner and Miner state that "Objectives ought to be set for every activity that a company thinks is important and the performance of which it wishes to watch and measure."[15] Table 7-2 shows how 1072 business managers rated certain goals as to their perceived importance and significance for company success.

Table 7-2 Evaluation of Corporate Goals by Business Managers

Type of Goal	Percent Rating as Highly Important	Percent Indicating Significant for Corporate Success
Organizational efficiency	81	71
High productivity	80	70
Profit maximization	72	70
Organizational growth	60	72
Industrial leadership	58	64
Organizational stability	58	54
Employee welfare	65	20
Social welfare	16	8

SOURCE: George W. England, "Organizational Goals and Expected Behavior of American Managers," *Academy of Management Journal*, vol. 10 (1967), pp. 107–117.

As indicated, the 1072 managers surveyed rated several goals besides profit as highly important and significant to corporate success. Note that this survey was made in 1967. Today, one would expect a much higher percentage to rank social-welfare goals as highly important.

Characteristics of Objectives

Characteristics of Effective Objectives. In order to make a genuine contribution to organizational success, objectives need to possess several characteristics.

First, objectives should be *specific* and *measurable*. For instance, the example Raia gave for a marketing objective was "to increase commercial sales to 85 percent and reduce military sales to 15 percent over the next two years." Compare this to such possible phrasing of the same idea as "to achieve a well-balanced proportion of sales in the near future." The latter is vague, leaving many crucial questions unanswered. The former tells people exactly what top management considers to be a well-balanced proportion of sales. By stating its objectives in specific, measurable terms whenever possible, management provides a clear reference point for subsequent decisions and for evaluation of progress. Middle managers will have little difficulty deciding whether to allocate more money to commercial advertising or to military marketing. It also will be easy to determine exactly how well the organization is doing with respect to its marketing objectives. The value of this becomes obvious when performing the control function.

Notice that the preceding example and others given not only specify exactly what the organization wants to accomplish but also *when* the result is to be attained. A *specific time horizon* is another characteristic of effective objectives.

Seemingly obvious, but often not adhered to in practice, is that an objective must be *attainable* if it is to facilitate organizational effectiveness. Trying to attain an objective beyond the organization's capabilities, either due to insufficient resources or external factors, can have disastrous consequences. RCA, for example, suffered enormous losses when it decided to become a major manufacturer of computers largely because it lacked the expertise to compete with IBM. Also, as stated by Steiner and Miner, objectives "are important motivators of people in organizations because, generally, people like to try to achieve the objectives set for the organization."[16] If objectives are not attainable, the employee's need for achievement is likely to be frustrated and motivation reduced. Furthermore, it is common practice to link compensation and promotions to goal attainment. Therefore, an unattainable objective may also impede the effectiveness of other means the organization uses to motivate its people.

Lastly, to be effective, the organization's multiple objectives must be *mutually supportive.* That is, actions and decisions required to attain one objective should not detract from the attainment of others. For example, an objective of maintaining inventory at a level of 1 percent of sales would not, for most firms, support an objective of fulfilling all orders within two weeks. Failure to make objectives mutually supportive tends to cause conflict between the units of the organization responsible for attaining the inconsistent objectives.

Long-Range versus Short-Range Objectives. An important characteristic of objectives is their time horizon, the amount of time in which the organization hopes to attain them. Objectives typically are formulated for time spans ranging from long to short. A *long-range objective,* according to Steiner, is one with a time horizon of roughly five years, sometimes longer for technically advanced companies.[17] A *short-range objective,* in most cases, is one the organization plans to attain within a year. *Medium-range objectives* have a 1 to 5 year time horizon.

Long-range objectives typically are broad in scope, and the organization formulates them first. Medium- and short-range objectives are then formulated to support the attainment of longer-range objectives to which they are related. Usually the shorter the time horizon of the objective, the narrower its focus. For example, a long-range productivity objective may be "to increase overall productivity by 25 percent within 5 years." Consistent with this, management would set a medium-range objective of increasing productivity by 10 percent within 2 years. It would also establish short-range objectives in such specific areas as inventory costs, employee training, plant improvement, more efficient use of existing facilities, management development, union negotiations, and so forth. These *must* support both the long-range objective, to which they are directly related, and other objectives of the organization. To continue our example, "to negotiate a union contract within one year that provides an appropriate bonus if an individual's productivity increases by 10 percent a year," would be a short-range objective that supports both the long-range productivity objective and human resource objectives.

FEATURE 7-3

The National Bank of Georgia Long-Range Corporate Objectives

1. Emphasize growth in profits, return on equity and return on assets.
2. Attain and maintain desirable quality, mix and interest-sensitive balance in assets and liabilities.
   a. Emphasize asset quality rather than asset quantity, placing emphasis on proper administration, analysis, documentation, review and audit.
   b. Maintain a prudent degree of liquidity in the balance sheet.
   c. Maintain a well balanced mix of sources of funds with emphasis on reliable core deposits.
   d. Maintain a strong capital base consistent with growth in assets.
3. Concentrate on providing a full range of quality services to the consumer market, the small to medium size commercial market and the correspondent bank market.
4. Utilize the resources of the bank to develop the full potential of the Trust Department.
5. Establish and convey a corporate image of a progressive, consistent, financially strong yet innovative bank staffed by competent, highly professional and customer-oriented people.

Objectives of Organizational Subunits. A large organization is composed of many different subunits. Each of these is an organization itself and therefore also needs objectives to function effectively. Typically, management formulates objectives of broader scope and longer range for higher levels of the organization. These serve as a foundation for setting objectives on lower levels.

In many organizations today managers are given the right to formulate objectives for their work unit, provided these objectives are consistent with those of the level above them. For example, top management would have an objective of increasing overall sales by 75 percent within five years. The sales managers of each major division in the company would set a consistent

6. Provide equal opportunity employment with a working environment and career development opportunities that will enable all officers and staff to achieve their fullest potential, receive recognition and fair compensation.
7. Continue to develop and retain competent, well-trained, in-depth management throughout the organization.
8. Maintain the highest standards of professional ethics, moral character and competence, both individually and corporately.
9. Communicate fully and effectively with officers and staff, directors, shareholders, and the investment community.
10. Adhere to sound accounting principles that ensure quality of earnings and full disclosure.
11. Continually practice expense control through efficient operations and implementation of cost saving opportunities.
12. Utilize effective management tools for purposes of short and long term planning, measurement of performance, and review of established goals and objectives.
13. Broaden the investor base in the bank's capital stock, both numerically and geographically.
14. Form a bank holding company, after good earnings trends have been established and capital structure is solidified, to acquire well-capitalized, profitable banks with strong growth potential.
15. Provide a pleasant working environment that results in a warm and friendly place in which to work and bank.

SOURCE: Courtesy of National Bank of Georgia.

short-range objective of increasing sales by 20 percent within one year. Regional sales managers would formulate a specific, attainable sales objective for each salesperson in their territory, based on past performance, that would lead to the overall increase of 20 percent.

When this process of formulating a consistent hierarchy of objectives throughout the organization is performed effectively, it can be a powerful force for coordination and unity of purpose. Each person in the organization knows what he or she is expected to accomplish. If each performs as planned, the organization will meet its overall, long-range objectives and attain its mission.

Guides to Decision Making and Action

Sound objectives are a critical component of effective planning, but they are not wholly adequate guidelines for decision making and behavior. An objective only states *what* the organization wants to accomplish and *when* it wants this desired result. *How* the objective is to be attained is addressed only in the general sense of defining what business the organization is in. This leaves enormous latitude. Even with the best of intentions, people responsible for meeting the objectives may easily choose courses of action or behave in ways that do not, in fact, facilitate attaining the objectives. To prevent such misdirection and misinterpretation, management should formulate additional plans and specific guidelines that support its objectives.

The underlying purpose of these guidelines is to channel future decisions and behavior to alternatives management considers conducive to its overall purpose. The idea is to increase cohesiveness of action, not lock people into an intellectual straightjacket. The major components of formal planning used to accomplish this are policies, strategies, procedures, rules, and budgets.

Policies

Policies are broad guides to action and decision making that facilitate attainment of objectives.

Generally formulated by top management for a long life, a policy establishes parameters within which future decisions on related matters are to be made. In the words of Steiner and Miner: "Policies may be thought of as codes that state the directions in which action may take place. . . . Policies direct action to the achievement of an objective or goal. They explain how aims are to be reached by prescribing guideposts to be followed. They are designed to secure a consistency of purpose and to avoid decisions which are short-sighted and based on expediency."[18]

A policy of offering equal job opportunity to minorities and women, for example, contributes to objectives for meeting societal obligations and making the best use of people. Having and enforcing such a policy helps prevent subordinate managers from deliberately or inadvertantly excluding women and minority candidates from consideration. It guides their thinking away from choosing an alternative on the basis of personal values and preferences and toward a decision consistent with organizational objectives.

Note that although policies channel decisions, they allow discretion. General Motors, for example, has a policy to minimize the amount of new tooling required to produce a new model. If you examine their cars closely, you will observe that many have identical trunks, doors, bumpers, or engines. Sometimes a new model Chevrolet will have parts used on the previous year's Buicks and Oldsmobiles. Clear evidence of the leeway in decision making this policy allows is that many people never notice the high degree of standardization within the GM family of cars. Similarly, the equal opportunity policy previously mentioned leaves a manager free to hire just about anyone, provided nobody is excluded simply on the basis of race, religion, or sex.

Strategies

Strategies are broad decisions to act and to allocate resources in certain ways in order to attain objectives.

A strategy is typically formulated by top management and chosen from among major alternative ways of achieving the organization's objectives. If you had an objective of traveling from New York to Los Angeles in the shortest possible time, for example, deciding to fly would be a strategy consistent with this objective. It eliminates from future consideration other forms of travel, but still allows considerable discretion. You could still choose when to fly and what airline to use, for example.

We illustrated a corporate strategy in Chapter 2 when we spoke of Fotomat Corporation's decision to increase its advertising budget significantly to create a perception that the company is a high quality film processor. Another strategy Fotomat is using to meet its sales objectives is to introduce a new product, videotapes.

Organizational strategies share much in common with those of sports such as football. They should; football teams are formal organizations. A football team's top management, the coach, would have a far easier job if the team could run over the opposition with every type of play. But it very seldom can. Until the recruiters manage to snare both a fast 250-pound running back and a quarterback with an accurate 50-yard pass, the coach must cope with opponents about equal in ability or a bit tougher than his team. To do so, he takes into account the strengths of his players, say a strong passing quarterback and a good receiver. And he analyzes the weaknesses of the other team, say a poor pass defense. His experience then leads him to decide upon a strategy for Saturday's game: keep the ball in the air.

In managerial terms, the coach made his team's objective, winning, more probable by choosing the strategy that made the most effective use of its limited resources in a given situation. The resources in this case, as they often are, were people. These people could have tried to win the game by running with the ball, by concentrating on defense, by passing a lot, or by allowing the quarterback complete discretion in choosing plays. The coach decided, however, to have the organization *act* in a certain way—primarily passing—and *to allocate* his human *resources* accordingly.

This strategic decision is typical in that it restricts the organization's efforts to a single, general line of action but still allows considerable discretion. The team, for instance, probably has several dozen different passing plays that can be used.

Tactics. Just as management formulates short-range objectives consistent with and facilitating the attainment of long-range objectives, it often must develop short-range strategies consistent with its broad, long-range strategies. These short-range strategies are referred to as **tactics**. A specific passing play, for example, is a tactic consistent with a passing strategy. Advertising in photographic magazines would be a tactic consistent with Fotomat's strategy for increasing its share of the 35mm processing market.

Some characteristics of tactics are:

1. Tactics are formulated in pursuit of strategy.
2. Whereas strategy is almost always formulated at the highest levels of management, tactics often are developed and implemented at middle-management levels.
3. Tactics have a shorter time range than strategies.
4. Whereas the results of strategies may not be fully seen for several years, tactical results tend to be quickly evident and easily related to specific actions.[19]

Factors in Selecting Strategies. Because of internal complexities and a changing environment, managers of large organizations must consider many factors when selecting a strategy:

1. The needs of its "customers" and how they are changing.
2. Limits and opportunities of the environment. This would include factors such as competitive, legal, technological, and sociocultural developments.
3. The organization's internal capabilities, its strengths and weaknesses.

These are essentially the same factors management considers when it formulates multiple objectives. Because strategies are refinements of those objectives, they involve the same basic elements and should consider them in a consistent fashion. An essential aspect of being consistent is that a strategy must further each objective to which it is subordinate. A governmental strategy of using secret police to eliminate dissidents, for example, is a logical means of preventing overthrow. However, even though preventing armed rebellion is one of its objectives, this strategy would be inconsistent with the overall expressed objectives of a democracy such as ours.

The Need for Multiple Strategies. Strategies specify how resources are to be allocated to attain objectives. Therefore, *every objective requires some form of strategy.* Each major subdivision should formulate written strategies for attaining its divisional objectives. These strategies may sometimes vary considerably and still contribute effectively to the objectives of the organization as a whole. Cadillac division's strategy of producing luxury cars contrasts sharply with Chevrolet's strategy of producing compact and moderately priced autos. Yet both of these strategies have proven successful in attaining the overall General Motors corporate objective of earning a profit from products related to the internal combustion engine.

Procedures

Organizations, like people, can benefit by applying their past experiences to future decisions. Recalling what happened in the past can help prevent repeating a mistake. Equally important, not repeating the analysis that led to a satisfactory decision saves time and prevents introduction of an error. Thus, when a decision-making situation tends to recur frequently, management often finds it desirable to reuse its time-proven way of doing things and evolve a standardized guide to action. When expressed formally, this guideline is called a procedure.

A procedure prescribes what action is to be taken in a specific situation.

Essentially, a procedure is a programmed decision that eliminates the need to "reinvent the wheel." Procedures usually outline a chronological sequence of activities to be performed in a specific situation. In general, the person performing a procedure is allowed little discretion and few alternatives.

Rules

When the successful execution of plans depends on a task being performed precisely, it may be desirable for management to eliminate *all* discretion. To meet its objectives of internal security, for example, the CIA must restrict employment to people who are extremely loyal and trustworthy. It therefore cannot allow managers to hire *anyone* without conducting an investigation of the person's background. Management also feels the need to eliminate choice when there is a relatively high probability that some people might behave in a way that will have negative effects. Many organizations, for example, require people to be at work for a specific time period, such as 9 A.M. to 5 P.M.

To cope with these minor, but important, situations where a high degree of conformity is needed to attain objectives, managers develop rules.

A rule specifies exactly what is to be done in a specific, single situation.

Rules differ from procedures in that they deal with a very specific and limited issue. Procedures, on the other hand, cope with situations that involve a sequence of several related actions.

Table 7-3 lists the major contributions rules and procedures make to attainment of organizational objectives.

Problems with Rules and Procedures. Sometimes workers perceive rules and procedures as stifling, or too restrictive, or fail to see their value. As a result, there may be rebellion against the rules, expressed as hostility to the organization or manager, or outright disobedience. If this happens, rules will detract from attaining objectives, whether or not they are inherently valid. The expedient solution to this rebellion would be to eliminate the

Table 7-3 How Rules and Procedures Contribute to Attainment of Objectives

Rules and Procedures:
1. Channel the actions of workers in a direction that, based on experience, has a high probability of being successful and contributing to objectives.
2. Improve efficiency by avoiding repetition of the process leading to a satisfactory decision.
3. Enable managers to predict exactly what subordinates will do in the situation covered.
4. Permit accurate comparisons with past performance or the performance of other groups. (Since the same task is being done the same way, it should be performed with equal or greater effectiveness each time.)

rules, but this probably would lead to the equal evil of the problems the rules were intended to prevent.

However, if one closely examines situations in which rules cause more disruption than they prevent, one often sees that the real source of problems is not the rules or procedures themselves. Rather, conflict arises because of the *way management presents rules* to workers.

Modern workers on even the lowest levels of the organization are relatively well-educated in comparison to their predecessors.[20] Moreover, American culture supports strongly the notion of a high degree of individual freedom. Thus workers are understandably reluctant to accept restrictions of any sort that are laid down as dictatorial edicts. Whereas at one time the boss's word went unquestioned, today subordinates usually insist on knowing *why* it is necessary to do things as stipulated by the rules or procedures.

Therefore, assuming the rules in question are valid and necessary, the best means of gaining compliance is to communicate their purpose to subordinates. In most cases, if a subordinate genuinely understands how and why the rules help the organization get its job done more effectively, conflict will be minimized, and they will be obeyed freely. If the manager can communicate how these rules and procedures help workers personally, they usually will be even more willing to comply. Incidentally, when managers take the trouble to convince rather than coerce workers into following regulations, they sometimes discover that the workers' way of doing a thing is more efficient than management's rule or procedure. This fact was illustrated by the example in Chapter 1 of the airplane wing-skin cutter who discovered a new procedure for his work that greatly improved manufacturing efficiency and productivity.

Budgets

As mentioned earlier, one of the main uses of planning is to *allocate resources* as effectively as possible. The types of plans discussed above only provide very general guidance in the area of allocation. They channel thinking and acting on matters related to the use of resources in directions management considers conducive to attaining objectives while leaving unresolved the fundamental issues of what resources are actually available and how, exactly, they should be used to attain objectives. Nor do the types of planning discussed thus far provide an answer to the basic question of what objectives are reasonably attainable, given the resources available. These matters are the nuts and bolts, the pragmatics, of planning.

To cope with what resources are available, managers use budgets, a planning tool that is wholly distinct from, but closely related to, the objectives-strategies-rules sequence.

> *A budget is a technique for allocating resources, expressed quantitatively, to attain objectives expressed in the same terms.*

Budgets are by far the most widely used component of formal planning. While many organizations never formally develop objectives and strategies in writing, the great majority use written budgets. In fact, you probably already are somewhat familiar with them, since many families and individuals budget to determine the best way of using a limited amount of money to obtain the necessities and extras of life.

Quantifying Resources and Objectives. The first step in budgeting, as indicated by its definition, is to *express numerically* both resources and formulated objectives. It is possible and in some situations common to use time units, such as hours or man-hours. One could also use simple, raw numbers, such as 6,000 square feet (in budgeting space). The unit most commonly used, however, is the dollar or its equivalent in local currency.

Benefits of Quantifying. However difficult it may be, assigning all resources and objectives a numerical value is a worthwhile, usually essential, aspect of organizational planning. Quantification makes it possible for the manager to visualize, compare, and combine the widely differing elements involved in organized endeavor.

To understand quantification, imagine you have a simple objective such as wanting to earn $3000 for a scholarship fund by holding a picnic. You know that you will need tables, food, advertising circulars, and printed tickets. With no idea of the relative value of these resources, you could only guess at an appropriate price for tickets and the number that must be sold. Leaving such critical matters to guesswork clearly would considerably reduce the chances of attaining your objective of $3000.

If you determine, however, that:

- Table rental will cost: $200.00
- Food will cost: $2.00 per person
- Promotion and tickets are: $100.00

You can easily see that it will be necessary to charge more than $2 per person for tickets. Then, if you decide that $5 would be a fair price, you can readily compute how many tickets must be sold to earn $3000:

> $3000 = ($N$ × $3) − $300, where N is the number of people and $3 the profit after deducting food costs.

Obviously, you must obtain 1100 paying customers to meet your objective. Expressing all factors in a convenient common unit such as dollars also makes it easier to answer many other significant questions about resource allocation and objectives. If we know how much money we have, for instance, we can determine how much we will be able to produce under various cost conditions. To continue our above illustration, if we had only $900 to invest in the picnic, we could serve only 600 meals. Or, working inversely, we can determine how much money we will need to meet our objective. To earn $3000, we would need to have available at least $2500 to cover minimal expenses. We can also determine how much we would earn at different sales levels. The profit from 600 tickets to our picnic would be $1500.

Overview of the Planning Process

In the preceding section we described the components of formal planning with respect to types of plans and mechanisms for guiding action and decision making. Another aspect of formal planning is *how* management objectively decides what its objectives and supporting plans should be. This involves two closely related activities: premising and forecasting. Management uses the former to define its present situation, the point at which it is starting. The latter, forecasting, is used to predict what *probably* will occur in the future. This includes where the organization should be if it follows a given course of action and what the environment should be like. The combination of these activities, if performed effectively, provides management with the information it needs to perform the planning function effectively in complex situations. Therefore, let us briefly describe premising and forecasting before summarizing the steps of the planning process.

Premising

In organizational planning, a **premise** is an *assumption* considered to be true that can be used as a reference point for decision making. "There are many people who, if allowed to get away with it, will often arrive at work late," for example, is a premise about human behavior. If management accepts it as true, it should logically establish rules governing working hours and penalties for breaking them.

Table 7-4 Internal Factors Important in Premising

1. *Resources available.* To plan, management must know the quantity and quality of critical resources available to the organization. These include money, plant and equipment, supplies, and people.

2. *Organizational structure.* The existing structure of the organization often determines which objectives and strategies will be easiest to undertake. A plan requiring a major change in structure to execute is almost always far more expensive and risky. Therefore, although structure is changeable, it usually is considered a "given."

3. *Existing plans.* As noted, plans should form a hierarchy, with subordinate plans contributing to broader ones. Therefore, the existing plans of the organization, particularly its broad objectives, strategies, and policies, are assumed to be static when formulating supporting plans. A strategy of concentrating on consumer products, for example, would be a premise leading to rejection of a tactic involving a new product aimed at industrial customers.

4. *Human behavior.* Conscious and unconscious managerial attitudes toward subordinates are premises that often strongly influence planning. A manager who assumes that workers are willing and able to take on added responsibility will, if possible, formulate plans that reflect this belief. One who believes that workers are inherently lazy probably will be pessimistic in planning productivity and formulate rigid rules and procedures to keep workers in line.

Table 7-5 External Factors Important in Premising

1. *General environment.* These are assumptions about prevailing economic conditions, social values, the political climate, the state of technology relevant to the organization, and legal constraints.

2. *Competitive environment.* These are assumptions about the organization's competitors, including who they are and their relative strengths. Related to this is the assumed demand for the organization's output.

3. *Resource Market.* These are assumptions about the availability and cost of resources required to attain objectives. They would include such things as interest rates, how many people in the immediate area are available for work, and how powerful unions are.

Internal and External Premises. As mentioned earlier, the underlying aim of premising is to define the current situation so that management can determine what the organization should do to be successful. Since factors both within the organization and in its environment affect success, management needs to make both *internal premises* and *external premises.* It makes the former by analyzing the organization, the latter by analyzing the environment. Table 7-4 lists the general areas of internal premises most important in planning. Table 7-5 does the same for external premises.

Tangible and Intangible Premises. Management uses premises as a basis for planning decisions on the assumption that they are, in fact, true. However, it is important for management to differentiate between tangible and intangible premises when planning. A *tangible premise* is one that can be verified objectively. Examples are: "We have $1 million cash in the bank"; "The cost of parts for our new product is $21.56 per unit at current market prices"; "Federal law requires the installation of emission control devices on all cars." *Intangible premises* cannot be verified objectively, either because they involve a prediction about the future, or because the situation is too complex to analyze fully. Examples are: "Sales will increase 10 percent next year"; "Improving working conditions will motivate our people to increase productivity by 15 percent"; "Social pressure will force government to reduce taxes during the 1980s."

Usually, tangible premises are considered facts. Management therefore can feel more secure about making a major commitment based on a tangible premise than it can when the premise is intangible. However, because both internal and external factors are *variables,* they are subject to change. All premises must be periodically evaluated to determine whether they are still a valid reference point for planning decisions.

Controllability. Another important consideration is how controllable the premise is. A highly controllable premise is one management can change readily. Examples are: most supporting plans; organizational structure to some degree; how much people are paid and, thereby, the relative ability of the organization to attract and keep people; and how much money is allocated for a given activity. Other premises can be partially controlled. Examples would be assumptions about the organization's market share and its relationship with labor unions. Some premises are based on factors over which even very powerful organizations have little or no control. These include what the population of a city will be in 20 years, whether taxes will increase, and whether or not there will be high inflation. In general, the more controllable a premise, the more it can be relied upon when planning. For example, the objective of installing a computerized record-keeping system is based on the premise that programmers will be available. By paying higher than average wages, management can virtually guarantee it will have programmers when they are needed.

Forecasting

Many premises, as noted above, are about conditions in the future over which management has little or no control. But assumptions about these situations are, nevertheless, required for many planning activities. Clearly, the better management's ability to predict future internal and environmental conditions in such situations, the better its chances of formulating attainable plans. In fact, early management writer Henri Fayol considered predicting the future and planning accordingly to be the very essence of management. In his view, all organizational plans were an amalgamation of several forecasts. Today, though still considered very important, forecasting plays a more limited role in the planning process.

Table 7-6 Types of Forecasts

1. Economic forecasts are made to predict both general economic conditions and sales for a particular company or product.
2. Technological forecasts predict what new technologies can be developed, when they can be developed, and how economically feasible they will be.
3. Competition forecasts predict the strategy and tactics of one's competitors.
4. Survey-research forecasts predict what will occur in complex situations by integrating knowledge from many different areas. For example, the future market for automobiles can only be evaluated by considering impending changes in economic conditions, social values, politics, technology, and pollution-control standards.
5. Social forecasting, now done by only a few very large companies, is used to predict changes in people's attitudes and societal conditions. Obviously, a firm that can correctly predict how people will feel about matters such as comfort, materialism, patriotism, or whether quality of life or medical care will change is going to have an advantage in planning new goods and services. It also can be advantageous in managing, especially in motivating. General Electric uses a complex social-political forecasting technique to improve its long-range planning in the area of industrial relations.

Forecasting is a technique that uses both past experiences and present assumptions about the future to predict what will occur. When forecasting is properly performed, the resulting forecast is a vision of the future that can reasonably be used as a premise for planning.

Forecasting today is a specialized field with several subspecialties. There are companies whose only business is making forecasts in a specific area. A notable example is the Gallup organization, which specializes in gathering and analyzing information that enables one to make predictions about preferences and outcomes on various political and social issues. Many firms and divisions of large businesses conduct highly sophisticated market research to forecast consumer acceptance of planned new products. These specialists have developed several specific techniques for making and improving the quality of forecasts. We will discuss some of them later in this book. Table 7-6 briefly describes five general types of forecasts often used in conjunction with organizational planning.

Steps in the Planning Process

Now that we have learned what the major components of organizational planning are and something about how organizations attempt to predict the future, let us consolidate our knowledge with an overview of the planning process. The process of selecting objectives and deciding what must be done to attain them can be viewed as consisting of seven interrelated steps. Illustrated in Figure 7-3 and described in this section, these are selecting a mission or purpose, analysis of internal capabilities, analysis of the environment, setting objectives, developing supporting plans, implementing plans, and controlling plans.

1. Selection of a Mission. The selection of a mission or the definition of the organization's purpose is the logical starting point of planning. Its mission is

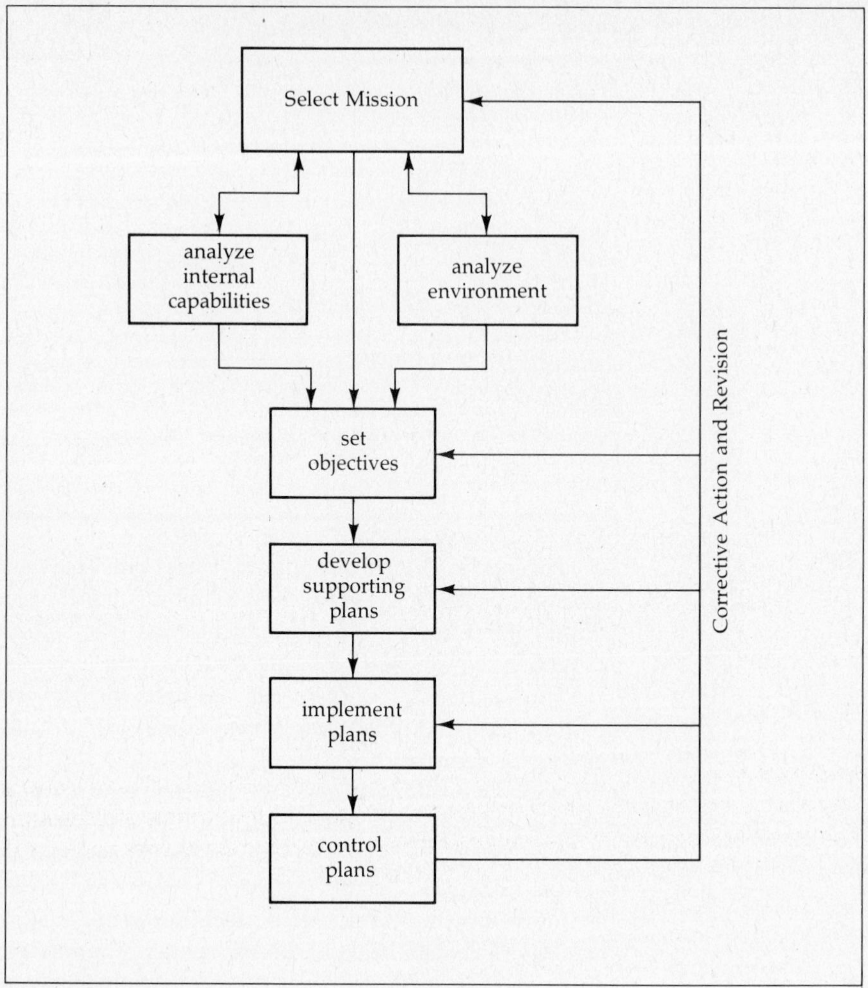

Figure 7-3 **Steps in the Planning Process**

the organization's overriding reason for existence and the foundation for all subsequent planning and other decisions. Whether a given course of action will contribute to attainment of the mission is the criterion on which all managerial decision making is based. However, although we say that selection of a mission is the starting point of organization because it provides members with a conscious, common objective, management needs to analyze the capabilities of the organization and its environment first in order to formulate a suitable statement of purpose.

2. Analysis of the Organization: Internal Capabilities. To determine what the organization can reasonably be expected to accomplish successfully,

Table 7-7 Analyzing Internal Capabilities

Marketing
1. How effective are we at selling and distributing our products or services?
Finance
1. How much cash do we have available now, and how much will be available to us in the future?
2. How much are we able to borrow, if necessary? How much money are we earning now, and how much can we expect to earn in the future?
Production
1. What can we produce with our current facilities and equipment?
2. Are our tools and methods of production efficient?
3. Are our costs of production too high?
4. Is the quality of our output adequate?
Human Resources
1. What technical and managerial skills do our people have?
2. Are we capable of training people to perform necessary tasks? How satisfied and motivated are our employees?

management must analyze its strengths and weaknesses. The purpose of doing so is to answer the fundamental question, "Where are we now?" This analysis involves honestly answering many difficult questions about the organization's capabilities in key areas. A few of the most important questions are listed in Table 7-7.

3. Analysis of the Environment: External Threats and Opportunities. Organizations, as we know, interact actively with their environment in a variety of ways. Therefore a necessary aspect of organizational planning is to analyze the threats and opportunities in the environment. These include: competitors, economic conditions, government regulations, laws, customers, technology, and sociocultural values. The rate at which these various factors affecting the organization are changing also must be taken into account. Therefore, this step requires forecasts of the environment. Several companies such as Berkey Photo, for example, suffered high losses because, although they correctly predicted a high customer demand for pocket calculators, they failed to correctly predict how rapidly technology would develop and new, strong competitors would enter the business.

4. Setting of Objectives. The setting-of-objectives phase begins with the establishment of long-range goals for the organization as a whole. Management then formulates medium- and short-range objectives for both the overall organization and each of its subunits that are consistent with and contribute to its long-range desired results.

5. Development of Supporting Plans. To improve the probability of attaining its objectives, management needs to create an extensive network of supports to guide action and decision making. These supports include policies, strategies, tactics, procedures, rules, and a variety of budgets. These facilitate attainment of objectives by increasing unity of purpose and limiting future decisions to alternatives management considers conducive to the organization's aims.

6. Implementation of the Plan. The aggregate of the preceding steps is the organization's plan for success and survival. But it is important to realize that the planning process does not stop here. The plan must be implemented. In the words of Peter Drucker:

> The best plan is *only* a plan, that is, good intentions, unless it *degenerates into work.* The distinction that marks a plan capable of producing results is the commitment of key people to work on specific tasks. The test of a plan is whether management actually commits resources to action which will bring results in the future. Unless such commitment is made, there are only promises and hopes, but no plan.[21]

Converting the plan to action is accomplished through the managerial functions of organizing and motivating, as described in following chapters. Communicating and leadership are also critical to effective implementation.

7. Control of the Plan. Planning, like every management function, is a process. It does not end with implementation. The last step in the planning process is controlling the plan, which is accomplished through the control function of management. Briefly, in controlling the plan management determines to what degree its plans have actually been implemented. Of special concern is how much progress the organization has made toward attaining each of its objectives. By gathering information on progress and evaluating results, management is able to determine whether its plans are resulting in the future management predicted for the organization. If the organization is not attaining its objectives as intended, controlling helps management determine why and enables it to take corrective action before serious problems arise.

Eventually, if the organization is successful, the controlling process will let management know that it soon will attain its objectives. Management then preserves the organization by selecting new, more ambitious objectives for it, perhaps even broadens its mission. Thus the cycle begins anew.

The preceding process, with appropriate modification, can be applied to each component of formal planning. Figure 7-4 illustrates how it could be applied to perform strategic planning in a large bank. This diagram seems to

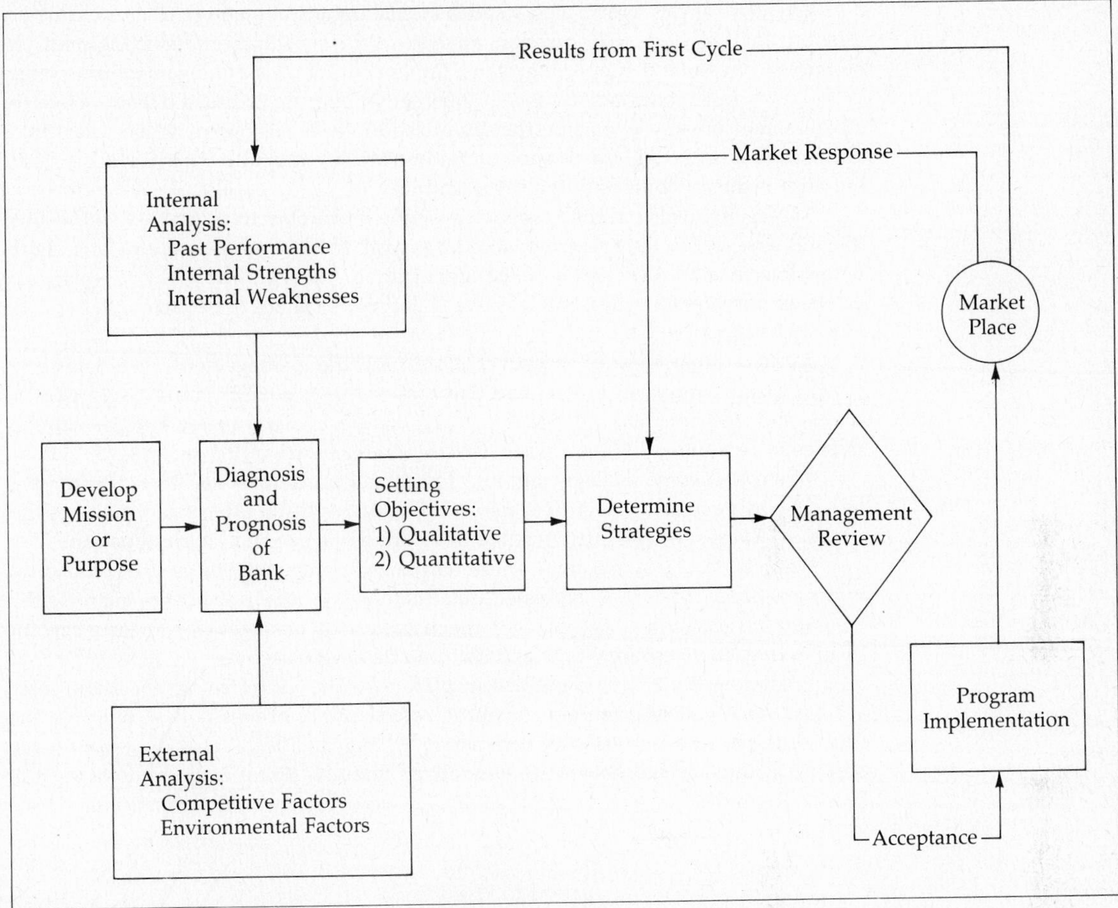

Figure 7-4 Strategic Planning in a Large Bank

have a major error: it shows the mission being developed before internal and external factors are analyzed. However, since strategies are intended to support fulfilling the organization's mission, the diagram correctly considers the mission a tangible, uncontrollable *premise.*

SUMMARY

Planning is the process of selecting objectives and deciding what should be done to attain them. The positive contribution that planning makes to both individual and organizational achievement has been clearly established.

There are seven interrelated steps in formal organizational planning: selecting a mission, analysis of the organization, analysis of the environment, selecting multiple objectives, developing supporting plans, implementing plans, and controlling plans.

An organization's mission is its fundamental purpose or broad overall objective. Management must look outside the organization, to its customers, when selecting a mission. To be effective, the mission should be broad enough to serve for many years but within the capabilities of the organization.

Management also needs to specify multiple broad objectives, desired end results, in every area of key importance. It should, as well, specify long-, medium-, and short-range objectives for every unit of the organization. These multiple objectives should be specific, preferably measurable, have a definite time span, be attainable, and be mutually supportive.

To make attainment of objectives more probable, management formulates supporting plans conducive to its aims. The first of these, policies, are broad guides to action and decision making. Strategies are broad decisions to act and allocate resources in certain ways. Short-range, specific strategies are called tactics.

When necessary, management also formulates procedures and rules. Procedures usually outline a chronological sequence of activities to be undertaken in a specific situation. Rules specify exactly what is to be done in a specific, single situation.

Budgets are the component of formal planning most widely used in practice. A budget allocates resources, expressed quantitatively, to attain objectives expressed in the same terms. Budgeting makes it much easier for management to visualize the relative impact of resources and activities on attaining objectives.

Predicting the future is implicit in planning. The future being uncertain, management must make assumptions about it, referred to as premises. Both tangible and intangible premises are used in forecasting what is likely to occur. Forecasting has become a sophisticated field, with specialized forecasts being made in areas such as economic conditions, technological advances, social change, and competition.

REVIEW QUESTIONS

1. Is there a difference between individual planning and organizational planning?
2. Describe these broad categories of formal planning: (a) policies, (b) strategies, (c) procedures, (d) rules, and (e) budgets.
3. Why is an organization's mission the basis for its existence?
4. How does an organization select its mission?
5. Why is there a difference between the mission of a nonprofit organization and the mission of a small organization?
6. Why do contemporary organizations need to have multiple objectives?
7. What are the characteristics of effective objectives?
8. Differentiate between policies, strategies, and objectives.
9. Briefly describe the difference between tangible and intangible premises.
10. How does an organization make forecasts?

DISCUSSION QUESTIONS

11. "Predicting the future is one of management's greatest challenges." Explain this statement in the context of today's postindustrial society.
12. How does the planning process differ in these three situations? A large multinational petroleum company? A large urban hospital? A small, rural college?
13. What effect does the internal and external environment have on the planning process?
14. "Failing to plan is planning to fail." From your experience, describe three organizations you are familiar with that follow this premise.
15. If you were the chairwoman of the board of a major utility, how would you effectively forecast the future?

CASE INCIDENT 1

The New Competitor

In a well-known industry producing consumer products, the production technology has progressed rapidly as has the industry's growth curve. The technology has progressed through stages of development and improvement.

The first level was not very sophisticated, being primarily conceived by persons with good mechanical ability. As the levels of improvement were introduced by competitors in the industry, it was becoming more apparent that the engineering education and experience was also improving. In fact, some firms were making great efforts to recruit and develop persons of that caliber.

Thus it was that firms seemed to progressively improve the technology of production as each new plant was added to the industry capacity. The technology was generally directed toward increasing output and improving quality control.

The stage of technology throughout most of the industry had moved through levels II and III and currently were at a comparative level of IV. The life cycle curve was approaching the maturity stage; the volume of growth was beginning to slow down and flatten out.

Charley Company has been contemplating a new plant for about three years and now has purchased land, approved architectural plans, and contracted for a beautiful building which will incorporate production technology at level V. The building is about half completed.

Tonight the president of Firm C reads in his local newspaper that a major competitor, Delta Company, headquartered 800 miles away, has announced plans for a new plant to be located in the adjacent county to Charley Company. It is reportedly to be operational within 12 months and incorporate technology at level VI—a dramatic improvement over previous developments. Charley Company's president is scheduled to leave the next night on an overseas business trip for ten days.

Questions

1. As president and general manager of Charley Company, what would be your concerns?
2. As the same executive, what would be the list of actions that you would take to the office the next morning?
3. As a consultant and close confidant to Charley Company's president, what would be your list of suggested actions?

SOURCE: Written by Dr. James R. Miller, Department of Management, Georgia State University.

CASE INCIDENT 2

The Heart Association

Usually, the planning process is associated with the business organization. Yet, planning serves as the basis for any type of successful organization. For example, the following was prepared by the American Heart Association, Georgia Affiliate. While it represents only one segment of a multi-planned endeavor, it does provide you with some insights on the application of planning in the nonbusiness environment.

After you've had a chance to study the AHA statement, how would you as a student of management evaluate it in terms of what you now know about planning, missions, and strategy? Specifically, how do you think you could improve the AHA statement?

AMERICAN HEART ASSOCIATION, GEORGIA AFFILIATE

MULTIDISCIPLINARY FIVE-YEAR GOALS AND OBJECTIVES TO DECREASE MORBIDITY AND MORTALITY FROM CARDIOVASCULAR DISEASE

THE PROBLEM

Cardiovascular diseases, most notably atherosclerosis, constitute the greatest health threat to the developed countries of the world. Although we have been privileged in this country to see a 24% reduction in the death rate over the past ten years, these diseases are still responsible for half the total deaths each year, and kill more Americans than all other causes combined. Economic costs and losses run into the billions. All ages, races, and social classes are affected. In Georgia, cardiovascular diseases accounted for 50.8% of all deaths from all causes during the most recent year for which statistics are available.

While it may be argued that "Everyone has to die of something," and "We all have to go *sometime*," the tragedy of cardiovascular disease is not the individual in his eighties who succumbs to a heart attack or stroke after a full life, but the man or woman struck down in the 30's, 40's, 50's . . . the "prime of life" years when these individuals are at their peak of productivity in their careers and personal lives. To give all our people a better chance at longer, fuller, and more productive lives is why the American Heart Association exists.

OUR MISSION

Our mission, then, is the reduction of premature death and disability from cardiovascular diseases. To accomplish this mission, we must identify methods that will result in a realistic approach to the problem and permit the Georgia Affiliate to focus its attention and resources in those areas in which it can make unique or substantial contributions toward the fulfillment of its mission.

OUR WEAPONS

Our first line of defense against cardiovascular disease must be an informed public. If the individual does not understand what he [or she] must do to preserve health and reduce his risk of cardiovascular disease, if he does not recognize when he needs outside help, and if he or members of his family are not prepared to take the appropriate steps to obtain this help, then all of the world's medical knowledge will be of little value. The educational process that would prepare an individual to help preserve his own health and reduce his risk should ideally begin in his youth when lifelong patterns are being formed, and continue throughout his adult life. Our role is twofold: Helping to build good health habits in the young, and serving as agents of change in adult health habits through public information and education programs designed to teach preservation of health and raise the general health consciousness of Georgians.

The second line of defense is comprised of those individuals or institutions to whom the patient first turns for help—the practicing physician, emergency medical services, the clinic or neighborhood health center, the hospital—and even at times the nonmedical person who is on the scene when an acute emergency occurs. In order to be effective, these individuals, institutions and services must not only be capable of providing high quality care, but must be prepared to do so in a manner that is acceptable and accessible to, and understood by, the public. Our programs in this area will address such things as professional education, health care standards (ACLS/BCLS for example), and public information regarding access to care and services.

Finally, our third line of defense—that which serves as the underpinning for the first two—is biomedical research to identify those factors (such as dietary fats, smoking, hypertension, etc.) that adversely affect human health and to devise methods for preventing, diagnosing, and treating these conditions and the diseases to which they contribute. In this regard, the Affiliate has a unique role to play, in that while we cannot invest the huge sums needed for large-scale clinical trials or epidemiological studies, we have an excellent mechanism for supporting young investigators who are just beginning their research careers, helping them gain the experience and results necessary to compete for larger grants in the national arena. The emphasis should be on the support of quality research projects having high merit ratings.

OUR STRATEGY

To adequately develop these lines of defense requires a programmed effort that first takes into consideration the fact that *the Heart Association cannot be all things to all people.* The Affiliate has limited resources in terms of money, volunteers, and staff, and the need for each of these resources always exceeds the supply. Since there are numerous programs and activities that are capable of improving cardiovascular health in Georgia to *some* degree, hard choices must be made regarding the disposition of these resources. This implies priority setting, which is made more efficient by the establishment and implementation of an Affiliate-wide, goal-oriented, long-range planning process. Such a process helps the Affiliate focus its resources on high yield, cost-effective projects that either help prevent the disease process, or provide ongoing relief and control, yielding the highest return on time and money invested.

TO SUMMARIZE:

OUR MISSION: The reduction of premature death and disability from cardiovascular disease.

OUR LINES OF DEFENSE:

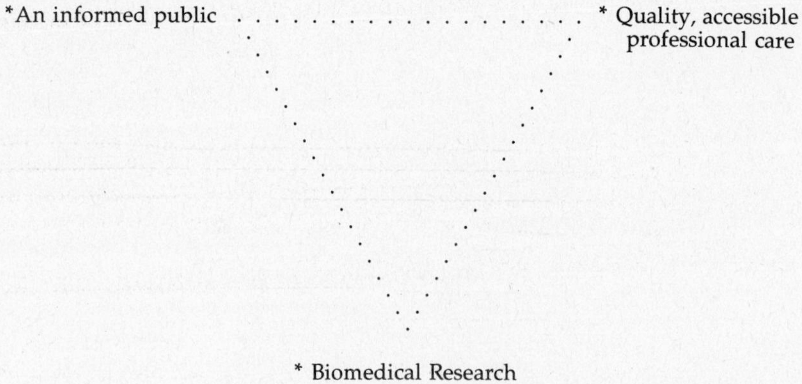

*An informed public . . . . * Quality, accessible professional care

* Biomedical Research

OUR TARGETS:

* 5 million Georgians
* Primary care physicians, nurses, and para-medical groups
* Patients and families of patients suffering from cardiovascular diseases

OUR METHODS: All means of communication to reach Georgians where they study, work, meet and live, through what they read, see and hear.

NOTES

1. "Take Charge Guy," *Wall Street Journal*, May 16, 1978, p. 1.
2. An interesting, though not scientific, book on the power of having goals and implementing them is Napoleon Hill's best-seller, *Think and Grow Rich*, rev. ed. (New York: Hawthorne, 1967). It contains stories of many famous people.
3. J. E. Bryan and E. A. Locke, "Goal Setting As a Means of Increasing Motivation," *Journal of Applied Psychology*, vol. 51 (1967), pp. 274–277.
4. G. P. Lathan and S. B. Kinne, III, "Goal Setting As a Means of Increasing the Performance of the Pulpwood Harvester," Atlanta: *American Pulpwood Association, Harvesting Research Project*, 1971.
5. G. P. Lathan and S. B. Kinne, III, "Improving Job Performance Through Training in Goal Setting," *Journal of Applied Psychology*, vol. 59 (1974), pp. 187–191.
6. R. Stagner, "Corporate Decision Making: An Empirical Study," *Journal of Applied Psychology*, vol. 53 (1969), pp. 1–13.
7. J. Eastlack, Jr. and P. McDonald, "CEO's Role in Corporate Growth," *Harvard Business Review*, May–June 1970, pp. 150–163.
8. S. S. Thune and R. J. House, "Where Long-Range Planning Pays Off," *Business Horizons*, vol. 13 (1970), pp. 81–87.
9. D. Herold, "Long-Range Planning and Organizational Performance: A Cross Validation Study," *Academy of Management Review*, March 1972, pp. 91–102.
10. R. L. Katz and D. Kahn, "Leadership Practices in Relation to Productivity and Morale," in D. Cartwright and A. Zandler, eds., *Group Dynamics—Research and Theory*, 2d. ed. (New York: Harper & Row, 1960), pp. 554–570.
11. A. C. Filley, R. J. House, and S. Kerr, *Managerial Process and Organizational Behavior*, 2d. ed. (Glenview, IL: Scott, Foresman and Co., 1976), p. 455–457.
12. Though very insightful at the time, by contemporary standards this is not a well-formulated mission because it is too vague. Perhaps today Vail would have said something like our mission is "to provide low-cost communication services to our present and future customers."
13. Peter F. Drucker, *Management: Tasks, Responsibilities, Practices* (New York: Harper & Row, 1973), p. 61.
14. Theodore Leavitt, "Marketing Myopia," in J. F. Chapman, ed., *Modern Marketing Strategy* (Cambridge, MA: Harvard University Press, 1964).
15. George A. Steiner and John B. Miner, *Management Policy and Strategy* (New York: Macmillan, 1977), p. 158.
16. Ibid.
17. George A. Steiner, *Top Management Planning* (New York: Macmillan, 1969).
18. Steiner and Miner, op. cit., p. 25.
19. Ibid., pp. 23–24.
20. In 1970, 80 percent of American young people were high-school graduates, as compared to only 16.5 percent in 1920. S. W. Ginzberg, "Changing American Economy and Labor Force," in Rosow, ed., *The Worker and the Job* (Englewood Cliffs, NJ: Prentice-Hall, 1974).
21. Drucker, op. cit., p. 128.

CHAPTER 8

Organizing Authority Relationships

In Chapter 3 we saw that specialized division of labor can greatly increase the work output of a group of people. However, to realize this potential, the people of an organization must be organized. Unless the relationships between people and organizational units are clearly established and their work is coordinated, the efficiencies of specialization will be lost. Delegation is the primary process by which managers establish formal relationships among people in an organization. Through delegation of authority and tasks, managers match people with work and decide which people will work together in a superior-subordinate relationship.

After reading this chapter, you should understand the following important terms and concepts:

- delegation
- responsibility
- authority
- parity principle
- power vs. authority
- line authority
- unity of command
- chain of command
- staff authority
- advisory authority
- concurrent authority
- functional authority
- types of staff

Delegation, Responsibility, and Authority

For plans to be implemented, someone obviously must *actually perform* each of the tasks required to attain the organization's objectives. Management therefore must determine an effective way to combine and coordinate the key variables of tasks and people. Setting objectives and supporting them with policies, strategies, procedures, and rules makes a contribution to meeting this need. Motivating and controlling, we will discover, also play crucial roles in insuring that people perform tasks effectively. However, organizing is the function most visibly and directly concerned with the systematic coordination of relationships among the many tasks of the organization and consequently the formal relationships among the people who perform them.

> ***Organizing*** *is the process of creating a structure for the organization that will enable its people to work together effectively toward its objectives.*

There are two major aspects to the organizing process. One is dividing the organization into subunits appropriate to its objectives and strategies. This is what many people mistakenly consider the entirety of the organizing process. We will explore it in the following chapter. Here our focus is on a far more fundamental, though often less tangible, aspect of organizing: *authority relationships.* These relationships, as we will learn, are the threads that link top management to the lowest levels of the work force and make possible the distribution and coordination of tasks.

The means by which management establishes authority relationships is delegation. One cannot understand the organizing process without first understanding delegation and the related concepts of authority and responsibility.

Delegation

As the term is used in management:

> ***Delegation*** *is the assignment of tasks and authority to a recipient who assumes responsibility for them.*

The critical role of delegation in organized endeavor is apparent from this definition. Delegation is the means by which management distributes among its people the work of the organization, the countless tasks that must be performed for objectives to be attained. If an essential task is not delegated to another person, the manager must perform it personally. This, of course, is clearly impossible in many cases because the manager's time and ability are limited. More important, as early management writer Mary Parker Follett observed, the essence of management is "getting work done through others." Therefore, in a very real sense, delegation is the act that makes one a manager.

Though fundamental for successful organized endeavor, delegation is one of the most misunderstood and misapplied concepts in managing. Not fully understanding the necessity of delegation, or what is required to make it effective, has caused many a brilliant entrepreneur to fail just when his organization grew large. To even begin to understand how to delegate effectively, a topic we will elaborate on later, one must understand the related concepts of responsibility and organizational authority.

Responsibility

In the context of delegation, **responsibility** is an obligation to perform tasks and account for their satisfactory completion. By obligation we mean that an individual is expected to fulfill certain job requirements when he or she accepts a position with the organization. In effect, the individual makes a contract with the organization to perform the tasks of the position in exchange for certain rewards. Being accountable means that the person is held answerable to the delegator for the results of the task to be performed.

For example, upon accepting a job as an assembly-line worker at Sony, a person might be assigned (delegated) the task of wiring circuit boards into television sets. By accepting the job and its rewards, the worker implicitly agrees to perform it in a manner satisfactory to Sony. To meet this responsibility, the worker would have to rewire a set, if he discovered he had made a mistake. Because he is held accountable for performing the task correctly, the worker must answer to his supervisor for any mistakes. The supervisor, although he should be tactful and considerate in doing so, has the right to demand an explanation or that the job be done over if performance is poor.

Inability to Delegate Responsibility. It is important to recognize that although delegation is wholly dependent on its acceptance, *responsibility* itself *cannot be delegated.*

The inability to delegate responsibility means *a manager cannot* shed responsibility by passing it on to a subordinate. Although a person assuming responsibility for a task need not perform it personally, he or she remains accountable for its satisfactory performance. This is easily seen in many work relationships. The head doctor of a surgical team delegates many important duties to nurses, for example. But, if the patient dies because the nurse gave him the wrong type of blood, the head surgeon is considered accountable and can be sued for malpractice. Similarly, if a sales representative does not attain her sales objective for the year and, as a result, the department does not meet its objective, the sales manager, not the representative, must answer to the head of marketing.

In very large organizations, unfortunately, top managers rarely speak to subordinates on lower levels who actually perform most of the organization's specific tasks. They are, nevertheless, responsible and accountable for them. If a junior engineer at General Motors makes a design error that eventually requires the company to recall 100,000 autos, one can safely bet that the vice-president of engineering will spend several nervous hours explaining why to the president. Perhaps the president himself will have to explain to the stockholders why he let earnings decline through this error. Even though the president of GM and that obscure engineer never met, the stockholders rightly hold the president accountable for everything related to GM's performance.

Former President Harry S. Truman indicated awareness of his ultimate responsibility for government with a now famous sign on his desk. It said: "The buck stops here." He is not the only U.S. president to feel this way. One of President Carter's first acts was to borrow that sign from the Truman Library.

The extent of their responsibility is one reason why managers, particularly those heading large corporations, are so highly paid. But it is doubtful that even a several-hundred-thousand dollar a year salary would lure an intelligent person to a top post if there were no way that person could influence the performance of all those people on whom his or her own success hinges. This brings us to a most important concept: organizational authority.

Organizational Authority

If a person is expected to do something for the organization, assume responsibility for the satisfactory completion of a task, the organization must supply the resources required. Management does this by delegating authority along with tasks.

> ***Authority*** *is the limited right to use the organization's resources and channel the efforts of some of its people to perform tasks.*

Authority is delegated to *a position, not the individual* who happens to hold it at the time. This is expressed by the old military saying that you salute the uniform, not the man. When an individual changes jobs, he or she loses the authority of the old job and picks up that of the new. For example, even though a Procter & Gamble sales manager is on a higher level of management when promoted to brand manager, she could no longer issue orders to her former subordinates in the sales department. However, because delegation is not possible unless there is a person in the position, it is very common to speak of delegating authority to the individual.

Contrasting Views of Authority. There are two views of the process by which authority is obtained. The classical view holds that authority is passed from higher to lower levels of the organization. In a business, for example, the credit manager attains her authority from the assistant controller, who attains his from the vice-president of finance, who attains hers from the president, who attains his from the board of directors. Taken even further, the board gets its authority from the stockholders, who get theirs from the institution of private property, which is based on the Constitution and laws of the country. This seems logical and consistent with the concept that authority is delegated by managers to their subordinates.

However, as Chester Barnard, a writer of the administrative school and former president of New Jersey Bell observed, a subordinate is able to reject a superior's requests. Based on this, Barnard formulated what is referred to as

FEATURE 8-1

Authority, Tasks, and Responsibilities of a Middle Manager

The plant manager is a pivotal figure in American industry and ranks among the most highly paid and valued of all middle managers. What's more, his responsibilities seem to be growing. "The able manufacturing man recognizes more and more that the name of the game is profit and loss," says R. J. Wytmar, president of Wytmar & Co., a Chicago recruiting firm that regularly surveys companies on the movement and duties of their executives. "In the past, all a manufacturing man had to do was to produce a product. Now he has to explain what it costs and why."

But when it comes to making major corporate decisions, the plant manager usually has little say. Some managers contend they don't want anything more than the chance to give a little advice. "It wouldn't be good business to do anything in the plant without asking the plant people," says Raymond Shelmire, manager for operations for three Johns-Manville Corp. glass-fiber plants in Defiance, Ohio. "But we already have a lot of responsibility, and I'm not sure we could do justice to the job if we took on any more."

Atlas's Mr. Hoffman says that he is content to "have enough input to affect the decisions concerning this plant." But making decisions, he says, is "the most challenging part of any job, and only the dullard doesn't want to be the top dog and make the top decisions."

Norman B. Keider, Atlas's president, rates Mr. Hoffman's chances of moving into upper management as "reasonable": one chance in three of becoming an Atlas executive, one in five of becoming a top manager at another Tyler subsidiary and one chance in 10 of moving into the corporate offices at Tyler.

As it is, it would seem that Mr. Hoffman's duties are considerable. They range from ordering the raw materials for dynamite, nitroglycerin, blasting caps and slurries (gelatinous ammonium nitrate-based explosives) to delivering the finished goods to customers in construction, mining and quarrying. He oversees the safety of 950 employees, the profitability of an operation that will report about $50 million in sales this year, the reliability of dangerous products and the general care and security of 500 buildings, a 2,700-acre wooded site and over a ton of stored explosives.

But while Atlas leaves all production policies up to Mr. Hoffman, it keeps the purse string policies for itself. Thus Mr. Hoffman was powerless this winter to hire a badly needed draftsman until Atlas authorized creating a new salaried position, a process that took over two months.

SOURCE: June Kronholz, *Wall Street Journal*, April 21, 1977, p. 1. Reprinted by permission of *The Wall Street Journal*,

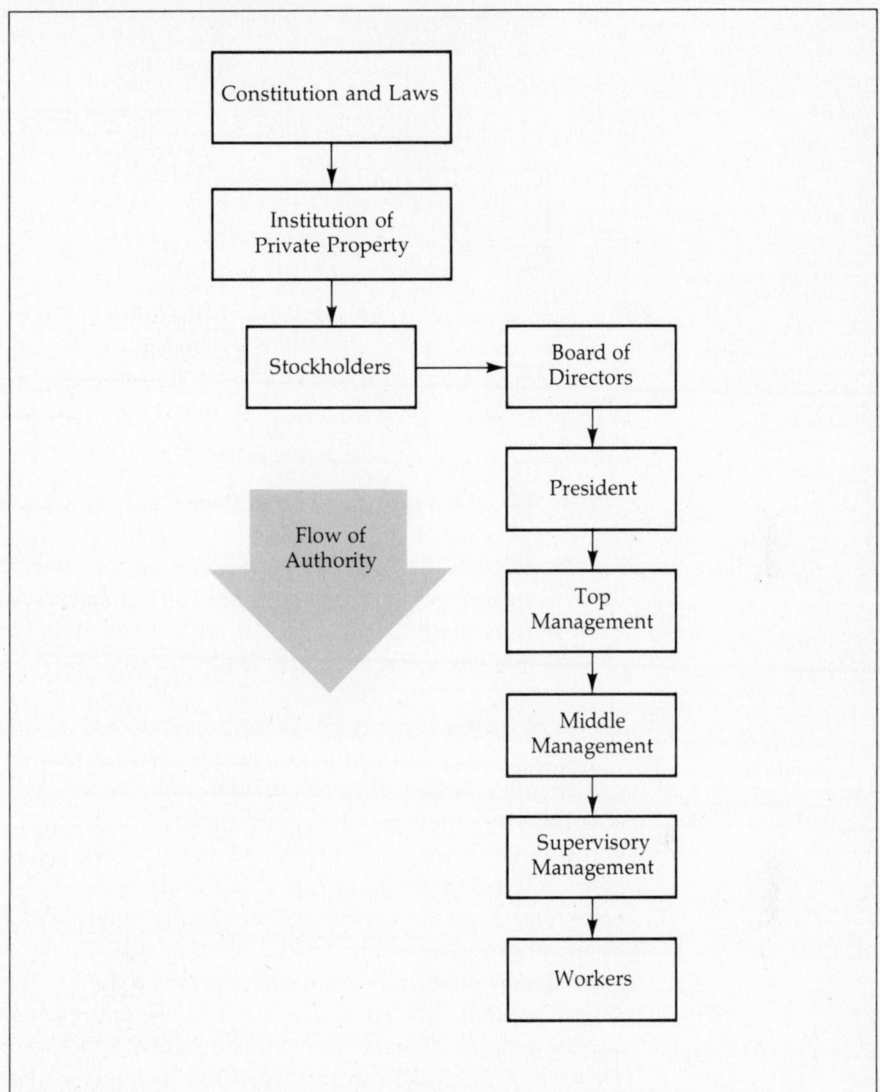

Figure 8-1 Classical View of Organizational Authority

the *acceptance* view of authority. He defined authority as "the character of a communication (order) in a formal organization by virtue of which it is accepted by a contributor to the organization as governing the action he contributes; that is, as governing or determining what he does or is not to do so far as the organization is concerned."[1] Thus, in Barnard's view, if a subordinate does not accept his manager's authority, it does not exist. The acceptance view is illustrated in Figure 8-2, which you should compare to the classical view illustrated in Figure 8-1.

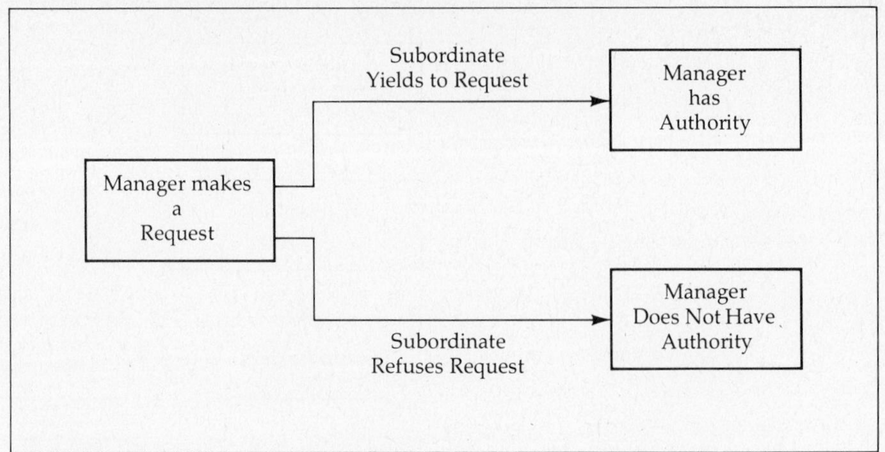

Figure 8-2 Acceptance View of Organizational Authority

As we will discover, Barnard's acceptance view acknowledges the existance of power, which often modifies the managers' ability to use the authority inherent in their position. In any event, whichever of these views is correct, it is clear that authority is always limited.

Limits of Authority. As our definition specified, authority is the *limited* right to use resources and command people. Within an organization, these limits are usually specified through written policies, procedures, rules, and job descriptions. Or they may be communicated orally to the subordinate. Persons going beyond these limits exceed their authority, even when doing so is absolutely necessary to perform delegated tasks. A worker authorized to operate only a certain machine, for example, would be exceeding his authority by using one assigned to another worker if his broke down. More obviously, a Congresswoman who uses office expense money for personal business exceeds the limits placed on her right to use government resources.

In general, the limits of authority grow wider as one moves up the organization. But even the authority of top managers is limited. The chairperson and president of a large, public company are accountable to stockholders. They must answer to those stockholders if expenditures seriously exceed the overall budget. Nor can top corporate officers give themselves a raise, a use of organizational resources, without the board of directors' approval. There also are many external limits to authority. Laws prevent managers from knowingly delegating duties that are likely to seriously harm workers, even if the organization has no policies in the area. The law also clearly forbids authorizing use of the organization's resources for bribery or, in most cases, political contributions.

Much of a manager's authority is derived from the traditions, mores, cultural patterns, and folkways of the society in which the organization functions. People obey the orders of a superior partially because it is socially acceptable behavior to do so. These factors limit authority as well as support it. Managers cannot delegate authority that conflicts with laws or cultural values, at least not for long. This means, of course, that they cannot delegate duties requiring such authority and expect them to be carried out. Sometimes this restriction impinges on the organization's plans. For example, several companies in recent years have decided to stop doing business in countries where bribery is essential. These companies find giving up the added profit preferable to forcing their managers to meet quotas by concealing payments and otherwise exceeding their legitimate authority.

It is important to realize, however, that limits placed on authority, either by the organization or its society, often are widely exceeded in practice. To better understand this, let us briefly examine the difference between authority and power.

Authority and Power. Authority and power are often confused with each other. Authority is defined as a delegated, limited right, inherent in a position to use organizational resources. **Power**, in contrast, is the ability to act or the capability to affect a situation. One can have power without having authority.

For example, because the treasurer has the right or authority to sign checks, he has the power or ability to transfer the firm's money to his own bank account. His authority, however, is limited to legitimate transactions. If the treasurer steals, the company's president has both the power and authority to fire him. However, if he plans ahead, a dishonest treasurer may have the power to escape legal authorities by fleeing to a foreign country in the company jet. To give a less extreme, but more typical example, an experienced sales representative may not have the authority to formulate a new sales strategy. However, if the vice-president of sales respects her expertise, she may have the power to sway the choice to the alternative she prefers.

Authority, in other words, determines what a person occupying a particular position has a *right* to do. Power determines what he or she *really can do.* The ways in which power is used can have a positive or negative effect on the organization. In later chapters we will learn that leadership is heavily dependent on power and people often use power to pursue organizational objectives more effectively.

Line and Staff Relationships

The preceding discussion was slightly oversimplified in order to stress the essential concepts of organizational authority. As we mentioned, authority is always limited. In some cases, these limits change the nature of authority so

FEATURE 8-2

Delegation, Responsibility, and Authority: An Illustration

The United States of America is a democratic governmental organization in which every citizen is a member and technically has an equal voice in all decisions. However, it being impractical for every citizen to participate actively in even most major decisions, our founding fathers created a system whereby citizens *delegate* people to represent them at the local, state, and national levels of government.

Our delegated representatives are *authorized* to make decisions for us but only within *limits* established by law. However, they are not expected to personally perform most of the services of government. We realize, for example, that the president will delegate the *task* of defense to the secretary of defense, who will delegate most of it to the chiefs of staff, and so on until some soldier physically performs each required specific job. Even though high governmental officials do not perform each task, they are still responsible for their satisfactory completion. If, for example, an economic advisor suggests to the head of the Federal Reserve Bank to raise interest rates in order to curb inflation, the head, not the advisor, is *held accountable* by the president if the tactic fails. The president, in turn, is held accountable by us.

Since we give the president full *authority*, within the *limits* of law, to use all of the *resources* of the United States government, and he *assumed responsibility* by accepting the office, he must answer to us for *any* failure of performance. When elections are held, responsible citizens exercise their power and authority by voting to replace delegates who failed to meet their responsibilities.

considerably that one must consider authority relationships as being of two general types. These are referred to as line authority and staff authority, which also is used in different forms.

Line Authority

Line authority is the authority that flows from a superior directly to a subordinate and through to other subordinates. In simple terms, it is line authority that provides the manager with institutionally supported power to command immediate subordinates toward desired ends. A manager with line authority also has the right to make certain decisions and act on certain matters without consulting others, within the limits set by the organization, by law, or by custom.

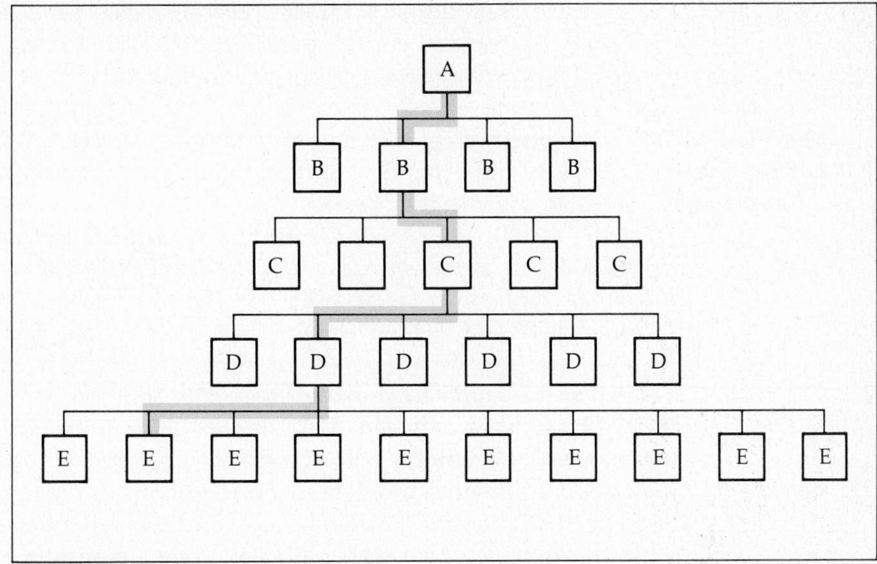

Figure 8-3 **Chain of Command**

For example, a hospital administrator with full line authority over its resources can use the hospital's money to purchase any item he or she deems necessary by just ordering payment through the treasurer. This administrator may also be able to decide which physicians ought to be hired and what the salary of each position is to be, as well as to choose heads of departments and set objectives for the hospital. Similarly, a sales manager can usually make the final decision on hiring new representatives, what the expense allowance of each sales person is, and tell sales people to call on certain customers.

Chain of Command. Delegation of line authority is what creates the organization's hierarchy of management levels. The process of creating a hierarchy is referred to as the *scalar process.* Because the authority to command people is usually passed on through the scalar process, the resulting hierarchy is called a **chain of command** or *scalar chain,* as illustrated in Figure 8-3. Probably the clearest example of chain of command is the hierarchy of military organizations. Soldiers of a given rank are easily distinguished from those on higher and lower levels by their uniforms and insignia, and the hierarchy is actually called the chain of command.

In most organizations, everyone from president to clerical workers wears essentially similar clothing, but a chain of command still exists. James Mooney, a former General Motors vice-president and a writer of the administrative school, made a historical analysis of military, government, business, and religious organizations. He found that all were based on a hierarchical system of superior-subordinate relationships.[2] We can therefore say that a chain of command created by delegation of line authority is a characteristic of all but the very smallest formal organizations.

The Need for Staff and Staff Authority

Before attempting to define staff authority, let us briefly review the origins of staff to understand why in some situations line authority alone will not meet an organization's needs.

According to Claude George, the concept of staff was first used methodically by the armies of Alexander the Great (336–323 B.C.).[3] It is very difficult, if not impossible, for an officer in the heat of battle to command his men effectively and to plan strategy at the same time. But since both planning and directing are absolutely essential to win any military operation, a way had to be found to provide them. The solution was to divide the task of winning wars between two varieties of military specialists: officers who planned and officers who commanded soldiers in battle. But this division caused a potential problem. Because soldiers are obligated to follow the orders of all officers, it would be easy for them to be thrown into confusion by a situation in which the orders issued by a planning officer conflicted with the orders of their direct superior.

To prevent this, Alexander's armies withheld the authority to command from planners and assigned these specialists to assist a high ranking officer in the line organization. The planners, in that way, could recommend strategy and have a good chance of it being followed by the troops, yet avoid the disruption of a confused chain of command. Since these planners were the assistants of a top officer, they were referred to as his staff. Officers who fought on the battle line, rightly enough, were called line officers. Military organizations today still use these designations.

Staff in Contemporary Organizations. For many years, the use of staff was relatively limited. But when technology soared and the environment grew more volatile and complex, many organizations required an increasing variety and degree of specialized expertise. A pharmaceutical firm, for example, needs chemists, physicians, quality-control technicians, computer programmers, educators to train its salesforce, and lawyers to ensure government regulations are met. The concept of staff was expanded and modified to meet organizations' needs. Consequently, today there are many types of staff and variations of staff authority.

Types of Staff

Staff performs so many different functions in contemporary organizations it is impossible to list them all. However, one can classify staff as being of two or three basic types with respect to the functions performed for the organization. The three **types of staff** are *advisory staff, service staff,* and *personal staff,* which sometimes is considered a variety of service staff. However, one should keep in mind that in practice the distinction among these types is

FEATURE 8-3

A Staff Manager's Job

Mr. Armbruster's employer is TRW Inc., and his title there is director of corporate planning. "But that isn't what I do," he says. "I always think about that little box quite awhile and then I put down 'engineer'—it isn't right either but it fits the space and people understand it."

Mr. Armbruster is a prime example of the fastest growing segment of today's corporate America: the middle management "knowledge specialist." Typically steeped in a narrow field of expertise, these specialists have little or no political clout in the executive suite and command few subordinates. They neither set corporate policy, as does top management, nor produce a salable product, as do workers on the assembly line. Their job responsibilities often baffle co-workers down the hall, let alone family and friends.

But while their contributions to the corporate weal may be invisible to outsiders, and to many insiders, sometimes even themselves, knowledge specialists are having a marked impact on how big business operates. More and more these anonymous managers are handling problems of information management, psychology, politics, ecology, law, social policy and other areas that were unknown or ignored in the executive office as recently as a decade ago.

As the responsibilities of these specialists expand, amoeba-fashion, to engulf practically every aspect of running a huge corporation, their collective influence becomes apparent. Middle managers are making most of the day-to-day operating decisions and also are making nearly all of the specialized studies and recommendations on which top management is basing its long-range decisions. As a result, "sometimes it appears that middle management is practically running the company," says Frederick A. Teague, a vice president at Booz Allen & Hamilton, the consulting firm.

Management recruiters say the hiring of knowledge specialists accounts for the bulk of the explosive growth in middle management over the past decade. (In fact, the growth has been so great that some companies have had to cut back, through firings, in recent years.) Although no industry-wide figures are available, recruiters say that what has happened at TRW is fairly typical. TRW's corporate staff has more than doubled in size in the past 10 years, to about 300 people, and nearly all of that growth has been among knowledge specialists.

Gardner Heidrick, co-chairman of Heidrick and Struggles, a Chicago-based management consulting and recruiting firm, notes that the demand for specialists in big companies has been building "ever since the Roosevelt

continues on page 250

FEATURE 8-3, continued

administration first created the need for a lot of lawyers and accountants in companies." In recent years, sharply increased government attention to corporate hiring and promotion policies, health and safety standards and pollution controls, along with the growth and increasing complexity of large corporations, has greatly increased demand on management and has spawned ever-growing amounts of paper work and the need for more experts to handle it.

Yet although these often "faceless" middle-management specialists collectively have considerable influence within a company, as individuals they often face the frustration of little or no supervisory authority and working with little visibility in a position that isn't well understood. It isn't always easy for a knowledge specialist to feel appreciated or to see a bright future ahead of him in such a position. A specialist must constantly be building his own expertise. Yet to rise very far in management, says James E. Dunlap, TRW's vice president of human relations, "the specialist has to somehow or other get broader and become more of a generalist."

Nowhere is the impact of an emergent corporate staff of specialists in widely diverse areas of expertise more evident than at TRW, an innovative multinational concern with $3 billion of annual sales, ranging from auto parts and electronics systems to aerospace and industrial products. TRW's knowledge specialists range the globe, giving money to orchestras, colleges and hospitals, arguing with tax officials in Singapore, lobbying elected officials in California and creating computer programs to do such things as automatically audit purchases and sales between divisions.

seldom sharp. It is not at all uncommon for a staff to perform both service and advisory functions.

Advisory Staff. If line management faces a problem requiring special skills, it can bring suitable specialists into the organization on either a temporary or permanent basis and thereby form an *advisory staff*. The function of these specialists is to advise line management in their area of expertise. The most common uses of advisory staff are in the areas of law, advanced or special technology, training and personnel development, and employee counseling.

Service Staff. In virtually any of the areas in which advisory staff are used, the function of staff can be, and often is, extended to the performance of services. Perhaps the best known and most frequent usage of service staff is the personnel department common to most large companies. The personnel department maintains employee records, locates potential job candidates and

As one example, TRW's human relations staff has grown to 20 from seven in 1967. One of its newest members is Paul D. Hubert, 41, the director of productivity projects. He is one of five behavioral specialists immersed in questions of how to restructure work to make jobs more efficient, more productive and more satisfying. Shirley A. Curry, 41, corporate manager of employee benefits, spent half of the past year supervising the preparation of new slides, booklets and memos required by the Employee Retirement Income Security Act of 1974.

TRW's finance staff is probably the most highly specialized arm of the corporate staff and numbers 92, up from 43 a decade ago. Dennis G. Tischler, 34, manager of international taxes, is one of three tax managers reporting to the director of taxes. Mr. Tischler and his seven tax specialists pay $100 million a year of TRW's taxes in 30 foreign countries and file TRW's federal tax return, a document that fills four two-inch binders and takes two man-years to prepare.

In the cramped little office where he daily pores over computer readouts, John Armbruster compares his work to the microwave oven his wife would like to buy. "I'm caught up here in providing something no one would miss if it weren't provided," he says.

Ruben F. Mettler, president and chief operating officer of TRW, calls Mr. Armbruster's contributions "very real and very large, but also diffuse and subtle." Over the past few years, he says, his work has had "a very positive effect on the bottom line," which rose 6% in 1974, 12% in 1975 and 28% in 1976, when net income was $133 million.

SOURCE: Richard Martin, *Wall Street Journal*, April 18, 1977, pp. 1, 23. Reprinted by permission of *The Wall Street Journal*,

screens them, and, in some instances, will supply line management with required personnel. This illustrates how a staff can have both advisory and service duties.

Other areas where service staff are used include public relations, market research, budgeting, planning, logistics, environmental-impact evaluation, and legal problems. These staff departments provide management with information necessary for effective decision making.

Personal Staff. *Personal staff,* a variation of service staff, which is formed whenever a manager hires a secretary or assistant to relieve the burden of mechanical work, is the most frequent use of staff. The duty of the personal staff is whatever the executive wishes done. The staff person has no authority in the organization. When he or she acts, it is in the name of the manager. We can indicate the presence of personal staff as a box to the side of the manager on the organizational chart, as is illustrated in Figure 8-4.

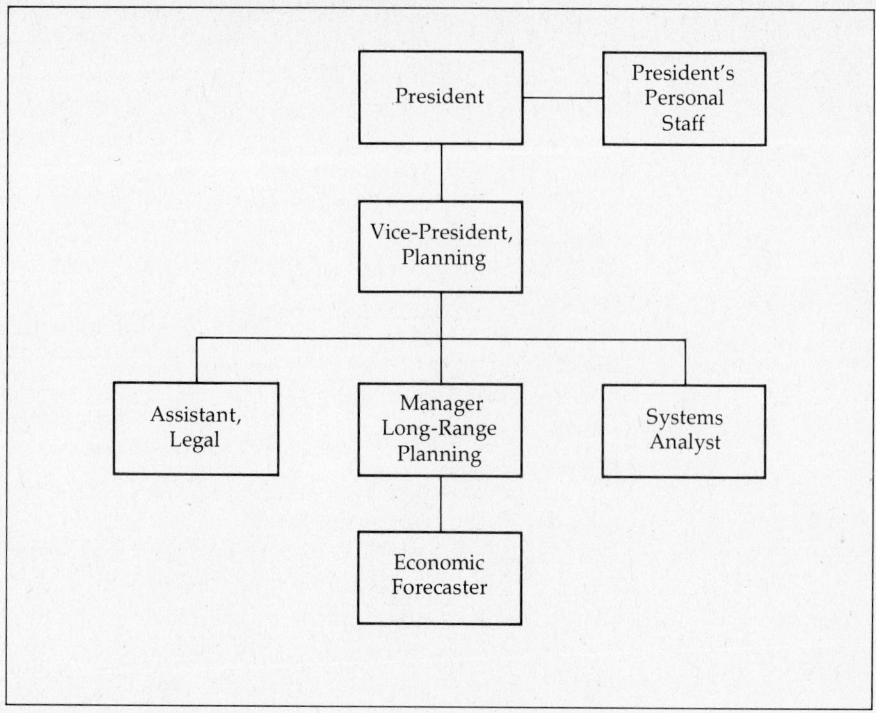

Figure 8-4 Personal Staff and Advisory/Service Staff
(Note that the Staff Vice-President has line authority within his own department.)

Although the personal staff has no formal authority, it can have great power. Through scheduling of appointments and filtering of communications, they may control access to the executive for whom they work. This may force persons lower than their boss in the hierarchy to curry the favors of the staff in order to have access to him or influence him. If the executive genuinely listens to or depends on personal staff for advice, the staff's power is greatly magnified. The personal secretaries of high executives occupy what in group-dynamics jargon is referred to as a position of centrality. They are frequently able to acquire power that far exceeds their formal authority.

Variations in Staff Authority

The advisory, service, and personal staff classifications describe staff according to its use. To understand the staff concept in contemporary organizations, one must also consider the nature of the authority delegated to staff. There is an exceptional range of authority delegated to staffs of every type. Staff authority can be highly limited, virtually purely advisory. Or, it can be so broad that the difference between line and staff is almost eliminated. We will now describe the major variations of staff authority and the reasons for their use.

FEATURE 8-4

The Power of Personal Staff

Anyone who has tried to get past the secretary of a top manager knows how powerful personal staff can be, even though they have no formal authority. There have been a number of instances, however, in which personal staff have accumulated so much power they have been able to almost take over an organization's operations. A famous example is the White House staff of Richard Nixon. These men used their official and close personal relationships to Mr. Nixon to prevent "undesirables" from having access to the president. Since such persons included a large percentage of Congress and even a few cabinet secretaries, the staff effectively had enormous influence over governmental decisions. They also tried to shield the president from information they felt would upset him. Although subsequent stories indicate otherwise, according to Mr. Nixon, his staff withheld information about the Watergate incident and its cover-up. Whether or not this was true, any president's personal staff has no line authority whatsoever in the United States government. All of their actions are made in the name of the president. Therefore, as Mr. Nixon fully acknowledged, the president is accountable for anything his staff does.

Advisory Authority. The authority of staff originally was limited to advising the line organization *only* when line initiated the request. When staff authority is restricted to advise only on request, line management is supposed to consult the advisory staff whenever its knowledge is applicable. But line managers are not obligated to do so. They can, if they choose, resolve the problem without even letting the staff know it exists.

This point is illustrated by an interview with Dr. Delmar Landel, chief psychologist at General Motors. Asked if GM executives follow the advice of the organizational development and research department, a staff activity, Dr. Landel replied, "To answer that question you first have to understand a little about how GM operates. It's a highly decentralized organization, in which the different operating units have a great deal of autonomy. The executive group here at headquarters provides us psychologists as a resource for the division. So it's pretty much up to them as to whether or not they choose to call on us for help or advice."[4]

When staff's authority is advisory, it often must spend time selling line managers on the worth of staff services and suggestions. Even if staff advice is sought and received, line managers can disregard it. This, of course, may prove rather frustrating to staff and lead to conflicts between line and staff, a serious problem we will discuss in Chapter 20.

Compulsory Consultation. Because staff may have difficulty getting line management to seek its advice, even when doing so is clearly in the organization's best interest, top management sometimes extends the authority of staff to *compulsory consultation*. When consultation is compulsory, line *must* discuss relevant situations with staff before taking action or bringing a proposal to top management. Line management is not, however, obligated to actually follow staff's advice.

A common example of compulsory consultation is the use of a market-research staff. In many organizations, the marketing department or production department must get an estimate of a proposed new product's sales potential from the marketing-research staff before proceeding. By conducting research, this staff provides a sales estimate which the line organization may or may not choose to accept. But company regulations call for the estimate to be made before top management will even consider approving the new product.

Concurrent Authority. Top management can further extend the authority of staff by giving it the right to disapprove line-management decisions with which staff does not agree. The aim of **concurrent authority** is to set up a system of checks to balance power and prevent major blunders. Not surprisingly, the most common use of concurrent authority is in governmental organizations. Both the House and the Senate, for example, must approve all laws before they become official statute. The president, too, has concurrent authority to a limited degree, but his veto can be overridden by the Congress.

Many companies use concurrent authority to control financial expenditures by requiring a double signature for all major purchases.

Functional Authority. A staff with **functional authority** can initiate as well as veto action in its area of expertise. In essence, the line authority of the organization's president is channeled through staff, giving it the right to act on certain matters. Thus, functional authority eliminates the distinction between line and staff for all practical purposes.

Functional authority is quite common today because complex contemporary organizations often require a high level of uniformity in areas such as accounting practices, labor relations, and employment testing. They also need to ensure, in certain situations, that staff expertise will, indeed, be used whenever it is needed. If every staff decision in these important areas had to be routed through line for implementation in a large organization, too much time would be wasted. On an organizational chart functional authority is designated with a dotted line.

Line Authority Within Staff. We have described the variations in authority that staff has with respect to the line organization. It is important to realize that in larger organizations today, a given staff may consist of many people. In such situations, the staff would be a department requiring more than one level of management. Thus, there would be a line organization and conventional chain of command within the staff. Naturally, managers within the staff hierarchy would have line authority with respect to their own subordinates, irrespective of the nature of the staff's authority relative to the organization as a whole (as was illustrated in Figure 8-4).

Organizing Authority Relationships Effectively

For the organization to attain its objectives and grow, management cannot afford to merely go through the motions of organizing authority relationships. It must perform this aspect of the management process as effectively as all others. Because the management functions are interdependent, ineffective delegation of tasks and authority will eventually cause problems in every other function. However, in order to genuinely understand all of the factors involved in organizing authority relationships effectively, one needs knowledge about structure and its relationship to other variables which we have not yet presented. Therefore, we will return to this topic later and focus on only a few fundamental concepts. The first of these is determining which activities ought to be line and which staff. The second concept is the role of line authority in coordination and some ways management can facilitate coordination through delegation. Last, but not least, we will discuss common obstacles to effective delegation and some ways in which management can overcome them.

Organizing Line and Staff Relationships

During organizing, management must decide if a given activity should be line or staff. This decision should be based on how fundamental and direct a contribution the activity makes to attainment of overall objectives. However, to think of staff activities as unessential to objectives is grossly incorrect. *All* activities should facilitate attaining objectives. If an activity does not, it should be eliminated, not made a staff function. The question, thus, is not whether there is a contribution but how directly related it is to the organization's primary mission.

Line activities properly are those concerned directly with creation, financing, and distribution of the organization's goods or services. Staff assists performance of these primary functions as a skilled nurse assists a surgeon during an operation. The surgeon probably could save the patient in an emergency without the nurse, but the risk is less and the work goes more smoothly because of the nurse's work. The nurse, on the other hand, cannot under any circumstance perform the operation successfully—attain their organizational objective—without the surgeon.

Naturally, what specific activities ought to be staff depends on the organization's mission, objectives, and strategies because structure, as a variable, is dependent on objectives. Or, as management writer Alfred Chandler once expressed it, "Structure follows strategy." Differences in objectives lead to fundamental differences in which structure is most appropriate. For example, in the majority of organizations legal services are clearly a staff activity. However, in a law firm attorneys are the backbone of the organization. Similarly, training is usually either a staff activity or simply one of the line manager's tasks. But in a college, teaching is the organization's primary activity. On the other hand, finance is a key activity for almost every organization and therefore a line area. However, the keeping of financial records, accounting, can be considered a staff activity because it is essentially an aid to financial management.

Line Authority and Coordination

Delegation of line authority and the resulting chain of command play a key role in the process of coordinating an organization. To begin, line authority "personalizes" and simplifies the relationship between subordinates and superiors. The recipient assumes personal responsibility for tasks and is accountable to the delegator personally for their satisfactory completion. If the subordinate runs into problems, he or she knows exactly to whom to turn for a solution. If the immediate superior cannot provide a solution, the problem can be passed up the chain of command in an orderly manner. Everybody knows exactly who can do what.

Of course, coordination is not an inevitable outcome of specifying line relationships. Unless, for example, there is a single person or very small group with the authority to make decisions of any type, every truly vital, difficult decision that arose could stop the organization dead in its tracks. If there is no point at which "the buck stops," there simply would be nobody who could say, "We've discussed this problem at length, now we must act. *This* is what we should do. . . ." In addition, the length of the chain of command and the tasks assigned to various positions on it must be appropriate to the situation at hand. These decisions involve many factors within the organization and environment, so we will hold off discussing them for later chapters.

Instead, we will present two concepts related to facilitating coordination and line authority that require no knowledge of contingency theory to understand. These are the principle of unity of command and the need to limit span of management.

Unity of Command. According to management historian Claude George, Jr., the concept of a formal chain of command was employed by the Hebrews as early as 1491 B.C.[5] Managers understood even then that for a chain of command to be effective, the relationship between subordinate and superior must be clear and simple. The best way to bring about clarity, the ancients saw, was for a subordinate to be accountable to and take orders from only *one* superior. This belief is now usually called the principle of unity of command. It may be the oldest expressed principle of organizing, for the Bible states that an individual should have only a single master.

According to the principle of **unity of command**, a person should receive authority from only one superior and should be accountable to only that person. Or, as professors Koontz and O'Donnell expressed it: "The more completely an individual has a reporting relationship to a single superior, the less the problem of conflict and the greater the feeling of personal responsibility for results."[6]

In an organization that abides by this principle, all formal communication must be routed along the chain of command. A person with a problem cannot go over the head of his or her immediate superior and speak to the top manager about it. Nor can the top manager issue an order to a low-level employee without going through managers at intermediate levels. Of course, due to power and informal relationships, even in organizations like the military that rigidly enforce the principle people will sometimes circumvent the chain of command. Also, if the chain of command is very long, adhering to the principle of unity of command could considerably slow down communication and decision making in some situations.

However, the principle of unity of command has proven its worth as a coordinating mechanism for centuries and in countless numbers of organizations. Henri Fayol included it among his fourteen principles of organizations. Therefore, with a few exceptions, such as the matrix structure described in the following chapter, most organizations try to use it.

Limiting Span of Management. Span of management, defined earlier as the number of people who report *directly* to a manager, is established through delegation of line authority. Technically, the top manager of an organization could decide to have everyone report directly to him or her instead of creating a chain of command. This is what a high-school football coach who calls in all plays from the bench does. Indeed, because top management is ultimately responsible for successful performance of all tasks no matter how many subordinate managers there are, it has a strong incentive to retain as much direct control over tasks as possible. In practice, however, failure to keep spans of management reasonably small makes coordination almost impossible.

Countless managers have learned the hard way the problems having too large a span of management can cause. One of the first to learn was Moses. As recounted in Exodus Chapter 18, when Moses first led the Israelites out of Egypt he tried to do all the managing himself. For a while things went as smoothly as could be expected on a long trek through the wilderness. But eventually, as often happens when a new venture grows into a large, established organization, some people got confused about the organization's purpose. There also was considerable bickering and other counter-productive behavior.

Since nobody except Moses was authorized to resolve problems, he got incredibly bogged down with trivia: "Moses sat to judge the people; and the people stood by Moses from the morning unto the evening." This made for a long work day. More important, nothing except judging was getting done—and that none too effectively.

Fortunately for the Israelites, Moses was open to sound advice. Jethro, Moses' father-in-law, diagnosed the problem as overly broad span of management and suggested creating additional levels of management:

> So Moses gave heed to the voice of his father-in-law and did all that he had said. Moses chose able men out of all Israel, and made them heads over the people, rulers of thousands, of hundreds, of fifties, and of tens. And they judged the people at all times; hard cases they brought to Moses, but any small matter they judged themselves.[7]

Management theorists have devoted considerable attention to determining just what the ideal span of management is. The administrative school was particularly concerned with the issue. A wide range of numbers was proposed, with a span of between seven and ten subordinates considered best by several writers. However, as we will discuss later, contemporary research indicates that the most appropriate span varies widely. Management level, the nature of the tasks being performed, the characteristics of subordinates, and the relative abilities of the manager all play a role in determining how many people a manager can directly supervise effectively.

What is clear is that unless spans of management are kept reasonably small, management will be unable to meet its responsibilities not only for coordination but also for control over performance and developing and motivating subordinates.

Obstacles to Effective Delegation

The expectations and obligations delegation creates can be a powerful force for harmony and unity of purpose. However, unless management makes a concerted effort to take into account the personalities and needs of recipients, the result may be considerable anxiety and problems for both manager and recipient.

Delegation is a form of communication exchange. The manager has duties that must be performed by subordinates. To perform them properly, subordinates must understand exactly what the manager wants. Delegation also involves motivation, influence, and leadership. The manager must get subordinates to actually perform their tasks effectively. As in all communication and influence processes, *both* parties are crucial to success. Recognizing this, William Newman listed several reasons why managers may be reluctant to delegate and why subordinates may choose to avoid added responsibility.[8]

Managerial Obstacles. Newman cites five reasons why managers may be reluctant to delegate:

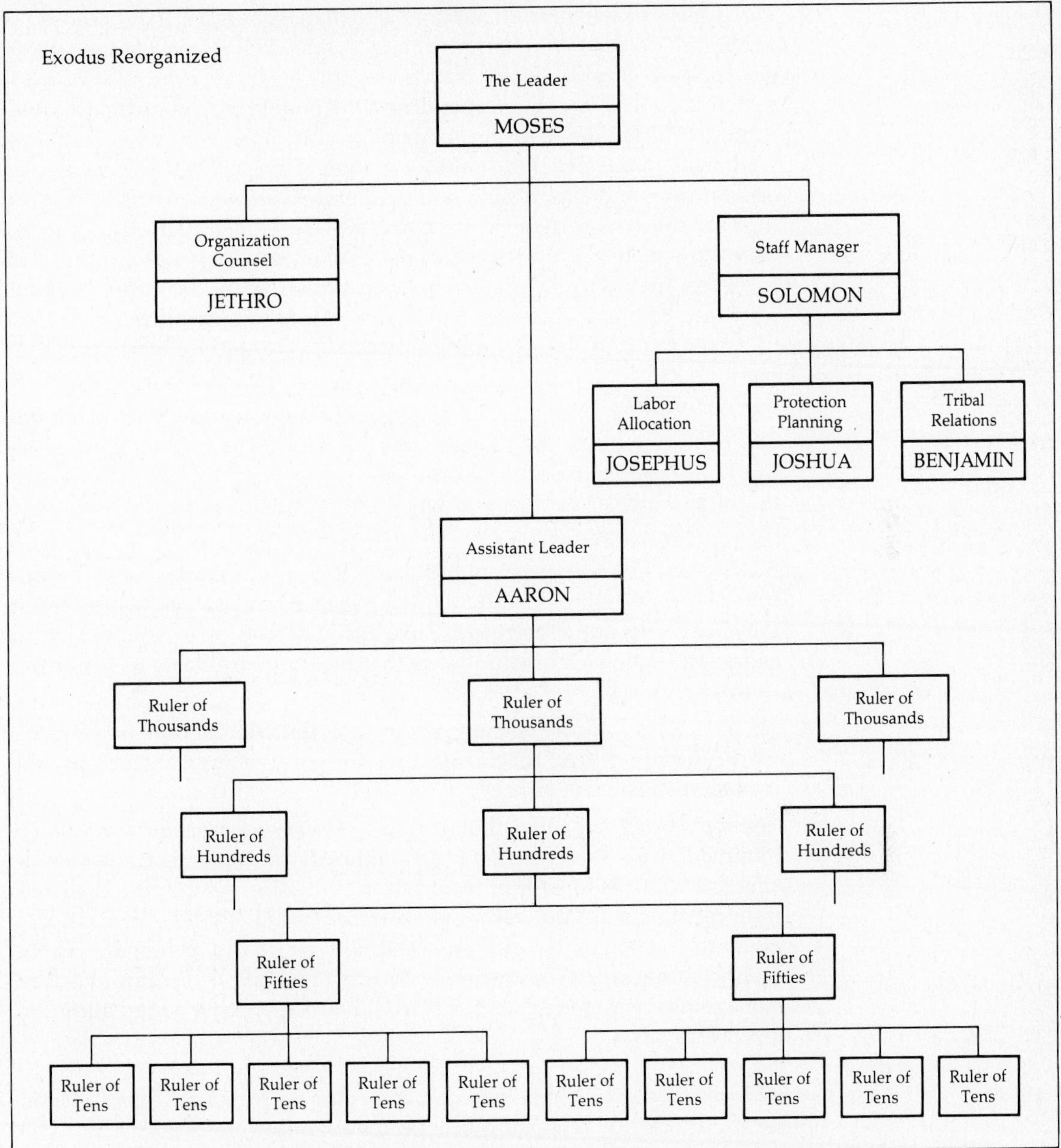

Figure 8-5 Moses and His Span of Management

Before reorganization Moses' span of management was in the thousands. After, it was three. Solomon also had a span of three. The ruler of hundreds is shown to have a span of two, the ruler of fifties, a span of five.

SOURCE: Reprinted by permission of the publisher, from *Organization*, by Ernest Dale (New York: American Management Association, 1967), p. 13.

1. *The "I can do it better myself fallacy."* The manager argues that because he or she can do the job better, he or she should do it instead of the subordinate. Two considerations may make this a fallacy even if it is true, which it often is not. First, spending time on a task a subordinate could perform, means the manager may not be able to perform other duties as well. The *overall* benefits could be greater if the manager concentrates on planning and supervision and deliberately allows the less important duty of the subordinate to be performed less than perfectly. Second, unless the manager allows subordinates to attempt new tasks and added authority they will be unable to develop their skills. Thus, by insisting on doing things themselves, managers may fail to meet their responsibility for training and grooming subordinates for promotion to management.
2. *Lack of ability to direct.* Some managers become so involved in day-to-day operations that they neglect the broader picture. Unable to grasp the long-range perspective of the work flow, they do not fully realize the importance of distributing work among subordinates.
3. *Lack of confidence in subordinates.* If managers act as though they lack confidence in subordinates, subordinates will in fact tend to lose confidence. They will lose initiative and feel a need to frequently ask if they are doing things correctly. This, of course, sets up a vicious cycle by aggravating the lack of confidence that made subordinates feel insecure in the first place.
4. *Aversion to risk.* Since managers are accountable for a subordinate's work, they may fear that delegating the job will cause problems the managers must answer for.
5. *Absence of selective controls to warn management of impending difficulty.* In conjunction with delegating added authority, management must create effective controls to supply feedback on subordinates' results. Feedback from controls helps guide the subordinate toward attaining goals. It also gives the manager the security of knowing that a problem will be caught before it blows up into a disaster. If controls are not effective, management has good cause to worry about delegating added authority to subordinates.

Subordinate Obstacles. Subordinates, according to Newman, avoid responsibility and block the delegation process for six major reasons:

1. The subordinate finds it easier to ask the boss what to do rather than figure out the problem.
2. The subordinate fears criticism for mistakes. Since greater responsibility increases the chances of making an error, the subordinate avoids it.
3. The subordinate lacks the information and resources needed to do the job successfully.

4. The subordinate already has, or believes he or she has, more work than he or she can do.
5. The subordinate lacks self-confidence.
6. The subordinate is not offered any positive incentives for assuming added responsibility.

Overcoming the Obstacles

The fact that delegation is often ineffectual even though just about everyone admits its importance is clear evidence of how difficult it is to overcome the obstacles. Several obstacles are deeply rooted in human behavior, consequences of individual psychology. Insecurity, aversion to risk, lack of self-confidence, inability to trust another to perform a task one is accountable for—are all prime examples. Psychological problems are the most difficult barriers of all to overcome: both managers and subordinates must take a hard look at themselves, recognize their own fears, and rise above them.

There is relatively little a subordinate can do to clear psychological blocks to delegation in a superior. Even consistently fine performance may be ignored by an overly anxious boss. (Keep in mind that a manager who cannot learn to delegate effectively places a ceiling on his or her own career.) However, there is a great deal that managers can do to improve their own performance and overcome causes for refusing added responsibility.

To begin, managers can create the kind of control system they need to feel secure about delegating a high degree of authority to subordinates. They can also identify and improve their leadership and influence skills. They can also overcome much of their subordinates' insecurity by expressing trust and confidence. You do not have to shout criticism at a person to point out deficiencies in performance. Perhaps the most important roads to effective delegation are clear communication, following the parity principle, and positive incentives.

Communication. When a subordinate does not perform tasks as management desires, the problem can be faulty communication. In the press to get things done, managers may quickly skim through what they expect. The subordinate may hesitate to ask questions for fear of looking stupid. Or, more commonly, the subordinate, too, is in a hurry to get on with the job. Consequently, both parties may *think* they understand what was assigned and what is expected. Later, often too late, the work is not done right and both are disappointed.

Parity Principle. For delegation to take place effectively, it is necessary for authority and responsibility to coincide; that is, management must delegate sufficient authority for an individual to be able to accomplish all tasks for which he or she has assumed responsibility. This is known as the **parity principle**. By corollary, a person can only be expected to assume responsibility for those tasks within his or her scope of delegated authority. For example, a marketing manager delegated the task of increasing sales of Radio Shack's home computers can only be expected to accept responsibility and accomplish the task if given authority to conduct an advertising campaign and provide motivational incentives to salespeople.

Unfortunately, the parity principle is often violated in practice. If you should find yourself in the situation of having responsibility for tasks that you do not have sufficient authority to perform satisfactorily, you should let your supervisor know as soon as possible and request a problem-solving session.

Incentives for Additional Responsibility. More responsibility usually means more work and more risk for the person assuming it. Many, if not most people, do not find these additions inherently attractive. The average person, reasonably enough, expects to be rewarded in some way. But, unfortunately, many organizations fail to back their loud wishes to extend the responsibility of subordinates with an incentive system that offers them positive rewards for assuming that burden. Current research strongly indicates that employees will be less motivated if they feel they are giving the organization more than they are getting. Consequently, the lack of positive incentives for assuming added responsibility may block otherwise sound attempts at authority dispersion.

These rewards can take almost any form. Additional pay, promotion opportunity, a fancier title, praise, added status, and more pleasant working conditions have all proven effective. The requisite is that the subordinate sees a clear link between assuming added responsibility and satisfying personal needs. It is equally important for top management to create an incentive system that rewards *managers* for delegating added authority successfully in accordance with organizational objectives.

SUMMARY

Delegation, the assignment of tasks and authority to a recipient who assumes responsibility for them, is the foundation of the organizing process. Responsibility, an obligation to perform tasks and account to a superior for their satisfactory completion cannot be delegated. Therefore, delegation has only been attempted until the recipient actually assumes responsibility.

Authority is the limited right to use the organization's resources to perform delegated tasks. When extended to the right to command people, it is more precisely termed line authority. Authority is limited by plans, procedures, rules, and oral orders of superiors, as well as by forces outside of the organization such as laws and cultural values. The limits of formal authority are often exceeded in practice because of power and informal organizations.

Delegation is unlikely to be effective unless management adheres to the parity principle, which holds that the extent of authority must coincide with what is needed to meet responsibilities and perform tasks.

Delegation of line authority results in a scalar process or chain of command. The number of persons reporting directly to a manager is that manager's span of management. Failure to limit the span to appropriate size results in confusion and overburdens the manager. One way of reducing the potential for confusion is to adhere to the principle of unity of command, which holds that a person should receive orders from and account to only one superior.

The concept of staff authority was developed to help organizations use experts without violating the principle of unity of command. Staff tasks can be described as advisory or service and are thought of as supporting those activities directly related to attaining objectives. Common types of staff are advisory, service, and personal.

Today staff authority ranges from being limited to advising on request, to compulsory consultation, to concurrent authority, to functional authority. The latter is close to line authority in scope. It also is common for line managers to have staff authority in certain areas, and the head of a staff has line authority over his or her subordinates.

Delegation is difficult to implement effectively. A number of obstacles in the form of mistaken notions or negative behaviors on the part of both managers and subordinates can cause delegation to break down.

REVIEW QUESTIONS

1. "Specialization contains the seeds of its own undoing." What are the implications of this statement for management?
2. Why is delegation fundamental to managing?
3. In effective management, tasks, responsibilities and authority are bonded together. What happens if any of these elements is eliminated or altered?
4. What is the difference between authority and power?
5. Define these important terms with regard to organizing people: parity principle, line authority, scalar process, and the principle of unity of command.
6. What are some common obstacles to effective delegation?
7. Describe the major types of staff.
8. What is the difference between advisory authority, concurrent authority, and functional authority?
9. What are the factors that determine whether authority is line or staff?
10. Why is effective two-way communication important in performing tasks that management desires?

DISCUSSION QUESTIONS

11. How does delegation differ in a democratic government from a communist government?
12. "The buck stops here." What ramifications does this statement have to supervisors, middle managers, and top managers?

13. If one of your employees goes beyond his or her limit of authority, what do you, the effective manager, do to rectify this situation?
14. Newman has cited five reasons why managers may be reluctant to delegate and six reasons why subordinates avoid responsibility and block delegation. Discuss these concepts in light of our postindustrial society.
15. What is the relationship between line and staff in a nonprofit organization?

CASE INCIDENT

The Emergency Room

Rounding a curve, and staying close to the right-hand side of the road, Bonnie Greene was driving home from school. Suddenly, a pickup truck was also on her side of the road and completely out of control. Bonnie's car was demolished and there was $4,000 damage done to the pickup. Fortunately, the driver of the truck, who was ticketed for reckless driving, was not injured. Bonnie Greene was not so fortunate and was rushed to Northwest Hospital's emergency room. There she was met by her mother, who had been contacted by one of the investigating officers.

Upon arriving at the hospital, Bonnie and Mrs. Greene were told to take a seat until the admissions clerk could get to them. Although able to walk, Bonnie was badly bruised and appeared to be in a state of shock. In particular, she constantly complained of head pains.

While the emergency room did not appear busy, it was almost two hours before Bonnie was admitted and examined. What really irritated Mrs. Greene was her feeling that staff members were indifferent and rude. When Mrs. Greene returned home she was still furious about the treatment her daughter had received from Northwest and decided she would share her feelings with the hospital administrator, M. J. Glenn.

M. J. Glenn was on vacation. Mrs. Greene was assured by his secretary that her complaints would be brought to his attention just as soon as he returned. In the meanwhile, nothing could be done.

Three weeks passed and there was still no response from Mr. Glenn. Mrs. Greene called again and finally got through to Mr. Glenn, who indicated that things had been hectic since he returned from his vacation, the first he had had in four years. After listening to Mrs. Greene, Mr. Glenn indicated that he had checked into the situation and had received a completely different story from the emergency room staff. He indicated that Mrs. Greene was probably just overreacting.

Mrs. Greene replied that if Mr. Glenn thought she was upset, he had a real treat coming when contacted by her attorney. Mr. Glenn said he would look into the situation again, but Mrs. Greene should understand that Northwest's emergency room was a leased operation, and he couldn't be held responsible for everything that went on.

Questions

1. How would you react to Mr. Glenn's reply that the emergency room was a leased operation, and he couldn't be held responsible for everything that went on?
2. If you were Mr. Glenn, how would you handle this situation?

NOTES

1. Chester A. Barnard, *The Functions of the Executive* (Cambridge, MA: Harvard University Press, 1938), p. 163.
2. James D. Mooney, *The Principles of Organization* (New York: Harper & Row, 1947).
3. Claude S. George, Jr., *The History of Management Thought* (Englewood Cliffs, NJ: Prentice-Hall, 1968).
4. "Industrial Psychology on the Line," *Psychology Today*, July 1978, p. 71.
5. George, op. cit.
6. Harold Koontz and Cyril O'Donnell, *Management: A Systems and Contingency Analysis of Managerial Functions*, 6th ed. (New York: McGraw-Hill Book Company, 1976), p. 444.
7. Exodus 18:21.
8. William H. Newman, "Overcoming Obstacles to Effective Delegation," *Management Review*, January 1956, pp. 36–41.

CHAPTER 9

Organizing Organizations

We saw in Chapter 3 how specialized division of labor is used to design tasks, enabling the organization to accomplish much more work than its members could as individuals. In Chapter 8 we learned how management uses delegation to create a thread of authority and responsibility that runs through the organization from top to bottom and to distribute tasks among its people. We will now study the alternatives management has for designing a structure for the organization as a whole that will enable it to execute its strategy, interact with its environment, and thereby attain its objectives effectively. We will describe the major variations of bureaucratic and nonbureaucratic structures in wide use today and also compare centralization and decentralization.

After reading this chapter, you should understand the following important terms and concepts:

bureaucracy
departmentation
functional departmentation
divisional organization
product departmentation
territorial departmentation
customer departmentation
mechanistic structure
adaptive or organic structure
project organization
matrix organization
free-form organization
centralization
decentralization

Organizing the Organization

In the last chapter we saw how management uses delegation to organize authority relationships and distribute tasks among the people of the organization. All managers must delegate to get work done through others, therefore organizing is a function all managers must perform, irrespective of their level. However, although the essential concept is still delegating to divide labor vertically and horizontally, deciding upon a structure for the organization as a whole is almost always a task performed by top management. Supervisors and middle managers assist by providing necessary information and, in larger organizations, by selecting a structure for their subunit consistent with that chosen by top management for the overall organization.

Management's broad objective in performing this function is to select the structure that is most appropriate in light of the organization's objectives, strategies, and other internal and external factors. The "best" structure is the one that best enables the organization to interact effectively with its environment, to effectively and efficiently channel the efforts of its people, to make efficient use of its resources, and thereby to meet the needs of its customers and attain its objectives.

Designing an Organizational Structure

Planning and Organization Design. Since the aim of organizing is to facilitate attaining objectives, the design of a structure clearly must be based on planning. In fact, some writers consider choosing an overall structure a strategic decision because it determines how the organization will generally channel effort to attain its broad objectives. But in our view organizing is a distinct function, so we consider it based on strategy, as opposed to being a strategy itself. This concept originated with Alfred Chandler. He analyzed how the organizational structures of Du Pont, General Motors, Standard Oil of New Jersey, and Sears changed over the years. Observing that these changes were related to changes in strategy and objectives, Chandler coined the now famous maxim, "Structure follows strategy."[1] The sequence in which an organization is designed, not surprisingly, parallels the sequence in which components of the planning process are formulated.

Steps in Designing an Organization. The order in which we presented concepts of organizing may have been misleading. Our discussions proceeded from tasks to authority relationships to, here, designing an overall structure. This order may have led you to think that organizations are organized from the bottom up; that is, tasks are designed first, the overall structure last. However, the exact opposite is true. According to classical organizing theory, with which most managers agree in this area, organizations should be designed from the top down. Management should select broad divisions first, design specific tasks last, just as broad objectives are formulated first, rules last in planning.

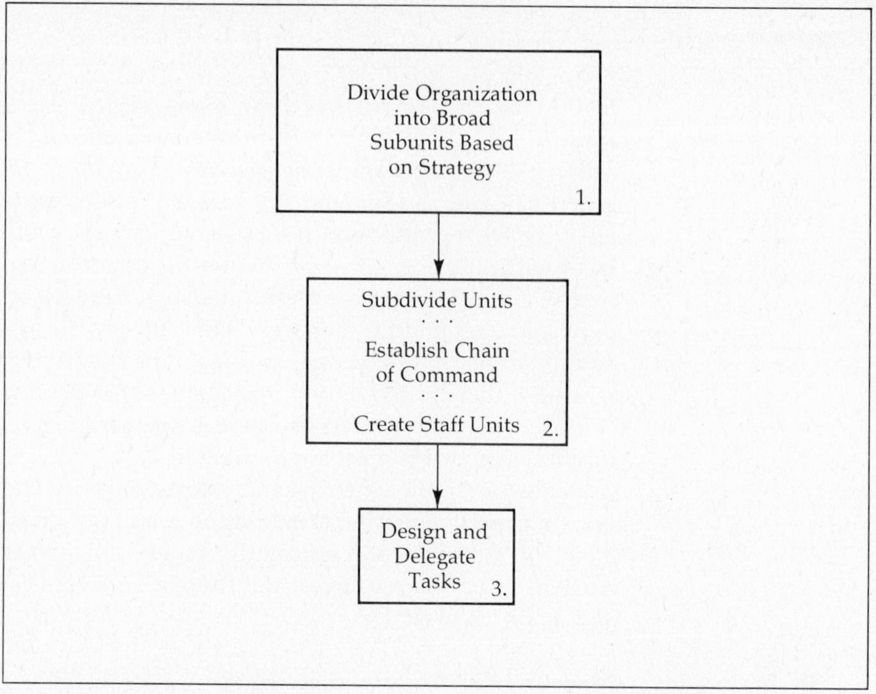

Figure 9-1 Steps in Designing an Organizational Structure

The sequence of steps, therefore, is:

1. Horizontally divide the organization into broad subunits corresponding to activities of critical importance in carrying out strategy. Decide which activities should be line and which staff.
2. Establish authority relationships between positions. Here management establishes the chain of command and, if necessary, further subdivides units to make more effective use of specialization and to avoid excessive spans of management.
3. Design jobs comprised of certain tasks and delegate these tasks to individuals. Management, strongly influenced by technology, designs specific tasks and ensures that each is assigned to a person who assumes responsibility for its satisfactory performance.

It is very important to realize that the resulting structure is not a static form, like the structure of a building. Since structure is based on plans, a major revision of plans may require a corresponding modification of structure. Indeed, in the ongoing organization, it might be more appropriate to refer to the process as *re*organizing because, like all the functions it is an unending cycle. Successful organizations today continuously assess the appropriateness of their structure and change it in accordance with the dictates

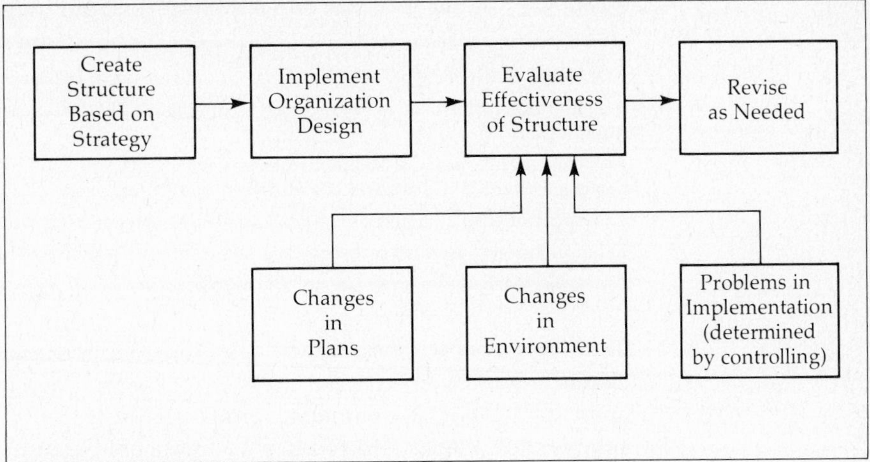

Figure 9-2 Changing Structure in Response to Environment and Strategy

of the environment, as determined through planning and controlling. Almost every issue of *Business Week* reports a major reorganization underway in some large company.

The remainder of this chapter describes the various alternatives for organizing an overall organization that have been successfully implemented to date. Each, as we shall learn, has characteristics that are suited to certain needs and situations. The order of presentation roughly corresponds to the order of development. Thus, we begin with bureaucracy, the first systematically thought out model for an organizational structure and still the predominant basic form of structure.

Bureaucracy

The word *bureaucracy* usually brings to mind visions of red tape, bungling, aimless activity, waiting an hour to register for a class that has been cancelled, and trying to fight city hall. These problems certainly do occur. However, the cause usually is not bureaucracy per se but faulty implementation, the inherent difficulties of large size, and behavior by individuals contrary to the organization's procedures and expressed objectives. As a concept, originally formulated by German sociologist Max Weber in the early 1900s, bureaucracy is, at least in the ideal, one of the worthiest ideas in history.

Weber's Model. It is important to understand that Weber's concept of bureaucracy did not describe actual organizations. Rather, Weber proposed bureaucracy as a normative model, an ideal that organizations should strive to attain. This is clear in Table 9-1, which summarizes what Weber considered the characteristics of what he termed a *rational* bureaucracy.[2]

Table 9-1 Characteristics of a Rational Bureaucracy

1. A clear-cut division of labor resulting in a host of specialized experts in each position.
2. A hierarchy of offices, with each lower one being controlled and supervised by a higher one.
3. A consistent system of abstract rules and standards which assures uniformity in the performance of all duties and coordination of various tasks.
4. A spirit of formalistic impersonality in which officials carry out the duties of their office.
5. Employment based on technical qualifications and protected from arbitrary dismissal.

Characteristics of Bureaucracy. In more modern language, a bureaucracy is characterized by specialized division of labor, a distinct management hierarchy and chain of command, formal planning, and employment based on competence. Weber referred to it as "rational" because decisions in a bureaucracy presumably are made objectively. The implication is that personal whims of the organization's owners and people are not to conflict with the objectives of the organization. (These ideas contrasted sharply with practices of most organizations prior to 1900.) Because it has a large, well-defined middle-management group, the organization chart of a bureaucracy resembles a pyramid, as illustrated in Figure 9-3.

If the description of a bureaucracy sounds familiar, it is because virtually everything we have said about organizations and management thus far primarily describes rational bureaucracies. The bureaucracy is often referred to as the traditional or classical organizational structure. The great majority of organizations today are a variation of bureaucracy. The reason for this long and widespread use is that the characteristics of bureaucratic structures are well suited to most business and service organizations and to governments of all types. Objectivity in decision making helps the well-managed bureaucracy adapt to change. Promotion based on competence helps provide a steady supply of high-caliber technical and managerial talent. Also, the concept of social equality implicit in bureaucracy is consistent with the expressed values of both democratic and communist countries. The American civil-service system, for example, is a bureaucracy that was originally created to curb political patronage and make government closer to the bureaucratic ideal. In sum, as management researcher John Child states, "Max Weber's analysis of bureaucracy continues to provide the single, most influential statement of the rationale of contemporary organizations."[3]

Departmentation

Useful as it is, the bureaucratic model cannot be applied without amplification and modification. Although organizations have much in common with

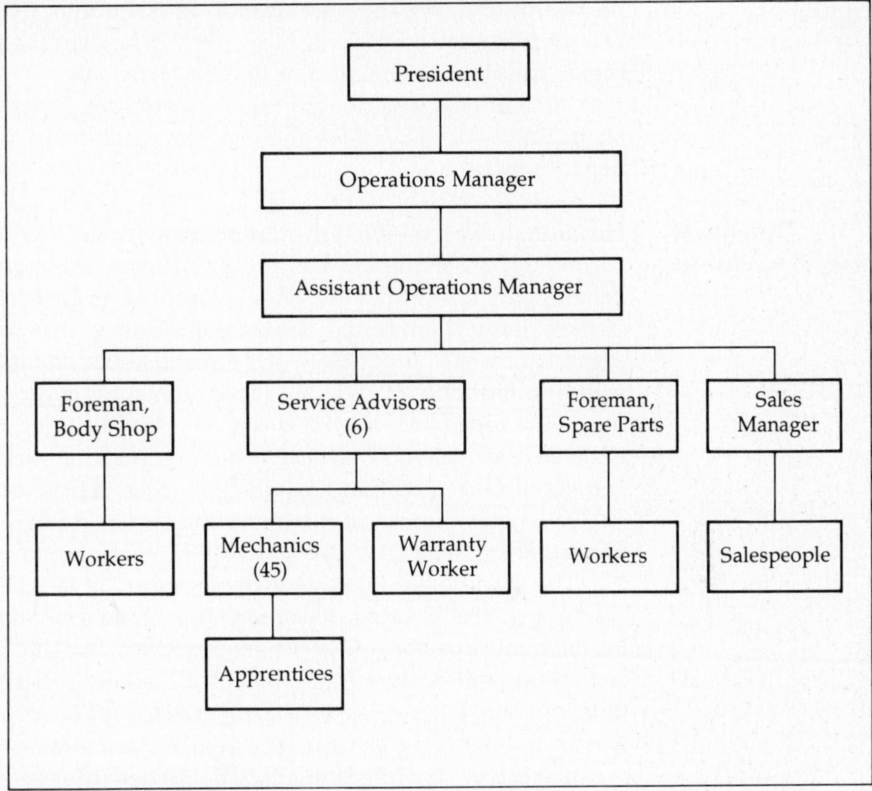

Figure 9-3 **Organization Chart of a Bureaucracy at an Automobile Dealership**

one another, they also differ in important ways. These differences clearly must be taken into account during organizing. For example, some organizations are large, some small. Some are large, but operate in only one main area, as IBM does in information processing and McDonald's in fast-food restaurants. Others, like Gulf and Western, are conglomerates that operate many disparate businesses such as films, publishing, hotels, and others under a single corporate umbrella. Some organizations, such as Federated Department Stores and Chrysler Corporation, directly serve the general public. Others, such as Container Corporation of America and Boeing, deal primarily with large organizations. Some very substantial organizations, such as New York City's government, operate in a very small geographic area, whereas others such as ITT, Exxon, and Coca Cola do business in almost every country in the world. A few organizations, big companies like Mobil Oil and General Motors and governments of developed nations, face almost all these situations simultaneously.

To cope with these differences in objectives, strategies, and situation, managers use various systems of departmentation. **Departmentation** is the process of dividing the organization into subunits. These are often referred to as departments, divisions, or sections. Whatever the unit is called, the process is still departmentation or *departmentalization.*

We will now describe the most widely used systems of departmentation, beginning with the earliest and simplest variation of bureaucracy, functional departmentation.

Functional Departmentation

Functional departmentation is sometimes called traditional or classical departmentation because it was the first organizing system to be studied and developed.[4] It is still very widely used by organizations that are not extremely large. **Functional departmentation** is the process of dividing the organization into units that each have distinct, dissimilar tasks and responsibilities. Basically, functional departmentation is grouping workers according to the broad task they perform. The specific lines of division correspond to those activities most critical to the organization. Because the organization is divided into units that have distinct tasks, functional departmentalization also facilitates the use of mass-production technology in manufacturing organizations.[5]

The traditional functional departments of a business are production, marketing, and finance. These are the broad activities or functions every business must perform to attain its objectives. Specific names vary, however, and traditional designations do not accurately describe the primary functions of some businesses, especially in the service sector. An airline, for example, is a service business that does no production work in the sense of manufacturing. Therefore, the functional departments of an airline company usually are called operations, sales, and finance. The variety of names is even greater in nonbusiness organizations. In an army one finds infantry, artillery, and armored divisions. Hospitals have departments of administration and medicine.

Derivative Departments. If the organization or a given department is very large, major departments can be subdivided functionally as well. These subdivisions are termed *derivative departments.* To continue our airline example, operations might be subdivided into derivative departments such as engineering, maintenance, ground operations, and flight operations. The essential idea is to make increased use of specialization and keep spans of management reasonably small. One must be careful, however, that the departments do not become more concerned about subunit objectives than overall objectives.[6]

The concept of derivative departments is applicable to all systems of organizational design. Figure 9-4 illustrates an organization with functional departments subdivided into derivative departments.

Application. The advantages and disadvantages of functional departmentation are summarized in Table 9-2. In brief, evidence indicates that functional departmentation is often useful for organizations with a limited product line

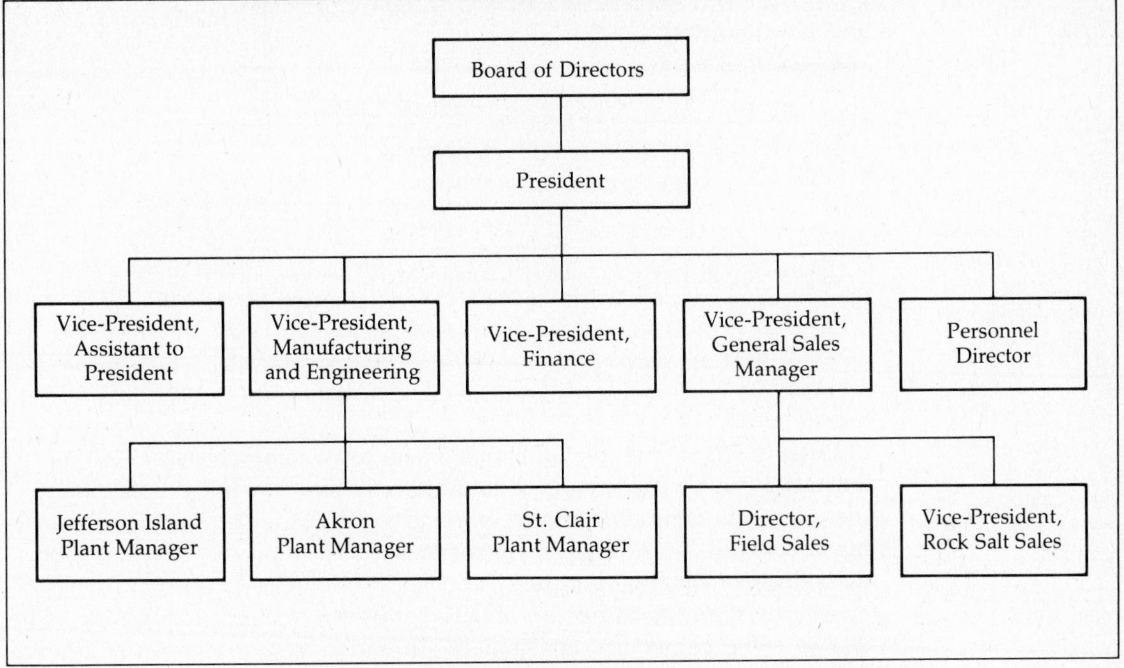

Figure 9-4 Abbreviated Organization Chart of Diamond Crystal Salt Company

This chart illustrates functional departmentation at the vice-president level. Note the derivative departments reporting to each vice-president. The personnel director has staff authority.

SOURCE: K. White, "Understanding The Company Organizational Chart," An AMA Research Study #56 (New York: American Management Association, Inc., 1963) pp. 158–159.

requiring the performance of standardized tasks and operating in a stable environment. Examples would be firms in the metals and materials and rubber industries. Functional departmentation is not appropriate for organizations with many product lines, or in a rapidly changing consumer or technological environment, or when operations are spread over a geographic area containing several different markets, cultures, or laws.[7] For these organizations, a divisional structure is more appropriate.

Divisional Departmentation

During the early twentieth century, astute managers like GM's Alfred Sloan, Jr. and his counterparts at Procter & Gamble, Du Pont, and Sears recognized that the traditional functional structure no longer met their needs. The size to which these organizations had grown and wanted to grow made it obvious that continued use of functional departmentation would cause problems. If an enormous firm tried to fit all of its operations within three or four major departments, it would have to subdivide those departments hundreds

Table 9-2 Advantages and Disadvantages of Functional Departmentation

Advantages
1. Facilitates attaining the benefits of specialization.
2. Facilitates use of mass-production technology.
Disadvantages
1. Departments may become more concerned with subunit objectives than overall objectives. This increases the potential for conflict between functional areas.
2. Chain of command becomes too long if organization is very large.

of times to reduce the span of management to an acceptable size. This would make the chain of command incredibly long and unwieldy. Also, many of these big companies had spread out over a very wide geographic area, making it difficult for a single manager to keep track of all activities, such as marketing, of a similar nature.

Further complicating the situation was the increased diversity of activities some companies engaged in. In earlier centuries even substantial firms like the East India Company were involved in only one or two types of businesses, but modern firms often operate many businesses of widely different character. This is especially true of conglomerates such as Gulf and Western, ITT, and Litton Industries.

Similarly, some firms had begun selling and producing products intended for several distinct customer groups. For example, DuPont was faced with an enormous loss of revenues when the end of World War I brought a halt to the munitions sales that were its mainstay. It clearly needed to broaden its customer base and effectively reach the general public and institutions as well as the government. A number of special situations also existed in industries such as steel where a particular technology was so critical that virtually the entire business revolved around it.

To cope with the new problems brought on by size, diversity, technology, and change, the managers of these far-sighted organizations developed three major new variations of divisional departmentation: product departmentation, customer departmentation, and territorial departmentation.

Product Departmentation. One of the most common ways in which businesses grow is by increasing the number of products they make and sell. If management is successful, several product lines may attain such high sales that they require a substantial organization themselves and become crucial to the organization's overall success. This was the problem that confronted pioneers of divisional organization like Procter & Gamble and Libbey, McNeil and Libbey. They coped with it through **product departmentation**,

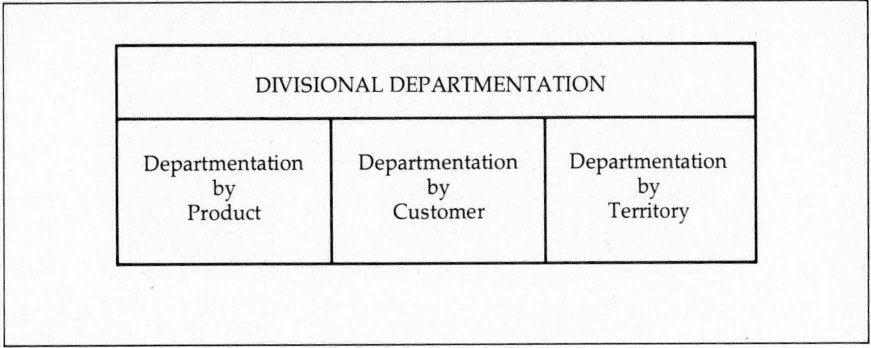

Figure 9-5 **Types of Divisional Departmentation**

organizing into divisions responsible for a major product line. The idea was so successful that it quickly spread to General Motors, General Foods, Lever Brothers, and Corning Glass. Today, most large manufacturers of consumer goods with diverse product lines employ departmentation by product.

Under product departmentation, a single manager, often referred to as the brand or product manager, is delegated authority over all activities required to produce and market that product or service for which he or she is responsible. The heads of derivative functional departments such as manufacturing, sales, and engineering would report to this product manager, as is illustrated in Figure 9-6.

Product departmentation enables a very large firm to devote as much attention to a product as a smaller company with only one or two products. As a result, according to a Harvard University study, firms using product departmentation tend to be more successful at creating and marketing new products than companies using other structures.[8] Perhaps because responsibility for profit is so clearly defined, product departmented organizations tend to have a good record for controlling costs and meeting deadlines. They also are able to respond more rapidly than functionally departmented firms to changes in the competitive, technical, and customer environments. An added benefit is that, because all activities are under the direction of a single manager, coordination is improved.

A potential disadvantage of product departmentation is increased costs resulting from duplication of activities. Each product department has its own functional departments. These may not be sufficiently large to make maximum use of facilities. This would be especially true of mass-production manufacturing plants and equipment that usually can be operated 24 hours a day.

Customer Departmentation. Some organizations sell a wide variety of goods or services that appeal to a few large groups of customers or markets, each of which has easily distinguished or special needs. If two or more of

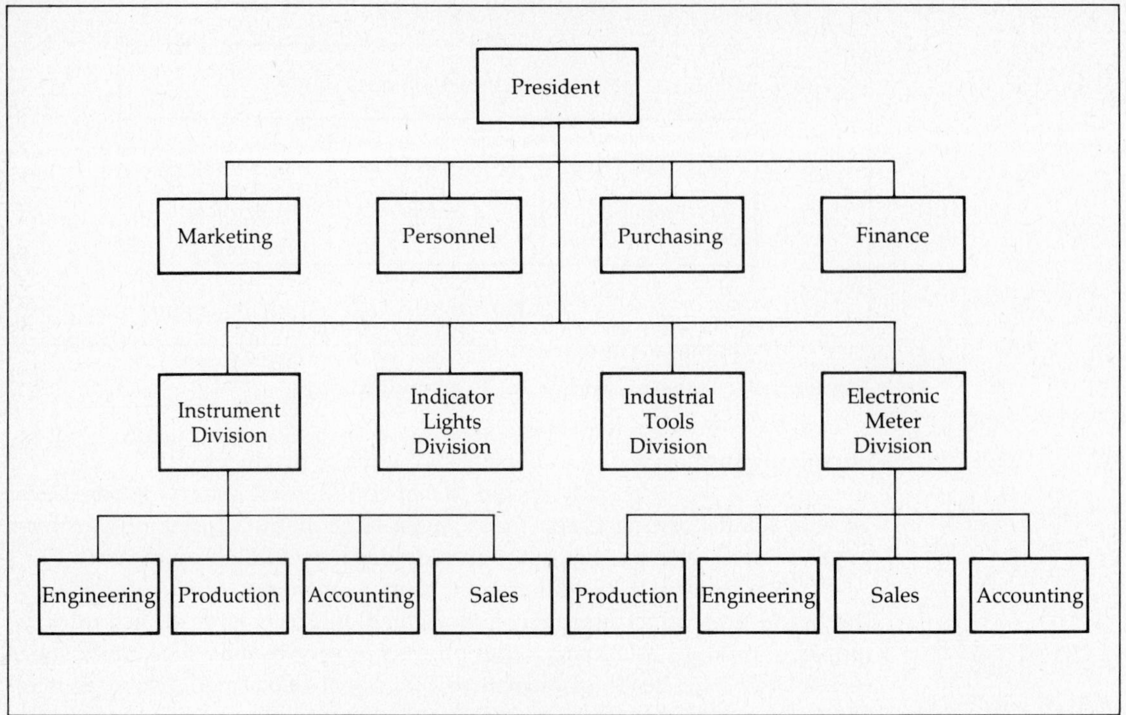

Figure 9-6 Departmentation by Product

SOURCE: H. Koontz and C. O'Donnell, *Management*, 6th ed., (New York: McGraw-Hill, 1976), p. 311. Used with permission of the McGraw-Hill Book Company, © 1976.

these customers become extremely important, the firm may choose to use **customer departmentation**, or organize divisions around customer groups, as illustrated in Figure 9-7. The purpose of doing so is to meet the needs of these customers as well as an organization that concentrates on only one customer group.

Large publishers, for example, have separate departments for adult trade (general reading) books, juvenile trade books, college texts, and elementary–high-school texts. Each of these customer-oriented divisions operates as an essentially independent company. Hence, each has its own editorial, marketing, finance, and production departments. Commercial banking is another field in which customer division is in widespread use. Here the major groups are retail or consumer (individuals), corporate, institutional (organizations like pension funds or universities), correspondent banking (other banks), trusts, and international. Departmentation by customer also is common in organizations that sell at both wholesale and retail. Hertz, Avis, and other major auto-rental firms have special departments for sales to individuals and for sales to fleets.

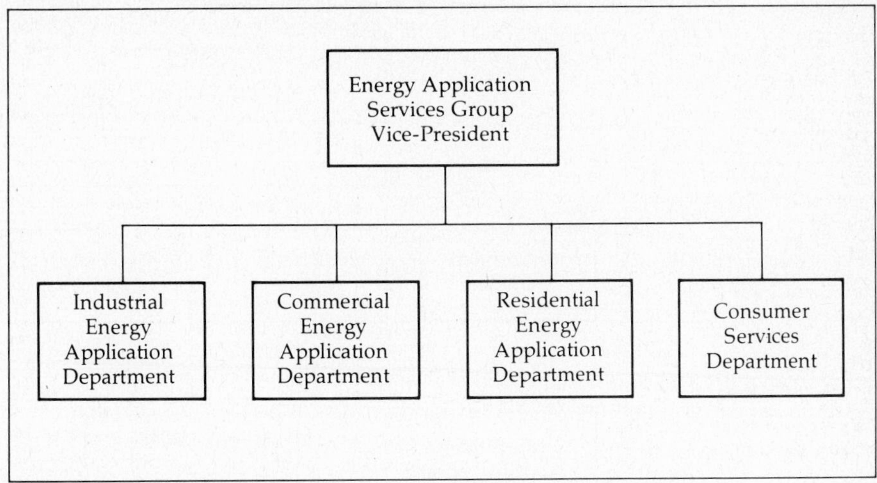

Figure 9-7 Departmentation by Customer

SOURCE: Public Information Department, Cleveland Electric Illuminating Co., Ohio, 1977. Used with permission.

Interestingly, although departmentation by customer usually is associated with businesses, some educational organizations are turning to it. It now is common to find special divisions for adult education, executive development, or personal enrichment in addition to the more conventional programs. Some experts feel that these new customers eventually may become the major source of revenue for higher-education organizations. Many people feel, as well, that the public would be better off if our governmental organizations became more customer centered.

The potential advantages and disadvantages of customer departmentation are similar to those of product departmentation, allowing for the difference in orientation.

Territorial Departmentation. When an organization operates over a wide geographic area, especially one international in scope, it may prove desirable to divide people along geographical lines, as illustrated in Figure 9-8. Division along geographic lines is termed **territorial departmentation**. Using a territorial system of division makes it easier for the organization to cope with variations in laws, local customs, and customer needs. It also shortens the lines of communication between the organization and its customers and between members of the organization.

A familiar example of territorial division is the sales organization of many large companies. Here we often find broad divisions, such as "East Coast," which in turn are divided into narrower ones, such as "Northeast," which are further divided into states or other units. In some companies territorial subdivisions can become extremely small. A Xerox Corporation rep-

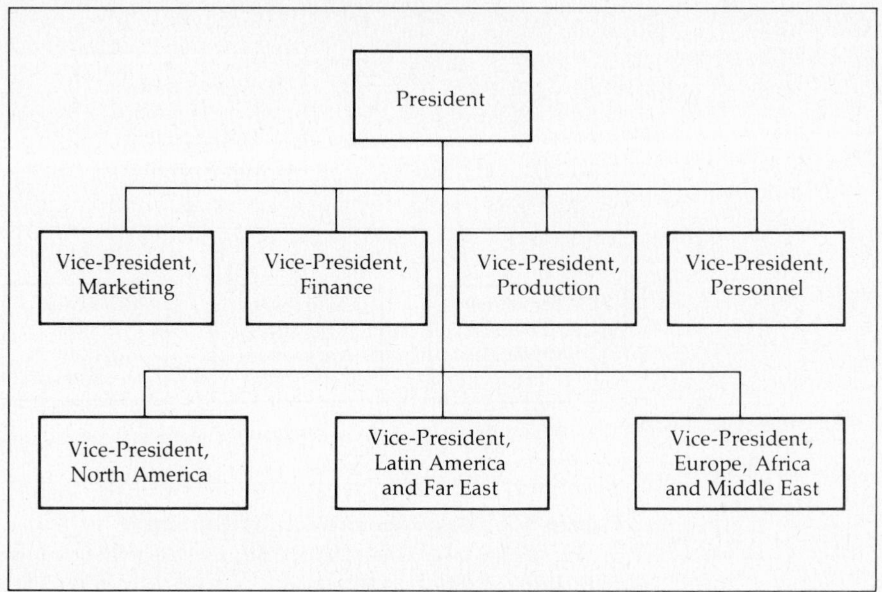

Figure 9-8 **Territorial Departmentation**

resentative in New York sometimes has a territory of only one or two blocks or a large building like the World Trade Center. Other companies, notably pharmaceutical firms and manufacturers of consumer package goods, form subsidiary companies on national lines and then departmentalize these on a functional or other basis.

A nonbusiness example of territorial organizing is the State Department of the United States. It operates embassies and consulates around the world. Many other government agencies, especially ones such as the Internal Revenue Service (IRS) that deal frequently with the public, also make use of territorial departmentation. Large accounting and management consulting firms also are usually organized by territory. The relative advantages and disadvantages of territorial departmentation are similar to those of product and customer structures.

Choice of Divisional Orientation. We stated earlier that the various forms of divisional departmentation have similar advantages and disadvantages. This is because the objective of all forms of divisional departmentation is to make the organization more effective in responding to specific factors in its environment. A customer orientation will facilitate coping with changes in products brought due to competition, technological advances, or customer demands. Territorial departmentation makes the organization more effective in dealing with differences in local cultures, laws, and markets as it expands geographically. Customer departmentation, of course, makes the organization more effective in meeting the needs of those customers on which it depends most heavily. The choice of a divisional orientation, therefore, would be based on which of these factors management judges to be most important in executing its strategy for attaining objectives.

Divisional departmentation in all its forms has clearly demonstrated its worth for many years in America. Beginning in the 1960s, widespread use of divisional departmentation spread to European business, which until then had primarily used traditional functional departmentation. By 1972 about 70 percent of 127 large European businesses, almost all of which used functional departmentation in 1960, had switched to divisional organization in order to respond more effectively to the changes in European business and social conditions.[9]

Composite Structures

Organizations, as you may already have realized, are not limited to the exclusive use of only one system of departmentation. If large enough, organizations can make appropriate use of every type of structure described thus far, as well as the more recently developed structures presented later in the chapter. The basic corporate structure of General Motors, for example, revolves around products, but these major divisions such as Cadillac, Buick, and Chevrolet are organized along functional lines. Each division has departments such as marketing, purchasing, engineering, and accounting.

The organization chart illustrated in Figure 9-9 shows product, functional, customer, and geographic divisions within a single product department of a large bank.

Adaptive Structures

Problems of Bureaucracy

As mentioned earlier, systems of departmentation, however sophisticated in application, are variations of bureaucracy. They adhere, or at least try to adhere, to the characteristics Weber cited. Consequently, they should reap the positive benefits of that form: clear chains of command, promotion of the most competent, objective decision making. Unfortunately, not only is the ideal bureaucracy a myth, but rational bureaucracy also has some inherent problems, as were noted by sociologist R. K. Merton.

Merton's Critique. Merton contends that, because they need to reduce variations of human behavior (demand for control), bureaucratic organizations tend to emphasize rule enforcement (emphasis on reliability).[10] This requires the formulation of standard procedures, rules, and regulations and the application of negative sanctions by supervisors to penalize inappropriate behavior by subordinates. Employees must closely follow their role prescriptions and make decisions within strict guidelines provided by the organization for objectives to be attained.

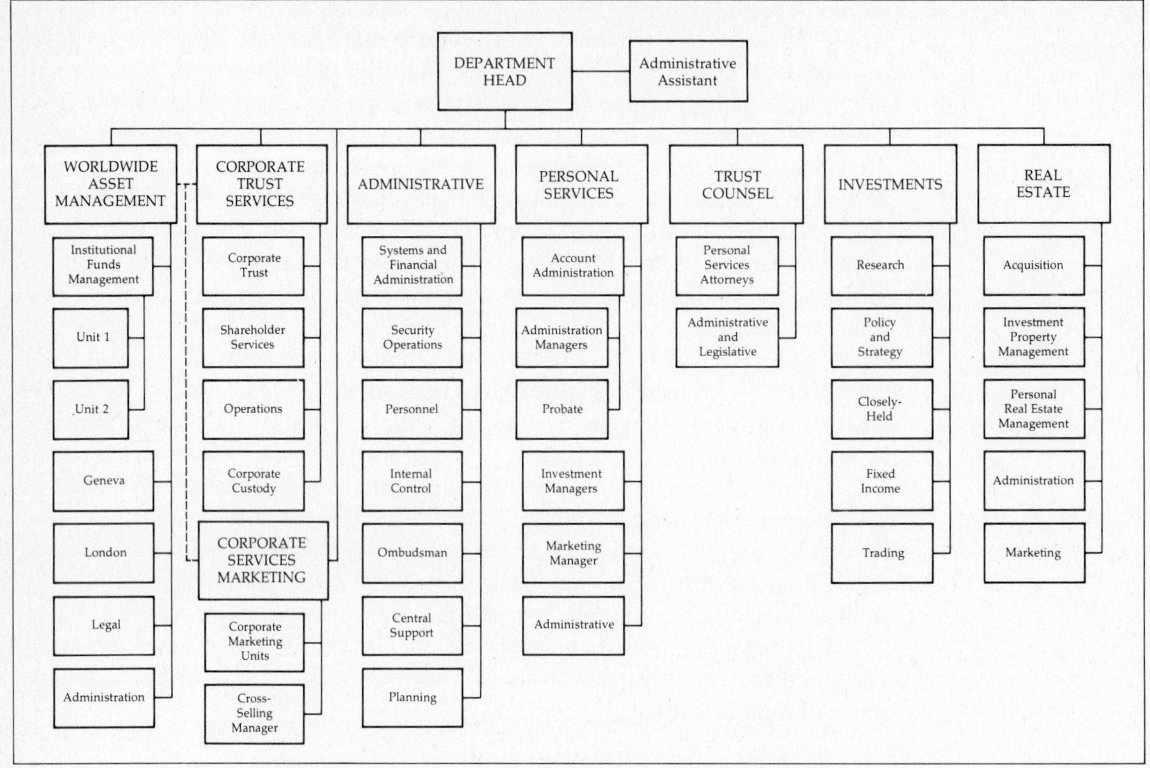

Figure 9-9 The First National Bank of Chicago Trust Department Organization

SOURCE: Courtesy of the First National Bank of Chicago.

This can be desirable; however, a number of unintended outcomes also follow. Since problems are investigated in terms of an organizational precedent, that is, past experience, there may not be a thorough search for alternatives in decision making. Reliance on present rules may lead to rigidity of behavior, which makes handling clients more difficult. This would occur when a person strictly follows the rule, even though that may not be the best response to the client's needs. When such difficulty does occur, the bureaucrat often defends his or her actions by pointing to the rules or guidelines. This could easily further aggravate the client. However, the bureaucrat is safe from negative sanctions because he or she has behaved correctly from the organization's official point of view. In other words, the person may do the right thing, but the result will be dysfunctional in terms of attaining the organization's objectives.

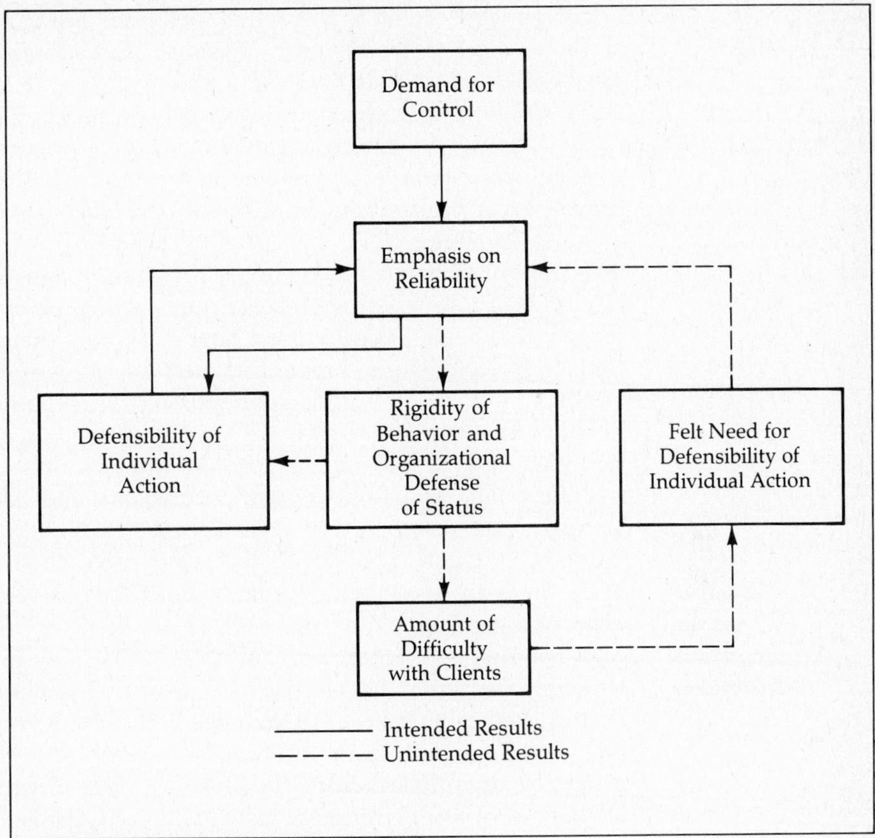

Figure 9-10 Simplified Merton Model
SOURCE: James G. March and Herbert A. Simon, *Organizations* (New York: John Wiley & Sons, Inc., 1958), p. 41.

The Merton model is depicted in Figure 9-10. In discussing it, management theorists Katz and Kahn stated that the Merton model applies primarily to organizational members who deal with the outside public. The same rigidity, however, can develop among employees. Increased problems in cooperation, communication, and coordination between parts of an organization can result from strict observance of rules. Another dysfunctional consequence of bureaucracy, according to Katz and Kahn, is "the lack of innovative and spontaneous behavior necessary for effective organizational functioning. An almost exclusive emphasis upon rule enforcement, with its resulting rigidity, can destroy this innovative aspect of organizational functioning."[11]

Change, Technology, and Bureaucracy. The many positive qualities of bureaucracy have, in most cases, outweighed the negative consequences. By developing ever more sophisticated variations and composites of departmentation to meet their changing objectives and strategies, many large, well-managed organizations have been able to stay with an essentially bureaucratic structure and prosper. However, particularly since the 1950s, certain organizations have entered a situation where change is so rapid, projects are so complicated, and technology moves so rapidly that the dysfunctional consequences of bureaucracy, as described by Merton and other critics, overcome its benefits.

We will elaborate on the impact of environmental change and technology on structure when we discuss the contingency approach to organizing later in this book. Basically what happens is that the orderliness of conventional departmentation, especially when the chain of command is long, may slow communication and decision making to the point where the organization can no longer effectively respond to change. In addition the organization may have to make such extensive use of sophisticated technology that the traditional mechanism of staff departments and staff authority no longer suffices.

Adaptive Versus Mechanistic Structures

Since the early 1960s, many organizations have developed new, more fluid types of organizational structure which are better suited to rapid change and high technology than are bureaucracies. These new forms of organizational structure are generally referred to as **adaptive structures** because they can be modified quickly to meet changes both in the environment and in the needs of the organization. Another widespread term for these more flexible designs is **organic structure**, an allusion to the structure's capacity to adapt to changes in its environment just as a living organism does. An adaptive or organic structure is not just a variation on bureaucracy, as is divisional departmentation. It is based on aims and assumptions radically different from those of bureaucracy.

Here is how Tom Burns and G. M. Stalker, British behavioral scientists who studied the relationship between structure and organizational success, compared organic structures to bureaucracies, which they referred to as **mechanistic structures**:

> In mechanistic systems the problems and tasks facing the concern as a whole are broken down into specialisms. Each individual pursues his task as something distinct from the real tasks of the concern as a whole, as if it were the subject of a subcontract. "Somebody at the top" is responsible for seeing to its relevance. The technical methods, duties, and powers attached to each functional role are precisely defined. Interaction within management tends to be vertical, i.e., between superior and subordinate. Operations and working behaviour are governed by instructions and decisions issued by superiors. This command hierarchy is maintained by the implicit assumption that all knowledge about the situation of the firm and its tasks is, or should be, available only to the head of the firm. Management, often visualized as the complex hierarchy familiar in organization charts, operates a simple control system, with information flowing up through a succession of amplifiers.

> Organic systems are adapted to unstable conditions, when problems and requirements for action arise which cannot be broken down and distributed among specialist roles within a clearly defined hierarchy. Individuals have to perform their special tasks in the light of their knowledge of the tasks of the firm as a whole. Jobs lose much of their formal definition in terms of methods, duties, and powers, which have to be redefined continually by interaction with others participating in a task. Interaction runs laterally as much as vertically. Communication between people of different ranks tends to resemble lateral consultation rather than vertical command. Omniscience can no longer be imputed to the head of the concern.[12]

It is important to realize that these newer organic organizational designs are not always more effective than mechanistic forms. As will be elaborated on later, organic designs are more appropriate for organizations operating in a rapidly changing environment, whereas mechanistic forms may be more appropriate in situations where the rate of change is relatively slow. Discussing this contingency concept, Wendell French and Cecil Bell state: "Theory and research suggest that neither the purely organic form nor the purely mechanistic form may be optimal under all circumstances, but there needs to be a good 'fit' between technology, tasks, internal and external environments, and the skills of the people in the organization."[13]

Moreover, as Burns and Stalker pointed out, these two forms are located at opposite ends of a continuum. They are not a dichotomy. Thus organizations fall between the two extremes, possessing characteristics of both mechanistic and organic structures to varying degrees. Also, it is common for subunits of an organization to be structured differently. You may find within a large organization subunits whose structure is mechanistic and others whose form is organic. Often, for example, management uses a highly mechanistic structure for production activities and an organic structure for the research and development department.

Two major variations of organic structure in use today are project organization and matrix organization.

Project Organization

The typical department head in a large bureaucracy has many different duties and is responsible for aspects of several different projects, services, or products. The head of a college publishing house, for instance, is responsible for production, editing, and marketing of dozens or even hundreds of individual titles each year. As a result of being spread out this way, it is inevitable that even a good manager will pay more attention to some activities than others. In the shuffle between these many responsibilities, some details invariably get lost and go undone. If each project is small and inexpensive relative to the overall organization's activities, this causes no major difficulty. While obviously undesirable, for example, it is not catastrophic for a large publisher if a few planned books are published late or never.

But, if individual projects are very large, failure to pay close attention to each could have drastic consequences. To cope with projects that are massive, but limited in duration—tasks such as building a dam, building and launching a moon rocket, designing and building a new weapons system—an increasing number of organizations have begun using project organizing.

The **project organization** is a *temporary* structure formed to accomplish a specific, well-defined objective. The idea is to gather together the best talent available to the organization in order to accomplish a complex project within established cost, time, and quality limits. When this project is completed, the project team disbands. Its members move on to a new project, return to their permanent "home" department in the organization, or, as sometimes happens, leave the parent organization.

The chief advantage of project organization is that it focuses effort on a single undertaking. Whereas a typical departmental manager must handle several projects simultaneously, the project manager can concentrate all effort on one.

There are several forms of project organization. In the so-called *pure* or *aggregate* project structure, the temporary group is in essence a scaled-down replica of the permanent functional structure. In this variant, the project manager has full line authority over team members and resources needed to accomplish the objective. The pure project structure is used only for extremely large tasks, such as space-vehicle construction. On less massive projects, the cost of duplicating services already available within the parent organization becomes prohibitively expensive. To cope with these smaller projects, the organization can use a project structure in which the project manager essentially serves as an advisory staff to a top manager. This high-level general manager coordinates the project through a conventional functional structure.

The most common version of project organization is sufficiently different from the forms just described to warrant a different name. This is the matrix structure.

Matrix Organization

The use of matrix structures was pioneered by medium-sized aerospace companies during the 1950s and 1960s. These firms were too small to use project organization economically. Yet, they were large enough for functional structures, in which integration does not take place until one reaches the top of the organization, to cause problems. In an effort to get the advantages of both forms, some companies such as General Electric, Equitable Life Insurance, TRW, Dow Corning, and Shell Oil experimented with the concept of a project structure overlayed on a permanent functional organization. The chart of such a structure, as shown in Figure 9-11, resembles a grid: hence the term *matrix.*

In a **matrix organization**, in contrast to project structures, team members are only on *loan* to the project head. They are responsible to both the project manager and the head of the functional department to which they are permanently assigned. The project manager exercises what is referred to as "project authority." This may vary from almost complete line authority on

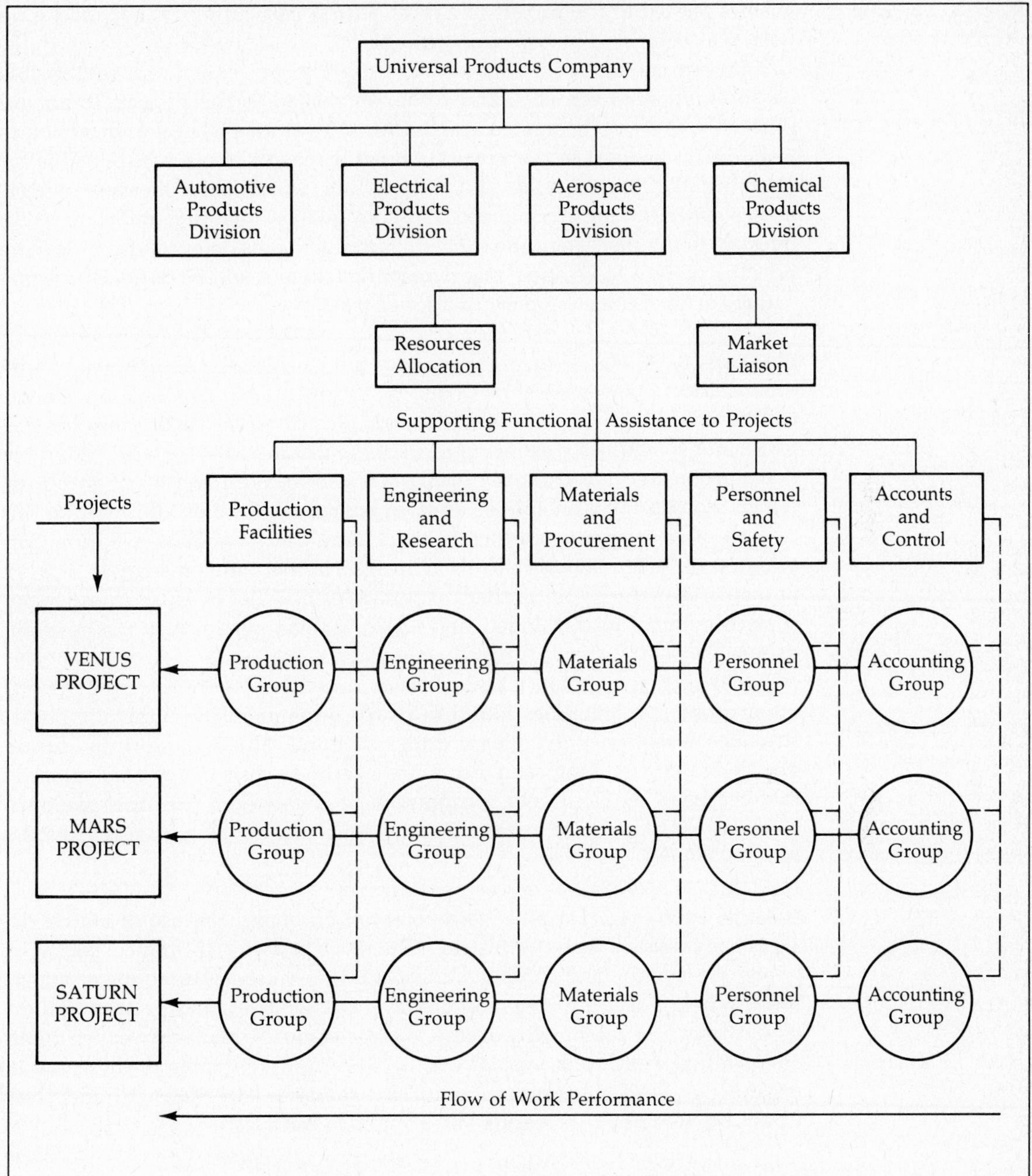

Figure 9-11 **Matrix Organization (Aerospace Division)**

SOURCE: John F. Mee, "Matrix Organizations," in *Business Horizons*, vol. 7 (Summer 1974), no. 2 pp. 70–72. © 1965 by the Foundation for the School of Business at Indiana University. Reprinted by permission.

matters related to the project to almost purely staff authority, depending on what was delegated by top management.

Project managers in a matrix organization, in general, are responsible for integration of activities and resources related to the project. To accomplish this, they are delegated full authority over all physical and monetary resources to be used in the project. Project managers also are responsible for planning the project, especially scheduling work. They measure performance as well to ensure that project's cost, quality, quantity, and time objectives are being met. The functional department heads delegate duties, decide how the work is to be done, and determine where it will be done. Functional managers also supervise performance of tasks.

Problems with Matrix Structures. Like the proverbial bed of roses, matrix organization's pluses are surrounded by thorns. As the September, 1976 Organizational Planning Bulletin of General Electric warns, "it's a complex, difficult, and sometimes frustrating form of organization to live with." Many of these problems stem from the horizontal and vertical overlay of authority, which violates the principle of unity of command. Studies indicate that this overlay often results in conflict.[14] John Humphrey, president of Forum Corporation of North America—a consulting firm that trains managers to work in matrix structures—states that "expectations may not be clear, interpersonal skills may not be developed, and working relationships may not be established."[15]

Management writers Stanley Davis and Paul Lawrence cited several other problems sometimes found in matrix structures. These include power struggles, a tendency to collapse under economic strain, conformity during group decision making, and excessive overhead costs. They also mention that because "people do not recognize a 'boss' to whom they feel responsible," there is a tendency toward anarchy, with functional managers grabbing for total control."[16]

Benefits of Matrix. Despite these potential problems, the use of matrix designs has spread to many industries. Chemical, banking, insurance, packaged goods, electronics, and computer companies now use it. Variations of matrix are also being used by hospitals, government agencies, and professional organizations. The reason why is easy to understand. Several early experimenters obtained exceptional results with it. *Results* are the name of the game in organizing, as in all management. The experiences of Shell Oil and Dow Chemical, described in Feature 9-1, are good examples.

Free-Form Organizations

Yet another approach to creating an adaptable organizational design is the free-form structure. A **free-form organization** does not have a consistent, set structure but rather is comprised of a number of different structures. Thus the overall organization takes on whatever form is best suited to its current

FEATURE 9-1

Matrix Organization at Shell Oil and Dow Chemical

Shell's chemical division was reorganized along matrix lines in 1970, a process that took several years. Six years later, 1976, the division's sales tripled, going from 523 million to 1.6 billion dollars. Profits over the same period went from near zero to 159 million dollars. This prompted Shell to reorganize its oil products division into a matrix structure as well.

Dow Chemical first became interested in matrix organization in 1968. "By spreading out decision making Dow Chemical executives hoped the company could handle more information and respond more quickly to changes in technology, market conditions, or government regulations, while at the same time relieving senior management of some of the decision-making burden." While these goals are difficult to measure, to a large extent Dow Chemical seems to have achieved them. Observes a market researcher for a competing chemical company: "Dow Chemical is a formidable competitor. They have a flat management that is able to make quick decisions, whereas we seem to have a system layered with a lot of personnel and overhead." Dow's sales and earnings, like Shell's, improved significantly. Sales rose an average of 15 percent a year, going from around $100 million in 1967 to $355 million in 1976. Net earnings over the same period quadrupled, going from $10.2 million to $43 million.

SOURCE: "How to Stop the Buck Short of the Top," *Business Week*, January 16, 1978, p. 83.

situation. One division of a firm may use product departmentation, another may organize functionally, and another may use a project or matrix design.

The corporate top-management group is responsible for long-range planning, policy formation, and coordination and control of the overall organization. Surrounding this central group is a number of companies that typically are treated as independent profit centers or virtually independent companies. These companies are almost completely autonomous with respect to operating decisions. Their responsibility to the parent company is primarily budgetary. They are expected to attain profitability objectives and hold spending within overall limits established by the core top-management group. How this responsibility is met is wholly at the discretion of the managers in charge of each respective profit center.

Conglomerates. The most widespread users of free-form organization are very large conglomerates, such as Textron, Martin-Marietta, ITT, Gulf and Western, and Fuqua Industries. These firms grow primarily by merger and acquisition, rather than by internal expansion. As a result they often become involved in business operations that are too diverse to fit comfortably within any one system of structure. Therefore corporate top management allows each subsidiary company's top management to select the structure most appropriate to its own particular needs.

Another major reason why conglomerates use free-form organization is that it enables them to add and shed activities quickly with minimal disruption. There is little interdependence among subsidiary companies, relative to that in typical departmentation. It would be unthinkable, for example, for a functionally departmented firm to eliminate its marketing department for poor performance. A free-form conglomerate, on the other hand, can sell a subsidiary that is performing poorly, or add one with good potential, and the change will be scarcely noticed by other operating divisions. This characteristic has also made the free-form structure popular with businesses in high-technology industries that must rapidly introduce new products and eliminate obsolete ones.

Centralized and Decentralized Organizations

As we have noted several times, there is no one "best" organizational structure. The best structure is the one most appropriate for the strategies and situation of the organization. In departmentation, the consideration is essentially how to divide labor horizontally, what kinds of tasks each unit should perform. Another important consideration in designing an organization structure is vertical division of labor. During organizing, top management must decide *where* in the hierarchy major decisions should be made. This decision affects the shape of the organizational structure and the decision-making effectiveness of management.

What we are referring to here is the relative amount of authority delegated to different positions in the structure. As we learned in our discussion of authority relationships, management must delegate at least enough authority for a subordinate to perform assigned tasks. Also, if the span of management becomes too large, line authority must be delegated and additional levels created to prevent loss of coordination. These, however, are very broad parameters. Within them there are many possibilities with respect to delegation of authority to make specific decisions.

Organizations in which top management retains authority to make most important decisions are termed **centralized**. A **decentralized organization** is one in which authority is distributed to lower levels. In a highly decentralized organization, managers below the top level have considerable discretion in specific areas.

Characteristics of Decentralization

In practice, no organization is either purely centralized or purely decentralized. Rather, these are extremes of a continuum, and organizations fall somewhere in between. They range from retaining most, if not all, authority to make important decisions at top levels to allowing levels below the top considerable decision-making authority. The difference is one of relative degree; that is, an organization can be described as centralized relative to other organizations or itself at a different time. For example, before U.S. Steel was reorganized in 1974, the company had two operating divisions and five sales divisions, none of which had profit responsibility. The new structure had five virtually independent profit centers. Top management, in other words, decentralized U.S. Steel by authorizing divisional managers to make crucial profit-loss decisions.

Several characteristics determine how decentralized an organization is relative to others. These are:

1. The number of decisions made at lower levels. If a larger number of decisions are made by subordinate managers, the organization is more decentralized.
2. The importance of decisions made at lower levels. In a decentralized organization, lower-level managers can make decisions involving substantial resources, increased manpower, or commit the organization to a new course of action.
3. The impact of decisions made at lower levels. If subordinate managers can make decisions that affect more than one function, the organization is probably decentralized.
4. The amount of checking on subordinates. In a highly decentralized organization, top management seldom reviews day-to-day decisions of subordinate managers. The presumption is that these decisions were made correctly. Evaluation is based on overall results, especially profitability and growth.

Within a single organization, certain divisions or activities may be more centralized than others. Store managers and franchise holders at McDonald's, for example, have almost complete authority over local personnel decisions and some authority over food purchases. Location decisions are made at an intermediate level in the McDonald's organization. And pricing and new product decisions are made at the highest levels. In a typical hospital, administrative functions tend to be highly centralized; but people in medical activities, particularly physicians, are given almost complete autonomy of action. Within a large university there may be considerable variation between departments on how much an instructor can alter the content of required courses.

When speaking of an organization as centralized or decentralized, one is really describing the extent to which major decisions are delegated to levels below top management in important areas such as pricing, product design and development, marketing, and matters related to performance of the divisional unit. Even in very decentralized organizations top management retains a number of decisions: setting overall objectives, strategic planning, corporate policy formulation, bargaining with unions, and development of financial and accounting systems. Clearly, it would be unwise to allow managers of one part of an organization to dictate how the whole organization should operate. Similarly, top management needs to retain control over the spending and strategies of its major divisions. As described in Chapter 11, General Dynamics Corporation suffered enormous losses because it decentralized highly without top management retaining authority over these important activities.

Although highly decentralized organizations do delegate some decision-making authority to middle-management levels, very major decisions in large companies are made only in positions that are high in the managerial hierarchy, at the divisional level.[17] This form of decentralization in large corporations is referred to as *federal decentralization.*

Factors Influencing Decentralization. Shortly after World War I, such companies as General Motors, Du Pont, Sears, and Standard Oil of New Jersey recognized potential problems in the functionally departmented, centralized structures they were then using. Although functional departmentation and centralized decision making had been effective in the past, as these companies expanded their product lines, entered new businesses, and began to operate internationally, management found that the number and complexity of decisions became too great for top management to make by itself. To continue growing and keep their key decision making effective, management of these firms saw that authority for certain important decisions would have to be delegated to lower levels in the hierarchy. Thus these organizations moved toward decentralized structures in which top management would concentrate on making decisions in the areas of long-range planning, allocation of corporate resources to the various divisions, and coordination and evaluation of the divisions. Divisional managers were delegated the right to make decisions in areas directly related to their specific product or service responsibilities.

This tendency to reorganize due to the company's strategy for expansion is the essence of Alfred Chandler's maxim, "structure follows strategy," which has received much research support.[18] Several other large companies moved toward a decentralized, divisional structure around the same time and for similar reasons: Union Carbide, Westinghouse Electric, U.S. Rubber, Goodrich, and the A & P grocery chain. However, as might be expected, the trend has not been universal, nor have all firms that adopted decentralized structures continued to move in that direction. As of 1976, for example, one of the early pioneers of decentralization, Sears, began to reorganize toward more centralization because of decreasing profitability. Whereas major purchasing and advertising decisions were once made by store or area managers, under the new structure they will be made at corporate headquarters. Sear's management feels that this will give it better control over spending and enable Sears to make better use of its size and purchasing power when negotiating with suppliers.[19]

Today, according to a comprehensive research study, the four most highly decentralized industries are transportation, chemicals, electrical manufacturing, and rubber. These industries are characterized by great product diversity and multinational operation, as compared to the more centralized food, machinery, paper, and metals industries.[20] Later in this book we will elaborate on the factors involved in the growth of decentralization, as well as other factors—such as rate of environmental change, technology, and size—that influence which organizational structure is likely to be most effective.

Advantages of Centralized and Decentralized Structures

Partly because it shows confidence in people's capacity to manage well, partly because it has often proven very successful, decentralization has many advocates today. One of the strongest and most influential is Peter Drucker, whose books on management are extremely popular with businesspeople. Drucker was among the first to study what may be the world's grandest effort to decentralize an organization: Alfred P. Sloan's reorganization of General Motors Corporation during the 1920s. Based on the apparent success of decentralization at GM, Sears, Standard Oil, General Electric, and Du Pont, Drucker states:

> A basic rule of organization is to build the *least possible* number of management levels and forge the shortest possible chain of command.[21]

Apparently, many managers agree. The majority of large American businesses are decentralized organizations. Their overall structure is based on the system of federal decentralization, which gives managers of major divisions almost complete autonomy over their own operations. However, even its strongest supporters recognize that decentralization is not the "right" answer all the time. Decentralization and centralization both have advantages and disadvantages, depending on characteristics of the external and internal variables. The major advantages of each are summarized in Table 9-3. The potential disadvantage of centralization is lost opportunity to attain the advantages of decentralization, and vice versa.

SUMMARY

When organizing the overall organization, management selects a structure based on its strategy that will best enable the organization to interact with its environment and attain its objectives effectively. Because both the environment and organizations

Table 9-3 Advantages of Centralization and Decentralization

Advantages of Centralization
1. Centralization improves the control and coordination of specialized, independent functions and decreases the number and magnitude of erroneous decisions by less experienced managers.
2. A strong, centralized management can prevent the sort of situation in which some divisions of the organizations expand at the expense of others or the organization as a whole.
3. Centralized management makes centralized staff expertise more economical and easier to use.
Advantages of Decentralization
1. Proponents of decentralization believe that extremely large organizations cannot be managed centrally because of the quantity of information required and the resulting complexity of decision making.
2. Decentralization gives decision-making authority to the manager closest to the situation and therefore most knowledgeable of its details.
3. Decentralization stimulates initiative and identification with the organization. Under decentralization, the largest full unit of organization is small enough for its manager to fully understand, fully control, and feel part of. The manager, thus, will feel the same enthusiasm for his or her unit that an independent entrepreneur feels for his or her own business.
4. Decentralization helps train younger managers for top posts by exposing them to making important decisions early in their career. This ensures that the organization will always have an adequate supply of management talent. The premise is that managers are made by experience, not born with the talent. Since the distance from top to bottom is shorter, decentralization encourages the aggressive young manager to stay with the firm and advance within it.

themselves are continuously changing, the organizational structure must be appraised and redesigned as necessary from the top down.

The majority of organizations today are bureaucracies. The traditional structure for a bureaucracy is functional departmentation, which divides the organization into units that each perform a specialized function. Production, marketing, and finance departments, or their equivalents in nonmanufacturing organizations, still serve many small organizations well. However, departmentalizing exclusively by function is too unwieldy for a large, diversified organization.

Just after World War I, several large businesses, realizing the limitations of functional organization, began to use divisional organization as the basis for their structure. The major variations of divisional organization are product departmentation, territorial departmentation, and customer departmentation. The choice is dependent on which of these factors is most important to the organization's strategy.

The many benefits of bureaucracy include clear-cut division of labor and hierarchy, promotion based on competence, and consistent rules and standards. Its potential dysfunctional consequences include rigidity of behavior, communication problems, and an inability to innovate quickly. If the organization is very large, or must cope with rapid change or complex technology, these problems increase in mag-

FEATURE 9-2

Organizing Big Business

The following excerpt describes how three big companies—General Electric, Liberty Mutual Insurance, and Johnson & Johnson—are organized and how their structures have changed in response to strategy and the environment. The organization charts shown are not actual ones but simplified modifications based on the author's analysis of these companies.

General Electric is not as large as General Motors, but it is a more complex company because it manufactures a wider range of products in a large number of organizational units. G.E. was one of the pioneers of decentralization and it made a great effort to adhere to the traditional principle of "authority should equal responsibility" by keeping control over staff at the operating level.

In the past decade, the balance of power has steadily shifted away from department managers toward the central office. New layers of top-level operating executives have been added and new functions and increased authority have been given to corporate staff members. Nevertheless, the organizational structure still gives considerable autonomy to line operations.

To understand General Electric's present organization (Figure 1), it first is necessary to examine its roots. Prior to 1968, G.E. was built around 10 product groups, with four or five product, consumer or geographic divisions under each. Across the bottom, under the divisions, more than 100 departments operated. They were (and still are) the key units at G.E.

Management's intention was to create small- to medium-sized businesses that department managers could wrap their arms around and run as their own. Their performance was measured against their budgets and profits. The main intention in decentralization was not to democratize the organization, but to create greater control at the operating level.

At that time, Group and Division Vice Presidents possessed little functional staff and acted primarily as advisors who periodically asked questions and evaluated performance. Most important, they played a central role in investment decisions. Headquarters staff "consultants" were available to give advice on such matters as marketing, engineering and manufacturing problems, but a line manager retained the right to refuse the staff's advice and go his own way.

The staff developed substantial power even in the absence of formal authority, since the consultants were physically located at corporate headquarters in New York and had easy access to top executives. A line manager

continues on page 294

FEATURE 9-2, continued

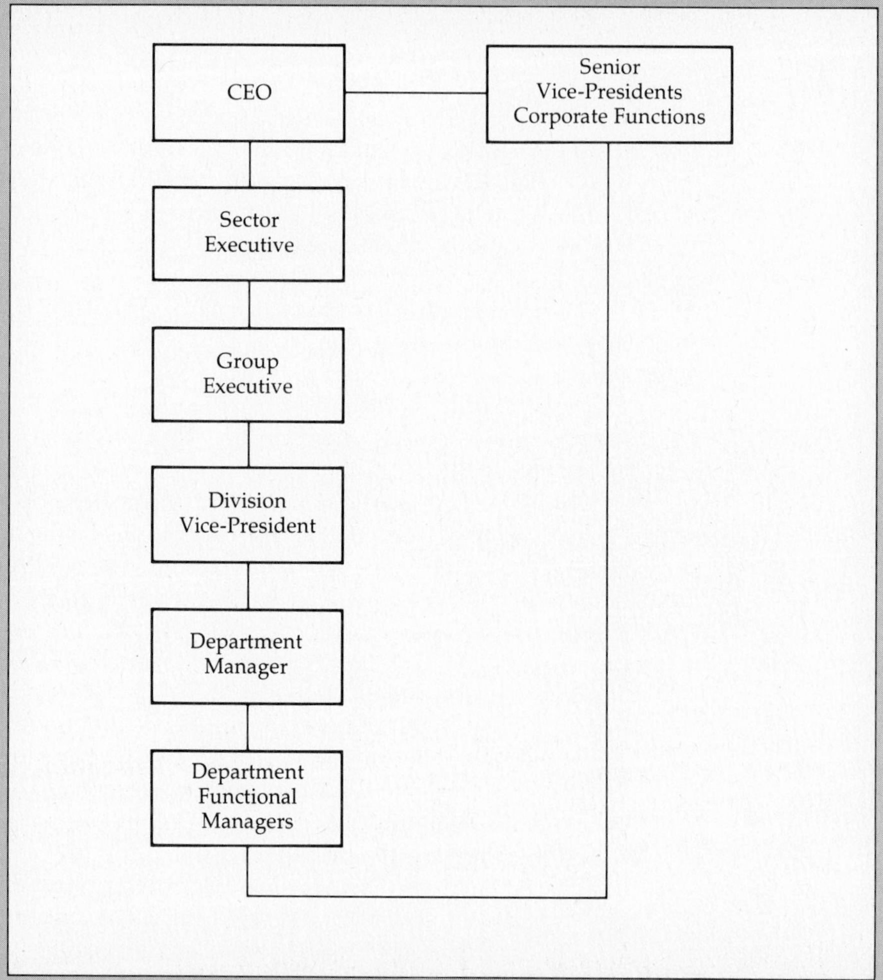

Figure 1 General Electric

who ignored a consultant's advice and then exceeded his budget or missed his profits was neck deep in trouble with top management.

The several functional staffs thus served a communication function similar to the finance organization at General Motors, links to help top management keep track of what is going on. Some central staff even referred to themselves as the "policemen" of the company—a phrase not likely to endear them to the line departments and divisions.

Modifications were made to G.E.'s structure after 1968 that mainly affected the top levels. First, three executive vice presidents were added to the

President's office to help monitor and integrate increasingly complex and diversified activities. This was a common phenomenon in the late 1960's and early 1970's; by adding some executives at the top, presidents had more experience and capacity to draw on in a flexible manner because the chain of command was ambiguous at the top.

Second, the corporate staff was strengthened. Dropping the term "services" from the vice presidential titles symbolically communicated that central staff members were more than just passive advisors or even traveling auditors. Some gained the authority of "compulsory consultation" because a group executive or division vice president might refuse to discuss a department manager's proposals unless the relevant corporate staff member had been consulted, or perhaps even given his approval. In such cases, staff would hold virtual veto power over departmental plans. In addition, new corporate staff units were created which were more oriented toward overall integration rather than helping or controlling the parts—units like "management and manpower development" and "research and development."

In 1973, further modifications were made elevating the executive vice presidents to vice chairmen of the board and placing them directly in the chain of command. The staff executives became senior vice presidents and additional integrative company titles appeared, such as "corporate development," "corporate strategic planning," and "technology planning and development." Many firms that had previously created multi-person executive offices had restored a more traditional chain of command, but the implications at General Electric appeared to be consistent with the original 1968 change—stronger management control.

Last year, the three vice chairmen were returned to the executive office and replaced in the chain of command with another layer of management, five Sector Executives.

G.E.'s "overlap" system with its multiple lines of communication was designed to strike an optimum balance between department manager autonomy and presidential office control. It is an uneasy balance, for the pendulum swings back and forth according to economic conditions and company performance. In good times, autonomy is greater as the department managers take advantage of opportunities. In bad times, the top's need to reduce expenses and eliminate fat tends to prevail. Clearly, the pendulum now is swinging toward control by the higher levels in order to promote better integration and coordination.

Liberty Mutual Insurance Company is a nationwide organization of 13,000 people providing all kinds of insurance to business and personal policyholders. In the home office in Boston, the Vice President of Finance is responsible for investment of funds from which insurance companies derive most of their profits. From a narrow business perspective, the rest of the organization exists to obtain money to loan and invest.

continues on page 296

FEATURE 9-2, continued

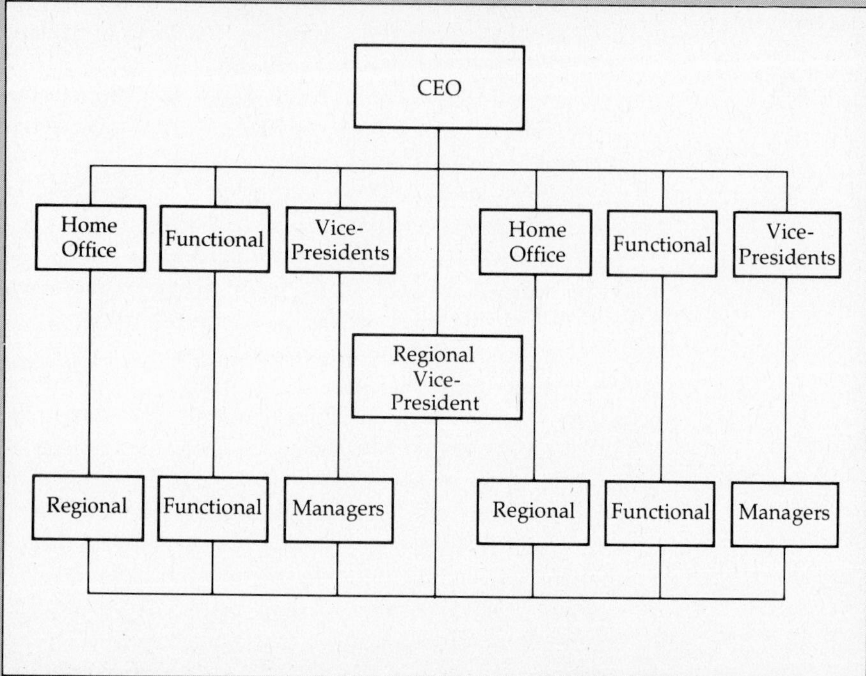

Figure 2 Liberty Mutual Insurance

The *underwriting* department designs policies, determines risks, sets premium rates and defines which policyholders are desirable. *Operations* is responsible for the physical completion of policies, data collection and office policy and procedure. *Claims* handles the investigation of accidents and payment to claimants. *Loss prevention* inspects policyholder property and helps to

nitude and may prevent it from attaining objectives. Some organizations have therefore begun to move away from a mechanistic, bureaucratic structure and have adopted an organic, adaptive structure.

The mostly widely used variations of adaptive organizational design are the project organization, matrix organization, and the free-form organization. Project and matrix structures have a temporary, special purpose structure overlayed on the permanent structure. This overlay of authority may lead to power struggles, conformity in group decisions, and excessive costs. But, because it can respond rapidly to change and make full use of specialized expertise, some organizations have achieved excellent results with matrix and project structures.

Free-form organization, used widely by conglomerates, consists of a parent company with subsidiary companies operated as separate profit centers. Each subsidiary

prevent accidents, thus reducing claims. *Sales* oversees the entire field force of sales managers and salesmen.

The distinction between line and staff is hazy. Each of the major functions in Liberty Mutual tends to consider itself of greatest importance. A sign in one sales office says, "Sales is not the most important department, it is the only department." Each home office department sets policy and procedures in its function that are applied in the various geographic areas by the regional functional managers.

The home office functional departments are powerful for good reason. Liberty Mutual is a national company selling insurance to national clients who expect a consistent level of service. A policyholder such as Sears must be confident that it will be treated equitably whether an accident occurs in Massachusetts, Oregon, or Georgia.

But because Liberty Mutual is nationwide, it also must be divided in geographic territories, and therein lies an awkward structural problem. Local functional managers—the claims manager or sales head of a particular office—each report to two superiors: the *regional* vice president and their home office *functional* vice president. To complicate matters further, it is not clear who is really the stronger superior. In the short run, the regional vice president evaluates the local functional manager's performance and then makes salary recommendations. In the long run, however, the manager's promotions depend more upon his relations with the functional specialists in Boston.

Liberty Mutual's organization (Figure 2) can be described as a "multiple-links" structure because regional personnel report through two chains of command. The regional vice president is to be an integrator who coordinates regional activities to sell insurance and provide service in his geographic area. He usually comes from a sales background and may even double as a regional sales manager. He is an important person, but he does not have

continues on page 298

uses the structure best suited to its needs. Subsidiaries are added or dropped by the parent firm in accordance with its strategy and objectives for growth. Many large organizations use a composite structure; that is, they use several of these alternative designs in combination.

Whatever the structure, management may choose to decentralize authority by allowing managers below the top level to make important organizational decisions. The potential advantages are improved vertical communication, improved decision making, increased managerial motivation and enthusiasm, and better-trained managers. However, centralization also has advantages that make it more appropriate for some organizations. These include economical use of staff, a high level of coordination and control of specialized activities, and curtailment of situations in which parts of the organization expand at the expense of the whole.

Feature 9-2, continued

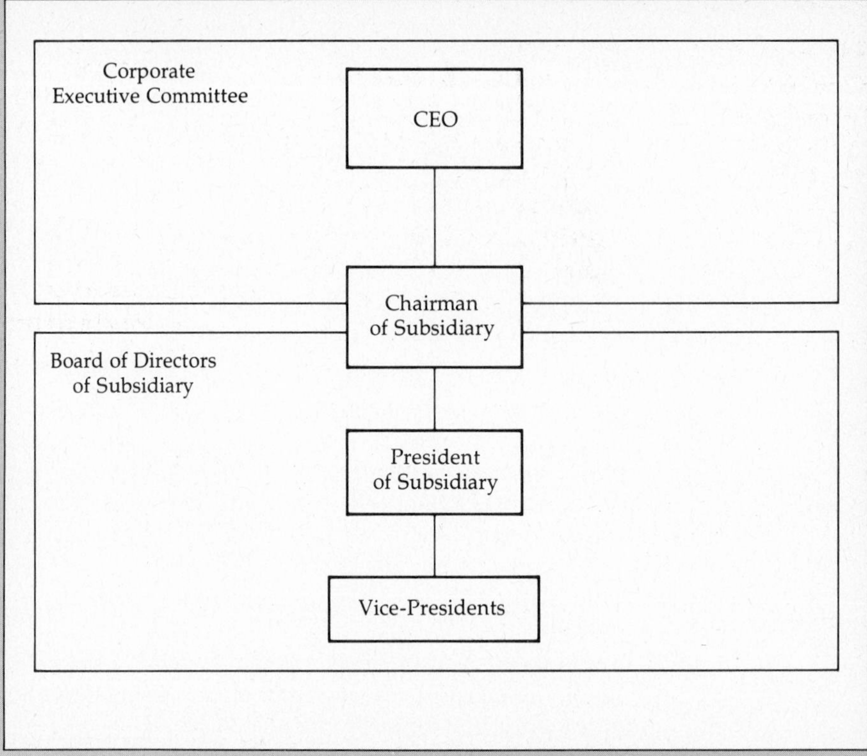

Figure 3 Johnson & Johnson

final authority over the functional managers who report to him. The regional vice president cannot, for example, order the regional claims manager to violate home office claims policy, but he can, when he thinks it is necessary, encourage the manager to depart from policy and agree to fight the home office if the manager is reprimanded.

The unity of command principle appears to be bent, if not broken, but it is done in order to balance the conflicting needs for standardized central policy and procedures on one hand and local effort and initiative on the other. The system succeeds only if the regional vice president enjoys the confidence of both the home office executives and his regional functional managers. . . . Thus, individual personality and style play a major role in defining effectiveness in Liberty Mutual's multiple-linking structure.

Johnson and Johnson is a conglomerate with more than 75 subsidiaries around the globe. Johnson and Johnson Domestic Operating Company produces the familiar "band-aids" and baby products. Ethicon manufactures surgical instruments and sutures; McNeil is a pharmaceutical firm; Stim-u-dents makes gum massagers. These are medical products, but other subsidiaries make sausage casings, cigarette filters and cellophane tape. The diversity of products and geography make the traditional chain of command impractical. The firm's solution: Divide and conquer.

The subsidiaries are divided into eight groupings (Figure 3), each headed by a person who is Chairman of the Board of the five to 20 companies in that group. Companies within each group typically share either geographic location or a similarity in product line.

Each subsidiary is organized as if it were an independent company, even though almost all are entirely owned by J&J and no stock exists in their names. The full-time salaried executives of each subsidiary constitute its board of directors.

The eight chairmen have offices at the corporate headquarters in New Brunswick, N.J., but they spend most of their time visiting their respective companies. None of them has much staff, and, in fact, the complement at headquarters is quite small. A visitor to a large Georgian building in New Brunswick, with powder blue carpeting and a Williamsburg chandelier, is informed that this is the office of the J&J Domestic Operating Company. The corporate headquarters is across the street in a nondescript converted factory.

This contrast is striking and symbolic. The central staff is small; no specialists continually travel among the subsidiaries as at General Electric; no financial organization knits the whole together as at General Motors. The integrating force has been mainly the president and the various chairmen.

Johnson and Johnson's system is termed "multiple role" because the chairmen are both line officers atop their respective subsidiaries and personal staff to the corporate president and chairman. The corporate officers utilize the chairmen as advisors and project leaders, as well as communication links to the subsidiaries. Thus, each chairman is expected to control and represent his subordinates while also being involved in corporate problem-solving.

The president of Ortho may argue that his net return on investment is greater than the return at the more mature Personal Products subsidiary, so he should be able to invest his own profits plus some from Personal Products. Or the president of Devro may argue that although his return on investment is not very good yet, future projections suggest that substantial investment now will pay off in the future. Thus, he wants someone else's profits when he has generated very little himself. The corporate executives and chairmen must reconcile these conflicting requests.

The system is intended to foster an overall corporate perspective while retaining independence among the subsidiaries. Nonetheless, it is not entirely successful because the weak central staff permits parochial views to predominate from time to time. Finance is fairly well controlled at the top

continues on page 300

FEATURE 9-2 continued

through the Vice President of Finance who has functional authority, but personnel and research present problems.

Since there is no strong central industrial relations staff, each subsidiary hires and promotes independently. This has caused the corporation to lose some good people. A young manager whose promotion is blocked at, say, a subsidiary in Rhode Island may leave J&J when, in fact, openings exist to suit him in New Jersey. Without a central staff, there was no way in the past for either him or the corporation to know. Recently, however, the corporation has developed a central personnel file and requires each subsidiary to report to other subsidiaries on openings before they are filled.

As at General Electric, there has been pressure toward increased centralization through enlarging corporate staff. Yet the overall structure has been and must remain decentralized to allow the companies to pursue their opportunities in diverse areas.

SOURCE: Ross A. Webber, "Staying Organized," *Wharton Magazine*, vol. 3 (Spring 1979): no. 3, pp. 19–23.

REVIEW QUESTIONS

1. What are the steps in designing an organizational structure?
2. What is the relationship between planning and structuring the overall organization?
3. What are the characteristics of a rational bureaucracy?
4. What are the major variations of departmentation in wide use today?
5. What potential problems did Merton identify in a bureaucracy?
6. Distinguish between organic and mechanistic structures.
7. Briefly define matrix, project, and free-form organization.
8. What characteristics determine how decentralized an organization is?
9. What are the relative advantages of centralized and decentralized organizations?
10. Illustrate a composite structure.

DISCUSSION QUESTIONS

11. What factors led to the development of divisional organization?
12. Using your own knowledge give some examples of organizations following Chandler's concept that structure follows strategy.

13. Give examples of situations in which each major variation of bureaucracy is appropriate.
14. Which do you feel is preferable: centralization or decentralization? Why?
15. Give an example of a situation in which a mechanistic structure might be preferable to an adaptive one and vice versa.

CASE INCIDENT

The School of Administration

"If you tell me one more time that management is a universal process, I think I'll throw you out of the meeting." Dr. Morton was upset not only with himself for making this statement to a colleague, but with Dr. Crasswell for trying to convince him of something that he felt just wasn't the case.

For the fourth straight day, the university had been holding open hearings dealing with a proposed reorganization of several departments in the Colleges of Arts and Sciences, Business, and Education. The university had just completed a five-year self-study, and one of the key recommendations was that all of those programs dealing with management and the administrative sciences be brought together in a single School of Administration. If this recommendation was implemented, it would have a significant impact on the Departments of Management and Hospital Administration, in the College of Business, Educational Administration in the College of Education, Political Science in the College of Arts and Sciences, as well as the newly created Institute of Governmental Institution which, as yet, was not housed in any particular College because of some lingering jurisdictional problems between the College of Business and the College of Arts and Sciences. As a result of this dispute, it was decided to have Public Administration report directly to the provost or executive vice-president.

According to Dr. Crasswell, who chaired the university structure segment of the self-study, this proposed School of Administration would bring together faculty, students, and programs concerned with management and the administrative sciences. According to Crasswell, this new school would eliminate course and program duplication, more effectively utilize faculty and staff, and provide a higher quality and more coherent program for students. Further, Crasswell reasoned, if all the experts are right, management is management regardless of an organization's essential purpose.

While many agreed with Crasswell, it appeared that Morton's sentiments would prevail; that is, "This is the system that has worked best for us. It should remain as is."

Questions

1. How would you respond to the argument that if it works, don't change it?
2. Why is reorganization both an intellectual and emotional problem?
3. Can you describe in detail how your university is organized?
4. Do you agree that management is a universal process? Explain your answer.

NOTES

1. Alfred P. Chandler, *Strategy and Structure: Chapters in the History of the American Industrial Enterprise* (Cambridge, MA: The MIT Press, 1962).
2. Max Weber, *Theory of Social and Economic Organization,* A. M. Henderson and T. Parsons trans. (London: Oxford University Press, 1921).
3. John Child, "Organizational Structure and Strategies of Control: A Replication of the Aston Study," *Administrative Science Quarterly,* vol. 17, no. 2 (June 1972), pp. 168–177.
4. Both Frederick W. Taylor and Henri Fayol were contemporaries of Weber and early strong proponents of functional departmentation and the concept of bureaucracy. Fayol's thoughts on functionalization are found in H. Fayol, *General and Industrial Administration* (London: Sir Isaac Pitman & Sons, 1949).
5. Arthur H. Walker and Jay Lorsch, "Organizational Choice: Product vs. Function," *Harvard Business Review,* November–December 1968, pp. 129–138.
6. Luther Gulick, "Notes on the Theory of Organization," in *Papers on the Science of Administration,* Luther Gulick and Lyndall F. Urwick eds. (New York: Institute of Public Administration, 1937), pp. 23–24.
7. Donald Marquis, "Ways of Organizing Projects," *Innovation,* no. 5, 1969.
8. E. Raymond Corey and Steven H. Star, *Organizational Strategy: A Marketing Approach* (Boston: Division of Research, Graduate School of Business Administration, Harvard University, 1970).
9. L. G. Franko, "The Move Toward a Multidivisional Structure in European Organizations," *Administrative Science Quarterly,* vol. 19 (December 1974), pp. 493–506.
10. R. K. Merton, *Social Theory and Social Structure* (New York: The Free Press, 1957).
11. Daniel Katz and Robert L. Kahn, *The Social Psychology of Organizations* (New York: John Wiley, 1966), p. 76.

12. Tom Burns and G. M. Stalker, *The Management of Innovation* (London: Tavistock Publications, Ltd., 1966), pp. 9–10.
13. Wendell L. French and Cecil H. Bell, Jr., *Organization Development*, 2d. ed. (Englewood Cliffs, NJ: Prentice-Hall, 1978), p. 224.
14. A. G. Butler, "Project Management: A Study in Organizational Conflict," *Academy of Management Journal*, no. 16 (1973), pp. 84–101; D. R. Kingdon, *Matrix Organization: Managing Information Technologies* (London: Tavistock Publications, Ltd., 1973); Jay A. Galbraith, *Organizational Design* (Reading, MA: Addison-Wesley, 1977).
15. "How to Stop the Buck Short of the Top," *Business Week*, January 16, 1978, p. 83.
16. Stanley M. Davis and Paul R. Lawrence, "Problems of Matrix Organizations," *Harvard Business Review*, May–June 1978, p. 132.
17. John B. Miner, *The Management Process*, 2d. ed. (New York: Macmillan, 1978), p. 281.
18. John Child, "Organizational Structure, Environment and Performance—The Role of Strategic Choice," *Sociology*, vol. 6 (1972), pp. 1–22; R. E. Miles, C. C. Snow, A. D. Meyer, and H. J. Coleman, Jr., "Organizational Strategy, Structure, and Process," *The Academy of Management Review*, vol. 3 (July 1978), pp. 546–562; R. J. Litschert and T. W. Bonham, "A Conceptual Model of Strategy Formation," *Academy of Management Review*, vol. 3 (April 1978), pp. 211–219.
19. "Sears Strategic About Face," *Business Week*, January 8, 1979.
20. L. E. Fouraker and J. M. Stopford, "Organizational Structure and Multinational Strategy," *Administrative Science Quarterly*, vol. 13 (1968), pp. 47–64.
21. Peter F. Drucker, *Management: Tasks, Responsibilities, Practices* (New York: Harper & Row, 1973), p. 546.
22. Cyril O'Donnell, "Group Rules for Using Committees," *Management Review*, vol. 50 (October 1961): no. 10, pp. 63–67.

CHAPTER 10

Motivating

Managers have always recognized the need to get people to perform the organization's work. However, throughout most of history they believed doing so was a simple matter of offering economic rewards. In this chapter we will learn why this usually proved successful, even though it is actually incorrect. In doing so we hope to dispel the lingering misconception that money will always get a person to work harder and also lay groundwork for contemporary views of motivation. The bulk of this chapter is devoted to the theories of motivating developed during the past 30 years. We will learn that determining what *really* drives people to exert maximum effort at work is difficult to determine and extremely complex. But, by understanding contemporary models of motivating, the manager can considerably improve his or her ability to get today's educated, affluent worker to perform the tasks required to attain the organization's objectives without resorting to crude manipulation.

After reading this chapter, you should understand the following important terms and concepts:

- motivating process
- motivating vs. manipulation
- carrot-and-stick motivation
- need
- primary needs
- secondary needs
- law of effect
- intrinsic rewards
- extrinsic rewards
- content theories of motivation
- process theories of motivation
- Maslow's Hierarchy of Needs
- McClelland's Need Theory
- Herzberg's Two-Factor Theory
- hygiene factors
- motivators
- expectancy theory
- equity theory
- Porter-Lawler Model

Motivating: Its Meaning and Evolution

By planning and organizing, management determines what is to be done by the organization, when it is to be done, how it is to be done, and who is supposed to do it. These decisions, when made effectively, enable management to coordinate the efforts of many people and harness the potential benefits of division of labor. Unfortunately, managers sometimes fall into the trap of believing that because a particular course of action or organizational structure works wonderfully on paper, it will work well in practice. Nothing could be farther from the truth. In order to *attain* objectives effectively, the manager clearly must *both coordinate work and get people to perform it.* Managers are popularly referred to as executives because the mainstay of their role is to ensure that the work of the organization is actually *executed.*

Managers translate decisions into actions through the essential managerial function of motivating. In its present managerial context:

> *Motivating is the process of moving oneself and others to work toward attainment of individual and organizational objectives.*

Motivation Versus Manipulation

Machiavellian Motivation. Some people think that motivation is just a euphemism for manipulation; that is, they believe that managers get work accomplished by psychologically pressuring people into doing things they do not really want to do. Unfortunately, this view has a sound basis in reality in some organizations. Ever since Machiavelli wrote *The Prince* in about 1514, a book often considered the first guide to leadership in a large organization, there have been managers who believe that those in command not only do but *should* get others to do their bidding by unscrupulously playing on greed and desire for power. Judging from the large sales of Anthony Jay's *Management and Machiavelli* and Michael Korda's *Power!,* 1970s best-sellers that updated Machiavellian techniques for use in contemporary organizations, outright manipulation still has many adherents.

We will not pretend, as some introductory management texts do, that manipulation, amorality, and the use of fear and economic pressure are unheard of in the modern organization. Nor will we claim that Machiavellian techniques are no longer effective. In *certain situations,* as described in our discussion of power and personal influence, manipulative threats and even crude force can lead to desired results.

However, although you should be aware of these tactics, you should not presume they represent the mainstream of management. The fact is that Machiavellian techniques are not often used in well-managed contemporary organizations. Interestingly, when used at all, pure psychological manipulation is generally confined to the ranks of management. Because of the power of organized labor and changes in accepted social values, managers of contemporary organizations rarely can successfully employ crude pressures to stimulate nonmanagerial subordinates to increase output.

Motivating Without Manipulating. For the simple reason that they are more effective in most situations, the theoretical approaches and applications of motivation described in this chapter have largely supplanted Machiavellian manipulation. The difference between manipulation and what we consider effective motivating is one of both attitude and approach. Manipulation is based on the assumption that people are driven primarily by greed and fear. The manipulative manager tries to get people to do his or her bidding, even though it may be clearly contrary to their own interests and needs.

Motivating in contemporary management thought and practice, in contrast, assumes that each person is a unique being with a complex set of continuously changing drives. It cannot be presumed, for example, that everyone is greedy for more money and power. Equally important, the thrust of contemporary motivating is toward creating a situation in which the individual can satisfy personal objectives by performing work that will lead to attainment of organizational objectives.

In sum, the manipulator assumes that in every interpersonal interaction there is a winner and a loser. In motivating, the manager tries to create a situation in which *everyone*—the subordinate, the manager, and the overall organization—wins.

Early Motivational Practices and Beliefs

Not surprisingly, the current nonmanipulative view of motivating emerged gradually over a period of many years. It is interesting that much of currently accepted management theory was developed in an effort to explain why certain techniques of practicing managers were more effective than others. Theoretical insights, that is, generally have come from observation and classification of successful practice. However, in motivation the reverse has largely held true. The discoveries of theorists and behavioral scientists have often pointed out ways of motivating more effectively *before* they occurred to the majority of practicing managers.

Difficulty of Understanding Motivation. In motivating the manager is not dealing with phenomena, such as technology and structural alternatives, that can be readily analyzed objectively to determine which alternative should be most effective. One cannot directly measure or observe what goes on in an individual's mind but must infer the mental process from the behavior manifested. This makes it easy to misinterpret the true cause of a particular behavior.

For example, one might, as Machiavelli would, interpret a manager's clawing desperately for a promotion to be indicative of a desire to earn more money or have more power. This could be so. But it is also possible that this person is striving so hard because of an unconscious desire for recognition or approval. As a child, this individual may have learned that striving and success would result in parental approval, and through reinforcement this behavior became an integral part of his personality.

The expression "the unconscious or subconscious mind" is commonplace today. Every college student is at least somewhat familiar with the concept. However, until the twentieth century was well underway only a few people had heard of Freud's postulates, and many of those disagreed with his radical ideas such as an event in childhood continuing to affect behavior in adulthood. Consequently, management's understanding of behavior at work, especially motivation, was subject to oversimplifications and misconceptions until the science of psychology developed sufficiently to address the specific problems of the workplace.

Importance of Early Practices. Although today it is widely accepted that the underlying assumptions of early approaches to motivation were incorrect, it is still important to understand them. To begin, although early managers grossly misunderstood human behavior, the techniques they used were, in their situation, often very effective. Because the techniques worked and were used for many hundreds of years, as opposed to the couple of decades current theories have been around, early attitudes on motivation are deeply embedded in our culture. Many managers, particularly ones without formal training, continue to be strongly influenced by them. It is quite possible you will encounter such practices at work.

Moreover, you may be tempted to succumb to the lure of their simple, pragmatic appeal. This probably would be a mistake. Subordinates in today's organizations are typically far better educated and more affluent than those of times past. Their motives, as a result, tend to be more complex and difficult for the manager to perceive accurately. Therefore, today it is often difficult to be an effective motivator without understanding at least a little about the "why" of motivation. Last but not least, we hope that a brief glimpse of history will help you better appreciate that effectiveness in motivation, as in all management, is related to the situation.

Carrot-and-Stick Motivation. Thousands of years before the word *motivation* entered the manager's lexicon, people were well aware of the possibility of deliberately influencing others to accomplish tasks for an organization. The primary technique used to accomplish this is now referred to as **carrot-and-stick motivation**, after the classic method of getting a donkey to move. The Bible, early histories, and even myths are filled with tales of kings dangling rewards before a prospective hero's eyes, or holding a sword over his head. However, king's daughters and treasure were offered only to a select few. The "carrots" offered for most work were barely edible. It was simply taken for granted that most people would be grateful for anything that kept them and their family alive another day.

This usually was quite true, even in Western nations in the late nineteenth century. During much of the Industrial Revolution, economic and social conditions in the English countryside were so hard that farmers flooded the cities and literally begged for the privilege of working 14 hours a day in filthy, dangerous factories at bare survival wages. When Adam Smith wrote *The Wealth of Nations*, life for the common person was even harder. His postulate of economic man, discussed earlier, was doubtless heavily influenced by observation of these harsh realities. In a situation where most people were struggling for survival, it was understandable for Smith to conclude that a person would always attempt to improve his economic condition when offered an opportunity to do so.

Despite advances in technology, the working person's lot still had not improved significantly when the scientific management school arose around 1910. However, Taylor and his contemporaries recognized the foolishness of starvation wages. They made carrot-and-stick motivation much more effective by objectively determining "a fair day's work" and actually rewarding those who produced more in proportion to their contribution. The increased productivity resulting from this motivational technique, in combination with more effective use of specialization and standardization, was dramatic. This great success left a good taste for carrot-and-stick motivation that continues to linger in the mouths of managers.

However, largely because of the effectiveness with which organizations used technology and specialization, life for the average person eventually began to improve. The more it did, the more managers found that the simple technique of offering an economic "carrot" would not always get people to work harder. This encouraged management to look for new solutions to the problem of motivation in the awakening field of psychology.

Management Becomes Aware of Psychology. Even as Taylor and Gilbreth wrote, news of Sigmund Freud's postulate of the unconscious mind was spreading through Europe and reaching America. However, the notion that man was not always rational was a radical one, and managers did not leap to embrace it immediately. Although there were earlier efforts to use psychology in management, it was the work of Elton Mayo that really made clear its potential benefits and the inadequacy of pure carrot-and-stick motivation.

Elton Mayo was one of the very few academics of his time with both a sound understanding of scientific management and training in psychology. He established his reputation in an experiment conducted in a Philadelphia textile mill between 1923 and 1924. Turnover in this mill's spinning department had reached 250 percent, whereas other departments had a turnover of between 5 and 6 percent. Financial incentives instituted by efficiency experts failed to affect this turnover and the department's low productivity, so the firm's president requested help from Mayo and his associates.

After carefully examining the situation, Mayo determined that the spinner's work allowed the men few opportunities to communicate with one another and that their job was held in low regard. He felt that the solution to the problem of turnover lay in changing working conditions, not increased rewards. With management's permission he experimented with the introduction of two ten-minute rest periods for the spinners. The results were immediate and dramatic. Turnover dropped, morale improved, and output increased tremendously. Later, when a supervisor decided to do away with the breaks, the situation reversed to the earlier state, proving that it was Mayo's innovation that had led to the improvement.

The spinner experiment confirmed Mayo's belief that it was important for managers to take into account the *psychology* of the worker, especially the notion of irrationality. He concluded that:

> What social and industrial research has not sufficiently realized as yet is that these minor irrationalities of the "average normal" person are cumulative in their effect. They may not cause "breakdown" in the individual but they do cause "breakdown" in the industry.[1]

However, Mayo himself did not fully realize the import of his discoveries, for psychology was still very much in its infancy.

The first truly major investigation of behavior in the workplace was the landmark Hawthorne experiments, conducted by Mayo and his associates during the late 1920s and discussed at length later in this book. The Hawthorne work began as an experiment in scientific management. It ended nearly eight years later with the realization that the human dimension, especially social interaction and groups, significantly affects individual productivity. The Hawthorne team's findings helped launch the human relations school, which dominated management thought until the mid-1950s.[2]

However, the Hawthorne experiments did not result in a model of motivation that adequately explained the drive to work. Psychological theories of work motivation were not developed until much later, beginning in the 1940s, and are still evolving.

Modern Motivational Theories

Because the systematic study of motivation from a psychological perspective is so new and complex, we are not yet able to determine *exactly* what motivates a person to work. However, due to research in human behavior at work, we are able to explain motivation in a general way and create pragmatic models of motivation in the workplace. These research findings are the primary focus of the remainder of this chapter.

Content Versus Process Theories. We have chosen to classify motivational theories within two categories: content theories and process theories. The **content theories** of motivation revolve around the identification of inward drives, referred to as needs, that *cause* people to act as they do. Under this heading we will describe the work of Abraham Maslow, David McClelland, and Frederick Herzberg. The more recent and sophisticated **process theories** revolve primarily around *how* people behave as they do, incorporating such factors as perception and learning. The major process theories we will cover are expectancy theory, equity theory, and the Porter-Lawler model of motivation.

It is important to understand that while these theories disagree on a number of matters, they are not mutually exclusive. The development of motivational theory has clearly been evolutionary rather than revolutionary. As we stated earlier, these are not just idle, ivory-tower theories. They can and have been applied effectively to the daily challenge of getting others to perform the work of the organization effectively. Therefore, in each case we will briefly point out the relevance of the theory to management practice.

Needs and Rewards

In order to understand either content or process theories, one must first understand the meaning of two concepts fundamental to both. These are needs and rewards.

Needs

Psychologists say a person has a **need** when that individual perceives a physiological or psychological deficiency. Although a particular person at a particular time may not have a need in the sense of perceiving it consciously, there are certain needs that every person has the potential to sense. The content theories represent efforts to classify these common human needs within specific categories. There is as yet no single uniformly accepted identification of specific needs. However, most psychologists would agree that needs can generally be classified as either primary or secondary.

Primary Versus Secondary Needs. **Primary needs** are physiological in nature and generally inborn. Examples include the needs for food, water, air, sleep, and sex. **Secondary needs** are social-psychological in nature. Examples are the needs for achievement, esteem, affection, power, and belonging. Whereas primary needs are genetically determined, secondary needs usually are learned through experience. Describing the development of secondary needs, Paul Lawrence and Jay Lorsch state:

> As the individual system strives to master problems, certain behaviors turn out to be consistently rewarding; that is, they provide solutions to the problems the individual faces. Consequently, the next time the individual needs to solve a problem he tries the same pattern again. Over time, as some of these patterns are consistently rewarding, the individual learns to rely on them.[3]

Because individuals have different learned experiences, secondary needs vary among people to a greater extent than primary needs.

Needs and Motivational Behavior. Needs cannot be directly observed or measured. Their existence must be inferred from a person's behavior. By observation of behavior, psychologists have determined that needs motivate, that is, cause people to act.

When a need is felt, it induces a drive state in the individual. Drives are deficiencies with direction. They are the behavioral outcome of a need and are focused on a goal. Goals, in this sense, are anything that is perceived as able to satisfy the need. After the individual attains the goal, the need is

FEATURE 10-1

Motivating at Jim Walter Corporation

Jim Walter Corporation is a conglomerate with sales of $1.7 billion and over 25,600 employees working in 112 plant locations.

Jim Walter is a people-oriented person and his company reflects and even stresses that. "Our biggest asset is people," he has said many, many times, and this day he restates the point. "You can pick up the paper almost any day and see where a number of big companies have had big trouble and I'd guess a good part of those troubles—though not necessarily all of them by any means—stem from that same word, people, or the lack of them."

The attitude is a lot more than words with Jim Walter. Known for a management philosophy that minimizes the middle layer, delegating authority broadly and demanding (and usually getting) goal-based performance, the company rewards its people in at least direct proportion to the responsibility assigned.

Walter makes it sound so simple: "We try to hire the best people we can, at a very good wage or other accommodation of income. Then we sit down and give them the responsibility of doing their jobs without making them have to go through layers of bureaucracy to get a decision.

SOURCE: Bernard Daley, "Jim Walter—The Man and the Corporation," *Sky*, May 1979, p. 36. This article has been reprinted through the courtesy of Halsey Publishing Co., publishers of Sky magazine.

either satisfied, partially satisfied, or not satisfied. For example, if you have a need for challenging work, this might drive you to attempt the goal of getting a challenging job. After getting the job, you may find that it is not actually as challenging as you thought it would be. This may induce you to work with less effort or seek another job that will, in fact, satisfy your need.

The degree of satisfaction obtained by attaining the goal affects the individual's behavior in related future situations. Generally, people tend to repeat behaviors they associate with satisfaction and avoid those associated with lack of satisfaction; this is known as the **law of effect**. To continue our example, if you learn that certain tasks usually satisfy your need for challenge, you will tend to seek out such tasks in the future, as is illustrated in Figure 10-1.

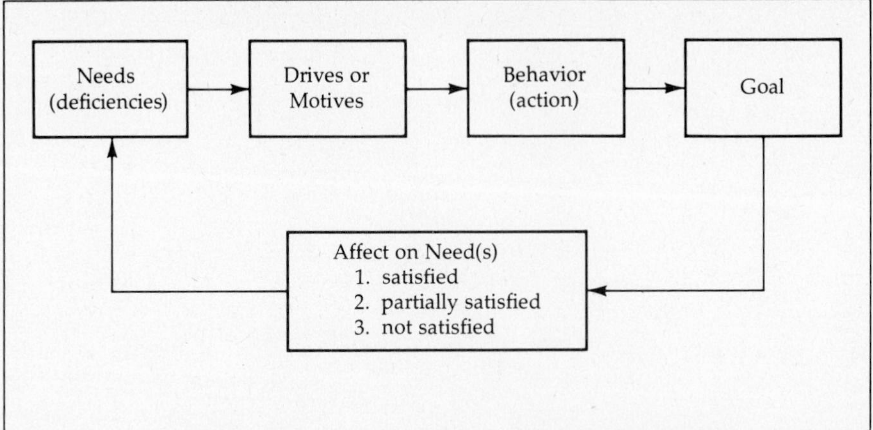

Figure 10-1 Simplified Model of Needs Motivating Behavior

Since needs induce a drive to attain a goal the individual perceives will satisfy the need, it follows that management should attempt to create situations that permit people to perceive they can satisfy their needs through behaviors conducive to attainment of the organization's goals. For example, recall the example in Chapter 3 describing how the introduction of longwall technology into coal mines broke up the independent work groups and deprived the workers of close interpersonal relationships. This is an example of a characteristic of the work situation and tasks affecting need satisfaction. The new technology also did not enable workers to gain a sense of completion and challenge because under the new method each worker only performed a small part of the total mining operation. Consequently, workers were unable to fully use their abilities. As a result, workers engaged in negative behaviors. Absenteeism and turnover increased, productivity decreased. To cope with these problems, management implemented the composite longwall method. This apparently satisfied the needs deprived by the longwall method by creating a situation in which technology did not conflict with individual goals. The problems dissipated.

Complexity of Need Motivation. It is important to note that not all workers have the high need for task completion and independence that the coal miners had. Just as all people have different thumbprints, all people are a unique composite of characteristics. It therefore follows that there is tremendous variation in people's specific needs, what goals a person will perceive as leading to satisfaction of a need, and how a person will behave to attain these goals. Discussing this, Stephen Carroll and Henry Tosi state:

> An individual's need structure is determined by his socialization, or early learning experiences, and thus there are many differences among individuals with respect to the needs that are important to them. More important, there are many ways in which a particular kind of need may be satisfied. For instance, one per-

son's ego needs may be satisfied by being recognized as the best worker in a department. Another may find this need satisfied by others' recognition of his dress style—being acknowledged as the sharpest dresser in his group.

The specific manner in which an individual satisfies a particular need is learned by reinforcement experiences early in life. We learn through experience that some situations are more desirable (rewarding) than others, and we seek these out. Other situations are ones we seek to avoid.[4]

Thus, creating jobs with more challenge and responsibility has a positive motivational effect on many, but by no means all, workers. You must always keep in mind the need for a contingency approach. There is no one best way to motivate. What works effectively with some people may prove an anathema to others.

Rewards

Throughout our discussion of motivation, we will refer to the use of rewards to motivate people to perform effectively. In motivation, the word *reward* has a much broader meaning than the images of money or pleasure it most often is associated with. A *reward* is anything an individual perceives as valuable. Since each individual's perceptions are different, what will be considered a reward and its relative value may differ widely among individuals. To give a simple example, whereas a suitcase filled with hundred-dollar bills would be perceived as a highly valuable reward by most people of civilized nations, the suitcase would probably be considered more valuable than the money by a primitive Tasaday tribesman of the Philippines. Similarly, an extremely wealthy person might perceive a few hours of genuine friendship as more valuable than even a large amount of money.

Intrinsic and Extrinsic Rewards. The manager is concerned with two general types of rewards: intrinsic and extrinsic. **Intrinsic rewards** are obtained through the work itself. Examples would be feelings of achievement, challenge, self-esteem, and the sense that one's work is meaningful. Friendship and social interaction arising through work are also considered intrinsic rewards. The most common means of providing intrinsic rewards is through design of working conditions and tasks. Volvo, for example, partially abandoned repetitive assembly line methods in one experimental plant in favor of teams for building cars in order to increase intrinsic rewards for its production people.

Extrinsic rewards are the type that most often come to mind when the word reward is heard. **Extrinsic rewards** are attained not from the work itself, but rather are granted by the organization. Examples of extrinsic organizational rewards are pay, promotion, status symbols such as a private office with a window, praise and recognition, and fringe benefits such as vacations, a company car, expense account, and insurance.

For management to determine whether and in what proportion it should use intrinsic and extrinsic rewards to motivate, it must determine what the needs of its workers are. This was the aim of the content theories.

FEATURE 10-2

Intrinsic Versus Extrinsic Rewards For Managers

Enjoyment of work, rather than money, motivates a surprising proportion of American business executives, says Paul R. Ray & Co., a leading executive recruiting firm.

In recent survey of 425 top level executives, the Ray company said that only half had any desire to retire before 65 and about 12 percent wanted to work at least until they are 70. This was the case although three-quarters of those replying could expect pensions equal to half or more of their highest annual salary.

Enjoyment of work apparently is enhanced by executive mobility and the challenge of a new job, the replies indicated. Eighty-six percent of those replying had been on their current jobs less than five years.

SOURCE: UPI, *Atlanta Journal*, Nov. 17, 1977, p. 16-D. Reprinted by permission.

Content Theories of Motivation

As mentioned above, the **content theories** of motivation are primarily efforts to identify the needs that drive people to act, particularly in the work setting. The work of three people has been particularly influential in laying this important groundwork for our current understanding of motivation, namely, Abraham Maslow, Frederick Herzberg, and David McClelland.

Maslow's Hierarchy of Needs

One of the first behavioral scientists to make management aware of the complexity of human needs and their effect on motivation was Abraham Maslow.[5] When forming his theory of motivation during the 1940s, Maslow acknowledged that people really have a great many needs. This concept was elaborated on by his contemporary, Harvard psychologist H. A. Murray.[6] However, Maslow felt that mankind's diverse needs could be condensed within the following five basic categories:

1. *Physiological* needs are the essentials of survival. They include food, water, shelter, rest, and sex.
2. *Safety and security* needs include the needs for protection against physical and psychological threats in the environment and confidence that physiological needs will be met in the future. Buying an insurance pol-

icy or seeking a secure job with a good pension plan are manifestations of security needs.

3. *Social* needs, sometimes called the need for *affiliation,* include a feeling of belonging, of being accepted by others, of interacting socially, and of receiving affection and support.
4. *Esteem* needs include self-respect, achievement, competence, respect of others, and recognition.
5. *Self-actualization* needs include fulfillment of one's potential and growth as a person.

Need Hierarchy and Motivation. Maslow's theory holds that these needs are arranged in a *prepotent hierarchy*, as illustrated in Figure 10-2. By this he meant that lower-level needs require satisfaction and thereby affect behavior before higher level needs have an effect on motivation. That is, according to Maslow, an individual will be motivated to satisfy the need that is prepotent, or most powerful for him or her, at a specific time. Before the next level need becomes the most powerful determinant of behavior, the lower-level need must first be satisfied. As psychologists Calvin Hall and Gardner Lindsey state in their explanation of Maslow's theory, "When the needs that have the greatest potency and priority are satisfied, the next needs in the hierarchy emerge and press for satisfaction. When these needs are satisfied, another step up the ladder of motives is taken."[7] Because one's potential expands as one grows as a person, the need for self-actualization can never really be fully satisfied. Therefore, the process of needs motivating behavior never ends.

For example, a starving person will first be motivated to find food, and only after eating will attempt to build a shelter. Once comfortable and secure, a person will be primarily motivated by the need for social contact, then will actively seek the respect of others. Only after the individual feels inwardly content and respected will he or she be primarily motivated by the need to grow to full potential. If the situation radically changes, the most prepotent need may change drastically. Just how swiftly and far one's primary needs can drop down the hierarchy and how powerful the lowest-level needs are is illustrated by the behavior of the survivors of a plane that crashed in the Andes in 1975. To stay alive, these normal people, some of them professionals, ate their deceased traveling companions.

However, it is important to realize, as Maslow acknowledged, that a need does not have to be totally satisfied before the next higher level begins to influence behavior. Thus, the levels in the hierarchy are not discrete steps. For example, people usually begin seeking affiliation long before their security needs are assured and often even before physiological needs are wholly satisfied. This is clearly illustrated by the high importance of social interaction and ritual in very primitive cultures of the Amazon jungle and parts of Africa, even though hunger and danger are always present.

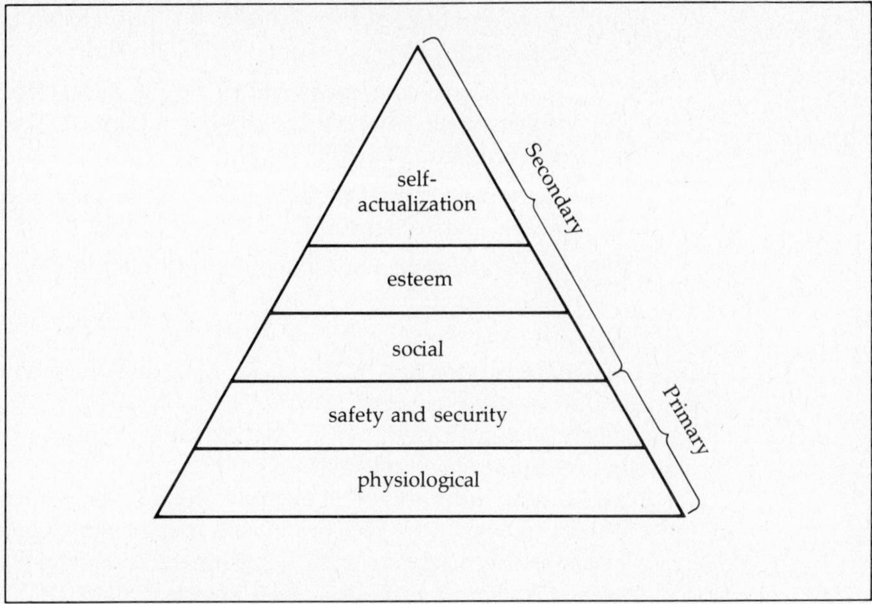

Figure 10-2 Maslow's Need Hierarchy

In other words, although at a given moment one need will predominate, a person may be simultaneously motivated by more than one need. Furthermore, as Maslow states, "We have spoken so far as if this hierarchy were a fixed order but actually it is not nearly as rigid as we may have implied. It is true that most of the people with whom we have worked seemed to have these basic needs in about the order that has been indicated. However, there have been a number of exceptions. There are some people in whom, for instance, self-esteem seems to be more important than love."[8]

Relevance in Management. Maslow's theory of human motivation made an extremely important contribution to management's understanding of the drive to work. It made managers aware that people are motivated by a wide variety of needs. In order to motivate a given individual, the manager must provide an opportunity to satisfy prepotent needs through behavior conducive to attaining organizational objectives. Not too long ago managers could motivate very effectively solely through economic incentives for performance because most people operated primarily on lower-need levels. Today the situation has changed. Because of generally higher wages and fringe benefits won through collective bargaining and governmental regulations such as the Occupational Health and Safety Act of 1970, even persons lowest in the organizational hierarchy are relatively high on Maslow's need hierarchy. As Terrence Mitchell states:

> In our society the physiological and safety needs play a relatively minor role for most people. Only the severely deprived and handicapped are dominated by

Table 10-1 Satisfying Higher-Level Needs of Workers

Social Needs
1. Design jobs that allow social interaction.
2. Create team spirit.
3. Conduct periodic meetings with all subordinates.
4. Do not attempt to stifle informal work groups that are not actually negative.
5. Provide outside social activities for organizational members.
Esteem Needs
1. Design more challenging tasks.
2. Provide positive feedback on performance.
3. Give recognition and encouragement for performance.
4. Involve subordinates in goal setting and decision making.
5. Delegate additional authority.
6. Give promotions.
7. Provide training and development that increases competency on the job.
Self-Actualization Needs
1. Provide training and development activities that increase a person's ability to make full use of potential.
2. Provide challenging, meaningful work that requires a person to use his or her full potential.
3. Encourage and develop creativity.

these lower-order needs. The obvious implication for organizational theorists is that higher-order needs should be better motivators than lower-order ones. This fact seems to be supported by surveys which ask employees what motivates them on the job.[9]

In sum, as a manager you need to carefully observe your subordinates' behavior to determine, as best you can, what their active needs are. Because these needs change over time, you cannot assume that a technique that once worked will continue to work. Table 10-1 lists some ways in which managers may be able to satisfy higher-level needs in the workplace.

Criticisms of Maslow's Theory. Although Maslow's theory of human needs seemed to provide managers with a useful description of the motivation process, subsequent tests have not totally substantiated it. Whereas people can be classified within broad categories of higher- and lower-level needs, a strict five-category hierarchy does not seem to exist. Nor has the concept of a prepotent hierarchy been totally supported. Gratification of one need does not automatically activate the next level as a motivator of performance.[10]

The major criticism of Maslow's theory is that it fails to take individual differences into account. Edward Lawler posits, in contrast, an individual need-preference hierarchy that is learned from past experience.[11] Thus, because of past experience, self-actualization may be a dominant need for one person, but another ostensibly similar person working in a similar capacity might be more influenced by esteem, social, or safety needs. Some people who were raised during the Depression, for example, continue to manifest motivation by safety needs even though they have attained considerable financial security.

In sum, as Mitchell states, "Managers must be aware of individual differences in reward preferences. What will motivate one subordinate will not work with another individual. Different people want different things, and managers must be sensitive to these needs if they want to motivate their subordinates."[12]

McClelland's Need Theory

Another motivational model, one stressing higher-level needs, is that of David McClelland who describes people in terms of three needs: power, achievement, and affiliation.

Power. The need for power is expressed as a desire to influence others. In relation to Maslow's hierarchy, power would fall somewhere between the needs for esteem and self-actualization. People with a need for power tend to exhibit behaviors such as outspokenness, forcefulness, willingness to engage in confrontation, and a tendency to stand by their original position. They often are persuasive speakers and demand a great deal from others. Management often attracts people with a need for power because of the many opportunities it offers to exercise and increase power.

Managers who are motivated by the need for power are not necessarily "power hungry" in the pejorative sense in which the expression is often used. Discussing different ways to exert one's power, McClelland states:

> Those individuals with the highest need for power, that is not expressed in a win-loss, dominance-submissive style, but a more socialized form of influence, should be groomed for advancement into higher managerial positions. Personal dominance may be effective in very small groups, but if a human leader wants to be effective in large groups, he must rely on much more subtle and socialized forms of influence. . . . The positive or socialized face of power is characterized by a concern for group goals, for finding those goals that will move men, for helping the group to formulate them, for taking some initiative in providing members of the group with the means for achieving such goals, and for giving group members a feeling of strength and competency they need to work hard for such goals.[13]

Achievement. The need for achievement would also fall between that for esteem and self-actualization. This need is satisfied not by the manifestations of success, which confer status, but with the *process* of carrying work to its successful completion.

Table 10-2 Herzberg's Hygiene Factors and Motivators

Hygiene Factors	Motivators
Company policy and administration	Achievement
Working conditions	Advancement
Pay	Recognition
Interpersonal relations with superiors, co-workers, and subordinates	Responsibility
Quality of supervision	Growth opportunities

Individuals with a high need for achievement generally will take moderate risks, like situations in which they can take personal responsibility for finding solutions to problems, and want concrete feedback on their performance. As McClelland points out, "No matter how high a person's need to achieve may be, he cannot succeed if he has no opportunities, if the organization keeps him from taking initiative, or does not reward him if he does."[14] Thus, if management wishes to motivate individuals operating on the achievement level, it should assign them tasks that involve a moderate degree of risk of failure, delegate to them enough authority to take initiative in completing their tasks, and give them periodic, specific feedback on their performance.

Affiliation. McClelland's affiliative motive is similar to Maslow's. The person is concerned with forming friendly relations with others, desire for companionship, and the desire to help others. People dominated by the affiliative need would be attracted to jobs that allow considerable social interaction. Managers of such individuals should create a climate that does not constrain interpersonal relations. A manager could also facilitate their need satisfaction by spending more time with such individuals and periodically bringing them together as a group.

Herzberg's Two-Factor Theory

During the late 1950s, Frederick Herzberg and his associates developed another need-based model of motivation. Herzberg's research team asked 200 engineers and accountants of a large paint company to respond to the questions: "Can you describe, in detail, when you felt exceptionally good about your job?" and "Can you describe, in detail, when you felt exceptionally bad about your job?"[15]

Herzberg found that the responses could be grouped within two general categories, which he called *hygiene* factors and *motivators.* These are described in Table 10-2.

The **hygiene factors** are primarily related to the environment in which work is performed whereas the **motivators** are primarily related to the nature of the work itself. According to Herzberg, hygiene factors result in dissatisfaction if they are not present or are inadequate. If they are adequate,

Maslow	Herzberg
Self-Actualization Esteem	Motivators
Social Safety and Security Physiological	Hygiene Factors

Figure 10-3 Comparison of Maslow's Needs and Herzberg's Factors

however, they do *not* induce motivation or give satisfaction. In contrast, if the motivators are absent or inadequate they do not result in dissatisfaction. If adequate, however, the motivators are the factors responsible for motivating workers and assuring job satisfaction.

Here is how Herzberg described the relationship between factors and motivation:

> The findings of these studies, along with collaboration from many other investigations using different procedures, suggests that the factors involved in producing job satisfaction (and motivation) are separate and distinct from the factors that lead to job dissatisfaction. Since separate factors need to be considered, depending on whether job satisfaction or dissatisfaction is being examined, it follows that these two feelings are not opposites of each other. The opposite of job satisfaction is not job dissatisfaction, but, rather, no job satisfaction; and, similarly, the opposite of job dissatisfaction is not job satisfaction, but no job dissatisfaction.[16]

Herzberg and Maslow. Herzberg's theory of motivation has much in common with Maslow's. Herzberg's hygiene factors correspond to the physiological, safety, and security needs of Maslow. His motivators are comparable to Maslow's higher-level needs, as illustrated in Figure 10-3. But Herzberg's theory, as noted, differs sharply on one score. Maslow would consider the hygiene factors as inducers of behavior. If a manager offers the opportunity to satisfy one of them, according to Maslow, the worker will exert increased effort as a result. Herzberg, on the other hand, feels that the hygiene factors come into play only when the worker perceives them as unfair or inadequate. Table 10-3 contrasts the content models of Maslow, Herzberg, and McClelland.

Relevance in Management. According to Herzberg's theory, providing employees with hygiene factors will not motivate them. It will only prevent

Table 10-3 Maslow, McClelland, and Herzberg Compared

Maslow
1. Divides needs into primary and secondary arranged in a prepotent hierarchy.
2. The lowest unsatisfied need on the hierarchy motivates behavior.
3. Once a need is satisfied, it no longer motivates.
McClelland
1. Focuses on higher-levels needs for achievement, power, and affiliation. Considers these most important today because lower needs are widely satisfied.
Herzberg
1. Divides needs into hygiene factors and motivators.
2. Holds that hygiene factors only prevent dissatisfaction.
3. Motivators, which correspond roughly to Maslow's higher-level needs and McGregor's needs, actively induce behavior.
4. To motivate, management must primarily concern itself with the nature of work itself.

dissatisfaction. In order to motivate, management must provide the motivators as well as the hygiene factors. Many organizations have attempted to implement the theory through job enrichment programs. In *job enrichment*, work is redesigned and expanded to make the job more personally rewarding to the worker. Job enrichment attempts to structure work so that it provides workers with one or more of the following: challenge, autonomy, variety, responsibility, and a sense of completion of a whole unit of work. Included among the several hundred firms that have undertaken job enrichment to combat the tedium and loss of productivity associated with extreme specialization are AT&T, American Airlines, and Texas Instruments. Although job enrichment is successful in many situations, we will see when we elaborate on it in Chapter 19 that it is not appropriate for all workers.

To apply Herzberg's theory effectively, management should, other factors permitting, present a menu of hygiene factors and especially motivators and allow employees to choose those of personal preference.

Criticisms of Herzberg. Although implemented effectively in several organizations Herzberg's theory has been subject to controversy. The major criticism focuses on his research methods. When people are asked to think of times they felt especially good or bad about their jobs, they tend to credit themselves and things in their control for satisfying experiences and blame others and things outside their control for dissatisfying experiences. Thus, the results Herzberg obtained were at least partially a result of the way he asked questions.

Summarizing their review of 31 studies on Herzberg's theory, House and Wigdor state, "A given factor can cause job satisfaction for one person and job dissatisfaction for another person, and vice-versa."[17] Therefore, either hygiene factors or motivators can be a source of motivation for people, depending on their needs. Since individuals have different needs, different factors will motivate different people.

In addition, Herzberg assumes a strong correlation between satisfaction and productivity, which other studies indicate does not always exist. Discussing this, Hellriegal and Slocum state:

> The lack of a strong relationship between job attitudes and performance is illustrated by employees who are highly satisfied with their jobs because they are able to socialize with coworkers, but who have a low motivation for performance. In other words, productivity is a secondary goal to other goals that employees are seeking at work. Increasing the motivators will not always lead to higher performance.[18]

For example, a person may love his job because he considers co-workers friends and the job therefore allows him to satisfy social needs. However, the person may consider talking to co-workers more important than getting work done. Therefore, his satisfaction will be high, but his performance will be low. Because social needs are so important, providing a motivator such as increased responsibility may not improve productivity or increase motivation for this individual. This would be especially true if co-workers perceive increased output as a violation of their norms.

These criticisms further illustrate the need to consider motivation from a contingency perspective. What motivates one person in a given situation may not work with a different person or situation. In sum, while Herzberg made an important contribution to understanding motivation, his theory did not consider enough situational variables. It became clear to subsequent researchers that to explain motivation at work one must consider many behavioral and environmental factors. This realization led to the development of the process theories.

Process Theories of Motivation

The content theories revolve around needs and related factors that energize behavior. Process theories view motivation from a different perspective. They describe what channels behavior toward goals and how people choose to behave as they do. Process theories do not dispute the existence of needs but contend behavior is not *solely* a function of needs. Behavior, according to *process theories,* is also a function of an individual's perceptions and expectations about a situation and the possible outcome of a given behavior.

There are three major process theories: expectancy theory, equity theory, and the Porter-Lawler model.

Expectancy Theory

Expectancy theory, often associated with the work of Victor Vroom, contends that having an active need is not the only requisite for an individual to be motivated to channel behavior toward a certain goal.[19] The individual must also expect that the behavior will, in fact, lead to satisfaction or get what is desired. **Expectancies** can be thought of as an individual's estimate of the probability that a certain event will occur. Most people expect, for example, that having a college degree will enable them to get a better job or that working hard will probably lead to promotion.

With respect to work motivation, expectancy theory stresses three factors: effort-performance, performance-outcome, and valence of outcome.

Effort-Performance Expectancies (E-P). This expectancy deals with the relationship between the amount of effort expended and performance or attainment of objectives. For example, a salesperson might expect that 10 more calls a week will result in a 15 percent sales increase. A manager might expect to receive a highly positive performance appraisal if a lot of effort is devoted to writing reports requested by superiors. A factory worker might expect that producing high quality goods with minimal waste of materials will earn him a high productivity rating. Of course, in all these examples, the individual may expect that the effort will *not* result in a certain level of performance. If people do not feel that there is a direct relationship between effort expended and subsequent performance, expectancy theory predicts motivation will decrease.

Performance-Outcome Expectancies (P-O). The second factor affecting motivation is the expectancy that a certain outcome, usually a reward, will result from a given level of performance. Continuing our above examples, a salesperson might expect that he will receive a 10 percent bonus or membership in an exclusive health club if sales increase by 15 percent. The manager may expect that as a result of being appraised as highly competent she will get a promotion and other added benefits. The factory worker might expect that attaining high productivity ratings will result in a pay raise or an opportunity to become a foreman.

As with the effort-performance expectancies, if the individual does not perceive a strong relationship between performance and desired outcome—in this case rewards—motivation to perform will decrease. Thus, even if the salesperson believes that making 10 more calls a day will increase sales 15 percent, he may not be motivated to make the calls if he believes that there is little likelihood of actually being rewarded for this performance. Similarly, if the person expects that performance will be rewarded, but does not expect that she can attain the required level of performance with reasonable effort, motivation will also decrease. This could occur because the individual has a poor self-concept, has not been adequately trained or groomed for the job, or because he or she does not have enough authority to accomplish the task.

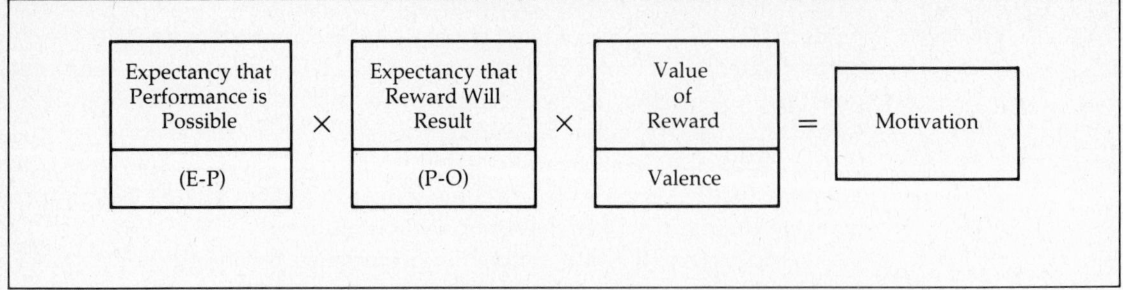

Figure 10-4 Vroom's Motivational Model

Valence of Outcome. The third factor affecting motivation in the expectancy model is the valence or value of the outcome or reward. *Valence* is the anticipated relative satisfaction or dissatisfaction that will result from a certain outcome. Because different individuals have different needs and preferences for rewards, the rewards being offered in exchange for performance may not be valued. Continuing our above examples, the individuals may be offered a pay increase for performance when what they really desire is a promotion, or more challenging work, or more recognition. If valence is low, the reward has little perceived value, expectancy theory predicts that motivation to perform will decrease.

It is not uncommon for management to offer rewards before assessing whether they are valued by employees. An interesting example of this occurred at an insurance company known to one of the authors. To motivate the salesmen, management offered a two-week trip to Hawaii for the salesman and his wife for making quota. Management was perplexed when some of the better salesmen sold less after the program was announced. The prospect of having to spend two weeks away with their wives, it turned out, was not considered a reward by all of the salesmen.

Relationship of Expectancies. As pointed out above, if *any* of the three links critical to motivation are low, motivation and subsequent performance will be low. This relationship can be expressed by the formula:

$$\text{Motivation} = \text{E-P} \times \text{P-O} \times \text{Valence}$$

This equation is illustrated in Figure 10-4.

Relevance in Management. Expectancy theory offers several suggestions to managers who wish to increase the motivation of the work force:

1. Because different people have different needs and therefore place a different value on a given reward, management should try to match offered rewards to the needs of the worker.

2. To motivate effectively, management must establish a firm relationship between performance and reward. Therefore, management should give rewards only for effective performance and withhold them for ineffective performance.
3. Managers should develop high, but realistic, expectations for their subordinates' performance and help subordinates perceive that they are capable of attaining this level of performance by exerting effort. How employees perceive themselves is affected by their manager's expectations about their behavior.

Discussing this, management writer and consultant Sterling Livingston states,

> The way managers treat their subordinates is subtly influenced by what they expect of them. If a manager's expectations are high, productivity is likely to be excellent. If his expectations are low, productivity is likely to be poor. It is as though there were a law that caused a subordinate's performance to rise or fall to meet his manager's expectations.
>
> The powerful influence of one person's expectations on another's behavior has long been recognized by physicians and behavioral scientists and, more recently, by teachers. But heretofore the importance of managerial expectations for the individual and group performance has not been widely understood."[20]

In addition, in order for an individual to expect that he or she can attain the level of performance required to obtain a valued reward, he or she must be delegated sufficient authority to accomplish the task and be provided with proper training so that his or her ability level is adequate.

Research generally supports expectancy theory.[21] However, some critics have called for expectancy theory research that takes individual and organizational contingencies into account.[22] Others feel that there is a need to clarify and refine technical, conceptual, and methodological issues.[23]

Equity Theory

Another explanation of how individuals channel and maintain their efforts toward goals is provided by equity theory.[24] **Equity theory** states that individuals subjectively determine the ratio of reward received to effort expended and compare this ratio to that of other people doing similar work. If the comparison indicates imbalance (inequity), the other person is perceived as obtaining greater reward for equivalent effort and the individual experiences psychological tension. As a result, the individual will be motivated to reduce the tension and restore a state of balance (equity).

Individuals can restore balance and a feeling of equity by either changing their effort level or trying to change the reward received. Thus, individuals who perceive themselves as underpaid in comparison to others may either reduce their effort or seek increased rewards. Similarly, people who perceive themselves as overpaid may tend to increase their effort. Research indicates that when people believe they are under-rewarded they generally

FEATURE 10-3

Motivating Young Workers

Young workers respond well to motivational programs, more companies find.

Six Flags, which operates amusement parks, bases its program on the view that teen-agers "do want rewards for a job well done and care about their work," says a company spokesman. The company sponsors sports activities and has frequent discussion sessions. Walt Disney World in Florida polls its young workers to find out what they want. "Usually it's more money," says a Disney official.

But the polls also show young workers want to know what's expected of them. Universal Studios, responding to that concern, puts out a newsletter designed specifically for its young tour guides. Los Angeles-based All-American Burger Inc. likes to encourage competition between night and day staffs, with winners getting cash bonuses.

SOURCE: *Wall Street Journal*, January 15, 1980, p. 1. Reprinted by permission of *The Wall Street Journal*,

decrease their effort. When they believe they are over-rewarded, they generally increase effort.[25]

Relevance in Management. Equity theory's implication for management is that unless people perceive their rewards as equitable they are likely to put forth less effort. However, perception of equitability is relative, not absolute. The individual compares himself to others in the organization or people doing similar work for other organizations. Since people may behave in unproductive ways if they perceive their rewards as unfair because people doing similar work receive greater rewards, employees should be made to understand why the difference exists. It should be made clear, for example, that the higher earning co-worker is paid more because his greater experience enables him to produce more. If the difference in reward is due to greater effectiveness, individuals receiving lesser rewards should be made to understand that when their performance reaches the level of the other person they will receive similar rewards.

Some organizations attempt to circumvent the problem of perceived inequity by maintaining a policy of keeping all salaries confidential. Unfortunately, this is not only very difficult to enforce, but may actually cause people to suspect inequities when they do not in fact exist. Also, by keeping the earnings of superiors secret, the organization may lose the positive moti-

FEATURE 10-4

Forms of Inequity Perceived by Workers

Results of a *Psychology Today* survey indicate that many minority, female, and handicapped people perceive that they are being unfairly treated on the job. This, according to equity theory, has serious implications for managers who need to motivate these people, who together comprise well over 60 percent of the national work force.

About 43 percent of the survey felt they had been victims of job discrimination within the past five years. The following is a breakdown of the reasons for discrimination and the forms that it took:

	Reasons for Discrimination				
Form of Discrimination	Sex	Race	Ethnic Origin or Religion	Age	Physical Handicap
Affirmative action guidelines led to my not being hired although I had sufficient qualifications.	18.0%	32.7%	24.1%	16.7%	31.0%
My salary was lower than for other workers doing comparable work.	48.5%	15.5%	17.2%	28.1%	17.2%
I was expected to do more work, different work, or less prestigious work than other workers who had similar jobs.	28.0%	21.8%	27.6%	25.1%	17.2%
I could not get the job for which my skills qualified me.	37.2%	34.5%	31.0%	44.8%	37.9%
I was not accepted or invited to participate in informal social activities like lunch or a drink after work.	12.8%	7.3%	19.0%	7.4%	6.9%
I was not encouraged or allowed to participate in in-house training programs.	16.2%	15.5%	12.1%	9.4%	6.9%
I did not have access to informal communication or sources of information relevant to my job.	25.3%	29.1%	43.1%	24.6%	34.5%

NOTE: Because respondents checked as many of the forms of discrimination as applied to them, all categories add up to more than 100%.

SOURCE: *Psychology Today*, May 1978, p. 65.

FEATURE 10-5

Motivation in a Nationalized Industry

Nationalized industries in prosperous nations have particular difficulty in motivating their workers to increase productivity. François Legrand, head of the state-owned *Société Nationale Industrielle Aerospatiele* (SNIAS), builder of the Concorde jet, is always seeking new ways to motivate his work force. Here is how he describes the problem, and an experimental solution used in the firm's helicopter division:

"In France now, workers get four weeks vacation in summer, plus another week off in the winter to go skiing. Most of them have reached a standard of living where they aren't really interested in making any more money." So much for "cheap" labor.

How do you motivate workers who aren't interested in more money? Legrand's solution: Try psychic rewards.

Borrowing from Volvo's Kalmar experimental factory in Sweden, Legrand recently introduced the concept of autonomous team assembly. A group of workers assembles a complete AStar from the ground up. There are no foremen, and workers can go to the canteen whenever they like. Legrand gives each team a production quota; filling the quota ahead of schedule means a team's members can repair to their favorite bistro, go skiing or to the beach.

To introduce competition among teams, Legrand uses the Japanese technique of posting teams' productivity rates in the hangars, all plotted against each other. It's still experimental, but there are signs it is working: SNIAS helicopters' 7,800 workers account for 21% of SNIAS' work force, but 26% of its revenues and probably a great deal more of its profits.

SOURCE: Lawrence Minard, "Vive l'helicoptere!" *Forbes*, April 16, 1979, p. 75. Reprinted by permission.

vational influence of the prospect of increased earnings through promotion, as indicated by expectancy theory.

The Porter-Lawler Model

Lyman Porter and Edward Lawler have developed a very comprehensive process theory of motivation that incorporates elements of both expectancy and equity theories.[26] Their model, shown in Figure 10-5, includes five variables: effort, perceptions, performance, rewards, and satisfaction. According

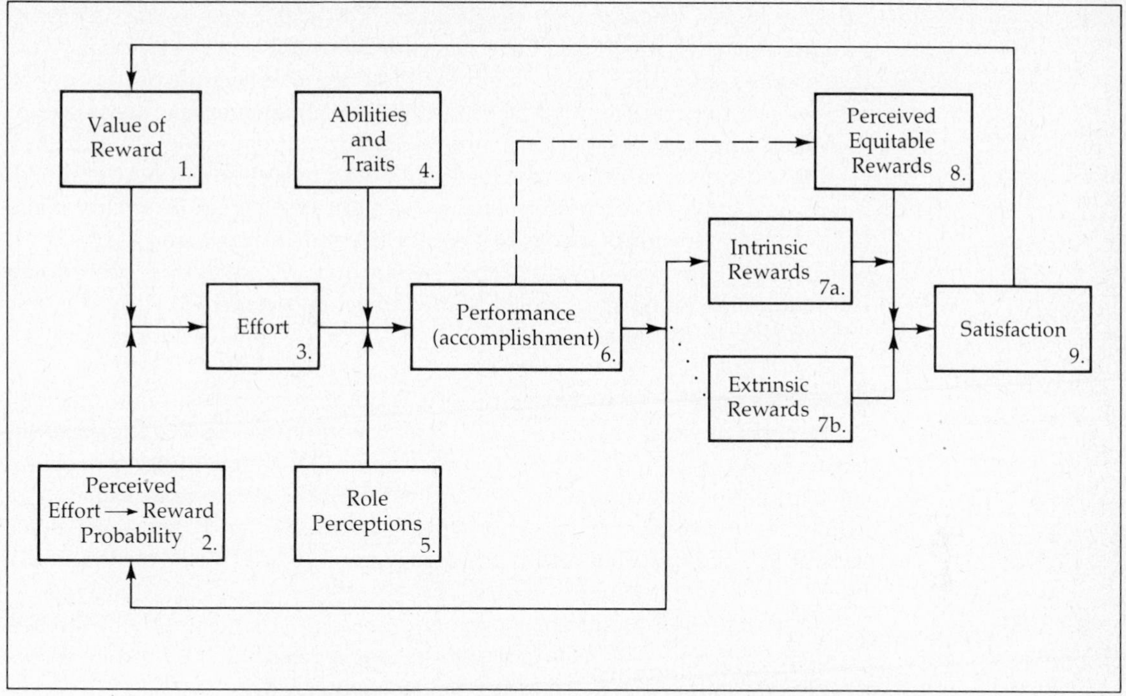

Figure 10-5 The Porter-and-Lawler Motivation Model

SOURCE: Lyman W. Porter and Edward E. Lawler, III, *Managerial Attitudes and Performance* (Homewood, IL: Richard D. Irwin, Inc., 1968), p. 165. Used with permission.

to Porter and Lawler, performance is dependent on an individual's effort, abilities, traits, and the person's perception of his or her role. Effort varies with the perceived value of the reward and the expectation that a certain level of effort will in fact result in a certain reward. Moreover, the theory establishes a relationship between rewards and performance. Namely, an individual satisfies needs through rewards received because of performance.

Let us go through the model step by step to better understand Porter and Lawler's explanation of motivation. The numbers in parentheses are from Figure 10-5, to which you should refer. According to the model, an individual's performance (6) is dependent on three variables: abilities and traits (4); role perceptions—how clearly the individual perceives and understands his or her role (5); and effort (3). Effort, in turn, is dependent on an individual's expectancy of the connection between effort and potential rewards (2) and the value of the reward to the individual. Attainment of the desired level of performance (6) may result in intrinsic rewards (7a) such as feelings of accomplishment, competence, and self-esteem, and extrinsic rewards (7b) such as praise from the subordinate's manager or work group, bonuses, and promotion.

The dotted line between performance and extrinsic rewards is used to indicate that there may not be a connection between one's performance and the rewards attained. This is because they are a reflection of the opportunities for rewards provided by the individual's manager and organization. A dashed line between performance and perceived equitable rewards (8) is used to indicate that individuals have their own perception of how equitable the reward attained for performance is, as indicated by equity theory. Satisfaction (9) is a result of perceived equity (8) and intrinsic and extrinsic rewards (7a,b) for performance. This satisfaction (9) gives the subordinate information about how valuable the reward actually is, which will affect perception of it in future situations.

Relevance in Management. One of the most important points made by Porter and Lawler is that *performance leads to satisfaction.* This is the exact opposite of the view held by many managers. Managers influenced by the early human relations theorists tend to believe that satisfaction leads to performance. In other words, happier workers work harder. Porter and Lawler, in contrast, contend that a sense of achievement leads to satisfaction and is likely to also increase performance.

Research tends to support Porter and Lawler's conclusion that high performance is a cause of high satisfaction, not a result of it. In other words, people feel satisfied because of high performance.[27] In sum, the Porter-Lawler model makes a major contribution to our understanding of motivation. It demonstrates that motivation is not a simple matter of cause and effect. It also shows how important it is to integrate effort, abilities, performance, rewards, satisfactions, and perceptions into a consistent system.

SUMMARY

Motivating, the process of moving oneself and others to work toward organizational objectives, is essential if managers are to implement decisions and convert plans into actual work.

Until the 1940s, most motivational practices were based on incorrect assumptions, such as Adam Smith's economic man. Yet, these techniques were effective then and sometimes are now because of the prevailing economic and social situation.

Modern theories of motivation are based on psychological research, which management became familiar with through the work of Elton Mayo who helped launch the behavioral school of management.

Content theories of motivation, such as those of Maslow, McClelland, and Herzberg, focus on identifying needs, which are perceived deficiencies that induce a drive to act. Human needs can be generally classified as primary or secondary. Primary needs are genetically determined. Secondary needs are usually learned.

Needs may be satisfied through rewards, which are anything perceived as valuable by the individual in question. Management deals with both extrinsic rewards, such as pay and promotion, and intrinsic rewards, such as a feeling of achievement, that are obtained through work itself.

According to Abraham Maslow, people have five basic needs—physiological, safety, social, achievement, and self-actualization—arranged in a prepotent hierarchy. A person is not motivated by the higher-level need until the one below is at least partially satisfied. However, the hierarchy is not absolutely rigid.

McClelland, believing Maslow's classification incomplete, described people in terms of needs for power, achievement, and affiliation.

Herzberg concluded that factors at work affecting need satisfaction, and therefore motivation, could be classified as either hygiene factors or motivators. The hygiene factors, which include pay, working conditions, interpersonal relations, and quality of supervision only prevent dissatisfaction. To actually motivate, management must provide motivators such as achievement, advancement, recognition, responsibility, and growth opportunities.

Process theories of motivation also hold that needs motivate, but primarily view motivation from the perspective of what channels behavior, taking into account factors such as perceptions, expectations, and learned behavior.

Expectancy theory holds that for an individual to be motivated to channel behavior toward a certain goal he or she must expect this behavior has a high probability of leading to need satisfaction or attainment of the goal. Motivation is a function of effort-performance expectancies, performance-outcome expectancies, and valence. The highest degree of motivation will occur when the individual believes that effort will definitely result in attainment of objectives, which will definitely result in a reward that is highly valued. If probability of attainment or receiving a reward is low, or the reward is perceived as having little value, motivation will decrease.

Equity theory holds that individuals subjectively determine the ratio of reward to effort and compare this to what they perceive that others receive for similar effort. A comparison indicating inequity results in psychological tension. Generally, if the person feels under-rewarded, effort will decrease. If the individual feels over-rewarded, he or she will put forth more effort.

The Porter-Lawler model, which includes research-proven aspects of previous theories, is one of the most comprehensive, well-accepted motivational theories yet developed. Porter and Lawler hold that motivation is a function of needs, expectancies, and perceived equity. Performance is dependent on effort, abilities, traits, and the individual's perception of his role. Effort varies with the perceived value of the reward and the expectancy it will be attained. According to Porter and Lawler, whose view is supported by research, performance leads to satisfaction, rather than vice versa, as human relations school theorists tended to believe.

REVIEW QUESTIONS

1. Distinguish between motivation and manipulation.
2. What is the major difference between content theories of motivation and process theories of motivation?
3. Explain the simplified model of needs motivating behavior.
4. What is the difference between intrinsic and extrinsic rewards?

5. In motivation, what role does the word reward play?
6. Discuss the three factors of expectancy theory with respect to work motivation: (a) effort-performance, (b) performance-outcome, (c) balance of outcome.
7. What is the relevance of expectancy theory to management?
8. What are the implications of equity theory for management?
9. Porter and Lawler state that "performance leads to satisfaction." What are the ramifications of this statement to management?
10. McClelland describes people in terms of three needs: power, achievement, and affiliation. What role do these needs play in McClelland's model of motivation?

DISCUSSION QUESTIONS

11. Since needs induce a drive to attain a goal, why does it follow that management should attempt to create situations that permit people to perceive that they can satisfy needs through behaviors conducive to attainment of the organization's goals?
12. How has motivation played a role in the development of management thought?
13. Compare and contrast Maslow's model of motivation with Herzberg's and McClelland's.
14. Describe a contemporary situation in which carrot-and-stick motivation might work effectively.
15. Select a motivational situation from your experience and show, step by step, how the Porter-Lawler model can be applied to it.

CASE INCIDENT 1

The Gift Wrap Department

An attractive wrap can transform even an ordinary gift into something truly exceptional. Stan Maxwell believed this and as manager of Edson's gift wrap department, he constantly strived to impress his staff with the idea that in many instances it was their handiwork which transformed the ordinary into the exceptional. To Maxwell, the gift wrap department was a very important part of Edson's image as a top of the line retailer.

Depending upon the time of the year, the gift wrap department would employ from 30 to 100 employees. Stan Maxwell had developed a training program for all new employees. The two-week training course duplicated real life situations and combined what Maxwell called gift wrap psychology with practical work. At the successful completion of this two-week program, certificates were presented to each graduate. Maxwell often boasted that his graduates could work anywhere. As a matter of fact, they could, and a Maxwell trained wrapper was welcomed by virtually any retailer in the city.

Stan Maxwell was especially proud of his close relationships with his staff. As a matter of fact, he considered them family. In building this sort of climate, Maxwell placed special emphasis on the recruitment and selection process and believed the right person, carefully trained, and supervised by someone who cares are the primary ingredients of an efficient gift wrap operation.

Last week, Barry Martin, an experienced wrapper and informal leader of the extremely busy downtown gift wrap location, told Maxwell that he needed a raise "right away." Martin indicated that the last 7 percent increase didn't even keep up with inflation. Maxwell said that absolutely nothing could be done on a "this minute" basis, but an overtime situation was developing this weekend and that if Martin worked Saturday and Sunday at premium pay, he would be making almost as much as he could make working five days at straight pay.

Barry Martin told Maxwell that he had better ways to spend his weekends.

Questions

1. If you were Stan Maxwell, how would you respond to Barry Martin?
2. As a manager, how do you determine what makes people tick?
3. Do you think Barry Martin might be expressing the feelings of other employees in the gift wrap department? Explain your answer.

CASE INCIDENT 2

Motivation in a Service Business Organization

Crawford & Company of Atlanta, Georgia, is the second largest, but the most profitable, firm in the field of insurance claims adjustment. The company services—for a fee—claims the large insurance companies are unable or unwilling to handle themselves. The majority of firms in this field are small mom-and-pop type operations. Here is what T. Gordy Germany, the chief executive officer, says about motivation.

Crawford adjusters are well educated (Crawford still hires only college graduates, though that may change), . . . mainly because they work harder. They work harder not because they're paid more (today a Crawford adjuster starts at $11,000 if he's lucky) but because their chances for one day making big money are much better than those of an insurance company adjuster.

"You'll work your tail off for the first five or ten years if you think you'll make a big chunk of change down the road," says Germany. "We've got 625 branch managers. Half receive 40% of their branches' profits. This year a substantial percentage of our managers will make over $50,000 and nearly 15% of those will make over $100,000. This is a good carrot."

But it is not an easy carrot to reach. Perhaps 90% of Crawford's adjusters quit within six months. "A lot of people can't say 'No' to little old ladies," Germany explains. "You're dealing with people who are mad. When my man goes to see the parents of some kid you ran over, they're not going to invite him in to have coffee. You're walking into a hornet's nest on almost everything you do.

"My son thinks I'm a slave driver," he goes on, "and I am. You've got to have a certain amount of that in you to make money today. Look: We buy a few cars and some desks. So if you've got four, five or ten people working and you can get them to produce two or three times their salary you're going to make money like a burglar." And he does.

SOURCE: *Forbes*, April 2, 1979, p. 65.

Questions

1. What motivational approach does Mr. Germany use?
2. Why do you feel Crawford has been so successful in its field?
3. Do you believe Mr. Germany has a good understanding of what motivates people? Why?
4. What would you recommend Mr. Germany do to increase the motivation of his adjusters and reduce the high turnover? Is it desirable to reduce turnover in Crawford & Company's situation?

NOTES

1. Elton Mayo, *The Human Problems of an Industrial Civilization* (Boston: Graduate School of Business Administration, Harvard, 1946).
2. Edgar Shein, *Organizational Psychology*, 2d. ed. (Englewood Cliffs, NJ: Prentice-Hall, 1970).
3. Paul Lawrence and Jay Lorsch, *Developing Organizations: Diagnosis and Action* (Reading, MA: Addison-Wesley, 1969), pp. 68–69.
4. Stephen J. Carroll and Henri L. Tosi, *Organizational Behavior* (Chicago: St. Claire Press, 1977), p. 80.
5. Abraham Maslow, "A Theory of Human Motivation," *Psychological Review*, no. 50 (1943), pp. 370–396.
6. H. A. Murray, *Explorations in Personality* (New York: Oxford University Press, 1968).
7. Calvin S. Hall and Gardner Lindsey, *Theories of Personality* (New York: John Wiley, 1957), p. 326.
8. Maslow, op. cit.
9. Terrence Mitchell, *People in Organizations* (New York: McGraw-Hill, 1978), p. 157.
10. M. A. Wahba and L. G. Bridgewell, "Maslow Reconsidered: A Review of Research on the Need Hierarchy Theory," *Organizational Behavior and Human Performance*, vol. 15 (1976), pp. 212–240.
11. Edward Lawler, *Motivation in Work Organizations* (Monterey, CA: Brooks/Cole, 1973).
12. Mitchell, op. cit.
13. David C. McClelland, "The Two Faces of Power," *Journal of International Affairs*, vol. 24 (1970), pp. 30–41.
14. Ibid, p. 30.
15. F. Herzberg, B. Mauser, and B. B. Snyderman, *The Motivation to Work* (New York: John Wiley, 1959).

16. Frederick Herzberg, "One More Time: How Do You Motivate Employees?" *Harvard Business Review*, January–February 1968, pp. 56–57.
17. Robert House and L. A. Wigdor, "Herzberg's Dual Factor Theory of Job Satisfaction and Motivation: A Review of the Evidence and a Criticism," *Personnel Psychology*, vol. 20 (1967), pp. 369–389.
18. Don Hellriegal and John W. Slocum, *Management: Contingency Approaches*, 2d. ed. (Reading, MA: Addison-Wesley, 1978), p. 346.
19. Victor H. Vroom, *Work and Motivation* (New York: Wiley, 1964); Lyman W. Porter and Edward E. Lawler, *Managerial Attitudes and Performance* (Homewood, IL: Richard D. Irwin, 1968).
20. J. S. Livingston, "Myth of the Well-Educated Manager," *Harvard Business Review*, vol. 49 (January–February 1971), pp. 79–89.
21. Terrence R. Mitchell, "Expectancy Models of Job Satisfaction, Occupational Preference and Effort: A Theoretical, Methodological, and Empirical Appraisal," *Psychological Bulletin*, vol. 81 (1974), pp. 1053–1077; Robert J. House, H. Jack Shapiro, and Mahmoud A. Wahba, "Expectancy Theory as a Predictor of Work Behavior and Attitudes: A Reevaluation of Empirical Evidence," *Decision Sciences*, vol. 5 (July), 1974, pp. 481–506.
22. Leon Reinharth and Mahmoud Wahba, "Expectancy Theory as a Predictor of Work Motivation, Effort Expenditure, and Job Performance," *Academy of Management Journal*, vol. 18 (1975), pp. 520–573; Henry T. Sims, Jr., Andrew D. Szilagyi, and Dale R. KcKemey, "Antecedents of Work Related Expectancies," *Academy of Management Journal*, vol. 19 (1976), pp. 547–559.
23. Terry Connolly, "Some Conceptual and Methodological Issues in Expectancy Models of Work Performance Motivation," *Academy of Management Review*, vol. 1 (1976), pp. 37–47.
24. David G. Kuhn, John W. Slocum, and Richard D. Chase, "Does Job Performance Affect Employee Satisfaction?" *Personnel Journal*, June 1971, pp. 455–459, 485; Jay R. Schuster, Barbara Clark, and Miles Rogers, "Testing Portions of the Porter-Lawler Model Regarding the Motivation of Pay," *Journal of Applied Psychology*, June 1971, 187–195; J. Stacey Adams, "Inequity in Social Exchange," in L. Berkowitz, ed., *Advances in Experimental Social Psychology*, 2d. ed. (New York: Academic Press, 1965), pp. 267–300.
25. Paul S. Goodman and Abraham Friedman, "An Examination of Adams's Theory of Inequity," *Administrative Sciences Quarterly*, vol. 16 (1971), pp. 271–288; Michael R. Carrell and John E. Dittrich, "Equity Theory: The Recent Literature, Methodological Considerations, and New Directions," *Academy of Management Review*, vol. 3 (April 1978), pp. 202–210.
26. Porter and Lawler, op. cit.
27. D. O. Jorgenson, M. D. Bennett, and R. D. Pritchard, "Effects of the Manipulation of a Performance-Reward Contingency on Behavior in a Simulated Work Setting," *Journal of Applied Psychology*, vol. 57 (1973), pp. 271–280.

CHAPTER 11

Controlling

In earlier chapters we frequently mentioned the uncertainties of managing and the need to consider management an unending process. Plans do not always work out as intended. People do not always accept delegation, nor can management always motivate them to work toward objectives. The environment is continuously changing, and the organization must adapt accordingly. You may therefore have begun to wonder how management determines whether it is, in fact, attaining its objectives, how it detects its own and its workers' mistakes, and how it determines when the organization needs to adapt. The answer is through the process of controlling. Controlling, in simple terms, is the process by which management determines whether its decisions are correct or need to be modified.

After reading this chapter, you should understand the following important terms and concepts:

- control process
- preliminary control
- concurrent control
- postaction control
- feedback
- standards
- performance indicator
- range of deviation
- exception principle
- control-oriented behavior
- management by objectives (MBO)

The Nature and Purpose of Controlling

Control, like power, is a word that evokes negative reactions. To many people control connotes restraint—the leash on a dog, coercion, confinement—images contrary to our ideal of individual liberty. Because of this preconception, controlling is one of the most misunderstood management functions. If asked to guess what control means to a manager, people often respond with something like keeping workers in line. This is correct in a sense. One aspect of control is indeed ensuring conformity of a sort. However, to think of controlling as simply restraining negative behavior and making everyone toe the line is to miss its primary purpose in management.

As a management function:

Controlling is the process of ensuring that the organization is attaining its objectives.

Controlling involves setting standards, measuring actual performance, and taking corrective action when performance deviates significantly from standards.

Why Control Is Necessary

Managers begin performing the control function the very moment they formulate objectives and establish an organization. An organization is a purposeful structure, and structure and purpose imply control. Objectives and plans establish boundaries for the organization and the work of its members. The organizing process refines and elaborates these limits by defining relationships between people, what each person's tasks are, and what authority each person is delegated.

These limits are essential, if the organization is to succeed. Without them chaos would reign, making group effort of any complexity virtually impossible to unify. Even more important, goals, plans, and structure give the organization direction by channeling and guiding work. Thus, control is an inherent outgrowth of organization. This is a major reason why Peter Drucker states, "The synonym for control is direction."[1]

Uncertainty. Although planning and organizing introduce an element of control, they do not meet the need for a specific managerial process of controlling. Because they deal with the future, plans are inevitably *uncertain.* The development of feasible plans and a sound structure in no way guarantees that the organization will attain its objectives and succeed. Plans and organizational designs are only a picture of what management would *like* the future to hold. Many things could prevent this "picture" from "developing" properly.

Changes in laws, social values, technology, competition, and other environmental variables could make plans that were feasible when formulated unobtainable at a later point in time. Henry Ford, for example, probably would have liked to sell only black Model T cars for as long as there was iron in the earth. But when Alfred P. Sloan took over General Motors and implemented new strategies, such as offering buyers a wide selection of auto designs, Ford's strategy no longer worked effectively. The environment of most contemporary organizations changes at a higher rate than that of Ford and GM during the first quarter of the century. Think of the impact pollution and safety regulations, competition from Europe and Japan, and the energy shortage have had on American auto manufacturers during the last ten years in relation to the changes they faced in earlier decades. In order to anticipate and react to change, organizations need an effective mechanism that can assess its impact on the organization.

In addition, even the best organizational design has some negative consequences. Specialized division of labor, for example, introduces problems of coordination, the potential for friction between work groups, and may lead to the design of jobs that people find dull and unmotivating. Consequently, a design that looks good on paper or proved successful in another time or place, may not accomplish as much as management hopes.

Adding to the inherent uncertainty of managing is that much of the organization's work is done by *people.* Unlike computers, people cannot be programmed to perform tasks with absolute precision. Despite the many recent advances in understanding behavior at work, managers are still a long, long way from being able to consistently predict accurately how people will respond to instructions, authority, and leadership. If management misjudges what motivates their people, they may choose to refuse delegation or even actively work against attaining the organization's objectives. For example, despite high pay in some auto assembly plants sabotage problems apparently result from boredom. Or, a breakdown in communication, often difficult to avoid in today's world of complex information and large organizations, might cause people to misunderstand what they are supposed to do. Personal problems, such as heavy traffic that morning, or a thousand other trivial reasons, could cause a usually reliable worker to have an exceptionally bad day. Finally, even the most willing person operating under the best possible conditions occasionally makes mistakes.

Compounding of Errors. Mistakes, problems in the internal variables, and misjudgment in predicting the future or people tend to compound in effect if not quickly corrected. By analogy, if you make an error when computing the balance in your checking account, you might later make the more serious mistake of bouncing a check, which could injure your relationship with a friend or business and damage your credit rating. The potential for such compounding of error is high for an organization because of the high degree of interdependency.

An especially vivid business example of this phenomenon of errors compounding is General Dynamics's experience with the Convair 880 commercial jet. Plans for the new plane were initially drawn up while General Dynamics was headed by its founder, Jay Hopkins. A brilliant leader and in many respects an excellent manager, Hopkins built the huge, decentralized defense firm and ran it by sheer force of personality. However, he failed to institute the sort of formal management information and control system usually needed by a giant firm competing in a volatile, high-technology industry. Hopkins instead depended on his own exceptional energy and the personal loyalty of division managers to keep tabs on his corporation's many activities. This worked rather well at General Dynamics until one of those unforeseeable strokes of fortune, cancer, took Hopkins's life in 1957.

Naturally, work on the Convair 880 did not halt with Jay Hopkins's death. Managers of that division, as might be expected, went ahead with the project. The first of their many risky decisions was to base cost estimates for the new plane on the premise of strong sales to Delta, United, and American Airlines, even though the only solid order was from Howard Hughes's TWA, which soon developed troubles of its own. As development progressed, it became apparent that these sales estimates were too high and projected costs were too low. Convair managers also found that major modifications would be needed to make the new plane's engine and airframe operational.

Thus, on several occasions managers of the division decided that it would be necessary to increase investment in the 880 project in order to not lose everything that had already been spent. In essence, Convair was gambling for double or nothing with hundreds of millions of dollars belonging to General Dynamics's stockholders.

Taking risks, of course, is unavoidable in business. However, in the case of Convair, the risks were not only enormous and based on fallacious premises, but also taken without the full knowledge of corporate top management. Due to the lack of an effective control system, Frank Pace, who replaced Hopkins as Chief Executive Officer (CEO), did not really know what was taking place in the Convair division. When information reached him, it usually was too late to do anything. General Dynamics top management often found itself in the awkward position of having to approve expenditures after they had already been made.

The last straw was the Convair division's decision to develop the 890, a significantly different aircraft, as a modification of the failing 880—without permission from the board of directors. The resulting expenses clearly informed top management that it had lost control of the company. Eventually new, more effective information and control systems were instituted. But they came too late to prevent General Dynamics from earning the dubious distinction of taking in 1961 what was then the biggest loss in corporate history: nearly half a billion dollars.[2]

The later debacles of Lockheed Corporation, which had to be assisted by the federal government, and W. T. Grant, whose bankruptcy will be discussed later, also have been attributed largely to poor controls. Less widely publicized are the countless failures of small firms headed by entrepreneurs who failed to understand the importance of controlling and allowed errors to compound to the point of bankruptcy or severe financial loss.

Prevent Crises. Even more common than going past the point of no return is the case where the organization survives, but perpetually moves from crisis to crisis. A striking number of experienced managers feel that this state of affairs is unavoidable in *their* business. Other firms, they feel, have an easier go of things while theirs is a hectic, fast-paced business, and there is no way to avoid continuously veering away from the brink just in the nick of time. Nothing could be further from the truth. While an occasional situation could become extreme too quickly to detect in time for the organization to plan how to cope with it, in most cases there is no need for crisis-to-crisis management.

The control function is the dimension of management that meets the need to identify problems and correct them *before* they reach crisis dimensions. As the *I Ching,* the Chinese *Book of Changes,* so wisely stated some 3000 years before anyone thought of a discipline of management:

> The superior man, when he sees what
> is good, moves toward it;
> and when he sees his errors, he
> turns from them.

One of the major reasons why controlling is imperative is to enable the organization to detect its errors and turn from them before they impair attaining objectives.

Encourage Success. Equally important is the need "to move toward what is good" (to paraphrase the *I Ching*), which is the positive side of the control process. By comparing actual performance to plans—answering the question, "How far have we come?"—management identifies the successes of the organization as well as its failures. In other words, an important use of controlling is to uncover which of the organization's activities contribute most effectively to attainment of overall objectives. This is how a small organization determines how to expand or contract and large conglomerates like Gulf and Western determine which of their affiliated companies should get greater resources and which should be sold or discontinued. By identifying its errors and successes management is able to adapt the organization to the demands of a dynamic environment quickly enough to make the greatest possible progress toward its broad objectives.

Pervasiveness of Controlling. As you should have gathered from the many important uses of control, it is a critical and complex function of management. One of the most important things you should realize about control is its pervasiveness. Control is *not* restricted to the province of the manager designated the "controller" and his or her assistants. *Every* manager, regard-

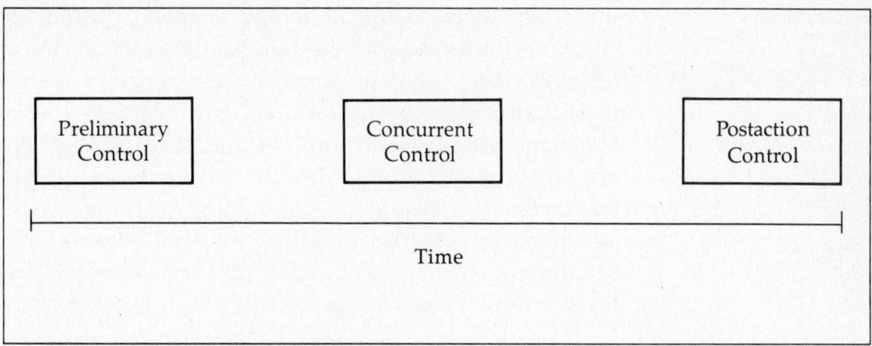

Figure 11-1 Time of Application for Primary Types of Control

less of level, must make control an integral part of his or her job, even if not specifically told to do so.

Controlling is a fundamental, interdependent aspect of the management process. Planning, organizing, and motivating cannot be wholly separated from controlling. In fact, they are an integral part of the organization's overall control system. This will become clearer as we discuss the three primary forms of control—preliminary, concurrent, and postaction. All of these primary forms of control are similar since the aim of each is to help ensure that actual results will be as close to desired results as possible. They differ in the time of application.

Preliminary Control

The control process resembles an iceberg in that a large part of it is not in open view. Some of an organization's most important controls are hidden within other functions of management. Planning and organizing, for example, although seldom recognized as control mechanisms, allow preliminary control over an organization's activities. (It is called preliminary because it takes place before actual work begins.)

The main means of preliminary control is carrying out—as opposed to creating—policies, procedures, and rules. Because policies and rules are created to support plans, which are devices to increase the probability of meeting objectives, enforcing them is a way of making certain that work will progress toward desired objectives. Similarly, writing clear job descriptions, effectively communicating objectives to subordinates, and staffing with qualified people are ways to increase the probability that the organizational structure will operate as planned. Organizations use preliminary control in three main areas: human resources, material resources, and financial resources.

Human Resources. As mentioned earlier, organizations exercise preliminary control over human resources by carefully identifying the skills needed to perform a job and by selecting people who appear best qualified to do these jobs. Establishing a minimum level of education or experience and checking the applicant's credentials help ensure that workers will be capable of performing their delegated duties. Setting compensation at an equitable level and administering psychological tests or conducting extensive prehiring interviews also can improve the probability of having competent workers. Most organizations continue to exercise preliminary control over human resources after hiring by conducting training. Training enables managers and workers to learn the skills they need before they actually begin work or to improve their current skills. This increases the probability that they will be able to perform as expected.

Materials. It clearly is impossible to make products of high quality from inferior raw materials. It also does little good to catch faulty materials after they have been used. Production firms therefore routinely exercise preliminary control over their material resources. They do so by establishing engineering standards for minimal quality and physically checking the material to make sure it conforms to these requirements. One means of preliminary control is selecting a supplier who has proved dependable when it comes to meeting specifications. Also related to preliminary control of material resources is maintaining inventories of raw material at a level that will prevent shortages, as will be discussed later.

Financial Resources. The principal tool for preliminary control of financial resources is the budget, which also serves a planning function. Budgets operate as a preliminary control mechanism by ensuring that cash will be available when it is needed by the organization. They also set parameters on spending that help prevent a department or the organization as a whole from exceeding the limits of its cash resources.

Concurrent Control

As its name implies, **concurrent control** operates while work is in progress. It most often is exercised over the work of subordinates and traditionally is the responsibility of immediate superiors. Regular checking of a subordinate's work, coupled with a discussion of problem areas and suggestions for improvement, helps prevent deviations that would be seriously detrimental if allowed to continue.

Concurrent control of this type is not literally concurrent, in the sense of being simultaneous with the work. Rather, concurrent control is based on the measurement of actual results *after* some work has been performed toward desired objectives. To accomplish this, management requires feedback.

Feedback. **Feedback**, in the sense we use the term here, is data about results. A simple example of feedback is telling subordinates specifically why what they did was undesirable when you see them make mistakes. Feedback systems enable managers to identify and correct the many unforeseen prob-

Table 11-1 All Feedback Systems

1. Have objectives
2. Use external resources
3. Process external resources for internal use
4. Monitor significant divergences from objectives
5. Correct divergences to attain objectives

lems that can cause an organization to deviate from the most effective route to its objectives.

Feedback control systems are not, however, a managerial invention. They are among the most common of natural phenomena: all living organisms depend on feedback control for survival. The maintenance of your internal body temperature at 98.6 degrees F is accomplished by an automatic, extremely complex feedback control system. You also use feedback control whenever you pick up an object with your hands. Your eyes sense where the object is and pass that information to your brain, which sends the appropriate impulses to reach, grasp, and lift to your muscles. As your hand moves toward the object, your eyes sense whether it is on course, and your brain continuously sends impulses to correct deviations. If you disrupt the system by closing your eyes when the object is small or moving, there is a strong possibility that your hand will miss because of lack of control.

All feedback systems, biological or organizational, as Table 11-1 illustrates, contain the same fundamental elements and operate on the same principle.

The thermostat and furnace that regulate the temperature of a house illustrate the operation of a typical simple feedback control system. The objective of this system, in which you function as the goal setter, is to maintain room temperature at a given level. The thermostat's thermometer acts as a sensor that is capable of monitoring and measuring an external factor, air temperature. A switch mechanism in the thermostat processes sensed information (an air temperature above or below the goal) and converts it into a form that the system can use to *induce action*, an electrical impulse to turn the furnace on or off. As long as air temperature remains below the desired level or goal, the thermostat continues to tell the furnace to stay on. When the sensor has gathered information indicating air temperature is at the desired level, it sends an impulse that turns the furnace off. The process is repeated whenever the temperature drops below the goal. In this way the thermostat and furnace act as a control system to correct deviations in the room's temperature. The system ensures that your overall objective of comfort will be met as long as it is working properly.

Limitations of Feedback Systems. The thermostat-furnace mechanism just described has a number of limitations common to all feedback systems. The accuracy of the sensing device defines its effectiveness. If the thermometer does not measure correctly, room air temperature will be off to a corresponding degree. Similarly, the system cannot react more quickly than the thermometer, the switch, and the furnace's capacity to provide heat allow. Also, the thermostat was designed to operate within a broader system, the climatic environment. It works on the presumption that some climatic force will always cause room air temperature to drop below the desired standard. Should the broader environment change, as it does in the summer, the system will be unable to maintain temperature at the desired level because it is unable to lower room temperature. If you wish to cope with the contingency of summer, you will need a more sophisticated control system, one that can select either heating or cooling. (This, of course, will be more expensive, so you may not be able to afford the better control system.)

Organizational Feedback Systems. The feedback control systems used in management are in many ways similar to the thermostat mechanism. Both process inputs to attain desired outputs. The inputs of an organizational feedback system are all of its resources: materials, money, and people. The output is goods or services. But there is one very major difference. A thermostat and furnace are a *closed loop* control system: they operate continuously and automatically without outside intervention. Most organizational feedback controls are *open loop* systems. An external element, the manager, regularly intervenes to change both the objectives of the system and its operation. Open loop controls are a virtual necessity in management because so many different variables affect the organization.

Both external and internal factors can cause deviations to which the system must respond in order to attain goals. Included among the internal factors are problems associated with any of the variables described in Chapter 3. External factors are literally anything in the environment that affects the organization: competition, new laws, technological change, general economic disruption, changes in cultural values, and others discussed earlier. It is possible to view much of management as an effort to maintain the organization as an effective feedback system that sustains output at set levels despite interference from internal and external forces of deviation. However, good management, as we have learned, goes far beyond merely maintaining the status quo and reacting to problems. Unless the organization continuously strives to adapt and improve by adopting a proactive orientation, it probably will not remain effective in the long run.

Postaction Control

Concurrent control employs feedback while work is in progress so that problems can be corrected before they become too costly and the desired level of objectives can be attained. *Postaction control* employs feedback after the work is completed. After the action being controlled has been completed, or a predetermined amount of time has passed, actual results are compared to desired results.

Although postaction control is applied too late to correct problems as they develop, as management professor William Newman states, it has two important functions. One is that postaction controls provide management with planning data if similar work is to be undertaken in the future. By comparing actual results with desired results, management is better able to determine how realistic its plans were. It also obtains information about problems and can formulate new plans that can overcome them in the future. The second function of postaction control is as an aid to motivation. If management bases motivational rewards on a certain level of performance, actual performance clearly must be measured fairly and accurately. In the words of Newman, measuring performance and giving appropriate rewards are necessary "to build future expectations about the close relationship between actual results and rewards."[3]

In the following section, which describes the control process in detail, we will see that controlling not only facilitates the identification and correction of problems in meeting established goals but also helps management decide when change is necessary.

The Control Process

There are three distinct stages in the control process. These are: setting standards, comparing performance to standards, and taking necessary corrective action. Each stage involves several activities.

Setting Standards

The first phase of the control process, setting standards, highlights how closely intertwined the planning and control functions are. **Standards** are specific objectives against which progress can be measured. They are an outgrowth of the planning process: all control standards ought to be derived from the organization's multiple objectives and strategies. Two essential characteristics distinguish objectives that can be used as standards, namely, a *time limit* and a *specific criterion that can be measured and compared to accomplished work*. To earn a profit of $1 million in 1983, or to hold absenteeism below 3 percent by 1985 are examples of objectives that can serve as control standards.

Performance Indicators. The specific, measurable criterion of $1 million and the time limit of one year are performance indicators. A **performance indicator** defines exactly what must be achieved to attain an objective. This enables the manager to compare *actual* work to *planned* productivity. As a result, management is able to answer the crucial question, "What do we have to do to reach our objective?" and its extension, "What remains to be done?" For instance, if management discovers that the firm has earned only $400,000

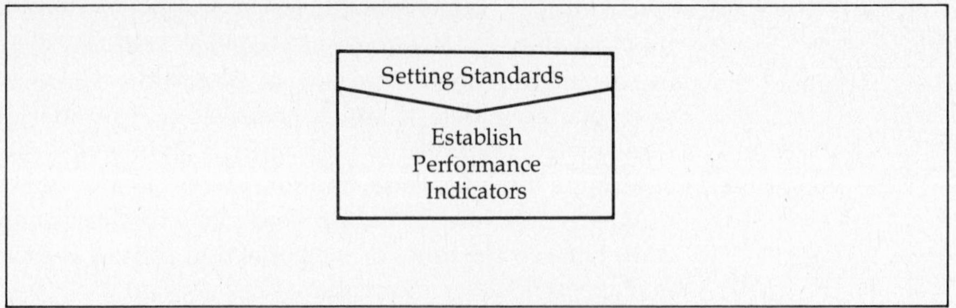

Figure 11-2 First Stage in the Control Process

during the first six months, it knows that the company will have to greatly step up productivity to meet the planned goal of $1 million by year's end.

It is relatively easy to establish performance indicators in such areas as profit, sales, and cost of materials because they are quantifiable. But several crucial organizational goals cannot readily be expressed numerically.

Improving morale, for example, is an objective that often seems difficult or impossible to quantify. One cannot rate morale accurately on a scale or reduce it to dollar equivalents. But effective organizations try to overcome the quantification difficulty. For example, one can obtain information about the mental state of workers through attitude surveys and interviews. Furthermore, some of these apparently unmeasurable objectives can be *indirectly* quantified by measuring manifestations of good and poor performance. Low labor turnover, for instance, is usually a manifestation of high satisfaction. Therefore, the turnover rate may be used as a performance indicator for setting standards in the area of satisfaction. For example, top management could establish its objective for the coming year as reducing turnover from 10 percent to 6 percent.

The danger in using manifestations instead of direct measurement is that other variables may affect the manifestation being measured. Low turnover, to continue our example, could reflect generally poor economic conditions rather than high satisfaction. In other words, people stay not because their needs are genuinely being met but because they believe it would be hard to get another job. As pointed out in our discussion of decision making, the manager must always be careful to distinguish between symptoms and true causes. It is essential for management to understand that many factors in the situation affect the outcome of a managerial action.

Inability to express a performance indicator directly in quantifiable terms should not, as it often is, be used as an excuse to avoid setting a control standard in the area. Even a subjective indicator, provided its limitations are recognized, is better than none at all. Without *some* form of performance indicator there can be no effective managerial control. The inevitable consequence of this is management by *reaction,* which is not really management but rather a knee-jerk response to situations already out of hand. Some otherwise excellently managed organizations have suffered severe problems because they failed to establish performance indicators in the difficult-to-measure areas of social responsibility and ethics.

One of the best-known examples of lack of performance indicators is the 1961 indictment of General Electric Company and several of its key executives for conspiracy to rig the prices of heavy equipment.[4] Because of its size and dominant position in the electronics industry, GE has always had to be extremely wary of violating antitrust laws. At the trial, Ralph Cordiner, then CEO of the company, produced written documents specifically instructing all GE divisions to avoid anything that might be construed as monopolistic business practice. He obviously believed that GE's policies on the subject were clear to all concerned. It was only after the fact—seven executives went to jail—that Mr. Cordiner discovered that he also should have established performance indicators to determine whether these policies were being followed.

What apparently happened was that GE, an early leader of the movement toward decentralization, had given the managers of its over 100 profit centers considerable autonomy. These managers were authorized, as they still are, to run their operations as they saw fit. However, they were under heavy pressure from top management to contribute respectable profits to the company. Unlike General Dynamics, General Electric had outstanding financial controls to ensure that they in fact did so. However, when it devised these financial controls, top management failed to also establish performance indicatiors for *how* profits were made. As a result, Mr. Cordiner had no way of knowing for certain whether divisional managers were actually adhering to corporate policies prohibiting price-fixing. Having no information, he was unable to take timely corrective action when some of his top managers experienced a moral failure and yielded to the temptation to look good by using questionable tactics to raise profits.

Comparing Performance to Standards

The second stage of the control process is comparing actual performance to the standards established earlier. In this phase the manager determines how well results have lived up to expectations. He or she also makes another crucial decision: how much variation from standards is permissible or relatively safe. The second stage concludes with an evaluation that should lead to an action decision. The several activities involved in the second phase often are the most visible aspect of a managerial control system. They are the range of deviation, measurement, communication, and evaluation.

Range of Deviation. The standard and its performance indicator are ways of providing the members of an organization with a clear, distinct target for their efforts. However, except in a few very specialized instances, it seldom is necessary or even desirable for the organization to hit that target precisely. One of the characteristics of a good control standard, in fact, is a realistic safety margin. For example, consider a large department store such as Macy's in New York that has sales in the hundreds of millions.

For convenience, let us assume that Macy's goal for the coming year is $365 million in sales, which equals $7 million a week. If sales for the second week in March are only $6.8 million, Macy's has little cause for alarm. Even though $200,000 is a shortfall that might bankrupt the average retailer, to Macy's it is a minor deviation from standards. Chances are that next week sales will exceed the budget by that amount or more. What matters is that the average sales week is $7 million, not every week. If Macy's had a control system that caused it to react to small variations in weekly sales by conducting a major promotion or firing a few salespeople, it would be impossible for management to concentrate on anything but controlling. Top management therefore establishes a **range of deviation**, an amount by which performance may deviate from plans without cause for concern. The owner of a small business can do the same, but the range will be less.

Deciding what the range of deviation should be is a critical issue. If too much deviation is allowed, problems could reach crisis dimensions. On the other hand, reacting to every minor variation would be so time-consuming and costly that the control system would overwhelm and disrupt the organization, preventing rather than facilitating attainment of objectives. In such situations, there would be a high degree of control, but the *control process* would be ineffective. A typical example of this is almost any situation where one has to go through an inordinate amount of red tape to get anything accomplished. Many government programs have been judged ineffective because more money is spent administering the system, making sure it is controlled, than on the services themselves.

Exception Principle. To be effective, controls must be economical. The benefits must exceed the costs of the control system. Costs of control include the time it takes managers and nonmanagers to collect, communicate, and analyze the information, any equipment used for control, and the costs for storage, transmission, and retrieval of control-related information. In the case of a business, if the profits realized from the investment in control do not exceed its costs, the controls would be uneconomical and counterproductive. One way management can increase the economic efficiency of its control system is by practicing *management by exception.* Often called the **exception principle**, this holds that only significant variations from standards should trigger the control system. By extension, operations that are inherently trivial should not even be measured.

The problem, of course, is to determine what a truly important deviation is. Immediate dollar value, the most obvious guideline, is not always sound. What is trivial in one situation may be drastic in another. For example, it would not really hurt General Motors for sales to be $1 million below projections in any given week. But failing to tightly control the quality of a 50-cent part could force GM to recall hundreds of thousands of autos at a later date.

Measurement of Results. Measuring results, determining how much progress toward meeting standards has been made, is usually the most troublesome and expensive aspect of controlling. To be effective, the system of measurement must be congruent with the activity being controlled. To begin, management must select a unit of measure that can be converted into the units in which the standard is expressed. Thus, if the standard is profit, measurement would be in the form of dollars or a percent, depending on how the standard was stated. If absenteeism or turnover is being controlled, the measurement would be in the form of a percentage of that. As a general rule, the standard will specifically state what should later be measured.

Selecting an appropriate unit is often the easiest part of making measurement contribute to attaining objectives, the true purpose of control. It is equally important for the speed, frequency, and accuracy of measurement to match the activity being measured. A pharmaceutical firm, for example, must exert exceptionally precise control over the quality of its products. Even a minuscule amount of contaminant could literally kill a customer. Therefore, a drug manufacturer's quality control measuring system must be extremely accurate and at least fast enough to catch a bad batch before it leaves the plant. However, despite the need for high quality measurement, a drug manufacturer cannot measure a high percentage of its output because testing destroys the medicine. Excessively frequent measurement would be so costly that few people would be able to afford the product. This effect would be contrary to the social and profit objectives of the pharmaceutical house. The company therefore only fully tests a random sample from each batch. In other words it measures only frequently enough to ensure a very high probability of safety.

Similarly, most organizations conduct audits (a control technique discussed later) and inventories of materials at infrequent intervals. If a manufacturer, for example, physically counted its materials every day it would know theft losses exactly. But the company would have no time to make anything! Therefore, most manufacturers conduct major inventories approximately every six months. They know from experience that this is a period over which losses due to theft or error probably will fall within an acceptable range of deviation. Banks, on the other hand, count all of their "merchandise" every day because money is an unusually tempting target for theft. But they only thoroughly audit their records at wide intervals, which is why embezzlers have sometimes been able to steal fortunes before detection.

Special applications of the computer have made measurement for control purposes much faster, cheaper, and more accurate. Computerized cash registers currently used by Sears and J. C. Penney now measure and tabulate both cash flow and inventory at the moment of purchase. Provided volume is high enough, this is a lot less expensive than the old method of record keeping and information processing.

However, *any* system of gathering and processing information is relatively expensive. The cost of measurement is often the single largest expense

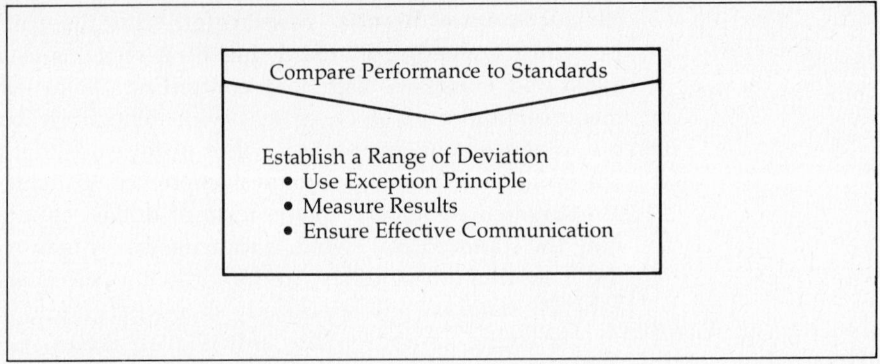

Figure 11-3 Second Stage in the Control Process

factor in the control process. It often determines whether a control is worthwhile. The manager thus must avoid the temptation to measure everything as accurately as possible. Doing so, by making the controls too expensive, would result in a control system whose costs outweigh its benefits. (In a business, the purpose of measurement is to increase profits, not find out exactly what is happening.)

Communication. Communication plays a key role in making control effective. For a control system to operate effectively, both standards and results must be communicated to appropriate people in the organization. This information obviously must be accurate. It also has to be timely and reach responsible people in a form that lends itself to decision making and action. It also is desirable to secure maximum understanding when standards are set. This requires effective communication between those who set the standards and those who are to attain them.

The major stumbling blocks in gathering and transmitting control information are various communication problems discussed earlier. While some information can be gathered and reported by machine, most involves some human interpretation. The human element introduces the potential for distortion of the information on which control decisions will be based. Distortion often becomes an especially acute problem when subjective assessments are unavoidable. Appraising management performance is a good example. The organization needs to know which of its managers are good and bad performers. But it is difficult to determine this effectively, particularly for lower-level managers who do not have profit and loss responsibility. However, by formulating specific objectives, managerial performance can be appraised with less distortion and more objectivity.

Once again, there is ample evidence to indicate that actively seeking the participation of people affected improves trust and communication, thereby making the control system more effective. Management by objectives, discussed later, is currently a popular way of involving managers in control.

FEATURE 11-1

Control at American Can Co.

Even now, few corporate controllers have been given as free a hand to organize and expand their departments as has Lionel N. Sterling, the 40-year-old senior vice-president and controller of American Can Co. And Sterling has made the most of it. Formerly in the control department of International Telephone & Telegraph Corp., he has succeeded in building one of the most far-flung controller departments to be found at any major company.

The center of Sterling's new control system is a monthly meeting that he and American Can's President William S. Woodside hold with each division head and division controller. "Our orientation and our reports are red-flag in nature," he says. Each divisional manager updates the annual forecast of earnings and cash flow, comparing them both with the annual budget and a five-year plan, which itself is updated every year. Any deviations from the budget are then discussed at length. More important, says Sterling, the division managers are asked to identify factors that might alter the forecast down the road.

The managers assess how much these factors could affect profits and determine just how likely it is that each of these factors will occur. This provides a probable range of error for each forecast. For example, the manager might think his division is close to a major cost-reducing breakthrough that could add $100,000 to a division's forecast of $1 million in earnings for the year. But if the manager believes there is a 75% chance that the breakthrough will occur, he would add $75,000 to his profit range.

Sterling also introduced an elaborate information-gathering system shortly after he arrived at American Can. Formerly, some of the operating areas of the company had their internal accounting records hooked up to a computer, but others did not. Sterling computerized all the divisions and set up a centralized system so that accounting information is transmitted as quickly to him as it is to the head of the division.

SOURCE: "The Controller: Inflation Gives Him More Clout with Management," *Business Week*, August 15, 1977, p. 90. Reprinted by permission.

Participation also can be effective on lower organizational levels. A paper product company with which one of the authors is familiar trained production workers to understand basic accounting and manufacturing economics concepts so that they would appreciate and comprehend the importance of meeting standards. The workers also learned about the standards of their competitors and why it was critical for them to be efficient and productive.

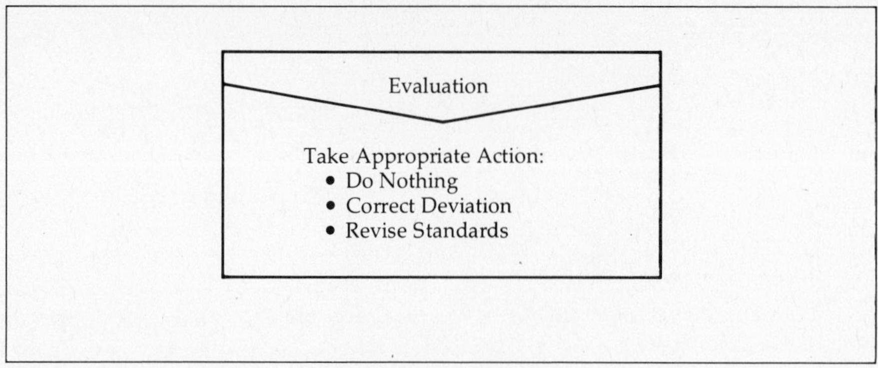

Figure 11-4 Third Stage in the Control Process

Sometimes it is even desirable to secure subordinate participation in the actual setting of standards, usually a management prerogative. One study showed that perceived participation in the decision-making and goal-setting phase of budgeting resulted in greater commitment to the organization and its goals.[5]

Great advances have been made in recent years in the communication of purely quantifiable information. It is now possible for the manager to receive crucial information in synthesized form, with key comparisons already made, almost as quickly as the organization receives the raw data. Some people believe that this new ability to process control information at exceptional speed is what makes possible the giant organizations of today. Certainly, there is no very large organization at present that does not use computers for control. We will discuss these new management information systems more fully in a later chapter.

Evaluation. The final phase of the comparison stage is evaluation of the information on results. The manager must decide whether the information is valid and whether it is significant. By *significant* it is meant both whether the information is applicable to the phenomenon under investigation and is genuinely important in decision making.

Sometimes evaluation is guided by organizational policy. Top management of a bank, for example, may request a loan officer to reject an application if the individual's current debts are already above a certain percentage of his or her income or assets. Or, in many situations, the range of deviation established earlier can serve as a guideline. However, managers must often use personal judgment to interpret the validity of information and the relationship between results and standards. In doing so, the manager must take into account risk and other factors influencing decision making. The objective of evaluation is to make a decision on whether action is necessary and, if so, what it should be.

Action

After evaluation, the manager must decide upon one of three courses of action: to do nothing, to correct the deviation, or to revise the standard.

Do Nothing. The primary purpose of control is to ensure that the management process is actually getting the organization to perform according to plan. Fortunately, things do not always go wrong. If the comparison of results to standards indicates that objectives are being attained, the best course of action may be do nothing. However, management cannot presume that what occurred during one time period will happen again. Even the most effective techniques will eventually be affected by change. Thus, if the control system shows that all is going well, management acts by again measuring performance and thereby repeating the control cycle.

Correct Deviation. A control system that does not provide a means of correcting significant deviations from standards before truly serious problems arise is valueless. Naturally, correction must focus on the true source of the problem. Ideally, the measuring stage should pinpoint the cause as well as the quantity of deviation from standards. This involves effective decision making. However, since much organizational work is the result of complex group effort, absolute precision in identifying the root of a problem may not always be possible. The focus of correction, in any event, should be getting an understanding of the causes of deviation and getting the organization back on course.

Management can take corrective action by making improvements in any of the internal variables, managerial functions, or processes. For example, management may feel the structure is the major variable causing the deviation between desired and actual results. Such was the case with the Gillette Company. After five straight years of declining earnings from the personal care division responsible for female products such as Adorn and Tame cream rinse and the toiletries division responsible for male products such as Right Guard and The Dry Look hairspray, top management concluded its structure needed revamping.

Because of changes in the social values of their customers, top management of Gillette Company decided that having both a personal care division and a toiletries division was no longer necessary. It decided to consolidate them into one division. Discussing these changes, Derwin F. Phillips, president of the new consolidated personal care division, a combination of the two previous divisions stated, "As men and women have come closer together in beautifying motivation, most of us came to realize that men and women weren't that different in what they wanted in a hair-care product." Phillips therefore felt that having separate divisions was too costly and constraining. For example, when the unisex marketing strategy for Ultra Max was formulated, both divisions struggled over which one would develop the product. This in-fighting and double overhead were the causes of the two divisions' lethargic performance according to top management.[6]

Whereas this example illustrates correction primarily through a major change in restructuring a large organization, it is important to stress that any of the internal variables may be a source of the problem. The effective manager realizes that several factors may be contributing to less than desired results.

Naturally, the manager cannot choose a particular corrective action just because it resolves the immediate problem at hand. All relevant internal variables and their interrelationships must be weighed before choosing an action. Because of the interrelationships between subunits of an organization, any major change will have an impact on every aspect of the organization. Therefore, the manager must take care that the "correction" does not cause more difficulties than it resolves. Professor John Kotter of Harvard University cited the following illustration of this potential problem:

> . . . the president of a high technology manufacturing firm once fired and replaced three directors of engineering in a period of just four years. In each case, he did so because the company's new product development process was not functioning well. He never really considered the possibility that other factors, some beyond the control of the engineering director, might be causing the problem. A subsequent diagnosis of this situation, by the corporate staff of the firm that acquired this manufacturing company, led to a very different conclusion. They decided that the process problems were being caused by a combination of factors, including some inappropriate informal norms, the lack of certain types of formal coordination arrangements, and some attitudes held by the key figure in the dominant coalition (the president). In support of their diagnosis, they found that the three former engineering directors were all pursuing successful careers elsewhere as heads of engineering in high technology manufacturing firms.[7]

Also, as hard as it may be at times, a dedicated manager tries not to make decisions because they are beneficial in the short run when the long-term consequences will be costly. For example, a few years ago the head of a company division experiencing low sales decided to lay off one-third of the work force. Analyzing the situation, the division head reasoned, "If the turndown continues, we will be in good shape to ride it out. If it isn't as bad as we think it will be, then after the holidays we can rehire many of the workers. Most important, my division will attain its last-quarter profit goals. Considering the kind of year it has been, that can get me a bonus and promotion."

This manager, who we'll call George, was highly commended for saving the company's profits. But within a year, his decision proved disastrous. A critical personnel strategy of the company was to avoid unionization, and thereby the costs associated with rigid work rules, restricted hiring and promotion, and strikes. Largely because of the layoff George implemented, the workers voted for union representation at the first opportunity. Thus, although George made his short-term profit objectives, the company as a whole lost one of its most important competitive advantages.

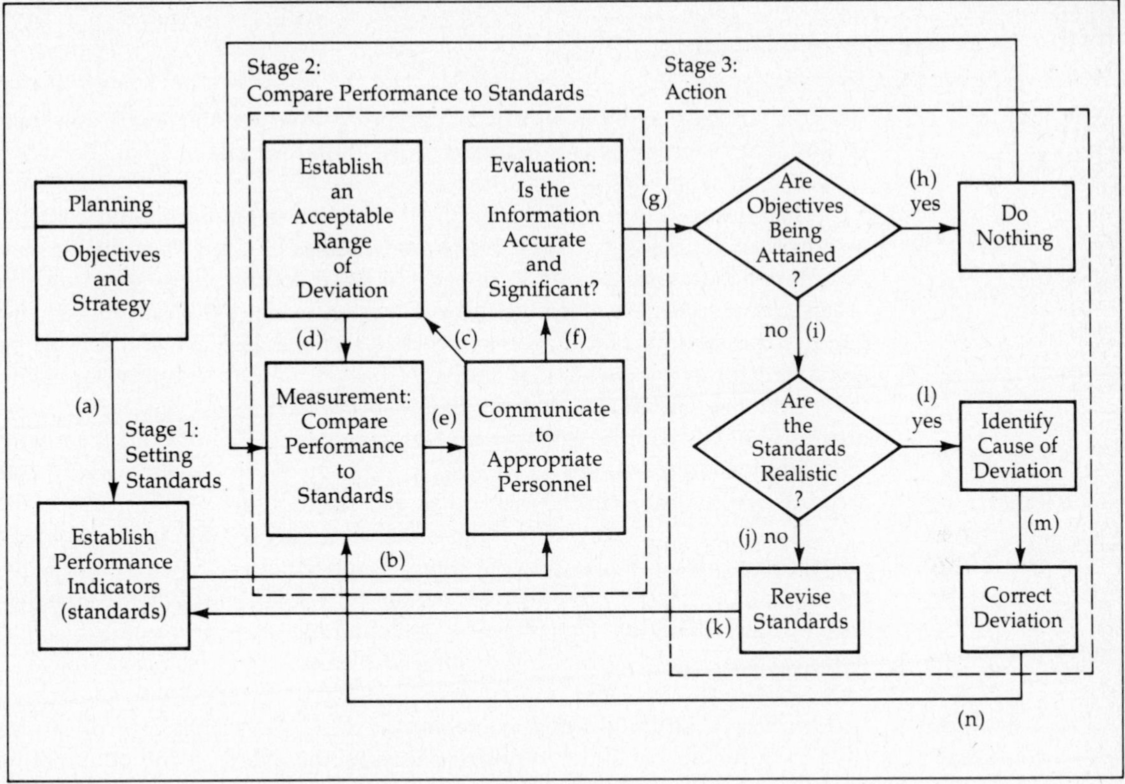

Figure 11-5 The Control Process
Letters correspond to the sequence of control activities.

Revision of Standards. Not all significant deviations from standards *should* be corrected. Sometimes the standard itself may be unrealistic because standards are based on plans, which are only *predictions* of the future. Standards must be reviewed whenever plans are revised.

It often is the control system that points out the need to revise plans. If, for example, almost the entire salesforce exceeded quota by 50 percent, the quota is probably too low to be a valid standard of satisfactory performance. A highly successful organization will frequently have to revise its standards upward. And, although this should not happen too often, at times a plan will prove overly optimistic and standards will have to be revised downward. Standards that are too difficult to attain can frustrate worker and manager needs for achievement, possibly decreasing their motivation. As with corrective action, the need for drastic revision of standards in either direction may be a symptom of problems in the control process itself or perhaps in the planning process.

Figure 11-5 is a comprehensive model of the control process.

Behavioral Aspects of Control

As with virtually every aspect of managing, people are an inextricable part of the control process. The manager must therefore take human behavior into account when designing controls.

That controlling has a strong, direct effect on behavior should come as no surprise. Management often deliberately makes its controls highly visible in order to influence people to behave in ways conducive to attaining the organization's desired objectives. For example, every bank employee who handles transactions is told in no uncertain terms that every dollar must be accounted for every day. The money often is counted by a supervisor as the teller watches. Similarly, that regular inspections will be made to ensure quality is never kept secret in manufacturing plants. People in a company who are authorized to spend money or sign checks know for certain that accounts will be thoroughly checked by outside auditors.

The underlying idea of making controls highly visible is not to catch mistakes and fraud, but to prevent them. Management hopes that, knowing the controls exist and are effective, people will consciously avoid mistakes and negative behavior. This increases the potential of control to make actual performance as close as possible to desired results.

Potential Negative Effects

Unfortunately, although most managers are well aware that control can be used to influence behavior in positive ways, some overlook the potential of control to cause unintended dysfunctional behavior. These negative effects are often a by-product of the control system's visibility.

Control-Oriented Behavior. People usually *know* that management is using controls to evaluate their performance. They realize that mistakes and outstanding performance in those areas in which management sets standards and most vigorously implements control techniques are the ones management is most likely to take into account when deciding upon rewards and punishment. Thus, the cliché that subordinates usually do what management "inspects" them to do often holds true.

Discussing this effect of control on behavior, one organizational behavior book states: "The very act of measuring influences the behavior of the people being measured. When superiors measure subordinate performance, they trigger a chain of cognitive and motivational effects. Subordinates tend to interpret the measurements as defining important aspects of the job. They respond by trying to make the measurements register at a level which will be rewarded."[8] Several studies confirm the tendency of employees to emphasize those areas which are measured and neglect those areas which are not measured.[9]

As mentioned earlier, a control can have positive impact on behavior. However, unless the control system is very carefully designed to take this tendency into account, it may encourage behavior that makes employees look good on control system measures but does not facilitate attainment of objectives.

An example of this problem sometimes occurs when salespeople are evaluated solely on the basis of sales volume. Experienced salespeople know that a call on an established account is more likely to generate a sale than a call on a new account. Therefore, if total dollars of sales are the only aspect of performance being evaluated, they may concentrate only on established customers and seldom make calls on prospects. If the company's overall objectives include increasing its market share, which can only be done by bringing in new accounts, this behavior clearly has negative consequences. It may lead to a loss of market share if competitors are successfully increasing their market share. Similarly, if salespeople are not evaluated on the basis of customer satisfaction and service as well as sales, they may ignore these vital functions. They may not, for instance, call customers after the order is placed to see if there have been problems, or respond to any such problems, or even inform customers of new products of potential interest because they have never been purchased in the past. In addition, if salespeople are not evaluated on the degree to which they supply the marketing department with information on company needs, they probably will not do so or only do so casually. This would make it far more difficult to attain important objectives in responding to changing needs of customers by developing attractive new products. In sum, one objective of the company would be met effectively, but the control would in the long run detract from attainment of overall objectives in many areas.

Research on management practices in the Soviet Union, which has recently begun experimenting with monetary rewards to stimulate productivity, also illustrates this problem. It was found that when managers were rewarded on the basis of production output, they attained production goals at the expense of operating repairs and preventive maintenance. This caused output in the following time period to drop, when it became necessary to attend to repair problems. This would not occur if operating repairs and maintenance were also used as control standards.[10]

Production of Invalid Information. Another potential behavioral effect of control is that it may influence people to give the organization invalid information. For example, when proposing a new project or budget, managers may overstate the cost of resources needed and understate revenues that will be generated. If top management habitually reduces budget requests when reviewing them (a control activity), this increases the chances that lower level managers will get the amount they actually want and need. Also, if managers are evaluated on the basis of how well they stick to budgeted limits, asking for too much money gives them some leeway to make mistakes and still look good. Similarly, managers may attempt to set objectives that are slightly lower than what they believe is attainable, thereby increasing the chances of actually attaining them—and looking good at evaluation time. The problem with this behavior, which often is well-intended, is that superiors do not really know what resources are needed and what the organization can attain. This may cause it to miss important opportunities for growth.

Behavioral Guidelines for Effective Control

Newman offers several recommendations for managers who wish to avoid unintended negative behaviors and thereby increase the effectiveness of the control function.[11] Newman's recommendations are as follows:

Set Meaningful and Accepted Standards. People should feel the standards used to evaluate them are relevant to their job and also should understand how they help the organization attain its broader objectives. If people believe that control standards are irrelevant or too nit-picking, they may ignore them, deliberately circumvent them, or experience frustration.

Management should also strive to have its standards genuinely accepted by the people affected. Some writers advocate participation in the setting of standards for the purpose of increasing acceptance.[12] One study found that perceived participation in decision making and objective setting during budgeting resulted in greater personal commitment to the organization and its objectives.[13] We will describe specific techniques for using participation in the setting of standards when we discuss zero-base budgeting and management by objectives.

Establish Two-Way Communication. If the subordinate perceives a problem with the control system, he or she should be able to discuss it openly without fear that his manager will resent it. Professor Newman states that each supervisor—from the president to the foreman—should have a frank discussion with his subordinates about the levels of expected results that will be used in each area of control. Such two-way communication will increase the chances of people accurately understanding the true purpose of controls and help to uncover flaws in the controls not apparent to upper level managers who designed them.

Avoid Overcontrol. Management should not inundate subordinates with so many controls that they compete for attention and result in confusion and frustration. A key question to ask about a proposed control is, "Is this necessary to prevent or warn of significant deviations from desired results?" In addition, superiors should not check subordinates' work too often or too closely, for this understandably can be annoying.

Set Tough but Attainable Standards. It is important to take motivation into account when establishing controls. A clear standard is often an aid to motivation because it tells people exactly what the organization expects them to achieve. However, according to the expectancy theory of motivation, people will only be motivated to work toward objectives they perceive to be attain-

FEATURE 11-2

Unnecessary Controls Reduce Effectiveness

The dethroning of Arthur R. Taylor as president of CBS Inc. is said to have resulted in part from his emphasis on placing tight controls on a business that depends far more on creative energy. Similarly, observers say the trouble that Franklin M. Jarman had at Genesco Inc., the apparel and retail store conglomerate, had a lot to do with his insistence on controls that straitjacketed operations. Jarman was ousted as Genesco's chief executive last January. Even J. C. Penney, well-known as a tightly managed company, is relaxing some of its controls because they have occasionally taken more of the employees' time than they are worth. "We are very aggressively trying to back off unnecessary controls," says Penney's Northam.

SOURCE: "The Controller: Inflation Gives Him More Clout with Management," *Business Week*, August 15, 1977, p. 85. Reprinted by permission.

able. Therefore, if the standard is perceived as unrealistically or unfairly high, it may demotivate workers. Similarly, standards that are too low may not be challenging enough. This might adversely affect the motivation of people with high, active needs for achievement. The effective manager is sensitive to differences in the needs and abilities of subordinates and sets standards that take them into account.

Reward Attainment of Standards. If management wants its people to be motivated to do their best for the organization, it should reward them for meeting performance standards. According to expectancy theory, there should be a clear relationship between performance and reward. If people do not perceive this, or feel the reward is not equitable, they may not work as hard in the future.

Characteristics of Effective Control

Human behavior, of course, is not the only factor determining the effectiveness of control. In order to fulfill their true purpose—facilitating attainment of objectives—controls must possess several important characteristics. Let us conclude this introduction to the control process by describing them.

Strategic

Plans are the basis of control. To be effective a control system must be strategic; that is, it must reflect and support the organization's established overall priorities. The relative difficulty of quantifying or measuring an activity except cost, should never be a criterion in deciding whether or not to institute a control mechanism. Activities that are not of strategic importance should be measured only infrequently and not even reported upon unless deviation is unusually severe. (Absolute control over trivia like minor expenses is meaningless and may even detract from attaining important objectives.) The rebellion over expense accounting that one observes in sales organizations is often the only way salespeople can communicate to management that requiring paperwork for small expenses is a nuisance, rather than a meaningful control.

Yet there must be an effective control for every activity that top management identifies as being of strategic significance, even if those activities are difficult to measure. Naturally, exactly which activities these are will vary for every organization. However, all organizations need effective controls when they have specific objectives in the areas listed on page 213 in Chapter 7.

Focus on Results

The ultimate aim of the control process is not to gather information, set standards, or identify problems. It is to attain objectives. Measuring and reporting, while important, are only a means to this end. If management wants control to be effective, it must keep these highly visible means from acquiring more importance than the organization's true objectives. It would be foolish, for example, to fire the company's best salesperson just because he or she never turns expense accounts in on time.

Moreover, one cannot claim the control system focuses on results unless it actually can get them. Having vast, accurate information on deficiencies is worthless, for example, unless that information is actually used to implement corrective action. This means that control information is only meaningful if it reaches those with sufficient authority to effect appropriate change. When controls fail to work, it is often the authority structure, not the measuring mechanism, that needs to be modified. Thus, controls must be integrated with other management functions to be effective.

In sum, the control process can only be said to be effective if the organization actually attains the objectives it desires and is able to formulate new objectives that will enable it to survive in the future.

Appropriate

To be effective the control must be appropriate to the activity being controlled. It must genuinely measure and evaluate what is of true importance. An inappropriate control may conceal, rather than reveal, critical information. For example, it is common practice to measure sales effectiveness by setting a quota against which actual dollar volume is compared. This may lead the firm down a primrose path to enormous losses because it is not sales but profits that really count. Many factors could lead to a quota being met without particularly good sales performance. The company might, for example, have offered unusually high discounts or provided an exceptionally high level of support service to get additional orders. Or, inflation may have caused prices to rise. In such situations, a firm could be losing money with every sale.

This problem with quotas is exactly what happened to Sears a few years ago. In an effort to reverse continued losses of market share, in 1977 Sears decided to use gross sales, rather than gross profit margin, as a performance standard. Store managers, in an effort to meet this standard, discounted merchandise heavily in order to increase volume. As a result, sales increased by 13 percent during the fourth quarter of 1977, but profits decreased by 36 percent. This, to say the least, is not what management intended when altering its standards. Sears soon concluded that its new system of control was inappropriate for what the firm genuinely wished to accomplish and have managers stress.

Timeliness

Because the objectives they are supposed to help attain have a time component, controls must be timely to be effective. Timeliness in control is not high speed or high frequency, but an interval of measurement and evaluation suitable to the phenomenon being controlled. The most appropriate time interval is determined by such factors as the time frame of the base plan, the rate of change, and the cost of measuring and reporting results.

A retail store, for example, may require reasonably accurate information on inventory levels on a weekly basis to ensure that it has enough merchandise on hand. However, an actual physical count of inventory, intended to control theft, would only have to be made quarterly. Similarly, a retailer needs to determine and check its sales on a daily basis to make deposits and control cash flow. But, occasionally, a retailer may need to measure sales on an hourly basis in order to determine peak and slack sales periods so that it has the right number of people on the sales floor at all times. This is one reason why, as you may have observed, computerized cash registers are often programmed to print time of sale on a receipt. Another is that knowing the time of sale enables management to determine who is responsible, in the event of error or poor service, giving it added control.

In addition, of course, a primary purpose of control is to correct deficiencies before they become serious. Therefore, an effective control system is one that gets relevant information to the right people before a crisis occurs.

Flexibility

If the unforeseen were predictable, there would be no need for controls. Controls, like plans, have to be flexible enough to absorb change. Moderate changes in plans should seldom require a severe change in the control system. For example, a company with a line of 100 products should use inventory control techniques that can accommodate a fairly substantial increase or decrease in the number of products and the amount of each kept on hand. Without a sufficient degree of flexibility, the control system will become incapable of coping with the very situations it is meant to handle.

For example, if a new cost factor such as the need to comply with a new law suddenly arises, unless the company can incorporate it within the existing control system it will be unable to keep track of costs.

Simplicity

The most effective controls are generally the simplest ones that will serve the purpose for which they are intended. Simple controls absorb less effort and are more economical. But most important, if the control system is too complex for the people who interact with it to understand and support, it cannot possibly be effective. Excessive complexity leads to confusion, a synonym for *lack* of control. To be effective, a control must be designed in accordance with the needs and abilities of the people who implement it and are affected by it.

There have been many instances of organizations going to great expense to develop elaborate controls that were never used because they were too complicated for the people who had to implement them. In the 1960s, for example, almost all the major New York banks tried to upgrade their control systems. The result was a flood of enormous, complex volumes that covered everything under the sun. All but one of these banks had to put aside their new manuals of control procedures because clerical personnel simply could not understand them.

The manager who developed the one usable procedures manual was no brighter or more literate than the others. His approach, however, showed a strong understanding of what makes controls and communication effective. This manager's "secret" was to test all instructions on his two teen-age daughters. If the girls, who knew nothing of banking, understood the procedure, the manager could be confident the bank's employees surely would.

Economy

It seldom is desirable to aim for perfection in control because the last increment of improvement often involves a disproportionate increase in cost and effort. For example, it is virtually certain that a percentage of shipments received by a company will be short. But, unless the material is very valuable or very easy to count, checking the content of every single box probably would cost much more than simply absorbing the loss.

It should never be forgotten that all costs to an organization should result in a net increase in benefits. The expense should bring the organization closer to attaining its objectives. Therefore, if the overall cost of a control exceeds the benefits that result, the organization would be better off with no control or a less thorough control. Since there are many hidden costs of control, such as work time and distraction of effort that could be allocated to other tasks, the ratio of cost to benefits usually must be rather low for the control to be economically justified.

Of course, to determine the true cost-benefit ratio of controls, one must consider the long run as well as the short. For example, it would not be worthwhile for most restaurants to control the costs of each item on the menu within a range of one cent. For McDonald's, however, that degree of control has contributed many million dollars in profits because one cent is both a significant percentage of price and it is multiplied by many billions of items sold.

If there is a firm rule of control, it would have to be that any control that costs more than it contributes to objectives results not in added control but misdirection, a synonym for lack of control.

Integrating Planning and Control: Management by Objectives

As we have noted, controlling is based on planning. For control to be effective, it must be thoroughly integrated with planning. Such integration is essential for the management process as a whole to be effective. A popular management technique with the potential to integrate planning and control in the difficult area of human resources is management by objectives, usually abbreviated MBO. MBO is a motivational technique as well, one that helps overcome some of the possible negative effects of control on behavior. The following description by Anthony Raia illustrates this underlying aim of integrating planning and control and also improving performance: "The emphasis (of MBO) is on trying to predict and influence the future rather than on responding and reacting by the seat of the pants. It is also a 'results-oriented' philosophy of management, one which emphasizes accomplishments and results. The focus is generally on change and on improving both individual and organizational effectiveness."[14]

Peter Drucker is credited with being the first to publicize MBO as an approach for increasing organizational effectiveness.[15] Drucker felt that every manager, from the highest to the lowest levels of the organization, should have clear objectives that support those of managers on the level above them, as illustrated in Figure 11-6. Drucker felt that adhering to this process would enable each manager to have a clear understanding of what the organization expected of him or her, of the organization's objectives, and of the objective of his or her supervisor. George Odiorne, another popular writer on MBO, also discusses this process.[16]

Douglas McGregor, another advocate of MBO, approached it from a different perspective. McGregor felt that an MBO approach is necessary because it enables managers to be evaluated on the basis of results, rather than personality traits. For example, telling a subordinate he has little initiative is not a very useful form of feedback. It is not specific enough for the subordinate to use for correcting performance deficits. In contrast, telling a subordinate that his output was 10 percent below the objective established six months ago provides a clear frame of reference, a standard, for controlling performance and discussing what problems seem to have occurred and what can be done to improve future performance. Therefore, McGregor suggests that every manager should establish specific performance objectives and the

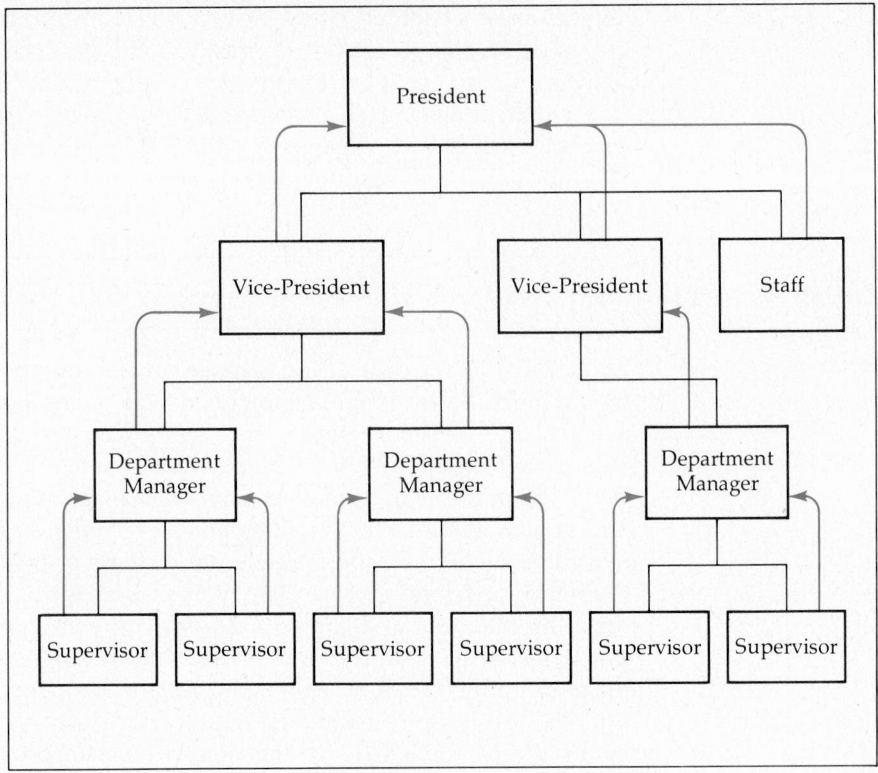

Figure 11-6 Hierarchy of Objectives in MBO
The objectives of each manager should support those of the immediate superior. The order in which objectives are formulated is from top to bottom on the chain of command.

means for attaining them in conjunction with his or her immediate superior. After a set period of time, the manager and subordinate could assess actual performance in comparison to these established objectives.

The MBO Process

Raia describes **management by objectives** as a process of four interdependent and interrelated steps:

1. The formulation of clear, concise statements of objectives
2. The development of realistic plans for their attainment
3. The systematic monitoring and measurement of performance and achievement and
4. The taking of corrective action necessary to achieve the planned results.[17]

Formulation of Objectives. The first step, formulation of objectives, follows the pattern of our discussion of the planning process and that illustrated in

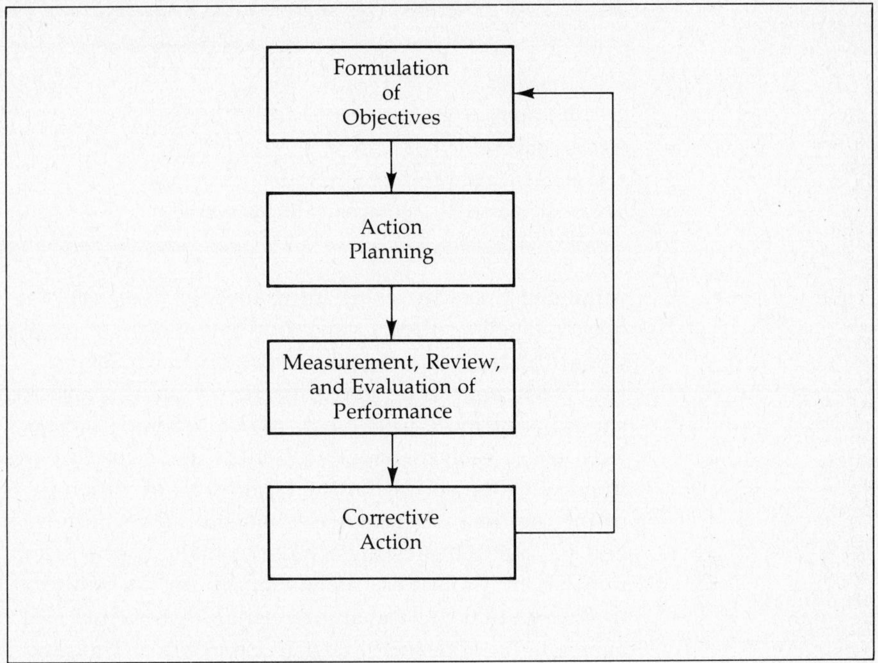

Figure 11-7 **Steps of the MBO Process**

Figure 11-7. After long- and short-range objectives are formulated by top management for the organization and their own work, they are formulated for persons on lower levels in descending order on the chain of command. Early writers such as Drucker and McGregor strongly believed that subordinate managers should actively participate in the formulation of their own objectives, basing their objectives on those of their superiors. This could be accomplished by a departmental meeting in which subordinates discuss the unit's objectives and projects for the coming year. Based on the information obtained, each subordinate would prepare a set of objectives for his own work unit. Then the departmental manager would discuss these subunit objectives with each subordinate and ensure that they are mutually supportive.

Research indicates, however, that maximum participation in the formulation of objectives does not always occur and is not always desirable. In an MBO-type program at General Electric it was found that managers accustomed to little participation did not perform better when there was high participation in objective setting.[18] Other studies indicate that the number of managers who actually participate in setting objectives decreases from higher to lower levels.[19] Carroll and Tosi, based on their experience with the Black & Decker Company, state, "The traditional concept of organizational structure and the decreasing discretion at lower levels of the organization impose a practical limitation on the nature and degree of involvement and

Table 11-2 General Areas in which Support from Managers is Needed

1. Information
2. Clarification of authority and responsibility relationships
3. Staff support
4. Horizontal and vertical coordination
5. Capital, materials, equipment, and manpower

influence that can result from an objective program."[20] Thus, managers at higher levels of the organization generally are more able to influence what their objectives will be than those on lower levels.

Whatever the degree of participation, the objectives of each subordinate should contribute to those of his or her superior. As Drucker states, the objectives "of each manager's job must be designed by the contribution he has to make to the success of the larger unit of which he is a part. The objectives of the district sales manager's job should be defined by the contribution he and his district sales force have to make to the sales department, the objectives of the project engineer's job by the contribution he, his engineers and draftsmen make to the engineering department."[21] If this is done each manager will understand "what is expected of him and why, what he will be measured against and how."[22]

Two-way communication is necessary when objectives are formulated to ensure that each person genuinely understands his or her respective objectives. In addition to clarifying performance expectations, two-way communication enables subordinates to convey to managers what they require to attain objectives. Table 11-2 lists the general areas in which subordinates require support from their managers to attain objectives. Figure 11-8 illustrates a typical MBO statement of objectives.

Action Planning. The second stage of the MBO process is action planning. According to Raia: "While a clear set of objectives reflects the 'ends' of managerial performance, well-conceived action plans provide the 'means' for their attainment. Action planning involves determining what, who, when, where, and how much is needed to achieve a given objective. It is a practical way of providing a connecting link between the statement of an objective and a more complete program of implementation."[23]

The development of action plans has the following benefits:

1. They are a means of assessing the feasibility of attaining objectives.
2. They help identify potential problem areas and unanticipated consequences.
3. They facilitate the search for better and more efficient ways to reach objectives.
4. They provide a framework for estimating costs and developing budgets, schedules and resources.

MANAGERIAL JOB OBJECTIVES

John Atkins	7/2	PLANT MANAGER
PREPARED BY THE MANAGER	DATE	MANAGER'S JOB TITLE
F. W. Crawford	7/2	PRESIDENT
REVIEWED BY HIS SUPERVISOR	DATE	SUPERVISOR'S JOB TITLE

STATEMENT OF OBJECTIVES COL. 1	P COL. 2	DATE COL. 3	OUTCOMES OR RESULTS COL. 4
1. To increase deliveries 98% of all scheduled delivery dates	A	6/31	
2. To reduce waste and spoilage to 3% of all raw materials used	A	6/31	
3. To reduce lost time due to accidents to 100 man-days/year	B	2/1	
4. To reduce operating cost to 10% below budget	A	1/15	
5. To install a quality control radioisotope system at a cost of less than $53,000	A	3/15	
6. To improve production scheduling and preventative maintenance so as to increase machine utilization time to 95% of capacity	B	10/1	
7. To complete the UCLA executive program this year	A	6/31	
8. To teach a university extension course in production management	B	6/31	

Figure 11-8 Managerial Job Objectives

This is a sample statement of job objectives for a manager participating in an MBO program. Column 2 indicates the relative priority of each objective. After the elapsed time period, actual results would be recorded in column 3, making it easy to compare the manager's actual performance with planned results.

SOURCE: Anthony P. Raia, *Management by Objectives* (Glenview, IL: Scott, Foresman and Company, 1974), p. 60.

5. They identify what work relationships and support are required.
6. They help identify the contingencies that should be taken into account for objectives to be attained.[24]

There are six steps in the action planning stage:

1. Specify the major tasks and activities required to attain objectives. For example, the activities required to attain the objective of reducing plant costs by 8 percent during the next year may be the development of production improvements by engineering and creating a human resource program to reduce absenteeism and improve the skills of the work force.
2. Establish the critical relationships between major activities. This essentially involves examining the activities from an overall perspective and constructing a schedule for performing them in the proper sequence.
3. Clarify roles and relationships and delegate appropriate authority for each activity.
4. Estimate time requirements for each major activity and subactivity.
5. Determine the resources required for each activity. It is essential for management to determine the costs of attaining objectives before attempting to implement them. Resource requirements would usually be determined and allocated through budgeting.
6. Verify deadlines and modify the action plan. After discussions with subordinates and other managers it often is necessary to modify the action plan to make it more realistic. Completion dates may have to be extended, resources increased or decreased, tasks rescheduled, and so on.

Review and Evaluation. The review and evaluation stage occurs after a specific, set time period has elapsed. Its purpose is to determine the degree to which objectives were attained, identify any problems and obstacles, determine the causes of problems, identify personal development needs, and reward effective performance. We elaborate on factors related to effective performance appraisal in our discussion of human resource management in a later chapter.

Corrective Action. The last step of the MBO process, taking corrective action, corresponds to the last step of the control process. Assuming objectives have not been attained, after ensuring that management has accurately identified the cause, they must decide what action to take to correct the deviation. If it is determined that the objectives set were unrealistically difficult, the level of expected performance may have to be decreased. It is quite possible that the reason for failure may lie not with the individual but some other organization variable, such as structure, tasks, or technology. If so, these will have to be changed as appropriate, taking into account the effect the change will have on other aspects of the organization.

If objectives have been attained, or in light of what has been determined during the review phase, the MBO process will begin anew with the setting of objectives for the upcoming time period.

Effectiveness of MBO Programs

MBO has many supporters and there are many examples of positive results from applying MBO. The overall validity of an MBO approach is supported by research in goal setting and feedback.

Research Foundation of MBO. There is a substantial body of research indicating that the performance of people who have specific goals to attain is superior to that of people when no goals are set or when people are asked to do their best.[25] Setting specific goals increases performance because the individual has clear expectations about what should be done. According to expectancy theory, if people clearly understand what they are expected to achieve, and perceive a strong likelihood (expectancy) that exerting a certain level of effort will enable them to attain this level of performance and receive an appropriate reward, their motivation to perform a task should increase.

There is also much research indicating that providing people with feedback about their performance increases future performance.[26] Life insurance agents who received periodic productivity bulletins and progress letters discussing their performance, improved their performance. Those who did not receive such feedback decreased their performance. A study at General Electric found that increasing the amount of feedback people received from their foremen increased the performance of workers. This study also showed that to be most effective such feedback should be specific, relevant, and timely.

Why MBO Programs Fail. Despite this support, MBO has many critics, and there are many instances in which MBO programs have failed.[27] One cause of failure is too much emphasis on participation in objective setting. Studies have shown that the use of participation motivates some individuals and increases their performance. However, other studies indicate that in some situations participation is not appropriate and does not always lead to increased performance.[28]

The more common and basic problem, however, is that management often fails to approach MBO in a comprehensive manner. For example, it may not modify the reward system to fairly reward attainment of objectives. Table 11-3 summarizes the common reasons why MBO programs have failed.

Table 11-3 Reasons Why MBO Programs Fail[29]

1. Lack of top management involvement and support. For an MBO program to succeed, it must have the complete support of top management.

2. Distortion of philosophy. MBO programs tend to be resisted when used as a "whip" to increase control over subordinates.

3. Difficulty setting objectives. Some jobs and areas of performance are hard to quantify and evaluate objectively.

4. Increased paperwork. Managers may resist the program because it adds to their paperwork burden.

5. Increased time pressure. To use an MBO program, the manager must learn to establish priorities and use time effectively.

6. Lack of relevant skills. Managers may not have the requisite skills for identifying objectives, planning, communication, and interpersonal interaction, such as coaching, counseling, and giving and receiving feedback.

7. Lack of individual motivation. Intrinsic and extrinsic rewards must be sufficient to motivate people to perform.

8. Poor integration with other systems. The objective setting and review phases must be performed in conjunction with other activities such as forecasting, budgeting, and other processes.

9. Inappropriate change strategies. The design and implementation of an MBO program must be carefully planned. Careful consideration must be given to the way the system is designed, how it is to be introduced, and who is to participate.

SUMMARY

Controlling is the process of ensuring that the organization is meeting its objectives. It is a necessary function because the future is uncertain and the organization needs to detect and correct problems before they become serious. An integral part of every manager's job, control can also be used to encourage success.

Preliminary control, usually in the form of carrying out policies, procedures, and rules, is used primarily in the areas of human resources, materials, and financial resources. Concurrent control operates while work is in progress and usually is exercised over the work of a subordinate by an immediate superior. Postaction control is applied after work is completed or a set time period has passed.

Concurrent and postactive control are both based on feedback. Organizational feedback control systems are open loop systems because an external element, the manager, intervenes to change both the objectives of the system and its operation.

The first step of the control process is setting standards, specific, measurable objectives with a time limit for attainment. Management needs standards in the form of performance indicators in all areas of critical importance, as defined by and based on its plans.

The second step, comparing performance to standards, begins with deciding upon a suitable range of deviation in accordance with the exception principle. Only significant variations from standards should trigger the control system, or it will become economical and unwieldy. Then comes measurement of results, usually the most troublesome and expensive aspect of control. After comparing the measured results with the standard, the manager is able to evaluate what sort of action is necessary.

The action phase can take the form of correction through improvements in the organization, revision of the standard, or doing nothing, in which case the process begins again with measurement.

Controls often strongly affect behavior, sometimes in unintended, negative ways. If management does not design controls appropriately, they may lead to control-oriented behavior in which people strive to meet control requirements rather than attain objectives. Or they can lead to production of invalid information. These potential problems can be overcome by setting meaningful, accepted standards, by establishing two-way communication, by avoiding over control, by setting tough but attainable standards, and by having effective rewards for attainment of standards.

To be effective, controls must be strategic, must focus on results, and must be appropriate, timely, flexible, simple, and economical.

Management by objectives (MBO) is a technique with the potential to integrate planning and control. Steps of the MBO process are: formulation of objectives, development of action plans, review and evaluation, and taking corrective action. For an MBO program to succeed, management must be careful not to use participation when it is not appropriate and to approach the program from a comprehensive perspective.

REVIEW QUESTIONS

1. What is the role of control in management?
2. What are the primary types of control from a time perspective?
3. What is feedback control?
4. What are the stages of the control process?
5. What is the relationship between planning and control?
6. Why does the manager have to be aware of the behavioral effects of controls?
7. Why is budgeting so helpful in management?
8. What are the distinguishing characteristics of a control standard?
9. Why is it so important to establish an appropriate range of deviation?
10. What are the characteristics of effective control?

DISCUSSION QUESTIONS

11. Describe the relationship between the planning and controlling processes, giving specific examples.
12. Work an organizational example through the control process model.
13. Describe an experience or a situation in which controls adversely affected behavior. How could this have been avoided?
14. How would controls in a decentralized and highly centralized organization differ?
15. Can management successfully use controls to force people to conform to organizational values?
16. Why must management take a comprehensive approach to MBO?
17. Give an example of how failure to consider interrelationships might cause an MBO program to fail.

CASE INCIDENT

Grant Manufacturing Company

Ben Carley came to Grant Manufacturing Company right out of college. Ben majored in management and this was his first full-time job, although he had worked for a number of organizations to pay for part of his school costs.

During his five years in college (Ben's working added an extra year), he took several courses in personnel. One course, Wage and Salary Administration, was particularly interesting to Ben and served as a basis for his first major job assignment at Grant Manufacturing, an in-depth review of the company's job evaluation program.

Jay Richards, Grant's personnel director, took great pride in having, as he put it, "graduated cum laude from the school of hard knocks." Richards was well liked by employees. But, after eighteen years adding a new name to personnel was, according to Richards, "a nice change of pace." In developing a basic understanding of Ben's new role, Richards thought it might be well to take a look at Grant's job evaluation system. "Actually," he remarked, "I never cared much for the program when Grant had it installed five years ago and this new job will give me an opportunity to see if my bias was rooted in fact." Therefore, Richards's desire to examine the company's job evaluation program resulted in Carley's assignment to the personnel department.

"Carley, I want to know all there is to know about a job evaluation program, and I expect you," said Richards, "to give me all the necessary information."

Carley got busy and noticed right away that the job evaluation program had received almost no attention since it had been installed. He was certain that new jobs had been added and that many of the job descriptions were no longer applicable. Further, he was especially troubled by a recent article in a business publication which indicated, according to Department of Labor figures, that nationwide employers failed to pay their workers $70 million in overtime.

Carley thought it might be well to share some of these early concerns with Mr. Richards and asked him if the company's compensation program was in compliance with the Fair Labor Standards Act.

Richards said he wasn't sure what the Act required, but he was certain the company's legal counsel was right on top of these matters.

Richards even asked Carley to call the lawyer to get his opinion.

When Carley got in touch with Alex Davison, the lawyer, to ask about company compliance with the Fair Labor Standards Act, Davison said, "How should I know? Until now, no one asked and I assumed you people knew what you were doing."

Carley told Richards about his conversation with the attorney. Further examination indicated that for the past two years, the company had been in direct violation of certain overtime provisions of the Fair Labor Standards Act.

According to Davison, one complaint to the Department of Labor by an unhappy employee could eventually cost the company $750,000, not including legal fees.

Questions

1. Relate the control function to this situation.
2. What action would you recommend that the Grant Company take? Why?
3. How do external factors affect internal systems and controls?

NOTES

1. Peter F. Drucker, *Management: Tasks, Responsibilities, Practices* (New York: Harper & Row, 1973).
2. Richard A. Smith, *Corporations in Crisis* (Garden City, NY: Doubleday, 1963), pp. 207–249.
3. William H. Newman, *Constructive Control: Design and Use of Control Systems* (Englewood Cliffs, NJ: Prentice-Hall, 1975), p. 33.
4. Smith, op. cit., pp. 113–166.
5. D. Searfoss and R. Monczka, "Perceived Participation in the Budget Process and Motivation to Achieve the Budget," *Academy of Management Journal*, December 1973, pp. 541–554.
6. "Gillette: A New Shampoo Aims for More of the Unisex Market," *Business Week*, April 3, 1978, pp. 96–97.
7. John P. Kotter, *Organizational Dynamics: Diagnosis and Intervention* (Reading, MA: Addison-Wesley, 1978), p. 30.
8. David R. Hampton, Charles E. Summer, and Ross A. Webber, *Organizational Behavior and the Practice of Management* (Glenview, IL: Scott, Foresman, 1973), pp. 531–532.
9. Frank J. Jasinski, "Use and Misuse of Efficiency Controls," *Harvard Business Review*, July–August 1956, pp. 105–112.
10. D. Granick, *The Red Executive* (Garden City, NY: Doubleday, 1960).
11. Newman, op. cit.
12. Newman, ibid.; G. H. Hofstede, *The Game of Budget Control* (London: Tavistock Publications, 1968).
13. Searfoss and Monczka, op. cit.
14. Anthony P. Raia, *Management by Objectives* (Glenview, IL: Scott, Foresman, 1974), p. 11.
15. Peter F. Drucker, *The Practice of Management* (New York: Harper & Row, 1954).
16. George S. Odiorne, *Management by Objectives* (New York: Pitman Publishing Corp., 1965).
17. Raia, op. cit.
18. H. H. Meyer, E. Kay, and J. R. P. French, "Split Roles in Performance Appraisal," *Harvard Business Review*, vol. 43 (1965), pp. 123–129.
19. Anthony P. Raia, "Management by Objectives in Theory and Practice," *Southern Journal of Business*, 1968, pp. 11–20.
20. Stephen J. Carroll, Jr. and Henry L. Tosi, Jr., *Management by Objectives* (New York: Macmillan, 1973), p. 31.
21. Drucker, op. cit., p. 128–129.
22. Ibid.

23. Raia, *Management by Objectives*, p. 17.
24. Ibid., pp. 68–69.
25. Edward A. Locke, "Toward a Theory of Task Motivation and Incentives," *Organizational Behavior and Human Performance*, vol. 3 (1968), pp. 157–189; Edward A. Locke, "Performance Goals as Determinants of Level of Performance in Boredom," *Journal of Applied Psychology*, vol. 51 (1967), pp. 120–130; J. F. Bryan and E. A. Locke, "Goal Setting As a Means of Increasing Motivation," *Journal of Applied Psychology*, vol. 51 (1967), pp. 274–277.
26. E. E. Smith and S. S. Knight, "Effects of Feedback on Insight and Problem Solving Efficiency in Training Groups," *Journal of Applied Psychology*, vol. 43 (1959), pp. 209–211; J. A. White, J. Antoninetti, and S. R. Wallace, "The Effect of Home Office Contact on Sales Performance," *Personnel Psychology*, vol. 7 (1954), pp. 381–384; L. Miller, "The Use of Knowledge of Results in Improving the Performance of Hourly Operators," *General Electric Company Behavioral Research Survey*, 1965; P. S. Hundal, "Knowledge of Performance As an Incentive in Repetitive Industrial Work," *Journal of Applied Psychology*, vol. 53 (1969), pp. 224–226.
27. See Drucker, Odiorne, and Carroll and Tosi books on MBO cited previously for examples.
28. Raia, *Management by Objectives*, pp. 149–151.
29. Raia, *Management by Objectives*, pp. 149–151.

Safari Land

SHEILA A. ADAMS
Department of Management, Arizona State University

With a deep sigh Wilbur Thompson put aside the financial reports he had been studying. An operating loss of more than $100,000 for his first full year of business seemed too discouraging to deal with at the moment. The veterinarian's report on the death of a second giraffe only partially covered the memo which told of another zebra found slaughtered, apparently by lions. He couldn't understand it. They had promised him that the lions, raised in captivity, would not harm the other animals so long as they were well fed. And, of course, they were. There lay the latest food bills to prove it! Yet, this was the third zebra attacked and killed in the last six months.

Promises! Everyone promised but somehow . . . There was the matter of the interstate which passed close to the entrance to his park. State officials had assured him it would be completed within three months after Safari Land was due to open. More than a year later no progress could be seen. Sure there was a new administration at the state house, and they were re-evaluating all projects, especially highway projects, in light of taxpayer resistance to more spending. And speaking of that new administration! After he had the solemn word of the previous Highway Department Administrator that an exit from the freeway at the county road which led to Safari Land would be provided, it now appeared that the new Administrator was reconsidering "his" exit along with several other proposals. If that exit were denied, his park was doomed!

But, perhaps the most disturbing news came in the letter he now held. This letter notified him of a suit against Safari Land, and against him, charging negligence. He remembered the Burtons. They had come through the park last summer. Despite warnings (posted frequently along the track) not to open car windows, one of the Burton children had rolled down a window and thrown a sandwich out. A lion ("Perhaps that's the one who's after the zebras," Thompson thought suddenly) swallowed the sandwich and leaped onto the hood of the stopped car, apparently seeking more food. Mr. Burton, in a panic, stepped hard on the accelerator and lost control of the lunging vehicle which swerved off the track crashing into a nearby tree. Although there were only minor injuries to the family members, the car was a total loss. The Burton's suit asked for $3 million—$10,000 in damages and $2,990,000 for mental anguish.

Mr. Thompson sighed again. "How could such a well-conceived idea have gone so sour," he wondered.

Nearly three years ago, Thompson chanced on the opportunity to buy a large piece of an abandoned oil field in Southern Texas at a bargain price. The oil exploration group which owned the land was fighting bankruptcy and converting assets to cash. Thompson, a former minor league baseball coach, was looking for a new venture since his athletic contract had not been renewed. His meager savings were fast becoming depleted and this looked like a golden opportunity. Remembering how much his family had enjoyed their trip to Africa several years ago, he believed an "open" park with animals moving freely while people remained in their vehicles would attract a great many visitors. Located only 15 miles west of Interstate 37 near the small town of Poco, Texas, the site was midway between the vacation and tourist attractions of San Antonio and Corpus Christi—about one and a half hours drive from either city.

Visitors to San Antonio could be enticed south to spend an extra day on an African Safari, while Corpus Christi tourists might stop on their way to or from that gulf city. Possibly arrangements could be made with the two cities to work up some tour packages so travelers might spend time in both cities sandwiching the animal park between. The possibilities and potentials were endless! Thompson's excitement led him to plunge his remaining savings and all the money he could raise into the venture. Much work would be required to achieve success. Financial backers would be needed, bids sought for construction, animals selected and transported, contracts made with feed companies, personnel recruited and trained, and dozens of other details considered. He agreed to purchase the land, provided earnest money to the sellers and began the long process of turning a piece of dry, barren southern Texas into a facsimile of his fond memories of Kenya.

Thompson put together a syndicate of five buyers who were looking for ways to tap the lucrative tourist trade. Americans were moving about in ever increasing numbers; longer vacation periods, the recreational vehicle's popularity, increasing disposable income all contributed to the success of nearly every tourist-related venture they had observed. With $1 million from each of them he purchased the land and from a procurement agent he had met in Africa he ordered an assortment of animals. The agent supplied lions, zebras, gazelles, giraffes, wildebeests, and a variety of monkeys to be delivered as soon as Thompson said the park was prepared for their arrival. The animals had been raised in captivity and Thompson was assured there would be no problems with the lions if they were well fed.

A 15-foot, vine-covered, barbed wire-topped fence was erected around the perimeter of the property. Thompson planted a large number of mature trees and shrubs, dug a 10-acre lake and graded a winding road through the park. Traveling at a very slow 5 to 10 miles per hour, it took a maximum of one hour to traverse the entire track. Visitors would be given instructions to remain in their vehicles driving along the well-marked trail through the park. Stopping to observe animals grazing or at play was acceptable but windows must remain closed while vehicles were in the park.

Admission to Safari Land was advertised as $5.50 for adults, $3.50 for children, with youngsters under two admitted free. A picnic area with tables and a small playground were separately fenced. Families would purchase tickets, drive slowly through the park, ending at the picnic area where children and adults could leave the vehicle and stretch their legs.

Questions

1. What was wrong with Thompson's plan?
2. Which of his problems could have been foreseen? How might they have been avoided?
3. What do you think of the location strategy for Safari Land?
4. What forecasting techniques could Thompson have used in developing his plan?
5. What should Thompson do now?

PART THREE CASE STUDY 2

Colonial Furniture

BY TIMOTHY S. MESCON

Department of Management, Arizona State University

Roger Russell enjoyed planning his first vacation in five years. He was going to take his family on a week-long visit to Disney World in Orlando, Florida. Roger's wife, Cathy, had insisted on the trip, and, after much deliberation, Roger consented. After all, he had just completed directing a successful United Way campaign in town, and the town council elections (for which he was a candidate for selectman) were a good five months away. Also, it had been a while since he had spent a great amount of time with his daughters, and a week during Christmas would be an ideal time for a trip to Florida.

Both Roger and Cathy had grown up in the picturesque town of Hillsborough, New Hampshire, not far from the Maine border. Throughout his youth, Roger had always maintained an interest in woodwork. For special occasions, he would often construct small tables, rockers, and other pieces of hand-crafted furniture for his family and friends. In fact, his work had gained such notoriety that some local merchants had expressed an interest in selling his furniture on consignment. Roger thought that someday he might be interested in making furniture for a living, but he did want to first finish his education and then enjoy himself for a while.

Following his graduation from Hillsborough High School, Roger packed his bags and traveled to Durham, New Hampshire, where the university was located. Roger did enjoy himself during college but also graduated with a bachelor's degree in business administration four years later. While interviewing on campus, Roger was offered a position as a quality control manager for a large furniture manufacturer in Boston. The excitement of "beantown," the thousands of young people, and the proximity of Boston to his home town, made such an offer very enticing. He had always wanted to live in Boston, and this opportunity coupled with his interest in furniture seemed to represent an ideal situation.

Roger enjoyed his work in Boston, but over the first few years he realized that consumers were not really "getting their money's worth." The furniture was of average quality and the drawers and backing were made from a process that compressed sawdust. This type of particle board is often found on low- to medium-priced furniture products, but the furniture from this plant was priced quite high. Roger believed that consumers were willing to pay the higher price in order to have top-grade furniture and that his company was not meeting that expectation. He attempted to upgrade the furniture quality by offering suggestions to his boss, the plant manager, about material sources and finishing techniques which could be utilized at small cost to the firm. His suggestions were always received courteously and the manager complimented him on his interest and enthusiasm. However, no changes in materials or process were ordered. Roger's dissatisfaction with his company's products and frustration with his boss grew.

On a visit to Hillsborough, Roger renewed his friendship with Cathy O'Sullivan, his high-school sweetheart. Cathy had attended the University of Massachusetts, majored in early childhood education, and was now a third-grade teacher at a local elementary school. As fate would have it, the two were engaged six months later. One weekend on another visit to Hillsborough, the two discussed their future. Cathy enjoyed their home town and felt that she would not be comfortable living in Boston. Recognizing this and aware of his increasing frustration with his present job, Roger made a few inquiries during the next few months about possible jobs with local businesses. Several companies offered him a position, including one woodworking firm, but somehow none of them seemed quite right to Roger. Either the salary was too low, the work required him to travel, or the job was too far removed from his love of woodwork.

Two months prior to their wedding date, Roger decided to work for himself, to open his own business. He leased a small abandoned warehouse in the downtown area, and with the money he saved along with a loan from his parents, decided to pursue his lifelong ambition: furniture construction.

The first year of marriage for Roger and Cathy was rough. The business expanded slowly, and the two used Cathy's income for living expenses. Starting with a work force of three, Colonial Furniture gained a solid local reputation. Roger purchased only precut maple, and in his warehouse he and his two employees constructed early American tables, chairs, desks, and rockers. Roger served as manager, assembler, quality control expert, salesman, and deliverer. Originally, Colonial Furniture was sold to merchants in the immediate area.

Gradually, the business grew. During the next five years, Roger's original fleet of 1 expanded to include 10 trucks and 10 full-time drivers. Roger now employed 3 full-time salespeople who traveled to Concord and Manchester, New Hampshire, Lawrence, Lowell, and Boston, Massachusetts; Providence, Rhode Island; and Portland, Maine. The original work force of 3 grew to 100.

As the business grew, Roger gradually removed himself from operations, and formulated a specific organizational structure that included: production, purchasing, quality control, sales, accounting, and maintenance. Roger realized the necessity of functionalizing his operation because of the rapid expansion of his business.

During a regularly scheduled weekly meeting with his managers, the production supervisor suggested that Roger might want to consider a four-day work week. The idea seemed novel to Roger, and during the next few months he began to query Colonial employees on their feelings about this idea.

Six months after the suggestion was made, two 10-hour shifts were created at Colonial, on a Monday through Thursday work week. Coinciding with this innovative development, Roger, utilizing the assistance of a wage and salary consultant instituted a companywide incentive program. The bonus plan provided for a 6-cent contribution for every piece of furniture manufactured, with a 9-cent surcharge or subtraction from the pool for substandard pieces. During the first year of the plan, Roger paid out $50,000 in bonus money to the 100 Colonial employees. Today, 5 years from the inception of Colonial Furniture, sales had increased a hundredfold from $50,000 to $5 million.

Questions

1. What forces led Roger to open his own business?
2. What activities did Roger perform during the early years of his business?
3. Draw an organizational chart showing the functional divisions of the present Colonial Furniture.
4. What activities outside the firm are related to Roger's position as owner/manager of Colonial?
5. How would you characterize Roger's relations with his employees?

PART FOUR

Group Dynamics and Leadership

It is important to realize that the management process as we described it applies to the creation and operation of the *formal* organization. As we mentioned in Chapter 1, within every formal organization there are *informal* organizations. Although management did not create these informal organizations, they are a real factor with which the manager must cope because informal organizations and other groups can strongly influence individual behavior and can affect the work performance of people. Also, however well management performs its functions, it is not possible to prescribe every relationship and interaction required to attain objectives in a dynamic, ongoing organization. Both manager and subordinate must frequently interact with people outside the organization and in other subunits not within a direct chain of command. Unless people can quickly obtain the cooperation of these individuals and groups on which they are in effect dependent, they cannot successfully perform their own tasks. To cope with these situations, the manager needs to understand the workings of groups and the process of leadership, the subjects of Part Four.

We begin in Chapter 12 with a discussion of group dynamics. This includes the development, characteristics, and management of informal organizations and also the effective management of small formal groups within the organization. Chapter 13 covers power and personal influence. These are the basis of leadership and the mechanisms by which the manager is able to influence the behavior of individuals and groups, whether or not the manager has formal authority over them. Chapter 14 extends the discussion of leadership by presenting the various approaches to leading effectively in an organization and by describing the evolution of leadership theory. To be genuinely effective, to get people to do their best for the organization, the manager needs to be an effective leader as well as an effective performer of the managerial functions.

An Interview with Christopher J. Gilbey

The ability to develop networks of informal associations and influence others over whom one has no formal authority is often critical in management. This is especially true in Chris Gilbey's industry—the volatile, highly-charged popular music business, where careers and fortunes can skyrocket or plummet in the space of a few weeks. When Chris arrived in Australia in 1972 he had no college degree, no management experience, and no money. His music background as a performer and songwriter who had made several records that never hit the charts would hardly be considered adequate for even a lowly management job. What Chris *did* have was a letter of introduction to the head of J. Albert & Son, one of the largest music publishing houses in the southern hemisphere. Somehow, as he explains it, Chris was able to convince Mr. Albert, "that my services were invaluable to him as a record producer. (I don't know if it was my experience that convinced him, or my gift of gab, or whether he was just impressed by my one and only suit—a white silk suit purchased extremely cheaply in the Far East, but nevertheless, exquisitely tailored)." Whatever it was, over the course of five years Chris worked his way up to head of promotions, then vice-president of Albert International. Twice a year Chris circled the globe in an effort, often successful, to build Albert's position in the industry and acquire rights to musical properties at favorable terms. Despite the obvious benefits of staying at the world's finest hotels and dining at great restaurants on an expense account, Chris wanted to try working on his own.

In 1977, he left Albert and formed a music publishing, management, and production company in partnership with another Australian record executive. When one of their acts became successful in Europe, Chris returned to his native England and opened a branch office. Unfortunately, recession sent the music industry into a severe downturn. Financial insecurity and a yearning for warm Australian sunshine led Chris to sell his interest in the firm and seek another corporate position. This time Chris had a sound background in the industry and was well known among music executives. Consequently, he received several offers. The one he accepted was from the ATV Music Group, a division of Lord Lew Grade's Associated Communications Corporation, a major firm in the entertainment industry. The assignment was to start and run a new subsidiary in Australia. At the time of this interview, Chris Gilbey had been Managing Director, the equivalent of President, of ATV Northern Songs for 18 months, and just formed a production division whose first release was a hit.

Author: You have worked for a relatively small company, started your own firm, and now work for a large firm. Why did you choose to work for a big company rather than continue on your own?

Gilbey: Large companies, of course, have many drawbacks. One has to answer to a multiplicity of people—international boards, presidents, directors, teams of auditors, and so on. Even if one becomes enormously powerful, there are always others who can call one to account. Nor are the potential financial rewards as attractive as those of an owner. But, once one has attained a certain level of financial stability, power becomes a far more important goal. The power of a large corporation's many millions of dollars can be used as a lever in the struggle for external power, glory, and money. Right now I have the best of all possible worlds. I run a small, closely knit operation that I set up myself along lines that I prefer, with the objective of building it into Australia's most important music company. While my current budget is not large, I can, if necessary, draw on substantial resources and have a built-in network of international affiliates. Also, because of the corporation's support, I am not overloaded with administrative work, as I was when working on my own. This allows me to become involved in aspects of the music business other than publishing. All in all, I find my current position and its potential far more exciting than the prospect of owning all the stock of a company that in the final analysis is not worth all that much.

Author: The music industry is extremely volatile. Could you comment on how change affects you and how you attempt to stay abreast of it?

Gilbey: We are in a business that is constantly looking for a new miracle product—another Elvis Presley or Beatles. Therefore, we tend to be highly attuned to change. In fact, the music industry is probably more aware of swings in public opinion and tastes than almost any other business. The sales charts published weekly in industry magazines enable us to continuously objectively evaluate our success and the appeal of our products against that of competitors. Despite all our market research and information, every so often there comes a point where change is imminent yet nobody recognizes this fact. We have all become too self-satisfied with our successes. This is the point at which a new company, with different ideas, is able to rise overnight and vie with the giant conglomerates. The reward is millions of dollars in immediate profits and a shot at becoming the new "hot" company of the industry, which enables one to attract more top artists and thereby make still more millions. My job and personal goal is to be the person who recognizes such a turning point—and effectively capitalizes on it. My present job puts me in an ideal position to do so. ATV Northern Songs is too new and too small a company to become complacent. Yet, if it seems that we have found the next Helen Reddy, the enormous resources of Associated Communications can be used to make the most of the opportunity.

Author: Given the high degree of uncertainty in predicting what will appeal to the public, how do you make decisions about which artists and projects to back? Is your decision making primarily subjective or objective?

Gilbey: Decision making about artists is a very personal task. In order to create a hit one has to mix a certain amount of objectivity—knowledge of the marketplace—with one's own subjective tastes. Perhaps most important is not deciding which artists to sign but knowing which records should *not* be released. Even the most talented performers and writers may sometimes produce work that is mediocre without realizing it at the time. In the final analysis, I would say that subjective opinion is most important in our industry. The people who make the right decisions either have tastes that correspond to those of the mass of consumers or an innate ability to recognize art. (I think I probably am among the former.)

Author: What do you do to minimize risk in your business decisions?

Gilbey: The music business is an inherently high-risk one. Only a few records become hits, many die without a trace. The most important way in which I personally minimize risk is to avoid "grey projects" and back only those songs and artists in which I have total faith. In the industry, the uncertainty of picking a hit is offset by the fact that the investment required to produce a record is relatively small in comparison to that of, say, films. Thus, one hit will pay for many losers.

Author: Do you feel that you have sufficient autonomy to perform your job as well as possible?

Gilbey: I certainly have enough authority to perform my job within the parameters established by my superiors. Naturally, it would be great to have a bigger budget and still more power and authority within the corporation. However, one has to walk before one runs. I am sure that once I demonstrate that I can deliver the goods, the company will take the point of view that I should be given more rope so that I can do a better job of hanging myself.

Author: What would you do with the rope?

Gilbey: I would very much like to develop my company into a total creative workshop for entertainment that produces not only hit songs, but hit records and hit movies. I am sure that this will all come in time. I see Australia, with its lower overhead and equal technology combined with a population that can be used as a test market, becoming the movie and music Mecca of the '80s in the same way that England set the tone of music in the '60s.

Author: Do you think you will be able to convince your superiors of this?

Gilbey: Selling ideas to others in the company is extremely difficult. My superiors are all overseas with their own values and their own marketplace. They tend to feel that outside views are parochial.

Author: How do you overcome this obstacle and influence others to accept your position?

Gilbey: My basic approach is to prove my product locally and use local success to enthuse my colleagues internationally. I never promote what I don't believe in. This, I think, helps build credibility. With respect to influencing people locally, I begin by using my assistant to do a soft sell. If that fails, I do a hard sell myself using whatever I have at my disposal—calling on old friendships, pulling in favors, anything legitimate. Contrary to popular opinion, we don't use bribes, call girls, or payola to influence people. My guiding principle, for what it's worth, is to view the business as a service industry in which not only the person I deal with immediately must be sold, but the next down the line, until one reaches the actual consumer. So what I often try to do is provide services that help retailers as well as wholesalers, thereby making it easier for the wholesalers to be successful with our product. If one does this consistently, people come to trust you, making influence easier in more difficult situations such as when one is promoting an unknown artist.

Author: Moving to a different topic, what motivates you to work the long hard hours you obviously must put in?

Gilbey: On one level, what motivates me is a need to become more successful in the way I define it personally. For me this means making the best possible deal in any negotiation, be it for the company or a mortgage for my house. The true motivation, though, is making stars out of ordinary people. I know this sounds corny and phony, but that's really the way it is for me.

Author: How do you motivate the people who work for you?

Gilbey: I feel that the people who work with me are a lot like I am. We're a team, and our rewards are directly proportional to our success as a unit. One thing I really try to do, though, is to anticipate people's needs and to advance them before they come asking for it. Having been forced many times in the past to "ask for a raise," I feel that this is the point at which the team spirit that makes a company successful fractures and is never repaired completely.

Author: In closing, if you were running the Associated Communications Corporation, what would you do differently?

Gilbey: That's a question I find a lot more difficult to answer than I would have a few years ago. Then I probably would have reeled off a dozen grand proposals. Now I realize that perspectives change as one rises and is able to see a broader segment of the company and the effect of outside influences upon it. From my current vantage point I don't feel that it is possible to make an intelligent judgement regarding the corporation as a whole. Also, it is hard to fault the job Lord Grade, who started the company and still runs it, has done. The company is very large and expanding rapidly while maintaining an extremely firm economic base, something very few firms in the entertainment industry can claim. My thoughts and concerns are not of what I *would* do if I were Lord Grade. I just try to concentrate on what I *can* do as Managing Director of ATV Northern Songs to make it a profitable arm of the corporation and a major force in the Australian entertainment industry.

CHAPTER 12

Group Dynamics

Throughout most of this book we have used the term *organization* when we actually meant *formal* organization. We also have stressed management of large, complex organizations. This may have given the misleading impression that organizations are wholly logical, deliberately created entities over which the effective manager had complete control or that management is applicable only to large groups. However, an organization is a social entity as well as a goal-attaining vehicle. It is a place where people interact and form relationships. As a result, within every formal organization there is a complex web of informal groups and informal organizations not created by management. These informal organizations often have a strong impact on performance and organizational effectiveness. Therefore, the effective manager must understand them and learn to cope with them. Also essential to effective management today is working effectively within small groups, such as committees and one's own immediate subordinates, deliberately created by management. These are the subjects of this chapter.

After reading this chapter, you should understand the following important terms and concepts:

group
informal organization
Hawthorne effect
why people join groups and informal organizations
grapevine
Homans's model
factors affecting group performance
problems and benefits of informal organizations
ad hoc committee
standing committee

Groups, Informal Organizations, and Their Importance

Human beings enjoy and seem to need the company of their own kind. Most of us actively seek interaction with other people. In many cases our encounters with others are brief. Like trains that pass in the night, we meet people and feel no lasting or important impact. When two or more people spend enough time in close physical proximity to each other, however, they gradually become *psychologically aware* of one another. The length of time is largely a function of the situation and how dependent on each other the people are. But the result of psychological awareness is basically the same, even though it may vary greatly in intensity. Awareness of what others think of and expect from them causes people to modify their behavior in some way that acknowledges the existence of a social relationship. When this happens, a casual gathering of people becomes a group.

Each of us belong to many groups. We are members of several family groups, including our immediate family, grandparents, cousins, in-laws, and so forth. Most people also belong to several friendship groups, a circle of people who see one another relatively regularly. Some of the groups with which we become affiliated are very short-lived. Their mission is simple, and the group disbands as soon as the mission is accomplished or the members lose interest in it. A few students who get together to study for an upcoming test would be an example. Other groups exist for many years and may come to exert considerable influence on their members or even their external environment. A high-school clique is an example of such a group.

Although this chapter is the first with the word *group* in its title, we have already discussed groups extensively. As defined by Martin Shaw, a **group** is, "two or more persons who are interacting with one another in such a manner that each person influences and is influenced by each other person."[1]

According to Shaw's definition, one can view an organization of any size as comprised of several groups. Management deliberately creates groups when it divides labor horizontally into subunits and vertically into levels of management. There may be over a dozen management levels in each of many departments of a large organization such as the United States Navy or U.S. Steel. A production department could be divided into subunits such as cutting, painting, and assembling. These subunits may be even further subdivided. For example, a cutting department work force could be organized into three different tasks, with ten to sixteen workers and a supervisor assigned to each. Thus, the large organization is composed of literally hundreds or even thousands of small groups.

Formal Groups Versus Informal Groups

These groups created *deliberately* by management through the organizing process are **formal groups**. However small, they are formal organizations whose primary function with respect to the organization as a whole is to perform specific tasks and attain certain specific objectives. There are two basic types of formal groups in an organization: command groups and committees.

Command Groups and Committees. A *command group* consists of a manager and the subordinates within his or her span of management. The company president and senior vice-presidents are a typical command group. So are the manufacturing manager and the managers for production, purchasing, and quality control, or a supervisor and his or her group of production workers. However, although they fall within his or her chain of command, production workers are not part of the firm president's command group because they do not report directly to the president. The second type of formal group, the committee, is described later in this chapter.

Informal Organizations. The formal organization is deliberately created by management, but once created it also is a social setting in which people interact in ways not prescribed by management. People from various subgroups mingle over coffee, during meetings, at lunch and after work. Out of this social interaction emerge many friendship groups, informal groups that together comprise the informal organization.

An **informal organization** is a spontaneously formed group of people who interact regularly for some identifiable purpose. These purposes, like the formal organization's mission, are the informal organization's reason for existence. We will describe them later, as reasons why people join groups and informal organizations. It is important to realize that there are many informal organizations within a large organization. Most of these are loosely interconnected in a sort of network. Therefore, some writers consider *the* informal organization to be a network of informal organizations.

Importance of Group Management. By now there should be no need to state that it is critical for managers to effectively manage each formal group with the organization. These groups are interdependent, the building blocks of the organization as a system. Unless the objectives of each subunit group are mutually supportive and attained effectively, the organization as a whole cannot effectively attain its overall objectives. Also, groups affect the behavior of individuals. Thus the better a manager understands the characteristics of groups, factors influencing their effectiveness, and the art of effective group management, the more likely he or she can improve the success of the subunit and organization.

Although not created by management, informal organizations are a very powerful force that, under certain conditions, may actually dominate the formal organization and negate the efforts of management. Moreover, informal organizations are very pervasive. What some managers fail to realize is that managers themselves often belong to one or more informal organizations. The phenomenon is not something associated solely with submanagerial workers.

FEATURE 12-1

Informal Groups and the Manager's Career

The first thing I would do if I were starting today is make sure I took part in the lunchtime activities. Lunch is the best business training ground the white male has yet invented. I would take and make opportunities to be included. It's a lot easier today than it was years ago when the men went their way and the secretaries went theirs.

Every day for half an hour to an hour a group of people get together and talk about the company's problems, some individual problems and how they were dealt with, who is difficult in the company, and how to handle that person. This day-to-day informal coaching is the most important conditioning the white male has received for traversing the corporate trails.

It's the best vantage point from which to get a full view of what's happening and how to deal with it.

Eileen M. DeCoursey
Vice President, Employee Relations
Johns-Manville Corporation
Denver, Colorado

SOURCE: Milton Rockmore, "Learning from Your Mistakes," *American Way*, June 1979, p. 124.

The groundwork for understanding informal groups was laid by a famous set of experiments conducted by Elton Mayo.[2] Though not without flaw, these famous experiments had an impact on management's understanding of behavior at work equivalent to Ford's impact on manufacturing procedures. Therefore, let us present these experiments before discussing the nature of the informal organization in more detail.

The Hawthorne Experiments

In November 1924 a group of researchers began an experiment at Western Electric Company's Hawthorne Works in Cicero, Illinois. Their original intent was to determine the relationship between physical working conditions and productivity, a logical extension of scientific management, the predominant school of that era. As often is the case with significant discoveries, the results did not turn out as expected. By accident, the researchers hit upon something far more important, that eventually led to development of the human relations school of management.

The Four Phases of Experiments. The first of what eventually became four phases of experiments was designed to determine the effect of lighting on productivity. Workers were divided into a control and an experimental group. Much to the researcher's surprise, when they increased illumination for the experimental group, the productivity of *both* groups increased. The same happened when illumination was decreased.

The researchers concluded that lighting had at most only a minor impact on productivity. They felt the experiment had been unsuccessful because of *factors that they had been unable to control.* It turned out that they were right, but for the wrong reasons.

Harvard's Elton Mayo, already prominent, joined the group for phase two, the Relay Assembly Test Room experiment. This time, a small group of six volunteers was isolated from the rest of the work force and given special pay as an incentive for participation. Workers were also allowed more freedom to converse than customary at the plant, and formed close relationships as a result. At first, the results accorded with hypothesis. When, for example, extra rest breaks were given productivity increased, which the researchers attributed to lessened fatigue. So the team kept making changes along these lines, such as shorter work days and weeks, and productivity kept on going up. But when the researchers restored the original conditions, productivity remained high.

According to management theory of the time, this should not have happened. But it did, so the participants were interviewed to find out why. The researchers eventually concluded that some *human element* had had a greater influence on work than technical and physical changes: "In brief, the increase in the output rate of girls in the Relay Assembly Test Room could not be related to any change in their physical conditions of work, whether experimentally induced or not. It could, however, be related to what can only be spoken of as the development of an organized social group and a particular and effective relation with its supervisors."[3]

The third phase of the experiments was originally intended to be a simple plan for improving supervision and thereby improving work attitudes. It mushroomed into an enormous program of over 20,000 interviews. A monumental amount of information was gathered on employee attitudes. As a result, the researchers learned that a person's performance and status in the organization were determined by both the individual *and* the work group. To study the effect of peers on performance, the researchers decided on a fourth experiment.

Called the Bank Wiring Observation Room experiment, the fourth phase was intended to determine the effect of an incentive pay plan based on *group* productivity. The researchers, using the premises of scientific management, reasonably hypothesized that faster workers, motivated by the desire to earn more, would push slower ones to improve output. They were again surprised.

What actually happened was that faster workers tended to reduce their productivity to conform to work standards set by the group. They did not want to be thought of as rate busters or as endangering the livelihood of a group member. As one worker put it: "We've only got so much work to do, you know. Now just suppose a person was doing 6,000 connections a day, . . . that's two whole sets. Now suppose that instead of just loafing around when he gets through he did two more rows on another set . . . Before long he would have an extra set done. Then where would you be? Somebody could be laid off."[4] Slower workers, however, did try to improve their output. They did not want to be thought of as "chiselers" by the rest of the group.

Findings of the Hawthorne Experimenters

The Hawthorne experiments generated so much data that many important findings resulted from them—too many to describe in detail here. The major findings were the importance of behavioral factors, the importance of the supervisory climate, and the Hawthorne effect.

Hawthorne Effect. One of the best-known results of the experiments was awareness of a phenomenon now referred to as the "**Hawthorne effect**." This is a condition in which newness, interest in the experiment, or extra attention lavished on the subject causes a distorted, overly favorable result. In essence, the subjects of the experiment try far harder than they normally would simply because they know they are part of an experiment.

Behavioral science researchers are now well aware of the Hawthorne effect and take pains in designing research to avoid it. However, it is still not unusual to discover after the fact that research findings were distorted by it. For example, many companies fall into the trap of skewing their market testing of new products by exerting more effort during the test than could be expected in normal practice. As a result, the new product may fail when it goes into full production because salespeople no longer treat it as special. Similarly, a new training program for improving communication and morale between managers and subordinates is often successful initially. However, as time passes, the managers may go back to their old practices because they no longer get the support and special attention received during the training period.

Supervisory Climate. The Hawthorne effect clearly influenced productivity, but it was not the only factor involved. In the view of the researchers, the *type of supervision* was another major cause of improvement. During the experiments, workers often were less closely supervised than usual. When supervision was carried out by regular foremen, it appears supervisors often did a much better job than usual because observation made them more conscious of what they were doing.

Discussing this, Blum and Naylor state, "Further questioning brought out the fact that freedom from rigid and excessive supervision was the most important factor in determining the girls' attitude toward their work. In other words, rest pauses, a free lunch, a shorter work week, and higher pay did not, in the minds of these girls, count as much as freedom from supervision."[5]

The realization that quality and type of supervision can strongly influence productivity awakened managerial interest in leadership. We will discuss what modern researchers have learned about the relationship between style of leadership and productivity in Chapter 14. When we do, we will see that some current findings question some of the postulates of the Hawthorne team. Nevertheless, it is undeniable that our current awareness of the enormous impact the first-level manager or supervisor has on the way people perceive themselves, their work, and their organization is partly a direct result of Hawthorne.

Relevance of Behavioral Factors. The original orientation of the Hawthorne experiments was rooted in scientific management. Just as Taylor and Gilbreth did, the researchers set out to determine the impact of *physical* factors on productivity. Subsequently, it turned out that Mayo's great finding at Hawthorne was that *social and psychological* factors influenced productivity more strongly than physical ones, assuming the design of tasks was already reasonably efficient. In simple terms, Mayo discovered that new patterns of social interaction emerged as a result of the experimentation. It was this *restructuring of social relationships,* not defined or controlled by management, that was the main cause of changes in productivity.

Hawthorne's Impact on Management. Long before Maslow theorized about human needs, the Hawthorne studies provided evidence that social relationships between co-workers have to be taken into account. The Hawthorne studies were the first time that behavioral sciences were systematically applied in order to improve organizational effectiveness. They demonstrated that workers have social needs in addition to the economic needs stressed by earlier writers. The organization became viewed as something more than a logical arrangement of workers performing tasks. Managers and researchers realized that it is also a social system in which individuals, formal groups, and informal groups interact. Referring to the Hawthorne studies, management writers Scott and Mitchell state, "These researchers argued convincingly that the best designed organization, according to the classical principles, may be confounded by small groups and by individuals who did not behave the way the rational prescriptions of economic man said they should behave."[6]

If we assess the research methodology of the Hawthorne studies against current standards, we would conclude that they suffer from limitations.[7] Still, largely as a result of behavioral science research that traces its roots to Mayo's experiments, today we have a far better understanding of the nature and dynamics of formal and informal groups in the workplace. The remainder of this chapter summarizes current knowledge and shows how to apply it to improve organizational effectiveness. Let us begin with a description of how the informal organization develops.

Development and Characteristics of Informal Organizations

How Informal Organizations Arise

The work environment is an especially favorable medium for group formation. The formal structure and tasks of the organization typically bring the same people into close physical proximity every day, often for years at a time. People who otherwise might not have met often come to spend more time with co-workers than their own family. Moreover, the nature of the tasks they perform in many cases forces them to communicate and interact with one another very frequently. As we have pointed out, members of an organization are dependent on one another in many ways. A natural result of this intense social interaction is the *spontaneous emergence* of informal organizations.

Informal organizations have much in common with the formal organizations on which they are superimposed. They are, in a word, organized. Like the formal organization, they have a hierarchy, leaders, and objectives. Emergent organizations also have unwritten rules, called *norms,* that serve as guidelines for members' behavior. These norms are enforced with rewards and sanctions. The crucial difference is that a formal organization is a *deliberate, conscious* creation. An informal organization is more a *spontaneous* response to unfulfilled, active individual needs. Figure 12-1 illustrates the difference in formation.

Whereas the structure and patterns of the formal organization are developed by conscious managerial planning, those of an informal organization arise from social interaction. Describing the process by which informal organizations develop, Leonard Sayles and George Strauss state:

> Employees form friendship groups based on their contact and common interest and these groups arise out of the life of the organization. Once these groups have been established, however, they develop a life of their own that is almost completely separate from the work process from which it arose. This is a dynamic self-generating process. Brought together by the formal organization, employees interact with one another. Increasing interaction builds favorable sentiments toward fellow group members. In turn, these sentiments become the foundation for an increased variety of activities, many not specified in the job description: special lunch arrangements, trading of job duties, fights with those outside the group, gambling on paycheck numbers, etc. And these increased opportunities for interaction build stronger bonds of identification. Then the group becomes something more than a mere collection of people. It develops a customary way of doing things—a set of stable characteristics that are hard to change. It becomes an organization in itself.[8]

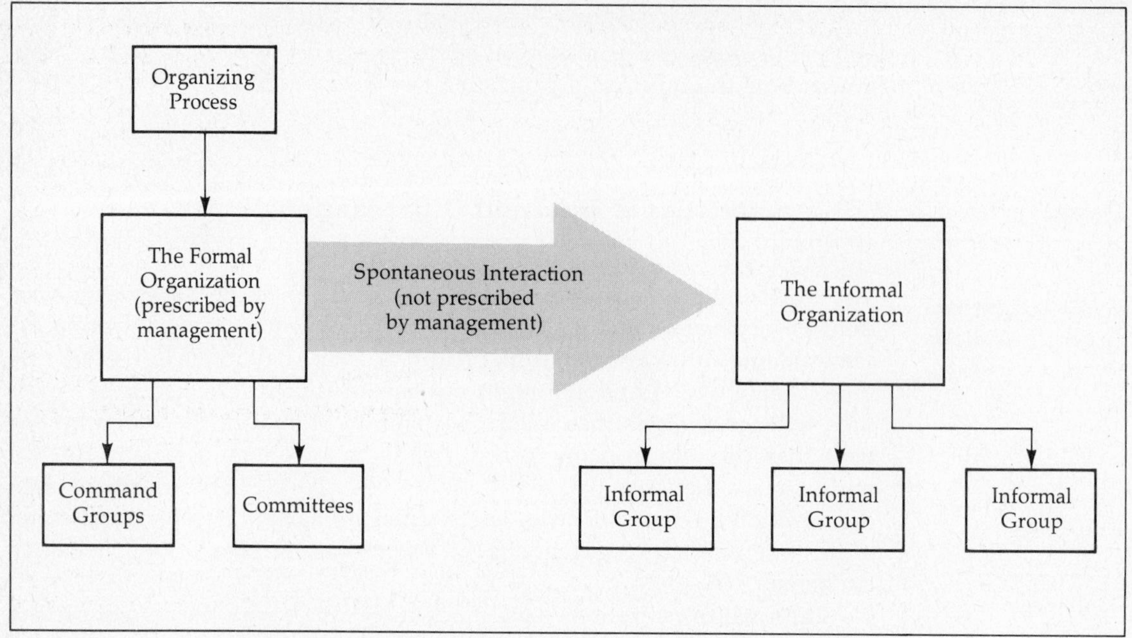

Figure 12-1 Growth of Formal and Informal Organizations

Why People Join Groups and Informal Organizations

People usually know why they have joined a formal organization. In general, they either want to accomplish its objectives or need the rewards such as income and prestige derived from the affiliation. People also join groups and informal organizations for distinct reasons. But they often are not consciously aware of what they are. As the Hawthorne experimenters realized, membership in informal groups may give people psychological benefits every bit as important to them as the salary paid by their employer. The most important reasons for joining a group are affiliation, assistance, protection, communication, and proximity and attraction.

Affiliation. The foremost reason for joining an informal group is to satisfy the need for affiliation, which is one of our strongest needs. Even before Hawthorne, Elton Mayo discovered through his early spinner experiment that people whose work provides no opportunity for social contact tend to be dissatisfied.[9] Yet, although the need for affiliation is widely recognized, few formal organizations make deliberate, specific provisions for social contact. Therefore, workers often are forced to turn to informal organizations to obtain it.

Assistance. Ideally, subordinates should feel free to seek advice and talk over problems with their immediate superior. When they cannot, usually the superior needs to examine his or her relationships with them. In any event, rightly or wrongly, many people believe that their superiors in the formal organization will think less of them for asking how to do certain tasks. Others fear criticism. Furthermore, every organization has a large number of unwritten rules. These govern small matters of procedure and propriety, such as how long a coffee break should be, how the boss feels about chatting and joking, what type of clothing is looked upon most favorably, and how strictly the rules are enforced. A worker understandably would hesitate to ask a superior for help on these matters.

People often prefer to resolve their need for assistance in such situations, as well as most others, through peers. For example, a new production worker would tend to ask another production worker for instructions. This causes new workers to seek participation in an established social group that includes experienced employees. Receiving assistance from a co-worker is valuable to both giver and receiver. The giver acquires prestige and self-esteem as a result of helping, the receiver gets the needed guidance. Thus, the need for assistance nurtures informal organizations in two ways.

Protection. People have always known that there is strength in unity. One of the primary reasons why prehistoric people formed tribes was for added protection against the hostilities of their environment. A sensed need for protection remains an important reason for joining certain groups. While there seldom is real physical danger in the workplace these days, early trade unions evolved from social groups who met in pubs to discuss management abuses. Today, members of informal organizations made up of lower-level workers protect one another from being caught at infringing rules. They do such things as punch time cards for one another and cover up errors. Or they may join forces to protest hazardous job conditions. Not surprisingly, this protective function assumes added importance when management is distrusted.

Managers, too, sometimes form informal organizations for protection. Their aim usually is to defend their area against encroachment by other subunits of the organization. Marketing people, for example, may try to gain prerogatives that might go to production or finance by informally gathering to plot against these "enemies." Students of management sometimes find it difficult to believe that such situations occur in many organizations. They *do,* and they clearly detract from attaining overall organizational objectives. This problem with informal organizations further illustrates the need to integrate objectives of subunits and direct their efforts for the good of the organization as a whole.

Communication. People like to know what is going on around them, especially if it affects their jobs. Yet, many formal organizations have relatively poor internal communication systems, and, of course, sometimes management deliberately withholds certain information from subordinates. Therefore, an important reason for joining informal organizations is to get hooked up to the informal communication channel, the grapevine. The grapevine, which we will discuss later in this chapter, also carries social gossip and other news that is unavailable from formal sources. This information may satisfy the individual's needs for psychological security and affiliation.

Proximity and Attraction. People often join informal groups simply to be close to people they consider attractive. Secretaries or engineers in a department, for example, often work in large rooms without partitions between desks. These people, partly because they perform similar work, have much in common with one another and are likely to consider each other attractive. As a result, they may have lunch together, discuss work and personal problems during coffee breaks, or petition management for higher salaries or better working conditions. The impact of proximity alone was illustrated by a study of air force bomber crews. The finding was that people tended to develop closer relationships to people stationed in their immediate vicinity than those stationed just a few yards away.[10] People are generally attracted to others whose characteristics they perceive will satisfy needs for affiliation, competence, security, esteem, and so on.[11]

Characteristics of Informal Organizations

The process by which an informal organization develops and the reasons why people join it give the informal organization characteristics both similar and dissimilar to those of the formal. Understanding these characteristics is a subject in itself, one we, unfortunately, are unable to describe in detail here. The following is a brief description of a few basic characteristics of informal organizations that are particularly relevant to management because they can strongly affect performance of the formal organization.

Social Control. As the Hawthorne team learned, the informal organization exerts social control over its members. Its primary mechanism for doing so is the establishment and enforcement of norms, group standards of acceptable and unacceptable behavior. The individual must conform to these norms to be accepted by the group and maintain his or her position within it. It is common, for example, for an informal organization to have well-defined values regarding dress, performance, acceptable types of work, and protocol. The group may use strong sanctions to enforce conformity to these norms. Those who do not conform may be ostracized. This is a severe and effective penalty when, as often is the case, a person depends on the informal organization for satisfaction of social needs.

The social control exerted by the informal organization can influence the member's motivation to work toward objectives of the formal organization. It also may influence the way the individual perceives managers and the fairness of managerial decisions. As William Scott states when discussing group norms, "These standards may be at odds with the values set by the formal organization so an individual may well find himself in a situation of conflicting demands."[12]

FEATURE 12-2

Informal Organization in Major League Baseball: An Example of Social Control

He eats alone. He travels alone. He rooms alone. He drinks alone. And, essentially, he works alone. He is effectively ostracized by his colleagues. Shunning, the Amish call it.

In a very real sense, 26-year-old National League rookie umpire Dave Pallone is an outcast. Alone in an existence which by its nature is lonely at best.

A couple of weeks ago in San Francisco, he opened his equipment bag to discover the tools of his trade—"The tools of ignorance," ironically—had been vandalized. The straps on his shinguards were slashed, his hatband ripped, his mask padlocked. The word "scab" had been scrawled across the bag.

A few days later, he was surrounded by six angry San Francisco Giants. His colleagues stood rooted at their stations. Not long ago, he was bumped three times by Chicago Manager Herman Franks. Again, his colleagues offered no assistance.

"I'll never talk to some of these guys . . . ever," says Pallone, one of the eight minor-league umpires hired by the majors during the strike lockout which kept veteran officials on picket-line duty the first month of the season.

"All 52 of the major-league umpires have a pact not to talk to us in the clubhouse or off the field . . . and they're abiding by it," Pallone says. "Once in a while, you'll hear a 'hello,' or someone will say 'do this' or 'do that.' But that's about it."

The 52 veteran umpires police their ranks vigorously. Recently, an American League umpire telephoned a member of the crew on which Pallone was working to warn him "about being friendly" to the rookie.

Pallone is braced against continuing ostracism.

"I thought maybe they would say, 'OK, it's over, we got what we want, let's forget it," he says. "But they haven't. I don't know what's going to happen.

"Maybe next year a few of them will talk to me."

SOURCE: Phil Musick, "Rookie Umpire Vows: 'No Way Will I Quit,' " *Atlanta Constitution*, July 31, 1979, pp. 1-D, 5-D.

Resistance to Change. Informal organizations tend to resist change. This tendency is partly because change may pose a very real threat to the survival of the informal organization. Restructuring, the introduction of new technology, expansion that would bring in many new employees, and so forth could easily result in the physical dispersal of group members, diminishing their opportunities for interaction and social need satisfaction. Or, such changes could enable rival groups to gain stature and power.

Because people respond not to what is objectively happening but to what they perceive to be occurring, a proposed change may be perceived by the group as far more threatening than it actually is. For example, a group of middle managers may resist introduction of a computer system because they fear it will make their jobs obsolete, when management really plans to give them added responsibility.

Resistance will develop whenever members perceive a threat to their experience of group identification, shared experiences, social need fulfillment, common interests, or positive sentiments. Management may be able to reduce this resistance to change by encouraging and permitting subordinates to participate in decision making, a topic discussed in later chapters.

Informal Leadership. Like formal organizations, informal ones have leaders. The informal leader acquires his or her position by gaining and exerting power over group members, just as the leader of the formal organization does. In fact, there is little effective difference in the means used by informal and formal leaders to exert influence. Thus much of the discussion of power and leadership in the following chapters also applies to informal leadership. The major exception is that the formal leader is backed by delegated formal authority and usually operates within a specific, delegated functional area. The informal leader relies much more on acceptance by the group and tends to stress people and relationships. The informal leader's sphere of influence may have little relationship to the divisional boundaries of the formal organization. Although sometimes the informal leader is also the formal group's leader, often he or she may be relatively low in the formal organization's hierarchy.

Factors that may enable a person to become a leader of an informal organization include age, seniority, technical competence, work location, freedom to move around the work area, and a responsive personality. The exact characteristics are determined by the values of the group. Thus, in some informal organizations being older will be perceived as a positive characteristic and in others it will not.

The informal leader has two primary functions: to help the group attain its goals and to maintain and enhance group life. Sometimes these functions are performed by different people. If so, the informal group will have two leaders. One dominates in matters related to performing group tasks, the other in social matters.[13]

Table 12-1 Typical Information Communicated by Grapevines

Upcoming layoffs on the production line
New company policy penalizing lateness
Changes in the organizational structure
Upcoming transfers and promotions
A detailed description of an argument between two managers at the last sales meeting
Who is dating whom after hours

Informal Communication: The Grapevine. Communication is vital to the survival of an informal organization. This communication takes place through an informal communication channel referred to as the **grapevine**. Keith Davis, who has done much research on communication in informal organizations, found that the term *grapevine* originated during the Civil War. The temporary telegraph lines strung from tree to tree by the Union and Confederate armies resembled grapevines. Messages transmitted on them often were garbled and confused. Eventually, it became common to attribute inaccurate messages and rumors to "the grapevine."

The grapevine's reputation for inaccuracy continues to this day. However, research studies indicate that the grapevine, the informal communication channel, is in fact accurate more often than not. Davis's research indicated that 80 to 99 percent of information communicated via the grapevine is accurate for noncontroversial company information. He suggests, however, that the level of accuracy would not be as high for personal or highly emotional information. Davis states: "People tend to think the grapevine is less accurate than it is because its errors are more dramatic and consequently more impressed on memory than its day-by-day routine accuracy."[14] Furthermore, irrespective of its accuracy, "All evidence shows that the grapevine is influential, either favorably or unfavorably."[15] Table 12-1 lists some typical information carried by organizational grapevines.

Managing the Informal Organization

Homans's Model

It is important for managers to realize that informal organizations interact dynamically with the formal organization. One of the first persons to discuss this factor and the formation of informal organizations was group theorist George Homans.[16] In Homans's model, which is illustrated in Figure 12-2, activities refer to the tasks people perform. People interact with each other when performing these tasks. These interactions, in turn, result in the development of sentiments, or positive and negative feelings toward one another

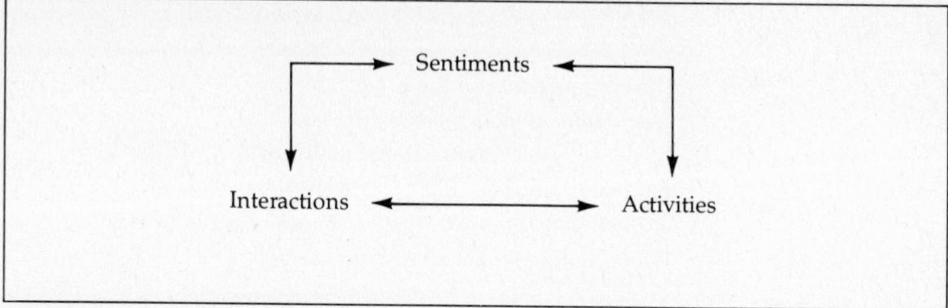

Figure 12-2 **Homans's Model**

and management. These sentiments influence the way in which people will perform their activities and interact in the future.

Besides helping show how informal organizations arise out of an action of management—the delegation of tasks—which leads to interaction, Homans's model illustrates the necessity of managing the informal organization. Because group sentiments influence both interactions and tasks they may also influence the performance of the formal organization. Depending on whether they are favorable or unfavorable, they may result in an increase or decrease in performance, absenteeism, turnover, grievances and other factors upon which organizational success is contingent. Hence, even though the informal organization is not created by management or fully under its control, it must be managed effectively for the organization to attain its objectives.

Problems and Benefits with Informal Organizations

One of the greatest and most common roadblocks preventing effective management of groups and informal organizations is perceiving them as inherently bad. The belief of some managers that an informal organization is a reflection of ineffective management is a dogmatic myth. The development of informal organizations, as we have seen, is a natural phenomenon, a pervasive component of every organization. Like so many other factors in management, informal organizations in actuality have both problems and benefits associated with them.

Problems with Informal Organizations. It is true that some informal groups may behave in ways that are counterproductive in terms of attaining formal objectives. The grapevine may spread rumors that are false and lead to negative attitudes toward management. The group's norms may cause performance to be below the objectives set by management. The tendency to resist change may impede needed innovation, as may the tendency toward conformity in informal organizations. However, such counterproductive behavior is often a reaction to the group's perception of how management is treating them. Group members perceive, correctly or not, that they are being treated inequitably and respond as any individual would to sensed unfairness.

FEATURE 12-3

How Women Managers Can Use the Informal Organization

Women working in a company should set up an informal system of relationships to support, inform and advise each other.

- *Why this is necessary:* Informal structures within an organization usually provide the best aid for becoming useful and productive and for identifying opportunities that lead to promotions. *But* these relationships in management are generally dominated by men. (There are more of them and they have been there longer.)
- *What the women's group could do:* Provide information about available jobs in various parts of the company. Locate and seek assistance from male managers who encourage and support women.
- *Obstacles to overcome when forming a group:* Limit damaging competition among women. Competent women can all move ahead. Assistance of *other* women may be crucial.

Some working women try to build up a secure position by doing a job in which they aren't dependent on anyone else. But a good *management* position is exactly the opposite. A manager must be able to delegate work, to be dependent on other people to do their assigned jobs and to assign those jobs in such a way that the person clearly knows what must be done. A manager must be able to provide assistance and support to subordinates. A manager must be able to coordinate and lead other people, to inspire confidence and trust by being confident of and trusting toward them. The informed women's group is a means of helping each woman learn those skills.

SOURCE: Reprinted from *Boardroom Reports*, July 15, 1977, p. 10, *Management's Source of Useful Information*, 500 Fifth Avenue, New York, NY 10036.

Potential Benefits of Informal Organizations. The visible negative behaviors of informal organizations sometimes blind managers to the many potential benefits of informal organizations. Since group membership is contingent on working for the organization, loyalty to the group may translate into loyalty to the organization. Many people refuse higher paying jobs with other companies because they are reluctant to give up the social ties developed at their present firm. It is possible for group objectives to be congruent with those of the formal organization and for the performance norms of the informal organization to be higher than performance objectives of the formal. For example, the intense team spirit characteristic of some organizations which results in a strong drive to succeed is often an outgrowth of informal relationships, not deliberate efforts by management. Even the grapevine may help the formal organization at times by supplementing the formal communication network.

By failing to work effectively with them, or engaging in actions to deliberately suppress informal organizations, managers often become unable to harness these potential benefits. In any event, whether a particular informal organization is harmful or beneficial, it exists and must be dealt with. Even if management disbands a particular group, another will surely arise—probably one with negative sentiments toward management. Consequently, the effective manager must learn to cope effectively with *both* the informal organizations and formal work groups.

Managing the Informal Organization

The solution proposed by earlier writers for coping with an informal organization was to destroy it. Management writers today focus on using the informal organization to help the formal organization attain its objectives. Scott and Davis offer the following suggestions for doing so:[17]

1. Recognize that the informal organization exists, and nothing can destroy it completely without also destroying the formal organization. Therefore, management should accept it, work with it, and not threaten its existence.
2. Listen to the opinions of informal leaders and group members. Discussing this, Davis writes, "Each manager needs to learn who the key informal leader is in any group and work with the leader to encourage leadership that furthers rather than hinders organizational objectives. When an informal leader is working against an employer, the leader's widespread influence can undermine motivation and job satisfaction."[18]
3. Consider possible negative effects on the informal organization before taking any action.
4. To decrease resistance to change by the informal organization, allow the group to participate in decision making.
5. Control the grapevine by promptly releasing accurate information.

Making Groups Effective

In addition to managing informal organizations in order to harness their potential benefits and curb their potential negative impact, management obviously must also make its command groups and committees effective. Since these formal groups are a deliberately created component of the formal organization, much of what we have presented about organizational manage-

FEATURE 12-4

Harnessing the Informal Organization

Romac Industries, a producer of waterworks pipes and fittings, adopted a most unusual method for determining pay raises. The stimulus was to avoid unionization. The result, though probably not deliberately intended, was an extremely effective use of the informal organization.

The system works like this: Romac, a 10-year-old company with about $3 million in annual sales, generally hires unskilled workers and starts them at $4.50 an hour. Within six months, they get about a dollar-an-hour wage increase from management.

After that, an employee desiring a raise "goes on the board." He fills out a form stating his current wage, the desired hourly increase—usually 40 cents to 80 cents—and why he thinks the raise is merited. His picture and request are posted on a bulletin board for at least five days so that other workers can observe the candidate's work habits before casting their votes. The majority rules.

The philosophy behind ballot-box raises is that workers will produce more when they know that their wages are directly dependent on how much they turn out. So every day, Romac posts the number of units each department produces per day and what each employee makes per hour.

"That way everyone can make an informed judgment about where they fit in the company, how much everybody is producing and who deserves a raise," explains Manford R. McNeil, the 52-year-old founder and president, whom the workers call "Mac." "They work with each other every day. They know better than I do who's producing and who's goofing off."

Apparently, few goof off. According to Joe Warner, the plant manager, units produced per man hour have increased about 44% since March 1977. "Of course, some of the increase is due to improved equipment and management's encouraging employee productivity, but I think the raise program has a lot to do with it," Mr. Warner says.

SOURCE: Rachel Bagey, "To Get a Pay Raise, a Worker at Romac Asks Other Workers," *Wall Street Journal*, September 9, 1979, p. 1. Reprinted by permission of *The Wall Street Journal*,

ment applies to them as well. Like the organization as a whole, groups require planning, organizing, motivating, and controlling to be effective.

Therefore, here we will focus on just the one aspect of small group performance that many managers find most problematic: facilitating group effectiveness during decision-making and problem-solving meetings. Depending on the characteristics of the group and the way in which it is conducted, a meeting can be an exercise in futility or an extremely effective tool for combining talent and experience and generating innovation. Before presenting some specific guidelines for making meetings effective, let us first note the general factors affecting the performance of a group.

Factors Affecting Group Performance

A group will be more or less effective in attaining its objectives depending on the following **factors affecting group performance**: size, composition, group norms, cohesiveness, conflict, status of members, and the functional roles of group members. These will be discussed in turn.

Size. The ideal size for a group has long been a matter of contention in management thought. Writers of the administrative management school thought that formal groups should be relatively small. R. C. Davis, for example, believed that groups with three to nine people are ideal. Keith Davis, a more contemporary writer who has done much research on groups, tends to agree. He feels that the preferred number is five.[19] Research indicates that the actual average size of group meetings ranges from five to eight members.[20]

Several studies indicate that groups with approximately five to eleven members generally make more accurate decisions than those not within this range.[21] Research has also found that groups of five people generally are characterized by greater member satisfaction than larger or smaller groups.[22] This seems to be because in groups of two or three members people may feel anxiety over their high level of visibility and responsibility. Groups with over five members, on the other hand, may increase inhibition about speaking before the group.

In general, as group size increases, communication becomes more difficult, and there is less agreement on common objectives and activities. Increased size also increases the tendency toward informal division into subgroups, which may have inconsistent goals, and the formation of cliques.

Composition. The composition of the group refers here to the degree of similarity in the members' personalities. A major reason for using a group to make a decision is to gain the benefits of diverse opinions. Thus, it is not surprising that research indicates a group composed of individuals that differ in personality traits are more effective than those whose members have similar personality traits.[23] As Miner points out, when "groups are constituted so as to contain members who are either very much alike or very different, the diverse groups produce more and better solutions. More viewpoints and perspectives are brought to bear."[24]

Group Norms. As the earliest researchers on groups in the workplace found, the norms of a group strongly affect the degree to which the group will work toward or against organizational objectives. This holds for both informal organizations and formal groups because all groups have norms that tacitly convey to members how they are expected to behave and perform. As one writer states,

> From the point of view of the organization, it can be said that norms may be of two particular natures: positive or negative. Positive norms are those that support the organization's goals and objectives and that foster behavior directed toward the achievement of these ends. Negative norms have just the opposite effect; they promote behavior that works against the organization's achieving its objectives. Norms that support hard work, loyalty, quality consciousness, or concern for customer satisfaction are examples of positive norms. Negative norms are those that sanction criticism of the company, theft, absenteeism, and low levels of productivity.[25]

Management must be careful to avoid a superficial interpretation of the group's norms. For instance, a group of executives who feel that always agreeing with the boss is sound behavior would appear to be exhibiting a high degree of loyalty. However, such a norm would in fact lead to the suppression of ideas and opinions that may be beneficial to the organization.

Cohesiveness. A group's cohesiveness is the degree to which members are attracted to each other and the group. A highly cohesive group is one in which members are highly attracted to one another, like each other, and perceive themselves to be similar. A high degree of cohesiveness can increase effectiveness, provided that the objectives of the group are consistent with those of the organization. This is because the cohesive group works well as a team.

Management may be able to increase positive cohesiveness by conducting periodic meetings that stress overall objectives of the group and enable each member to perceive his or her contribution to attainment of these objectives. Of course, if the group's objectives differ from those of the organization, a high level of cohesiveness would adversely affect performance from the organization's standpoint. This was demonstrated by the bank wiring room experiment at Hawthorne.

A potential negative consequence of high cohesiveness is groupthink.[26] *Groupthink* is the tendency for individuals to suppress their real views on an issue in order to avoid disrupting the group's harmony. Members feel that dissent will disrupt the group's sense of belongingness and therefore should be avoided. The result is decreased performance in problem solving because all relevant information and alternative solutions are not discussed or evaluated. When groupthink occurs, there is an increased chance for a mediocre decision, one that offends nobody.

Conflict. We stated earlier that diversity usually improves group performance. However, diversity also increases the potential for conflict. Naturally, although a spirited exchange of opinions is helpful, infighting and other manifestations of outright conflict are detrimental. The causes of conflict in small groups and techniques for resolving it are the same as for other units of the organization. Therefore, we will discuss them later in this book.

Status of Group Members. An individual can acquire status in an organization or group for a number of reasons, including seniority, job title, location of office, educational background, social skills, information, and expertise. These factors will increase or decrease status depending on the values and norms of the group. Studies have shown that members with high status are more able to influence group decisions than those with low status.[27] This does not always lead to increased effectiveness.

A person who has only worked for the company a short while may have better ideas and more expertise relevant to the task than the person who has high status because of many years' seniority with the company. The same could hold for a departmental manager, who may have lower status than the person with the title of vice-president. To make effective decisions, it is essential for all relevant information to be considered and for all ideas to be weighed objectively. Thus, for the group to perform effectively it may be necessary for the higher status members to make a concerted effort to prevent their ideas from dominating the group.

Functional Roles of Group Members. The way individuals behave in a group is a critical factor affecting group performance. For the group to perform effectively, its members need to behave appropriately with respect to both carrying out objectives and interacting socially. Thus, there are two functional role orientations required for an effective group setting. The first, task roles, are concerned with selecting and carrying out a group task. Maintenance roles refer to behaviors related to strengthening and maintaining group life and activities. These behaviors are summarized in Table 12-2.

Guidelines for Effective Meetings

Studies such as those of Mintzberg have shown that managers spend much time attending meetings. The factors previously cited as affecting the general performance of groups also apply to meetings. Leland Bradford offers the following guidelines for increasing the effectiveness of meetings:[28]

1. Formulate specific objectives for the meeting and review them briefly at the start of the meeting.
2. Ensure that there is an open flow of communication among group members.
3. Use members' resources fully and encourage participation. The competence, expertise, information, and ideas of *all* members should be brought to bear.

Table 12-2 Behaviors in a Group

Task Roles
1. *Initiating activity:* proposing solutions, suggesting new ideas, new definitions of the problem, new attack on the problem, or new organization of material
2. *Seeking information:* asking for clarification of suggestions, requesting additional information or facts
3. *Seeking information:* looking for an expression of feeling about something from the members, seeking clarification of values, suggestions or ideas
4. *Giving information:* offering facts or generalizations, relating one's own experience to the group problem to illustrate points
5. *Giving opinion:* stating an opinion or belief concerning a suggestion or one of the several suggestions, particularly concerning its value rather than just its factual basis.
6. *Elaborating:* clarifying, giving examples or developing meanings, trying to envision how a proposal might work if adopted
7. *Coordinating:* showing relationships among various ideas or suggestions, trying to pull ideas and suggestions together, trying to draw together activities of various subgroups or members
8. *Summarizing:* pulling together related ideas or suggestions, restating suggestions after the group has discussed them
Maintenance Roles
1. *Encouraging:* being friendly, warm, responsive to others, praising others in their ideas, agreeing with and accepting contributions of others
2. *Gate keeping:* trying to make it possible for another member to make a suggestion to the group by saying, "We haven't heard anything from Jim yet" or suggesting limited talking time to everyone so that all will have a chance to be heard
3. *Standard setting:* expressing standards for the group to use in choosing its content or procedures or in evaluating its decisions, reminding group to avoid decisions which conflict with group standards
4. *Following:* going along with the decisions of the group, thoughtfully accepting ideas of others, serving as audience during group discussion
5. *Expressing group feelings:* summarizing what group feeling is sensed to be, describing reactions of the group to ideas or solutions

SOURCE: "Role Functions in a Group," *The 1976 Handbook for Group Facilitators* (La Jolla, CA: University Associates, 1976), pp. 136–137.

4. There should be a climate of trust so members feel free to comment openly and tactfully on views and ideas with which they disagree.
5. Conflict should be viewed as a positive force and be managed effectively.

Avoiding Groupthink. A group meeting intended to gain the benefits of diversity of opinion cannot be successful unless groupthink is circumvented. To decrease the potential for groupthink, the leader of the meeting should: (1) convey to group members that they should feel free to express any opinions or doubts they have about anything being discussed; (2) appoint one member to play the role of devil's advocate; (3) be able to accept differences of opinion and criticisms as constructive comments.

The Management of Committees

A *committee* is a group within the organization delegated authority for a particular duty or group of duties. Sometimes committees are referred to as boards, task forces, commissions, or teams. But in all cases, it is *group* decision making and action that distinguishes the committee from other organizing systems.

Three out of four jokes about bad management seem to contain the word committee. Yet, the use of committees is definitely on the rise. This is partly because the committee is compatible with any major system of organizing, partly because of the increasingly technical nature of business decisions. But the main reason why committees have not become outmoded is that a correctly used committee is a highly effective tool for accomplishing certain objectives.

Types of Committees

There are two general types of committees, *ad hoc* and *standing.*

An **ad hoc committee** is a temporary group formed for a particular purpose. (*Ad hoc* is a Latin term meaning "for this.") The production manager might form an ad hoc committee to identify production problems and alternative ways of correcting them. Congress frequently forms ad hoc committees to study special problems or handle sensitive matters. The Warren Commission assigned to investigate President Kennedy's assassination is an example. After an ad hoc committee completes its work, it disbands.

A **standing committee** is a permanent group within the organization with a particular purpose. The most frequent use of standing committees is to advise the organization in areas of continuing importance. A familiar and very widely used example of a standing committee is the board of directors. The board of a large business frequently is divided into standing committees such as the audit committee, the finance committee, and the executive committee. Reporting to the president of a large company are often committees on policy, planning, grievances, and salary review, among others.

At lower levels of management, committees could be created for such tasks as: cost reduction, improvements on the production line, social affairs, improving relationships between departments.

Authority and Committees

Within many organizations there are, in addition to the above, informal committees. These are groups organized outside of the formal organization to cope with a sensed problem. For example, four production workers may decide to meet for 20 minutes to discuss problems that are occurring in the production process. Like all informal work groups these may help or hinder the organization. Whichever is the case, they operate only because they have obtained power, not because they have authority.

The authority of a committee is delegated by management, exactly as is the authority of individuals. Like individuals, committees must account to the delegator for performance of their duties. However, because a committee is a group, individual accountability is diminished. Committees can have either line or staff authority. The majority have staff authority. The Cabinet and National Security Council, for example, are standing committees with staff authority in the federal government delegated by and accountable to the president of the United States.

The board of directors, on the other hand, is a standing committee with line authority in the organization. The board not only advises the president but can also take action to implement its decisions through the line organization. When a committee has line authority, as does the board, it is called a *plural executive.* Very large businesses sometimes use plural executives in addition to the board to formulate and implement important policies and major spending proposals. The Communist party of the Soviet Union has a plural executive, the *troika,* in its chain of command.

When to Use Committees

Like any management tool, a committee will only be effective if all or most factors in the situation favor its use. Most management theorists advocate a committee only when a group could do the job better than an individual or when it would be risky for the organization to give any single individual total power. The following are situations where the use of committee organization may be desirable:

1. When the problem is one that requires considerable expertise in a specific area. A committee can be used to advise the executive responsible for the decision. In today's complex, rapidly changing environment, it is unreasonable to expect a top-level manager of a diversified enterprise to keep abreast of all the details affecting the organization. Advice from a committee on all pros and cons of a new and complex area, especially one in which the firm has never been involved, can be extremely useful. Examples of such a situation would include the decisions to enter a new market, develop a new product line, acquire or merge with another company, raise a large amount of capital for expansion, and respond to social or legal pressure to modify major policies.
2. When a decision is almost certain to be highly unpopular in the organization. A committee can be used to diffuse resentment and responsibility. The board of trustees of a university will frequently make unpopular decisions that would expose the president or chancellor to unpleasant social pressure.
3. When it would improve morale to have group participation in the decision. Occasionally a decision would disrupt morale if it were forced on

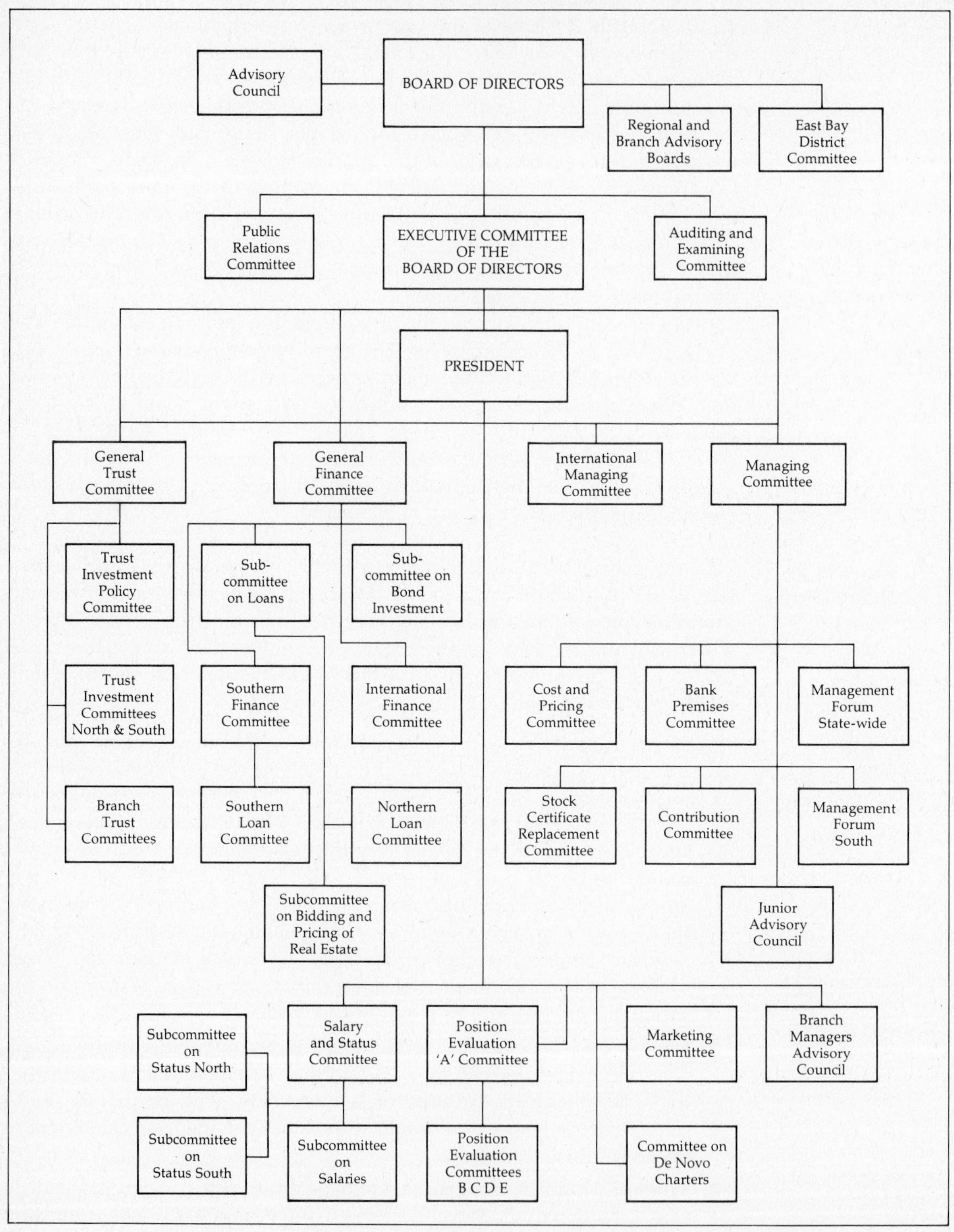
Advisory Council
BOARD OF DIRECTORS
Regional and Branch Advisory Boards
East Bay District Committee
Public Relations Committee
EXECUTIVE COMMITTEE OF THE BOARD OF DIRECTORS
Auditing and Examining Committee
PRESIDENT
General Trust Committee
General Finance Committee
International Managing Committee
Managing Committee
Trust Investment Policy Committee
Sub-committee on Loans
Sub-committee on Bond Investment
Trust Investment Committees North & South
Southern Finance Committee
International Finance Committee
Cost and Pricing Committee
Bank Premises Committee
Management Forum State-wide
Branch Trust Committees
Southern Loan Committee
Northern Loan Committee
Stock Certificate Replacement Committee
Contribution Committee
Management Forum South
Subcommittee on Bidding and Pricing of Real Estate
Junior Advisory Council
Subcommittee on Status North
Salary and Status Committee
Position Evaluation 'A' Committee
Marketing Committee
Branch Managers Advisory Council
Subcommittee on Status South
Subcommittee on Salaries
Position Evaluation Committees B C D E
Committee on De Novo Charters

subordinates without consulting them. In these situations, management can use a committee to bring subordinates into the decision-making process.

4. When there is a need to coordinate the work of diverse departments in the organization. A committee brings managers together and helps them gain a better understanding of their role.
5. When it is undesirable to give full power to a single individual. Spreading authority over members of a committee can help an organization avoid mistakes in crucial areas and relieve pressure on top management. Insurance companies often use a committee to evaluate and approve investments because of the large sums of money involved and the need to ensure that conservative tactics are being used.

When Not to Use Committees

The committee's notoriety for ineffectiveness often is traceable to misuse. Committees are subject to mismanagement and overuse. Below are some common abuses of committees and situations where an individual would perform more effectively than a group.

1. When the committee's authority and responsibilities are not clearly defined. In this case it will face the same problems as an individual in a similar situation. Before forming a committee, management must decide exactly what its purpose is:

- Just diagnose the problem?
- Submit a list of solutions with pros and cons?
- Recommend a single course of action?
- Actually implement its decision? (To do so, the committee must have line authority.)

2. When the committee is too large or too small. There is a tendency to add members to a committee for political expediency, rather than because

---

Figure 12-3 Committee Organization in a Large Bank

This bank has supplemented its management organization structure with a large number of committees and subcommittees. All these groups exert influence on management policy and decision making, and certain committees, such as the position evaluation committee, actually make decisions. Others, such as the advisory council of the board of directors and the regional and branch advisory boards, operate only in an advisory capacity. Likewise, the general trust committee concerns itself only with policy decisions, while the trust investment and branch trust committees make actual decisions. Most of the committees have as their members senior or other key managers from all the important departments and divisions of the company. The junior advisory council, however, consists of lower-level managers or those about to be placed in a managerial capacity. While it carries on important analyses and projects and advises senior management groups, its primary purpose is training junior managers for future increased responsibilities in the bank.

SOURCE: Koontz and O'Donnell, *Management: A Systems and Contingency Analysis of Managerial Functions*, 6th edition (New York: McGraw-Hill, 1976), pp. 412–413. Reprinted by permission.

the person would genuinely contribute. The optimal size for a committee is 5 to 10. Involving fewer than five people may be insufficient for gaining the full benefits of diversified opinion. More than 10 people is unwieldy and makes it difficult for all members to fully participate.[29]

3. When the committee wastes time. C. Northcote Parkinson noted that committees tend to spend more time on matters easily understood by all members than they do on highly complex issues. This is because many people are reluctant to demonstrate ignorance by speaking out on an unfamiliar or controversial subject. Hence, committees sometimes haggle endlessly on trivial matters yet make crucial decisions in a matter of minutes. Parkinson calls this the "law of triviality": "The time spent on any item of the agenda will be in inverse proportion to the sum involved."[30] Time is a costly resource. A committee that wastes it on trivia may not be worthwhile.
4. When rapid decision making and implementation is crucial. No group can act as quickly and decisively as a competent single individual. Recognition of this is why the president of the United States cannot declare war but is given authority to use the armed forces in the defense of the nation in any way he sees fit for a limited period.
5. When compromise leads to mediocrity. A group decision seldom is unanimous. If dissent is strong, the compromise decision that everyone can live with usually reflects the lowest common denominator of the group.
6. When the committee costs more than it is worth. Obviously, the manpower cost of making a group decision far exceeds that of an individual choice. Top management must therefore consider how much money the problem really involves before assigning it to a committee.
7. When conformity results, causing the committee to not critically assess ideas of fellow members. A group can become overly enthusiastic about a project as easily as it becomes too cautious. Individuals may suppress their doubts in the face of this enthusiasm, fearing their colleagues will consider them poor "team players."

In addition to the preceding, it must be kept in mind that committees are groups. Therefore, all the characteristics, processes, and problems of groups also pertain to them.

SUMMARY

A group is two or more people who interact with one another in such a manner that each person influences and is influenced by each other person. An organization often contains many formal and informal groups.

The two basic types of formal groups are command groups, which consist of a manager and his or her immediate subordinates, and committees or task forces. These small groups must be managed effectively because they are the building blocks of the organization.

Informal organizations emerge out of the social interaction that is an inevitable part of a formal organization. An informal organization is a spontaneously formed group of people who interact regularly for some identifiable purpose.

The impact of informal organizations and groups was brought to management's attention by the Hawthorne experiments of Elton Mayo. An impetus for the human relations school, they demonstrated that an organization is a social system. Another discovery was the Hawthorne effect, a condition in which newness or extra attention causes a distorted, overly favorable result in an experiment.

People join groups and organizations for affiliation, assistance, protection, and communication.

Primary characteristics of informal organizations are social control, resistance to change, the existence of informal leaders, and a communication network referred to as the grapevine. The grapevine is far more accurate, at least for nonemotional information, than commonly believed. Homans's model illustrates that the informal organization interacts dynamically with the formal, affecting performance of tasks and the way people perceive their jobs and management.

Problems associated with informal organizations include causing performance to fall below managerial standards, spreading false rumors, and a tendency to resist change. Potential benefits include increased loyalty to the organization, high team spirit, and higher productivity when group norms exceed formal standards.

Management cannot eradicate informal organizations, but it can manage them to harness their potential advantages and curb their disadvantages. To do so management should accept the informal organization and work with it, listen to the opinions of informal leaders and group members, consider the effect of actions on the informal organization, allow the group to participate in decision making, and control the grapevine by promptly releasing information.

Small groups play an essential role in organizational success. Factors influencing the performance of a group include size, composition, group norms, cohesiveness, degree of conflict, status of group members, and functional roles of group members. The most effective group would be one of a size suited to its task, composed of heterogeneous personality types, with norms favoring work toward organizational objectives, with team spirit, a healthy level of conflict, not dominated by high status members, and good performance of both task and maintenance roles.

A meeting will usually be more effective if its leader formulates specific objectives for it, ensures open communication, uses the resources of all members, builds a climate of trust, and manages conflict effectively. Also, an effort must be made to avoid groupthink.

Committees are widely used to fill gaps in the organizational structure and ensure that essential tasks not clearly part of any department's responsibilities are performed, to coordinate departments, and to perform special functions. Standing committees are permanent; ad hoc, temporary. If the committee has line authority it is called a plural executive.

Committees are most useful in situations where either the problem requires special expertise, the decision to be made is likely to be unpopular, morale would be improved by group decision making, when it is necessary to coordinate the work of diverse units, or when it is undesirable to give full power to a single individual.

REVIEW QUESTIONS

1. Define groups and informal organization.
2. What did the Hawthorne experiment contribute to management thought?
3. How do informal groups and organizations arise?
4. Why do people join groups?
5. List the characteristics of a group.
6. What is a grapevine and why is it important to informal organizations?
7. What are some benefits and problems of informal organizations?
8. What are the principal types of committees?
9. When should committees be used?
10. What factors affect the performance of a group?

DISCUSSION QUESTIONS

11. Describe an example of group cohesiveness working against a formal organization.
12. How do you feel management should respond to the grapevine?
13. How could you use the informal organization to advance your own career?
14. What can a manager do to effectively manage groups and informal organizations?

CASE INCIDENT

Readi-Range

Maybe not the biggest but the best. For the past thirty years Readi-Range placed great emphasis on quality gas and electric kitchen ranges. Today the company is recognized as a producer of first-class products. Perhaps this is why Bill Neel, Readi-Range's marketing vice-president, was so disturbed by customer complaints about the early American model, a range designed to capitalize on the country's bicentennial celebration. Apparently the range's wooden handle was not holding up, and it was this handle that helped give this model its uniqueness.

When Bill Neel shared his concern with Harley Thompson, vice-president of manufacturing, Thompson replied that, as usual, the folks in sales were blowing things out of proportion. Neel assured Thompson that this wasn't the case and that he, Neel, was not crying wolf, but that the wolf was really at the door and ready to break in. In order to prove his point, Neel invited Thompson to attend the next customers' meeting and gather some information firsthand.

Twice a year, special meetings were held for Readi-Range's biggest customers. At these meetings, new models were introduced, and customers, in this case primarily department and furniture stores, were invited to look at the new range and to discuss sales promotions, product problems, and other matters pertaining to their relationship with Readi-Range.

Thompson accepted, and at the customers' meeting heard Norman Jackson, one of Readi-Range's most important customers say, "the next time Readi-Range ships me an early American range with a defective handle is when I start looking for another vendor."

Jackson's comment caught Thompson's attention, since Jackson had bought 2000 units last year from Readi-Range.

When Thompson saw Neel after the meeting, he said Jackson had made a believer of him. "Now," Thompson said, "I'm going to have to convince my people."

Questions

1. In terms of informal organization, how would you interpret Thompson's comment about convincing "my people."
2. If you were Thompson, what would you do?
3. As a student of management, what does this incident indicate about formal-informal organization relationships?

NOTES

1. Marvin E. Shaw, *Group Dynamics: The Psychology of Small Group Behavior* (New York: McGraw-Hill, 1971), p. 10.
2. Elton Mayo, *The Human Problems of an Industrial Civilization* (New York: Macmillan, 1933), chapters 3–5.
3. Ibid., p. 74.
4. F. J. Roethlisberger and William J. Dickson, *Management and the Worker* (Cambridge, MA: Harvard University Press, 1949), p. 419.
5. Milton L. Blum and James C. Naylor, *Industrial Psychology* (New York: Harper & Row, 1968), p. 313.
6. William G. Scott and T. R. Mitchell, *Organization Theory: A Structural and Behavioral Analysis* (Homewood, IL: Richard D. Irwin, 1972), p. 28.
7. Alex Carey, "The Hawthorne Studies: A Radical Criticism," *American Sociological Review*, June 1967, pp. 403–414.
8. Leonard S. Sayles and George Strauss, *Human Behavior in Organizations* (Englewood Cliffs, N.J.: Prentice-Hall, 1966), p. 89.
9. Elton Mayo, "Irrationality and Revery," *Journal of Personnel Research*, March 1923.
10. D. M. Kipnis, "Interaction Between Members of Bomber Crews As a Determinant of Sociometric Choice," *Human Relations*, vol. 10 (1957), pp. 263–270.
11. Lawrence S. Wrightsman, *Social Psychology in the Seventies* (Monterey, CA: Brooks/Cole, 1972), pp. 418–419.
12. William Scott, "Organization Theory: An Overview and Appraisal," *Academy of Management Journal*, vol. 4 (1961), pp. 7–26.

13. Kenneth D. Benne and Paul Sheats, "Functional Roles of Group Members," *Journal of Social Issues*, vol. 4 (1948), pp. 41–49.
14. Keith Davis, *Human Behavior at Work* (New York: McGraw-Hill, 1977).
15. Ibid., pp. 280–282.
16. George C. Homans, *The Human Group* (New York: Harcourt Brace Jovanovich, 1950).
17. Scott, op. cit.; Davis, op. cit.
18. Davis, op. cit., p. 273.
19. R. C. Davis, *Fundamentals of Top Management* (New York: Harper & Row, 1951); Keith Davis, *Human Relations in Business* (New York: McGraw-Hill Book Company, 1957).
20. R. Tillman, "Problems in Review: Committees on Trial," *Harvard Business Review*, vol. 38 (1960), pp. 6–8.
21. G. E. Manners, Jr., "Another Look at Group Size, Group Problem Solving, and Member Consensus," *Academy of Management Journal*, vol. 18 (1975): no. 4, pp. 715–724; E. J. Thomas and C. F. Fink, "Effects of Group Size," *Psychological Bulletin*, vol. 60 (1963), pp. 371–384.
22. R. Hackman and N. Vidmar, "Effects of Size and Task Type on Group Performance and Member Reactions," *Sociometry*, vol. 33 (1970), pp. 37–54; P. E. Slater, "Contrasting Correlates of Group Size," *Sociometry*, vol. 21 (1958), pp. 129–139.
23. L. R. Hoffman, "Homogeneity of Member Personality and Its Effect on Group Problem Solving," *Journal of Abnormal and Social Psychology*, vol. 58 (1959), pp. 27–32; L. R. Hoffman and N. R. Maier, "Quality and Acceptance of Problem Solutions by Members of Homogeneous and Heterogeneous Groups," *Journal of Abnormal and Social Psychology*, vol. 62 (1961), pp. 401–407; E. E. Chiselli and T. M. Lodahl, "Patterns of Managerial Traits and Group Effectiveness," *Journal of Abnormal and Social Psychology*, vol. 57 (1958), pp. 61–66.
24. John B. Miner, *The Management Process* (New York: Macmillan, 1973), pp. 194–195.
25. Mark Alexander, "Organizational Norms," *1977 Annual Handbook for Group Facilitators* (La Jolla, CA: University Associates, 1977), p. 123.
26. Irving Janis, *Group Think* (Reading, MA: Addison-Wesley, 1972).
27. P. A. Collaros and L. R. Anderson, "Effect of Perceived Expertness Upon Creativity of Members of Brainstorming Groups," *Journal of Applied Psychology*, vol. 53 (1969), pp. 159–163; E. P. Torrance, "Some Consequences of Power Differences on Decision Making in Permanent and Temporary Three-Man Groups," in *Small Groups: Studies in Social Interaction*, eds. A. P. Hare, E. F. Borgatta, and R. F. Bells, (New York: Alfred A. Knopf, 1955), pp. 482–491.
28. Leland P. Bradford, *Making Meetings Work* (La Jolla, CA: University Associates, 1976).
29. Cyril O'Donnell, "Group Rules for Using Committees," *Management Review*, vol. 50 (October 1961): no. 10, pp. 63–67.
30. Cyril N. Parkinson, *Parkinson's Law and Other Studies in Administration* (Boston: Houghton-Mifflin, 1957).

CHAPTER **13**

Power and Personal Influence: Their Role in Leadership

We learned in the last chapter that groups and informal organizations can strongly influence individual behavior and organizational performance. The manager clearly needs to direct the groups' efforts—and that of all individuals—toward objectives, even though these relationships may fall outside those prescribed by management. The basic primary mechanism for accomplishing this direction is leadership and the distinct but closely related concepts of power and personal influence. This chapter concentrates on power and influence to lay a foundation for our more extended discussion of leadership approaches. Just as the degree of delegated authority determines what a manager has the right to do in the formal organization, a person's relative power determines what he or she is able to do in informal as well as formal relationships. Many people perceive power as being a bit dirty, but as we shall soon learn, power is necessary for organizational success.

After reading this chapter, you should understand the following important terms and concepts:

- difference between leading and managing
- organizational leader
- influence
- power
- need for power in management
- coercive power
- reward power
- expert power
- referent power
- traditional or legitimate power
- charisma
- rational faith
- situational nature of power
- power of persuasion and participation
- dependency and power

Power, Influence, and the Managerial Leader

Business students are often surprised by the low regard some practicing managers have for academic theories of management. It is fine, these critics argue, to talk of organizing, planning, motivating, and control. Studying why certain practices work and speculation about what *should* be the best way to handle the manager's job is an interesting intellectual exercise. However, management theories have never been famous for causing action. When you step out of the ivory tower into the real world, the manager's job boils down to getting someone else to do something the way *you* want it done. What really counts, these critics feel, is the effective use of leadership, influence, and power.

This view considerably predates the concept of professional management. The theme of Nicolo Machiavelli's famous work, *The Prince*, published in the 1600s, is that raw power and outright manipulation are the best means to run a state. The popularity of Anthony Jay's *Management and Machiavelli* and Michael Korda's *Power!*[1] illustrates how enduring and pervasive it is even today.

As often is the case with opinions that have endured and grown widespread, there is validity to the argument that power and leadership are the most significant tools for managing effectively.[2] However, anyone who thinks that leadership *alone* is the answer is short-sighted. All functions of management must be performed for a complex organization to attain objectives effectively. Like communicating and decision making, leading is an activity that pervades all of management. Planning, organizing, motivating, and controlling cannot be performed effectively without effective managerial leadership.

Organizational Leadership

Leading Versus Managing. Although leadership is an essential ingredient of effective management, effective leaders are not necessarily effective managers. A leader succeeds whenever he or she successfully influences others. Unquestionably effective leadership sometimes can be a hindrance to the formal organization. This happens, for example, when a powerful informal leader gets the work group to restrict its output or produce poor quality goods or services. As Filley, House, and Kerr state **the difference between leading and managing**: "Management can be defined as a process, mental and physical, whereby subordinates are brought to execute prescribed formal duties and to accomplish certain given objectives. Leadership, in contrast, is a process whereby one person exerts influence over the members of a group."[3]

An example of an extremely effective leader who eventually proved to be a poor manager was Adolf Hitler. While Hitler managed to convince millions to follow him, he did not manage well enough to attain his organizational objective of world supremacy for Germany. A manager is successful only when the *organization* attains its objectives.

Also, the manager achieves that status through a deliberate act of the formal organization, the delegation of authority. Leaders, on the other hand, cannot be created at will by the organization, although the ability to lead can be increased through delegation of authority. While people in an organization are conscious of who managers are, followers sometimes do not realize they are being led. Finally, leaders are not limited by restrictions to authority and structural boundaries. It is quite common for a manager to be a leader of people with no connection at all to his or her formal position in the hierarchy. It is even possible, as we shall soon learn, for subordinates to lead their superiors in certain situations.

Organizational Leadership Defined. Our primary concern in this book is the **organizational leader**, a person who must *both* lead and manage effectively. The organizational leader's objective is to influence others to do the work of the organization. Many writers have attempted to pin down in their definitions of organizational leadership what special ingredient the leader contributes. Katz and Kahn, for instance, saw leadership as "the influential increment over and above mechanical compliance with the routine directives of the organization."[4] Peter Drucker carries this line of thought even further in his definition:

> Leadership is the lifting of a man's vision to higher sights, the raising of a man's performance to a higher standard, the building of man's personality beyond its normal limitations.[5]

Our definition of leadership in its managerial context is:

> *Leadership is the ability to influence individuals and groups to work toward attaining organizational objectives.*

In the next chapter, we shall explore at length the various approaches or styles managers can adopt to lead effectively, their relative benefits, and the impact of the situation on leadership. However, for that discussion to be meaningful, it is necessary to first grasp how leadership operates and what it is that enables a person to energize others to act. Thus, in this chapter our attention focuses on the underlying elements of leadership: influence and power.

Influence and Power

Influence is "any behavior on the part of one individual which alters the behavior, attitudes, feelings, and so on, of another."[6] The specific means whereby one person can influence another might range from a request whispered softly in the ear to a knife against the throat. The equivalent of the latter in an organizational setting would be a threat of firing.

A person can also strongly influence others through ideas alone. Karl Marx, who had no formal authority in any political organization and never personally used violence, had an incalculable influence on the course of the twentieth century. Managers need to influence in a way that is highly predictable and leads not just to acceptance of an idea, but to action—actual work toward the organization's objectives. To influence and lead effectively, the manager must develop and use *power*.

Power. Power has had a bad public image ever since Lord Acton said, "Power tends to corrupt and absolute power corrupts absolutely." Most people associate power with violence, strength, and aggression. This is an understandable attitude. Indeed, brute force often does underly power, even in genteel societies such as our own that frown on violence outside of sports and television. But force is not a requisite for power. In fact, as we will soon discover, the fist—even when gloved in velvet—in certain circumstances may diminish rather than increase power. As we define it:

Power is the ability to influence the behavior of others.

The manager **needs power** in addition to formal authority because of his dependency on people both within and outside his chain of command.

Dependency and the Manager. Every manager is dependent upon superiors, subordinates, and peers in several parts of the organization. Without the cooperation of these people, the manager cannot perform his or her duties effectively. Many managers also are directly dependent upon outside individuals and organizations, such as suppliers, customers, competitors, regulating agencies, and unions. In an ideal world, all of these people and forces would willingly cooperate to give the manager whatever is necessary to get the job done and meet the organization's objectives. The real world, unfortunately, is not so idyllic.

Even when a manager clearly has the authority to direct a subordinate's efforts, it is not always possible to do so. As Chester Barnard observed and as we noted in our discussion of authority, the subordinate can reject the manager's request, thereby effectively eliminating his authority. Modern workers are generally more educated and less willing to comply with traditional authority than their predecessors. Even if this problem does not exist, managers are often highly dependent on people over whom they have no formal authority at all. Line management, for example, has become increasingly dependent on staff over which it has no control for information and services. Staff, in some situations, has only advisory authority and must depend on line to get suggestions implemented.

This dependency on factors and people that cannot be directly controlled is a leading cause of executive frustration. More than feelings are at stake, however. If the manager cannot deal with these many "uncontrollable" forces effectively, he or she cannot perform his or her own job, which will necessarily decrease individual and organizational effectiveness.

Power and influence, the tools of leadership, are virtually the only means the manager has to cope with these situations. Unless the manager has sufficient power to influence those on whom his performance is dependent, he simply cannot obtain the resources needed to formulate and attain objectives through others. Thus, although often abused, power is a requisite for organizational success. As sociologist Robert Biersted states, "Power stands behind every organization and sustains its structure. Without power there is no organization and without power there is no order."[7]

The Power Balance

The concept of dependency also illustrates the incorrectness of another common impression about power. Many people feel that having power infers an ability to impose one's will irrespective of the feelings, desires, and abilities of the other person. If this were true, the appointed leaders of the organization, managers, would always have the power to influence at least their own subordinates. However, it is now widely recognized that influence and power depend as much on the person being influenced and the situation as on the leader's ability. Absolute power does not exist because nobody can influence all people in all situations.

In an organizational setting, for example, power is only partially determined by the hierarchy. The important determinant of how much power one has in a given situation is not the degree of formal authority, but the degree to which the other person is dependent. The more dependent the other person, the greater one's power. This can be expressed by saying the power person A has to influence person B is equal to person B's dependency on person A:[8]

$$P\,A_b = D\,B_a$$

Power of Subordinates. For example, managers usually have power over subordinates because they are dependent on the manager for such things as raises, work assignments, promotions, increased authority, social need fulfillment, and so on. However, in some situations the subordinate has power over the manager because the manager is dependent on him or her for such things as information needed to make decisions, informal contacts with people in other subunits whose cooperation the manager needs, the influence the subordinate may have over fellow workers, and the ability of the subordinate to perform tasks. A good example of subordinates having considerable power over management is the extremely favorable contracts popular entertainers and sports figures are able to obtain. Management obviously would prefer not to pay salaries in excess of a million dollars, far more than they themselves usually earn, to any individual. However, they have little choice because the organization and, therefore, themselves are highly dependent on these individuals in order to attain their sales objectives and competition for popular sports figures is very great.

Summarizing the factors that confer power to subordinates, David Mechanic states,

> To the extent that a person is dependent on another, he or she is potentially subject to the other person's power. Within organizations one makes others dependent upon him by controlling access to information, persons, and instrumentalities which I shall define as follows:
>
> Information includes knowledge of the organization, knowledge about persons, knowledge about norms, procedures, techniques, and so forth.
>
> Persons include anyone within the organization or anyone outside the organization upon whom the organization is dependent.
>
> Instrumentalities include any aspect of the physical plant of the organization or its resources (equipment, machines, money, and so on).[9]

Research has verified that subordinates have power. In one study hospital attendants were found to have power because ward physicians were dependent on them. This dependence was due to the physician's short tenure, low interest in administration, and the large amount of administrative work required. As a result, there was a tacit negotiation that gave the attendants increased power over decision making concerning patients in exchange for performing some of the doctor's administrative tasks. If the physician did not honor this understanding, the attendants withheld information, disobeyed orders, and generally failed to cooperate. This made it difficult for the doctor to handle paperwork and obtain updated medical information required for daily treatments.[10]

Another study found that prison guards were somewhat dependent on inmates. Although guards could report inmates for disobedience, frequent reports would convey to prison officials that the guards were unable to maintain order and command obedience. Therefore, the guards allowed some rule violations in exchange for more overall cooperative behavior.[11]

The manager must realize that because subordinates often have power, using all the power at his or her disposal unilaterally may cause subordinates to respond by demonstrating their own power. This can result in wasted effort and decreased goal attainment. An effective manager therefore tries to maintain a reasonable balance of power, enough to accomplish objectives, but not so much as to cause subordinates to feel powerless and rebellious. This balance is illustrated in Figure 13-1.

David McClelland, whose research suggests that effective managers have a high need for power, also observes that effective managers do not express power in a dominant-submissive manner.[12] Rather, the positive, or socialized, face of power is characterized by concern for group objectives, helping the group formulate them, providing the group with the means to attain them, and providing group members with support and a feeling of competence.

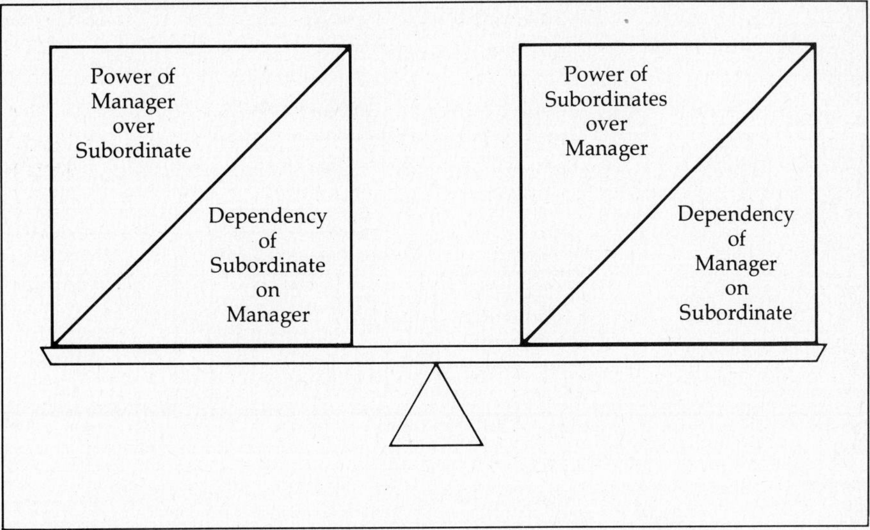

Figure 13-1 Balancing Managerial and Subordinate Power

SOURCE: Adapted from D. A. Nadler, J. R. Hackman, and E. E. Lawler, *Managing Organizational Behavior* (Boston: Little, Brown and Co., 1979), p. 164. Reprinted by permission.

Forms of Power and Influence

We have already pointed out that to lead one must influence and to influence effectively one must have a base of power. Common sense leads us to understand that to have power one must appear able to control something of importance to the follower, something that will create dependency and cause him or her to act as desired. The one "something" we all have in common are the basic needs identified by Maslow: physiological, safety, social, esteem, and self-actualization. Recall our discussion of motivation, and you should readily perceive that power must somehow be based on an appeal to the follower's active needs.

All forms of influence induce people to follow another's wishes by fulfilling or preventing fulfillment of unsatisfied needs, or they induce the follower to *expect* that a need will or will not be satisfied, depending on how the follower behaves. As we have discussed, people develop expectations about what may occur as a result of behaving a certain way. After behaving this way, the person perceives the results of the behavior on his or her need state. The leader also perceives the effect of the influence attempt on the prospective follower's behavior. As a result, the leader and the follower learn to behave in a similar or different manner in the future. This process of leader-subordinate influence is illustrated in Figure 13-2.

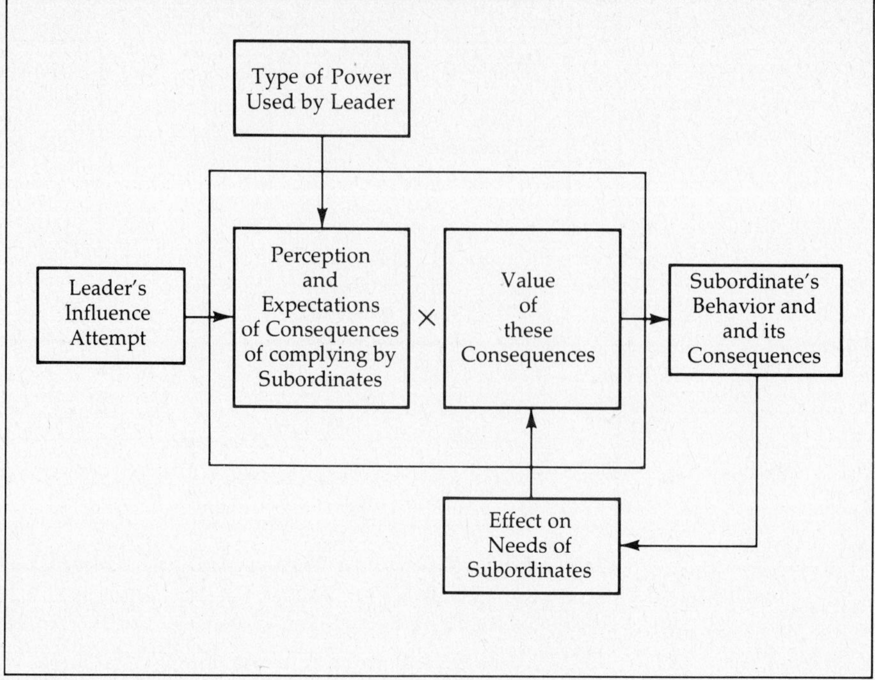

Figure 13-2 Leader-Subordinate Influence Model

SOURCE: Adapted from David Nadler, J. Richard Hackman, and Edward Lawler, *Managing Organizational Behavior* (Boston: Little, Brown and Co., 1979), p. 162. Reprinted by permission.

Bases of Power

There are many ways power can be accomplished, many forms power can take. French and Raven, researchers in the area of power and leadership, came up with one very popular classification of the bases of power.[13] According to them, there are five primary forms of power:

- *Coercive power* is based on fear. The follower believes that the influencer has the ability to punish in a way that will prevent satisfaction of an active need or will be otherwise unpleasant.
- *Reward power* is based on the follower's belief that the influencer has the ability to satisfy an active need or give pleasure.
- *Expert power* is based on the follower's belief that the influencer has special knowledge that will satisfy a need of the follower.
- *Referent power* is based on characteristics or attributes of the influencer that cause the follower to be strongly attracted to or identify with the influencer.
- *Legitimate power* is based on the follower's values. The follower believes that the influencer has the right to give orders and that it is his or her duty to obey. He or she follows because tradition teaches that obedience

FEATURE 13-1

Machiavellian Business

Proof that Machiavelli's ideas are still influential are the following suggestions from Professor Arthur J. Kover of Cornell University who teaches a graduate course nicknamed Machiavellian Business.

If you want power (either to tell others what to do or to protect yourself from others who may seek to direct your future), the first rule is: *get power as quickly as you can*. Get into a position where *you* make the decisions. That means you assert your decision-making role as quickly as possible. You must balance this aggressive stance with a concession of diffidence to the real power in the organization. Done stupidly, it comes across as subservience; done with wit, it's strategic positioning. The subordinate who learns his boss' weakness and complements him by filling in those weaknesses, does a service to the boss, the organization—and to himself. It quickly places him in a position of being in control of a function important to the boss and the organization, and that's a source of power.

General rule: Never make an enemy if you can avoid it. The business world is too small. An enemy today may be your superior tomorrow. In some situations, that rule may be hard to follow.

Example: You and your colleague are under consideration for a promotion. You get it. He either quits or stays on and hates you. *How to defuse that hate and get his cooperation:* Follow the primary rule of getting power as quickly as you can, only this time confer the power on your colleague who is now your subordinate. Share some of your power with him, give him new responsibilities, and thus a reason to be beholden (and loyal) to you. Otherwise, he'll wait for the appropriate time and stab you in the back.

Another example: When firing someone, take the onus off yourself. Don't limit the failure to *his* shortcomings—make it a mutual shortcoming, including the organization's failure to meet his needs. And then give him time and support in finding a new job. If done right, he'll emerge unscarred (that's important), and you'll remain his friend.

There are literally hundreds of Machiavellian techniques, from memo-writing to making selective enemies for solidifying a position of power. Be aware that they all involve an element of risk. Don't be afraid to use them at appropriate moments when it's to your advantage. And use them to *protect* as well as to assault.

SOURCE: Arthur J. Kover, *Boardroom's Business Secrets* (New York: Boardroom Reports, 1977), p. 5. Reprinted from Boardroom Reports, Inc., Management's Source of Useful Information, 500 Fifth Avenue, New York, New York 10036.

will lead to satisfaction of the follower's needs. Therefore, legitimate power is often referred to as *traditional power.* Legitimate power would be operating when a subordinate obeys a manager's directives simply because he or she is superior in the organizational hierarchy. All managers exert legitimate power because they are delegated formal authority over others.

These bases of power are the means whereby the organizational leader can get others to work toward the objectives of the organization. They are also, of course, the means whereby informal leaders can work against the organization. Each will now be discussed in detail.

Coercive Power: Influence Through Fear

Coercive power, influence through fear, is what most people have in mind when they criticize power. Fear invariably evokes violent images: a loaded gun, threats of torture, a fist in the face. But if physical pain were the only mechanism for fear and coercion, its use in organizations would have disappeared when emancipation took away Simon Legree's whip. Brutality is often the medium of fear, but it is never the message. When fear turns the stomach, it is because a fundamental need, usually survival or safety, is directly threatened.

Coercive techniques will convey power whenever a person genuinely wants something and believes another is able to take it. The life of oneself or a loved one is an obvious example, but there are many less extreme ones. Many people suffer severe, continuous anxiety over losing security, love, or esteem. Therefore, even in nonviolent situations, fear is a common reason why people consciously or unconsciously allow themselves to be influenced.

Fear in the Workplace. The workplace can be especially rich in opportunities to develop power through fear and coercion because so many of our needs are satisfied there. Fear of losing one's job, for example, sometimes seems almost instinctive. Under certain circumstances, fear is so easy to use and so apparently effective—even a mild threat of firing, taking away some authority, or demotion generally gets immediate results—that some managers rely on it. When subordinates are effectively protected from crude, outright threats of this sort, management can use subtler techniques to create fear.

Ohio Bell, for instance, came up with a particularly creative technique that clearly demonstrates how far one can go from violence and still use fear effectively. All Ohio Bell did was show employees a movie. This film was a simulated newscast set in the year 1984. In it Congress was about to nationalize the phone system because it was going broke and unable to provide adequate service. Countless Bell employees would lose their jobs as a result. The anchorman concludes with a message that would have saved the company, if only workers had heeded it years ago (the current present): "a full day's work for a full day's pay." Bell calculated that increased productivity resulting from this film saved them $29 million over three years.

Fear and Managers. The blue-collar worker was once the primary target of fear-oriented techniques. Their overuse by managers did much to stimulate union membership. Now, by using coercive techniques of their own, unions have often succeeded in sheltering their members so well that it can be difficult to fire a union member for even justifiable reasons. Consequently, these days managers often seem more susceptible to influence through fear than their subordinates.

The high demand for competent, experienced managers usually makes crude threats of firing ineffective. Instead of the desired effect, it sometimes results in nothing more than a commission for an employment agency and a long, tedious search for a decent replacement. The more frequently used method of arousing a manager's fear is not through the wallet but the ego. Because they often operate on the esteem level, managers tend to fear humiliation. To avoid overkill, humiliation is typically spooned out to executives in small, barely visible doses: a casual mention by the manager, for example, that Susan already made her quota; implying the new person might be better for the promotion to vice-president; assignment of a low-status job nobody else wants; assignment of a less attractive office. These are but a few ways in which a manager can be made to fear that he may not be quite as good as he thinks he is and therefore ought to work a bit harder.[14]

Drawbacks of Influence by Fear. We have seen that fear can be and is used in modern organizations. But it is not used often because in the long run fear can be a very expensive means of influence. W. T. Grant's bankruptcy, one of the largest in history, graphically illustrates that fear ultimately is counterproductive and should be discouraged.

W. T. Grant, one of the world's largest retailers until 1975, knew it was having a problem with consumer credit, which was handled at the store manager level. Grant's choice of a solution was to set up a program of negative incentives, called Steak and Beans, for its store managers. Managers who failed to meet their quotas were subjected to such indignities as a custard pie in the face, being forced to push a peanut with their noses, having to run around their store backwards, and having their ties cut in half. All, of course, in public. Not surprisingly, most store managers began to meet their quotas almost immediately. Yet, despite these apparent improvements, Grant's kept going deeper and deeper in the red. The new top management team brought in by the company's creditors found one reason why. Store managers, knowing that Grant's controls and budgets were ineffectual, had avoided humiliation by simply falsifying their records.[15]

Fear failed to attain objectives at Grant's for the same reason coercive power fails most managers: lack of credibility and high cost. Fear is a deterrent only if there is a reasonably high probability of being caught at misbehavior. It, therefore, must be coupled with an effective control system. But, as discussed earlier, effective controls can be difficult to construct and expensive even under the best of circumstances. When coercion is the main base of power, it is almost impossible to maintain credible controls at less than prohibitive cost because the tendency for people to make a conscious effort to deceive the organization significantly increases.

Even if it is possible to institute effective controls at reasonable cost, the best possible result of influence by fear is minimally adequate performance. Because the person is given no opportunity to satisfy higher needs through work, he or she may seek their satisfaction elsewhere. Studies indicate that organizations that use coercive power heavily tend to be characterized by lower productivity and lower quality of output.[16] One study of office managers using coercive power indicated dissatisfaction among the salesmen.[17]

Organizations characterized by heavy use of fear probably cannot survive over the long term in a private enterprise, open-society environment. Our extensive presentation of fear techniques is not an endorsement, but rather a simple recognition of the realities of many organizations. Note that even the world of academia that has so strongly criticized power by coercion is occasionally guilty of using fear. "Publish or perish" is a threat most professors take quite seriously.

Reward Power: Influence Through Positive Reinforcement

The offering of rewards is one of the oldest and often most effective means of influencing others. *Reward power* influences by positively reinforcing behavior desired by the leader. The follower accepts influence because he or she expects to receive some form of reward in exchange for doing what the leader wishes. Or, in the view of expectancy motivational theory, the follower perceives that there is a high likelihood of receiving an extrinsic or intrinsic reward that will satisfy an active need, and also feels able to do what the leader desires.

As noted in our discussion of motivation, people have unique personalities and needs. Therefore, what one person perceives to be a valuable reward may not be perceived as such by another person or even by the same person in another situation. To effectively influence behavior, a reward must be perceived as sufficiently valuable. In other words, the follower must perceive the reward as an equitable exchange for acceptance of influence. This perceived fairness is reward power's major advantage over negative coercive techniques. People clearly are more likely to exert extra effort, as opposed to minimal performance, when they feel a fair, commensurate reward will be forthcoming.

Drawbacks of Reward Power. Reward power, in a sense, would always work, provided the manager were able to both correctly identify what followers perceive as rewarding and actually offer them this reward. However, in practice there are many constraints on a manager's ability to offer rewards.

Every organization has limited resources and can only budget so much for personnel rewards. Also, the manager's authority to offer incentives is limited by policies and procedures. In some cases there may be external limits, such as those imposed by a union contract, on what rewards can be offered for certain types of work. Increasing the difficulty of using reward power, of course, is that it often is very difficult to correctly identify what will be perceived as rewarding. Neither money nor increased job challenge are panaceas for influencing behavior in the workplace. The effective manager therefore learns to augment the use of reward power with other means of influence.

Legitimate Power: Influence Through Tradition

If all history is weighed, tradition would have to be considered the most common way to influence. To influence with tradition, the leader uses his legitimate and reward power to appeal to the follower's needs for safety and affiliation. The method will only work, however, if the follower has internalized values that make him believe the leader is able to satisfy those needs. Influence by tradition, therefore, is only possible when the norms of the organization's external culture support the view that following a superior is desirable behavior.

Western cultural tradition has reinforced the power of superiors for thousands of years. Almost all of us have been conditioned to obey people in certain positions. Few people, for example, have the courage to argue with a police officer giving an order. Although some younger workers today seem less predisposed to authority figures,[18] others still do what the boss says, right or wrong, just because "He's the boss, isn't he?" You probably have often done things you considered unpleasant just because your parents, whose traditional authority is deeply ingrained, told you to do them.

Tradition is particularly important to formal organizations. Ability to reward and punish reinforces the manager's power to give orders. But it would be extremely time consuming and awkward, not to mention expensive, if management had to constantly offer rewards each time it needed to get workers to follow an order. Thus, to a large degree, the smooth operation of organizations directly results from subordinates' willingness to accept the authority—legitimate power—of managers because of tradition. Tradition also continues to be a widespread and effective form of managerial influence because, unlike fear, it offers a positive reward: need satisfaction. When a person accepts influence based on tradition, he or she receives in return a sense of becoming an accepted member of a social group. This sense of belonging and identity may satisfy social needs and provide genuine security, which satisfies safety needs, as well.

An interesting, subtle appeal of tradition for some people is that it can eliminate or greatly simplify decision making. In a strong tradition system, questions of right and wrong are very clearly defined. The follower can shift the blame for unpleasant actions and decisions from himself to the leader or the system. Instead of having to justify his or her position when asked why things must be done a certain way, a person can simply reply, like Tevye in *Fiddler on the Roof*, "Tradition."

Tradition is an attractive influence mechanism for the organization as well as the leader. It has the big advantage of being impersonal. The follower responds not to the person but to the position. This adds stability, for the organization is not dependent on the life or abilities of a single individual. Giving the greatest rewards to those who best obey the system rather than the truly competent reinforces the organization's ability to use tradition to extract obedience from its members. Another feature is that influence by tradition is fast and predictable.

Drawbacks of Tradition. Tradition, interestingly, often explains in a single word why some proven concepts of management theory described in this book are not always widely used in practice. Merit-based rewards are a good example. Although almost everyone agrees that merit is the best criterion for awarding increased pay and promotion, seniority is, in fact, used far more often. It is easy to understand why. Seniority is easy to compute, wholly objective, and accrues equally to all. Because seniority has been used so long, many people have a vested interest in it. Having put in long years under a seniority system to rise to their present position, these people see switching to pure merit not only as unfair but as a serious threat. They therefore use the power they have acquired to maintain the status quo, even though it may not be in the best interest of the organization or society.

Tradition would work against the organization, for example, when a young manager who suggests an improvement is told, "We've always done it this way, and it's worked so far." Such an attitude can be a much greater problem than is generally realized. As discussed in Chapter 4, organizations must adapt to changes in their environment. This may require changes within the organization itself in the form of new policies, strategies, methods of organizing, and so forth. Therefore those organizations that persistently fall back on tradition as an argument against doing things differently may eventually face the same fate that befell the dinosaurs.

Declining Effectiveness of Tradition. Although tradition has historically been a very effective means of influence, its effectiveness seems to have declined in recent years. Several research studies indicate that response to authority figures has changed. Miner found that student attitudes favoring authority figures declined between 1960 and 1974.[19] Ondrack's studies also found a steady decrease in the authoritarian scores of college students since the 1960s. Students proved increasingly less willing to comply with the wishes of a person just because they were told to do so.[20] Pragmatic evidence of this trend among students is that during the 1960s they began to seriously question the right of universities to establish course requirements. Another vivid example of the reduced power of tradition is that thousands of American men refused the draft or deserted the army because they felt the Viet Nam war was unjust. Even some blue-collar workers today balk and argue over performing jobs they consider ridiculous. The boss's order alone is not a good enough reason any longer.

There are no completely satisfactory explanations for why younger Americans are not as readily influenced by tradition as their parents. Walton cites such factors as the rising level of wealth and security, the rising educational level, the shifting emphasis from individualism to social commitment, and the declining emphasis on socialized obedience in schools, families, and churches.[21] The underlying cause, however, must be that younger people do not perceive as strong a link between traditional values and rewards and their own need satisfaction. This may be because tradition is most effective with people motivated primarily by security and affiliation needs, while prosperity and increased leisure have raised the average need level to motivation by competence, esteem, and achievement. Or, perhaps our modern institutions have undermined their own traditional power base by failing to consistently reward good followers and punish those who engage in nonconformist behavior. Whatever the cause, it seems to be increasingly necessary for the organizational leader to rely on other influence mechanisms.

Referent Power: Influence by Charisma

Charismatic influence is not based on logic or long tradition, but on blind faith in the leader's ability. To influence through **charisma**, the leader uses referent power. This causes the follower to identify with or be strongly attracted to the leader by appealing to needs for affiliation and esteem. Unlike the generally impersonal, position-related influence of tradition, charismatic influence is virtually wholly personal. Even though they may never have met, in the follower's perception the relationship with the leader is almost one to one. The follower may perceive himself or herself as having much in common with the leader. On a subconscious level, the follower also expects that obedience will probably make him more like the leader, or at least a respected associate.

A good example of a charismatic leader is Muhammad Ali. Being an outstanding boxer certainly is not a logical cause for a person to be heeded by millions of people, as Ali is. Because of his charismatic personality, people feel a much stronger bond with Ali than with other champion fighters, such as Joe Frazier.

A manager perceived as charismatic because he or she is very supportive or dynamic is also able to use referent power. Managers with referent power often serve as powerful role models for subordinates' behavior. Evidence of this would be a subordinate imitating the manager's style and mannerisms. Referent power can be very effective for a manager. As Nadler, Hackman, and Lawler state, "For a respected and admired supervisor, referent power may suffice: subordinates may comply because they like and identify with their boss."[22]

FEATURE 13-2

Referent Power in Politics: The Situational Nature of Charisma

Politics is a field in which charisma is particularly important and helpful. Some of the most charismatic leaders in history have been national political leaders. But, as the following examples show, even the greatest of them did not possess charisma throughout their lives, nor were they always able to influence everyone.

Winston Churchill stumbled often on his rise to power before World War II, and his government was voted out of office as soon as it ended. But during those years when England's very survival was at stake, Britons made incredible sacrifices just because Churchill asked it of them. Across the Channel from England, around the time Churchill first became a force in politics, a very different person struck a responsive chord in the German peoples. Hitler's ravings of the master race, while sneered at by the rest of the world, deeply appealed to the esteem needs of Germans, whose pride still suffered from the humiliation of losing World War I. Hitler was surely one of the most charismatic people of all time, for his leadership feats were monumental, considering his humble origins. Yet, when the war turned against them, Hitler's influence over the German General Staff faded and had all but disappeared by the time he shot himself.

At around the same time, a man with very different traits was exerting enormous influence over the American people, namely, Franklin D. Roosevelt, perhaps the most charismatic president in American history. Comparison of F.D.R. with a later charismatic president, John F. Kennedy, highlights the limitations of charisma. During the 1960s, John F. Kennedy stirred the hearts of the American people, especially the young. But Congress was not similarly moved by his charisma and fought him so hard that many now consider Kennedy an ineffectual president. If these examples have yet to convince you that charisma is situational, imagine how few students and parents were notably moved by the magic of Golda Meir, the charismatic former premier of Israel, while she was a school teacher in Milwaukee.

Expert Power: Influence Through Rational Faith

Influence is through **rational faith** when the follower perceives that the influencer has special expertise that can satisfy an active need. Because of the leader's expertise, the follower accepts on faith the validity of his or her knowledge. Influence is considered rational in this case because the follower's decision to obey is conscious and logical.

A good example of influence by rational faith is the relationship most people have with their physician. Doctors occasionally use fear, but they cannot really coerce a patient into accepting treatment. We follow our doctor's orders because we believe that he has the knowledge and ability to cure and prevent illness. However, because we lack knowledge of medicine ourselves, we do not know for a fact that our doctor is capable of meeting our needs. So we are, in truth, really accepting his influence because we have faith in the expertise of the medical profession.

A person could exert expert power in an organization when he or she has information or ideas that others perceive will help the organization or subunit to attain an objective or make a better decision. Often the others may perceive that they need the expert's knowledge to further their personal objectives. Research has shown that if a group of people are told that one of them is an expert in the area, the group tends to follow that person's suggestions. This is true even when this person does not actually have the purported expertise.[23]

The tendency of subordinates to perceive their manager as an expert may have negative consequences in group decision making. Discussing this, Steiner and Miner state that a manager "may go into a meeting with his subordinates in search of information and alternatives for dealing with the problem that he poses and come out with the solution that he has in mind himself originally."[24] As Nadler, Hackman, and Lawler point out, "For some complex and highly technical tasks, subordinates may have more task-relevant expertise than the supervisor."[25] Thus, if you as a manager allow subordinates to perceive you as "the expert," they may not share their information with you. This would probably result in a less effective decision.

Technology and Size. The increased complexity of technology has accelerated the use of rational faith as an influence mechanism in modern organizations. Managers today are unable to fully understand many of the details of all operations crucial to their business. Few really know, for instance, how to program a computer to provide planning and control information. They must therefore accept on faith an expert's word that their data system is truly providing them with accurate information in the most efficient way possible. Large size has an effect similar to that of technology. Top management of a very large organization is often so far from the actual activities that in many instances it must trust the information provided by lower level managers, at least in the short run. The widespread acceptance of rational influence caused by technology and magnitude is a major cause of the proliferation of specialized staff.

Rational faith explains why staff can have very real influence in an organization, even though it may have no formal line authority. If staff has a history of being right, the line manager usually will accept its word without question and use the power conferred by line authority to relay staff decisions to the rest of the organization. In doing so, the line manager is really acting to satisfy his or her own needs. By accepting staff influence on rational faith, the line manager frees the time otherwise needed to check each staff recommendation thoroughly. The line manager can use this time for other activities, and perhaps also attain satisfaction of higher needs because of the intrinsic rewards of more challenging tasks. By implication, complete refusal to accept the advice of staff experts on faith may indicate that the line manager is more concerned with security than higher needs.

You yourself are likely to be strongly influenced by rational faith during the early period of your first management job. Those first days doubtless will remind you of the bewilderment of registering for your first college course. So you probably will accept on faith much of what you are told by experienced subordinates.

Limitations of Rational Faith. Rational faith is far less stable than the blind faith by which the charismatic leader influences. It also is slower. If the expert turns out to be wrong, it no longer is rational to follow the advice, so his or her influence decreases. Also, whereas a charismatic leader may be able to generate faith in his or her abilities with a single speech, in most cases rational faith takes time to build up. Staff, for example, sometimes must spend years proving itself before line management accepts its influence without question.

This does not mean, however, that rational faith is weaker than other forms of influence. Note that in several of the instances just mentioned, the influence of rational faith caused an inversion in the superior-subordinate power balance. Because the manager needed the information and recommendations of the subordinate, the subordinate's power increased. At least temporarily, the subordinate may have more power than the manager in a particular situation.

Persuasion and Participation

All of the bases have the potential to convey power, provided the situation is suitable. However, as we have often pointed out, many characteristics of the environment in which organizations operate have undergone considerable change in recent decades. People have become more educated on the average. Some organizations and subunits of larger organizations, especially in high technology fields like aerospace, electronics, and chemicals, are made up almost entirely of people holding advanced degrees. It is even more common to find work units where almost everybody is a college graduate. This increased level of education has in many cases eliminated the intellectual gap between leader and followers that prevailed for centuries. Social and monetary differences between people, too, have diminished over the years.

FEATURE 13-3

The Power of Delegation

The following excerpt from an interview with Michael Maccoby, author of the best seller, *The Gamesman*, shows how giving away power can actually increase power.

I know a manager, Maccoby says, who called in his staff and said: "I plan to offer a formal class after hours here at the plant. The subject: How to do *my* job. Anyone interested in learning that is welcome to attend."

The manager invested much time in the classes—preparing course material, reading lists, etc.

Result: Most of the staff took the course, and after a few months many of them had actually picked up portions of his job. Within a short time, he found he was "managing" and not running around doing errands, as he had before.

By giving away "power," Maccoby explains, that executive had actually gained an enormous amount of power: His staff trusted him, and he trusted them, so he could give them more responsible work to do—freeing him to undertake new, more difficult projects. The staff knew, for example, that the boss wasn't trying to hold them back, so they worked harder at everything they did. Motivation became automatic.

The concept, Maccoby says, can work practically anywhere in a company: The foreman offering classes to line workers; a v.p. of finance offering courses to high-level clerks, or the president offering classes to his immediate staff.

SOURCE: "Michael Maccoby: Emminent Psychologist Talks Business Management," *Boardroom Reports*, 1976, p. 8. Reprinted from Boardroom Reports Inc., Management's Source of Useful Information, 500 Fifth Avenue, New York, New York 10036.

Consequently, it has become increasingly difficult to base power on solely coercion, reward, tradition, charisma, or even expertise.

As the abilities of the follower have come closer to those of the leader, it has become increasingly necessary to actively seek the cooperation of the follower in order to influence. Two forms of influence that can induce the active cooperation of the follower are persuasion and participation. Contemporary managers can become more effective organizational leaders by developing skill in these forms of influence.

Influence by Persuasion

It is not necessary for a person to be able to punish or reward, to have the magic of charisma or even overwhelming expertise, in order to influence another. One of the most effective influence methods is **persuasion**, the effective communication of one's viewpoint. Like rational faith, persuasion is based on both referent and expert power. The difference is that the follower consciously believes he fully understands what he is doing and why. The leader who influences by persuasion does not *tell* the follower what to do. He or she *sells* the follower on doing something.

The leader using persuasion tacitly admits that the follower has some degree of power that can decrease the leader's ability to act. In other words, he acknowledges his dependency on the follower. For example, if a marketing manager wishes to reorganize the sales department, it is wise for him to acknowledge that the salespeople are capable of resisting the change in a way that might significantly affect output. Thus, although the manager may have the authority to impose a new organizational structure without consulting subordinates, it would probably be more realistic and effective to hold a meeting to allow them to express their opinions and explain why the change is desirable.

By actively soliciting agreement, the leader makes a strong appeal to the follower's esteem needs. If the follower also has needs for competence and power, the force of influence by persuasion is even greater. This is because the leader has acknowledged the follower's competence and the follower senses that he shares the leader's power. Persuasion influences by convincing the potential follower that doing what the leader wants will satisfy his or her own needs, whatever they may be. The leader can use either logical or emotional appeals to do this. Effective persuaders usually use both to varying degrees, depending on their sense of the listener's mood.

A clear and familiar example of persuasive influence is the relationship between a salesperson and a customer. A life insurance salesperson, for example, interweaves logical arguments for building an estate with an emotional appeal to the prospect's needs for security. Although seldom so obvious, everyone engages in selling in the figurative sense by trying to influence others. This is particularly true in organizations, especially when one has no formal authority over the other person or is unable to offer rewards.

Effective Persuasion. A number of factors affect the ability to influence by persuasion. The leader must have credibility. The argument must be within the intellectual grasp of the follower, yet not insult his or her intelligence. The objective of the leader should not run contrary to deeply held values of the follower. For example, if the leader's objective is to increase productivity by redesigning work, the leader's ability to persuade subordinates this is desirable will be minimal if they do not value increased job challenge or monetary rewards. It also is helpful for the influencer to have behaviors and personality traits that appeal to the follower. Many an argument and sale

Table 13-1 Using Persuasive Influence More Effectively

Make an active effort to identify the underlying needs of the listener and direct the appeal to those needs.
Begin the presentation with a position the listener is certain to find agreeable.
Attempt to establish an image of high credibility and trustworthiness.
Ask for a little more than one actually wants or needs. (One often must make concessions to persuade, and by asking more to begin with, you increase the chances of winding up with what you really want. This technique may backfire if one asks too much.)
Talk in terms of the listener's interests, rather than one's own. Frequent repetition of the word *you* seems to help the listener perceive the relationship between his or her own needs and doing what the influencer wants.
If more than one viewpoint is being presented, try to speak last, for the last argument has the best chance of influencing the audience.

have been lost because the prospective follower rejected the person, not the message or product.

Table 13-1 summarizes some techniques for using persuasive influence effectively.

Advantages and Disadvantages of Persuasive Influence. The major disadvantages of using persuasion to influence are slowness and uncertainty. It obviously takes far more time and effort to convince someone than to issue an order backed by coercive power, tradition, or charisma. No matter how much effort is put forth, one is never sure that the listener will accept influence. In addition, influence by persuasion, unlike the other forms, is a one-time event. The leader who relies on persuasion must begin anew every time he or she wishes to influence, which adds to the time spent on the influence process. The gains of influence by persuasion, however, often so outweigh these disadvantages that leaders with fear, reward, charisma, or tradition at their disposal often prefer to use persuasion.

To begin, using persuasion does not mean giving up other available tools of influence. Charisma, for instance, assists persuasion by helping the listener identify with the leader. Traditional influence and positive rewards enhance persuasion by giving the leader credibility. If the follower knows the leader has the ability to coerce but choses not to use it, the power of persuasion may be greatly amplified by reinforcement of esteem needs. Should persuasion fail, the leader with other means can fall back on them to influence. When persuasion succeeds, the leader's ability to influence by rational faith or blind faith increases. In fact, as often happens in the line-staff relationship, continued success with persuasion can actually endow one with the ability to influence by rational faith.

The biggest advantages of using persuasion instead of another means of influence are seen in organizations. The objective of the organizational leader, you should recall, is to get subordinates to do the work of the organi-

FEATURE 13-4

Comparison of Different Methods of Influence

Face-to-Face Methods	What They Can Influence	Advantages	Drawbacks
Exercise obligation-based power.	Behavior within zone that the other perceives as legitimate in light of the obligation.	Quick. Requires no outlay of tangible resources.	If the request is outside the acceptable zone, it will fail; if it is too far outside, others might see it as illegitimate.
Exercise power based on perceived expertise.	Attitudes and behavior within the zone of perceived expertise.	Quick. Requires no outlay of tangible resources.	If the request is outside the acceptable zone, it will fail; if it is too far outside, others might see it as illegitimate.
Exercise power based on identification with a manager.	Attitudes and behavior that are not in conflict with the ideals that underlie the identification.	Quick. Requires no expenditure of limited resources.	Restricted to influence attempts that are not in conflict with the ideals that underlie the identification.
Exercise power based on perceived dependence.	Wide range of behavior that can be monitored.	Quick. Can often succeed when other methods fail.	Repeated influence attempts encourage the other to gain power over the influencer.

zation as effectively as possible. A person given an order backed by coercion will usually follow orders, but do little more than meet minimal requirements. Sometimes coercive techniques will seem effective when used, but problems may occur weeks or months later in the implementation stage. A person influenced through persuasion, on the other hand, often may not need to be checked up on and is likely to try to exceed minimal requirements because the work is perceived to lead to personal need satisfaction on many levels. These advantages of persuasion, however, are only potential gains. In some situations, as discussed in the next chapter, coercion may be more effective than persuasion in attaining organizational objectives.

Influence Through Participation

Influence through participation goes even further than persuasion in recognizing the power and abilities of the follower. The leader makes no effort to impose his or her will or even opinions on the follower. Instead of convincing the follower to accept the leader's preconceived goal, the leader simply

Face-to-Face Methods	What They Can Influence	Advantages	Drawbacks
Coercively exercise power based on perceived dependence.	Wide range of behavior that can be easily monitored.	Quick. Can often succeed when other methods fail.	Invites retaliation. Very risky.
Use persuasion.	Very wide range of attitudes and behavior.	Can produce internalized motivation that does not require monitoring. Requires no power or outlay of scarce material resources.	Can be very time consuming. Requires other person to listen.
Combine these methods.	Depends on the exact combination.	Can be more potent and less risky than using a single method.	More costly than using a single method.
Indirect Methods	**What They Can Influence**	**Advantages**	**Drawbacks**
Manipulate the other's environment by using any or all of the face-to-face methods.	Wide range of behavior and attitudes.	Can succeed when face-to-face methods fail.	Can be time consuming. Is complex to implement. Is very risky, especially if used frequently.
Change the forces that continuously act on the individual: formal organizational arrangements; informal social arrangements; technology; resources available; statement of organizational goals.	Wide range of behavior and attitudes on a continuous basis.	Has continuous influence, not just a one-shot effect. Can have a very powerful impact.	Often requires a considerable power outlay to achieve.

SOURCE: J. P. Kotter, "Power, Dependence, and Effective Management," *Harvard Business Review*, July–August 1977, p. 133.

guides and facilitates the free exchange of information. The expert power of both leader and follower combine to form a joint position in which both truly believe. Influence results because people energized by high-level needs tend to work hardest toward an objective that they have had a hand in formulating. Joint determination, however, can influence the leader as much as it does the follower.

Participation clearly appeals to higher-level needs for power, competence, achievement, and self-actualization. It can only be used, therefore, if such needs are active motivators and if the follower can be counted on to work toward goals of his or her own choosing.

A landmark study of the effectiveness of participation was conducted in a garment factory during the 1940s. It found that when workers were allowed to participate in designing proposed changes in their jobs, the result was less resistance to these changes, higher production efficiency, and less turnover in comparison to workers not allowed to participate.[26] Other studies have indicated that participation has a positive effect on job satisfaction and productivity.[27] Consequently, writers of the behavioral school of management, such as Douglas McGregor and Rensis Likert, became strong advocates of participative management.

Unfortunately, participation did not prove the panacea it first seemed to be. Other studies have shown that participation is not appropriate for all situations.[28] Workers with less tolerance for ambiguity, lower preference for individualism, and those who do not feel uncomfortable in strongly controlled authoritarian situations may work best in a less participative, more directive supervisory situation. Other writers whose work is discussed in the next chapter have identified several situational factors that determine the relative appropriateness of participative influence.

Putting aside the question of inherent appropriateness, one reason why participation is not extensively used may be that managers resist giving up their traditional powers and prerogatives. This might be true because some people are undoubtedly attracted to managerial work by the opportunities it offers for satisfying a need for power. Such satisfaction, of course, is more probable when one has the ability to issue orders and compel their execution. We will explore the potential applications and pros and cons of participative influence more fully when we discuss the participative style of management.

Influence in Operation

Fear, reward, tradition, charisma, rational faith, persuasion, and participation are the tools managers can use to influence by appealing to the follower's needs. But even the very rare leader who has all of these mechanisms at his or her disposal must take other factors into account. Having power is not enough; it must be strong enough to influence others to work, preferably to work enthusiastically, toward goals. For this, several conditions must be met. These conditions are summarized in Table 13-2.

Influence will be greatest when the follower values the need appealed to highly, considers satisfaction or deprivation certain, and thinks that his or her efforts will surely meet the leader's expectations. Conversely, if any of these elements are missing, the power of the influencer diminishes or even disappears.

To better understand how the influence process works in practice let us examine a typical situation. John Turlock was the manager of production for a small tool-making company. In its plant there were 85 production workers, with 5 production supervisors each responsible for about 17 workers.

John had just returned from an annual objective-setting meeting with top management. One of his objectives was to decrease material wastage in

Table 13-2 How to Use Influence Effectively

1. The need appealed to must be active and strong.
2. The person being influenced must perceive the influencer as the source of some degree of need satisfaction or deprivation.
3. The person being influenced must consider the probability reasonably high that following will lead to need satisfaction or deprivation.
4. The person being influenced must believe that his or her effort has a good chance of meeting the leader's expectations.

the next year from 5.6 percent to 4.5 percent. Although John had a number of ideas to reduce wastage, he realized that it was important to gain the commitment of the work force, if the objective were to be attained. Thus, instead of calling a meeting with the five supervisors to tell them of his desires or informing everybody in the plant by memo, he decided to use a participative approach.

He first called a meeting with his supervisors and fully explained the situation. John was careful to explain how each tenth of a percentage point of material wastage added significantly to the cost of the product. In addition, he explained how competitive the industry had become and how it was essential for the plant to be as efficient as possible without resorting to any speedups or other practices he considered unethical.

After allowing for discussion and clarification, John said that although he had some ideas, he wanted the supervisors to come up with a number of ways to reduce material wastage. He then asked each supervisor to have a group problem-solving discussion with his or her workers and come up with as many ideas as possible. After this occurred, he suggested that each supervisor choose two of the workers who are informal leaders in their group to attend a meeting to discuss their group's ideas with the representatives and the supervisors from the other groups.

Two weeks later the five supervisors, ten workers, and the plant manager met for four hours. The result of this procedure was six additional ideas that had not occurred to the supervisors or plant manager. In addition, the workers throughout the plant were committed to the objective since they participated in the discussion and the generation of ideas. By the end of the year, material wastage decreased from 5.6 percent to 3.9 percent, which far surpassed the objective of 4.5 percent.

SUMMARY

Leadership, a linking process critical to effective management, is the ability to influence others to work toward objectives. To lead, to influence others, one needs to develop power.

Power, which is the ability to influence the behavior of others, is necessary for organizational effectiveness. This is because managers are highly dependent on many people both within and outside of the organization over whom they have little or no direct control.

There are several possible bases of power: coercion, reward, expertise, referent, legitimate. One can also influence others through rational faith, participation, and persuasion. The effectiveness of any form of power is contingent on whether the follower perceives that the leader can satisfy or deprive satisfaction of an active need and the situation. Thus, each technique has both advantages and drawbacks, and nobody can lead all people in all situations.

Coercive power influences through fear. It can only be effective if coupled with an excellent control system, which makes it very expensive. Also, fear gets only minimally acceptable performance at best, so it is seldom a desirable influence mechanism. Reward power, which influences through positive sanctions, is far better because it offers positive incentives, but it is difficult to determine what an effective reward is in some instances.

Traditional or legitimate power influences through appeal to culturally instilled values and is the most widely used form of power. However, due to changing values, tradition seems to be diminishing in effectiveness today.

Charisma, influence through referent power, is what most people associate with extremely dynamic leaders. The follower identifies with or is strongly attracted to the leader and has blind faith in the leader's abilities.

Expert power, influence through rational faith, has become increasingly widespread and effective due to increasing technological complexity. With changing social values, organizational leaders today have often come to find persuasion and participation the most effective means of influencing both nonmanagers, peers, and those outside the organization.

While slower and more uncertain than other forms of power, participation and persuasion seem to increase organizational effectiveness in situations where followers are motivated by higher-level needs, especially if the task is one that is relatively unstructured and calls for creativity.

In general, influence will be strongest when the follower highly values the need the leader appeals to, considers satisfaction or deprivation of the need a certain outcome of obedience or disobedience, and believes there is a high probability that effort will meet the leader's expectations.

REVIEW QUESTIONS

1. What is the difference between leading and managing?
2. What is the relationship between power, influence, and leadership?
3. Define power.
4. Briefly describe the bases of power identified by French and Raven.
5. What is charisma and how can managers use it?
6. What is rational faith and how is it most often used in organizations?
7. What are some advantages and disadvantages of persuasion?
8. How do other influence means help the manager influence through persuasion?

9. Why do relatively few organizations today think fear is an effective means of influence?
10. Briefly describe the concept of the balance of power between managers and subordinates.

DISCUSSION QUESTIONS

11. What environmental factors have caused tradition to become a less effective means of influence than it once was?
12. What is the fallacy in Lord Acton's statement, "Absolute power corrupts absolutely?"
13. How have changes in technology and size affected leadership and power in contemporary organizations?
14. "Objectives of the leader should not run contrary to deeply held values of the follower." Justify this statement.
15. As a lower-level manager, how could you influence top management to adopt one of your ideas?

CASE INCIDENT

My Own Shop

Gregg Walter was 33 years old. On many occasions, he felt that he had been in business for all of these 33 years. Walter's parents had been in the grocery business, and the family lived in an apartment right above their neighborhood store.

As long as he could remember, Gregg watched his mother and father work together in building this business. His parents were well liked by those in the neighborhood, and Walter's Grocery was one of the few remaining small stores that would extend credit to customers who were "a little short."

Gregg's parents put in 17-hour days, six days a week. Yet, they never complained. To Mr. and Mrs. Walter, as is the case with so many immigrants, the United States was still the land of unlimited opportunity.

From the time he was a little boy, Gregg worked in the store. He did whatever had to be done, whether it was cleaning up or delivering groceries. It was strictly a total family operation.

Although they all worked hard, Mr. Walter always reminded Gregg that they made a good living, and having their own store was much better than working for somebody else. While Gregg liked the idea of being your own boss, he thought perhaps that the price paid by his parents for this sort of social and economic independence was a bit too steep.

During his senior year in high school, Gregg's parents decided to retire. Over the years, they were careful and made some successful real estate investments. Mr. and Mrs. Walter were 55 years old when this decision was made.

Gregg went off to college and earned an undergraduate degree in business. While in college he met and married Marge Mannix who had a similar ambition to establish a successful career.

After graduation Gregg decided to accept a job with a major food processor. Gregg felt that he could be a corporate entrepreneur in much the same way that his parents were small business entrepreneurs.

"The chance of a lifetime," Gregg explained to his father. "It's a golden opportunity to run my own shop and put into practice all of those principles I learned from you and Mom as well as the more theoretical knowledge I learned in college."

Gregg could hardly wait to share the good news with his wife who was returning that evening from a business trip. Gregg had just been offered the district manager's position in Portland, Oregon, and while it meant he had to move, he was ready.

That evening Marge Walter arrived home from her trip. She had been in Baton Rouge inspecting her company's new plant.

When Gregg told Marge about his promotion and transfer, she said, "that's great, but what do I do about my own business career?"

Questions

1. How would you relate the various concepts of power to Gregg's desire to run his own shop? Can you do this, that is, run your own shop in a corporate structure?
2. How might the environment affect one's need for power and autonomy?
3. How do you think Gregg and Marge could resolve what appears to be a conflict in careers?

NOTES

1. Anthony Jay, *Management and Machiavelli* (New York: Holt, Rinehart and Winston, 1967). Michael Korda, *Power!* (New York: Random House, 1975).
2. Henry Mintzberg, *The Nature of Managerial Work* (New York: Harper & Row, 1973); David C. McClelland, "The Two Faces of Power," *Journal of International Affairs*, vol. 24 (1970), pp. 40–41.
3. Alan C. Filley, Robert J. House, and Stephen Kerr, *Managerial Process and Organizational Behavior*, 2d. ed. (Glenview, IL: Scott, Foresman, 1976), p. 211.
4. David Katz and Robert L. Kahn, *The Social Psychology of Organizations* (New York: Wiley, 1966), chap. 11.
5. Peter F. Drucker, *The Practice of Management* (New York: Harper & Row, 1954), pp. 159–160.
6. John B. Miner, *The Management Process* (New York: Macmillan, 1973).
7. Robert Biersted, "An Analysis of Social Power," *American Sociological Review*, vol. 15 (December 1950), pp. 730–736.
8. R. M. Emerson, "Power-Dependency Relations," *American Sociological Review*, vol. 27 (1962), pp. 31–40.

9. David Mechanic, "Sources of Power of Lower Participants in Complex Organizations," *Administrative Science Quarterly*, vol. 7 (1962): no. 2, p. 350.
10. Thomas J. Scheff, "Control over Policy by Attendants in a Mental Hospital," *Journal of Health and Human Behavior*, vol. 2 (1961), pp. 93–105.
11. G. M. Sykes, "The Corruption of Authority and Rehabilitation," in *Complex Organizations*, A. Etzione, ed. (New York: The Free Press, 1961), pp. 191–197.
12. David C. McClelland, *Power: The Inner Experience* (New York: Irvington, 1975); David C. McClelland, "The Two Faces of Power," *Journal of International Affairs*, vol. 24 (1970): no. 1, p. 30.
13. J. R. P. French and B. H. Raven, "The Bases of Social Power," in *Studies in Social Power*, ed. Dorwin Cartwright (Ann Arbor: University of Michigan Press, 1959).
14. For specific anecdotes about power in the executive suite, and how to use it, see Korda, *Power!*
15. *The Wall Street Journal*, January 18, 1977.
16. K. R. Student, "Supervisory Influence and Work Group Performance," *Journal of Applied Psychology*, vol. 52 (1968), pp. 188–199.
17. J. G. Bachman, C. G. Smith, and J. A. Slesinger, "Control, Performance, and Job Satisfaction: An Analysis of Structural and Individual Effects," *Journal of Personality and Social Psychology*, vol. 4 (1966), pp. 122–136.
18. Daniel A. Ondrack, "Attitudes Toward Authority," *Personnel Administration*, May 1971, pp. 8–17.
19. John B. Miner, *The Human Constraint* (Washington, D.C.: BNA Books, 1974).
20. Ondrack, op. cit.
21. Richard E. Walton, "How to Counter Alienation in the Plant," *Harvard Business Review*, vol. 50 (November-December 1972).
22. David Nadler, Richard Hackman, and Edward Lawler, *Managing Organizational Behavior* (Boston: Little Brown, 1979), p. 161.
23. P. A. Collaros and L. R. Anderson, "Effects of Perceived Expertness Upon Creativity of Brainstorming Groups," *Journal of Applied Psychology*, vol. 53 (1969), pp. 159–163.
24. George A. Steiner and John B. Miner, *Management Policy and Strategy* (New York: Macmillan, 1977), p. 268.
25. Nadler, Hackman, and Lawler, op. cit., p. 161.
26. L. Coch and J. R. P. French, "Overcoming Resistance to Change," *Human Relations*, vol. 1 (1948), pp. 512–533.
27. Alfred Marrow, David Bowers, and Stanley Seashore, *Management by Participation* (New York: Harper & Row, 1967); A. Lowin, "Participative Decision Making: A Model, Literature Critique, and Prescription for Research," *Organizational Behavior and Human Performance*, vol. 3 (1968), pp. 68–106; Carlene Roberts, R. E. Miles, and L. V. Blankenship, "Organizational Leadership, Satisfaction, and Productivity: A Comparative Analysis," *Academy of Management Journal*, vol. 11 (1968), pp. 401–414; M. Patchen, *Participation, Achievement, and Involvement on the Job* (Englewood Cliffs, NJ: Prentice-Hall, 1970); Rensis Likert, *New Patterns of Management* (New York: McGraw-Hill, 1967).
28. Paul Lawrence and Jay Lorsch, *Developing Organizations: Diagnosis and Action* (Reading, MA: Addison-Wesley, 1969); J. W. Lorsch and J. J. Morse, *Organizations and Their Members: A Contingency Approach* (New York: Harper & Row, 1974).

CHAPTER 14

Leadership: Style, Situation, and Effectiveness

We learned in Chapter 13 that managerial leaders need power to get the best from their people and that there are many potentially effective ways of influencing people. What leadership methods are, in fact, effective in today's organizations? How should *managerial* leaders behave in order to get subordinates to put forth their best effort toward attaining organizational objectives? These are the questions tackled in this chapter, which primarily concentrates on what researchers have discovered about styles of managerial leadership.

After reading this chapter you should understand the following important terms and concepts:

- leadership style
- autocratic or authoritarian leadership
- Theory X and Theory Y
- democratic leadership
- laissez-faire leadership
- employee-centered vs. job-centered style
- Likert's four systems
- two dimensional approach to leadership style
- the relationship among leadership style, satisfaction, and productivity
- Fiedler's contingency model of leadership
- path-goal leadership
- Vroom-Yetton decision-making model

Overview of Leadership Theory

We learned in Chapter 13 that there are several means by which one can influence others and lead them. We also noted that effective leadership and effective management are not synonymous. Unanswered was the important question of how *should* a manager behave as a leader? Which means of influence and which patterns of behavior are most effective in leading others to attain organizational objectives?

These are complex questions. Like so many management questions, their answers are not readily apparent. The development of leadership theory, which seeks to identify and predict which leadership characteristics are most effective and why, has been evolutionary. Behavioral scientists have taken three basic approaches to determine the significant factors in effective leadership. Described briefly in the following sections, these are the trait approach, the behavioral approach, and the situational approach.

Trait Approach

Leadership first became a subject of research at the turn of the twentieth century, the same period in which management was first studied. However, it was between 1930 and 1950 that the study of leadership was first undertaken on a large, systematic scale. These early studies focused on identifying the *traits* or personal characteristics of effective leaders. According to the *traitist theory of leadership*, also known as the *great man theory*, the best leaders have a certain set of characteristics in common. By extension, if these traits could be identified, people could learn to develop them and thereby become effective leaders. Some of the traits linked to effective leadership were intelligence, knowledge, physical appearance, integrity, good judgment, high initiative, social and economic background, and self-confidence.

Inability to Find Common Traits. In the 1940s, researchers began to examine the accumulated evidence on the relationship between personality traits and leadership. Unfortunately, although hundreds of studies were conducted, no consensus was reached on a set of traits that invariably distinguished a great leader. One study found that only about 5 percent of leadership traits were commented on in four or more investigations.[1] A comprehensive review of leadership research by Stogdill in 1948 affirmed that traitist studies continued to produce contradictory findings. He did find that leaders tended to excel in such factors as intelligence, scholarship, dependability, responsibility, activity, social participation, and socioeconomic status. However, Stogdill also found that the traits of effective leaders tended to vary with the situation. He eventually concluded, as most behavioral scientists today would agree, that "A person does not become a leader by virtue of the possession of some combination of traits."[2]

Importance of Traits. The discovery that no common set of traits can be identified in all effective leaders has often been cited as evidence that leadership effectiveness is entirely situational. However, Stogdill himself feels that this view tends to underemphasize the personal nature of leadership. He states that there is strong evidence that different skills and traits are required in different situations. Although not advocating a return to the traitist approach, Stogdill concludes, "the pattern of personal characteristics of the leader must bear some relevant relationship to the characteristics, activities, and goals of the followers."[3]

Behavioral Approach

Disenchantment with trait theories of leadership grew strong around the same time the behavioral school of management came to influence management thought. Thus, not surprisingly, the second approach to the study of leadership focused on the behavior of the leader. According to the *behavioral approach to leadership*, it is not the characteristics of the leader but rather the way the leader behaves toward followers that determines effectiveness.

An outgrowth of the behavioral approach was the classification of leadership styles or patterns of behavior. This was an important contribution and a helpful means of understanding the complexities of leadership. Therefore, in the following section of this chapter we will elaborate on the concept of style of leadership and describe such major categories as the autocratic, democratic, laissez-faire, job-centered, and employee-centered styles.

The basic shortcoming of the behavioral approach was the tendency to assume that there is a single "best" style of leadership. Usually, writers of the behavioral school tended to perceive leaders who behaved democratically and showed consideration as being most effective in contemporary organizations. However, as one group of writers states in summarizing findings of this approach, "There is no 'best' style of leadership. It is highly likely that an effective style depends on the nature of the situation and that when a situation changes the appropriate style changes also."[4]

Situational Approach

Neither the trait nor the behavioral approach was able to uncover a consistent relationship between the leader's traits or behavior and effectiveness. This does not mean that traits and behavior are unimportant in leadership. They are, as we will learn, critical components of success. However, more recent research demonstrated that additional factors may play a determining role in leadership effectiveness. These situational factors include the needs and characteristics of followers, the nature of the task, environmental pressures and demands, and how much information is available to the leader.

Therefore, contemporary leadership theory has moved toward a situational or contingency approach. Modern researchers have tried to determine which styles and traits are most appropriate in various situations. Their findings indicate that, just as different organizational structures are more appropriate in certain situations, different ways of leading are more or less appropriate depending on the characteristics of the overall situation. This

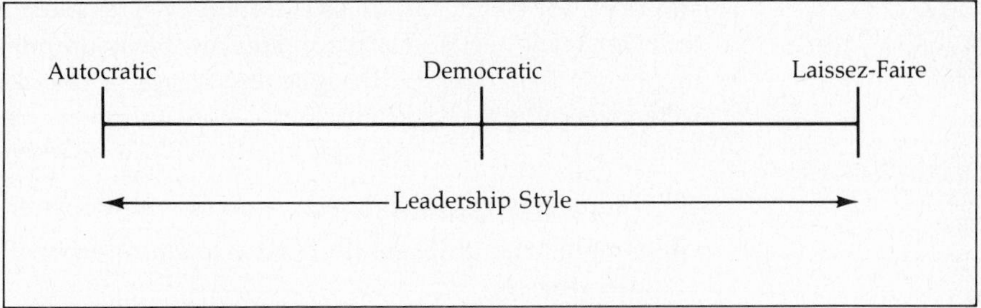

Figure 14-1 Autocratic–Laissez-Faire Continuum

means that the manager-leader must be able to behave in different ways in different situations.

However, in order to understand why a situational approach to leadership is necessary, it is first necessary to lay some groundwork. Let us begin with the concept of style of leadership.

Leadership Styles

As just mentioned, the behavioral approach to leadership made a significant contribution by analyzing and classifying styles of leadership in terms of how the leader behaves toward subordinates. Just as each individual has a more or less consistent overall personality and behavior pattern, each leader tends to behave toward subordinates in a relatively consistent way. **Leadership style,** in a managerial context, is the general way a leader behaves toward subordinates in order to attain objectives. The degree to which a manager delegates authority, the modes of power a manager employs, and his or her relative concern for human relationships or task orientation all tend to reflect the manager's leadership style.

Each organization is a unique combination of individuals, tasks, and objectives. Each manager has a unique personality and set of abilities. Therefore, styles of leadership do not actually fall precisely within the descriptive categories we will present. Rather, a given leader's style falls somewhere on a continuum. There are two commonly used systems for defining the parameters of this continuum. The traditional system classifies style as ranging from autocratic on one extreme to laissez-faire on the other. The second classifies the dimensions of leadership style as ranging from employee-centered to job-centered. Figure 14-1 illustrates the autocratic–laissez-faire continuum.

Autocratic Leadership

The autocratic managerial leader is highly authoritarian. The **autocratic leader** has enough of a base of power to impose his or her will on followers and does not hesitate to do so if necessary. The autocrat deliberately appeals to lower-level needs of subordinates on the assumption that this is the level on which they operate. Douglas McGregor, a noted scholar of leadership, called the autocrat's presumptions about followers **Theory X**. According to Theory X:

1. People inherently dislike work and when possible will avoid it.
2. People have little ambition, tend to shun responsibility, and prefer to be directed.
3. Above all, people want security.
4. It is necessary to use coercion, control, and threats of punishment to get people to work.[5]

Because of these assumptions, the autocrat characteristically tends to centralize authority. The leader structures the work of subordinates to the greatest possible degree and allows them little latitude in making decisions. The autocrat also closely supervises all work under his or her jurisdiction and exerts psychological pressure, often by threat of punishment, to ensure performance.

Benevolent Autocracy. When the autocrat avoids negative coercive power and instead primarily uses reward power to influence, he or she is called a *benevolent autocrat.* Although still an authoritarian leader, the benevolent autocrat shows active concern for the feelings and welfare of subordinates. He or she may even go as far as allowing or encouraging their participation in planning. But he or she retains the actual power to make and execute decisions. And, however benevolent, he or she betrays his or her autocratic style by rigidly structuring work and strictly enforcing a large body of rules that tightly control employee behavior.

Democratic Leadership

The democratic style leader's assumptions about subordinates differ radically from those of the autocrat. McGregor labeled these assumptions of the democratic leader **Theory Y**, which holds that:

1. Work is a natural phenomenon; and if the conditions are favorable, people will not only accept responsibility, they will seek it.
2. If people are committed to organizational objectives, they will exercise self-direction and self-control.
3. Commitment is a function of the rewards associated with goal attainment.
4. The capacity for creativity in problem solving is widely distributed in the population, and the intellectual potentialities of the average human being are only partially utilized.[6]

Because of these assumptions, the democratic-style leader prefers influence mechanisms that appeal to higher-level needs for belongingness, challenge, autonomy, and self-actualization. In all cases, the true democratic leader avoids imposing his or her will on subordinates.

Organizations in which the democratic style prevails are characterized by highly decentralized authority. Subordinates actively share in decision making and enjoy wide latitude in executing tasks. Often, after explaining the organization's objectives, the manager allows subordinates to define their own objectives consistent with those the manager must attain. Instead of constantly checking on people's work while it is in progress, supervisors usually wait until the task has been completed before making an evaluation. (Of course, for this to work it must be coupled with a highly effective control system.) The leader spends a relatively high percentage of time acting as a liaison to ensure that the work group's objectives mesh with those of the organization as a whole and that the group receives adequate resources.

Since the democratic manager assumes that people are motivated by higher-level needs for social interaction, achievement and self-actualization, he or she tries to make subordinates' duties challenging. In a sense, he or she tries to create a situation in which people motivate themselves to some degree because their work is intrinsically rewarding. The highly democratic manager also makes subordinates understand that they are to solve most problems without seeking approval or assistance. But the manager is careful to create a climate of openness and trust so that, if subordinates do need help, they will not be afraid to approach the manager. To accomplish this, the manager practices two-way communication and plays a developmental and guidance role. He or she tries to give subordinates insight into organizational problems, provide them with adequate information, and show them how to seek and evaluate alternative courses of action.

Laissez-faire Leadership. Leaders whose style is on the point farthest opposite autocracy on the continuum illustrated in Figure 14-1 are referred to as free-rein or laissez-faire leaders. *Laissez-faire* is a French expression meaning "leave it alone." The free-rein manager does just that. Subordinates are given virtually total freedom to select their own objectives and monitor their own work. In **laissez-faire leadership** influence is virtually exclusively by participation. True laissez-faire leadership, in the view of some writers, is "non-leadership" because the "leader" has almost no influence over the group. This makes it difficult to distinguish the leader from the followers. Thus, while a few very specialized task teams and committees may approach laissez-faire leadership, in actual practice the free-rein style is probably a descriptive ideal that does not really exist.

Lewin's Research. Perhaps the earliest study of leadership style effectiveness was that conducted by Curt Lewin and his associates.[7] The subjects of Lewin's investigations were ten-year-old boys. These boys were grouped into several recreational clubs, each of which was supervised by an adult trained in either democratic, authoritarian, or laissez-faire leadership. Au-

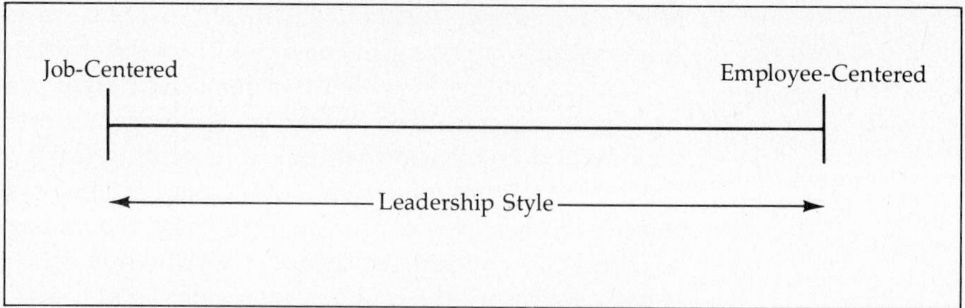

Figure 14-2 Likert's Leadership Style Continuum

thoritarian leadership was characterized by a high degree of unilateral leader power; the leader determined all policies of the group; no power was shared with the group. Democratic leadership was characterized by power sharing and participative decision making; responsibility was spread rather than concentrated. Laissez-faire leadership was characterized by a minimum of leader participation; the group had complete freedom to make its own decisions.

Lewin's landmark study found that authoritarian leadership resulted in a greater quantity of work than democratic leadership. However, this was offset by less work motivation, originality, friendliness in the group, and group-mindedness, a greater amount of aggressiveness expressed both toward the leader and other group members, more suppressed discontent, and more dependent and submissive behavior. Compared to democratic leadership, laissez-faire leadership resulted in less work, work of poorer quality, more play, and a preference for a democratic leader expressed in interviews. As we will learn, later research studies do not totally support these findings.

Job-Centered and Employee-Centered Leadership

The autocratic versus democratic continuum is one possible way to classify leadership style. Rensis Likert and his associates at the University of Michigan came up with an alternative system by comparing high performance groups to low performance groups within various organizations. They felt that the leadership style of managers could explain the difference in effectiveness. In their system, the basis for distinguishing leadership style is the manager's perceptions about such factors as motivation, communication, direction of information flow, decision making and control, and how objectives are set. Similar to McGregor's Theory X-Theory Y continuum, leaders of high and low performing groups were categorized on a continuum ranging from being extremely job-centered (Theory X) to extremely employee-centered (Theory Y). This system is illustrated in Figure 14-2.

Job-Centered Leaders. The **job-centered manager**, also referred to as task-oriented, is primarily concerned with the design of work and the development of rewards to increase productivity. The classic example of a job-cen-

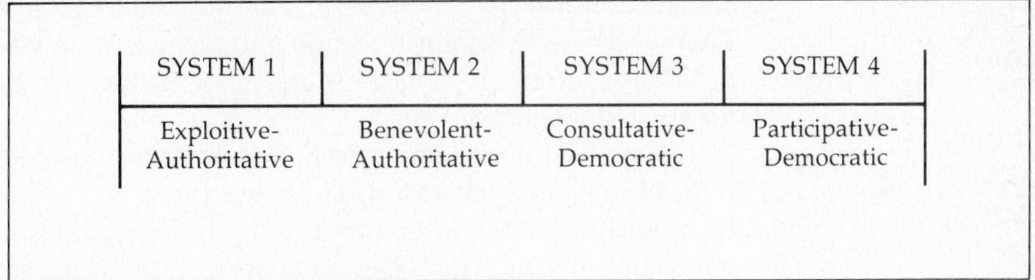

Figure 14-3 Likert's Systems

tered manager is Frederick W. Taylor. As discussed earlier, Taylor structured work according to engineering principles of efficiency and financially rewarded workers who exceeded a quota determined by careful measurement of potential output.

Employee-Centered Leaders. The primary concern of the **employee-centered manager**, in contrast, is with people. He or she focuses on improving performance through improving human relations. The employee-centered leader emphasizes supportive relationships, allows maximum participation in decision making, stays away from detailed supervision, and sets high performance goals for the work unit. He or she actively considers the needs of subordinates, helps them with problems, and encourages them to grow and develop. In essence, the employee-centered manager's behavior is similar to that of the participative style leader.

Likert concluded from his research that management style was invariably *either* job- *or* employee-centered. No managers were found who exhibited both of these qualities to any significant degree. The findings also suggested that an employee-centered style improved performance in almost all cases.[8] Later research, as we will learn, disputes these conclusions.

Likert's Four Systems

Another outgrowth of Likert's research on leadership was the postulate that four basic systems of management style exist.[9] Likert intended these four systems, illustrated in Figure 14-3, to serve as a guide that would help clarify the concept of leadership behavior. We present them here largely to help you understand that there are intermediate points of the management style continuum.

Likert described the system 1 manager as "exploitive-authoritative." These managers have the characteristics of the autocratic leader, as described earlier. System 2 management was referred to as "benevolent-authoritative." These leaders communicate in a condescending way to subordinates, but they allow a limited amount of decision making by subordinates. Motivation is by rewards and some use of punishment. In general, the system 2 leader corresponds to the benevolent autocrat. The system 3 manager, called "consultative," shows considerable, but not total, confidence in subordinates. There is two-way communication and some trust between superiors and subordinates. Important decisions are made at the top, but many specific ones are made by subordinates.

System 4 management, called "participative-group," is the style Likert found to be most successful. These managers have total confidence and trust in subordinates. Superior-subordinate relationships are friendly and characterized by mutual trust. Decision making is highly decentralized. Communication is both two-way and lateral. The system 4 manager corresponds to the participative (Theory Y) style manager described earlier. Also system 4 managers are highly employee-centered, in contrast to system 1 managers, who are highly job-centered.

Likert's research indicated that supervisors with the best records of performance focused their primary attention on the human aspects of their subordinates' problems, creating supportive relationships, building effective work groups, and setting high performance objectives. They used a group style of supervision instead of the traditional style of individual discussions with a subordinate. Discussing the benefits of this style for a sales organization, Likert states, "new appeals, new markets, and new strategies of selling, when discovered by any individual salesman, are shared promptly with the group and improved and perfected by them. . . . man-to-man interactions in the meetings, dominated by the manager, do not create group loyalty and have a far less favorable impact upon the salesman's motivations than do group interaction and decision meetings."[10] Other researchers have found similar results. However, as we will learn, later research again indicates that Likert's conclusions are not valid and applicable in all situations.

Two-Dimensional Views of Leadership Style

The findings of Likert and the work of McGregor gave a strong impetus to the participative style of management. Many practicing managers, however, were disappointed by the seemingly poor results of switching to employee-centered and participative styles. A group at the Ohio State University Bureau of Business Research, beginning in 1945, made an exhaustive study of leadership and found one reason why. According to their findings, there was a grave flaw in the concept of classifying leaders as being *either* job-centered *or* employee-centered. They discovered that while an autocrat is never also a democratic leader, it is very possible for a manager to be highly concerned with the job itself and still show a great deal of concern for human relations.

The Ohio State group came up with a system whereby leader behavior was classified along two dimensions—structure and consideration:

> *Consideration* includes behavior indicating mutual trust, respect, and a certain warmth and rapport between the supervisor and his group. This does not mean that this dimension reflects a superficial "pat-on-the-back," "first name calling" kind of human relations behavior. This dimension appears to emphasize a deeper concern for group members' needs and includes such behavior as allow-

> ing subordinates more participation in decision making and encouraging more two-way communication. *Structure* includes behavior in which the supervisor organizes and defines group activities and his relation to the group. Thus, he defines the role he expects each member to assume, assigns tasks, plans ahead, establishes ways of getting things done and pushes for production. This dimension seems to emphasize overt attempts to achieve organizational goals.[11]

The highest performance was associated with leaders who ranked strongly in *both* areas.[12] However, later research indicated this finding could not be generally applied to all situations.[13]

Managerial Grid. The promising concept of a two-dimensional approach to leadership effectiveness was modified and popularized by Blake and Mouton who constructed a grid that classifies leader-managers as having five basic styles.[14] As Figure 14-4 shows, the vertical axis of their grid ranks "concern for people" on a 1–9 scale. The horizontal axis does the same with "concern for production." A manager's style is determined by both of these factors. Blake and Mouton described the middle and four corner positions as:

1,1. *Impoverished:* the leader's effort is the minimum needed to get work done well enough to keep from getting fired.

1,9. *Country Club:* the leader concentrates on good, warm human relations, but has little concern for task efficiency.

9,1. *Task:* the leader is highly concerned with task efficiency, but has little regard for subordinates' morale.

5,5. *Middle of the Road:* the leader attains an adequate level of performance by balancing efficiency with reasonably good morale.

9,9. *Team:* the leader, by high consideration and effective guidance, gets workers committed to the goals of the organization. This leads to high morale and high efficiency.

Blake and Mouton assumed that the most effective style of leadership was the behavior of the 9,9 team leader. This person, they felt, combined a high degree of consideration for his or her subordinates with similar concern for productivity. They realized that it is difficult to define team leadership in many jobs. But they believed that with training and awareness of the goal all managers could move toward a 9,9 style and thereby become more effective.

Style, Satisfaction, and Productivity

The Leadership Style Debate

Ever since autocratic and employee-centered styles were first distinguished from each other, a debate has raged over which is better. Adherents of both

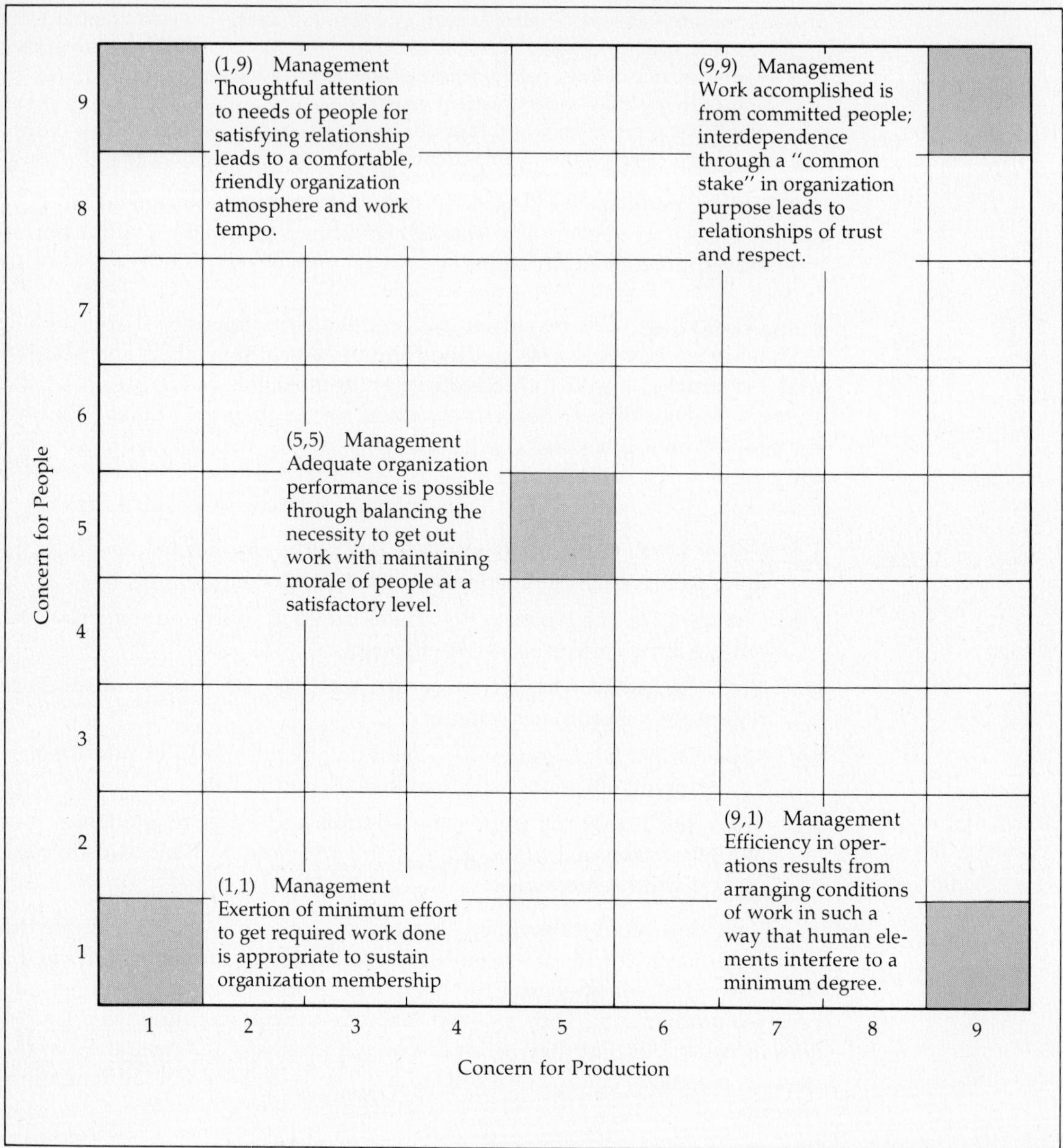

Figure 14-4 The Managerial Grid

SOURCE: Robert R. Blake and Jane S. Mouton, *The Managerial Grid* (Houston: Gulf Publishing Company, 1964), p. 10

sides have tended to act as though the issue were clear-cut: either one or the other had to be right. Advocates of a human relations approach dismissed autocrats as reactionaries using a style that changes in society and technology had made invalid. Those choosing traditional methods claimed that the new school was making unwarranted assumptions about the nature of people, creating anxiety by forcing tough decisions on people not equipped to handle them and by meddling in private affairs instead of concentrating on the job of managing. The specific arguments of both camps are varied and numerous, but we can reduce them to a few key differences of view on the best route to organizational effectiveness.

Autocratic View. Those favoring autocratic and job-centered techniques, in addition to their Theory X presumptions, contend that:

1. An autocratic style, especially benevolent autocracy, is inherently more efficient because it reinforces the leader's unilateral power and thereby increases his or her ability to influence subordinates to work toward objectives.
2. A job-centered focus yields maximum productivity because a manager cannot change human nature but can do a great deal to make work more efficient.

Authoritarians basically see the following relationship between leadership style and productivity as always holding true:

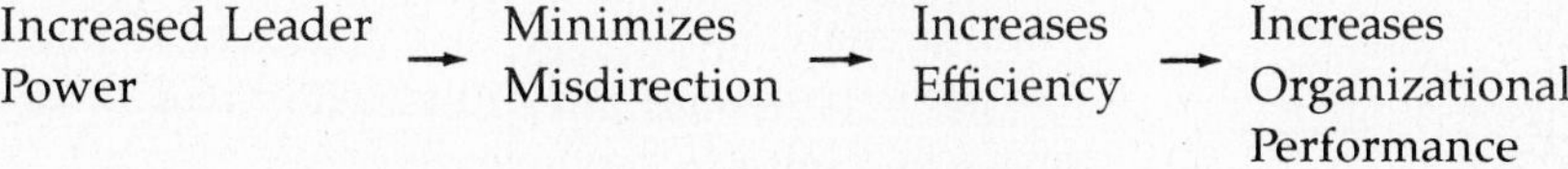

Human Relations View. Supporters of participative, employee-centered leadership, in addition to their Theory Y presumptions, believe that:

1. If not recognized and tapped, the power of the follower is great enough to undermine the leader's influence and cause organizational problems.
2. An employee-centered approach yields maximum productivity because those closest to the work are most capable of redesigning it for greater efficiency. Artificially enforced efficiency, instituted by experts from above, is often fought so hard that gains are lost.

Those who contend that a participative or employee-centered approach is always preferable to an authoritarian style also believe that there is a causal relation between satisfaction and productivity. The assumption is that:

Leadership Style —(Affects)→ Satisfaction —(Affects)→ Organizational Performance

The basic contention is that a participative style, when implemented correctly, always improves satisfaction and that increased satisfaction always leads to increased productivity.

Satisfaction and Productivity

Research on Leadership. Both the autocratic view and the human-relations view understandably have won many converts. However, it now seems clear that both sides have been guilty of excess, claiming more than evidence justifies.[15] For example, early proponents of democratic leadership contended that it was always more effective than authoritarian leadership when followers operated at a high-need level.

However, there are many well-documented cases of the more moderate, but still authoritarian, benevolent autocratic style proving extremely effective in these situations. Thomas Watson, Jr. had a reputation for being a tyrannical manager. Yet, he made IBM Corporation the world's leading high technology corporation, a reputation that tends to refute the premise that a basically authoritarian style is less effective with mature, highly educated subordinates. The same was true of the great football coach, Vince Lombardi. So, the autocratic style cannot be wholly dismissed as outdated.

The democratic style also has attractions, successes, and shortcomings. Since warm human relations and freedom to act are more pleasant than cold engineering calculations and rigid job structuring, the employee-centered approach is inherently attractive to many people. Without question, many organizational problems would be solved if improved human relations and participation inevitably led to increased satisfaction and higher productivity. Unfortunately, it does not. Researchers have found situations in which there was participation and low satisfaction and situations where there was high satisfaction but low productivity.[16]

For example, a foreman may allow production workers to participate in decisions about the way work is performed. However, if they do not have active needs for challenge or esteem, they may not sense need satisfaction from the foreman's style. They may, in fact, feel threatened. In another situation, people might receive satisfaction from the friendly atmosphere of the workplace, and as a result spend so much time socializing that they are not productive.

Clearly the true relationship among leadership style, satisfaction and productivity can only be determined by continued extensive empirical research. Fortunately, the area has recently received considerable attention.

Summary of Research on Leadership, Satisfaction, and Productivity

In summary form, research on the **relationship among satisfaction, leadership style, and productivity** indicates that:

- A democratic and employee-centered style does lead to higher satisfaction in many situations.[17]
- A democratic style may lower satisfaction in situations where followers operate on a low need level. Participation does, however, tend to have a

positive effect on the satisfaction of most people above the blue-collar level. There are also instances where it has proven successful with even relatively unskilled workers.[18]

- High satisfaction seems to reduce turnover, absenteeism, and accidents. This usually, but not always, increases productivity. However, low turnover does not necessarily indicate high satisfaction.[19]
- Higher morale and greater job satisfaction does not *always* improve productivity.[20]

Some researchers even contend that instead of high satisfaction leading to high productivity, the reverse is true. Namely, good performance, if rewarded, leads to higher satisfaction. In fact, Lawler and Porter state:

> If we assume, as seems to be reasonable in terms of motivation theory, that rewards cause satisfaction, and that in some cases performance produces reward, then it is possible that the relationship found between satisfaction and performance comes about through the action of a third variable—reward. Briefly stated, good performance may lead to rewards, which in turn lead to satisfaction; this formulation then would say that satisfaction, rather than causing performance, as was previously assumed, is caused by it.[21]

Therefore, according to this position, a manager's leadership style will only affect the satisfaction of subordinates if two conditions are met:

1. The style results in increased productivity.
2. The increased productivity is rewarded, which then leads to increased satisfaction.

However, further research is needed to validate this interesting view.

In sum, the research we have discussed thus far has failed to uncover a uniform relationship between leadership style and productivity.[22] This indicates that *no* single leadership style is always superior. In leadership, as in performing the management functions, the effective, proactionary manager needs to consider the *situation* in order to determine which course of action is most appropriate.

Contingency Approaches to Effective Leadership

The inability of earlier researchers to find a consistent relationship among leadership style, satisfaction, and productivity strongly indicated that some other factor or factors were at work. To find these factors, theorists began to look beyond the leader and follower and consider the situation as a whole. As often is the case in management research, this has proven difficult. However, three contingency models of leadership developed to date have made a significant contribution to understanding the complexities of the leadership process. These are Fiedler's contingency model of leadership, the path-goal approach, and the Vroom-Yetton leadership decision model.

Fiedler's Contingency Model of Leadership

As we have discussed, early attempts to explain leadership effectiveness concentrated on one dimension of leader behavior, such as job-centeredness. Later work, such as Blake and Mouton's managerial grid, examined two dimensions. But even this improvement focused primarily on the leader's behavior and did not take other variables into account. Fiedler's model made a significant contribution by identifying three factors of the situation that influence leadership effectiveness.[23] These are:

1. *Leader-member relations.* This includes degree of loyalty shown by subordinates, followers' confidence in the leader, and how attractive the leader personally is to followers.
2. *Task structure.* This refers to the degree to which the duties of subordinates are routine, well-defined, and structured, as opposed to being ambiguous and unstructured.
3. *Position power.* This refers to the amount of legitimate power associated with the leader's position, which affects the capacity to reward and the level of support the leader receives from the formal organization.

Effectiveness in Different Situations. Various combinations of these three dimensions yield eight potential leadership situations. These are illustrated in Figure 14-5 along with the style Fiedler found most effective in each instance.

Note that of the eight potential situations, number one is most favorable for the leader. Here, the task is highly structured and both position power and leader-follower relations are high, maximizing the capacity to influence. Situation 8, in contrast, is the least favorable because both position power and relations are poor, and the task is low in structure. Interestingly, Fiedler's findings indicate that the most effective leadership style in *both* of these extreme situations is task-oriented. This apparent inconsistency can be explained logically.

The potential advantages of task-oriented leadership are speed of action and decision making, unity of purpose, and a high degree of control over the work of subordinates. Thus, in a technical sense, the autocratic style is inherently an efficient means of attaining organizational objectives—provided followers cooperate enthusiastically with the leader. A task-oriented style is appropriate in this situation because leader-member relations are already good. Therefore the manager does not need to spend much time on these relationships. In addition, because the manager has considerable power and the task is routine, subordinates should comply with the manager's directions and need little assistance. Therefore, the manager's role in this situation is to state what must be accomplished.

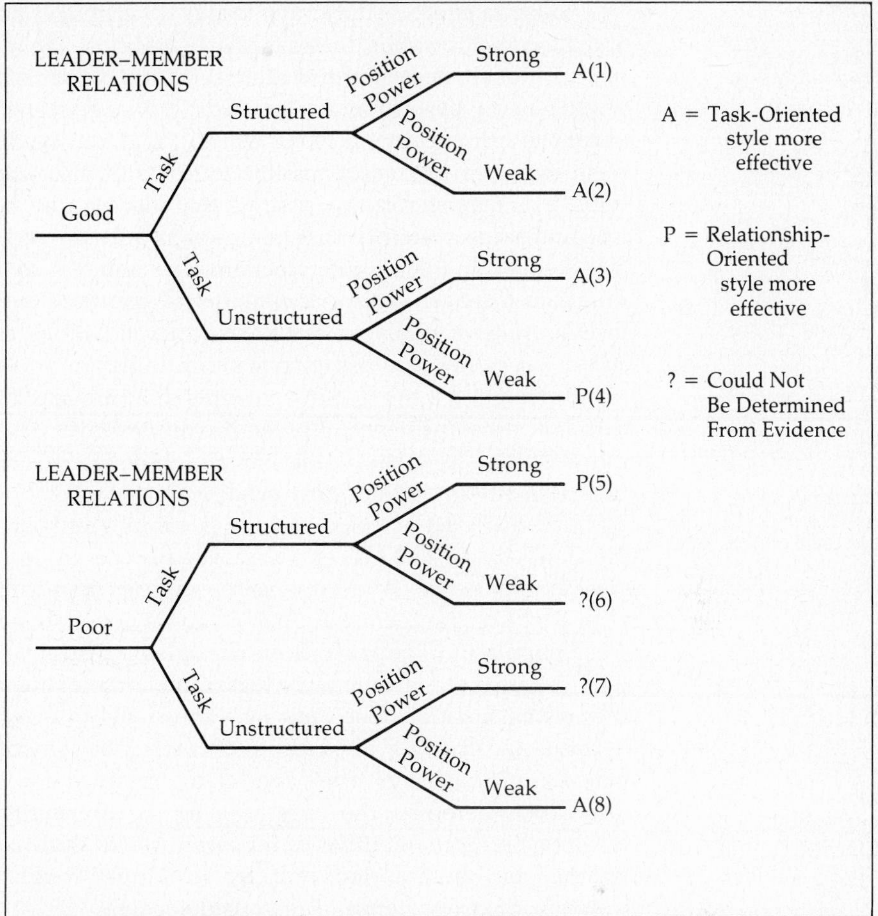

Figure 14-5 **Effectiveness in Various Situations, As Determined by Fiedler's Research**

Because situation 1 is the relatively rare case in which the leader carries a big stick but is still well liked, the potential drawbacks of authoritarian tactics and coercive/reward based power are minimal. Followers do not, for example, try to circumvent the control system or get away with doing just minimally acceptable work. Hence, especially where the work does not require a high level of creativity, the leader can actually realize the potential, often-cited efficiencies of a task-oriented style.

However, a manager should not equate a task-oriented style with being a dictator or abusing subordinates. If he or she takes such an approach, the potential for employee resentment, distrust, lack of cooperation, and commitment to informal groups with objectives counter to management's would probably be high. These factors, in turn, probably would make leadership ineffective.

To be an effective autocratic leader the manager needs to structure work and allocate it to subordinates fairly. In addition, the manager needs to make most, if not all, decisions and exercise a high degree of control to ensure that work is being performed to standards. It is not necessary for the manager to order subordinates about like a World War II marine drill sergeant to accomplish this. Nor is it even possible to do so in most contemporary organizations. The manager cannot assume that just because he or she has a certain title and some authority that he or she is a leader and automatically will be followed. Also, even if an autocratic style happens to be effective at a given time, the manager cannot assume it will continue to be effective. The genuinely effective manager recognizes that situations change over time and adapts his or her leadership style accordingly.

In situation 8 the leader's power is so minimal that followers will almost certainly resist influence, if given the opportunity. The authoritarian style is most effective here because it maximizes the leader's direct control, an absolute necessity to prevent total misdirection of effort.

The dilemma of green junior officers in Viet Nam is an excellent example. A newly arrived officer was scorned by his troops because of his lack of combat experience. And, obviously, sending men through jungles infested with Viet Cong snipers and booby traps is not a job that increases one's personal popularity. The few officers that tried a basically participative approach were laughed at—if they were lucky and smart enough to perceive the realities of the situation. The ones who continued to insist on "gung ho Army" heroism and trusting the guys to do their jobs sometimes learned the hard way about "fragging," the "accidental" tossing of a handgrenade in their direction. Therefore, the only way for an inexperienced officer to begin meeting his responsibilities to the army was to show concern for the lives of his men but remain aloof and, by working through a respected sergeant, insist on strict obedience to reasonable orders.

Relationship-oriented styles, according to Fiedler, seem to be most effective in situations that are moderately favorable to the leader. In these situations, the leader does not have enough power to win whole-hearted cooperation from followers. But, unlike the unfortunate situation 8 example, followers do not actively seek out opportunities to rebel. In most cases, followers are generally inclined to do what the leader wants if given reason and opportunity to do so. If the leader attempts a highly task-oriented approach, he or she runs the risk of antagonizing followers and thereby causing the potential drawbacks of that style to emerge. This would erode the leader's influence.

A relationship-oriented style, on the other hand, is likely to increase the leader's capacity to influence. Showing concern for subordinates' welfare, in effect, would improve leader-follower relations. Secondly, provided subordinates are motivated by higher-level needs, using a relationship-oriented style may enable the leader to stimulate followers to become personally involved with the work. This would be ideal, because a self-directed work force reduces the need for close, stringent supervision, and yet there is minimal risk of loss of control.

Research on Fiedler's Model. As summarized by three prominent management professors, research evidence indicates: "while leaders characterized by both leadership behaviors have been found to be more effective than others in several studies, there is also evidence that both leader behaviors [task or relationship] are not always effective and that their effects vary, depending on situational factors."[24]

Although the Fiedler model made a major contribution to the understanding of leadership by focusing on situational factors related to effectiveness, it has not been universally accepted.[25] "It is not clear whether the basic problem is in the overall construction of the theory or the measure used to tap it. In any event it is apparent that managers are much more changeable in their motives and personality, and much more flexible in their behaviors and styles, than the theory predicts."[26]

That Fiedler's model is not totally supported should not be interpreted as meaning it is of little value in managing. Quite the contrary! By determining that a task-oriented style is most appropriate in situations that are highly favorable or highly unfavorable, and that a relationship-oriented style is most effective in situations that are moderately favorable, Fiedler has built a foundation for future situational views of leadership. As Albanese states, Fiedler's contingency approach "is a very nice way of emphasizing the importance of the interactions of the leader, followers and the situation. The approach cautions against the simplistic notion that there is one best leadership style—regardless of the circumstances. Furthermore, information gathered from numerous studies suggests that the contingency approach can have practical implications for the recruitment, selection, and placement of leaders. Clearly, the contingency approach has made and continues to make a major contribution to the understanding of leadership."[27]

Belief in the inherent validity and necessity of a contingency approach to leadership is reflected in the more recent leadership effectiveness models of Mitchell and House and Vroom and Yetton.

Path-Goal Leadership

Another contingency model of leadership, similar in some ways to Fiedler's and sharing much in common with the expectancy theory of motivation, is that developed by Mitchell and House.[28] Called the **path-goal approach**, it also stresses the need for managers to use the leadership style most appropriate to the situation. According to the path-goal approach, managers can influence subordinates to attain goals by affecting the paths to their goals. Some ways by which a manager can influence the paths or means to goals are:

1. Clarifying what is expected
2. Being supportive, playing a coaching role, and reducing frustrating barriers

FEATURE 14-1

Managerial Implications of Fiedler's Contingency Leadership

If you think about the contingency approach to leadership, you should realize that according to it leadership has the potential to be improved by changing *any* of the variables. This premise has broad implications for management. It opens up avenues to effectiveness never touched upon by views of leadership that concentrated on the leader-follower relationship. For instance, organizations could improve their overall leadership by:

- Restructuring work groups along lines of personal compatibility. Matching workers who prefer direction with leaders who prefer a task-oriented style, for example, would improve leader-follower relations.
- Redesigning work to make it more or less structured. This would tip the situation toward task-oriented or relationship-oriented styles, as management preferred. Or, unstructuring the task could make it practical to move toward a more relationship-oriented style if that were more appealing to the work force.
- Modifying leader position power. An increased ability to reward would facilitate use of a task-oriented style. Reducing position power could prod task-oriented managers toward a more relationship-oriented style better suited to the organization's workers and objectives.

Other factors, such as cost or technology, may make such modifications difficult or wholly impractical. Leadership, like every other process of managing, is but one aspect of the effort to attain objectives.

3. Directing subordinates toward goal attainment
4. Arousing those subordinate needs over which the manager has some control and is able to satisfy
5. Satisfying subordinate needs when the goal is attained

House discusses two styles of leadership in his model: supportive and instrumental. Supportive leadership is similar to employee-centered or relationship-oriented leadership. Instrumental leadership is similar to job-centered or task-oriented leadership. "Supportive leadership is demonstrated by a friendly and approachable leader who shows concern for the status, well-being, and needs of subordinates. A supportive leader does little things to make work more pleasant, treats members as equals, and is friendly and approachable. Instrumental leadership is demonstrated by letting subordinates know what is expected of them, giving specific guidance as to what should be done and how it should be done, making the leader's part in the group understood, scheduling work to be done, maintaining definite standards of performance, and asking that group members follow standards and regulations."[29]

The leadership style that is most appropriate and that which subordinates will prefer is dependent on two situational factors: personal characteristics of subordinates and environmental pressures and demands.

Characteristics of Subordinates. When subordinates are characterized by a high need for self-esteem and affiliation, a supportive (or employee-centered or relationship-oriented) style is most appropriate. However, if subordinates have a high need for autonomy or self-actualization, they are likely to prefer an instrumental (task-oriented) style. Because their primary desire is to focus their efforts on the task and achieve, they prefer a manager to tell them what is expected and leave them on their own to accomplish it.

Another personal characteristic affecting the appropriateness of a leadership style is a subordinate's belief that he or she has an effect on the environment. Behavioral scientists refer to this characteristic as *locus of control.*[30] Basically, locus of control refers to the degree to which an individual believes that his or her actions can influence what happens to him or her. Individuals who believe their actions do, in fact, influence their environment prefer a participative style. Those who believe that they have little effect on events that occur around them, that things happen because of fate or luck, prefer an authoritarian or instrumental style.[31]

Environmental Pressures. In situations where the nature of the task is somewhat ambiguous, an instrumental style that provides direction is preferable and will increase satisfaction and productivity. However, for unambiguous tasks that are already structured, adding more structure through an instrumental style will be perceived as overcontrol. A supportive style would therefore be more appropriate. Similarly, if the task is already inherently satisfying to the subordinate, a supportive style would add little. However, if the task is somewhat unsatisfying, a supportive style is more appropriate.

As with Fiedler's model, future research is needed to validate the path-goal approach. Discussing this, Reitz states, "Like contingency theory Path-Goal theory is a promising approach to understanding the complexities of leadership effectiveness but much more research is needed to refine and validate the theory."[32]

Table 14-1 Five Styles Leaders Can Use to Make a Decision

1. You solve the problem or make the decision yourself, using information available to you at that time.

2. You obtain the necessary information from your subordinate(s), then decide on the solution to the problem yourself. You may or may not tell your subordinates what the problem is in getting the information from them. The role played by your subordinates in making the decision is clearly one of providing the necessary information to you, rather than generating or evaluating alternative solutions.

3. You share the problem with relevant subordinates individually, getting their ideas and suggestions without bringing them together as a group. Then *you* make the decision that may or may not reflect your subordinates' influence.

4. You share the problem with your subordinates as a group, collectively obtaining their ideas and suggestions. Then *you* make the decision that may or may not reflect your subordinates' influence.

5. You share a problem with your subordinates as a group. Together you generate and evaluate alternatives and attempt to reach agreement (consensus) on a solution. Your role is much like that of chairman. You do not try to influence the group to adopt "your" solution, and you are willing to accept and implement any solution that has the support of the entire group.

SOURCE: Victor H. Vroom, "A New Look at Managerial Decision Making," *Organizational Dynamics*, vol. 1: no. 4 (Spring 1973), p. 67.

Table 14-2 Problem Attributes in the Vroom-Yetton Model

1. The importance of the quality of the decision.

2. The extent to which the leader possesses sufficient information/expertise to make a high-quality decision by him- or herself.

3. The extent to which the problem is structured.

4. The extent to which acceptance or commitment on the part of subordinates is critical to the effective implementation of the decision.

5. The prior probability that the leader's autocratic decision will receive acceptance by subordinates.

6. The extent to which subordinates are motivated to attain the organizational goals as represented in the objectives explicit in the statement of the problem.

7. The extent to which subordinates are likely to be in conflict over preferred solutions.

SOURCE: Victor H. Vroom, "A New Look at Managerial Decision Making," *Organizational Dynamics*, vol. 1, no. 4 (Spring 1973), p. 67.

Vroom-Yetton Leadership Decision Model

Yet another contingency model of leadership is that formulated by Victor Vroom and Phillip Yetton.[33] The **Vroom-Yetton leadership decision model**, as its name implies focuses on the decision-making process. According to Vroom and Yetton, there are five possible styles a manager can use to make a decision. These are described in Table 14-1.

Seven situational factors or problem attributes, as listed in Table 14-2 determine which of these five styles will be most appropriate. Figure 14-6

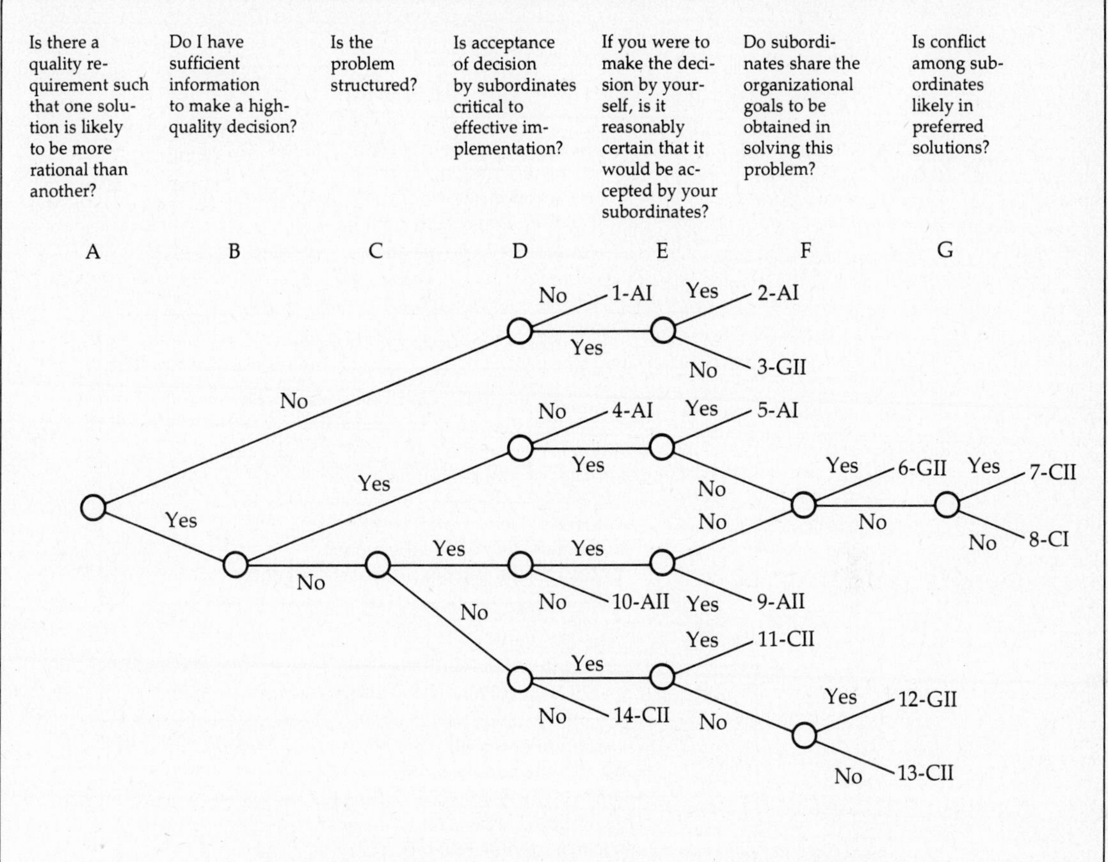

Figure 14-6 Vroom-Yetton Leadership Decision Model

SOURCE: Victor H. Vroom, "A New Look at Managerial Decision Making," *Organizational Dynamics*, vol. 1 (Spring 1973): No. 4, p. 70. © 1973 by AMACOM. Reproduced by permission.

illustrates important questions about these seven situational factors and presents a flow chart describing the most appropriate leadership style. After answering each of the questions defining situational factors, one eventually determines the most appropriate style, as shown in Figure 14-6.

Although the Vroom-Yetton model differs from both Fiedler's model and the path-goal approach because of its focus on decision making, it is similar to both in stressing that there is no one best style for influencing subordinates. The most appropriate style varies with the changing characteristics of the decision-making situation. As with the other contingency theories, the Vroom-Yetton model needs further refinement and research.[34] The general approaches to leadership we have described are summarized in Figure 14-7.

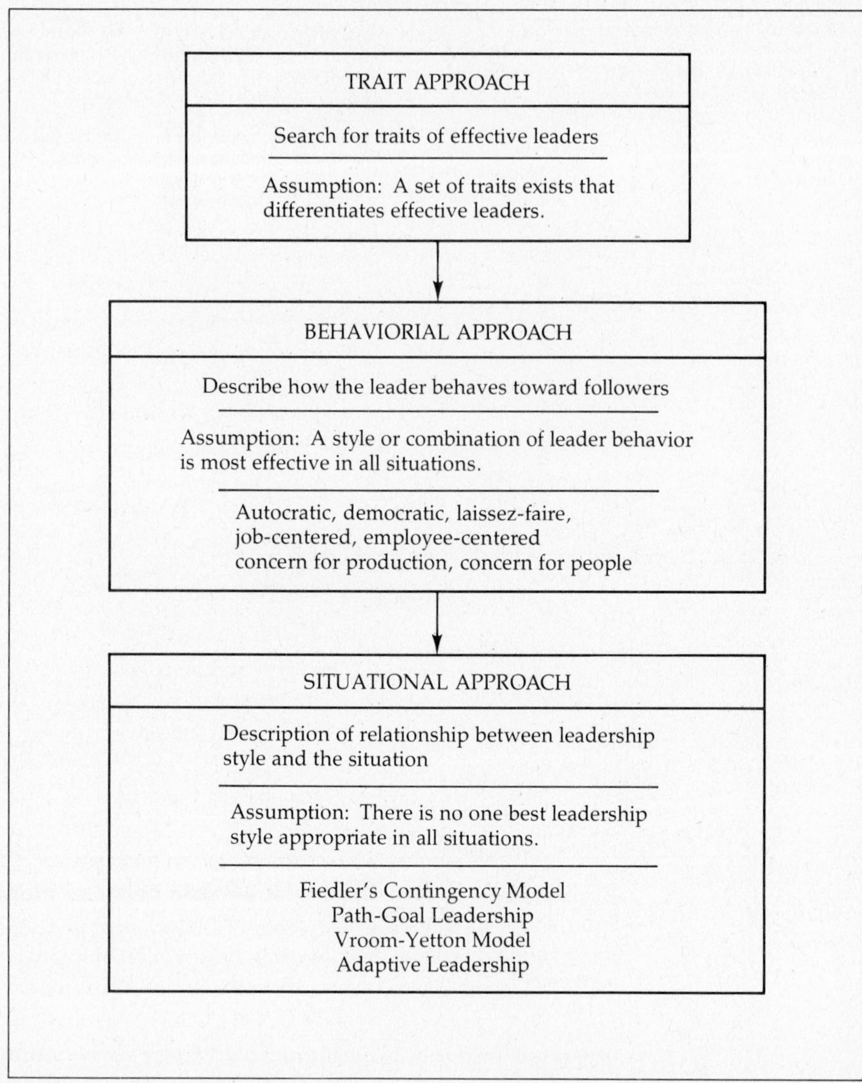

Figure 14-7 Evolution of Approaches to the Study of Leadership

Technology, Managerial Level, and Organizational Variables

Though not yet proven by research, it seems reasonable that several variables not included or given little stress by the three contingency models we have described also may affect leadership. Based on what has been learned about factors affecting organizational effectiveness in general, leadership effectiveness is probably influenced by technology, managerial level, and other organizational variables. Technology, as we have learned, is closely related to tasks, which Fiedler considers. Managerial level is partly included in

Fiedler's model under position power. However, here we refer to the nature of managerial work at different levels, rather than differences of authority. Under organizational variables affecting leadership are such factors as objectives, existing structure, and existing degree of decentralization.

Technology and Leadership. Technology can severely restrict, perhaps even dictate, a manager's leadership style. This is clearly seen when one considers a mass-production assembly-line situation. On an assembly line, technology determines what must be done and exactly when. Even a slight variation can result in a major decline in productivity. Moreover, this technology can only be altered at great expense, so it is unchanging and beyond the working manager's control. On a day-to-day basis, therefore, there is no point in seeking worker participation in decisions. In fact, allowing workers any latitude in routine decision making would be inherently counterproductive. Thus in situations where structure is crucial to successful completion of the task, the manager has little choice in leadership style. A job-centered, task-oriented style is the only one that has a reasonable chance of being effective.

When technology is a dominant factor in effectiveness, as it is for mass-production firms, first-line supervisors often play a very small leadership role. Technology, in essence, so limits the decision-making potential that the supervisor may be more of a technical specialist or expediter than a manager.

Assembly lines are not the only situations where technology and an inherent need for structure dictate leadership style. An effective leader of a surgical team must be highly authoritarian and task-oriented. While a chief surgeon may consult others before and after an operation, during the operation itself speed and precision are so crucial that the only possible style of leadership approaches total domination of followers by the leader. Clearly, if the team leader took time out to have subordinates participate in each decision and be warmly supportive of their help, the patient might die. In this task situation, it is obvious that an effort to build strong human relations while work is in progress would be exceptionally poor leadership.

Note, however, that building a climate of positive, trustful human relationships generally must be accomplished before the organization is in a high-pressure or crisis situation. An already well-established climate of trust between managers and subordinates should make subordinates more responsive to the leadership style management needs to employ. In organizations that have such a climate, what appears to be rote response to autocratic demands may actually be teamwork honed to a fine edge.

One of the authors was told of an example of this type of teamwork during a management-development workshop he conducted. Some managers at the workshop were employed by semi-conductor electronics firms in northern California, an industry characterized by rapid technological change and high competition. The high rate of change made it necessary for these firms to respond very rapidly in order to fill customer orders on short notice. As a result, the managers felt that it was essential to issue autocratic directives to ensure the product met customer specifications and delivery demands. They pointed out, however, that this leadership style was effective largely because they had first carefully built a climate of trust so that workers would respond quickly during high pressure situations.

Managerial Level. Besides having widely varying amounts of power attached to them, different management positions also have unique characteristics and requirements. Typically, managers lower in the hierarchy have more precisely defined objectives than top managers. They also have less discretionary control over the way they spend their time.[35] These differences in the nature of the management task impose restrictions on leadership behavior in much the same way technology does.

A supervisory-level manager, for instance a loading-dock foreman, has very specific duties and responsibilities. He or she must see that trucks are loaded, unloaded, and dispatched in an orderly manner. Most of his or her time is spent responding to requests for service from the organization and from incoming truckers. In this job, effectiveness is measured by the speed and accuracy with which these requests are filled. The need for speed and precision imposes structure on the work and requires the foreman to issue orders to subordinates at a rapid pace, one too fast to allow for consultation. Furthermore, because much of the work is manual and uncomplicated, the span of management can be very wide. This prevents him or her from devoting time to each subordinate's problems and development, even if he or she were inclined toward strengthening human relations. To a casual observer the first-level manager sometimes appears to be just another worker.

A company president, in contrast, has very general responsibilities and almost total discretion over how he or she spends his or her time. Compared with those of a typical supervisor, the decisions of a top manager are fewer in number, but much more complex. Time pressure is not as great because many of these decisions are long range and the top manager can set his or her own deadlines. In addition, few of these decisions can be made without consulting subordinates, at least to the extent of getting needed information. Analysis of a top executive's day usually reveals that most of it is spent on meetings and other forms of interpersonal communication.[36]

Furthermore, the people who report directly to a top manager tend to be self-directed and require little supervision. A top level manager therefore does not need to spend much time issuing directives or checking on work.[37] Thus, the top manager can afford to spend time and effort on the development and other personal needs of immediate subordinates. In fact, such development may be one of the top manager's specific organizational responsibilities.

Therefore, because of the nature of his or her work, much of the activity that is an inherent part of a top manager's tasks is associated with a participative and relationship-oriented style of leadership. This means, of course, that positive human relations and wise use of participation can be a decided asset in many top management situations. People who reach the top usually do so because they capitalize on all opportunities to improve their effectiveness and the effectiveness of others. This may explain why some researchers, such as Douglas McGregor, whose studies focused primarily on chief executives (presumably the most skillful organizational leaders), concluded that a participative style is usually most effective.

However, as we know, not all effective top managers refrain from authoritarian practices. History is full of examples of complete tyrants who were incredibly effective at getting others to work for their organizations. Certainly nobody associates Henry Ford, Napoleon Bonaparte, Joseph Stalin, General George Patton, or John D. Rockefeller with permissiveness and strong consideration for subordinates' feelings and thoughts. But their overwhelming achievements force us to consider them outstanding leaders, in the particular situations they operated within.

Organizational Variables. One of the points we have tried to stress in this book is the interdependence characteristic of organizations. To attain objectives effectively, it is necessary to be consistent in one's approach to the goal. Leadership is no exception. One cannot, for example, hope to successfully implement a highly participative style in an organization that has an elaborate, extensive system of procedures and rules. Allowing the high level of freedom associated with participation would necessarily lead to violation of some of these rules and thereby diminish their effectiveness. One way around this would be to seek participation in formulating rules and procedures. But it is not always possible or desirable to do so. The mission and objectives of some organizations simply cannot be attained unless certain activities are performed exactly as planned. Most mass-production and continuous process operations, for instance, must use engineering efficiency techniques to hold costs at a minimum in order to remain competitive. Establishing duties and responsibilities through participation might make jobs more pleasant and the work force more satisfied, but it would reduce profitability below acceptable levels.

Similarly, participative, relationship-oriented styles are inappropriate in mechanistic organizations. The high degree of structure inherent in a mechanistic design so strongly influences subordinate behavior that the impact of leader behavior is minimal in comparison. In addition, research indicates that workers in high performing, mechanistic organizations have a low tolerance for ambiguity in their work environment and prefer structure and a directive leadership style.[38] Thus, the most effective leadership style in this situation would probably be basically task oriented. The leader should simply do his or her best to get work performed as desired by top management. The reverse, of course, would be true in an organically structured firm. Authoritarian leadership styles are contrary to the concept of highly decentralized authority and the diffusion of influence to lower levels of the organization.

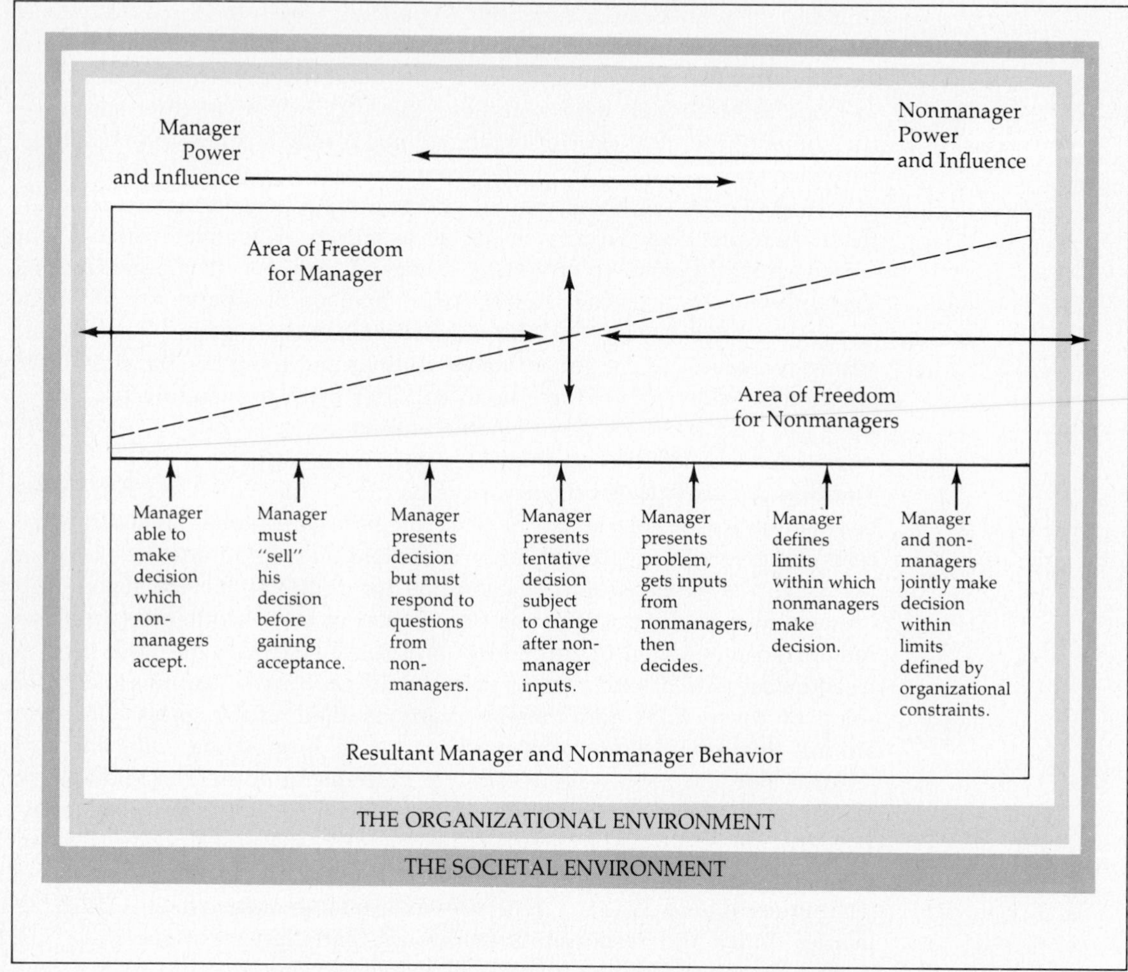

Figure 14-8 Revised Continuum of Manager-Nonmanager Behavior

SOURCE: Robert Tannenbaum and Warren H. Schmidt, "How to Choose a Leadership Pattern," *Harvard Business Review*, May-June 1973, p. 167.

External Variables

In 1958 Tannenbaum and Schmidt published a now classic article entitled "How to Choose a Leadership Pattern." In the retrospective commentary added when the article was reprinted in 1973, they made a substantial change, one consistent with open-systems theory and stimulated by the social turmoil of the 1960s. The following excerpt explains the change in their own words. Figure 14-8 illustrates the exhibit to which they refer.

> Our thoughts on the question of leadership have prompted us to design a new behavior continuum in which the total area of freedom shared by manager and

> nonmanagers is constantly redefined by interactions between them and the forces in the environment.
>
> The arrows in the exhibit indicate the continual flow of interdependent influence among systems and people. The points on the continuum designate the types of manager and nonmanager behavior that become possible with any given amount of freedom available to each. The new continuum is both more complex and more dynamic than the 1958 version, reflecting the organizational and societal realities of 1973.[39]

Exactly what the forces in the environment are and the degree to which they affect leader effectiveness has not yet been established by empirical research. It seems logical, however, that they would be the same forces influencing effectiveness of the other managerial functions, especially motivating and organizing.

For example, to be effective, managerial leadership must not deviate markedly from societal and cultural values. The social changes of the 1960s that partly prompted Tannenbaum and Schmidt to rethink their model tended to reduce the effectiveness of autocratic behavior and increase that of participative leadership. Research shows there are vast differences in what will work in different countries, a strong consideration in today's world of multinational corporations.[40] Europeans typically are more influenced by tradition and receptive to autocratic leadership than Americans. On the other hand, while Japanese culture strongly favors tradition and loyalty, the Japanese make extensive and effective use of participation in decision making.

Legal and governmental variables also affect leadership. New laws restricting what employers can do to dissenters have eroded the power bases of those who rely on coercion to influence. This necessarily diminishes the effectiveness of authoritarian tactics because subordinates know the leader cannot compel compliance. The presence of a strong union has a similar impact on leadership, although basically authoritarian leadership continues to prevail in manufacturing and even within unions themselves.

It should be especially interesting to see what impact the increasing numbers of women and minority members within both managerial and nonmanagerial ranks will have upon leadership patterns. Thus far there have been so few women and blacks in high managerial positions that nobody can objectively state what style they should adopt.

Need for Adaptive Leadership. The various situational models also drive home the need for a *flexible* approach to leadership. To evaluate the situation accurately, one must maintain an open mind about both subordinate abilities and one's own, the nature of the task, needs, power, and the quality of information. Even so appealing and human an attitude as the one McGregor described as Theory Y is still a presumption, not an objective evaluation of the facts at hand. Furthermore, even with an open mind, it is all too easy to make an erroneous judgment about people, so the manager must always be prepared to reevaluate his or her judgments and, if necessary, change style accordingly.

Also, few people attracted to a management career are content with having the same job for years on end. Most actively seek promotion to positions of greater responsibility. Thus, a manager who picks a style and adheres to it rigidly because it proved successful in the past, may be unable to lead effectively in the different situation of a higher-level job in which immediate subordinates are all highly achievement-oriented managers. Much the same would happen if, as often occurs, the manager is transferred from a department with highly structured tasks to one with highly unstructured, creative tasks.

The manager who wishes to lead as effectively as possible, to get the best out of his people, throughout his or her career cannot afford to have *one* style of leadership. Rather, the manager must learn to use whichever style, technique, and basis of influence is best suited to the immediate situation. If one were forced to give a name to the "best" mode of leadership, it would have to be *adaptive*, or as Argyris aptly stated, "reality-centered."

Describing reality-centered leadership, Argyris states it involves a leadership style which

> develops along a whole range of patterns. Also, decision rules are developed to serve as guideposts as to how and when leadership patterns are changed. . . . If one examines the literature on leadership, there has been a trend indicated that what is considered to be "effective" leadership varies with the situation. . . . no one leadership style is to be considered the most effective. . . . Consequently, effective leaders were those who were able to behave in many different leadership styles depending on the requirements of reality.[41]

SUMMARY

The three major approaches to the study of leadership have been the trait approach, behavioral approach, and situational or contingency approach.

Writers of the behavioral approach made an important contribution by classifying leadership style, the general way in which the leader behaves toward subordinates. Leadership style can be classified on a continuum ranging from autocratic to laissez-faire. The highly authoritarian autocrat often uses coercion, reward, or tradition to impose his or her will on subordinates. The autocrat's presumptions, which McGregor termed Theory X, indicate little regard for their capacities. The participative or democratic style leader, whose assumptions McGregor called Theory Y, prefers to influence through persuasion, rational faith, or charisma and avoids imposing his or her will on subordinates. The laissez-faire leader gives subordinates virtually complete freedom.

One can also, as Likert did, classify leaders as job-centered or employee-centered. The job-centered leader is concerned with designing work for maximum productivity and developing rewards to stimulate people to work harder. The employee-centered leader tries to get people to perform their best by improving human relations. To give a better picture of the range of styles on the continuum, Likert also came up with the postulate of four systems of management style.

A group at Ohio State developed a two-dimensional model of leadership behavior. They classified managers with respect to consideration and structure, finding the most effective to be strong in both these areas. Blake and Mouton elaborated on this concept with their managerial grid. They found that the "team leader," the manager whose style demonstrated strong concern for people and equally strong concern for productivity to be most effective.

While an employee-centered style does increase satisfaction in many cases, it does not necessarily increase productivity. According to research, there seems to be no firm, uniform relationship between leadership style and productivity. Because factors other than leader behavior and traits apparently can have a determining effect on leader effectiveness, it is now widely accepted that leadership effectiveness is situational.

Three contingency models of leadership have influenced management thought. Fiedler's contingency model, the first, considered three variables: leader-member relations, task structure, and position power. House and Mitchell's path-goal approach focused on what the leader could and did do to facilitate the path or means by which subordinates attain goals. Vroom and Yetton's model focused on leader decision making, considering five decision behaviors and seven potential situations. Although none of these theories has been totally supported by research, it seems clear that the concept that managers must adopt a leadership style consistent with the situation at hand is correct. There is no one best way to lead.

Other variables that may influence leader effectiveness are technology, managerial level, and organizational variables. When technology necessitates a high degree of structure, it severely restricts leader behavior. Because the nature of managerial work is different on different levels of the hierarchy, a style that proved effective on the supervisory level may be wholly inappropriate in a middle management or top management position. No leadership style can be effective unless it is consistent with the goals and existing structure of the organization.

More recently it has become clear that external forces also have a determining influence on leader effectiveness. Exactly what these forces are and their relative impact has not yet been determined. But it seems logical that the managerial leader of today must consider social and cultural factors when choosing a style.

The contingency view of leadership points out several new ways of improving leader effectiveness. One could restructure work groups to make members psychologically compatible with the leader, redesign work, or modify position power, for example. Above all, it is now clear that to be effective in today's rapidly changing world, a manager's leadership style must be adaptable, what Argyris calls "reality-centered."

REVIEW QUESTIONS

1. What are the three major approaches to the study of leadership?
2. Compare autocratic, democratic, laissez-faire, job-centered, and employee-centered leadership styles.
3. Describe the key differences between the Theory X and Theory Y manager.

4. What were Likert's four systems of management style?
5. Describe the two-dimensional leadership model proposed by the Ohio State group.
6. Describe the Blake and Mouton model of leadership. What style of leadership did these researchers consider to be most effective?
7. What seems to be the basic relationship among style, satisfaction, and productivity?
8. Describe Fiedler's contingency model of leadership.
9. Describe the path-goal model of leadership.
10. Describe the Vroom-Yetton model of leadership.

DISCUSSION QUESTIONS

11. Show through an example why a democratic, employee-centered style of leadership is not always effective.
12. Why would different styles of leadership be appropriate for different subunits of the organization? Give examples.
13. Compare and contrast the three situational models of leadership presented in the chapter.
14. Given the changes that are now taking place in our society, both cultural and technological, what style of leadership do you think will likely be most effective during the 1980s?
15. How does environmental volatility affect leadership style? Give examples.

CASE INCIDENT

Ashley Manufacturing

Ashley Manufacturing was a family-owned company located in a predominantly rural area. For over 50 years it had been a successful manufacturer of farm machinery and equipment. Tom Ashley, the company's founder, still dropped in a few days each week although he was 87 years old. The company was run by Tom Ashley, Jr.

Fifteen years ago, the workers at Ashley were unionized although there had never been a strike or any real labor trouble. Tom Ashley, Jr., felt that the union served no purpose and that the company and the workers would be better off without it. This view was not shared by the company's labor lawyer, Dan Wilson, who felt that it would be best just to leave things as they were. After all, he explained, there had been no trouble with the union and no real demands. "Why stir things up?" Dan wanted to know.

To Tom Ashley, Jr., and to his father, the union presence was a distasteful annoyance, and they hoped that the union might be eventually decertified. The thought of possible decertification was rekindled after Tom, Jr., returned from a conference dealing with how to manage a nonunion company.

Tom was especially impressed with one of the program instructors who was a labor relations consultant. After discussing the conference with Dan Wilson, Tom decided to contact Pete Hill, a labor relations consultant, about the situation at Ashley Manufacturing. Hill explained that decertification was the exception, not the rule, and that Dan Wilson's recommendation to leave things alone might be the wisest course to follow.

Tom Ashley was adamant, and suggested he wasn't about to "roll over and play dead for the union or anyone else." He insisted that "the union contributed nothing and that the employees would probably like to stop paying dues for nothing."

Pete Hill asked Ashley about relationships between first-level managers and employees. He was assured that Ashley's supervisors were experienced professionals who came up through the ranks and knew what they were doing. Hill suggested that he'd like to meet with the supervisors for the purpose of assessing the situation for himself and to collect some data about how they, that is, the supervisors or first-level managers perceived their roles.

Ashley agreed and Hill met with the company's 15 first-level supervisors. He was surprised to discover that length of service with Ashley ranged from 8 to 46 years. Indeed, they were an experienced group.

Hill asked the supervisors to participate in a survey in which they were asked to describe what they considered to be their major problems. The following items were most frequently mentioned:

1. Down time on machinery and equipment
2. Plant Layout
3. Inventory control

Hill immediately was impressed by the fact that most of the responses dealt with the technical dimensions of work and had relatively little to do with the human aspects. Hill asked Ron Walker, a 26-year veteran of Ashley and a highly experienced supervisor why there were so few comments from the supervisors about people problems. Walker replied, "We don't have time for people problems. That's the shop steward's job."

Questions

1. How would you describe the leadership or management style at Ashley Manufacturing?
2. What role do the union and shop steward appear to play?
3. If you were Pete Hill, what kind of advice would you give to Tom Ashley, Jr.?

NOTES

1. C. Bird, *Social Psychology* (Englewood Cliffs, NJ: Prentice-Hall, 1940).
2. Ralph M. Stogdill, "Personal Factors Associated with Leadership: A Survey of Literature," *Journal of Psychology*, vol. 25 (1948), pp. 35–71.
3. Ralph M. Stogdill, *Handbook of Leadership* (New York: The Free Press, 1974).
4. F. E. Finch, H. R. Jones, and J. A. Litterer, *Managing for Organizational Effectiveness: An Experiential Approach* (New York: McGraw-Hill, 1976), p. 94.

5. Douglas McGregor, *The Human Side of Enterprise* (New York: McGraw-Hill, 1960), pp. 33–34.
6. Ibid, pp. 47–48.
7. Curt Lewin, R. Lippett, and R. K. White, "Patterns of Aggressive Behavior in Experimentally Created Social Climates," *Journal of Social Psychology,* vol. 10 (1939), pp. 271–301.
8. Rensis Likert, *New Patterns of Management* (New York: McGraw-Hill, 1961), p. 7.
9. Rensis Likert, *The Human Organization* (New York: McGraw-Hill, 1967).
10. Ibid, p. 57.
11. Edwin A. Fleishman and Edwin F. Harris, "Patterns of Leadership Behavior Related to Employee Grievances and Turnover," *Personnel Psychology,* vol. 15 (1962), pp. 43–44.
12. For additional information see: Abraham K. Korman, "Consideration, Initiating Structure, and Organizational Criteria—A Review," *Personnel Psychology,* vol. 19 (Winter 1966), pp. 349–61; Andrew W. Halpin, *The Leadership Behavior of School Superintendents* (Chicago: Midwest Administration Center, The University of Chicago, 1959); R. M. Stogdill and A. E. Coons, *Leader Behavior: Its Description and Measurement* (Columbus: Ohio State University Press, 1957); Don Hellriegal and John W. Slocum, Jr., *Management: Contingency Approaches* (Reading, MA: Addison-Wesley, 1978), pp. 384–385.
13. A. C. Filley, R. J. House, and S. Kerr, *Managerial Process and Organizational Behavior* (Glenview, IL: Scott, Foresman, 1976), p. 234.
14. Robert R. Blake and Jane S. Mouton, *The Managerial Grid* (Houston: Gulf Publishing Company, 1964).
15. Stogdill, *Handbook of Leadership,* (op. cit.).
16. Ibid, p. 370; Victor H. Vroom and Phillip W. Yetton, *Leadership and Decision Making* (Pittsburg: University of Pittsburg Press, 1973).
17. Stogdill, *Handbook;* J. K. White and R. H. Ruh, "Effects of Personal Values on the Relationship between Participation and Job Attitudes," *Administrative Science Quarterly,* vol. 18: no. 4, (December 1973), pp. 506–14.
18. Victor H. Vroom, *Work and Motivation* (New York: Wiley, 1964); D. G. Kuhn, J. W. Slocum, Jr. and R. B. Chase, "Does Job Performance Affect Job Satisfaction?" *Personnel Journal,* vol. 50: no. 6 (June 1971), p. 455.
19. I. C. Ross and A. Zander, "Need Satisfaction and Employee Turnover," *Personnel Psychology,* vol. 10 (Autumn 1957), p. 327.
20. Ibid; F. Friedlander, "Motivation to Work and Organizational Performance," *Journal of Applied Psychology,* vol. 50 (1966): no. 2, pp. 143–152.
21. Edward E. Lawler, III and Lyman W. Porter, "The Effect of Performance on Job Satisfaction," *Industrial Relations,* vol. 7 (1967), p. 22.
22. R. L. Kahn, "Productivity and Job Satisfaction," *Personnel Psychology,* vol. 13 (1960): no. 3, pp. 275–287.
23. Fred E. Fiedler, *A Theory of Leadership Effectiveness* (New York: McGraw-Hill Book Company, 1967).
24. A. C. Filley, R. J. House and S. Kerr, *Managerial Process and Organizational Behavior* (Glenview, IL: Scott, Foresman and Company, 1976), p. 234.
25. A. Ashour, "The Contingency Model of Leader Effectiveness: An Evaluation," *Organizational Behavior and Human Performance,* vol. 9 (1972), pp. 339–355; Stogdill, *Handbook,* p. 82.

26. John B. Miner, *The Management Process*, 2d ed. (New York: Macmillan, 1978), p. 419.
27. Robert Albanese, *Managing Toward Accountability for Performance* (Homewood, IL: Richard D. Irwin, 1978), p. 382.
28. Robert J. House, "A Path-Goal Theory of Leader Effectiveness," *Administrative Science Quarterly*, vol. 16: no. 3 (September 1971), pp. 321–338; Robert J. House and Terrance R. Mitchell, "Path-Goal Theory of Leadership," *Journal of Contemporary Business*, vol. 3: no. 4 (Autumn 1974), pp. 81–97.
29. Hellriegal and Slocum, *Management: Contingency Approaches*, pp. 384–385.
30. Julien D. Rotter, "External Control and Internal Control," *Psychology Today*, June 1971, pp. 28–33.
31. Carl R. Anderson and C. E. Schneider, "Locus of Control, Leader Behavior and Leader Performance Among Management Students," *Academy of Management Journal*, vol. 21 (1978), pp. 690–698; Terrance R. Mitchell, C. M. Smyser, and S. E. Leed, "Locus of Control: Supervision and Work Satisfaction," *Academy of Management Journal*, vol. 18 (1975), pp. 623–630.
32. H. Joseph Reitz, *Behavior in Organizations* (Homewood, IL: Richard D. Irwin, 1977), p. 535.
33. Vroom and Yetton, *Leadership and Decision Making*, op. cit.
34. R. H. G. Fields, "A Critique of the Vroom-Yetton Contingency Model of Leadership Behavior," *Academy of Management Review*, vol. 4 (1979), pp. 249–257.
35. Ross A. Webber, *Time and Management* (New York: D. Van Nostrand Company, 1972).
36. Henry Mintzberg, *The Nature of Managerial Work* (New York: Harper & Row, Publishers, 1973), pp. 202–208. This cites several studies on how executives, particularly top executives, spend their time.
37. Rosemary M. Stewart, "The Manager's Job: Discretion versus Demand," *Organizational Dynamics*, vol. 2 (1974): no. 3, p. 67.
38. Jay W. Lorsch and John J. Morse, *Organizations and Their Members: A Contingency Approach* (New York: Harper & Row, 1974).
39. Robert Tannenbaum and Warren H. Schmidt, "How to Choose a Leadership Pattern," *Harvard Business Review*, May–June 1973, p. 168.
40. Ibid.
41. Chris Argyris, *Integrating the Individual and the Organization* (New York: Wiley, 1964), pp. 214–215.

PART FOUR CASE STUDY

Mid-South Airlines

TIMOTHY S. MESCON

Department of Management, Arizona State University

Paul Stephenson was a "go-getter." In college at the University of Southern Mississippi, Paul was involved in many activities. He was captain of the wrestling team and a standout performer for four years. He was president of Tau Kappa Epsilon fraternity. A management major, Paul obtained two summer internships with Alatoona Ship Building Company in Mobile, Alabama. His first summer in Mobile, Paul interned as an apprentice welder. The next summer Paul worked as an assistant to the manager of the industrial relations department. Paul was a member of Sigma Iota Epsilon (SIE) management honorary, Beta Gamma Sigma business honorary, and was also a member of the student chapter of the American Society of Personnel Administrators (ASPA).

Two years ago, fresh out of the University of Southern Mississippi, Paul had accepted a job as a ramp service agent with Mid-South Airlines. Mid-South is a large regional carrier headquartered in Memphis, Tennessee. While a starting salary of $11,500 per year was not overly enticing to Paul, opportunities for advancement and travel were abundant and tailor-made for any individual willing to work hard and desirous of visiting many exciting and glamorous places at little expense.

The job of a ramp service agent at Mid-South is quite similar to the same position at most airlines. Ramp service agents or ramp rats as they are affectionately called, are responsible for transporting, loading, and unloading baggage, freight, and mail. Increasing migration to the sunbelt helped spur Mid-South's growth in recent years, creating a number of new supervisory and middle-level management positions within the organization. Although Mid-South required all new management candidates to start on the ramp, Paul recognized the fact that there was much room for advancement in this rapidly growing airline and foresaw a bright future with Mid-South.

Following an eight-week orientation program at corporate headquarters, Paul was assigned to the company's Gulfport/Biloxi, Mississippi station. The Gulfport area is an appealing vacation spot, situated on the Gulf of Mexico. Vacationers generally enjoy the sun, the surf, golfing, and tennis facilities available at many fine resort hotels in the area. In recent years legislators in the Mississippi house had curtailed illegal waste dumping practices and open sewage lines in the gulf, and tourism was once again "king" in the area. The national hotel chains had recently built sizable facilities in Gulfport, and the general economy in the area was strengthening daily.

Initially, Paul was delighted to be located in his home state, not far from his family. However, he quickly realized that visibility and mobility were lacking at this station. The pace was slow and so was advancement. After 18 months on the job in Gulfport he applied for a transfer to the Memphis station. Paul's manager, Ed Wiley, hated to grant the transfer request since Paul had, indeed, been an outstanding performer. Ed did realize, however, that there was limited job mobility at the Gulfport station, so with great reluctance he forwarded the request to company headquarters. Six months later Paul was on the job in Memphis.

Paul was assigned to a team at the airport that was comprised of a number of older agents high on the seniority list at Mid-South. Additionally, Paul was assigned to the "banker's shift": 8:30 a.m. to 5:00 p.m. Delighted with his transfer, Paul decided to begin his personal campaign directed toward his first promotion. About one week on the job, Mike Chappuis, one of the older workers kidded Paul about working too hard. Mike was 55 years old, had been with Mid-South for 25 years, and was looked upon by his fellow co-workers as a friendly, likable fellow. Paul laughed off Mike's suggestion, but a few days later Tim Harvey and Stuart Green, two other co-workers, also hinted that Paul was working too hard and should slow down a bit. This gentle ribbing continued for about one month, but Paul simply ignored the taunts and remained as dedicated and as committed to maximum achievement and visibility as ever.

One afternoon, as each of the five flights situated in Paul's section prepared for departure, a late call came into the office requesting that flight 289 to Knoxville be held for a special air freight delivery. A dozen laboratory mice ordered by the psychology department at the University of Tennessee had arrived from Chattanooga, and due to the nature of the experiment being conducted on these mice, special delivery of the cargo was required. Such requests were not at all unusual. Planes were often held for laboratory animals, human organs destined for transplantation, mail, or emergency freight deliveries. Mike Chappuis received the call and asked Paul to signal to the pilot to hold the plane. Additionally, Mike asked Paul to open the forward luggage bin and wait by the plane for the mice to arrive. Paul raced out to the plane, signalled the pilot, opened the bin, and hopped in the pressurized baggage section of the DC-9 in order to protect his ears from the annoying whine of the jet engines. John Tavormina, another veteran on the job, walked over to the bin and told Paul the delivery was on its way.

Paul heard a truck drive up, the bin door slam shut, and the engines start up. Flight 289 destined for Knoxville was given clearance by the tower to taxi out to runway B.

Questions

1. Obtain a suitable definition for the term, "rate buster."
2. Analyze the formal communication network in force at Mid-South.
3. Analyze the informal communication network in force at Mid-South.
4. As Paul's immediate supervisor, how would you have prevented such an occurrence?

PART FIVE

Decision-Making Aids and Techniques: The Management Science Approach

In performing the management functions, the manager is really *making decisions* about planning, organizing, motivating, and controlling and implementing them through other people. Decision making, as we noted in Chapter 6, is a linking process that pervades all of management. All of the schools and management approaches we have described have attempted to help the manager make better, more objective decisions. However, the approach most closely and specifically associated with decision making techniques is the management science or quantitative school.

In this part we will examine the management science approach and related quantitative aids for decision making. Techniques in this area have become extremely sophisticated and complex. To fully understand and actually apply them often requires a background in relatively advanced mathematics or engineering. In contemporary organizations these techniques are usually used by staff specialists to generate information, develop alternative solutions, and to evaluate alternative courses of action to facilitate line management decisions regarding planning and control.

Therefore, our presentation will be largely descriptive. Our overall objective is to give you a basic understanding of how management science techniques can be used to improve decision making, a general idea of the major types of techniques and their uses, and the limitations of management science.

An Interview with Isabel Ramos

Selecting managers for these interviews was one of our most difficult decisions. Lack of space made it impossible to even attempt a true cross-section of management. The need to represent the small business entrepreneur, however, was clear. Over 90 percent of American private enterprise firms are small businesses operated by their owners. These firms employ nearly 60 percent of all private sector workers, even though 98 percent of them have fewer than 50 employees. Therefore, although few of them ever become rich or famous, small business managers like Isabel Ramos play a major role in our society.

Were she not a woman from a minority group, Isabel would be rather typical of the millions of American owner/managers. The eldest of four daughters, she immigrated to Florida from Cuba at age eight. Soon after graduating from community college, where she studied fashion merchandising, Isabel married and took a trainee job with a large department store. Less than a year later, pregnancy forced her to resign. An intense, active woman, Isabel did not find the life of homemaker to her liking. A year after the birth of her second child, she went back to work, again for a department store. However, because of the break in her career, she was forced to accept a clerk's job at a salary lower than she was earning fresh out of school. By her own admission, Isabel resented this and was an indifferent employee who argued with her boss too often for her own good. At age 30, she had an opportunity to open a small boutique and took it. At the time of this interview, Isabel Ramos had recently opened a second and larger store.

Author: What made you decide to start your own business?

Ramos: I am not the kind of woman who can be happy staying at home all day. I need to go out and work and do things. But I was never happy working at the department store. I thought it was unfair that I was paid so little. Also, I like to do things my way, so I was always getting my boss mad. I knew it was only a matter of time before he would fire me, and if that happened it would be back to cleaning house. That's when I got the idea of having my own store.

Author: Why did you pick the clothing business?

Ramos: Well, you know, I studied fashion merchandising in school and I had worked in stores, so I thought I knew enough about the business. I didn't discover how ignorant I was until after we opened. Also, I had almost no money to invest, but one of my uncles was a manufacturer's representative for some good fashion houses so I was able to get most of my starting inventory on credit.

Author: You couldn't have been all that ignorant. Most new businesses fail, and you have already managed to open a second store. How do you account for your success?

Ramos: Luck. And having a lot of relatives who were embarrassed to visit the store without buying something.

Author: Seriously, it couldn't have been all luck.

Ramos: No, but I really was very lucky at first. I opened just when wealthy Latin American tourists began to come over in big numbers, and there weren't very many stores selling the type of clothes I do where the owners spoke Spanish. About the only smart thing I did in the beginning was ask a lot of questions. I pestered everybody I could get to listen for advice about starting a store. There were only two things anybody agreed on: get the best location and the best accountant you can. That's what I did, and it was enough to save me from all the other mistakes.

Author: Has being a business woman, putting in the hours you must, caused you problems with your family?

Ramos: I am lucky in this, too. In Cuba it would have been unthinkable for a woman from a good family to work. The way the older people make it sound, everybody was a professional or a millionaire with a mansion and a hundred servants. But when we first came to America, we had no money, and it was accepted that women had to help make ends meet. Also, my husband is not the old-fashioned type. He went to college and he can understand my need to be more than a housewife. He didn't like the idea of the store at first, but once it happened he gave me all the support he could. The one part that bothers me is not spending enough time with the children. But we have a very close family, and my mother and sisters take good care of them while I work. One of the main reasons I opened the second store is so I could afford to hire enough people to get away from the counter for a few hours around dinner.

Author: How do you find having more employees, having to rely on others to get work done?

Ramos: It is very difficult for me to trust somebody else with my store. It's my nature to want to do everything myself, and I always worry when I am not there that something will go wrong. I know this is wrong, but it is a very hard thing to control because so much of me is in this business. I've gotten much better since I opened the second store. After a few weeks of going crazy running from one to the other all day long, I made my best salesgirl manager of the old store. The sales are still good, so I have to admit the store can get along without me standing behind the counter all day long.

Author: How would you rate yourself as a boss?

Ramos: I don't know; probably not very well. But I must not be too bad because I have had very few people leave me. I think what has helped me the most as a boss is remembering how much I hated working in the department store, especially not making what I felt I was worth. Every girl who works for me gets a commission besides her salary. Not enough to get rich, but a bit more than most retail store people in this area make. I also try to be considerate of their feelings and problems.

Author: Do you want to expand, or are you content with the two stores you have?

Ramos: I used to always say that I never wanted to get big and have all that responsibility. I suppose I was afraid I couldn't handle it. But I've become much more confident in the last year or so. The routine of working behind the counter is beginning to get a little boring. So I think I'd eventually like to have four or five shops and concentrate on the fun part of the business, buying.

Author: One of the points we stress in our book is that a manager has to take the world outside into account when making decisions. Do you feel this is necessary and actually do it?

Ramos: I'm not too sure exactly what you mean, but I think so. I always check on what my competition is doing, and I read the fashion magazines from cover to cover so I know what the trends are. In this business you have to stay on top of what's new, or people will stop dropping in to browse regularly.

Author: Do you decide what to stock mainly by intuition or some other way?

Ramos: Well, you have to have good intuition about what will sell. But if I just bought according to my own tastes I'd go broke. I've always really paid attention to people's reactions as they walk around the store. Not buying tells you almost as much about your merchandise as a sale. If I see twenty women get excited about a dress on the rack and not even try it on after seeing the price tag, I try to find something similar at a lower price.

Author: People who run big businesses frequently complain about governmental meddling and paperwork. How do you, as a small business manager, feel about this?

Ramos: America has been very good to me and my family. The government helped us so much when we first came. So it's hard for me to say anything bad about it. But I don't think it is right that a little business like mine has to fill out so many reports and papers that it needs a lawyer to make sure everything is right.

CHAPTER 15

Management Science Models and Decision-Making Techniques

Effective decision making is a requisite for performing the managerial functions. It therefore is not surprising that decision making has itself become the focal point of a school of management. The management science school strives to improve organizational effectiveness by increasing management's ability to make sound, objective decisions in situations of extreme complexity. Through models and quantitative techniques, management science has attempted to bring the discipline closer to being a true science. Developments in computer technology have made it increasingly more successful in doing so. In this chapter we will describe the characteristics of management science, modeling, types of models, and a few widely used decision-making and forecasting techniques. Our objective is not to show how to actually apply these methods, which is a course in itself. Rather, our objective is to give you an appreciation of what management science can do.

After reading this chapter, you should understand the following important terms and concepts:

management science
model
scientific method
game theory
queueing models
inventory models
linear programming
simulation
economic analysis
payoff matrix
decision tree
time series analysis
causal models
jury of opinion
sales force composite
customer expectation method
Delphi technique

Modeling and Management Science

Origins and Characteristics of Management Science

As we learned in our discussion of management history, the concept that scientific principles could be used to improve organizational effectiveness arose while management was still in its infancy as a discipline. Systematic application of the scientific method to management problems was the underpinning of the scientific management movement. The origins of the school of management currently referred to as management science, however, are very recent. It began in England during World War II with a team of scientists assigned to solve complex military problems such as the optimal location for civil defense facilities and gun sites, the optimal depth to explode antisubmarine charges, and the optimal size for a convoy of supply ships. During the 1950s and 1960s, the methodology developed by these pioneers was refined, converted to numerous specific techniques, and applied with increasing frequency and success to a wide range of industrial problems and decision situations.

The central focus of the management science approach "is to provide managers of the organization with a scientific basis for solving problems involving the interaction of components of the organization in the best interest of the organization as a whole."[1] This focus is important to all organizations, but particularly difficult to accomplish in large organizations due to the high degree of specialization. As Churchman, Ackoff, and Arnoff state:

> In an organization each functional unit (division, department, or section) has a part of the whole job to perform. Each part is necessary for the accomplishment of the *over-all objectives* of the organization. A result of this division of labor, however, is that each functional unit develops objectives of its own. For example, the production department generally assumes the objectives of minimizing the cost of production and maximizing production volume. The marketing department tries to minimize the cost of unit sales and maximize sales volume. The finance department attempts to optimize the capital investment policy of the business. The personnel department tries to hire good people at minimum cost, and to retain them, etc. These objectives are not always consistent; in fact, they frequently come into direct conflict with one another.[2]

Staff specialists trained in management science techniques attempt to assess the trade-offs involved in these different objectives and identify alternative solutions that provide a balance among objectives that conflict. Understanding the management science approach will help you communicate more effectively with staff specialists and work with them to develop effective solutions to organizational problems.

Today, one often finds the terms "management science," "decision science," "systems analysis," "systems sciences," and, most frequently, "operations research" used interchangeably. This overlap of terminology extends to the quantitative techniques that have been developed. Many writers would consider certain of the techniques that we classify under operations management and planning and control aids in later chapters as management science techniques. Whatever terminology one prefers, the distinguishing characteristics of **management science** as an approach are:

1. Use of the scientific method
2. A systems orientation
3. The use of models

Scientific Method. The fundamental procedure for all scientific investigation, first applied in management by the scientific management school, the **scientific method** consists of three steps:

1. *Observation.* This is objectively gathering information about the problem and situation and analyzing it. If the manager is concerned with the relationship between demand for products and inventory level, for example, he or she must assess how inventory levels vary under different conditions of demand. (Today, this and most other aspects of scientific analysis are usually performed by staff specialists in large organizations.)
2. *Hypothesis.* This is what the manager *believes* will occur, based on the observations. In making a hypothesis, the investigator identifies available alternatives, their consequences on the situation, and makes a prediction. The aim is to establish a relationship between the components of the problem. If, for instance, observation indicates that inventory will be depleted if demand during the month increases by 10 percent, the manager might hypothesize that increasing inventory by a certain amount would prevent the running out of inventory in such situations.
3. *Verification.* In the third phase the investigator verifies the hypothesis by observing the results of the decision. To continue our example, the manager might actually increase inventory by the amount recommended by a staff specialist. If the firm neither runs out of inventory nor carries too much stock, the hypothesis would be considered correct. If there is still a shortage when demand increases, or so much stock is kept on hand that inventory costs become prohibitive, the hypothesis would be considered invalid. Should this happen, the manager needs to return to step one and add the information gathered during verification and other information, and then formulate a different hypothesis.

When applying the scientific method to management problems, it is necessary to keep in mind that the organization is an open system. We have discussed this second aspect of the management science approach often. The last, *models,* are often needed because of the complexity of management problems and the difficulty of conducting experiments in real-life situations.

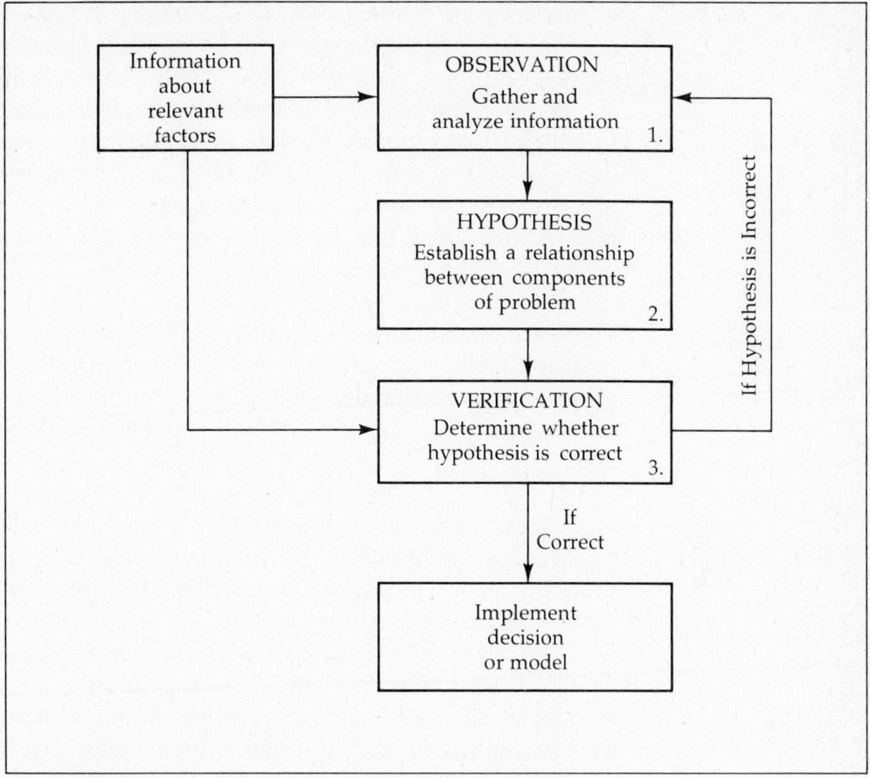

Figure 15-1 The Scientific Method in Management

Modeling and Management Science. Modeling is the concept around which much of our discussion will revolve. The reason for this extends beyond giving you a better understanding of the management science approach. The management science school's most visible and perhaps greatest contribution is the development of models that permit objective decisions to be made in situations too complex for casual evaluation of alternatives. Many of these models are too sophisticated for the average manager to use personally. However, without a basic understanding of models, a manager will be ill-equipped and hesitant to use their results. This may lead to using guesswork or trial and error to make a haphazard decision when proven techniques exist for making it quickly and accurately.

What a Model Is

Although certain types of management science models are so complex a computer is required to use them, the concept of a model is simple. As defined by Shannon, "A **model** is a representation of an object, system, or idea in some form other than that of the entity itself."[3] An organization chart, for example, is a model that represents the structure of the organization. All of the theories of management presented in this book are models of the operation of an organization or a subsystem of it. As you will soon discover, there are many other examples of models with which you are already familiar.

A key characteristic of a model is that it simplifies the real-life situation to which it corresponds. Because its form is less complex and the irrelevant data clouding a real-world problem is eliminated, a model often improves management's ability to understand and solve the problem at hand. A model also provides a systematic vehicle for decision makers to focus their own judgment and experience and that of experts.

Reasons for Modeling

There are many excellent reasons for using a model, rather than attempting to deal directly with the real world. These include the inherent complexity of many organizational situations, the inability to conduct real-world experiments even when experimentation is needed, and the future orientation of management.

Complexity. Like all management schools, the management science approach strives to be useful in solving real-world organizational problems. It therefore seems incongruous that one could improve one's ability to cope with reality by substituting a model for it. But, as we have learned, the real world of organizations is extremely complex. The actual number of variables involved in a given problem is virtually infinite, far too great for each to be taken fully into account. Consequently, in many situations it is necessary for the manager to limit the problem's dimensions, to simplify the real world to the point where it becomes comprehensible.

Experimentation. There are many managerial situations in which it is desirable to experiment and test alternative solutions to a problem. Foolish, indeed, would be the management of a firm that committed millions of dollars to a new product without first determining experimentally that it would function as intended and probably be accepted by customers. Some of this experimentation can and should be carried out in a real-world setting. When Boeing designs a new aircraft, Datsun a new automobile, IBM a new computer model, they always build a prototype and test it under actual conditions before going into full production. But direct experimentation of this type is very costly and time consuming. Imagine how expensive an automobile would be, or how little innovation there would be, if General Motors actually built and tested each of the thousands of parts conceptualized as potential improvements by its engineers.

There are countless critical decision-making situations in which alternatives need to be evaluated logically but experimentation with the real world is wholly impractical. For example, when Volkswagen decided to build a manufacturing plant in the United States, it had to choose a location with an adequate labor supply, favorable tax climate, and economically suited from the standpoint of obtaining materials and shipping out finished cars. It also had to determine the optimal sequence for assembling the thousands of parts in a Rabbit, which parts it should make itself rather than purchase, and what quantity of each part should be kept on hand. Obviously, it could not solve these problems by building an experimental version of each possible plant location and setup.

Future Orientation of Management. The last, but not least, reason for models is that so much of management involves the future. One cannot observe or experiment directly on a phenomenon that does not yet exist and never may. Thus, however much managers may wish to consider only the real and tangible, eventually they must turn to visualization and inferences. Modeling is the only systematic way yet developed for visualizing patterns in the future and determining the potential outcomes of alternative solutions so that they can be compared objectively.

In summation, as David B. Hertz states, "The manager must find ways of choosing among alternatives for allocating his resources, for sequencing activities that he and others will carry out, and for acquiring new and different people and physical resources. To do this, he must rely on some reasonable descriptions of the character and stability of the environment in which the consequences of decisions will unfold, both in the short- and the long-term future. He must face up to the patterns of uncertainty in these environments that are both inevitable and unpredictable."[4]

Management science models are the most powerful tool for accomplishing these objectives and overcoming a host of other problems related to decision making in complex situations.

Types of Models

There are a great number of models from which a manager can choose the one best suited to the problem at hand. Before describing some of the specific models most widely used by contemporary organizations and the problems to which they can be applied, let us briefly discuss the three basic types of models. These are physical models, analogue models, and mathematical models.

Physical Models. A *physical model* represents what is being studied with a scale-up or scale-down description of the object or system. As Shannon states, "The distinguishing characteristic of a physical (also sometimes called iconic) model is that it in some sense 'looks like' the entity being modeled."[5]

Examples of physical models are blueprints of a plant showing spatial relationships, a scaled down actual model of a plant, and a designer's illustration of a new car to 1/25 scale. A physical model like a blueprint makes it easy to visualize and determine whether a given type of machinery will physically fit within the space planned and to solve related problems, such as where doors should be positioned to facilitate the flow of people and materials. Automobile and airplane manufacturers always build scale-down physical replicas of new vehicles to test certain physical characteristics such

FEATURE 15-1

How a Staff Manager's Models Help Management at TRW

Mr. Armbruster is an intense, fussy man with dark, piercing eyes and nervous hands that are constantly drawing diagrams in the air. He worked summers in TRW's mail room while he was earning a degree in mechanical engineering at Case Western Reserve University. During six years in the Air Force he immersed himself in analytical research work and statistics. He earned a master's degree in industrial engineering and management at Oklahoma State University and later added an MBA degree in marketing and finance from Case Western. The advanced degrees, he believes, helped him "avoid being pigeonholed as a computer jock" early in his career at TRW.

That career began in 1965 as a reliability engineer in TRW's aircraft propulsion group. But that wasn't what he really wanted, so in 1967 he applied for a computer modeling job on the corporate staff and got it.

Computer modeling was then in its infancy as a forecasting tool for making long-range strategic decisions and for separating internal growth expectations from forecasts based on growth through acquisitions. A series of top-echelon memos and meetings had created the job. TRW's founder, Simon Ramo, in a 1966 memo first cited the need to start plotting mathematical growth curves that would project TRW's financial and operating results far into the future under different economic conditions. By the time Mr. Armbruster had been appointed a year later, the scope of the job had broadened considerably, but it was still very fuzzy.

"I've been doing about the same kind of work since 1967, but I've been doing it in a lot of different offices, because they didn't quite know where to put me," he says. First it was the data processing department, then the controller's office, then with the vice president of finance. "That was the first real recognition of the nature of my work," says Mr. Armbruster. His next boss was the vice president, economist, another step up in status. In 1973 a new post was created, vice president, corporate planning and development, and Mr. Armbruster has been director in this office ever since.

Mr. Armbruster's salary is in the $40,000 to $50,000 range, and he participates in TRW's management incentive bonus program, which is based on annual profit gains. "I don't know where the topside is on this job," he says. "I think I could have a very fulfilling career right here."

Certainly, the moves he has made so far have been significant. "It isn't uncommon to find people like me stagnating in an accounting department somewhere," says Mr. Armbruster. "My product isn't something that can be pushed up through an organization. Top management has to understand it and want it enough to reach down and get it."

The main product Mr. Armbruster and his young MBA assistant, John Keogh, produce is TRW's "top-down forecast," a half-inch sheaf of typewritten pages, financial tables, charts and graphs that is delivered to Mr. Mettler three times a year. It forecasts key financial and operating data, including profits, working capital requirements and return on assets as far as five years ahead and separates TRW's sales into 15 different business areas.

"The object is to be able to understand how much of TRW's performance is really under the control of management and how much is subject to the vagaries of the economy," says Mr. Armbruster. "It gives top management an idea of what's possible under five or six different conditions. They can select the preferable future and see what actions to take to attempt to reach various goals, rather than just let the corporation meander off on its own."

For instance, "Rube (Mr. Mettler, the president) can look at the forecast and tell an operating guy: 'Forget those plans, that business is strictly at the mercy of the economy. Use your creative management time to concentrate on this business, where what you do can make a difference,' " says Mr. Armbruster. "We've found that management can exercise far more control over a company's fate than was thought possible before."

Over the past three years, the short-term quarter-to-quarter portion of the top-down forecast has come closer to forecasting actual operating profits than have the traditional "bottom-up" forecasts prepared quarterly by the operating divisions.

The forecast doesn't just spring out of the computer room 250 feet down the hall where Mr. Armbruster spends a big chunk of his day. Building the various computer models that make the forecast possible has been a painstaking research and development process. The forecast still is evolving, growing more detailed and refined all the time. "The data that are generated to meet federal requirements, the SEC, IRS, EPA or whoever, usually are not the most useful data for running a company, so we have to go out and develop most of our own," he says.

That takes lots of time on the phone, "digging out stuff like how many pumps they moved out the door last quarter," he says. Sometimes it requires personal visits to operating divisions' financial staffs "to make friends and convince them to pull the stuff I need out of their archives," says Mr. Armbruster. "The people down below are very sensitive about requests from the corporate staff for data that are going to require their time and effort to put together. It's always a question of how far can I go without stepping on the toes of the operating people."

The quality of the information is a constant worry. "We're trying to look at the future with pretty flaky data sometimes," he says. "I have a high tolerance for ambiguity, but sometimes it gets very frustrating to never be sure

continues on page 494

FEATURE 15-1 continued

what's out there." He has built up his credibility carefully over the years, "and I guard it very jealously," he says. Still, bad information sometimes gets into a forecast because of aberrations caused by internal reorganizations, acquisitions and accounting changes over the years, and it can make things hot for an operating man who is meeting with top management. Recently a division vice president "phoned and really chewed my ear for a long while because I had bad data," says Mr. Armbruster.

Another worry is time. Mr. Armbruster, his assistant, Mr. Keogh, and TRW's econometrician, Van Bussmann, have spent about 80% of their time working together as a team lately in an effort to meet top management's increasing requests for more and faster information. "We're in danger of being loved to death," says Mr. Armbruster. "We just can't keep up with everything we want to do." Instead of going to lunch, he often sneaks off to the computer to run his own analyses.

Mr. Armbruster concedes that some of the time pressures he feels are self-imposed. "Sometimes if I didn't generate some particular report nobody would miss it because they don't even know it's coming," he says. "But I know it ought to be done and I feel like I've got to."

SOURCE: Richard Martin, "The Managers," *The Wall Street Journal*, April 18, 1977, p. 1. Reprinted by permission of *The Wall Street Journal*,

as wind drag. The model, being an identical replica, should respond as the proposed new car or plane, but obviously costs much less than building a full-scale prototype.

Analogue Models. *Analogue models* represent the object under study with a substitute that behaves as the real object does, although it does not look like the real object. A graph illustrating the trade-offs between production volume and cost, as illustrated in Figure 15-2, is an analogue model. It illustrates the effect of different production levels on costs. Another example of an analogue model is an organization chart. By constructing a chart, management can readily visualize chains of command and the formal relationship between individuals and activities. This analogue model is clearly a much simpler and more effective way of perceiving and communicating the complex interrelationships of a large organizational structure than, say, listing who reports to whom.

Mathematical Models. *Mathematical models,* also known as symbolic models, use symbols to describe the properties or characteristics of an object or event. An example of both a mathematical model and the power of models in helping us understand extremely complex problems is Einstein's famous

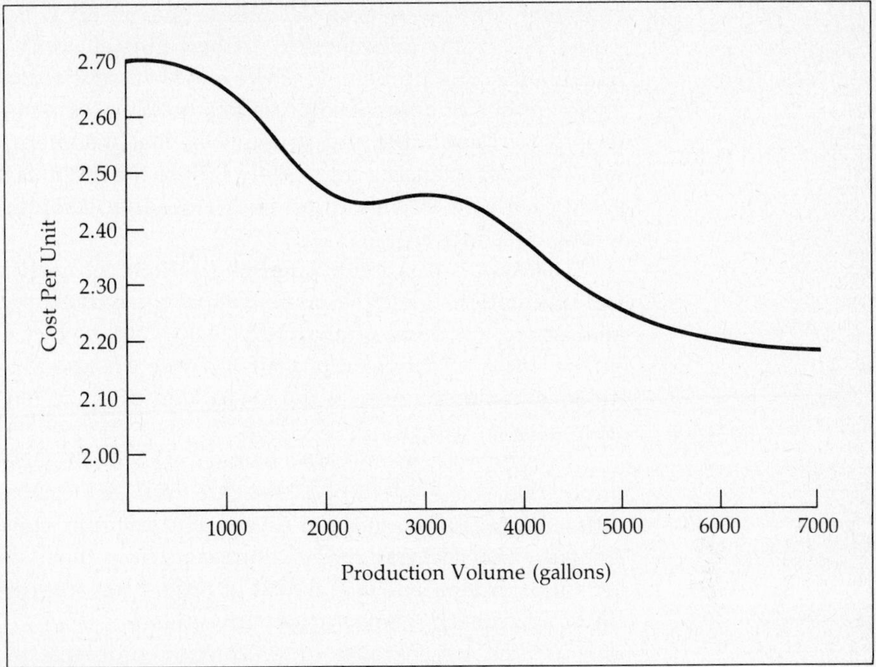

Figure 15-2 An Analogue Model

This analogue model shows the relationship between the volume of paint produced and the cost per gallon.

formula, $E = mc^2$. If Einstein had not been able to construct this mathematical model in which symbols are substituted for reality, it is extremely unlikely that physicists would have even a remote idea of the relationship between matter and energy.

Mathematical models are probably the type used most often for organizational decision making. For example, in place of the analogue model illustrated in Figure 15-2, one could illustrate the relationship between production volume and cost with the model $C = PV(0.1) + 2500$. This shows that cost, represented by the symbol "C," is equal to the production level (PV) multiplied by 0.1, plus 2500. We will discuss some commonly used mathematical models later in the chapter. First, let us examine the basic steps in the model-building process.

The Model-Building Process

Model building, like management, is a process. The basic steps of the model-building process are: problem formulation, model construction, model validation, implementation, and operation.

Problem Formulation. The first and most critical step in building a model capable of providing a *correct* solution to a managerial problem is *problem formulation*. Performing the mathematics correctly or using a sophisticated computer will be of no avail unless the problem itself is accurately diagnosed. According to Shannon, "Albert Einstein once stated that the proper formulation of a problem was even more essential than its solution. To find an acceptable or optimal solution to a problem, one must first know what the problem is. As simple and apparent as that statement may sound, too many management scientists completely ignore the obvious. Millions of dollars are spent each year in coming up with elegant and sophisticated answers to the wrong questions."[6]

Discussing this issue, Charles J. Hitch formerly of the Department of Defense states, "It is my experience that the hardest problems for the systems analyst are not those of analytical technique. In fact, the techniques we use in the office of the Secretary of Defense are usually simple and old fashioned. What distinguishes the useful and productive analyst is his ability to formulate (or design) the problem."[7]

Furthermore, just because managers know they have a problem does not imply they have identified the true problem. Managers must be able to differentiate symptoms from causes. For example, consider a pharmaceutical company that received many complaints from retail stores regarding the late arrival of orders. The late arrival of orders was not the true problem but the tip of an iceberg. Upon further investigation it was discovered that the orders arrived late because of production problems in the company's three chemical manufacturing plants. This, in turn, was caused by certain needed chemical supplies and spare machine parts being out of stock. This, in turn, was caused by poor forecasting of the demand for raw materials and spare machine parts.

Model Construction. After correctly formulating the problem, the next step of the process is to construct the model. In doing so, the model builder must determine the model's primary objective, what output specification or information the model is intended to provide to help management alleviate the problem. To continue the preceding example, the information wanted would be an accurate specification of when raw material and spare parts should be ordered and how much should be ordered.

In addition to specifying its primary objectives, the management scientist must determine what information is needed to construct a model that will meet these objectives and yield the desired output. In our example, necessary information would be an accurate forecast of demand for each chemical product, the percentage of chemical supplies in each product, the estimated life of machine parts, how long these parts have been used, and so on.

It is possible, often probable, that this necessary information is scattered among many sources. As one writer states when discussing the need to obtain information and views from many people throughout the organization, "A production problem should not be attacked strictly from the viewpoint of the manufacturing and control departments but also from the viewpoints of those in personnel, sales, mechanical and electrical engineering departments, the maintenance division, and the experimental laboratory."[8]

Other factors that must be considered in constructing a model are cost and human response. A model that costs more than the problem it is intended to solve obviously makes no contribution to attaining organizational objectives. Similarly, an extremely complex model may be perceived as a threat by eventual users and be rejected by them. Thus, to construct an effective model, managers and management scientists must work together and communicate their respective needs to each other. The management science school recognizes these potential problems.

Testing the Model. After the model is constructed, it must be tested. One aspect of testing is to determine the degree to which the model corresponds to the real-world situation. The management scientist must determine whether all relevant components of the real situation are incorporated in the model. This, of course, may be difficult to accomplish if the problem is very complex. As we have often noted, many models of management, on testing, were found insufficient because they did not include all relevant variables. Herzberg's model of motivation, for example, failed to take an individual's expectations into account. Naturally, the better the model approximates the real world, the better its potential for helping the manager make a good decision, assuming the model does not become too complex to be used.

The second aspect of testing involves determining the degree to which the model's output actually helps management cope with the problem. To continue our example, if the pharmaceutical firm's model provided management with valid information on how frequently and in what quantities materials and spare parts should be ordered, it would be considered useful because this information should enable management to take effective corrective action regarding the delays.

A good way of testing a model is to apply it to a past situation. The pharmaceutical firm could use its model to solve the inventory problem of the past three years. If the model is accurate, working out the inventory problem with the actual quantities and timing should yield the actual results that led to delays. Management could also determine whether this information, if it had been available, would have helped prevent production problems and delays.

Implementation. After the model has passed testing, it is ready to be implemented. As Shannon explains, no management science model "can be considered successfully completed until it has been accepted, understood, and used."[9] This explanation sounds obvious, but often is one of the most troublesome aspects of the model-building practice. One study of corporate-level operations research groups found that only about 60 percent of management science models were completely or mostly implemented.[10] A primary reason for lack of implementation is that the managers who are to use the model may fear it or not understand it.

If management science models are constructed by staff specialists (and they usually are), the managers who are to use them should participate in the analysis of the problem and output specifications. In addition, these managers should be trained to use the model, including how the model functions and what its potential uses and limitations are.

Model Updating. Even if the model is successfully implemented, it almost certainly will have to be modified. Management may discover that the output's form is not as clear as they would prefer or that additional output would be desirable. If the organization's objectives change in a way that affects decision criteria, the model will have to be modified accordingly. Similarly, changes in the external environment such as new customers, suppliers, or technology might invalidate the assumptions and information on which the model is based.

Common Problems with Modeling

Like all tools and techniques in management, management science models are fallible. Their effectiveness may be diminished by a number of potential problems. The most common of these problems involve invalid assumptions, information limitations, fear by users, poor implementation, and excessive cost.

Invalid Assumptions. All models are based on certain assumptions or premises. These may be tangible premises, such as the cost of labor for the next six months will be $200,000. If so, they can be verified objectively and have a high probability of being accurate. Or, some of the assumptions may be intangible, not objectively verifiable. Sales will increase by 10 percent next year is an example of an assumption that is not verifiable. One does not know for certain whether this, in fact, will occur. Since these assumptions are a basis for the model, its accuracy is dependent on their accuracy. A model cannot be used to project inventory requirements, for example, unless sales projections for the coming period are accurate.

In addition to assumptions about the components of the model, managers make assumptions about the relationships within the model. For example, a model intended to help decide how many gallons of different types of paint to produce would probably include an assumption about the relationship between selling price and profit, as well as assumptions about cost of materials and labor. The model's accuracy is also determined by the accuracy of these relationships.

Information Limitations. A major cause of invalid assumptions and other problems is information limitations, which affect both the building and use of models. The accuracy of any model is by necessity determined by the accuracy of information related to the problem. When the situation is extremely complex, the management scientist may not be able to incorporate or obtain information on all relevant factors. If the environment is volatile, information about it must be updated rapidly, which may or may not be possible or practical. Sometimes the model builder may ignore relevant aspects of the problem because they are not measurable. For example, a model for determining the effectiveness of a new technology would be misleading if it only incorporated information on decreased costs relative to increased specialization. The difficult-to-predict-and-measure impact of worker attitudes also affect productivity. If workers dislike the new process, increased costs due to absenteeism, high turnover, and production bottlenecks could prevent the increases in productivity from materializing.

In general, model building is most difficult under conditions of uncertainty. When necessary information is too uncertain to be obtained objectively, managers might be better off relying on past experience, intuition, consulting others, and sound judgment.

Fear by Users. A model cannot be considered effective unless it is used. A primary reason for not implementing a model is that the managers who use it may not have an adequate understanding of the results and therefore fear it.[11] A survey of production vice-presidents of Fortune 500 firms corroborated that the greatest barrier to the use of management science models was the vice-presidents' own lack of knowledge.[12]

To combat potential fear, one group of researchers concluded that quantitative staff specialists should direct considerably more of their time toward educating managers in the capabilities and use of models.[13] Managers should be trained to use them, and top management should stress how the model contributes to the organization's success and how it increases managers' capability to plan and control effectively.

Poor Implementation. Various studies have found that the state of the art of management science modeling techniques exceeds that of implementing them.[14] As mentioned previously, one cause is fear. Others are lack of knowledge and resistance to change. This problem reinforces the desirability of staff specialists' seeking the participation of users while constructing the model. When people have an opportunity to discuss and gain an understanding of an issue, technique, or proposed change, their resistance to it generally decreases.

Cost. As with all management techniques, a model's benefits must outweigh its costs. In determining the model's costs, management should include staff and line manager's time spent on construction and information gathering, training costs and time, and the cost of information processing and storage.

An Overview of Management Science Models

The number of different, specific management science models is almost as great as the number of specific problems they were developed to cope with. The following is a general description of some of the most widely used types. Our goal is not to explain how to apply them, for that is a course in itself, but to help you better understand the capabilities of management science models and the types of decisions to which they can be applied. This understanding should enable you to better communicate your problem needs to staff specialists and give you a basic understanding of how their proposed models and techniques can assist your decision making.

Game Theory. One of the most important variables affecting the success of an organization is its competition. Clearly, the ability to predict the actions of competitors would be advantageous for any organization. **Game theory** is a modeling technique for assessing the impact of a decision on one's competitors.

Game theory was originally developed by the military so that strategy could take potential responses of the enemy into account. In business today, game theory models are used to predict how competitors will respond to price changes, new promotional campaigns, introduction of an additional service, product modifications, and new products. If management determined through game theory that, if they increased prices, competitors would not also do so, they probably would decide against the increase to avoid being in an unfavorable competitive position.

Game theory is not used as frequently as the other models we describe. Real-world situations, unfortunately, often are too complex and fast changing to predict accurately how competitors will respond to another firm's specific tactics. However, game theory is useful for determining which are the most important factors to consider in a competitive decision-making situation.[15] This information is important because it enables management to consider additional variables or factors that may affect the situation and thereby make a more effective decision than would otherwise be possible.

Queueing Models. **Queueing** or **waiting-line models** are used to determine the optimal number of service facilities in light of demand for them. Some situations where queueing-line models might be useful are people calling an airline for reservations and information, data waiting for computer processing, equipment waiting for a repairman, grocery shoppers waiting to be checked out, trucks waiting to unload at a warehouse, bank customers waiting for available tellers. If, for example, customers have to wait too long for a bank teller, they may decide to do business elsewhere. Similarly, if trucks have to wait too long to unload, they cannot make as many deliveries in a day. Thus, the fundamental problem is balancing the costs of additional facilities—more people unloading trucks, more tellers, more airline reservation clerks—against the costs of less than optimal service—trucks unable to make extra stops because of long lines unloading, customers choosing to deal with a different bank or airline because of service delays.

According to Donald R. Plane and Gary A. Kochenberger, "The most important reason for service facilities to fall short of the demand for these facilities is that there is a short-term variation in the rate at which customers arrive for service, as well as a short-term variation in the time required to provide the service. This leads to idle capacity at some point in time, and periods of waiting lines at other points in time, although there might be ample capacity if there were complete control over arrivals, so that a schedule could be arranged."[16] Queueing models provide management with information regarding the optimal number of service facilities to have in order to balance the trade-offs between the costs of having too few or too many facilities.

Inventory Models. **Inventory models** are used to determine optimal timing and quantities for orders of resources and what quantity of a product should be stored. All organizations must maintain some inventory to ensure that production and sales are not delayed. A dry cleaner needs an adequate supply of chemicals, a hospital an adequate supply of medicines, a manufacturing firm an adequate supply of raw materials, parts, work in progress, and finished products.

The basic or objective of an inventory model is to minimize the negative cost trade-offs associated with inventories. These costs are of three basic types: ordering costs, holding costs, and shortage costs. Shortage costs are those related to running out of inventory. They include not being able to sell a product or service when otherwise possible and the costs of idle production time, such as having to pay people when they are not working. Keeping a large inventory of needed materials would ensure against incurring these shortage costs. Buying large quantities of required inventory materials would, in most cases, also minimize ordering costs because the firm might receive quantity purchase discounts and perform less paperwork. However, these potential benefits of a large inventory are offset by holding costs such as storage expenses, handling, interest, insurance, breakage, theft, and taxes. In addition, management must consider the opportunity cost of tying up funds in inventory that could be used for more productive investments, such as stocks, bonds, or bank deposits. Several specific models have been developed to help management determine when and how much inventory to order and what stock of work in progress and finished products should be maintained.[17]

Linear Programming. **Linear programming** models are used to determine the optimal way to allocate scarce resources among competing demands. They are among the most widely used management science models. Accord-

Table 15-1 Typical Production-Management Applications of Linear Programming

Aggregate production planning: Finding the minimum cost production schedule, including rate change costs, given constraints on size of work force and inventory levels

Product planning: Finding the optimum product mix where several products have different costs and resource requirements (e.g., finding the optimum blend of constituents for gasolines, paints, human diets, animal feeds)

Product routing: Finding the optimum routing for a product which must be processed sequentially through several machine centers, with each machine in a center having its own cost and output characteristics

Process control: Minimizing the amount of scrap material generated by cutting steel, leather, or fabric from a roll or sheet of stock material

Inventory control: Finding the optimum combination of products to stock in a warehouse or store

Aggregate production planning: Finding the minimum cost production schedule, taking into account inventory carrying costs, overtime costs, and subcontracting costs

Distribution scheduling: Finding the optimum shipping schedule for distributing products between factories and warehouses or warehouses and retailers

Plant location studies: Finding the optimum location of a new plant by evaluating shipping costs between alternative locations and supply and demand sources

Scheduling: Minimum cost assignment of trucks to pickup points and ships to berths

Worker assignments: Minimum cost assignment of men to machines and to jobs

Materials handling: Finding the minimum cost routings of material handling devices (e.g., forklift trucks) between departments in a plant and of hauling materials from a supply yard to work sites by trucks, with each truck having different capacity and performance capabilities

SOURCE: Richard B. Chase and Nicholas J. Aquilano, *Production and Operations Management* (Homewood, IL: Irwin, 1973), p. 244. © 1973 by Richard D. Irwin, Inc.

ing to a survey of production vice-presidents of Fortune 500 firms, linear programming and inventory models are the two most frequently used in industry.[18] They usually are used by staff specialists to solve production problems. Some typical production management applications of linear programming are listed in Table 15-1.

The following example illustrates a simple situation in which linear programming might be used to make a decision. A production manager has to decide how many gallons of each of three types of paint should be produced in order to earn the highest profit. The decision is subject to several constraints:

1. There are only 40,000 pounds of chemicals available—10,000 pounds of chemical A, 18,000 pounds of chemical B, and 12,000 pounds of chemical C.
2. Total machine time available for production is 30,000 hours.
3. One gallon of type 1 paint requires 1 pound of chemical A, ¾ pound of chemical B, and 1½ pounds of chemical C, and ⅛ hour of machine time. One gallon of type 2 paint requires 1 pound of chemical A, ½ pound of

	1 Gallon Type 1	1 Gallon Type 2	1 Gallon Type 3	Total Amount of Resource
Chemicals	1 A	1 A	1 ¼ A	10,000 A
	¾ B	½ B	1 ¼ B	18,000 B
	1 ½ C	¾ C	½ C	12,000 C
Machine Time	⅛ hr	¼ hr	⅙ hr	30,000 hrs
Profit	$.80	$.65	$1.25	

Figure 15-3 Illustration of Linear Programming
This is an illustration of how one would use linear programming to determine how to solve the paint-mixing problem described in the text.

chemical B, and ¾ pound of chemical C, and ¼ hour of machine time. One gallon of type 3 paint requires 1¼ pounds of chemical A, ¼ pound of chemical B, and ½ pound of chemical C, and ⅙ hour of machine time.

4. The net profit from selling a gallon of paint of types 1, 2, and 3 is $.80, $.65, and $1.25 respectively.

This problem is illustrated in Figure 15-3. By using a linear programming (LP) model, the manager could determine what quantities of each type of paint to produce, given the chemicals and machine time available and the contribution each type makes to profit. Without such a model, it would be extremely difficult to make an optimal decision in even this relatively simple situation.

Simulation. All of the models described thus far involve simulation in the broad sense because they all substitute a model for reality. However, as a modeling technique, **simulation** refers specifically to the process of designing a model of the real-world situation and using *experimentation* to determine from it how the real situation behaves. As N. Paul Loomba states, "The basic idea of simulation is to utilize *some device* to *imitate* a real-life system in order to study and understand its properties, behavior, and operating characteristics."[19] A wind tunnel is an example of a physical simulation model used to test the characteristics of proposed new aircraft and automobiles. In this or later business courses you may get an opportunity to hone your decision-making skills on one of the complex computerized business simulation games.

Simulation is used in situations too complex for a mathematical technique like linear programming. This may be caused by there being a large number of variables, certain relationships between variables being difficult or impossible to analyze mathematically, or a high degree of uncertainty.[20]

Simulation, in sum, is often a practical way to substitute a model for the actual system or a full-scale prototype. As Claude McMillan and Richard F. Gonzales note, "Experimentation with actual or pilot systems is costly and time consuming, and relevant variables are not always subject to control."[21] By experimenting with a model of the real system, one is able to investigate how the system might respond if certain changes are made or certain things occur, without having to actually observe the real system. If the results of experimentation with the simulation model indicate the modification is an improvement, the manager can more confidently decide to implement the corresponding change in the real system.

Economic Analysis. Few managers would fail to perceive simulation as a modeling technique. Many never think of economic analysis, clearly the most widely used of all techniques, as a form of model building. Under **economic analysis** fall all of the many methods for evaluating costs and benefits and the relative profitability of a business activity. A typical economic model is break-even analysis, the symbolic method for determining the point at which total revenue equals total costs and thereby the point at which a venture is profitable. Other economic analysis models are used to determine return on investment, net present value of a firm, and the return on a shareholder's equity in the firm. In fact, the majority of accounting techniques would be considered economic analysis models of the firm's performance and financial condition. We shall elaborate on economic analysis in Chapter 17, Financial Planning and Control Techniques.

Decision-Making Techniques

Almost every decision-making method used in management could technically be considered a variation on modeling. However, by custom the term *model* is usually restricted to the general types of techniques we just described and their many specific variations. There are, in addition to modeling a number of techniques intended to help the manager objectively reach a decision by determining which of several alternatives should contribute most to objectives. Under this heading fall the widely used techniques of the payoff matrix and decision trees, described in the following sections. To facilitate the use of these techniques and generally improve the quality of decisions management uses forecasting. The most common forecasting methods are also discussed in this section. Our aim, again, is to convey a general understanding of these aids, rather than teach how to apply them.

The Payoff Matrix

The crux of most managerial decision making is choosing the best of several alternatives, given established decision criteria. (You may wish to review the discussion of decision-making constraints and criteria in Chapter 6.) The *payoff matrix* is one of several techniques in the area of statistical decision theory that can help managers choose from among alternatives. It is particularly useful for determining which strategy should make the greatest overall contribution to attainment of objectives.

According to N. Paul Loomba, "A payoff represents a monetary reward or utility that is a consequence of a specific strategy *in conjunction* with a given state of nature. When payoffs are arranged in the form of a table (or matrix), we obtain a payoff matrix,"[22] as illustrated in Figure 15-4. The phrase "in conjunction with a given state of nature" is critical to understanding when a payoff matrix can be used and when a decision made with one is likely to be sound. It means, very basically, that the payoff is contingent upon a certain event actually occurring. If that event or state of nature does not in fact occur, the payoff will necessarily be different.

In general, a payoff matrix is useful when:

1. There are a reasonably limited number of alternatives or strategies to choose from.
2. What may occur is not known with certainty.
3. The results of the decision depend on which alternative is chosen and what events actually occur.

In addition, the manager needs to be able to reasonably determine the probability that relevant events will occur and to be able to compute expected value.

Probability. Managers seldom enjoy the luxury of complete certainty. Nor do they often have to operate under conditions of absolute uncertainty. In most decision-making situations, the manager must evaluate the probability, or likelihood, of an event occurring. To review our earlier discussion, probability ranges from 1.0 when the event is certain to occur, to 0 when the event is certain not to occur. Probability can be determined objectively, as it is in establishing the betting odds for a roulette table. Or it may be based on historical trends or a subjective assessment by the managers involved, based on their experience in similar situations.

If probability were not taken into account, the decision would always be skewed in favor of the most optimistic outcome. For example, citing the evidence that the investors in a successful motion picture can make a 500 percent return, whereas investing in a chain of stores at best would result in a

	PROBABILITY: STATES OF NATURE:	.1 FOG	.9 CLEAR
Strategy 1:	Plane	+$2,000	+$4,500
Strategy 2:	Train	+$3,000	+$3,000

"Let us imagine that a salesman is faced with the question of whether to fly or take a train to an out-of-town customer's location. If the weather permits, he can fly in 2 hours portal to portal, whereas the train will take him 7 hours. If he takes the train, he will lose a day at his present location that he estimates could be used to generate $1,500 in sales. He has also estimated that the out-of-town customer will give him an order for $3,000 if he makes a personal call. Should he plan to go by plane but then be grounded by fog, he will be unable to visit in person and will be forced to use the telephone. This will reduce the size of the out-of-town order to $500, but he will still be able to get the $1,500 at the present location.

The data in the matrix shown above reflect these estimates for the different outcomes. In addition, some guesses are presented concerning the probabilities of fog (which will ground the flight but not affect the train) and clear weather. We see that an estimate of one in ten chances of fog occurring has been supplied. Further, the matrix shows that with Strategy 1 (taking the plane), if the weather is clear (.9 probability, or 9 chances in 10), the salesman estimates his sales will be $4,500 (referred to as an outcome). The other three outcomes can be explained in similar ways."

Figure 15-4 Payoff Matrix

SOURCE: Martin K. Storr and Irving Stein, *The Practice of Management Science* (Englewood Cliffs, NJ: Prenctice-Hall, Inc. 1976), p. 1. Reprinted by permission.

20 percent return, would lead to always deciding in favor of films. However, if one also takes into account that the probability of a film being extremely successful is rather low, but the probability of a chain of stores earning a 20 percent return is very high, investing in stores becomes comparatively attractive. Or, to give a simpler illustration, a long shot at the races pays more because it probably will pay nothing.

Expected Value. Probability plays a direct role in determining expected value, a central concept of the payoff matrix. The expected value of an alternative or strategy is the sum of possible values multiplied by their respective probabilities. For example, if you feel that the strategy of investing in an ice cream stand has a 0.5 probability of earning an annual profit of $5,000, a 0.2 probability of earning $10,000, and a 0.3 probability of earning $3,000, the expected value is:

$$\$5{,}000(0.5) + \$10{,}000(0.2) + \$3{,}000(0.3) = \$5{,}400$$

By determining the expected value of each alternative and arranging them in a matrix, the manager can easily perceive which choice is most attractive in light of the decision criteria. This, of course, will be the one with the highest expected value. Research indicates that when accurate probabilities are established, decision trees and payoff matrices result in better decisions than those made using traditional approaches.[23] The use of a payoff matrix to solve a specific problem is illustrated in Figure 15-4.

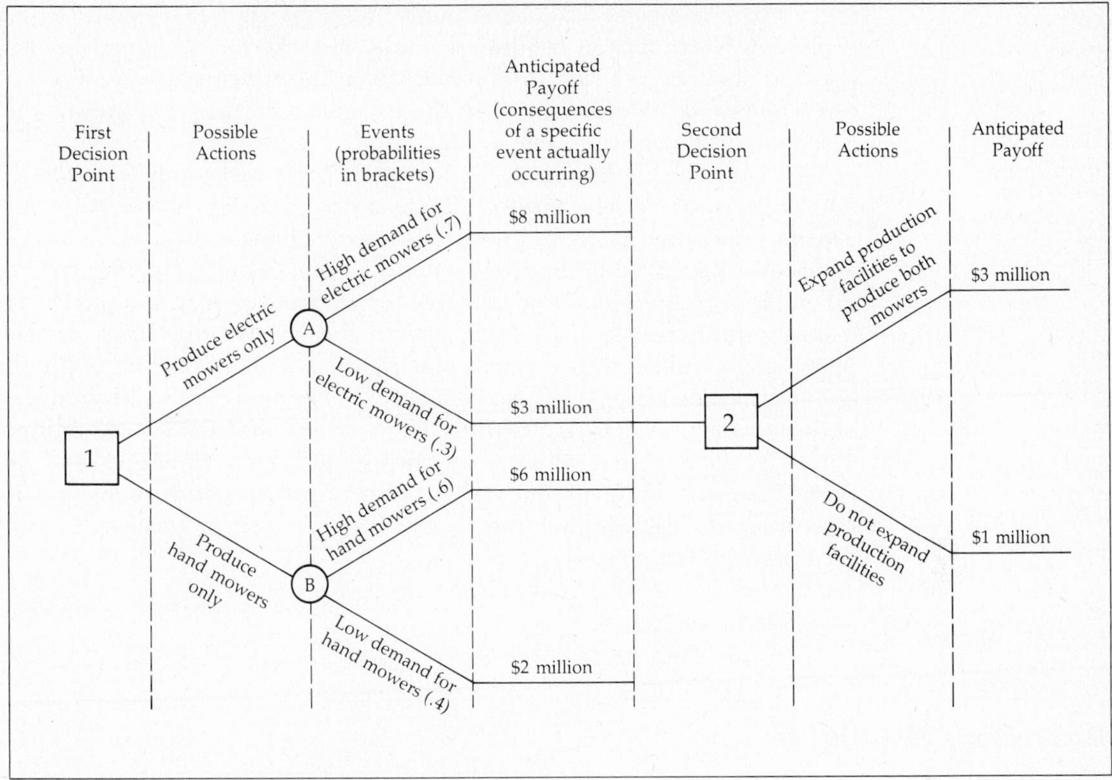

Figure 15-5 Decision Tree

Decision Trees

Decision trees are another popular management science technique for choosing the best alternative course of action. "A decision tree is a schematic representation of a decision problem."[24] Like the payoff matrix, a decision tree allows a manager "to consider various courses of action, assign financial results to them, modify these results by their probability, and then make comparisons."[25] The concept of expected value is also integral to decision trees.

Decision trees can be used in situations such as the one illustrated for the payoff matrix in which it is assumed that the data on outcomes, probabilities, and so on do not affect any later decisions. Here the manager is making a single decision. However, decision trees can also be developed for the more complex situation in which the outcome of a decision affects later decisions. Thus, the decision tree is a useful tool for making sequential decisions.

Figure 15-5 illustrates the use of a decision tree to solve a problem involving a sequential decision. The production vice-president of a company that is currently producing electric lawnmowers believes that the market for hand mowers is growing. He must decide whether to change over to production of handmowers and, if this is done, whether or not to continue producing electric mowers. Producing both types of mowers would require expansion of production facilities. In order to make this decision, the manager has obtained relevant information about the anticipated payoff of various actions and the probabilities of these events occurring. This information is shown on the decision tree, as indicated in Figure 15-5.

In using the decision tree, the manager works backwards from the second decision point. The most desirable decision at the second point is to expand production facilities and produce both mowers. This is because its anticipated payoff ($3 million) is greater than that of not expanding facilities ($1 million), *if* there is a low demand for electric mowers at point A. The manager continues to work back toward the current time (first decision point) and calculates the expected value for the alternative actions of producing electric mowers or hand mowers only. The expected value of producing only electric mowers is $6.5 million (0.7 × $8 million + 0.3 × $3 million). Similarly, the expected value of producing hand mowers only is $4.4 million. Thus, expanding production facilities to produce both mowers is the most desirable decision because its anticipated payoff is greatest, if events occur as expected.

Forecasting Techniques

The management science methods just described are used to resolve problems with known parameters. Each is based on a set of assumptions about an existing condition. In essence, the reasoning is that if X, Y, and Z are true, then the decision that will contribute most to attainment of objectives is alternative B. This is useful in many, perhaps the majority, of organizational decision-making situations. However, there are many situations in which the manager does not know at the outset what conditions are, what the possible alternatives are, and is unable to even approximate probabilities. This is because the problem involves some knowledge of *future* events. General Motors, for example, cannot make decisions about what sort of automobiles to produce in 1988 without some information about what social, economic, and technological conditions are likely to prevail at that time. Concern with the future is most pronounced during the planning process, particularly when selecting objectives.

The future, of course, can never be known with certainty. There are, nevertheless, a number of techniques that have proven themselves effective in forecasting what will occur in the many areas identified in our chapter on the planning process. These forecasting techniques all use both past experience and present assumptions about the future to predict what will occur.

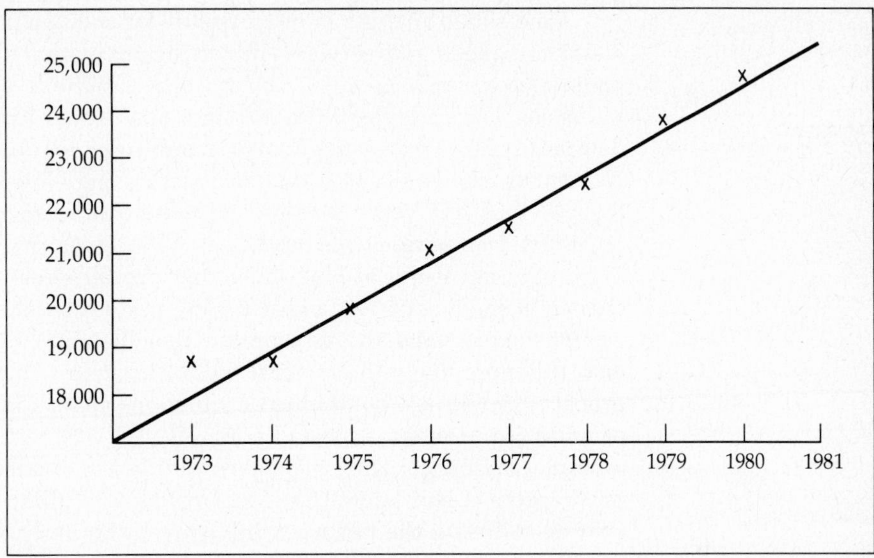

Figure 15-6 Time Series Analysis

This figure illustrates the use of time series analysis to assess tractor sales for 1981 based on sales between 1973 and 1980. (It should be noted that this figure is an analogue model of anticipated sales. Actually performing time series analysis involves advanced mathematical calculations.)

Their aim is to produce assumptions or premises that are a sound basis for planning and decision making.

Forecasting techniques are of two general types: qualitative and quantitative.

Quantitative Forecasting Techniques

Quantitative techniques can be used for forecasting when past activities can be assumed to be a trend that can be projected into the future and when there is sufficient information for a trend or relationships to be considered statistically valid. In addition managers must know how to use the quantitative model, and the benefits of better decision making should more than offset the costs of development.

Two typical quantitative forecasting techniques are time series analysis and causal modeling.

Time Series Analysis. Sometimes called trend projection, time series analysis is based on the assumption that what has occurred in the past is a good indication of what will occur in the future. Time series analysis is a technique for identifying historical patterns or trends and extending them into the future. This can be done by means of a table or by plotting past events on a graph, as illustrated in Figure 15-6.

Time series analysis is often useful for such activities as projecting demand for goods and services, projecting inventory needs, predicting sales patterns that are characterized by seasonal variations, and predicting personnel needs. For example, if the manager of a Burger King restaurant wants to determine how many pounds of hamburger to order for the month of November, she could base this decision on the November sales figures for the previous five years. Analysis of these figures might show that the demand for hamburgers historically is 10% lower in November because of Thanksgiving. It might also show that overall sales for the store have increased at the rate of 19% a year for the past four years.

The more valid the assumption that the future will be similar to the past, the more likely the forecast will be accurate. Thus, time series analysis probably would not be helpful in situations characterized by a high degree of volatility or when a major known change has occurred. To continue our example, the Burger King manager could not predict November demand for hamburgers if she knew that McDonald's was going to open a restaurant next door during the last week in October. Similarly, the Bell System could use time series analysis to predict the demand for Yellow Pages advertising in the coming year because it is in a stable business with essentially no competition. However, Ralph Lauren probably could not use it to predict Christmas season demand for a new line of designer shirts because the high fashion clothing industry is extremely competitive and consumer tastes can change radically from year to year.

Causal Modeling. Causal modeling is the most sophisticated and mathematically complex quantitative forecasting techniques in use today. It is used in situations involving more than one variable. Personal income, population changes, and the prevailing interest rate for mortgages, for example, affect the future demand for new, single family houses. **Causal modeling** attempts to forecast what will occur in such situations by studying the statistical relationship between the factor under consideration and the other variables. A causal model might reveal, for example, that each time mortgage rates increase by 1 percent, the demand for new housing decreases by 5 percent.

In statistical jargon, this relationship is referred to as a correlation. The more "perfect" the correlation, the better the model's ability to forecast. A "perfect" correlation (1.000) is one in which historically the relationship has *always* held true. If the demand for color television sets, for example, *always* decreased by 10 percent when the Gross National Product decreased by 4 percent, one could reasonably forecast that this would occur again in the future. Corning Glass, in fact, uses a causal model to forecast demand for its television picture tubes.[26]

The most sophisticated of all causal models are the econometric models developed to predict movements in the economy, such as the Wharton Model of the University of Pennsylvania. These models consist of thousands of equations and must be run on a very sophisticated computer. The cost is so high that even a very large business must subscribe to an econometric model, rather than develop its own. Despite this sophistication, causal models are not always right, as clearly evident by the federal government's inability to accurately predict the impact of various actions on the economy.

Qualitative Forecasting Techniques

As we have pointed out, to use quantitative techniques for forecasting one needs sufficient information to establish a trend or a statistically valid relationship between variables. When the amount of information is insufficient, or management does not understand the sophisticated technique, or when a quantitative model would be too expensive, management can use qualitative techniques for forecasting. In qualitative forecasting, the prediction of the future is made by soliciting the opinions of experts. Four widely used qualitative forecasting methods are a jury of opinion, the sales force composite, the customer expectation method, and the Delphi method.

Jury of Opinion. A **jury of opinion** is a method of forecasting in which the opinions of experts in relevant areas are combined and averaged. For example, to forecast profitability for a new computer model, Control Data Corporation might provide its divisional managers for production, marketing, and finance with all the background information available and ask their opinion of probable sales and margins. An informal variation on this method would be a group brainstorming session, in which members first try to generate as many ideas as possible. Only after all ideas are presented are any evaluated. This can be time consuming but often is helpful when the organization needs many new ideas and alternatives.

Sales Force Composite. Experienced salespeople are often excellent at predicting future demand. They know the customers intimately and can take their recent actions into account more quickly than one could build a quantitative model. Also, a good salesperson often has a "feel" for the market that may actually be more accurate than quantitative projections. The **sales force composite** method takes advantage of this expertise and judgment by combining the opinions of the sales manager and select personnel to forecast sales for a specific time period.

Customer Expectation Method. As one would surmise from its name, the **customer expectation model** is a forecast based on a survey of the organization's customers. The customers are asked to estimate their own future needs and requirements. By assembling all the data thus obtained and allowing for over or underestimation based on experience, management can often accurately forecast overall demand.

Delphi Technique. The Delphi technique is a more formal version of the jury of opinion method. It was originally developed by the Rand Corporation to forecast military events.[27] The **Delphi technique** is basically a pro-

FEATURE 15-2

How to Make Useful Business Forecasts

Forecasts are useful for business plans and operations only if the components of the forecast are carefully thought out and the limitations of the forecast are frankly acknowledged.

Here are some ways to do it right:

- Ask what use will be made of the forecast, what decisions will be based on it. This determines how precise the forecast must be. Some decisions are dangerous to make, even if the probable error in the forecast is less than 10%. Other decisions can be made comfortably with a much wider margin of error.
- Identify developments which *must* take place for the forecast to be valid. Then conservatively estimate the likelihood that these events will take place.
- Identify the components going into the forecast. Be clear about data sources.
- Determine how valuable past history is in making a forecast. Are changes so fast-paced that the forecast will be useless? Do similar products (or developments) give you a basis for making an accurate forecast for your product? Is solid information on past history easy to obtain or expensive?
- Determine how the forecast should be broken down. In sales forecasting it may be useful to identify parts of markets (growing customers, stable customers, big and little customers, likelihood of new customers, etc.)

SOURCE: *Boardroom Reports,* August 15, 1977, p. 10 from *An Executive's Guide to Forecasting,* John C. Chambers, Satinder K. Mullick, Donald D. Smith (New York: John Wiley & Sons, 1974). Reprinted from Boardroom Reports, Inc. Management's Source of Useful Information.

cedure to systematically enable a panel of experts to arrive at a consensus. Experts from a wide variety of related fields fill out a detailed questionnaire about the problem under consideration. They also develop written opinions. The experts are given a summary of the responses and asked to reconsider their prediction and, if it is out of line with others, to explain why. This procedure is repeated, usually three or four times, until a consensus prediction is reached.

The anonymity of the experts is an important element. It helps avoid the potential for groupthink and for status, interpersonal conflict or social needs to color the experts' opinions. Despite some questions about its reliability, since the outcome is obviously affected by which particular experts are consulted, the Delphi technique has been used successfully to forecast everything from future sales of a product to changes in complex phenomena such as social patterns and advanced technology.

SUMMARY

Management science strives to improve decision making through use of the scientific method, a systems orientation, and models.

A model is a representation of a system, idea, or object in a form different from the actual entity. Using a model is often necessary in management because of the complexity of organizations, inability to experiment directly on the real world, and the need to cope with the future.

The basic types of management science models are physical models, analogue models, and mathematical or symbolic models.

The first step in building a model is problem formulation. Unless the correct problem is diagnosed, the model cannot improve effectiveness. Subsequent steps are construction of the model, testing, implementation, and updating.

Game theory is a modeling technique for assessing the impact of an action on competitors. Queueing models are used to determine the optimal number of service facilities in light of demand. Inventory models help managers determine optimal timing and quantities for ordering resources and what quantity of finished products should be kept on hand. Linear programming models can be used to determine the optimal way to allocate scarce resources among competing demands. Simulation is a technique in which a device that imitates the real world is used to study its behavior and operation. Economic analysis comprises the wide variety of quantitative techniques used to determine the economic condition of an organization or the relative feasibility of an economic transaction.

Common causes of problems in modeling are the use of invalid assumptions, information limitations, fear by users, poor implementation, and excessive cost.

The payoff matrix is a useful decision-making technique for determining which alternative strategy will make the greatest overall contribution to objectives. To develop a payoff matrix, one needs to determine the expected value of outcomes, which is the sum of possible values multiplied by their respective probabilities.

Decision trees represent a problem schematically. They allow alternatives to be compared visually. Decision trees can be used in the more complex situation where the outcome of a decision affects later decisions.

Forecasting is used to identify alternatives and the probability they will occur. Typical quantitative forecasting techniques are time series analysis and causal modeling. Qualitative forecasting techniques include the jury of opinion, sales force composite, customer expectation method, and the Delphi technique.

REVIEW QUESTIONS

1. What are the three distinguishing characteristics of the management science approach?
2. Discuss these three different types of models: physical, analogue, and mathematical.
3. Describe the steps in the model-building process.
4. Discuss these problems in model building: information limitation, fear by users, poor implementation, and cost.
5. Briefly describe the management science models discussed in the chapter.
6. Discuss these specific techniques that exist to facilitate managerial decision-making: payoff matrix, expected values, and decision tree.
7. What is forecasting?
8. Discuss these two typical quantitative forecasting techniques: time series analysis and causal modeling.
9. Discuss these four widely used qualitative forecasting techniques: jury of opinion, the sales force composite, the customer expectation method, and the Delphi method.
10. How can a manager make useful business forecasts?

DISCUSSION QUESTIONS

11. Integrate the various definitions of a model discussed in the chapter and develop your own definition of a model.
12. Compare and contrast qualitative and quantitative forecasting.
13. David B. Hertz states, "The manager must find ways of choosing among alternatives for allocating his resources, for sequencing activities that he and others will carry out, and for acquiring new and different people and physical resources." How will the modern-day manager meet this challenge?
14. Discuss the various human and technical components a manager must be aware of in developing a model.
15. How can a manager overcome the numerous problems inherent in model building?

CASE INCIDENT

The Stadium Forecaster

As Operations Manager for Metro Stadium, Kathy McRae made a number of decisions for each stadium event that were sensitive to the anticipated attendance at the event. For example, it was Kathy's responsibility to decide how many concession stands to open and how many ushers and vendors to have on duty.

When Kathy first took the job, she relied heavily on subjective estimates to forecast attendance at each event. Often she called the management of the sports team or entertainment group involved in the event to obtain their estimate. After a year, however, Kathy had become very dissatisfied with this subjective approach to forecasting. One reason was that it took too much time to get estimates from other people. But the biggest problem was that everyone involved in making the estimates, including Kathy, seemed to have a tendency to overestimate attendance. As a result, the stadium was over-staffed and over-stocked with supplies for most events, leading to unnecessary costs.

Kathy resolved to investigate other, more objective methods of forecasting attendance. She determined, however, that any method she adopted must possess two characteristics:

1. Once the technique is developed, it must be quick and easy to apply for each event.
2. The technique must operate with data that is available just 24 hours before the event.

Upon reviewing the forecasting chapter of her old operations management text, Kathy felt sure that a causal model would be an appropriate method. This would involve developing a mathematical relationship of the form:

$$A = c_0 + c_1X_1 + c_2X_2 + \cdots + c_nX_n$$

where A is the attendance forecast, and each X is a variable believed to affect attendance. The c's are constants that are determined by statistical analysis of historical data. Given the values of the causal variables (X's) for a specific event, the model could be used to calculate a forecast for attendance (A).

Kathy realized that different models would have to be developed for different types of events. She decided to start by developing a causal model for baseball games. The first step was to identify causal variables (X's) for inclusion in the model. It occurred to Kathy that one such variable would be the number of tickets that had been sold 24 hours before the game.

Questions

1. Why do you suppose there was a tendency to overestimate attendance when subjective forecasting methods were used?
2. Will a causal model possess the two desired characteristics that Kathy had specified?
3. Can you suggest other causal variables to be included in the model to forecast attendance at baseball games? Remember that the data for each causal variable must be available at least 24 hours before the game.
4. What dangers do you see in using a causal model to forecast attendance at stadium events? What can be done to minimize the dangers?

SOURCE: Written by Dr. Thomas B. Clark, Associate Professor of Management, Georgia State University

NOTES

1. C. West Churchman, R. L. Ackoff, and E. L. Arnoff, *Introduction to Operations Research* (New York: Wiley, 1957), p. 6.
2. Ibid., p. 4.

3. Robert E. Shannon, *Systems Simulation: The Art and Science* (Englewood Cliffs, NJ: Prentice-Hall, 1975), p. 4.
4. David B. Hertz, "The Changing Field of Management Science," in *Contemporary Management*, Joseph W. McGuire (Englewood Cliffs, NJ: Prentice-Hall, 1974), pp. 95–96.
5. Shannon, op. cit., p. 8.
6. Shannon, op. cit., p. 25.
7. Charles J. Hitch, *Decision Making for Defense* (Berkeley, CA: University of California Press, 1967).
8. J. M. F. Roccaferrera, *Operations Research Models for Business and Industry* (Chicago: South-Western, 1963), p. 28.
9. Shannon, op. cit., p. 32.
10. Efram Turbin, "A Sample of Operations Research on the Corporate Level," *Operations Research*, vol. 2 (1972), pp. 708–721.
11. A. H. Rubinstein, "Some Organizational Factors Related to the Effectiveness of Management Science Groups in Industry," *Management Science*, vol. 15 (1967).
12. Thad B. Green, W. B. Newsome, and S. R. Jones, "A Survey of the Applications of Quantitative Techniques to Production/Operations Management in Large Corporations," *Academy of Management Journal*, vol. 20 (1977), p. 670.
13. Ibid.
14. R. V. Brown, "Do Managers Find Decision Theory Useful?" *Harvard Business Review*, vol. 48 (1970), pp. 78–79; C. W. Churchman, "Managerial Acceptance of Scientific Decisions," *California Management Review*, vol. 7 (1964), pp. 31–38; D. G. Malcolm, "On the Need for Improvement in Implementation of O.R.," *Management Science*, vol. 11 (1965); Green, Newsome, and Jones, op. cit., pp. 669–676.
15. Shiv K. Gupta and John M. Gozzolino, *Fundamentals of Operations Research for Management* (San Francisco: Holden-Day, 1974), pp. 265–291.
16. Donald R. Plane and Gary A. Rochenberger, *Operations Research for Managerial Decisions* (Homewood, IL: Irwin, 1972), p. 173.
17. Richard B. Chase and Nicholas J. Acquilano, *Production and Operations Management* (Homewood, IL: Irwin, 1973), pp. 313–376.
18. Green, Newsome, and Jones, op. cit.
19. N. Paul Loomba, *Management: A Quantitative Perspective* (New York: Macmillan, 1978), p. 394.
20. Claude McMillan and R. F. Gonzales, *Systems Analysis: A Computer Approach to Decision Models* (Homewood, IL: Irwin, 1973), p. 21.
21. Ibid., p. 20.
22. Loomba, op. cit., p. 50.
23. J. W. Hill, A. R. Bass and H. Rosen, "The Prediction of Complex Organizational Behavior: A Comparison of Decision Theory with More Traditional Techniques," *Organizational Behavior and Human Performance*, vol. 5 (1970), pp. 449–462.
24. Loomba, op. cit., p. 119.
25. Edward A. McCreary, "How to Grow a Decision Tree," *Think Magazine*, March–April 1967, pp. 13–18.
26. John C. Chambers, S. K. Mullick, and D. Smith, "How to Choose the Right Forecasting Technique," *Harvard Business Review*, July–August 1971, pp. 45–74.
27. Lesley Albertson and T. Cutler, "Delphi," *Futures*, vol. 8 (1976): no. 5, pp. 397–404.

CHAPTER 16

Operations Management and Management Information Systems

A major focus of management since its inception has been finding ways of making the organization's production of goods and services as effective and efficient as possible. Consequently, one of the most important specialties of contemporary management is the field known as operations management. In this chapter, we describe the operations manager's primary concerns and a few of the techniques for scheduling complex operations. Less obvious than the need to manage production systems, but equally important is the need to manage information. Accurate, sufficient, timely information, as noted earlier, is essential for objective decision making. In larger organizations, problems related to information are monumental. To solve them and be able to make the decisions necessary for the organization to succeed, in recent years management has paid increasingly more attention to the development of management information systems. In this chapter we also discuss what an MIS is, the steps in designing one, and what should be done to make an MIS effective.

After reading this chapter, you should understand the following important terms and concepts:

- operations management
- major phases of operations management
- production planning and control
- aggregate planning
- inventory control
- quality control
- Gantt chart
- milestone chart
- PERT/CPM
- critical path
- slack
- MIS
- steps in designing an MIS

Operations Management

The term *production* is one many people associate primarily with manufacturing organizations. The reason is obvious: these organizations are the ones that literally *produce* goods. Obvious, too, is their need for techniques to increase efficiency, economy, and quality of their operations. However, as we have so often stressed, *all* organizations are productive systems. Organizations whose output is intangible services such as life insurance, education, law enforcement, or health care also need to be concerned with productivity. Moreover the technological changes and increased complexity that have so strongly affected many manufacturing concerns also influence many organizations in other fields. Thus the management specialty once known as production management because it was applied almost exclusively in manufacturing is now referred to as operations management.

Operations management is the management of activities specifically related either directly or indirectly to the organization's production of goods or services. Or, as described by Richard B. Chase and Nicholas J. Aquilano, it is "the performance of activities entailed in selecting, designing, operating, controlling, and updating production systems."[1]

The production functions or systems of Burger King, for example, include all of the operations required to convert raw food and packaging materials into the product delivered to the customer. The production functions of a bank would include all of the processing required to maintain customer accounts, handle transactions with the Federal Reserve Bank, and control cash. Operations management techniques would be used by a hospital to facilitate checking patients in, billing, efficient scheduling of operating rooms and diagnostic equipment, and maintaining high quality patient care. Operations management extends to other organizational decisions as well. Table 16-1 illustrates the variety of decision areas to which operations management might be applied. Because operations management is becoming increasingly important to an organization's success, all people planning to enter management should have a basic understanding of it, regardless of what functional area they plan to work in.

The practices and techniques of operations management are drawn from many sources. Considered a modern specialty, its roots actually go far back in management history. Interest in techniques to improve the efficiency of production operations was integral to the Industrial Revolution. Extreme specialization of labor, the use of standardization and mechanization, and the moving assembly line could all be considered applications of operations management. They unquestionably greatly complicated the production function and made necessary its systematic management. The scientific management school, particularly Frederick Taylor and the Gilbreths, concentrated almost exclusively on managing operations, although they never used the

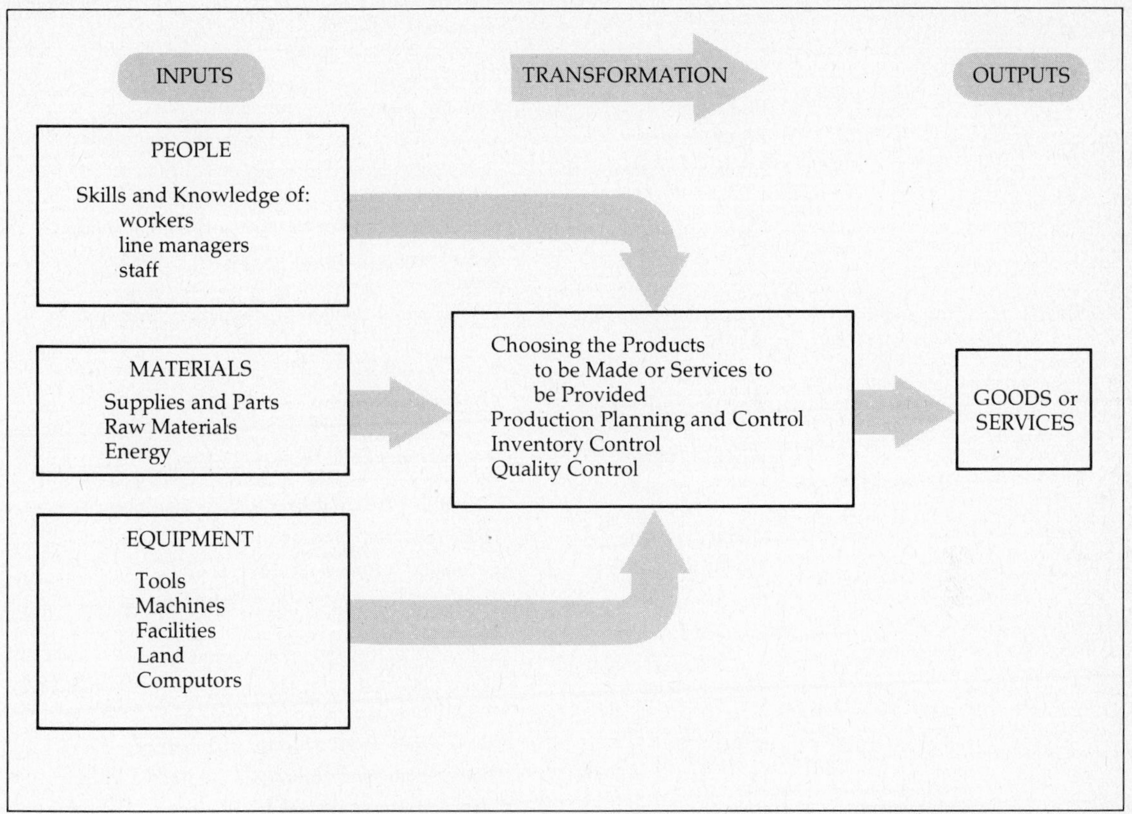

Figure 16-1 The Operations System

To produce goods or services, the organization must create and implement an operations system that transforms inputs such as people, materials, and equipment into the outputs specified by its objectives.

SOURCE: Adapted from H. E. Fearon, W. A. Ruch, P. G. Decker, R. R. Reck, V. G. Reuter, and C. D. Wieters, *Fundamentals of Production/Operations Management* (St. Paul, Minn.: West, 1979), p. 2. Reprinted by permission.

term. The operations research techniques of the management science school described in the previous chapter are an important aspect of operations management. Other components of modern operations management come from the engineering profession.

Because much of operations management does require an understanding of engineering and advanced mathematics, our aim in this chapter is to convey a general understanding of what the field is and give a few examples of operations management techniques for improving organizational effectiveness. Let us begin with the general activities, or phases, of operations management.

Table 16-1 Decisions and Alternatives in Operations Management

Decision area	*Decision*	*Alternatives*
Plant and equipment	Span of process	Make or buy
	Plant size	One big plant or several smaller ones
	Plant location	Locate near markets or locate near materials
	Investment decisions	Invest mainly in buildings or equipment or inventories or research
	Choice of equipment	General-purpose or special-purpose equipment
	Kind of tooling	Temporary, minimum tooling or "production tooling"
Production planning and control	Frequency of inventory taking	Few or many breaks in production for buffer stocks
	Inventory size	High inventory or a lower inventory
	Degree of inventory control	Control in great detail or in lesser detail
	What to control	Controls designed to minimize machine downtime or labor cost or time in process, or to maximize output of particular products or material usage
	Quality control	High reliability and quality or low costs
	Use of standards	Formal or informal or none at all
Labor and staffing	Job specialization	Highly specialized or not highly specialized
	Supervision	Technically trained first-line supervisors or nontechnically trained supervisors
	Wage system	Many job grades or few job grades; incentive wages or hourly wages
	Supervision	Close supervision or loose supervision
	Industrial engineers	Many or few such men
Product design/engineering	Size of product line	Many customer specials or few specials or none at all
	Design stability	Frozen design or many engineering change orders
	Technological risk	Use of new processes unproved by competitors or follow-the-leader policy
	Engineering	Complete packaged design or design-as-you-go approach
	Use of manufacturing engineering	Few or many manufacturing engineers
Organization and management	Kind of organization	Functional or product focus or geographical or other
	Executive use of time	High involvement in investment or production planning or cost control or quality control or other activities
	Degree of risk assumed	Decisions based on much or little information
	Use of staff	Large or small staff group
	Executive style	Much or little involvement in detail; authoritarian or nondirective style; much or little contact with organization

SOURCE: Wickham Skinner, "Manufacturing—Missing Link in Corporate Strategy," *Harvard Business Review*, vol. 47 (May–June 1969), p. 141.

Steps in Operations Management

Since its purpose is effectively managing the productive subsystem of an overall organization, operations management involves the entire management process as we have described it. Also, the management of operations must be integrated with that of the organization as a whole and contribute to its overall objectives. In a business, for example, the ultimate purpose of operations management is not maximum efficiency of production, but to increase profitability and better meet other objectives. However, because operations management involves specific, somewhat specialized activities, it is useful to describe its steps in terms more specific than planning, organizing, and so forth.

Based on Chase and Aquilano's definition, the **major phases of operations management** are selecting, designing, operating, controlling, and updating. The following is an overview of each.

Selecting. The operations manager's first decisions involve selecting the specific processes by which desired goods are to be made or services performed. According to Chase and Aquilano, selecting consists of "a series of decisions encompassing the theoretical feasibility of making the product, the general nature of the processing system, the specific equipment to be employed, and the specific routing through which the equipment must flow."[2] They identify four basic types of selecting decisions:

1. *Major technological choice:* Can the product be made? Does the technology exist?
2. *Minor technological choice:* What production process is most desirable?
3. *Specific component choice:* What equipment should be used?
4. *Process flow choice:* What should the sequence of activities be and how should the product be routed through facilities?

These decisions are described more fully in Table 16-2.

Service organizations also must make selection decisions in these areas. For example, banks increased the efficiency of customer service operations by modifying their process flow. Instead of having separate lines for each teller, they switched to the procedure of having customers wait in a single line for the next available teller. (This decision probably was made by means of a queueing model as described earlier.) They also have improved customer service through direct applications of technology, such as automated tellers that allow people to make transactions at any time.

McDonald's management, a leader in applying operations management to the service sector, would have made the four basic selection decisions, beginning by determining whether the technology existed to make fast-food products such as hamburgers and french fries. Mr. Kroc, its founder, then had to choose between an automated, assembly-line type of production process, or "custom making" each hamburger as most restaurants do. Consistent with his objectives, he chose the former. Then, McDonald's had to make

Table 16-2 Decisions in Process Selection

General-Process Decision	Decision Problem	Decision Variables	Decision Aids
Major technological choice	Transformation potential	Product choice Laws of physics, chemistry, etc. State of scientific knowledge	Technical specialists
Minor technological choice	Selecting among alternative transformation processes	State of the art in equipment and techniques Environmental factors such as ecological and legal constraints Primary task of organization General financial and market strength	R&D reports Technical specialists Organizational objectives Long-run market forecasts Mathematical programs Simulation
Specific component choice	Selecting specific equipment	Existing facilities Cost of equipment alternatives Desired output level	Industry reports Investment analysis, including make-or-buy, break-even, and present-value methods Medium-range forecasts
Process flow choice	Selecting production routings	Existing layout Homogeneity of products Equipment characteristics	Product specifications Assembly charts Route sheets Flow process charts Equipment manuals Engineering handbooks

SOURCE: Richard B. Chase and Nicholas J. Aquilano, *Production and Operations Management* (Homewood, IL: Irwin, 1973), p. 91.

specific component choices, decide exactly which pieces of equipment to use. This decision had long-term ramifications that later worked to McDonald's advantage. McDonald's decided to prepare hamburgers on a grill, whereas Burger King elected to use a broiler.[3] When McDonald's decided to increase sales volume by offering breakfast, it could do so without a massive technology change because eggs and pancakes could also be cooked on a grill. Burger King could not do so. This illustrates how operations management and technology can affect other aspects of managing, such as planning. Then, based on these decisions, management worked out specific procedures for preparing food and processing customer orders.

Designing. In designing, the operations manager determines what methods should be used to produce the product or service. Design decisions are strongly affected by the organization's objectives and the degree to which technology determines productivity. They include the design of jobs that will enable the chosen technology to be used efficiently. This should result in low production costs, high productivity, low waste of materials or products, and a desirable level of quality. However, management also must take motivation into account. As discussed earlier, some people respond adversely to routine, simple, repetitive tasks. This response may result in added costs due to absenteeism, high turnover, lower productivity, poor quality, or even deliberate sabotage that offset the potential benefits of highly specialized tasks.

Many job design decisions are affected by another important aspect of design. These are decisions on the layout of facilities. They include how machines, equipment, required materials, storage areas, and work stations should be arranged to facilitate production efficiency. Closely related is the design of the process flow, the procedure for producing the good or service. Process flow can be diagrammed on a chart, as illustrated in Figure 16-2.

Another major aspect of designing is the development of controls to ensure that production operations will meet standards. This includes the development of work standards through analysis of the job and the establishment of quality standards. The requisites for control of operations and the potential pitfalls are essentially the same as those for the general management function of controlling.

Operating. One category of operating decisions is related to making the long- and short-term level of output consistent with forecasted demand. These decisions, naturally, reflect the organization's long- and short-range objectives. The operations manager probably will find the forecasting techniques described in the previous chapter useful. Depending on the situation, he or she almost certainly will use one or more models, such as inventory models, queueing models, or linear programming to improve the quality of operating decisions. For example, running out of a critical, inexpensive part could cost an organization hundreds of thousands of dollars if it resulted in periods of idleness or missed orders.

The other category of operating decisions involves scheduling work operations and allocating workers in light of short-term demand. Allocation decisions can be made with a queueing model. Later in this chapter we will describe techniques for scheduling simple and complex operations.

Controlling. In controlling, management ensures that the operating system is attaining desired results. The operations manager obtains information on output quantity and quality, amount of materials and labor employed, inventory levels, quality of input, and so on. The manager compares this information with established standards, determines whether there is a significant deviation, what its causes are, and what action should be taken to correct it. The specific mechanisms for controlling operations, as noted above, were developed during the designing stage. The similarity to managerial control in general is obvious.

Updating. In the updating stage, management revises the operating system in accordance with changes in such variables as customer demand and preferences, competition, technological change, changes in organizational objec-

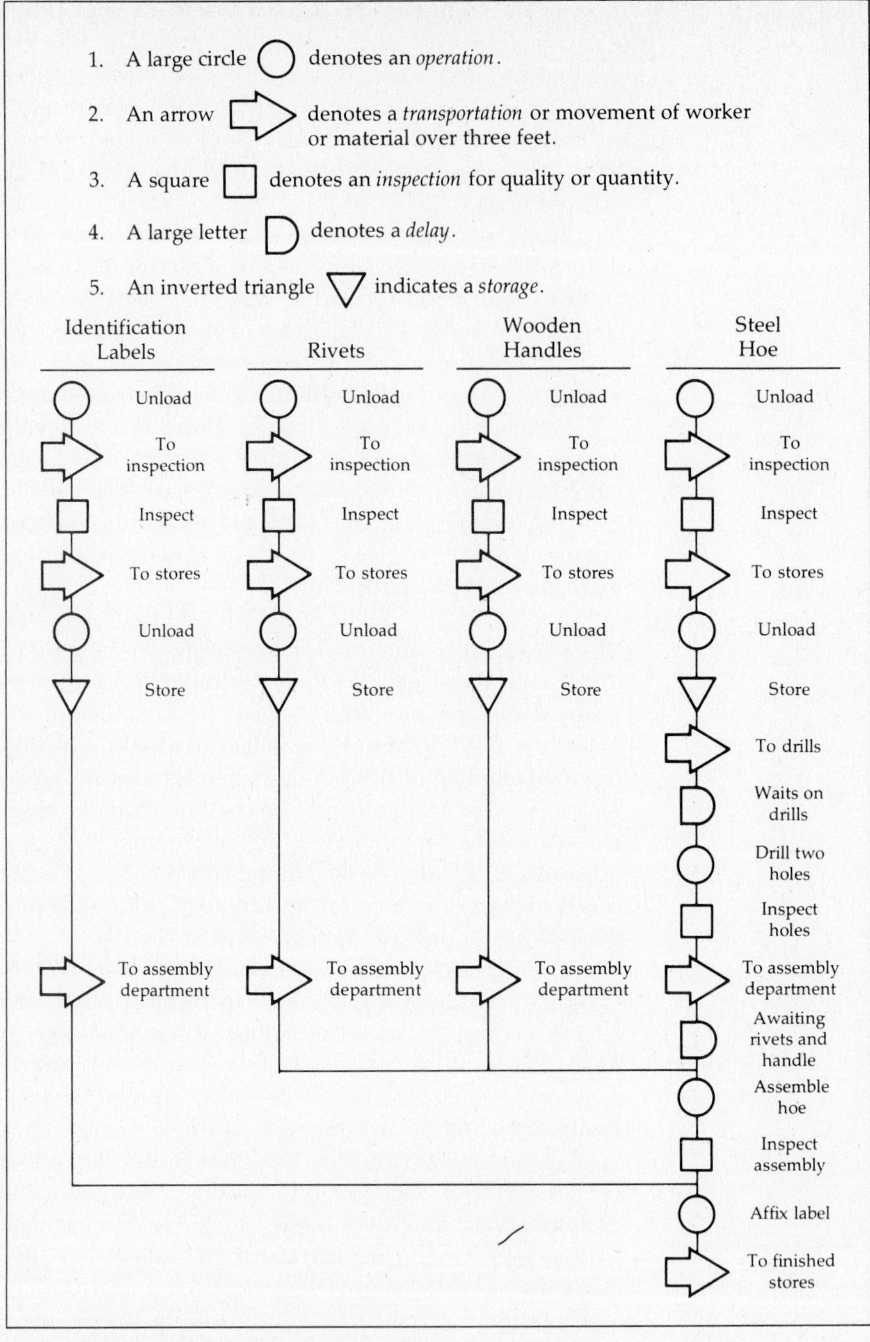

Figure 16-2 Process Flow Chart

The five symbols illustrated in this figure are commonly used to construct process charts such as this one which demonstrates the procedure for assembling a garden hoe.

SOURCE: Reproduced by permission from *Fundamentals of Production/Operations Management* by Fearon et al., copyright © 1979, West Publishing Company. All rights reserved.

tives or structure, and changes in the number or qualifications of available personnel. For example, when the major fast-food chains such as McDonald's and Burger King grew to the point where the market was nearly saturated, their major avenue of sales growth became additions to the menu. Operating systems that once produced only hamburgers and french fries had to be revised to produce breakfast foods and more complex sandwiches. They also had to be modified to improve the quality of products due to increased competition. Burger King, for example, recently installed computer-controlled frying machines costing $1000 each to compete with McDonald's high-quality fries. Burger King also designed new equipment so their milkshakes would not be slushy, and they modified packaging to keep Whoppers warmer.[4]

Planning and Control of Operations

All of the management functions must be performed effectively if the productive system is to attain its objectives. Motivating and organizing are critical to the success of a production organization, even when technology is the primary determinant of output. However, the functions of primary concern in operations management are planning and control. Most operations management techniques revolve around planning and controlling activities related to production, inventory, and quality.

Production Planning and Control. In planning and controlling production, the specific objective is to produce a level of output equal to anticipated demand at the lowest possible cost. To accomplish this, the manager performs aggregate planning, resource allocation, and activities scheduling.

Aggregate planning is a series of decisions to determine what level of output to produce for a given time period. It begins with a forecast of demand for the organization's products or services. Then management determines costs of operations, including those for labor, materials, energy, inventory, and technology. Since organizations using systematic operations management usually produce many products, with fluctuating demands for each, that can be made in several different ways, the manager is likely to be faced with a wide range of decisions and alternatives.

Some of the questions that must be answered in aggregate planning, according to Elwood Buffa, are "to what extent should inventory be used to absorb the fluctuations in demand that will occur over the next six to twelve months. Why not absorb these fluctuations by simply varying the size of the work force? Why not maintain a fairly stable work force size and absorb fluctuations by changing production rates through varying work hours . . . . Should the firm purposely not meet all demands . . . ?"[5]

Many alternatives are not clear-cut but have positive features and negative trade-offs. According to one group of writers, "Since the objective is to allocate workers, machines, and materials effectively, the typical strategy in making aggregate plans is to determine the most economical balance between labor costs and inventory costs at varying levels of production activity."[6] Changes in the labor force, for example, create costs associated with overtime, hiring, layoffs, and possible lower productivity. The costs associated with increasing or decreasing inventory were described in the previous chapter.

In practice, operations managers usually try to strike a balance among viable alternatives, rather than committing themselves to a single tactical plan for production. In smaller organizations these decisions can be made with charts and graphs, as they were in the past. However, a number of sophisticated mathematical and simulation techniques for aggregate planning have been developed recently.

Based on aggregate planning, the operations manager decides upon the optimal way to allocate resources such as labor, materials, and technology needed to meet the determined output level. This may involve determining whether new people should be hired, overtime allotted, how work should be distributed, what the sequence of work should be, and what and how frequently to order. Accomplishing this requires information exchange and close coordination between operations managers and the organization's personnel and purchasing departments.

Next, the manager must schedule the many activities involved in producing the product or service. He or she must determine what work will be performed and when, and the timing of each stage of the production operation. Gantt charts, milestone charts, and networking techniques, described later in this chapter, facilitate coping with the complexities of scheduling. Figure 16-3 illustrates these complexities.

Inventory Control. Among the usual responsibilities of the operations manager is planning and controlling the organization's inventory. Inventory includes both inputs of production such as raw materials, supplies, and component parts and outputs such as work in progress and finished products. Using **inventory models** to assess cost trade-offs, the operations manager determines when to order and in what quantity.

According to Chase and Aquilano, inventory planning and control has five purposes:

1. To maintain independence of operations
2. To meet variations in product demand
3. To allow flexibility in production scheduling
4. To provide a safeguard for variation in raw material delivery time
5. To take advantage of economic purchase order size.[7]

To these we would add holding inventory costs at the minimum level consistent with attaining organizational objectives and preventing shrinkage, the loss of inventory through theft and mishandling.

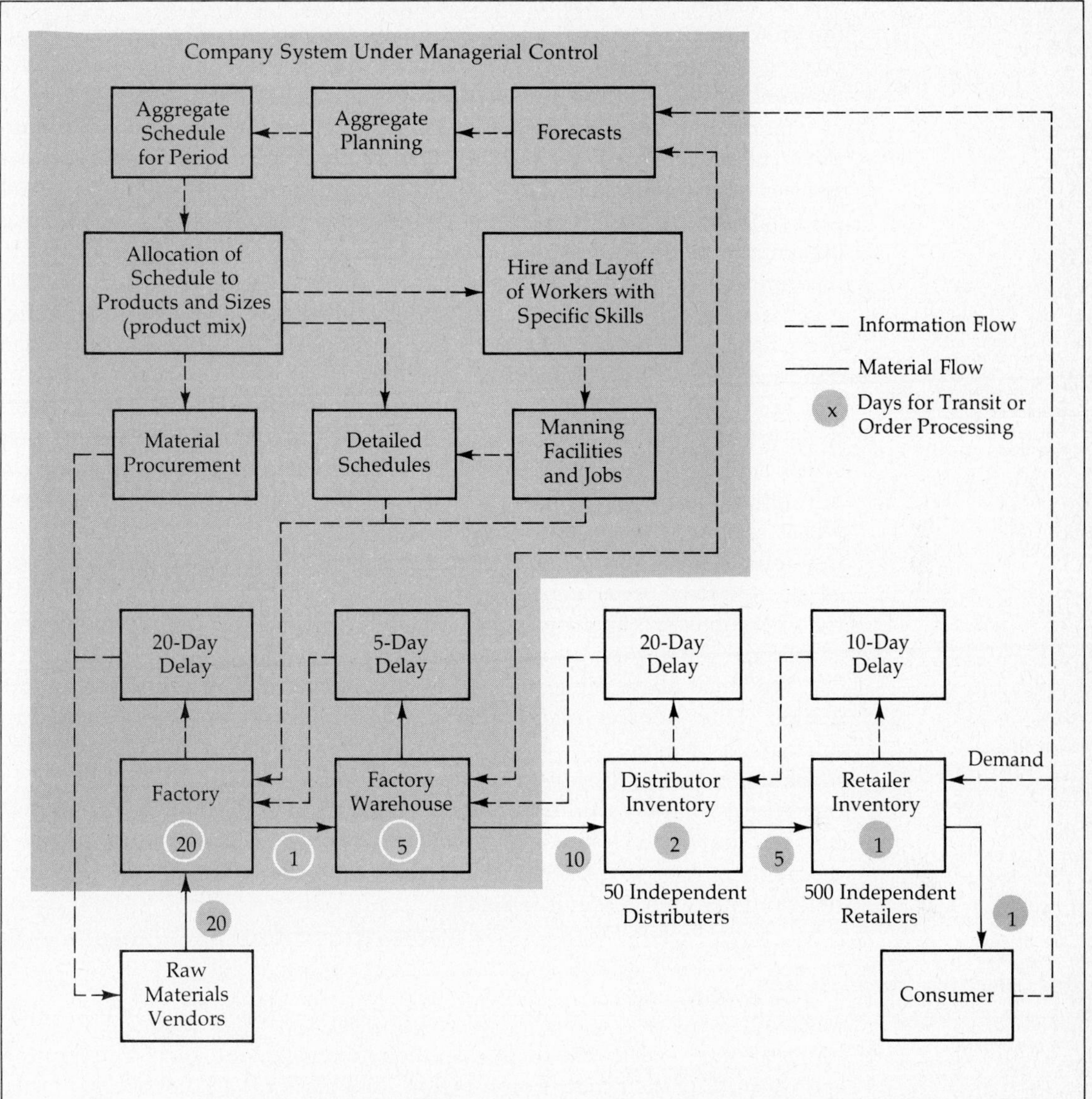

Figure 16-3 The Complexity of Production Planning and Control

SOURCE: Elwood S. Buffa, *Basic Production Management*, 2d. ed. (New York: John Wiley & Sons, Inc., 1975), p. 533.

Quality Planning and Control. "Quality is a characteristic of a product (or service), as is its size, shape, or composition. Specifically, it is a characteristic that determines its value in the marketplace and how well it will perform the functions for which it was designed. The quality of a product is expressed as a standard, and the quality of specific units of the product are measured in terms of the degree of conformance with the standard."[8]

Buffa identifies three phases in planning and controlling quality of output.[9] The first of these, the responsibility of top management, is establishing policies on output quality. To make these decisions, management needs information on customer needs, the quality level of competitor's output, and the impact differences in quality will have on profitability. It is critical to determine what level of quality is necessary and desired by customers. Too much quality can affect profitability and sales as strongly as too little. Many firms have discovered that customers did not feel they needed the added quality and were unwilling to pay for it.

Based on the policies established by top management, the next phase is to design the product accordingly. The person responsible for design issues specifications for overall quality and that of materials and components. A new school building, for example, must be able to withstand hurricane force winds, last many years, and resist fire. Accordingly, its designer must specify minimum quality and quantity of steel supports and the specific composition of concrete to be used. Increasing quality usually means increasing costs, and the operations manager must consider this trade-off and remain within the constraints established by management.

The third phase is maintaining quality during the actual production operation. This involves inspections of the production process, the product during production, and the product after production. Samples of the finished product will be tested to ensure they meet quality specifications. In many cases, the organization will extend quality control after the product has been purchased because problems often occur while a product is stored, distributed, or installed. IBM, for example, thoroughly tests a new computer several times after it is put in service.

Scheduling Techniques

As mentioned earlier, much of operations management involves planning and controlling the production function. Scheduling is a major aspect of this. In any operation such as mass-production manufacturing, admitting patients to a hospital, producing a television series, or building an apartment complex, the scheduling and coordinating of activities is often a primary determinant of overall economy and efficiency. For example, the enormous gain in productivity associated with assembly-line mass production can only be realized if the many component tasks are performed at the correct time and in an optimal sequence. The cost of shutting down a large assembly operation because a necessary part does not arrive on schedule would be unthinkably high.

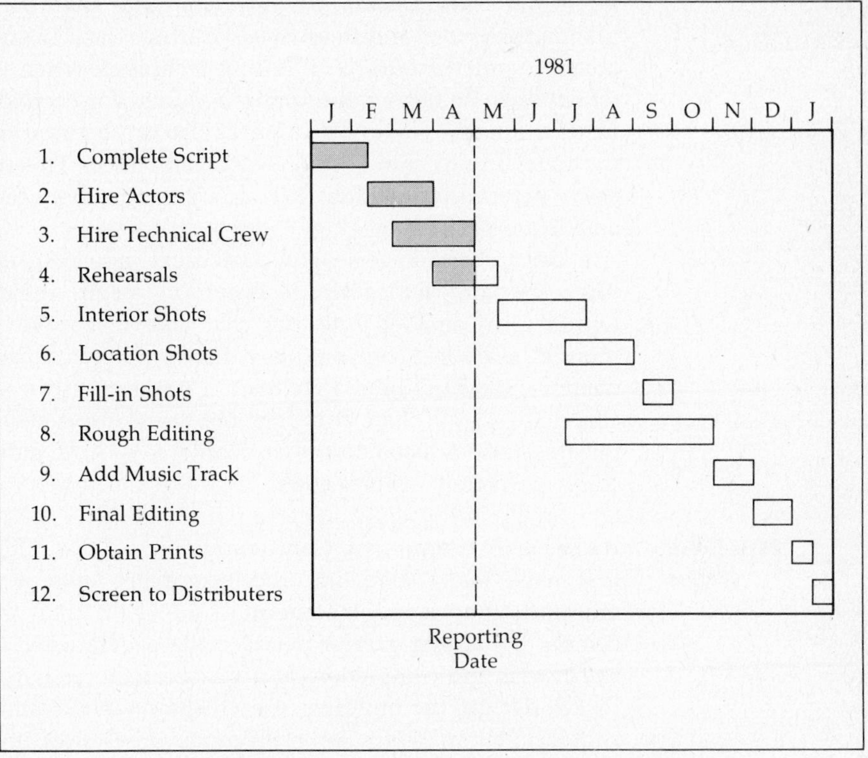

Figure 16-4 Simplified Gantt Chart for Producing a Motion Picture

Several techniques have been developed to facilitate scheduling of operations. The most popular of these planning and control aids are: Gantt charts, milestone charts, and network models.

Gantt Chart

Invented by management pioneer H. L. Gantt in about 1910, the Gantt Chart remains a widely used planning and control technique for nonrepetitive operations. A **Gantt chart** portrays graphically the planned and actual progress of work over a period of time. It can be used for almost any time related activity. The most popular usages are in machine shops, in intermittent production, in construction, and other tasks that are essentially one-of-a-kind in nature.

A typical Gantt chart is shown in Figure 16-4. In it time appears on the upper horizontal axis. The series of operations that must be performed are listed on the vertical axis. By filling in the bars as appropriate one can show how much progress has been made. For example, activity four is scheduled to be worked on from April through May and was about 50 percent complete by the end of April and therefore a couple of weeks behind schedule.

Advantages and Disadvantages. The Gantt chart makes it easy to visualize planned activities and their time requirements. This makes it a simple, inexpensive, and very useful planning technique when there is uncertainty in scheduling. By noting man-hours required for each job, the Gantt chart can be used for manpower planning. It also can be used for control by filling in the time line to show actual work completed. This allows the manager to easily determine whether there is a variation between planned completion and actual performance.

Gantt charts have several drawbacks, however, that limit their application, especially as a control technique. To begin, the chart is unable to cope with highly detailed activities that take place over long time spans. Although, moreover, one assumes that completed work has met quality and quantity standards, these factors are not explicitly considered by the Gantt chart. The Gantt chart also does not point out dependent relationships between activities listed on the horizontal axis. And, most important, the Gantt chart completely ignores costs.

Milestone Chart

As has been mentioned, Gantt charts cannot deal effectively with activities that have many elements and take place over a long time span. The milestone chart is an elaboration of the Gantt chart that resolves this shortcoming by adding greater detail to the events listed on the vertical axis. A *milestone* is the completion of a phase of the activity. In building a moon rocket, design, the building of each component, testing of each component, and installation might be appropriate milestones in the larger activity of constructing a guidance system. (NASA used milestone charting to plan and control the Apollo project.)

Figure 16-5 illustrates a simple milestone chart. On it, the milestones are designated by numbered triangles at appropriate points along the time bar. Naturally, a table such as the one in Figure 16-5 must accompany the chart to clarify the meaning of these numbers. A more typical milestone chart would include about 30 major activities and as many as a hundred triangles to represent milestones. When a milestone is actually completed, its triangle is inverted and placed below the time bar, as illustrated.

As you can see, the **milestone chart** contains many more checkpoints than the Gantt chart and allows the manager to easily and specifically compare actual progress to plans. This is what gives the milestone chart its greater advantages for control purposes.

Advantages and Disadvantages. Other than the capacity for greater detail, the milestone chart has about the same advantages and disadvantages as the Gantt chart. Like the Gantt chart, it cannot handle the important factor of costs. Since the schedule may have been met by taking extraordinary measures that added significantly to costs, this shortcoming may cause the observer to gain a deceptive impression of the project's overall control status.

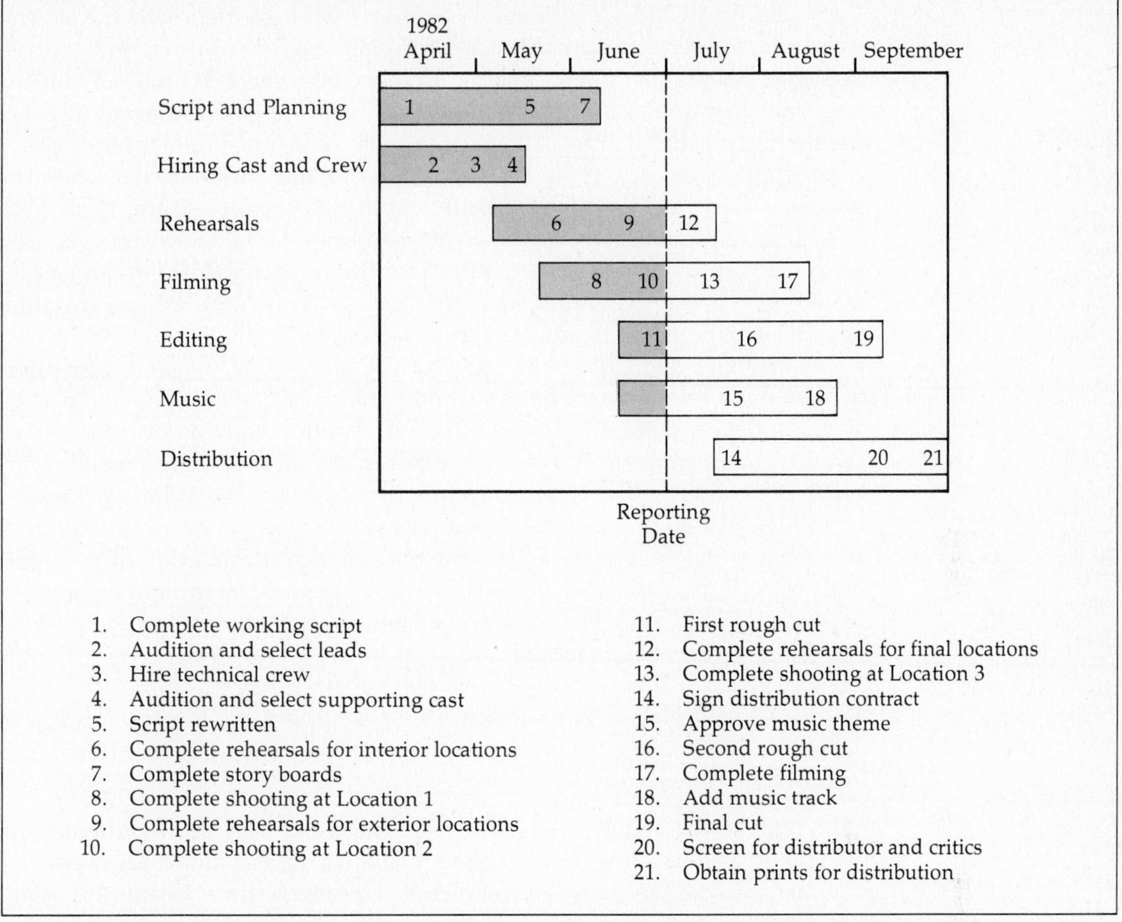

Figure 16-5 Simplified Milestone Chart for a Motion Picture

Network Models: PERT and CPM

Gantt and milestone charts both represent major activities on separate horizontal lines. This makes it difficult to determine from them whether there is a sequential relationship between these activities. To resolve this problem, a number of planning and control techniques were developed that are referred to as *time-event networks.*

PERT (an acronym for Program Evaluation and Review Technique) was developed in 1958 by the management consulting firm of Booz Allen & Hamilton for the United States Navy. It was used to plan and control the Polaris missile project in an effort to reduce the time originally forecasted for its completion. The **Critical Path Method, CPM,** was developed by Du Pont in 1957 to facilitate the scheduling of maintenance in chemical plants.

PERT and CPM are essentially similar.[10] Both of them and the several variations of each are primarily used for planning, scheduling, and controlling complex projects. The primary difference between PERT and CPM is the way time requirements for components of the project are estimated. PERT is used when it is difficult to estimate accurately how much time is required for component stages of a project. This type of situation often occurs when the project is new, as the Polaris missile and Apollo projects were. In a PERT model, time estimates are based on probabilities. CPM, in contrast, is used for projects in which the time required for the component stages can be estimated with greater certainty. Usually, this occurs because the organization has had experience with similar types of projects.

Both PERT and CPM have proven to be useful aids. By providing information about relationships between components of a project, they help management decide what to do, when to do it, and in what sequence operations should be performed to complete a project in the most efficient possible way. PERT is credited with reducing completion time for the Polaris project by two years. Although most often used for managing large, nonrepetitive projects, such as the development of weapons systems, construction of stadiums, highways, ships, computer systems, shopping centers, apartment complexes, and so on, PERT and CPM can also be applied to smaller, less complex projects, such as the one illustrated in Figure 16-6.

Steps in Developing a Time-Event Network. There are four basic steps in developing a time-event network model, such as the simple CPM model illustrated in Figure 16-6:

1. Analyze the component tasks of the project. These are represented on the model as *events* and *activities.* Depicted with a circle, an event is a specific task that must be completed at a specific time. Events are essentially the same as milestones. An activity, depicted with an arrow, corresponds to the amount of time or resources required to proceed from one event to another. The amount of time required is written above the line of the arrow. In Figure 16-6, for example, activity A requires 3 hours. The units, such as hours, must be consistent throughout the network, of course.
2. Construct a time network by determining the sequence of events and activities required to complete the project. In doing so, one must ensure that each activity is preceded by events and activities logically required to perform it and followed by those that it is required for. For example, activity E, removing the old compressor, cannot be performed until the fan has been pulled out and removed.
3. Estimate the time required for each activity. In a PERT network, because time is based on probabilities, three times would be shown: optimistic time, pessimistic time, and most likely time. Based on a weighted aver-

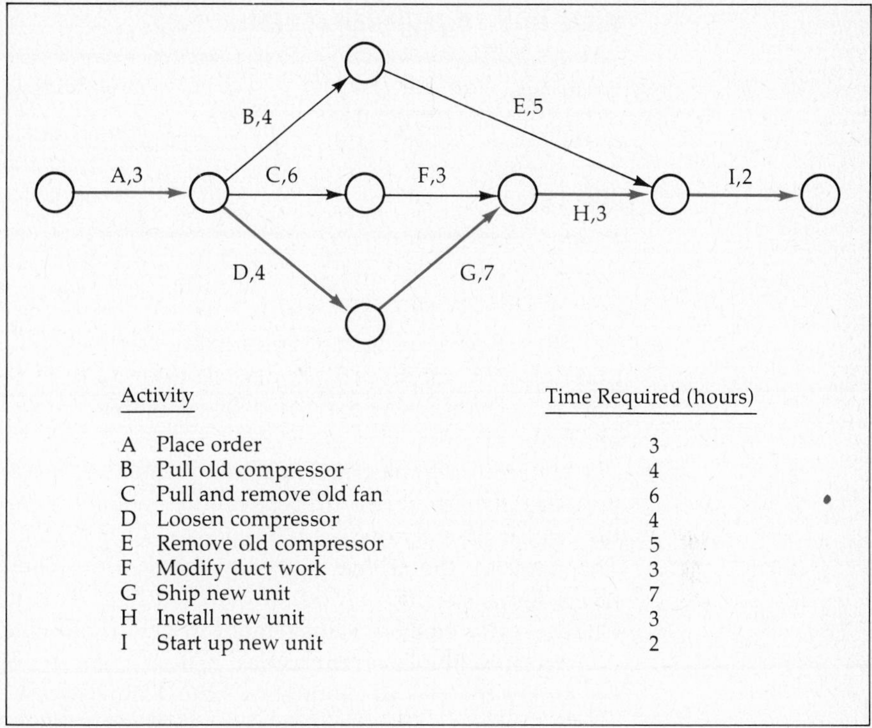

Activity		Time Required (hours)
A	Place order	3
B	Pull old compressor	4
C	Pull and remove old fan	6
D	Loosen compressor	4
E	Remove old compressor	5
F	Modify duct work	3
G	Ship new unit	7
H	Install new unit	3
I	Start up new unit	2

Figure 16-6 CPM Network Model

This figure illustrates the procedure for removing an ineffective compressor and installing a new compressor in an industrial air-conditioning system.

SOURCE: From Everett E. Adam, Jr. and Ronald J. Ebert, *Production and Operations Management* (Englewood Cliffs, NJ: Prentice-Hall, Inc., 1978), p. 463.

age of these, an expected time is calculated for each activity. The CPM model in Figure 16-6 shows only one time because there is a high degree of certainty about how much time each activity will require.

4. Determine the critical path and slack time. Determining time estimates for each activity enables the network designer to calculate the critical path, which can be thought of in two ways. From a time perspective, the **critical path** is the longest path through the network from start to completion. It also is the sequence of activities that, if completed in order, will result in the project being completed in the shortest possible time. If an event on the critical path is delayed, then the project as a whole will be delayed, which would affect the organization's ability to attain its related objectives. The critical path is illustrated with a shaded arrow. Table 16-3 shows how it was derived by computing the completion times for the three possible paths through the network.

Table 16-3 Calculation of Critical Path

Possible Paths	Time Required
A, B, E, I	3 + 4 + 5 + 2 = 14
A, C, F, H, I	3 + 6 + 3 + 3 + 2 = 17
A, D, G, H, I	3 + 4 + 7 + 3 + 2 = 19 (critical path)

After determining the critical path, the manager can compute the **slack** time for each activity. "Slack may be thought of as the amount of time the start of a given event may be delayed without delaying completion of the entire project."[11]

Determining the critical path and respective slack times for each activity provides management with particularly valuable information. An activity on the critical path cannot be delayed without delaying the project as a whole. Those not on the critical path have slack time. Therefore, they can be delayed for a specific period of time without any negative consequences. Knowing this enables management to determine when resources should be diverted to activities on the critical path in order to prevent delays and possibly reduce the overall completion time. Knowledge of critical path and slack is also very helpful in performing control while the project is underway. For example, if management determines that an activity with three weeks of slack is two weeks behind schedule, it will not need to take costly corrective action such as having people work overtime. On the other hand, if an activity on the critical path falls behind schedule, management knows that it will have to transfer or increase resources in order to meet schedules and attain objectives.

Advantages and Disadvantages. Probably the biggest benefit of network models such as PERT and CPM is that their comprehensiveness forces managers to plan operations in thorough detail. Also, by clarifying the time relationship and interdependency of key events and activities, they facilitate economic, effective control. As mentioned earlier, the best use of PERT is for nonrepetitive operations for which time and cost are uncertain but can be determined within a range of probability. CPM would be used when time requirements are known with relative certainty. If the operation is not extremely complex, a PERT chart can be designed by hand and is relatively inexpensive. If the operation is extremely complex, however, a computerized PERT system must be used. The costs of such a system must be weighed against its potential benefits prior to implementation.

The major drawback of PERT is that, like its predecessors, it does not directly incorporate cost factors. However, a modification known as PERT/Cost can partly overcome this shortcoming. This system involves estimating the cost of each activity and comparing it to the actual cost of completion, a cumbersome and difficult procedure. The associated cost data is not shown on the network chart but in an amplifying report, usually tabulated by computer. On less complex, hand-drawn PERT charts, cost and manpower data can be penciled in as convenient.

Management Information Systems (MIS)

Management science models and decision-making techniques enable contemporary managers to choose the most desirable alternative in situations of extreme complexity. Operations management techniques permit effective, efficient planning and control of the most sophisticated productive systems. However, the potential usefulness of these techniques, and of all managerial decision making, is highly dependent on timely, accurate, relevant *information.* Without such information on the existing situation and results, the manager cannot make an objective decision or determine whether the outcome of previous decisions conforms to plans.

Need for a Formal Information System

Much information used in day-to-day decision making is gathered informally. The manager observes subordinates, speaks with colleagues and customers, and reads newspapers and business periodicals. From these much useful knowledge is acquired, but far from enough information for the decision-making needs of even a small organization. The quantity of information generated by an organization and relevant to its success and the rate at which this information changes make it necessary for management to use *formal* methods for gathering and handling information.

Quantity of Information. Information quantity and problems increase dramatically as organizations grow larger. However, even a relatively small organization must cope with much more information than commonly realized. Consider a moderate size retail chain of twenty stores with annual sales of $10 million. The firm may have 300 employees working on an hourly basis at several different pay rates. Each week, management must determine how much each should be payed based on time cards, issue checks, and withhold the correct amount for taxes. The firm may deal with hundreds of different suppliers and process thousands of orders a year. The inventory on hand may consist of several hundred different items; the amount of each may fluctuate constantly and need to be controlled. In addition, there are tens of thousands of customer transactions each year that alter the amount of inventory and cash on hand. Then there is information related to the external environment: laws, trade regulations, government forms, competitors' actions, and so on. Thus, the management of even this relatively small firm must cope with well over a million items of information a year. The information flow of a really large organization with hundreds of thousands of employees, thousands of different products, and billions of dollars of inventory defies comprehension.

Change. The quantity of activities about which information is needed is only the tip of the iceberg. In most cases it is not much of a problem in itself. The real difficulty stems from change. The resources of an organization are in a continuous state of flux. At any given moment there will be more or less inventory, cash, accounts receivable, and accounts payable. Personnel join and leave the organization. Adoption of new technology may change the rate at which materials are absorbed and output is produced. If the external environment is turbulent, events critical to the organization's survival may occur with stunning speed. If management does not receive information about these changes in time, the result could be disastrous.

Coping with this information flow and quantity in a way that enables management to make effective decisions and guide the organization to success is the purpose of a management information system, commonly abbreviated to MIS.

What a Management Information System Is

Many definitions of MIS have been proposed[12] and have caused considerable confusion and misunderstanding. We define a **management information system** as a formal system for providing management with information necessary for decision making.

The MIS should make available information on the past, the present, and the anticipated future. It should encompass all relevant events within the organization and its external environment. The overall purpose of an MIS is to facilitate effective implementation of the planning, controlling, and operation functions. Its most important task is to deliver the right information to the right people at the right time.

Misconceptions of MIS. To understand what an MIS is, one should be aware of what it is not. To begin, an MIS is not a single, comprehensive, integrated system for meeting all of management's information needs. While such a system might be desirable, given the complexities of organizational reality, the probability of creating one is low. Rather, an organization's MIS consists of a series of information systems that cope with a specific decision area.

A second fallacy is that an MIS invariably involves the use of a computer. Recent advances in data processing technology have, indeed, made an enormous contribution to the development of management information systems. Certain types of MIS would not be possible without the speed and accuracy of computers. However, management needed information and a system for obtaining it long before computers were invented and the numerical majority of organizations still cannot afford them. The MIS of a smaller organization and much of that of a large one consists of reports and documents produced without the aid of a computer. A weekly sales report, a mar-

FEATURE 16-1

The Need for Effective Information Management

NEW YORK (UPI)—The paperless office is being held out as an ideal for the future but it can come about only if people in business and government learn how to manage information a lot better than they do now.

That is one of the ideas advanced at the National Information Conference and Exposition in Washington in mid-April.

Several speakers contended that solving the pitfalls of information management may be of greater concern to the United States than declining productivity or meeting capital formation needs because solving both those problems depends on data management.

Failure to make information readily available has enchained mankind before as Lancelot Hogben demonstrated in his famous book "Mathematics for the Millions" in the 1930s. He showed that by monopolizing the knowledge of how to measure things, the priestly class was able to maintain political and social dominance over even kings and emperors for thousands of years.

"Information is power and we'd better realize that the ability to use the electronic computer creates even more power in the world than the possession of nuclear weapons," says James G. Kolleger, president of Environmental Information Center, Inc., who was chairman of the show. . . .

But, said Kolleger and Paul Doebler, a New York management consultant who also was a coordinator of the show in Washington, there are many other trenchant examples showing that knowing how to get information out of computer banks promptly can prevent disaster and cut Gordian knots on the path to progress. . . .

A big utility company keeps its vital records in a cave regarded as secure against even nuclear air attack. But a recent audit shows the company's data retrieval system is so chaotic that 40 per cent of the stored documents can't be found. They have been destroyed, misindexed or just never put in the cave. The utility is in serious trouble.

A congressional committee working on an issue that can affect the lives of nearly all Americans finds itself similarly stymied. Mountains of data have been gathered and stored but the system for retrieving them is so inefficient that the most important index file simply has disappeared. So the committee proceeds to reach its finding on the basis of incomplete and badly digested information. At the last moment the lost file is recovered. To their

continues on page 538

FEATURE 16-1, continued

chagrin, the committee members find they were about to commit a monumental blooper.

"The real cause of this kind of chaos is that we start in most information systems at the wrong end—people who know about hardware or people who know about software are in control," Kolleger said. "We ought to start with the people who know about people, who understand the problem to be attacked in human terms."

By that, he said, he means management and scientists should tell the computer experts and software experts in no uncertain terms what they have to accomplish and refuse to let the hardware and software people dictate terms and conditions to them. There will be little or no progress towards proper information management until this happens, Kolleger and Doebler agreed.

"The crying need," Kolleger added, "is for information management that rightly treats information as a precious resource." He said that in most companies and government organizations, information services and functions are diffused throughout the organization haphazardly and are so poorly executed they are relatively inefficient."

A solution of this problem will require a lot more coordination than presently is customary—particularly in support services for libraries, print shops, mail rooms, word processing centers, forms control units, art and photography departments and the main computer center. People engaged in information service do not seem to realize that, for the system to work, they must be prepared to serve any arm of the company, even the most remote, not just their own little bailiwick.

SOURCE: Leroy Pope, "Information Is Power," UPI, in *Atlanta Journal and Constitution*, May 15, 1977.

ket research study of competition's market share, the daily news summary prepared by the CIA for the president, supervisor's reports of machine downtime, and the computer-generated summary of quarterly sales of major divisions used by AT&T top management are all examples of an MIS in operation.

Designing an MIS

It cannot be overemphasized that the intent of an MIS is *not* simply to generate and process information. The MIS must be *user-oriented*. That is, the information it processes must serve the needs of the managers who receive it. In designing an information system, management must keep in mind that the information needs of managers vary, depending on both their level in the hierarchy and functional responsibilities.

Table 16-4 Information Requirements by Decision Category

Characteristics of Information	Operational Control	Management Control	Strategic Planning
Source	Largely internal	→	External
Scope	Well defined, narrow	→	Very wide
Level of Aggregation	Detailed	→	Aggregate
Time Horizon	Historical	→	Future
Currency	Highly current	→	Quite old
Required Accuracy	High	→	Low
Frequency of Use	Very frequent	→	Infrequent

SOURCE: G. Anthony Gorry and Michael S. Scott Morton, "A Framework for Management Information Systems," *Sloan Management Review*, vol. 13 (Fall 1971), p. 58.

MIS and Managerial Activity. Discussing the differing information needs of managers, Robert N. Anthony classifies managerial activities within three categories:

- *Strategic planning* is "the process of deciding on objectives of the organization, on changes in these objectives, on the resources used to attain these objectives, and on the policies that are to govern the acquisition, use, and disposition of these resources."[13]
- *Management control* is "the process by which managers assure that resources are obtained and used effectively and efficiently in the accomplishment of the organization's objectives."[14]
- *Operational control* is "the process of assuring that specific tasks are carried out effectively and efficiently."[15]

These activity categories correspond roughly to the responsibilities of top management, middle management, and supervisory management. According to Gorry and Morton, the MIS should provide information suited to the differing requirements of each activity identified by Anthony.[16] This is illustrated in Table 16-4.

For example, the strategic planning activities of top management primarily involve future interactions between the organization and its external environment. Thus top management requires information from external sources. This information should not be overly detailed and should be sufficiently broad in scope to indicate trends. Extreme accuracy is not a requisite. A forecast of demand for economy automobiles in 1985 that is off by $10 million would not significantly reduce the effectiveness of General Motors's strategic planning.

Management control information is required by both top managers and middle managers. It, of course, must come from both internal and external sources. For example, top management needs information on both the performance of its major divisions and that of competing organizations. A middle manager would require information about productivity, expenditures, turnover, and perhaps changes in customer demand or technology. This information must be more detailed, narrower in scope, and more accurate than that required for strategic planning. It also should be generated at more frequent intervals because the time horizon of decisions is shorter.

Information for operating control, which is concerned with day-to-day activities, needs to be very accurate, narrow in scope, and current. It should come almost exclusively from internal sources. For example, a first-line supervisor needs to know exactly how many hours each person works each day, exactly what output is on a daily or weekly basis, and precisely how much material is used and wasted.

In addition, managers need information specifically related to their specific functional activities. The marketing manager needs information on sales, customer preferences, competitive advantages of new products, and research costs, for example. Detailed information on engineering specifications of a new product, which is vital to the head of production and the organization, is not essential to marketing decisions. Indeed, if the MIS provided such information regularly, it might impede the marketing manager's decision making by absorbing time and increasing confusion.

Environment and MIS. The environment in which the organization operates also must be taken into account. According to Henderson and McDaniel environmental volatility and uncertainty determine which ways of generating information are most suitable.[17]

They describe four primary ways of generating information: introspection, interaction, reports, and analysis. Introspection is an individual's own information resources: education, experience, background, and other learned knowledge. Interaction involves a meeting between two or more people in which information is exchanged. Reports include letters, data files, and formal studies. Analysis refers to the generation of information through the use of quantitative models and decision-making techniques.

In environments characterized by minimal volatility and uncertainty, many decisions can be programmed and made through established procedures. This permits a proportionally greater use of nonpersonal information sources such as reports and analysis. Organizations operating in more volatile environments also require reports and analysis. However, because many decisions are nonroutine and uncertain, they should use more information from personal sources such as interaction and introspection. Heavy use of such sources requires management to pay special attention to behavioral factors such as groupthink, conflict, and informal status relationships that often affect the quantity and quality of information.

Steps in Designing an MIS. There are several opinions on how a management information system should be designed. Our description is based on the views of Russell Ackoff. He considers the design of an MIS to be a five-step process:[18]

1. Analysis of the decision system. The process begins by identifying all decisions for which information is required. The needs of every level and functional area must be considered.
2. Analysis of information requirements. In this stage, management determines what type of information is required for each decision, as described above.
3. Aggregation of decisions. If a separate information system were required for each decision, the MIS would be hopelessly complex. According to Ackoff, "Decisions with the same or largely overlapping informational requirements should be grouped together as a single manager's task. This will reduce the information a manager requires to do his job and is likely to increase his understanding of it."[19] In other words, the MIS must be coordinated and integrated with the organizational structure. Having related decisions made by one manager or group of managers significantly streamlines the MIS.
4. Design of information processing. This is the step in which the actual system for collecting, storing, transmitting, and retrieving information is developed. If a computer is to be used, data processing people will participate. Figure 16-7 illustrates an information processing design.
5. Design and control of the control system. Building and implementing controls that will evaluate information generated by the MIS and permit identification and correction of deficiencies is an essential last step. It also will be necessary to modify the MIS in accordance with changes in the situation. As Professor Ackoff states, "It must be assumed that the system that is being designed will be deficient in many and significant ways. Therefore it is necessary to identify the ways in which it may be deficient, to design procedures for detecting its deficiencies, and for correcting the system so as to remove them. Hence, the system should be designed to be flexible and adaptive."[20]

Making MIS Effective

In covering the design of management information systems, we also pointed out some requisites for making them effective, such as ensuring that the type of information is suited to the manager's decision needs. Unfortunately, a host of potential problems can prevent even what appears to be a well-designed MIS from operating effectively. The intended users may not understand the system or may fear it, and reject its use. Or the system may prove too costly. The following are some suggestions for overcoming these problems and others so that a new MIS will prove effective in practice, not just on paper.

Involve Users in Design. Sophisticated, computerized management information systems are usually designed by staff specialists and outside consul-

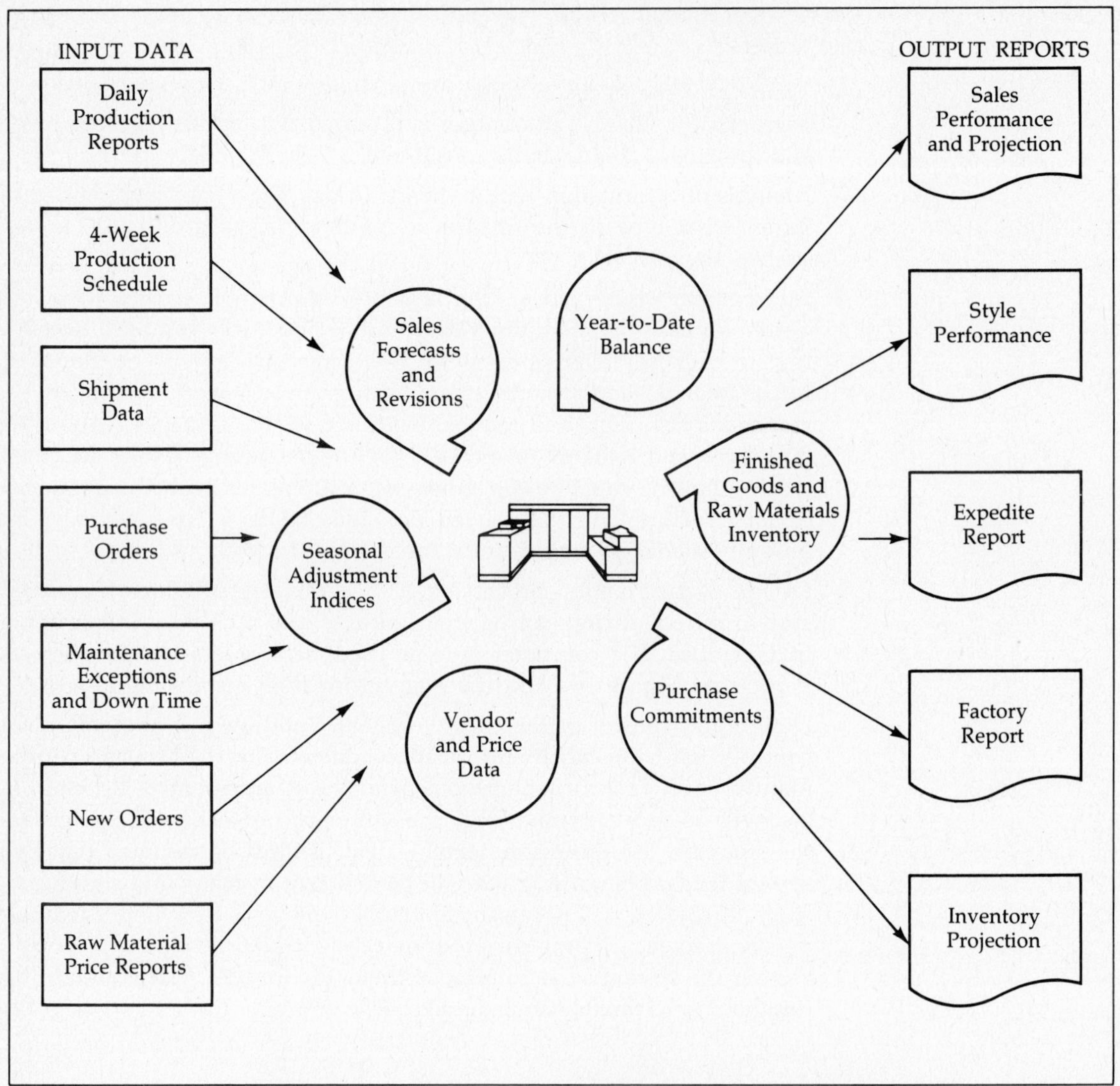

Figure 16-7 Able Manufacturing Company—Detail of Information Flow Showing Selected High-Level Reports

SOURCE: J. W. Konvalinka and H. G. Trentin, "Management Information Systems," *Management Services*, September-October 1965, p. 31.

tants. For the MIS to be effective in practice it is crucial for these specialists to involve the managers who will use it in the system's design. These users are the one who best know what the critical decisions are and what information is needed to make them. If they do not have some input during design, the system may fail to provide needed information or may inundate manage-

FEATURE 16-2

Banks Cut Costs with Information Management

The nation's top three banks not only control about one-third the assets of the nation's top 50 banks, they also are moguls of information management. And the three—Bank of America, Citicorp, and Chase Manhattan—often are at the leading edge of office automation, just as they were front-runners when computers were coming of age.

By tying word processors together with communications, BOA hopes to undercut a clerical wage rate that was swelling by over 10% a year in the early 1970s. In the last three years, a company spokesman says, the bank has saved $4.5 million through its WP efforts; hard and "soft" savings in 1978 were expected to hit $6 million.

Citibank, the nation's second largest and a hotbed of experimentation in white-collar automation, may well be the first bank to arrive at "tomorrow's office." The bank itself has called for the elimination of paper entirely from its back office support operations, a feat that could occur during the early 1980s.

One of the specific paths to this goal is a computer-assisted microfilm system in which microfilm provides data storage and the computer the wherewithal for rapid retrieval.

Citibank has also installed three microfilm systems made by Microform that use computer-assisted retrieval. A $1 million system bought in 1976 is saving $100,000 a year.

SOURCE: "Productivity and Information Management," *Fortune*, March 12, 1979, p. 40 (an advertisement prepared by International Data Corporation).

ment with too much or irrelevant information. Also, as we have noted in other chapters, involving people responsible for implementation usually decreases resistance to change, something implicit in a new MIS.

Training of Users. Resistance to change also will be decreased by thoroughly training managers in the uses of the system. Training should reduce the fear of the unknown that a complex MIS will induce. Most importantly, training will enable managers to make full use of the system's capabilities and help them avoid the pitfalls of its limitations. Without training, managers may consider themselves at the mercy of technicians and feel that the

MIS controls them, rather than vice versa. This would lead to resentment and resistance to use.

Cost Effectiveness. An MIS cannot be considered effective unless the benefits derived from it clearly outweigh the costs. The best MIS is not necessarily the one that provides the most information and the highest level of accuracy and speed. It is the one that provides the specific amount and quality of information management needs at the lowest possible cost. The costs of an MIS go far beyond those for specialists and data processing equipment. They include time spent on design, installation, and training, and the time and other costs associated with gathering, absorbing, and processing information.

Concentration on Relevant Information. One of the biggest problems associated with new MIS technology is the ease of producing too much information. Information overload impairs decision making as much as too little information does. Drowned in irrelevant facts, the manager may overlook important information or be unable to digest it quickly enough for timely decision making. Therefore, a well-designed MIS selectively supplies managers with only the type of information suited to their activities. Whenever possible, information will be condensed as much as possible to permit rapid absorption.

Testing and Technical Personnel. If the MIS is computer-based, the organization must staff itself with an adequate number of technical experts and operators. These specialists must be integrated within the organization as a whole and made to understand that their ultimate responsibility is to help attain its objectives, not make machines run smoothly. Also, new computers and programs are notorious for bugs. All manufacturers strongly recommend they be tested for accuracy by being run in tandem with other systems before relying on them.

Updating. As with most management aids, the MIS is affected by changes in both the external and internal environments. A change in organizational structure usually means that certain information will have to be distributed differently. For example, if top management moves toward increased decentralization, the MIS will have to be modified to provide lower-level managers with reports and other information formerly routed only to top management. Similarly, a change in objectives, such as deciding to produce a new product, means the MIS must be updated and changed to provide information about new customers and competitors. If governmental organizations impose new requirements for taxation, product safety, consumer information, job discrimination, and the like, the MIS will have to be updated to acquire, store, compile, and distribute the information required.

SUMMARY

Operations management is the management of activities related to the organization's production functions.

The five steps in operations management are selecting, designing, operating, controlling, and updating.

Operations management is particularly concerned with the planning and control functions as they pertain to operations, particularly planning and control of production, inventory, and quality.

Production planning and control involves aggregate planning, resource allocation, and activities scheduling. Inventory must be planned and controlled to prevent disruptions of production, meet variations in demand, and attain purchasing economies. Quality control involves setting policies on quality, establishing quality specifications in design, and inspection and testing of output during production and after it.

A Gantt chart is a widely used scheduling technique for nonrepetitive operations. It portrays planned and actual progress of work over a period of time graphically. Milestone charts can deal with activities with many elements taking place over a long span of time. They show more detail than a Gantt chart. Time-event network models such as PERT and CPM can be used for scheduling, planning, and control of operations in which there is a sequential relationship between activities. They enable the manager to readily determine the critical path, the sequence of activities that will take longest, and activities in which there is slack.

Management needs a formal information system because of the quantity of information and its rate of change. An MIS is a formal system for providing management with the information necessary for decision making.

The information needs of managers vary with hierarchy level and functional area. The external environment determines which ways of generating information are more appropriate. An MIS should be designed to take these differences into account and provide only the type and quality of information actually needed.

Steps in designing an MIS are analysis of the decision system, analysis of information requirements, aggregation of decisions, design of information processing, and design and control of the control system.

To make MIS effective, management should involve users in design, train users, make the system cost effective, concentrate on providing relevant, selective information, obtain required technical staff, test the MIS before relying on it, and update it in accordance with internal and external change.

REVIEW QUESTIONS

1. What is operations management and what is its relationship to the organization as a system?
2. What are the basic steps in managing operations?
3. What is aggregate planning?
4. What are some of the major considerations in designing an operation?
5. What is the purpose of inventory planning and control?

6. What is quality control and the steps used in attaining it?
7. Differentiate among Gantt charts, milestone charts, and network models.
8. When is PERT preferable to CPM?
9. What is an MIS, and why is it necessary?
10. What are the steps in designing a management information system?

DISCUSSION QUESTIONS

11. Describe some ways in which the information needs of managers vary depending on their position in the organization.
12. Illustrate how the environment affects the MIS and its design.
13. Prepare a simple milestone chart for your career, beginning at the present.
14. As a marketing manager, how might you be able to use the expertise of operations management specialists?
15. There are many people who believe that the paperless office will become a reality during the 1980s. By examining advertisements in business periodicals or other sources, identify several technological advances that may make this possible.

CASE INCIDENT

A Critical Mistake

"What do you mean, your crew is installing ductwork on the seventh floor of the east wing? That's got two weeks of slack time! It's the sixth floor of the west wing that's critical! For crying out loud, Prestwood, this job is a month behind schedule, and you are holding up plumbers and electricians on 6-W, because your men are working on the wrong activity. Don't you even care anymore?"

"Yes, Mr. Nelson, I care very much. I guess I am just buffaloed by this new CPM scheduling system."

"I'm coming out to the site to talk to you, Prestwood. Meanwhile, get your men over to 6-W on the double."

Roy Nelson slammed down his office telephone, grabbed his coat and briefcase, and headed for his car. He had been with Mullins Construction Company for 16 years and was now the project manager on the Wright Memorial Hospital job. Nelson had been the primary advocate for implementing a computerized CPM system for scheduling and controlling construction work. He remembered some comments he had made at a committee meeting when the system was under consideration. "It will bring us out of the dark ages. I guarantee you that it will improve our performance and save us a bundle of money." Now he was beginning to wonder whether the move to the CPM system had been a mistake. The system itself was working fine in a technical sense, but Nelson was not getting the results he expected and normally received from some of his key people.

Bill Prestwood had always been a conscientious and reliable HVAC (heating, ventilation, and air conditioning) foreman. Since the CPM system had been installed, however, Bill had seemed almost totally incompetent as a manager. His mistakes were causing serious problems on the Wright Memorial job. As he drove to the site, Roy Nelson even considered the possibility that Bill's errors might be deliberate; that he might be attempting to sabotage the hospital job or the CPM system. "Oh, that's a ridiculous thought," Nelson said to himself as he parked his car next to the office trailer.

Roy found Bill Prestwood on 6-W getting his crew started on the critical ductwork activity. "Bill, I hope we can figure out what our problem has been for the last several months. We have never had this kind of trouble before."

"I don't like these foul-ups any more than you do, Mr. Nelson."

"Okay, Bill. First, let's take a look at the weekly CPM printout that you received from my office last Monday. Where is it?"

"I think it's in the trunk of my car."

"The trunk of your car? What good is it to you in the trunk of your car? You should have that printout with you at all times! You don't leave your working drawings in the trunk of your car, do you?"

"No sir. But I understand the working drawings, and they don't keep changing from week to week. To be honest with you, that CPM printout means nothing to me. It is just a huge array of meaningless numbers."

"You got your copy of the CPM System Manual, didn't you?" demanded Nelson.

"Yes, I got all 300 pages of it."

"And you attended the seminar where I explained the system, didn't you?"

"I was there all right."

"Well then, what the . . ."

"Mr. Nelson, I have been a darn good HVAC foreman for you for eight years. If you want good foremen to lug a 20-pound computer printout around the job site, I suggest you issue each of us a wheelbarrow. As for me, I'm tired of taking orders I don't understand from a computer and then being blamed for mistakes. I think I would rather work for a company where people make the decisions and communicate with each other in plain English! Find yourself another HVAC foreman."

Questions

1. Was it a mistake to implement the computerized CPM system at Mullins Construction Company? Why or why not?
2. How do you explain the problem that Roy Nelson is having with Bill Prestwood? Could the problem have been avoided? How?
3. Can you identify any specific problems in the design of the CPM system itself? How could the problems be alleviated?
4. What should Roy Nelson do now?

SOURCE: Written by Dr. Thomas B. Clark, Associate Professor of Management, Georgia State University.

NOTES

1. Richard B. Chase and Nicholas J. Aquilano, *Production and Operations Management* (Homewood, IL: Irwin, 1973), p. 10.
2. Ibid., p. 90.

3. "Whopper War: Burger King Begins Big Hamburger Fight Against McDonald's," *Wall Street Journal*, April 5, 1978, pp. 1 and 13.
4. Ibid.
5. Elwood S. Buffa, *Basic Production Management*, 2d ed. (New York: Wiley, 1975), p. 486.
6. Chase and Aquilano, op. cit., p. 74.
7. Ibid.
8. Buffa, op. cit. p. 486.
9. Buffa, op. cit., pp. 486–487.
10. Chase and Aquilano, op. cit., p. 81.
11. Ibid., p. 507. We have not discussed how to compute slack time because we feel this topic is beyond the scope of a management principles text. Those readers who are interested should consult one of the operations management texts cited.
12. John Dearden, "MIS Is a Mirage," *Harvard Business Review*, January–February 1972, p. 90.
13. G. Anthony Gorry and Michael Scott Morton, "A Framework for Management Information Systems," *Sloan Management Review*, vol. 13 (Fall 1971), p. 57. This framework was originally developed in Robert N. Anthony, *Planning and Control Systems* (Boston: Harvard University, Graduate School of Business Administration, 1965).
14. Ibid.
15. Ibid.
16. Ibid.
17. J. C. Henderson and R. R. McDaniel, "A Network Model for Personalized Information Systems," Working Paper Series, 76-5 (Columbus, Ohio: College of Administrative Science, Ohio State University, 1976).
18. Russell E. Ackoff, "Management Misinformation Systems," *Management Science*, December 1967, p. 147.
19. Ibid., p. 154.
20. Ibid.

CHAPTER 17

Financial Planning and Control Techniques

An organization's need to keep track of its resources was recognized early in history and has remained in the forefront of managers' minds ever since. With the development of management and its allied disciplines, accounting and finance, came a wide variety of techniques specifically intended to facilitate planning and control. Moreover, these techniques, which once dealt exclusively with financial resources, have been expanded and refined to be applied to difficult areas such as human resources and social responsibility. Today, the most widespread application of quantitative techniques in day-to-day management practice is in the area of planning and control. The objective of this chapter is to give you a general understanding of the quantitative techniques you are most likely to encounter.

After reading this chapter, you should understand the following important terms and concepts:

budget development
revenue and expense budgets
product, material, and time budgets
fixed vs. flexible budgets
zero-base budgets
income statement
ratio analysis
liquidity
current ratio
leverage ratio
return on investment (ROI)
profit margin on sales
audit
internal vs. external audit
management audit
social audit
human resource accounting
break-even point

Many of the techniques of operations management and decision making described in the two preceding chapters would correctly be considered planning and control techniques. In this chapter we concentrate on the more general techniques, those used by nearly all organizations and many managers. For convenience, we will classify them under two main headings:

1. *Budgeting.* This is the most widely used of all planning and controlling aids. Almost all organizations use budgets to allocate resources according to plans and to determine whether resources were, in fact, used as intended.
2. *Financial planning and controlling aids.* These are tools and techniques for evaluating and predicting the financial status of the organization and its relative effectiveness as a user of resources. Included here are income statements, ratio analysis, and break-even analysis. Also described is auditing, a tool whose use is rapidly spreading to nonfinancial uses.

Budgeting

Because they often are prepared by an organization's financial staff, many people think of budgets as a purely financial tool. But budgets are, in truth, a wide-ranging management tool, not just a technique for manipulating numbers.

> *A budget is a plan that expresses expected results in quantitative terms. It also serves as a control standard for the allocation of resources and the evaluation of performance.*

As we can see from its definition, the budget has distinct purposes for both planning and control. It is a plan because the budget forecasts the allocation of resources and the results of work based on the organization's multiple objectives. A budget can simultaneously serve a control purpose because by measuring an activity over a specific time period it meets the requirements for a control standard. Moreover, planning and control are only the primary management uses of budgeting. Its other uses and ramifications affect the entire spectrum of the management process.

Uses of Budgeting

Budgeting is without question the most widely used technique for planning, controlling, and coordinating the activities of an organization. Some of the most significant uses of budgeting are:

1. *Integration and comparison of all operations.* In preparing a comprehensive budget, management converts all resources and planned output to dollars. This uniform unit of measure—a common denominator—permits radically different operations to be compared to one another. The bud-

get thus facilitates integration of plans by making it easy to see the relationship between plans and supporting subplans. The resources allocated to every subplan must equal what was allotted for the overall plan. Similarly, a firm's projected total output cannot exceed the sum of the projections for the output of each part.

2. *Allocates resources.* One of management's most important responsibilities is to allocate resources in a way that will lead to the attainment of objectives. The budget is its technique for doing this.
3. *Guides decision making.* The parameters established by the budget channel decisions of subordinate managers in the direction desired by top management. If the budget is enforced, no subordinate manager can spend more than top management allocated to his or her activity.
4. *Emphasizes profit and major objectives.* The budget of a business is constructed in a way that draws attention to profit, an essential objective for many organizations. A good budget for a nonprofit organization will similarly stress its primary objectives, such as delivering the greatest service at a set cost.
5. *Control.* The budget serves as a standard against which actual expenditure of resources can be compared to planned allocations. It also is a standard for comparing actual performance to planned output. Actually, as we will see below, there are many different budgets used for this purpose.
6. *Motivation.* Meeting a budget is an objective standard for evaluation. Organizations therefore often reward those who meet or improve upon budget standards. This makes budgets a useful tool for motivating managers to pay close heed to organizational objectives. (However, as pointed out in our discussion of control, the possibility of control-oriented behavior must be taken into account. Managers may become motivated to stay with their budget exactly when the organization would better meet its objectives if they spent more or less.)

Budget Development

Because budgets are guidelines for allocating resources to attain objectives, budget development usually begins after annual objectives have been formulated for each subunit of the organization. Budget development is usually performed by line management. Staff managers assist by providing information, services, and technical expertise, as required.

Development Process. Some companies continue to follow the older practice of the budget being developed by top management and the controller and imposed on lower levels of management with little consultation or communication. However, most companies today allow those managers accountable for results to prepare at least a preliminary budget for their own area. These preliminary budgets almost always have to be approved by the preparer's immediate superior, because of the widespread tendency to overstate

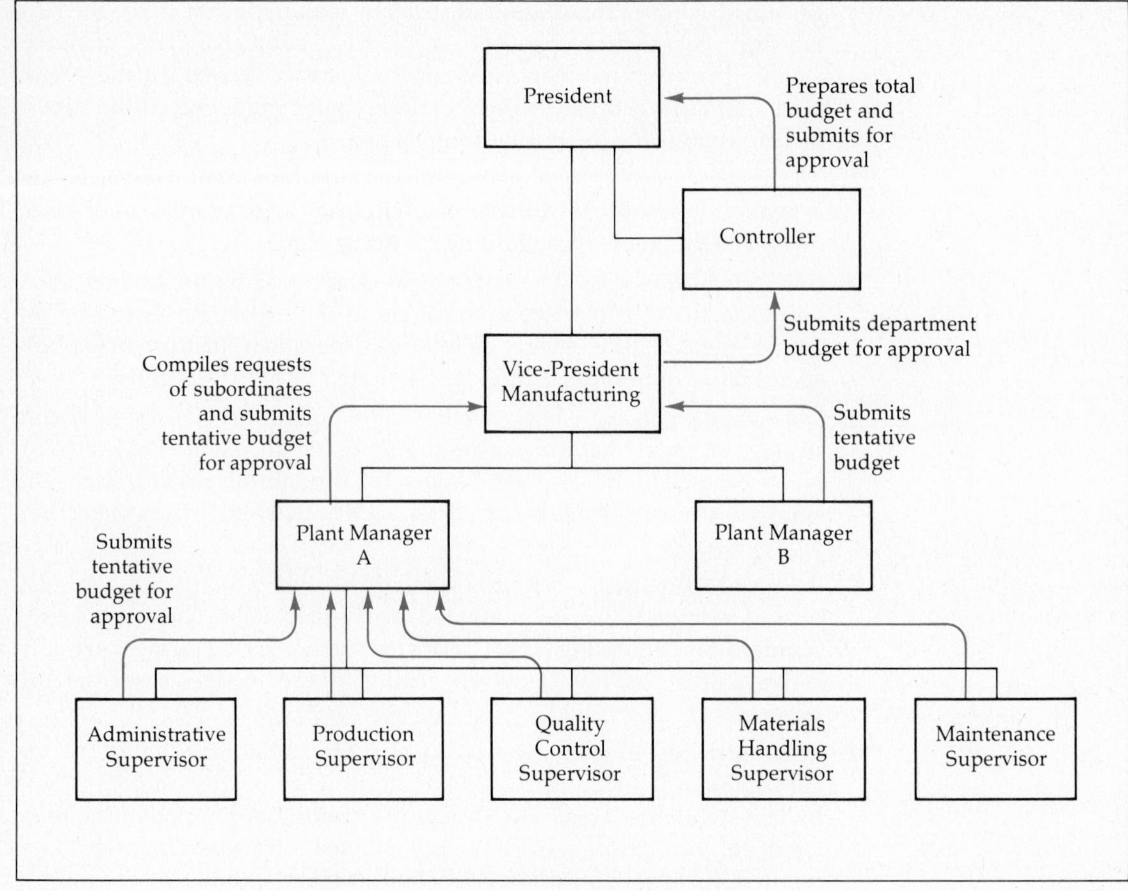

Figure 17-1 Budget Development Process

resource needs. The immediate superior prepares a budget for the broader area he or she is accountable for, based on the preliminary budgets of all subordinates. This is approved by the next level of management. This process is continued to the top management level. Eventually, the budgets for each subunit are consolidated by the controller or budget director. He or she then submits the consolidated budget package to the president or board of directors for approval.[1] Figure 17-1 illustrates this process.

Budget Departments and Committees. In larger organizations there is often a budget department or budget committee responsible for budget preparation and coordination. Budget departments are most widely used by divisionally organized firms. The department manager generally reports to the controller. The budget department is basically a staff unit that provides information and technical assistance to divisional managers and integrates the divisional budgets into a comprehensive package for top management approval. The department may also perform control activities, such as reporting discrepancies between actual performance and budgeted allocations.

Budget committees are generally composed of top-level managers from each functional area of the organization. Their primary function is to screen departmental budgets, reconcile differences of opinion on allocation of resources, reject, modify, or approve specific budget requests, and submit a consolidated budget to the president or board of directors for approval.

Types of Budgets

Since budgets have so many potential applications, it should not be surprising that managers have developed over the years a wide range of budgeting techniques to handle the special problems of their organization. There are dozens of types of budgets, each designed to meet a specific need. Some of the more common budgets are described in the following sections.

Revenue and Expense Budgets. This, the most common form of business budget, compares overall revenue and overall allocations. The revenue portion includes all income the firm plans to receive from its operations. The expense side tabulates the costs that it will incur to obtain these revenues, such as labor, rent, materials, and interest.

Cash Budget. The cash budget is a forecast of how much cash the organization will have on hand and how much it will need to meet expenses. Its purpose is to provide the organization with funds to meet its commitments but avoid having large amounts of cash be idle for extended periods.

Capital Expenditure Budget. This budget is an expression of the firm's long-term strategic objectives. It allocates capital expenditures, investments that normally are recouped over a long period of time. It helps warrant that productive facilities, such as expensive machinery and buildings, remain efficient and competitive while avoiding tying up a large percentage of the firm's resources in these assets that cannot readily be converted to cash.

Production, Material, and Time Budgets. Although for overall planning and control the organization needs to convert everything to dollar units, physical units are more useful for many operations. Production objectives, for example, are more relevant to supervisors when expressed as units produced. And staffing needs are more conveniently expressed in terms of man-days or man-hours. Therefore, in the areas of production, material usage, and labor time, most organizations prepare supplemental budgets in units relevant to the activity. For example, each foreman on a Zenith television assembly line might be budgeted to produce 100 sets per day, using 80 man-hours of labor. In the budgets of top management these figures would be converted to dollar equivalents like an output of $25,000 at a labor cost of $800.

Program Budgets. Until fairly recently, most governmental organizations used budgets that were subdivided into elements for the agency as a whole. The labor department, for example, would be allocated money for staff, rent, materials, and so forth. As government grew and added more and more functions and activities, this method of budgeting began to cause problems. Legislators could not determine exactly what it was they were funding. An increase of the budget could be and often was used for a program the lawmaker did not support. It also was impossible to determine which services and programs were most effective from a cost standpoint. To resolve this situation and regain a measure of control, since the 1950s governmental agencies have begun using program budgets.

A *program budget*, instead of allocating resources to an organization, allocates them to its programs. A program in this case is the collective activities needed to attain a specific objective. The defense department, instead of receiving a general budget for military readiness, now gets many different budgets. The development of a new weapons system like the cruise missile, for example, requires a separate program budget that must be approved by Congress. An elaboration of the program budget, the programming-planning-budgeting system (PPBS), developed by the Rand Corporation, was first used by the defense department under Secretary Robert McNamara in 1961. President Johnson ordered all government agencies to begin to implement PPBS in 1965.

The chief advantage of the program budget is that it focuses attention on the cost-benefit relationship. It forces government agencies to think through proposed programs and makes it harder to conceal inefficient ones. However, the program technique greatly complicates the budgeting process because so many specific cost factors must be considered to arrive at an overall figure. Therefore, despite reform pressure, organizations have been slow to adopt them.

Product Budgets. The **product budget** is very similar to the program budget in concept: it allocates resources and expenses on a product-by-product basis. The principal users are manufacturing organizations. A product budget allows such businesses to compare the cost effectiveness of various major products and weed out those that do not contribute profit in proportion to the resources they absorb.

Note the interrelationship between program or product budgeting, a planning and control mechanism, and organizational structure. It is important that the budgeting system is consistent with and contributes to the effectiveness of the structural design chosen by management. A company like Procter & Gamble that is organized along product lines, using its famous brand manager system of authority distribution, ought to (and does) use product budgeting to plan and control at the divisional level. Similarly, program budgeting is the logical technique to use in conjunction with new, adaptive structures such as project and matrix organization. This further il-

FEATURE 17-1

Budget for a Manufacturing Department

	Budget
Materials	$210,000
Labor	119,000
Labor loaned to Department 11	17,000
Department costs:	
Supervision	21,000
Indirect materials	14,300
Repairs and maintenance	2,100
Equipment operating cost	3,400
Depreciation, equipment	4,000
Allocated plant costs:	
Superintendence	19,500
Heat, light, and power	3,700
Taxes and insurance	5,400
Other plant occupancy cost	5,000
Depreciation, plant	7,000
Total cost	$431,400

SOURCE: Carl L. Moore and Robert K. Jaedicke, *Managerial Accounting*, 5th ed. (Cincinnati: South-Western, 1980), p. 55.

lustrates how altering one aspect of the organization may require adjustments in seemingly unrelated areas of its management.

Fixed and Flexible Budgets

The types of budgets we have just described were classified by their content. We can also classify budgets along another dimension as being flexible or fixed. This system amplifies rather than substitutes for the content description. For example, we could describe a budget as a flexible revenue budget or a fixed program budget.

Fixed Budgets. The **fixed budget** is the form familiar to most people. It is based on a forecast for an upcoming time period, hence it sometimes is referred to as a *forecast budget*. This forecast is not adjusted to reflect actual activity during the time period. Actual results—such as actual revenues or expenses—are compared to it after the entire time period has passed.

The budgets of governmental agencies usually are fixed. They are based on an appropriation given in response to the agency's forecast of needs for programs, hence are sometimes referred to as appropriation budgets. Should an unforeseen event occur, say a hurricane, war, or recession, the governmental organization cannot normally reallocate budgeted resources and expenses to cope with this actual activity. The responsible legislative body must specifically authorize a supplemental appropriation. Congress, for example, regularly does so when there is a natural disaster.

The type of fixed budget most often used by businesses is sometimes referred to as a *managed budget* because it is fixed by management for an upcoming fiscal period. Management uses fixed budgets to limit spending in areas where needs are highly predictable. Some activities that commonly would have a fixed budget are research and development, public relations, advertising, and new furniture for the executive offices. These budgets can, of course, be changed if management wishes. However, even if there is a sudden change in plans or available revenues, there is no provision for an automatic adjustment in the budget.

Flexible Budgets. **Flexible budgets,** on the other hand, are set up to adjust automatically to reflect actual activity. A common version of the flexible budget is the *engineering standard* or *standard cost* budget. These are used for repetitive production situations where costs are known from long past experience or readily established by time and motion study. To understand how a flexible budget works, let's look at such a situation, the assembly of pocket calculators.

The company determines by measurement that it should take an average of 10 minutes to assemble a calculator. The figure 10 minutes and the labor costs associated with it become a performance standard—the standard cost—against which actual work is compared. If, for instance, only four calculators were produced in a given hour, actual production for that hour would be considered low performance. When the firm uses a flexible budget, this standard cost becomes the budget's base. If 50 calculators are built, the time budgeted for labor would be 10 hours. If 55 calculators were actually assembled, the labor budget would be 11 hours.

The difference between fixed and flexible budgets becomes clear when we consider how a change in plans affects the evaluation of a deviation. Assume that we have a flexible budget and originally planned to assemble 1000 calculators in a given week. However, because orders failed to materialize, the plan was changed to call for only 900 calculators. Actual output for the week was 905 units at a labor cost of 185 hours. Had we a fixed budget, comparison of results to expectations for the week would have shown actual labor costs of 185 hours against planned expenses of 200 hours. This gives the erroneous impression that workers were unusually productive or that the labor standard is too low. But because we have a flexible budget, the amount of time allocated for production is automatically adjusted to reflect the change in plans. Instead of 200 hours, it is 180 hours. When we evaluate results against our flexible budget we see that actual output was below standard, not above.

This ability to respond to changes in plans and thereby permit a more accurate interpretation of results is the main reason why flexible budgets are considered preferable when they can be used. Results will appear to deviate from plans (a budget is a plan) for one of three causes:

1. Inefficiency: work should have met expectations but for some reason did not.
2. The standard was inaccurate and needs to be revised upward or downward.
3. Plans changed during the operation, and the standard was not adjusted to compensate.

Using a flexible budget wholly eliminates this third possible cause for an apparent variation. Thus the flexible budget makes it easier for management to determine whether corrective action is necessary and what it should be. Note that in our calculator example, if management had been using a fixed budget, it would not even have recognized that there was a productivity shortfall, unless some manager caught it through personal observation.

Zero-Base Budgeting

In ongoing organizations budgets for the upcoming time period are very often based on those for the current one. Managers simply add or subtract a certain percentage of the total to reflect planned changes. Unfortunately, under this traditional system it is far more common to add to than to decrease expenditures. This is especially true in public organizations, which do not have the restraining factor of having to earn a profit. But, in all organizations there is a tendency to equate power and the amount of money one is authorized to spend. Managers with the biggest budgets usually are perceived as the organization chart indicates. Therefore, some managers are understandably reluctant to voluntarily cut back their expenses, especially if they are given no specific incentive to do so. The result, after a few years, can be an incredible mushrooming of budget size with little actual increase in productivity.

The new technique of **zero-base budgeting** (ZBB) is an effort to counter this tendency for budgets to increase out of proportion to true need. Pioneered by Texas Instruments in 1970, ZBB is now used by hundreds of companies, many states, and dozens of cities. President Carter began converting the federal budget to ZBB in 1978, largely because of the positive experience he had with ZBB while governor of Georgia.

The underlying concept of ZBB is simple and logical. ZBB assumes that each year the manager starts with a budget of $0 and must base all monetary requests on justifiable program needs. Starting at the lowest practical level in the organization, managers build a budget for the upcoming year as if they were starting completely from scratch. Each manager identifies the services and major expenses for which he or she is responsible. A corporate communications manager, for example, might need money for a typing pool, writers, supplies, information storage, and computer time. The manager then writes a brief outline, called a *decision package* in ZBB jargon, that itemizes how much each item costs and justifies its necessity.

The decision package usually stipulates the minimum level of resources needed to maintain services at current levels. It also may include a description of what additional services could be provided if additional resources were made available. In addition, the decision package may examine alternative approaches not being used, such as buying services from an outside contractor instead of having them performed by employees. After ranking all of their decision packages by priority, the managers give them to their superiors, who go through the same procedure on a broader scale.

Advantages and Disadvantages of ZBB. The major advantages of ZBB are that it:

1. Focuses the budget process on a comprehensive analysis of objectives and needs
2. Combines planning and budgeting into a single process
3. Causes managers at every level to evaluate in detail the cost effectiveness of their operations
4. Expands management participation in planning and budgeting

In sum, ZBB genuinely integrates planning and control and allows subordinate managers meaningful participation in what hitherto had been top management planning and control. In the words of Jim McIntyre, when deputy director of the Office of Budget and Management, "Managers have some say in how to use resources, rather than simply having a financial officer say, 'This is it, here's what you've got to spend this year.' "[2]

ZBB has also led to considerable savings at some companies. Ford Motor Company claims that it saved them millions of dollars. Westinghouse Electric saved $4.2 million in overhead costs in 1976 as a result of an 8 month trial of ZBB. Xerox Corporation attributed much of a 13 percent profit increase in the fourth quarter of 1976 to ZBB.[3]

The main problem organizations have encountered with ZBB is an increased amount of paperwork and time devoted to budgeting. For example, the documents for justifying to Congress the navy's operations and maintenance budget usually is about 150 pages long. A 1977 experiment in zero basing this $10 billion budget resulted in justification documents being nearly 2000 pages long. However, organizations with more experience with ZBB have found this drawback may be alleviated by increasing the size of the smallest decision package and regulating paperwork. At Southern California Edison, the minimum decision package allowed in 1977 was $10,000, for example. And Texas Instruments requires all decision packages to be presented on one page of paper. There also seems to be a rapid decline in the amount of time and work required to implement ZBB after the first experience with it.

Is ZBB New? There is a question in the minds of some managers as to whether ZBB is really something new. According to William L. Strong of Firestone Tire and Rubber Company, it is "an old idea dressed up in a new name—trying to justify every dollar is implicit now at most companies."[4] Peter Pyrrh, whose book *Zero Base Budgeting* gave the concept a big boost agrees that "there's absolutely nothing new conceptually in ZBB—it's merely common sense." However, he goes on to point out, "this is a radical departure from traditional budget practice."[5] In summation, it probably would be fair to say that most well-managed organizations have always tried to justify the necessity of all budget expenses. However, until the advent of ZBB it often has been difficult to put this objective into consistent practice. ZBB, in effect, is a promising tool for controlling that critical control aid, the budget.

Financial Planning and Control Aids

Perhaps because money is so visible, so apparently valuable, and so easily measured, the first financial control aids were developed so long ago their origins are uncertain. Clay tablets dating back to 3,000 B.C., among the oldest writings translated, contain accounts of wealth and goods. Some historians even believe that the original purpose of written language was to keep track of trade transactions. Whether or not this is so, we know for a fact that formal techniques for financial control were in widespread use hundreds of years before management became a recognized discipline.

The first technique clearly and specifically used for controlling monetary expenditures was double-entry bookkeeping, invented in 1494 by the Italian monk Pacioli to determine whether voyages to the New World were profitable. The concept of recording every transaction twice in order to prevent thievery and catch mathematical errors is so effective it is still the backbone of modern business accounting. However, double-entry bookkeeping is not enough to meet the financial planning and control needs of contemporary, large organizations. As organizations grew in size and complexity, management sought out new tools for evaluating its financial status.

This is most understandable. The financial state of an organization is one of the most accurate indicators of its overall effectiveness. Unlike phenomena such as leadership, morale, and satisfaction, a firm's financial condition can be measured objectively and expressed relatively precisely. Furthermore, indicators such as profitability and return on investment provide an objective means of comparing the effectiveness of different firms and dissimilar activities within a company. Since earning a reasonable profit is a major objective of a private enterprise business, those firms that are most profitable on a long-term basis without contributing to societal problems usually are considered the most effective.

FEATURE 17-2

Income Statement and Balance Sheet

Texasgulf, Inc., Consolidated Statement of Income (amounts in thousands)

	Three Months Ended September 30		Nine Months Ended September 30		Twelve Months Ended September 30	
	1979	1978	1979	1978	1979	1978
Sales	$ 191,323	$ 157,210	$ 568,946	$ 431,319	$ 739,880	$ 555,295
Royalties, Interest and Other Income	4,551	1,989	8,517	4,878	10,262	7,024
	195,874	159,199	577,463	436,197	750,142	562,319
Costs and Expenses						
Operating, delivery and other related costs and expenses, including exploration	130,575	128,164	401,746	345,384	537,577	447,488
Selling, general and administrative	8,667	4,363	25,303	16,503	33,710	22,765
Interest	9,272	9,077	25,674	26,199	34,520	34,420
Income Taxes	15,450	4,750	41,200	13,000	45,800	14,425
	163,964	146,354	493,923	401,086	651,607	519,098
Net Income	$ 31,910	$ 12,845	$ 83,540	$ 35,111	$ 98,535	$ 43,221
Net Income Per Common Share						
Primary	$0.94	$0.34	$2.44	$0.92	$2.85	$1.11
Fully Diluted	$0.87	$0.36	$2.28	$0.98	$2.69	$1.21
Dividends Per Share						
Common	$0.30	$0.30	$0.90	$0.90	$1.20	$1.20
Preferred	$0.75	$0.75	$2.25	$2.25	$3.00	$3.00

One cannot, however, consider just total dollars earned or potentially earnable when evaluating an organization's financial effectiveness. It often is far more important to determine how much it has accomplished or will accomplish with the resources *available*. This is a problem addressed by ratio analysis and break-even analysis, which we will discuss shortly. First, let us describe one of the most widely used techniques for reporting the firm's financial state: the income statement.

Income Statement

Part of the planning process is expressing a specific profit objective for upcoming time periods. A company might plan, for example, to earn $25,000 during the first quarter of the year or $100,000 during the whole year. This objective serves as a control standard that can be used to evaluate the organization's performance. By obtaining feedback on results, management can

Consolidated Balance Sheet (amounts in thousands)

	September 30 1979	December 31 1978
Assets		
Cash and short term investments	$ 42,396	$19,594
Accounts receivable	130,853	121,981
Inventories	235,400	238,362
Total Current Assets	408,649	379,937
Investments, advances and other assets	103,739	102,421
Property, plant and equipment, net	1,054,404	1,031,427
	$1,566,792	$1,513,785
Liabilities and Stockholders' Equity		
Short term loans payable	$—	$ 53,500
Current maturities of long term debt	4,821	5,154
Accounts payable and accrued liabilities	93,143	76,765
Income taxes payable	31,021	3,995
Deferred income taxes applicable to current assets	7,450	7,450
Total Current Liabilities	136,435	146,864
Long term debt, less current maturities	353,751	357,350
Income taxes and other non-current liabilities	28,863	23,006
Deferred income taxes	224,179	220,164
Stockholders' equity	823,564	766,401
	$1,566,792	$1,513,785

The accompanying statements, which should be read in conjunction with the Consolidated Financial Statements included in the Annual Report to shareholders, have been prepared in the ordinary course of business for the purpose of providing information with respect to the interim period ended September 30, 1979 and are subject to audit at the close of the year.

SOURCE: Third Quarter Report, Texasgulf, Inc. Stamford, Conn.

compare its actual profitability with planned profitability. This enables it to determine whether there has been a significant deviation from desired results. Management determines actual profitability for a given time period by preparing an income statement, one of the most widely used of all financial reports.

The **income statement** is a report of revenues and expenses for a particular time period, usually a year or a quarter. Each important element of the firm's operations is reported on a separate line, as shown in Feature 17-2. Major expense elements include such things as cost of goods sold, administrative expenses, selling expenses, and depreciation. Under revenues would appear receipts from sales and other sources of income, such as interest. Interest costs and taxes, although technically expenses, are usually placed on separate lines near the bottom of the income statement. The last line is always net profit or loss, with a parenthesis used to indicate a loss.

The reason for placing important items on separate lines is to make it easier to identify areas of success and difficulty. By comparing its figures under each heading to those of similar firms, management can determine which areas it excells in and where it could use improvement. If profits fell below the planned goal, for example, a quick glance at the statement might enable management to identify the general cause. For instance, top management might see that sales and materials costs were exactly as planned, but the cost of labor was higher than anticipated. This is obviously not enough information to act on immediately. But it does help narrow the problem to manageable dimensions, one of the most difficult parts of problem solving.

Management can also use the information on the statement and that used to compile it to gain further insight into the firm's effectiveness. The accumulated experience of thousands of businesses indicates that relationships between major items on the income statement are often more useful guidelines for evaluation than raw dollar amounts. These relationships are typically expressed as *ratios*. The ratios most often analyzed for planning and control purposes are described in the following section.

Ratio Analysis

Ratio analysis is one of the most widely used methods for determining how effective an organization is relative to others in various important areas. A **ratio** is the proportional relationship between two numerically expressed factors, such as sales and profits. A ratio can be expressed as a percentage (20%), a fraction (1/5), or a proportion (1:5). Very often, the "1" is understood and the ratio is expressed as a single number, "5" to continue our example. The form of expression is based on custom or convenience and does not affect the meaning of the relationship between the factors.

Some of the ratios most useful to managers wanting to determine the relative financial health of their organization are liquidity ratios, leverage ratios, and profitability ratios. In the latter category fall return on investment, return on net worth, and profit margin on sales.

Liquidity Ratios. **Liquidity** is the degree to which a firm's assets are in the form of cash or readily convertible to cash. The more liquid a firm, the better able it is to pay short-term obligations such as debt payments, supply orders, salaries, and taxes on time. A firm with low liquidity could be forced to sell or mortgage its long-term assets, such as real estate or heavy equipment, to meet immediate obligations. This eventually will probably severely impair its long-term performance and thereby its future ability to pay creditors. Therefore, firms with relatively little liquidity are usually considered poor credit risks.

On the other hand, a firm that is *too* liquid—has too much cash—probably is not being aggressive enough in expanding or not getting the best return on its assets. This could cause serious problems in the long run. Montgomery Ward, for example, was once America's leading retail firm. It lost this position to Sears largely because Ward's CEO, believing another depression was on the way, insisted on hoarding cash during the period of rapid business expansion that followed World War II.

The most common liquidity ratio is the **current ratio,** which is current assets (cash or financial instruments readily convertible to cash, such as certificates of deposit, accounts receivables, and inventory) divided by current liabilities. For example, if a firm has current assets of $5 million and current liabilities of $2.5 million, its current ratio is 2. In other words, its current assets are two times greater than its current liabilities, so it could easily pay these debts. A current ratio of 2:1, it happens, is considered standard for most businesses.

Leverage Ratios. **Leverage ratios,** often called *debt ratios,* measure the degree to which an organization is financed by borrowed funds. Here, we are concerned with *total* debt and *total* assets, rather than immediate obligations and liquid assets. Thus, the simplest debt ratio is total debt divided by total assets. It most often is expressed as a percentage. For example, if a firm's assets are worth $20 million and all of its liabilities, including bonds, are $8 million, then debt is 40 percent of assets.

Leveraging, using borrowed money to expand, is an accepted business practice. It is a particularly important tactic for firms that grow through acquisition rather than internal expansion. All of the large conglomerates, such as Litton Industries and Gulf and Western, so prominent in American business today are highly leveraged. However, a firm that is very highly leveraged usually depends on a high volume of business to maintain a high level of profitability and meet its current obligations. This is because of the high level of fixed costs associated with interest costs of debt, which give such firms higher break-even points. Therefore, it may fare poorly when there is even a moderate economic recession. This could severely affect investor confidence in the firm. For example, when Litton Industries, dean of the conglomerates, reported its first quarterly earnings decline of a decade in 1968, within a month Litton stock dropped to half of its 1967 peak price.

The most immediate importance of the debt ratio, however, is that banks and other major lenders use it to determine whether to lend money for capital expansion. If a firm's debt ratio is significantly higher than that of firms in the same industry, it probably will be considered a poor risk for a large loan. This is one reason why Chrysler Corporation had to ask the federal government to guarantee its loans in 1979.

Liquidity and leverage ratios are primarily used by investors, financial officers, and top management. Most managers have relatively little authority over decisions that directly affect these ratios. On a day-to-day level, the average manager is usually more concerned with the profitability ratios described in the following section.

Return on Investment (ROI). When comparing the effectiveness of organizations in attaining their objectives it usually is unfair to consider only total profits. Doing so would necessarily imply that the firms with the highest profits are always the most effective, which is not true. Far more significant is how much the firm has earned compared to the assets used to produce those earnings. To obtain this valuable information on their organization's relative effectiveness, management computes the firm's return on investment, often abbreviated ROI. **Return on investment**, also frequently referred to as *ROA (return on assets)*, is the ratio of operating profits (profit before taxes and interest charges) to total assets.

In the Du Pont system of financial analysis, which popularized the use of ROI, the ROI is calculated by the following formula:

$$\text{ROI} = \frac{\text{sales}}{\text{investment}} \times \frac{\text{profit}}{\text{sales}}$$

Traditionally, ROI is expressed as a percentage.

The ROI or ROA is usually computed for both the company as a whole and for each of its key activities. By comparing its ROI to that of a competing firm, management determines how effectively it has used its resources relative to its competition. As with most financial ratios, a relatively small numerical difference is very significant. A book publisher with an ROI of 15 percent, for example, would be considered far more successful than one with an ROI of 11 percent. Similarly, comparing the ROIs of activities to one another helps management determine which of its operations most effectively uses resources to generate profits. An operation, product, or division whose ROI is lower than others in the firm should be investigated to decide whether there is a correctable problem or whether the firm would be better off eliminating that activity and allocating its resources to a more productive one.

What is considered a good ROI varies widely among industries and even activities within an industry. Therefore, the ROI is only valid as a measure of relative effectiveness when the activities compared are similar or the firms directly competitive. Also, several factors could distort a firm's ROI in a given year. For example, a large capital investment such as the purchase of a factory or computer often would lower the ROI for a time. By merely changing accounting procedures to shift expenses into another year a firm could increase its "paper" profits and thereby its ROI. However, in general a business venture with a long-term or expected ROI lower than the prevailing interest rate for bonds or savings deposits usually would be considered an unattractive investment.

Many firms establish a minimal projected ROI for new projects. Because of the risks inherent in any new venture, this figure usually is somewhat higher than the firm's current overall ROI. While it certainly makes sense to weigh a proposed project's profit potential, establishing a rigid, overly conservative ROI requirement for new ventures can cause the firm to miss important opportunities for expansion. For, example, for many years Du

Pont would not consider a new product with a projected ROI of under 20 percent. Because of this policy they turned down both the Polaroid Land camera and xerography. The lesson, of course, is that management cannot ever predict the future with complete accuracy: being too cautious is almost as bad as being too ambitious.

Return on Net Worth. Another technique for assessing profitability is to compute the *return on net worth ratio* which is net profit divided by stockholder's equity. (Net profit is profit after interest and taxes but before dividend payments. This is what is commonly reported on newspaper financial pages.) The return on net worth ratio, too, is commonly expressed as a percentage. *Stockholder's equity* is the funds shareholder's have invested in the business plus the accumulated profits not paid out in dividends but retained for use in the business. Or, from another viewpoint, shareholder's equity is what would theoretically be left in the way of assets if a firm paid off all of its liabilities such as long-term debt, wages, and accounts payable. The more profitable a firm, and the greater the percentage of earnings retained, the more rapidly shareholder's equity will grow. If there are no profits, shareholder's equity will either remain the same or decrease in value.

Profit Margin on Sales. The **profit margin on sales ratio** is computed by dividing net profit after taxes by the total amount of sales. For example, if a firm earns a net profit of $100,000 on sales of $1 million, its profit margin on sales would be 10 percent.

This ratio helps management avoid the common pitfall of investing most heavily in activities that generate the greatest sales volume, rather than those that are genuinely most profitable. Besides permitting comparison of activities within a firm, it also can be used to determine effectiveness relative to the competition. A firm with a ratio lower than that prevailing in its industry probably has a problem requiring corrective action because it is spending more than its competitors to earn the same profit. Again, however, there are wide variations on what is an attractive ratio when one crosses industry lines. Service businesses often have a profit margin on sales of over 25 percent, while that of supermarkets is usually less than 1 percent.

Interpreting Ratios and Other Financial Analysis Aids. Ratio analysis and other financial analysis aids are valuable because they enable management to objectively compare current performance of the company, division, or department to past performance, performance of competitors, or performance of other units of the organization. For example, management may discover that its profits increased 14 percent over last year, or that its return on investment is the third highest in its industry, or that the profitability of a given division is consistently below that of others. This information is particularly helpful for control. It also may be used to determine the causes of greater or lesser effectiveness, and thereby help management formulate plans to sustain or improve the overall effectiveness of the organization.

When determining and analyzing ratios, however, management must be aware of the potential for distortion. To begin, because a ratio is a relationship between two numbers, if one is unusually large or unusually small, the ratio could easily be considerably skewed by a minor error. Thus, it is imperative to examine not just the ratio but also the underlying figures. It also is usually necessary to examine several ratios in order to get a solid over-picture of the firm being analyzed before drawing conclusions. Just because one ratio is out of line does not mean they all are. Finally, one must take environmental factors into account. For example, a sales increase of 12 percent may seem respectable, but would actually be rather poor if inflation were over 10 percent.

The information obtained through ratio analysis and other techniques is, of course, only useful for planning and control if it is accurate. To determine whether such information is accurate, distorted, or manipulated, management uses auditing, a special procedure that is independent of the management process.

Auditing

Auditing is one of the few management techniques used almost exclusively for control. An **audit** is an official verification of accounts, records, or performance by an objective, independent examiner. The underlying purpose of an audit is to check the organization's control mechanisms. It helps management ensure that the information on which control is based is reported accurately and prepared properly.

Audits traditionally dealt only with financial data. This is why we discuss them under financial planning and controlling aids. However, today the use of auditing has expanded to many others areas. We will discuss the four main types of audits used by contemporary organizations: external, internal, management, and social.

External Audit. An **external audit** is an examination and evaluation of the firm's financial accounts and transactions by an outside accounting firm. The outside accountant is almost always a group of certified public accountants (CPAs). These external auditors verify important items on the company's income statement and related records in great detail. They often go as far as physically counting inventory and cash. The auditor's aim is to determine whether assets and liabilities have been accurately reported. After completing its audit, the CPA firm will issue a statement that evaluates the audited company's financial statements with respect to accuracy, consistency, and conformity with accepted accounting practices.

Because a CPA could lose his or her license and be severely penalized for deliberately misreporting findings or even just making an avoidable mistake, the credibility of an external audit by an established CPA firm is very high. Therefore, both outside investors and the company's own management are vitally interested in the auditor's report. In fact, to protect stockholders, the federal government requires publicly owned companies to have periodic audits by a qualified CPA. The CPA's evaluation in such cases is usually printed in the annual report issued to stockholders.

Internal Audit. As its name implies, an **internal audit** is conducted by the company's own staff. In addition to the same financial reports examined by external auditors, the internal audit group may examine other areas of operations. For example, it might verify the quality of reports, feedback, and so forth. The findings are presented to top management, which uses them to evaluate the firm's control mechanisms. In the aftermath of Watergate, internal audits were used to uncover illegal political contributions and payoffs in foreign countries that had been reported as legitimate expenses.

Management Audit. A **management audit** is an objective evaluation of the organization's management performance. Management audits come in a variety of forms. They may be conducted internally, in which case they are called *self-audits,* or they may be conducted by a team of outside specialists, such as a management consulting firm, or even the company's outside directors. Furthermore, a given management audit could cover just a relatively limited area, such as decision making. Or, it might range across the entire spectrum of the firm's management activities. As with any audit, the purpose of a management audit is to ensure that the company is being run the way management intends and that operations are at optimal performance levels. Often, the management audit serves as a basis for a major change in strategy or organizational structure.

Few firms can spare the extensive staff time required to perform a really thorough self-audit. Therefore, the current trend is toward externally conducted management audits. The best known of these is the management audit conducted by the American Institute of Management (A.I.M.). It is important to keep in mind that like many relatively new techniques, management audits such as those conducted by A.I.M. cannot be considered foolproof or wholly accurate. Some companies that A.I.M. rated excellent later suffered serious losses due to poor preparation for technological or competitive changes. Perhaps the practical usefulness of management audits will improve if, as has been discussed for some years, a certified management audit with standards like those of CPA audits is developed.

Social Audit. Well-managed organizations today make a concerted effort to meet their responsibilities to society. Many companies have written objectives and policies in this area. However, social goals are perhaps the most difficult of all to appraise objectively. Therefore, even excellent, well-intentioned firms have tended not to have formal controls over them. The result sometimes has been problems such as those encountered by General Electric, as described earlier. To gain control and ensure that societal objectives are actually being met, an increasing number of large organizations have begun using the social audit. The social audit represents management's best effort to date to develop a calculus for evaluating the firm's contributions to society. That is, the **social audit** is an attempt to measure, monitor, and evaluate the organization's performance with respect to its social programs and social objectives.[6]

In the words of Keith Davis and Robert Blomstrom: "A social audit is a systematic study and evaluation of an organization's social performance, as distinguished from its economic performance. It is concerned with possible influences on the social quality of life instead of the economic quality of life. The social audit leads to social performance."[7]

Discussing the reason for and need for a social audit these authors state that the potential benefits of the social audit are:

1. It gives management the information it needs to evaluate the effectiveness of programs related to affirmative action, ecology, community development, and the like.
2. Since managers tend to direct attention to those activities for which reports and evaluation are required, the existence of a social audit tends to promote active concern for meeting social performance goals.
3. It provides information that enables management to compare the relative effectiveness of different social programs.
4. It enables management to provide information to external groups that make demands on the firm for social performance.

A natural, evolutionary step in the battle to make social objectives fully operational, the social audit has received much attention from consumer groups. It probably will become increasingly important in coming years.

Human Resource Accounting

Another relatively new technique for increasing the validity of reports on the organization's status is **human resource accounting**. Since the late 1960s critics have contended that traditional financial and accounting methods make no provision for recording the value of the organization's human resources on the balance sheet. Consequently, traditional income statements may lead to a misinterpretation of the organization's true assets.

Elaborating on this issue, one group of writers states,

> Firms also make investment in human assets. Costs are incurred in recruiting, hiring, training, and developing people as individual employees and as members of viable interacting organizational groups. Furthermore, investments are made in building favorable relationships with external human resources such as customers, suppliers, and creditors. Although such expenditures are made to develop future service potential, conventional accounting practice assigns such costs to the 'expense' classification, which, by definition, assumes they have no value to the firm beyond the current accounting year.

> For this reason human assets do not normally appear on corporate balance sheets, nor are changes in these assets reflected on statements of corporate income. Thus, conventional accounting statements may conceal significant changes in the condition of the firm's unrecognized human assets. In fact, favorable performance may be recorded when human resources are actually being liquidated. If people are treated abusively in an effort to generate more production, short-term profits may be derived through liquidation of the firm's organizational assets. If product quality is reduced, immediate gain may be made at the expense of customer-loyalty assets.[8]

These writers state that the value of a firm's human resources usually have a value of 3 to 5 times payroll expenditures or 15 to 20 times earnings. Because of this considerable value of human assets, organizations must develop an accounting system "that will reflect the current condition of and changes in the firm's human assets."[9]

Break-Even Analysis

It is important to recognize that, while very useful, income statements and ratios only tell the manager what has *already* happened. The same is true of auditing. In order to plan for profitability, the manager must try to determine what is *going* to happen. The most widely used method of determining whether a given activity will be profitable, if all goes according to plan, is break-even analysis.

The **break-even point** (BEP) is the point at which total revenue (TR) equals total costs (TC). To determine BEP, one must take into account three major factors. These are the selling price per unit, variable costs per unit, and total fixed costs. The price per unit (P) is how much revenue the firm will receive for each unit of goods or services it sells. A college publishing company, for example, receives 80 percent of a book's retail price: its P for a $10 book, therefore, would be $8.

Variable costs per unit (VC) are the actual expenses directly attributable to producing each unit of output. For a college textbook, these would be the costs of paper, covers, printing, binding, and distribution, as well as royalties paid to the author. Naturally, the total of variable costs will increase as output increases. Fixed costs are those that, at least in the short run, will remain constant, irrespective of output. The major items in the total fixed costs (TFC) of a college text are editing, artwork, and composition (setting type). In addition, part of the administrative, tax, insurance, depreciation, and rental expenses of the publishing house would be allocated as a fixed cost according to a formula established by management. Continuing our example, let us assume that the fixed costs associated with publishing a book are $200,000.

Selling price minus variable costs gives the contribution to profit per unit sold. Thus, with a selling price of $10 and a variable cost of $6, the contribution to profit per book sold is $4. This, in turn, enables management to determine how many books must be sold to cover its fixed costs of $200,000. By dividing $200,000 by $4, it is readily seen that 50,000 books must be sold for the project to actually be profitable. This can be expressed in equation form as follows:

At break even

$$\text{TFC} = \text{BEP (Break-even volume)} \times (\text{P} - \text{VC})$$

or

$$\text{BEP (Break-even volume)} = \frac{\text{TFC}}{\text{P} - \text{VC}}$$

Using the same data, we get the same results with this formula as we did before:

Unit price (P) = \$10
Variable costs (VC) = \$6
Total fixed costs (TFC) = \$200,000
Therefore:

$$\text{BEP} = \frac{\text{TFC}}{\text{P} - \text{VC}} = \frac{200{,}000}{10 - 6} = \frac{200{,}000}{4} = 50{,}000 \text{ units}$$

Uses of BE Analysis. Computing the break-even point, although a relatively easy operation, yields a great deal of useful information. By coordinating the BEP figure with a sales estimate, ideally obtained through market research, the manager can immediately see whether the project will be profitable as planned and approximately how risky it will be. If our publisher's market research showed a sales potential of 80,000 copies, the text would be quite profitable and involve relatively little risk. A projection of only 35,000 copies sold, however, would indicate the project is highly risky.

One can also easily see the impact on profits that would result from changing one or more variables. For example, if the publisher increased P by \$1 to \$11, the BEP would fall to 40,000 units, as it would for a corresponding change in VC. Thus, BE analysis helps point out alternative approaches that could be more attractive to the firm. Publishers manage to produce scholarly texts with markets much smaller than those of introductory texts by paying lower royalties and by not using a second printing color. This alternative cuts TFC and VC to a level less than half that for an introductory text. Note, however, that this reduces the visual appeal of a book, which may cause potential customers to select a more attractive competitor and thereby reduce sales below the break-even point.

After the product's sales results and actual costs are in, management can return to the break-even model for control evaluation. Actual variable or fixed costs above those used to compute BEP would indicate the need for corrective action. However, very often this action would be reexamining the basis for predicting the figures. Like all predictions and plans, those used in break-even analysis can easily be wrong, often for reasons beyond the manager's control. During the early 1970s, for example, many publishers faced a profit squeeze because of a sudden, unforeseen jump in the price of paper that could not be completely passed on to consumers.

Although we used only one example for illustration, break-even volume can be computed for almost any product or service whose costs can be determined. This would include numbers of airline seats that must be filled, customers required by a restaurant, or sales of a new model car.

SUMMARY

A budget is a planning aid that expresses expected results in quantitative terms and serves as a control standard for the allocation of resources and the evaluation of performance.

Major types of budgets include revenue and expense, cash, capital expenditure, production, material, and time, program, and product budgets.

A fixed budget is not adjusted to reflect activity during the time period. A flexible budget, in contrast, is designed to automatically reflect actual activity that has a significant impact on expenses or revenues.

Zero-base budgeting is a new concept intended to help counter the common tendency for budgets to increase out of proportion to true need. Each key manager develops a decision package justifying all budget needs, instead of simply adjusting the previous period budget by a certain percentage. These decision packages are reviewed and combined to develop a budget for the organization as a whole.

The income statement is a report of revenues and expenses for a specific time period, usually a year or a quarter. Each important element of the firm's operations is reported on a separate line, making it easy to spot areas of success and difficulty.

Ratio analysis is used to determine how effective an organization is relative to others in several important areas. Liquidity ratios such as the current ratio show the degree to which a firm's assets are cash or easily converted to cash. Leverage ratios show the degree to which an organization is financed by borrowed funds. ROI is the ratio of net profits to total assets. The return on net worth ratio shows company investors how much they are earning. The profit margin on sales ratio helps management avoid the pitfall of concentrating on operations with high sales but low relative profits. Ratios are often difficult to interpret accurately.

Auditing is a technique used exclusively for control. An audit is an official verification of accounts, records, or performance by an independent examiner. External audits are conducted by people outside the firm, often a CPA firm. Internal audits are conducted by the organization's own staff to evaluate the control system. A management audit is an objective appraisal of management performance in key areas. Social audits are now being used by some organizations to ensure that social responsibility objectives are being met.

Human resource accounting is a new technique for evaluating the hidden but important asset of human resources.

Break-even analysis is used to determine whether an activity is or will be profitable. The BEP is equal to total fixed costs divided by unit price less variable costs.

REVIEW QUESTIONS

1. Why can a budget serve as both a planning and controlling aid?
2. What are the major types of budgets?
3. What is the difference between a fixed and flexible budget?
4. How does zero-base budgeting differ from the conventional way in which budgets are developed?
5. What is an income statement?
6. What are the uses and limitations of ratio analysis?
7. What are the major types of ratios and their uses?
8. What is an audit, and what purpose does it serve?
9. What is break-even analysis and what is its primary use?
10. Why is human resource accounting important in determining the firm's true status?

DISCUSSION QUESTIONS

11. What factors should one be aware of when interpreting financial statements and ratios?
12. Find a true example of a situation in which figures were made to "lie."
13. Apply break-even analysis to a simple business idea of yours.
14. Keith Davis and Robert Blomstrom think that a social audit leads to social performance. Discuss the implication of this belief in contemporary management.
15. Describe some ways in which use of budgeting can help a manager perform the motivating function effectively.

CASE INCIDENT

The Blue Lake Meeting

For the past two days, 33 key management and staff members of the Department of Public Resources had been meeting at Blue Lake Lodge. Edna Wiley, head of the department, had been with the state for almost 13 years and had been the Department of Public Resources' top administrator for the past 2 years. Her formal training included a masters degree in public administration, and it was generally agreed that her prospects for growth and advancement were excellent.

The Blue Lake Lodge meeting was one of a series of seminars that resulted from public pressure to make governmental agencies more effective and efficient. Ever since California's Proposition 13, federal and state employees were being made constantly aware of growing public concern about waste and inefficiency. In essence, the tax-paying citizen was now more knowledgeable and concerned.

The major theme of the Blue Lake meeting was better organization through better budgeting. Topics included a general review of the management process, planning-control relationships, and budgeting for organizational survival. The program staff was comprised of in-house people, two representatives of a major accounting firm, and a management professor from the state university.

At the closing session, the state's lieutenant governor spoke to the group and indicated that this was "a brand new ball game," and they would be expected to run their various departments as if they were in business for themselves.

Edna Wiley was excited and enthused. At long last, she felt, there was an opportunity to bury the old ways and adopt those policies and procedures that could lead to more effective operations. Edna approached the task of developing next year's budget proposal with renewed vigor and submitted her recommendations to her superior, Clarence Dickson. Edna was particularly proud of her budget, since she was requesting 12 percent less than she did last year. Careful analysis and consultation with key staff personnel in her department led to significant cuts in the travel and equipment areas.

About a week after Wiley sent in her budget for review, she received a call from Dickson. Dickson wanted to know if Edna had lost control of her senses. Dickson, who had introduced the lieutenant governor at the Blue Lake meeting, told Edna he didn't appreciate the kind of budget recommendations that would make them all look bad. Dickson said if everyone asked for less, people would get the impression that they weren't doing enough. "The name of the game," said Dickson, "is more." He suggested that Wiley restudy her recommendations and come up with a more realistic budget.

Questions

1. If you were Edna Wiley, what would you now do? Why?
2. Explain Clarence Dickson's position about asking for more.
3. What do you think was the real purpose of the Blue Lake meeting?

NOTES

1. W. Becker Selvin and D. Green, Jr., "Budgeting and Employee Behavior," *Journal of Business*, vol. 35 (1962), pp. 392–402.
2. "What it Means to Build a Budget from Zero," *Business Week*, April 18, 1977, p. 160.
3. Ibid, p. 164.
4. Ibid.
5. Ibid.
6. Keith Davis and Robert L. Blomstrom, "Implementing the Social Audit in an Organization," *Business and Society Review*, vol. 16 (1975), pp. 13–18.
7. Ibid, p. 13.
8. R. Lee Brummet, Eric Flamholtz, and William C. Pyle, "Human Resource Accounting in Industry," *Personnel Administration*, July–August 1969, pp. 34–46.
9. Ibid, p. 34.

PART FIVE CASE STUDY

Sports World, Inc.

TIMOTHY S. MESCON AND
Department of Management, Arizona State University
GEORGE S. VOZIKIS
Department of Management, Northern Texas State University

"Specials . . . brought customers into the stores, where they frequently found these items out of stock."

"Most of my managers are ex-jocks. That's the type of person that attracts my customers. The public has the misconception that if the store personnel have strong athletic backgrounds, they must know merchandising. I'd like to find the ex-athlete that knows this business. Hell, I'm happy to get two years out of my managers. Their role in my company only calls for them to keep my customers happy."

Jed Harrison, owner of Sports World, Inc. is a self-made man. At age 17, Jed dropped out of high school and enlisted in the marines. Jed was initially assigned to the supply division at Camp Lejeune, North Carolina. Jed enjoyed his work and enjoyed the challenge. After two years in the service, he completed the requirement for the G.E.D. (general education degree). The next year he was promoted to corporal and made the decision to pursue a career in the military. Three years later Jed was promoted to supply division sergeant. Years of managing supply operations at the base had given Jed invaluable insight into budgeting operations, ordering procedures, and materials handling and distribution. Jed enjoyed the marines, but decided to leave when his 20 years were up. In 1973 Jed made the decision to leave the military and return home to St. Louis, Missouri. In St. Louis Jed went to work as a salesman for Howard's, a large local department store chain, with five stores in the metropolitan St. Louis area. For three years Jed worked in the sporting goods department at Howard's. While he was content with his job, it became quite evident to him that even with his military experience, without a college degree his chances for promotion at Howard's were quite slim. Additionally, he noticed that at that time in St. Louis, there were few specialty sporting goods stores that carried a tremendous variety of equipment. Also, Jed had always been uncomfortable taking orders from others.

So, with $8000 he had saved, his military pension, and a $50,000 guaranteed loan from the Small Business Administration Jed bought out an old sporting goods store in downtown St. Louis.

An avid golf and tennis player, Jed decided to buy substantial merchandise in these two areas. Slowly, Jed built up a loyal following. He enlarged the original store, and opened up a second shop in a northeast St. Louis suburb. During the first five years of operation, Jed gradually shifted toward buying solely golf and tennis equipment, accessories, clothing, and shoes. His Sports World, Inc., stores had rapidly become quite popular with the local golf and tennis market.

Jed's brother-in-law, Russ Williams, and sister, Eileen, lived in Atlanta, Georgia. Russ had a thriving legal practice that now included three partners. Over the years Russ and Jed had become close friends. Quite frequently Russ, Jed, and Eileen met at a popular golf and tennis resort for a relaxing weekend. They particularly liked to visit Pinehurst in North Carolina, Callaway Gardens in Georgia, or Hilton Head, South Carolina. Russ had some capital to invest and suggested to Jed that he look into the growing Atlanta market for expansion. Following a year of negotiations and site investigations, Jed opened two stores in Atlanta and a third store in northwest St. Louis.

Jed realized that he could no longer control the five stores alone, so he appointed the two original managers from his St. Louis stores as vice-presidents. One moved to Atlanta, the other remained in St. Louis. Jed hand-

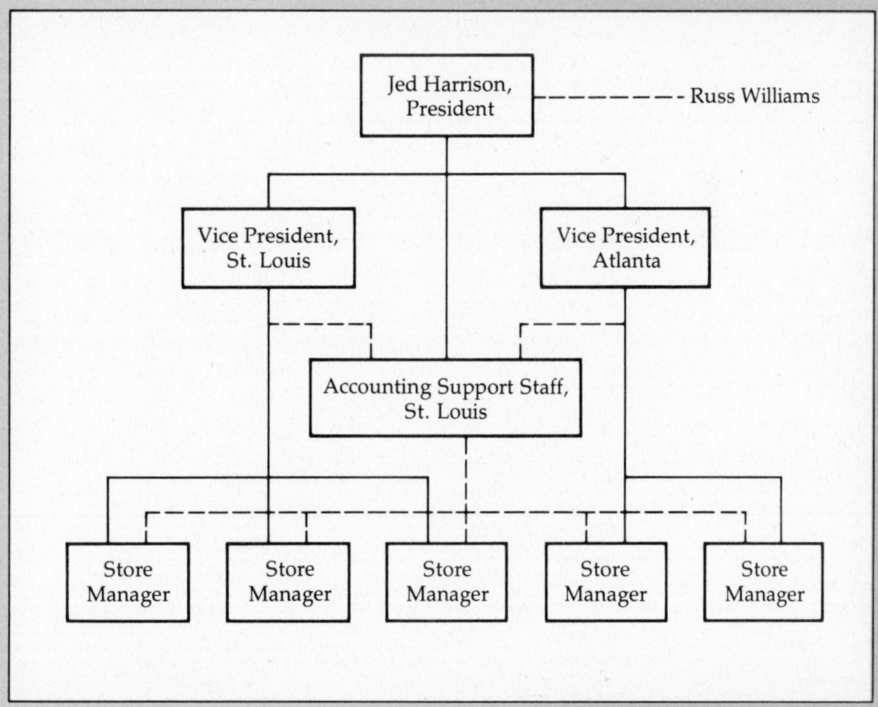

picked each of the store managers in St. Louis and flew to Atlanta to do the same. The two Atlanta stores were situated in affluent suburban areas of the city.

The stores in Atlanta were off to a slow but steady start. The third St. Louis store was not achieving Jed's expected level of sales, but he felt that it was simply a matter of time. Purchasing for all the Sports World's stores was done centrally by Jed. Jed traveled to a number of merchandise marts that previewed the latest fashions in golf and tennis wear. He enjoyed these trips and generally traveled to shows eight weeks a year. In addition, Jed visited the Atlanta stores once a month to examine the progress being made. While a great deal of the stores' merchandise was purchased at the trade stores, many distributors and salespeople visited Jed weekly in the original St. Louis store.

Jed also handled advertising for the five stores. Specials on tennis balls ($1.80/can) and tennis shoes ($15.95/pair) brought customers into the stores where they frequently found these items out of stock. Additionally, when one store in a city was having particularly good luck with a line, Jed would order an intrastore transfer of that product.

One week both Atlanta stores ran out of a popular line of Wilson tennis rackets. The managers called Jed, pleading for more rackets. Jed apologized and said that his orders are filled once every six weeks and that his hands were tied.

Two days later, full-page ads appeared in the Saturday and Sunday editions of the *Atlanta Journal*. The ads offered the same line of Wilson rackets that were no longer in inventory on sale at 25 percent off list price.

Questions

1. How was decision making conducted at Sports World, Inc.?
2. In this case did Jed's military experience prove to be a help or a hindrance?
3. Evaluate the corporate structure of Sports World, Inc.
4. What suggestions could you make to Jed for revising his management techniques?

PART SIX

Making Management Effective

In each of the preceding chapters we tried to point out as often as feasible that the effective manager considers the organization as an open system and management as a process of interrelated activities. Although we can state that decision making, communicating, leading, planning, organizing, motivating, and controlling are all required to formulate and attain objectives in any type of organization, and that all organizations share many characteristics in common, there also are wide variations among organizations. The major internal variables differ for each organization. Similarly, each organization faces a somewhat unique external environment, one that is dynamic, changing over time.

Therefore, while the management process may be fundamentally the same, there are no specific techniques or rules of managing applicable to all organizations at all points in time. Moreover, any time the manager changes one particular aspect of the organization, all other aspects will be affected to some degree. The ripples of change flow outward, as ripples do when a rock is thrown into a pond. The bigger the change, the greater and more enduring its impact on other parts of the organization will be.

Although we attempted to point out these interactions and interrelationships, there was so much material to cover on each topic that we may have slighted this important issue. Therefore, in this concluding part we will place particular stress on interrelationships and contingency considerations as we expand our knowledge of management.

Each topic covered is especially strongly affected by external and internal variables. In Chapter 18 we explore the critical topic of human resource management, a field that probably will become even more important in the 1980s. We will learn some of the methods and considerations in staffing the organization with people able to perform the tasks required and able to formulate and attain its objectives and in helping the people become as productive as possible. Human resource management involves not only motivating but also every management function. It involves planning to determine what the organization's human resource needs are and controlling to evaluate performance and identify people for promotion. Organizing decisions are particularly important. One of the major thrusts in contemporary human resource management, as we will learn, involves altering the organizational structure, redesigning work to increase its intrinsic rewards.

In Chapter 19 we will focus primarily on the contingencies that determine which organizational design is most appropriate for the organization and its subunits. Here we will blend our knowledge of the management process with what we have learned about the external and internal variables.

Finally, in Chapter 20 we will conclude our introduction to management with a discussion of the critical concepts of conflict and change. We will learn that conflict exists in even the best-managed organizations, and that, provided it is managed effectively, conflict can actually play a positive role in organized endeavor. We also will learn about methods and techniques the manager can use to be proactive, a need to which we have often referred. By learning to manage change, the manager enables the organization to adapt successfully to its environment and take advantage of opportunities it offers.

An Interview with Sheila Trifari

Sheila Trifari is Senior Vice President and General Manager of the International Division of Southeast First National Bank of Miami, Florida. Her job is one many would envy, for it involves frequent international travel to all corners of the world. Fluent in Spanish, French, and Portuguese, with an MBA and over 15 years of successful experience in international finance, she is unquestionably well qualified to hold it. Sheila Trifari differs in several ways from the other managers we have interviewed. Beginning with the obvious, she is a woman—one of the most highly placed women in the field of international banking. Second, Ms. Trifari is a true professional career manager. She achieved her position by working her way up the organizational ladder, as opposed to starting her own firm. Her formal management education and training are clearly reflected in her comments. Also, at the time of this interview, Ms. Trifari had not yet reached the top management level. Her perspective is that of an upper middle manager of a substantial, but not enormous, business organization. She is close enough to the top to understand the needs and problems of the organization as a whole, but not quite high enough to implement all of her personal preferences.

Author: Could you briefly describe your current job?

Trifari: In order to describe my job, let me put it into context. The bank has been international for a long time by virtue of its deposits. However, not so on the assets side [the bank's loans and investments]. That's because until 1974 the market in Florida was so lucrative that virtually everything the marketing officers touched turned to gold. Because the management at that time was not wholly familiar with international, they quite logically and rightly preferred to stick to their own state. Then the recession of 1974 came, and the next two years or so were spent working out the problems. By this time, management realized the situation in Florida was changing. There was a great deal of tourism from Latin America and foreign investment coming in, and trade increasing. At that time, a conscious decision was made that for the Southeast organization the international business, both on the liability and asset sides, would be important. My function has really been to build up primarily the asset side and develop for us expertise in our main market, which is Latin America. The last two years have been spent building the infrastructure to accomplish that, particularly the human resources needed to carry on a very aggressive, but prudent, program in building international assets and liabilities.

Author: About how many people report to you?

Trifari: Well, right now that's a little hard to say because there have been changes on changes. The bank is moving from being a multi-bank holding company whereby we had 42 banks each with its own board and president into a one bank holding company, and there have been about four major reorganizations and probably more are coming. I started out with operations, personal banking, and corporate banking departments. The way it's being restructured, operations has been consolidated, with both domestic and international reporting to an operations head. The personal international division is now reporting to a head of personal banking. So I would say that now I've got about 12 officers reporting to me and a staff of about 15. I report to an executive vice-president in charge of all corporate lending.

Author: How much latitude are you allowed in decision making?

Trifari: Very broad; very wide in the sense that there's so much to do in the organization. It's one of those organizations where you touch something and it brings up three questions and each one of those brings up four other matters. So I would say I've got very wide, broad, decision-making power. Of course, I try to keep my superiors informed as well as the people who work with me about what's happening. But it's not a structured environment. In fact, that's what I personally like about it.

Author: Are you able to set the objectives for international banking?

Trifari: Yes. I set the objectives. Then we go over them with the entire group. My deputy then bases his own on mine, and we have an integrated MBO system.

Author: The MBO system that you use, does it basically come from the top down or from the bottom up?

Trifari: In the organization, from the bottom up. In my own division I prefer to do it from the top down and from the bottom up. In other words, we have it go down and then come back, with constant feedback. I don't think there is enough definition from the top as to where we're going to do it any other way at this time.

Author: If there is little definition from above, how do you make your objectives mesh with those of the organization?

Trifari: [Jokingly] I just hope that they are right. Seriously, I don't really know my boss's objectives. You see, we have a lot of people coming in from outside. My boss has only been here three months. He hasn't really had much of a chance to get into his job and see what he's doing, so I can't put the blame upstairs. But as we move I would like to see things coming on down. I believe in a very open style of management because I think that people really do like to know, "What are we all supposed to be doing, and how does my area fit into it?"

Author: Isn't that kind of a strange situation, not knowing what the overall objectives are?

Trifari: Yes, but I think that working in an organization you can sort of extrapolate and, of course, you talk about what you're doing. For instance, I've gone over all of my objectives with my boss, and he understands them. So, even though it isn't done on a formal basis, it takes place on an informal basis.

Author: Is your performance appraised on the basis of your objectives?

Trifari: Yes, but this is really the first year that it's going to be formally appraised. The organization has had MBO, but it hasn't followed up. In other words, everybody does it, but then what? I think that in order to have a successful integrated MBO program, you've got to have constant review to determine if you are really doing what you're supposed to be doing. And if there are changes in the environment, you've got to review and update your objectives.

Author: You've often worked in countries where the prevailing attitudes about the proper role of women are quite different than they are here. How has that affected your ability to perform your job?

Trifari: I've had no problems. If you come in and establish pretty quickly that you have the credentials to do the job and you've got the credibility and backing of your organization, I think people will accept you as an individual. In Latin America, if anything, people went out of their way to be warmer and friendlier to me because I was a woman. Even in Japan, where I was the first woman they had dealt with on my level, there were no problems, perhaps because the Japanese I worked with had lived abroad and realized there are different rules in other societies.

Author: If you were running Southeast Banks, are there any major changes you would implement in the strategies or structure of the bank?

Trifari: I think that right now one doesn't see what either the strategies or the structure are going to be because we're in such a fluid situation. This is in great part due to the changes in legislation. It's only in the last year that the legislature has permitted mergers within the county and now state-wide consolidation. So the corporation is in a very fluid situation. Right now we are using a matrix system, and I sometimes wonder if we are mature enough for it. I would like to see the responsibilities of individual managers defined better. I'd also provide more information about where the corporation is going. I'd try to improve communication.

Author: Do you think that you are using communication technology available effectively?

Trifari: I think that we need a lot more management information, I really do. That's part of the problems we have. We weren't really prepared for sudden consolidation. There is not enough information, you have to spend too much time gathering it, and the quality isn't there. Just as an example, I don't get our risk report [report of existing loans and investments] until about six weeks after the end of the month. Now, I have a good feel for what our assets are because I have to sign everything. But that's a hell of a way to do it. I really need to get the risk report immediately.

Author: What changes and opportunities do you foresee for banking in the 1980s?

Trifari: I think the banking industry is going to undergo unprecedented change. There's no question that during the 1980s there's going to be some form of nationwide banking. The big banks, Citicorp, Bank of America, and various others will survive because of their size. But what's going to happen to a Manufacturer's Hanover or Banker's Trust? What niche are they going to carve out for themselves? That is the question. I think that the competitive forces and the economic forces are going to force banks to decide, "What do we want to do?" And that's where the opportunities lie. As always, the ones that will benefit are those organizations that anticipate change and plan ahead.

Author: In closing, what do you feel enabled you to become a senior vice-president, a corporate level relatively few women have reached?

Trifari: I'm 38, and I've always been committed to a career. I enjoy working. That's what turns me on. A lot of women have not been able to do that. They've taken time out for families, or they felt that the time and effort you have to put in to develop a career just wasn't worth it. So I think the primary factor has been my commitment. I've always enjoyed work, and I think I've had some breaks. I've met the right people at the right time. Each job I had opened up new horizons, and I said to myself, "Gee, I've gotten this far. What about *this* far?"

CHAPTER 18

Human Resource Management

The importance of people has been stressed throughout this book. In this chapter we will focus specifically on effectively managing people, the organization's human resources. We begin with planning human resource needs, recruiting, and selecting the best people for the organization's work. Then we discuss developing human resources through such techniques as training and management development. This is followed by how management can improve the quality of work life to increase satisfaction and, hopefully, productivity. Last, we discuss stress, its causes, and how it can be overcome.

After reading this chapter, you should understand the following important terms and concepts:

human resource planning
job analysis
job description
recruiting
selection
tests
assessment centers
organizational socialization
quality of work life
cafeteria system of compensation
redesigning work
job enrichment
job enlargement
job depth
job scope
stress

Despite the lack of consensus on what it takes for management and the organization to be successful, there are few who would disagree that people are the key ingredient. Without people, there is no organization. Without the *right* people, no organization can attain its objectives and survive. Thus, although the human relations school may have attached excessive importance to the human variable as a determinant in certain situations, managing human resources is without question one of the most important aspects of management.

In larger organizations, specific responsibility for overall management of human resources is held by professionally trained personnel specialists, usually within a staff department. For these specialists to contribute effectively to organizational objectives, they must be knowledgeable and competent in their own field and also well informed about the needs of line management. Moreover, unless line managers understand the scope, potential, and limitations of human resource management techniques, they will be unable to fully use the services of personnel specialists. It therefore is important for all managers to understand and appreciate the techniques and developments of human resource management.

Human Resource Planning, Recruiting, and Selecting

The logical starting point of human resource management is planning. The next step is finding the sort of people the organization needs and then deciding who is to be selected to join it.

Human Resource Planning

When management formulates objectives for the organization, it must also determine what resources will be required to attain them. The needs for money, materials, and equipment are obvious. Few managers overlook them during planning. The necessity for people, the organization's *human* resources, is also seemingly obvious. But unfortunately human resource planning often is not conducted formally or given the degree of attention its importance warrants.

Human resource planning is basically the application of the planning process to staffing and personnel related problems. For convenience, it can be considered as having three stages:

1. Assessment of present supply
2. Assessment of future needs
3. Development of a human resource program to meet future needs

Present Supply. Human resource planning in the ongoing organization logically begins with an assessment of present supply. Management must

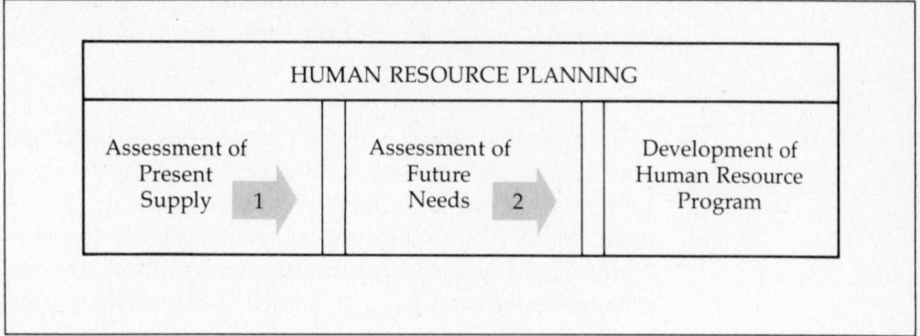

Figure 18-1 Human Resource Planning

determine how many people are involved in the performance of each task required for each of its specific objectives. Complicating this is the high degree of interdependence in many organizations. For example, preparing and placing a single television commercial might involve over 100 people in a large advertising agency. So simple an activity as handling baggage involves many different people at an airline.

Management, in addition, must evaluate the quality of its people. To accomplish this some organizations, such as AT&T, RCA, IBM, Rockwell International, and the U.S. Army have developed a **skills inventory**. This is a written record of the skills of their white- and blue-collar employees and the numbers of people possessing various skills.[1]

Future Needs. This stage of human resource planning is projecting personnel required to attain long- and short-term objectives. For example, if Control Data Corporation, a manufacturer of large computers, were to decide to enter the home computer market and become a leader by 1986, management would have to incorporate in its planning the hiring of research and development personnel with microcomputer expertise and marketing and sales personnel familiar with consumer electronics. Similarly, if the management of your local department store plans a promotional special on linens during the first week in January, it must also determine how many additional sales people will be required to handle the larger customer flow. Naturally, for a major organizational change such as the opening of a new plant or introduction of a major new product, the assessment of future personnel needs is a complex and critical task. In such situations the external labor market must be assessed to determine whether workers are available.

Development of a Human Resource Program. After management has determined what its needs will be, it must develop a program for meeting them. The needs, in essence, are objectives. The program is the means of accomplishing them. The human resource program would consist of a specific timetable and the determination of specific actions required to attract, hire, train, or promote the people required to attain organizational objectives.

Legal Considerations. As we pointed out earlier, legal constraints are a variable that must be taken into account during the planning process. This is particularly true in human resource planning. OSHA (Occupational Safety and Health Act), for example, sets standards for safety in many industries. Title VII of the 1964 Civil Rights Act prohibits discrimination on the basis of race, color, sex, religion, or national origin. The Equal Pay Act of 1963 prohibits wage discrimination based on sex. The Age Discrimination Act of 1967 prohibits discrimination against the elderly. There are countless other federal regulations and each state also regulates how management can act in many situations. Union contracts also frequently impose legal restraints on human resource programs by restricting who can be promoted, what work certain people can perform, and so on.

Job Analysis. For management to hire appropriate people, it must know in detail what tasks must be performed effectively and what the personal and social characteristics of the work are. These determinations are accomplished through **job analysis**.

There are several methods for analyzing jobs.[2] One is to observe the workers and formally identify and record the tasks and activities performed. A second method is obtaining such information by interviewing the worker or supervisor. This, of course, would probably be less accurate due to perceptual distortion. A third method is to have the worker fill out a questionnaire or write a description of the job and its requirements. The information obtained through job analysis is the foundation for most subsequent human resource planning, recruiting, and other concerns. Its most immediate use is to create a **job description**. This is a summary of the major tasks, skill requirements, and authority of the different types of jobs in the organization. Each major category of job, such as secretary, shipping clerk, advertising manager, or systems analyst would require a different description. Feature 18-1 illustrates a typical job description.

Recruiting

Recruiting is the building of a pool of candidates for each job from which the organization can select the most appropriate. The amount of recruiting required is largely a function of the difference between future needs and current personnel supply, taking into account such factors as retirement, turnover, termination, and expansion into new fields of endeavor. Organizations usually recruit from both external and internal sources.

External means of recruiting would include placing ads in newspapers and trade magazines, using an employment agency or executive search firm, and sending recruiters to college campuses. Some organizations make it known that people in their community are welcome to come by the personnel office and apply for future vacancies.

FEATURE 18-1

Job Description and Specifications for a Personnel Manager

Job Description

General Description

Performs responsible administrative work managing personnel activities of a large state agency or institution. Work involves responsibility for the planning and administration of a personnel program which includes recruitment, examination, selection, evaluation, appointment, promotion, transfer, and recommended change of status of agency employees, and a system of communication for disseminating necessary information to workers. Works under general supervision, exercising initiative and independent judgment in the performance of assigned tasks.

Examples of Work Performed

Participates in overall planning and policy making to provide effective and uniform personnel services.

Communicates policy through organization levels by bulletin, meetings, and personal contact.

Interviews applicants, evaluates qualifications, classifies applications.

Recruits and screens applicants to fill vacancies and reviews applications of qualified persons.

Confers with supervisors on personnel matters, including placement problems, retention or release of probationary employees, transfers, demotions, and dismissals of permanent employees.

Supervises administration of tests.

Initiates personnel training activities and coordinates these activities with work of officials and supervisors.

Establishes effective service rating system, trains unit supervisors in making employee evaluations.

Maintains employee personnel files.

Supervises a group of employees directly and through subordinates.

Performs related work as assigned.

Job Specifications

General Qualification Requirements

Experience and training

Should have considerable experience in personnel administration.

Education

Graduation from a four-year college or university, with major work in education and personnel administration.

Knowledge, skills, and abilities

Considerable knowledge of principles and practices of personnel administration; selection and assignment of personnel; job evaluation.

SOURCE: William F. Glueck, *Personnel: A Diagnostic Approach*, rev. ed. (Dallas: Business Publications, 1978), p. 108. © 1978 by Business Publications, Inc.

Most organizations prefer to recruit from within to the greatest degree possible. Promoting from within is less costly than an external source and also tends to increase employee loyalty, morale, and motivation. As we might expect from the expectancy theory of motivation, if people believe that the company is very likely to fill promotions from within based on how effectively people work, they should be motivated to work more effectively. A potential disadvantage of promoting exclusively from within is that qualified people with fresh viewpoints are not being brought into the organization, which may cause stagnation in thinking.

A popular technique for internal recruiting is to post job openings and encourage qualified people to apply. Some organizations have a policy requiring that all employees be notified of any job opening within the company and be given an opportunity to apply before outsiders are considered. An excellent internal source of recruits is encouraging employees to refer friends. Some organizations pay their employees a bonus for referrals who are hired.

Recruiting Problems. The major problem area in recruiting stems from the recruiter's desire to "sell" the company. Because of this, the recruiter may overstate the positive aspects of the job and company and gloss over or minimize problem areas. As a result, the job candidate may develop unreasonable expectations. Studies indicate that creating unreasonable expectations prior to hiring results in increased dissatisfaction and turnover.[3] To cope with this problem certain companies, such as Texas Instruments and New England Bell, have designed a program called Realistic Job Previews (RJP) to give candidates both sides of the story. These programs have significantly reduced dissatisfaction and turnover.[4]

Selection

In the selection phase of human resource planning and development, management chooses the most appropriate candidates from the pool of applicants created by recruiting. In most cases, the person chosen should be the one who appears to have the best qualifications to perform the actual job being filled, as opposed to the candidate who may seem most promotable. An objective selection decision may be based on the candidate's education, skill level, past experience, and personal characteristics, as appropriate. When the job is one for which technical knowledge is the primary determinant of performance, such as research scientist, education and scientific background would probably be most important. For management positions, particularly those on higher levels, interpersonal skills and the "chemistry" between the candidate and superiors and subordinates is critical. Effective recruiting and selection is a form of preliminary control over the quality of human resources.

The three most widely used methods of gathering information for selection decisions are testing, interviews, and assessment centers.

Tests. Behavioral scientists have developed a variety of tests that attempt to predict how effectively a candidate will be able to perform a given job. One type of selection test measures the ability to perform tasks relevant to the job. Examples would be a typing and shorthand test, demonstrating ability to operate a machine, and having the candidate make an oral or written presentation to demonstrate verbal ability. Another type of test measures psychological characteristics such as intelligence, motivation, drive, open-mindedness, self-confidence, emotional stability, and attention to detail. For a test to be useful in selection, there must be a significant relationship between a high score and job performance; that is, management must evaluate its tests to determine whether people who did well on them did in fact turn out to be more effective on the job than those with lower scores. Failure to conform to the testing guidelines established by the Equal Employment Opportunity Commission can result in legal action by workers who can claim the organization's personnel practices are discriminatory.

Similar requirements also apply to the use of application forms for selection. Although not a true test of ability or psychological characteristics, application forms have been successfully used to differentiate between more and less qualified people.[5] For example, specific information requested on the application regarding years of past experience, salary history, amount of education, type of school attended, hobbies, etc. may be used to select applicants, if these background factors can differentiate effective from less effective employees already working for the organization.

Assessment Centers. Assessment centers were first developed during World War II to screen and assess agents for the OSS, the forerunner of the CIA. AT&T was the first private company to use an assessment center as an aid in selecting managers and sales personnel. Today, several large firms such as J. C. Penney, General Electric, Sears, and IBM use them, typically for selection of candidates for promotion.

An assessment center measures ability to perform job-related tasks through simulation techniques. One, the "in-basket," places the candidate in the role of manager of a fictitious company who has three hours to decide how to respond to a variety of letters, memos, and information. During this time the candidate must make decisions, communicate with subordinates in writing, delegate authority, set up meetings, assign priorities, and so on. Another technique is a leaderless simulated organization meeting. The candidates are rated on such characteristics as verbal ability, persuasiveness, and interpersonal skills. Some other assessment center techniques are making oral presentations to groups, role playing, intelligence and psychological tests, and formal interviews.

Studies show that assessment centers are excellent predictors of job performance.[6] However, they are very costly and therefore usually used only by large, successful companies.

Interviews. Interviews are by far the most widely used selection technique. Even nonmanagerial workers are seldom hired without at least one interview. The selection of a high-level manager may involve dozens of interviews over the course of several months. However, studies have found a number of problems that occur during interviews which decrease their effectiveness as a selection tool.[7]

Many of these problems are perceptual and psychological in origin. For example, there is a tendency to make a decision about the candidate based on the first impression and disregard or misinterpret what is said during the rest of the interview. Another mistake is to evaluate an applicant relative to the person interviewed immediately before. If the earlier person was particularly poor, a mediocre candidate may be rated good or very good. There is also a tendency for interviewers to rate more favorably candidates whose appearance, social attitudes, and mannerisms are most like their own.

Studies show that structured interviews in which questions and responses are standardized and recorded increase accuracy.[8] Also, to effectively predict job performance, an interview must focus on information specifically related to the job. Stressing this, John B. Miner and Mary Miner state, "If an interviewer knows a lot about the job he is interviewing for and what kinds of people tend to succeed in it, he or she will be more objective and the results will be better."[9]

Some general recommendations for effective interviewing are:

1. Create rapport with the candidate and allow him or her to feel comfortable.
2. Focus on job requirements throughout the interview.
3. Don't evaluate on first impressions. Wait until all information is on hand.
4. Have a set of structured questions that all applicants will be asked. However, be flexible enough to explore other issues that arise.

Human Resource Development

At one time, staffing and personnel activities focused almost exclusively on recruiting and selecting. The idea was that once you found the right people, they would be able to get the job done. Modern, well-managed organizations now recognize that acquiring appropriate people is only the beginning of human resource management. Whereas most of an organization's resources are material objects that usually depreciate in value over time, its human resources can and should appreciate substantially in value as years pass. Thus, for the good of both the organization and its employees as individuals, management should undertake a systematic program to develop its human resources to full potential.

A successful human resource development program will result in a work force better able and better motivated to perform the tasks of the organization. Hence, productivity should increase, which in turn means that the organization's human resources have increased in value. For example, if a training program enabled assembly workers to increase output by 10 percent with no increase in costs, the organization's return on its investment in people would be that much greater.

Now we will discuss a number of techniques for developing people's potential: performance appraisal, use of the reward system, training and development, and career management. The first step in making the new person as productive as possible, however, is proper orientation and socialization.

Orientation and Socialization

If management wants the new employee to be successful on the job, it must keep in mind that organizations are social systems and that each person is a unique being. When the newly hired person arrives, he or she brings the attitudes and expectations acquired through past personal and work experiences. These may or may not mesh with the prevailing social and work characteristics of the new position. For example, the new person's last boss may have been highly authoritarian and strongly preferred written communication. He may therefore believe that it is desirable to send memos rather than pick up the telephone, even though the new superior in fact prefers oral communication.

Commenting on this, Carroll and Tosi state, "Thus, more often than not, the typical organization member has a set of expectations about his job which are somewhat unrealistic in terms of the organization's expectations. A period of adjustment and change takes place, and gradually the organization's expectations become better known to the individual and management becomes more aware of the individual's expectations."[10] During this adjustment period, the individual acquires new work attitudes through organizational socialization. Edgar Schein defines **organizational socialization** as "the process of 'learning the ropes,' the process of being indoctrinated and trained, the process of being taught what is important in an organization or some subunit thereof."[11]

Organizations employ a number of devices, both formal and informal, to socialize an individual. Formally, the organization provides the individual with information about itself during recruitment in an effort to ensure that the new candidate's expectations are realistic. This is often followed by training in specific skills and what is considered effective performance. Rules, procedures, and guidance from superiors are additional formal ways of socializing people in an organization. From informal work groups, as discussed earlier, the new individual learns the unwritten rules of the organization, who the managers with the most true power are, what the real chances for promotion and reward are, and what fellow workers consider to be an appropriate level of performance. As mentioned earlier, the informal group's norms, attitudes, and values can either support or work against the objectives and attitudes of the formal organization.

If the manager does not make an active effort to socialize new subordinates, they may become disappointed due to unrealistic expectations, assume that what occurred at their last job is appropriate behavior, or make other incorrect assumptions about the work. The manager should also keep in mind that what the new individual learns through socialization may come as a shock. A study of college graduates hired by a large auto manufacturer found that in comparison with those who stayed with the company, people who were terminated found most of the characteristics of the job worse than they had initially expected.[12]

Another study found a strong relationship between the amount of challenge new management trainees received and their subsequent career progress. Those individuals whose initial tasks were demanding and challenging developed high performance standards and were better prepared for future assignments than those given less challenging tasks. The former group was also promoted more rapidly.[13]

It is important to realize, however, that there are limits to what can be taught through organizational socialization. As Carroll and Tosi went on to state, " . . . the stereotyped idea of an individual being simply a pawn molded by an organization is not an appropriate way to view reality. It certainly is true that individuals are shaped by their organizational environments. However, organizations must, of necessity, adapt to the needs and values of various individuals or their very existence is threatened. Unless an organization can continue to secure the services of new members, it will atrophy and die."[14]

Performance Appraisal

Assuming the individual is adequately socialized, the logical first step in developing human resources is to determine how effectively people are performing at present. This is the purpose of performance appraisal, which can be thought of as an extension of the control function. As you should recall, the control process involves setting standards, measurement of results to determine deviation from standards, and corrective action, if needed. Similarly, performance appraisal requires managers to gather information on how effective each individual is at accomplishing delegated duties. Communicating this information to subordinates enables them to know how well they are doing and to correct less than acceptable behavior. Performance appraisal also permits management to identify the outstanding performers and in effect raise their performance standards by promoting them to more challenging positions.

In basic terms, however, performance appraisal serves three general purposes: administrative, informational, and motivational.

FEATURE 18-2

How American Workers Feel About Their Jobs

In May 1978, *Psychology Today* magazine summarized the results of an intensive survey of worker attitudes conducted under the supervision of Patricia A. Renwick and Edward E. Lawler. A total of 23,008 people responded to the questionnaire, and a representative sample of 2,300 were analyzed. Because of the size of this sample, the tables below almost certainly are a valid indication of the feelings of workers in the areas described. It should be noted, however, that the respondents were on average significantly better educated and better paid than the average U.S. worker. Therefore, the results more closely reflect views of managerial, professional, technical, and clerical workers than operatives of equipment and unskilled workers.

"All in all, I am satisfied with my job."

Strongly disagree	7.8%
Disagree	10.6%
Slightly disagree	7.5%
Neither agree nor disagree	5.7%
Slightly agree	15.1%
Agree	35.6%
Strongly agree	17.6%

"How satisfied are you with each of the following aspects of your job? And how important to you is each of them?" [Respondents were asked to choose among different degrees of importance and satisfaction for each job feature. Based on averages of their responses, the numbers below rank each from 1 (most important to the group or most often satisfying) to 18 (least important or least often satisfying).]

	Importance	Satisfaction
Chances to do something that make you feel good about yourself	1	8
Chances to accomplish something worthwhile	2	6
Chances to learn new things	3	10
Opportunity to develop your skills and abilities	4	12
The amount of freedom you have on your job	5	2

continues on page 594

FEATURE 18-2, continued

	Importance	Satisfaction
Chances you have to do things you do best	6	11
The resources you have to do your job	7	9
The respect you receive from people you work with	8	3
Amount of information you get about your job performance	9	17
Your chances for taking part in making decisions	10	14
The amount of job security you have	11	5
Amount of pay you get	12	16
The way you are treated by the people you work with	13	4
The friendliness of people you work with	14	1
Amount of praise you get for job well done	15	15
The amount of fringe benefits you get	16	7
Chances for getting a promotion	17	18
Physical surroundings of your job	18	13

"If you would continue to work, what is the one most important reason?"

	Male	Female
I enjoy what I do on my job.	29.0%	28.6%
I derive the major part of my identity from my job.	25.8%	27.5%
Work keeps me from being bored.	17.4%	18.2%
My work is important and valuable to others.	13.9%	10.8%
I enjoy the company of my coworkers.	5.3%	8.1%
I would feel guilty if I did not contribute to society through gainful employment.	4.4%	3.4%
I would continue out of habit.	4.2%	3.4%

SOURCE: *Psychology Today*, May 1978, pp. 56 and 57. © 1978 Ziff-Davis Publishing Co.

Administrative Functions. Every organization has a continuous need to evaluate its personnel in order to make administrative decisions regarding promotion, transfer, and termination. Promotion helps the organization by enabling it to use a person to full potential. It helps the individual by satisfying needs for achievement, challenge, and self-esteem. Transfer may be used to give a person a broader range of experience or because management feels he or she will be more effective in a different job. Sometimes transfer is used when a person is not performing effectively, but due to longevity and past contributions management feels termination would be unethical. A transfer in such situations puts the poor performer in a position where he or she can still make a contribution, but will not block the career progress of a high performing younger person or actually impede the attainment of organizational objectives. In situations where an individual has been given feedback and sufficient opportunity to improve performance, but is unwilling or unable to meet the organization's standards, termination is necessary for organizational objectives to be met. Whatever the administrative situation, a logical decision clearly cannot be made without an effective means of appraising performance.

Informational Functions. Performance appraisal is also needed to provide people with information about their relative level of performance. When done correctly, the individual will learn not only whether his or her performance is acceptable, but also specifically what strengths and weaknesses he or she has and which areas could be improved.

Motivational Functions. Performance appraisal is also an important means of motivating people. By identifying strong performers, management is able to reward them fairly with praise, pay, and promotion. Consistent, positive reinforcement for behavior associated with high performance should lead to similar behavior in the future. As you may have already realized, the informational, administrative, and motivational functions of performance appraisal are interrelated. That is, information leading to an administrative decision to promote a person should have a positive effect on motivating a person to perform well.

Making Performance Appraisal Effective. A recent survey found that over 90 percent of companies have some type of appraisal system, but several factors determine whether performance appraisal is effective.[15] To begin, most often a subordinate's performance is evaluated by his or her immediate superior. Therefore, this superior must be capable of evaluating performance accurately and not base appraisal on personal feelings toward the subordinate. The superior must also be able to communicate the appraisal to the subordinate. This can be quite difficult when performance is poor, especially if the superior has never been trained in techniques for communicating. Because of these potential problems formal appraisal systems may be resisted by managers.[16]

Intensive studies of performance appraisal at General Electric led to several significant conclusions.[17] One is that criticism is not an effective way for a manager to communicate information on performance deficits to subordinates. Criticism often results in defensive behavior. The subordinate becomes more concerned with defending himself than with the problem areas and means of improving performance. As one group of writers states, "The individual must be open to feedback and willing to discuss his or her performance in a non-defensive manner for a useful appraisal to take place."[18] This makes it necessary for the superior to create a relaxed, nonthreatening climate in which subordinates feel able to discuss their performance problems openly.

The manager must fully understand the difference between criticism and providing feedback on performance. Criticism is usually one-way communication delivered in harsh tones of voice. To provide effective feedback one must permit a two-way, problem-solving discussion on the areas where improvement is needed. For example, instead of saying, "Your performance for the last two months has been terrible," one could say, "John, our acceptable standard for wastage is 2 percent of materials used. Over the past two months your wastage level has been 5 percent. Why do you think this happened?" Note that phrasing feedback in this way permits management to determine whether it was the individual or some other factor that caused poor performance.

A second conclusion of the General Electric study was that giving subordinates information on their performance only once or twice a year is not very useful. Scheduling formal appraisal sessions once or twice a year is necessary. However, appraisal should also take place whenever necessary, as a day-to-day activity, or at least as often as the situation warrants. If the subordinate is working on a new, short-term project, performance should be appraised two or three times a month. If a subordinate has little confidence in his abilities, the manager may want to discuss good performance every few days to build his or her self-concept. With experienced, confident, proven performers, the manager may wish to intervene only as often as needed to maintain control.

A third finding of the General Electric studies was that performance and salary should not be discussed at the same time. Rather, a subordinate's strengths and weaknesses should be discussed in a separate session from the discussion of the administrative ramifications of performance.

Douglas McGregor strongly advocates a results-oriented approach to performance appraisal.[19] According to him, traditional appraisals are inadequate because they focus on personality traits such as cooperativeness, initiative, reliability, attitude, and so on. This forces the manager to be judgmental rather than objective. Also, telling a subordinate that he or she is not very cooperative or has a bad attitude provides little information about what he or she is specifically doing wrong and should do differently. Instead, according to McGregor, the manager and subordinate should set mutually agreeable

Table 18-1 Ambiguous Versus Behavioral Job Objectives

Ambiguous Job Objectives	Terminal Behavior Job Objectives
1. To demonstrate satisfactory ability on the job and perform at required standards	1. To operate the press such that a minimum of 120 pieces are produced correctly each hour, with no more than 1 incorrect (defective) piece produced in any hour
2. To develop a positive attitude toward the work and to be dependable	2. To give evidence of willingness to perform the job by not being absent from work except for those reasons and on those days specified by the union agreement; and by being at the proper work place when the shift bell sounds
3. To be able to communicate effectively with subordinates	3. To notify each division head of all changes in the budget by written memo to each no later than one day after notification of such change reaches your desk

SOURCE: Craig Schneier, "Content Validity: The Necessity of a Behavioral Job Description," *The Personnel Administrator*, February 1976. Reprinted by permission.

objectives that will serve as a standard for future appraisals. When specific objectives cannot be set, the manager should provide the subordinate with information that describes desirable behavior, as opposed to personality traits or ambiguous job objectives. An example of this is shown in Table 18-1.

As we have mentioned briefly, two-way communication is desirable for performance appraisal to be most effective. The employee must be able to freely discuss why performance was substandard, what may have caused this, and how he or she will attempt to correct the problem. Finally, a manager should attempt to perceive subordinates' performance with as little bias as possible. "For example, when asked to rate subordinates in a number of traits (such as dependability and attitude) supervisor ratings show a 'halo effect' such that a given subordinate tends to be rated the same on all traits even though that individual may actually be higher on some than others. It has also been shown that some supervisors tend to rate everyone high, while others rate everyone low, a fact that further serves to reduce the accuracy and usefulness of performance ratings."[20]

Training and Development

Organizations have a continuous need to improve the overall quality of their human resources. One way of accomplishing this is by recruiting and selecting more qualified and capable people as new employees. This alone, however, will not suffice. Management should also undertake a systematic program to build the skills of its current employees and help them grow to full potential within the organization. Its primary means of accomplishing this is through training and development programs.

Training is teaching employees skills that will make them more effective in their current jobs. Development refers to building skills and abilities that the employee will need to perform effectively in a future position. The ultimate objective of both training and development is to ensure that the organization will always have a sufficient number of people with the skills and abilities needed to attain the organization's objectives.

The importance of training is widely recognized. Unfortunately, however, many managers fail to appreciate the complexities involved. As one writer states, "Training programs, unfortunately, are sometimes developed and applied without sufficient analysis and planning. Training may be undertaken because 'It's the thing to do,' imitating other firms in the area which have begun to use some particular program; the pattern is copied almost as if it were the latest fashion, without considering carefully whether the new style really fits the needs of the situation."[21]

There are three basic situations in which training generally is useful and needed. The first is when a person first joins the organization. The second is when an employee is assigned to a different position or given new tasks to perform. The third is when appraisal reveals that a person lacks certain skills required to perform the job effectively.

Requisites for Effective Training. A detailed discussion of training program design is beyond the scope of this book. Training has become a large, specialized field. The specific techniques are many and must be tailored to the job and organization. The following, however, are some general requirements for a training program to be effective:

1. People should be motivated to learn. They should understand the objectives of the program and how it will improve their effectiveness and thereby their own need satisfaction.
2. Management should create a climate conducive to learning. This includes encouragement, active involvement of the trainees in the process, a supportive attitude on the part of the trainer, and a willingness to answer questions. The physical setting may also be important. Some organizations find it desirable to conduct training in special centers, rather than on the premises of the organization.
3. If the skills taught are complex, training should be broken into sequential stages. The trainee should be given an opportunity to practice the skills acquired at each step before proceeding to the next phase of the sequence.
4. Trainees should receive feedback on their performance and positive reinforcement for learning. This can come in the form of praise and recog-

nition from the trainer. Or, as some of the new computerized teaching systems permit, immediate, direct feedback when a problem has been solved correctly.[22]

Management Development

Both training and development should be employed at all levels of the organization. However, in practice systematic development programs are most often used to groom managers for promotion. As with training, considerable analysis and planning are required for management development to be successful.

The organization must first determine through performance appraisal what the abilities of its present managers are. Then, through job analysis, management should determine what skills and abilities are needed to perform each line and staff job in the organization. This enables the organization to determine which of its managers are best qualified to fill each position and which require training and development. After these determinations, management should construct a timetable for developing specific individuals who probably will be promoted or transferred.

Development and Motivation. Managerial development, of course, is primarily undertaken to ensure that managers have the skills needed to attain organizational objectives. Another consideration, not unrelated to this, is the need to provide satisfaction of higher level needs for achievement, challenge, and self-actualization. Unfortunately, some organizations do not provide sufficient opportunities to satisfy these needs through additional responsibility and promotion. One study found that recent MBA graduates reported a large discrepancy between their expectations for personal growth and development opportunities and what the companies actually provided. When these expectations were important, the people usually quit.[23] Management turnover is, needless to say, very undesirable because of the high cost of recruiting managers and integrating them into the organization. Replacing an employee can cost several times his or her monthly salary.

Techniques for Management Development. Management development can take place through lectures, small group discussions, case studies, readings, business games, and role playing. Courses in management and the many seminars on special topics given each year are, of course, variations on management development. Job rotation is also a widely used technique for development. By rotating a junior-level manager through various departments for periods of three months to a year, the organization gives the new manager exposure to a wide range of activities. As a result, the young manager should become aware of the various problems of different departments, the need for coordination, the informal organization, and the interrelationships between objectives of different subunits of the organization. This knowledge is vital to success in higher level positions and useful for even lower level ones.

An important means of developing managers is through the work they perform. Some firms assign new managers work that is so trivial that they become dissatisfied. "Recognizing this problem, some companies such as AT&T, Procter & Gamble, and Ford have developed programs in which prospective managers are given relatively challenging assignments at the very outset—problems which will test their ingenuity but presumably not go beyond their capacity to solve. Typically, such assignments initially concern responsible operating activities and, after a year or so, require leading an ongoing work team."[24]

Career Management

An extension of management development, career management programs have been developed by a variety of companies and consulting firms since the 1970s. One writer describes career management as a formal program "designed to develop programs or paths by which employees progress in the organization, that helps them develop themselves to their fullest capacity, and that makes the best use of their talents from the organization's point of view."[25] Career management programs help the organization use its people to full potential and helps the individuals achieve their capacities to the fullest.

A formal career management program encourages people to perceive their employment with the organization as "a meaningful series of positions that contribute to the organization and to his or her own development."[26] This is important because studies indicate that people usually have a rather passive attitude toward their careers. They tend to allow important career decisions to be initiated by others, rather than basing them on their own interests, needs, and goals.[27] According to writers and researchers in the field, career management programs result in greater commitment to the organization, increased motivation and productivity, and less turnover and underutilization of employees.[28]

Improving the Quality of Work Life

One of the most important recent developments in human resource management has been the creation of formal programs and techniques to improve the quality of work life. J. Lloyd Suttle defines **quality of work life** as "the degree to which members of a work organization are able to satisfy important personal needs through their experiences in the organization."[29]

In the United States, emphasis on improving the quality of work life has been stimulated by several recently established public and private institutions such as the National Quality of Work Center, the Work in America Institute, the Ohio Quality of Work Center, and the Center for Quality of Work Life at UCLA. According to Suttle, "organized labor has also exhibited a growing interest not only in encouraging but also in participating in the design of organizational change activity aimed at improving the quality of work life. As further evidence of this attention or perhaps as a result of it, one recent reviewer has estimated that more than 2000 public and private enterprises, including business and nonprofit organizations and also state and local governments, are currently involved in some formal change activity aimed at improving the quality of work life. The number of individual plants, offices, and work places where such activities are underway is perhaps many times that number."[30] Moreover, interest in quality of work life has spread to other Western industrialized nations.

Quality of work life can be improved by changing any organizational variable that affects people.[31] This includes techniques we have already discussed, such as decentralization of authority, training, management development, career management programs, effective performance appraisal, learning to manage conflict and change, and training managers to be more effective at communication and intergroup relations. All of these attempt to provide people with added opportunities to satisfy active personal needs while also making the organization more effective at attaining its objectives.

In the remainder of this chapter we will elaborate on three particularly significant areas affecting quality of work life: the reward system, work redesign, and stress.

The Reward System

The type and quantity of rewards offered by the organization are critical to the quality of work life. Research indicates that rewards influence the decisions people make regarding whether they should join the organization, how much they should produce, absenteeism, and when and if they should quit.[32] Many studies have found that absenteeism and turnover are directly related to satisfaction with extrinsic rewards.[33] When the workplace is pleasant and provides need satisfaction, absenteeism tends to be low. When it is unpleasant, absenteeism will significantly increase.

Money and Motivation. Money is the most obvious way in which the organization rewards its people. The controversy over the extent to which money is capable of motivating people to perform more effectively goes back to the rise of the human relations movement. Human relationists contended that a person's social needs were of primary importance, as opposed to the scientific management view that economic rewards would always increase motivation.

Although Frederic Herzberg concluded that most people view pay as a hygiene factor that prevents dissatisfaction, many behavioral scientists feel that money can serve as a motivator in certain situations. One writer states that "Applying Maslow's need theory to pay leads to the conclusion that pay can serve many needs—physiological, security, and recognition . . . In studies of motivation, Frederick Herzberg found that often money is a hygiene factor—that is, it did not affect behavior. If pay could be tied more directly to performance, however, it *could* become a motivator of behavior."[34]

This view has received research support from behavioral scientists investigating expectancy theory.[35] They have found that pay will lead to greater performance provided certain conditions exist. The first is that the person must place a high value on pay. The second is that the person must expect that pay and performance are related, that increased performance will lead to increased pay. It is clearly desirable for employees to perceive a link between pay and performance. However, studies have shown that while managers often claim to pay on the basis of performance, they actually primarily compensate on the basis of seniority and attendance, not merit.[36]

Edward Lawler offers the following suggestion for establishing a relationship between pay and performance:

> Each person's pay would be divided into three components. One part would be for the job the employee is doing, and everybody who holds a similar job would get the same amount. A second part of the pay package would be determined by seniority and cost-of-living factors; everybody in the company would receive this, and the amount would be automatically adjusted each year. The third part of the package, however, would not be automatic; it would be individualized so that the amount paid would be based upon each person's performance during the immediately preceding period. The poor performer in the organization should find that this part of his or her pay package is minimal, while the good performer should find that this part of his or her pay is at least as great as the other two parts combined. This would not be a raise, however, since it could vary from year to year, depending on the individual's performance during the last performance period. Salary increases or raises would come only with changes in responsibility, cost of living, or seniority. The merit portion of the pay package would be highly variable, so that if a person's performance fell off, his or her pay would also be decreased by a cut in the size of the merit pay. The purpose of this kind of system is, of course, to make a large proportion of an individual's pay depend upon performance during the current period. Thus, performance is chronologically tied to large changes in pay.[37]

Fringe Benefits. Long before the term *quality of work life* was coined, organizations attempted to improve it by augmenting monetary rewards with fringe benefits. Today, it is virtually taken for granted that fringe benefits such as vacations, sick leave, health and life insurance, and pension plans are part of any permanent job. The traditional approach to fringe benefits has been to offer all employees at the same organizational level the same benefits. However, this does not take into account differences among people.

Research clearly shows that benefits valued by one employee are not necessarily valued by others.[38] The perceived value of benefits is affected by such factors as age, marital status, and family size. For example, persons with large families are usually highly concerned with comprehensive medical benefits and life insurance. Older people tend to be more concerned with retirement benefits, younger ones with immediate cash. Recognizing this, some organizations have developed what is referred to as a **cafeteria system**

of compensation. The employee is permitted to select, within limits, a package most appropriate for him or her personally.

Although there are clear benefits to cafeteria compensation, there are also some drawbacks. The overall cost of benefits is higher because of increased administrative costs and because benefits such as insurance are less expensive when purchased in large amounts. Another problem is the need to educate employees about the options available to them and how they affect the person both currently and in the future. However, TRW implemented a cafeteria program in 1974 and found that employees are able to make informed choices when given sufficient information and that most wished changes in their benefits when offered the opportunity to have them.[39]

Work Redesign

Much of early management thought revolved around designing tasks to take maximum advantage of specialized division of labor, technology, and automation. As the American worker grew more prosperous, and cultural and societal values changed, industry began to experience problems related to the nature of work. Increasing numbers of people began to find highly specialized, repetitive tasks boring and demotivating. Absenteeism and turnover increased and there were even instances of sabotage. Consequently, the productivity gains one normally would realize from high specialization diminished significantly. To correct this problem, a number of progressive firms began experimenting with **redesigning work** so that it would provide greater intrinsic rewards and more opportunity to satisfy higher level needs for achievement, challenge, and self-actualization. The hope of management, of course, was that the increased satisfaction resulting from these changes would improve productivity and reduce the costs associated with absenteeism, turnover, and poor quality.

Job Enrichment and Job Enlargement. The two most widely used methods of work design are referred to as job enrichment and job enlargement. These methods involve increasing the amount of job scope or job depth.

Job scope is the number of different operations a worker performs and how frequently these are repeated. Job scope is referred to as *narrow* if the person performs only a few operations which are repeated frequently. Assembly-line jobs are a typical example. When job scope is wide, a person performs many different operations and repeats them infrequently. A short order cook's job is usually wide in scope relative to the job of the person who cooks hamburgers at a Burger King.

Job depth is the relative amount of influence a worker has over the job itself and the work environment. This would include such factors as the amount of autonomy the worker has in planning and performing the work, setting work pace, and relative participation in decision making. A laboratory assistant's job would have low depth if it were restricted to setting up chemicals and equipment and cleaning the lab. It would have high depth if

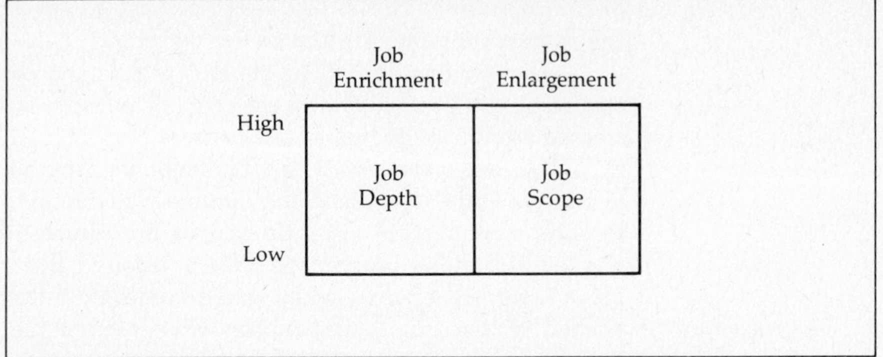

Figure 18-2 Comparison of Job Enrichment and Job Enlargement

the assistant could also order chemicals and equipment, perform some basic experiments, and prepare reports of results.

Jobs can be redesigned by changing either or both the job depth and job scope. **Job enlargement** refers to redesigning work to increase job scope. **Job enrichment** refers to redesigning work to increase job depth. The difference is illustrated in Figure 18-2.

When Work Redesign Is Desirable. Improving motivation and productivity through work redesign is another concept strongly based on Herzberg's two-factor theory of motivation. Herzberg's studies, as you should recall, concluded that work itself was a motivator, money was primarily a hygiene factor. It therefore seemed logical to management theorists and practitioners that changing work to increase the intrinsic rewards it offered should increase motivation and productivity. This, unfortunately, did not always prove true. Later studies of motivation (cited in Chapter 10) indicated that Herzberg's theory is not valid for all people and all situations. Therefore, job redesign is only appropriate for individuals and organizations with certain characteristics. These characteristics are summarized in a model originally developed by Richard Hackman and Greg Oldham. Based on a review of work redesign research, this model is illustrated in Figure 18-3.

According to Hackman and Oldham, there are three psychological states that determine a person's job satisfaction and motivation. The first, *experienced meaningfulness of work*, is the extent to which the person perceives work as important, valuable, and worthwhile. *Experienced responsibility* is the extent to which an individual feels both responsible and accountable for the results of his own work. *Knowledge of results* is the degree to which a person attains from the work an understanding of how effectively they are performing. Those jobs designed to allow *certain* individuals to experience these three states to a high degree should result in: high motivation from the job itself, high quality work performance, high satisfaction with the work, and low absenteeism and turnover.

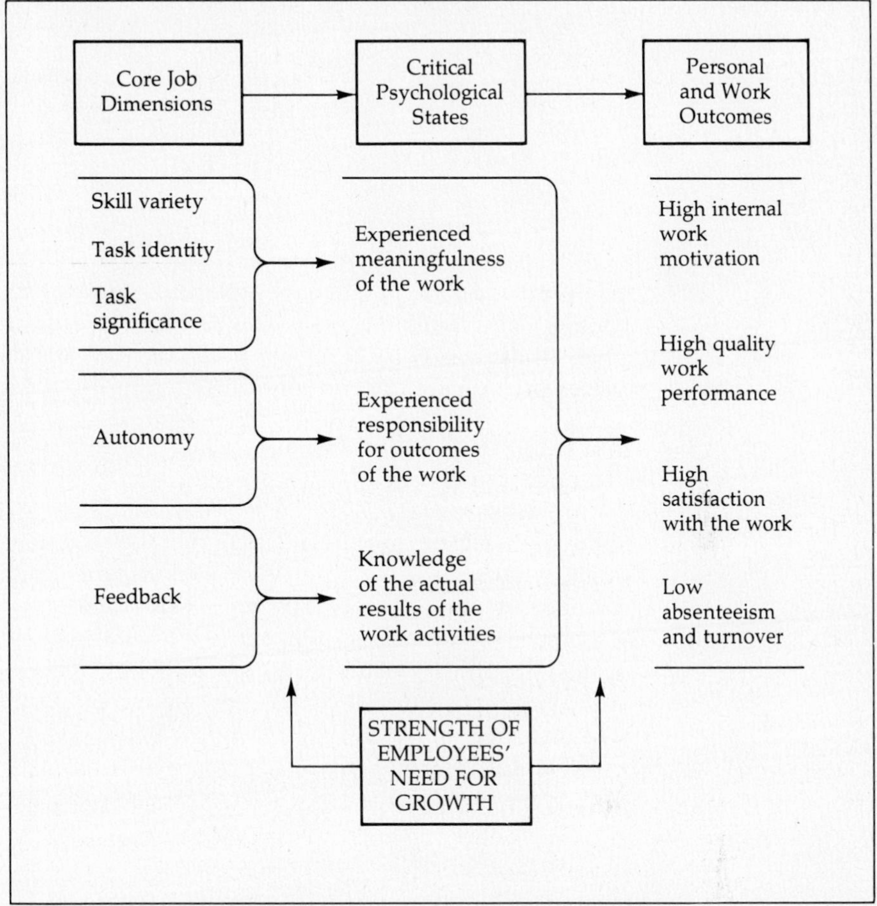

Figure 18-3 Job Characteristics Model of Work Motivation

Adapted from Hackman, Oldham, Janson, and Purdy, "A New Strategy for Job Enrichment," *California Management Review,* vol. 17 (1975): no. 4. © 1975 by the Regents of the University of California. Reprinted by permission.

Figure 18-3 illustrates the key core job dimensions that allow an individual to experience these three psychological states. As illustrated, experienced meaningfulness of work can be attained by giving a person more skill variety, task identity, and task significance. Experienced responsibility for the outcome of work can be attained by giving the individual more autonomy. Allowing the individual to obtain more feedback from work increases knowledge of the actual results of work. However, it is important to keep in mind that not all individuals respond favorably to such changes. As noted in our discussions of motivation, people have varying needs, attitudes, and expectations related to their work. Research has shown that those individuals with strong needs for growth, achievement, and esteem usually respond

FEATURE 18-3

Work Redesign Combined with Participation

One of the nation's more successful and advanced programs to improve the quality of work life in a manufacturing organization is at the General Motors Delco Remy battery factory in Fitzgerald, Ga. As the article indicates, GM's management has skillfully blended together work redesign, participation, training, and incentives.

In Fitzgerald they don't punch the timeclock, and they do have the "team concept."

As explained by personnel's Jones, the plant is divided into 30 teams, each responsible for running a section of the factory. Each team meets once a week, when members might figure out vacation schedules, lodge complaints about equipment or conditions to the team leader they elected, and decide if a member has learned all the team's work tasks and should be permitted to move to another team doing a different job.

The first two moves carry wage rate increases, illustrating the premium GM places on mobility.

The goal is combatting boredom, which can be frustrating and disruptive, as well as keeping a work force in which most everyone can do all the jobs in the plant.

"Each team must have some movement during the year," Jones said. "We've never said how much."

Similarly, the teams know production expectations, and decide themselves when they need to work overtime to keep up. But a team will be prodded by management if it isn't making the grade.

Jones said the battery plant has only slight problems with discipline and absenteeism, which has become seriously troublesome at many GM plants.

SOURCE: Marcia Kunstel, " 'Southern Hospitality' Keeps Union Out at GM," *Atlanta Journal and Constitution*, October 8, 1979.

favorably to job enrichment.[40] When individuals are not strongly motivated by higher level needs, job enrichment attempts are not as successful.

Technology also may influence whether job redesign is appropriate. Organizations employing mass-production technology are much more limited than those using unit-production technology in their ability to redesign jobs. The costs of redesigning work often outweigh the anticipated benefits for mass-production firms. In general: "Where the technology is not very flexible and involves major investments of capital, the cost of change may be great. One of the best opportunities for innovative job design is where a new work setting (a new plant, office, or facility) is being designed. In fact, some of the more notable work design experiments have involved such new settings."[41]

Applications and Results. Work redesign programs have been implemented by many major companies, including AT&T, Texas Instruments, Motorola, Procter & Gamble, General Foods, Corning Glass Works, Maytag, General Tire and Rubber, Buick, Banker's Trust, and Merrill Lynch. In one, laboratory technicians felt their technical ability and experience was not being utilized because the scientists refused to delegate anything other than routine work. After implementing a program where laboratory technicians were involved in planning projects and experiments, and given additional opportunity to assist in work planning and project setting, the quality of their monthly reports significantly improved compared to a group not exposed to the program. Another program involved sales representatives of three British companies. One group's jobs were changed to give them the responsibility to determine how frequently to call their customers. They were no longer required to write reports on every customer, and they were authorized to make immediate settlements of up to $250 for customer complaints. Those sales representatives given the enriched jobs increased their sales by 19 percent.[42]

Texas Instruments implemented a program where the janitorial service workers were allowed to decide how work would be divided and set up their own work schedules and standards. As a result, the number of required workers decreased from 120 to 71, turnover was reduced from 100 percent to 10 percent, and cleanliness improved.[43] The Buick Motor Division of General Motors implemented a work redesign program where the workers' jobs were expanded to include quality control concerns. Buick management feels this program was a significant factor in reducing petty grievances to zero, reducing the number of required rework cases, and improving productivity by 13 percent.[44]

Although there is not enough research evidence to make firm conclusions about work redesign programs, studies do show that work redesign generally results in improved job satisfaction, lower absenteeism and turnover, and improved product quality.[45] Productivity, however, has been found not to increase in most cases. This is probably because of the efficiency associated with extreme specialization of work.

Although these results indicate that increased organizational effectiveness occurs through the implementation of work redesign programs, there are those who criticize such programs. One criticism contends that worker satisfaction should not be given priority over economic efficiency. One group of writers states, "If changes in technology and hardware to improve the quality of work life are to be made, they must also promise higher profits."[46] Other writers state that "many workers do not feel alienated from their jobs and do not desire more responsibility or involvement at their work places."[47] In addition, these writers also state that, "attempts to enrich jobs are often frustrated by union constraints in the form of restrictive job descriptions, tenure requirements, craft jurisdictions, and general mistrust."[48] Thus, management should refrain from work redesign until they determine whether *their* employees are positively predisposed to it. In some programs, employees were given more variety, autonomy, and challenge than they desired. The results were poor performance and angry employees.[49]

Managing Stress

In this chapter we have discussed a number of techniques for managing human resources effectively. By using them appropriately, management can increase both the well-being of its people and the productivity of the organization. But even in the most progressive and well-managed organization, there are always situations and job characteristics that sometimes affect people adversely and induce a feeling of stress. Excessive stress may be highly debilitating to the individual and therefore to the organization. Thus, it is yet another factor the astute manager must understand and learn to cope with in order to be fully effective.

What Stress Is

Stress is among the most common human emotions. We all experience it at times. For you, stress may have surfaced as an empty feeling in the pit of your stomach as you stood up to give a presentation in class. Or, perhaps, you have noticed yourself becoming more irritable and less able to sleep during exam week. Minor stress is unavoidable and harmless. It is *excessive* stress that causes problems for individuals and organizations. As Dr. Carl Albrecht, author of *Stress and the Manager*, notes: "Stress is a natural part of human functioning. . . . We must learn to tell the difference between a reasonable degree of stress and too much stress . . . a zero stress condition is impossible."[50]

The type of **stress** managers are concerned with is a response characterized by excessive psychological or physiological strain. Research indicates that the physiological signs of stress include ulcers, migraine headaches, hypertension, backache, arthritis, asthma, and heart disease. Psychological manifestations include irritability, loss of appetite, depression, and reduced interest in interpersonal and sexual relations.[51]

In addition to decreasing an individual's effectiveness and well-being, excessive stress is costly to organizations. As Dr. Albrecht states, "It is now clear that many of the employee problems that cost money and performance as well as employee health and well-being originate in physiological stress.

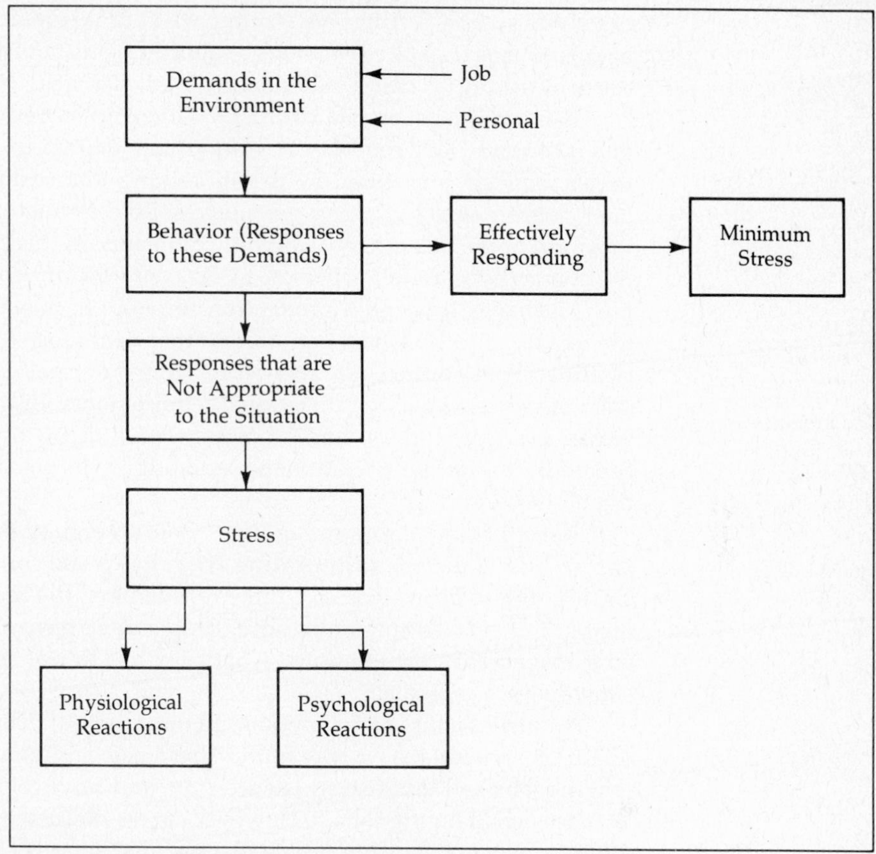

Figure 18-4 A Model of the Stress Response

Stress directly and indirectly adds to the cost of doing business, and it detracts from the quality of working life for a very large number of American workers."[52]

Causes of Stress

There are two general causes of stress that affect people within the organization. One cause is factors related to work and the practices of the organization. The other is events in the individual's personal life that affect work performance.

Organizational Factors. A common, understandable cause of stress in organizations is having too much work to complete in a specific time. Discussing this factor, Dr. Albrecht states, "The worker simply has been assigned an unreasonable number of tasks or an unreasonable level of production to accomplish in a given period. This practice usually causes anxiety, frustration, and a sense of hopelessness and loss of reward. But an underload can cause exactly the same feelings. A worker without adequate work to do usually begins to feel frustrated, anxious about his worth and position in the social order of the organization, and distinctly unrewarded."[53]

A second factor is role conflict.[54] Role conflict results when a worker is given contradictory requests. A worker may be told to be responsive to customer requests, and when he is seen talking to a customer, he may be told later not to neglect stocking the shelves. Role conflict can also occur from a violation of the principle of unity of command. In this case, two managers in the hierarchy may tell a person to do contradictory things. For example, a plant manager may tell a production foreman to maximize output whereas the quality control supervisor stresses that adherence to quality standards is essential. Role conflict can also result from informal group norms being at odds with the formal organizational requirements. In this situation, an individual may feel tension and anxiety because of his or her desire to be accepted by the group on one hand, and adhere to management's request on the other hand.

A third factor is role ambiguity.[55] Role ambiguity results when a worker has unclear expectations regarding what he or she should do or how he or she is going to be evaluated. Unlike role conflict, the requests are not contradictory but evasive and ambiguous. People must have a good understanding of management's expectations, what they are to do, and how they will be subsequently evaluated.

A fourth factor is job boredom. In one study of 2000 male workers in 23 different occupations, it was found that those individuals with more challenging jobs had less anxiety, depression, and physical illnesses than people with less challenging jobs.[56] However, as we discussed earlier, people have different needs regarding job challenge, and what is challenging or boring for one person may not necessarily be so for other people.

In addition to these factors, physical conditions such as inadequate temperature, poor lighting, excessive noise, and so on can induce stress. Research has also found that inadequate authority-responsibility relationships, poor channels of organizational communication, and unreasonable interpersonal demands can also induce stress.[57]

Personal Factors. Work is a major aspect of most people's lives. But, of course, everyone engages in many activities unrelated to the organization. The events in one's private life are also potential causes of stress that may result in lessened performance. Table 18-2 is a scale showing the relative stress caused by several common events. Thomas Holmes and Richard Rahe, who developed this scale, found that people with a cumulative score of over 300 had an approximately 80 percent chance of experiencing excessive physiological or psychological stress.[58] Note that positive life events such as promotion and earning much more money can cause as much or more stress as negative events.

Table 18-2 The Social Readjustment Rating Scale

Instructions: Check off each of these life events that has happened to you during the previous year. Total the associated points. A score of 150 or less means a relatively low amount of life change and a low susceptibility to stress-induced health breakdown in the next two years. A score above 300 raises the odds to about 80 percent, according to the Holmes-Rahe statistical prediction model.

Life Event	Mean Value
1. Death of spouse	100
2. Divorce	73
3. Marital separation from mate	65
4. Detention in jail or other institution	63
5. Death of a close family member	63
6. Major personal injury or illness	53
7. Marriage	50
8. Being fired at work	47
9. Marital reconciliation with mate	45
10. Retirement from work	45
11. Major change in the health or behavior of a family member	44
12. Pregnancy	40
13. Sexual difficulties	39
14. Gaining a new family member (e.g., through birth, adoption, oldster moving in, etc.)	39
15. Major business readjustment (e.g., merger, reorganization, bankruptcy, etc.)	39
16. Major change in financial state (e.g., a lot worse off or a lot better off than usual)	38
17. Death of a close friend	37
18. Changing to a different line of work	36
19. Major change in the number of arguments with spouse (e.g., either a lot more or a lot less than usual regarding child-rearing, personal habits, etc.)	35
20. Taking on a mortgage greater than $10,000 (e.g., purchasing a home, business, etc.)	31
21. Foreclosure on a mortgage or loan	30
22. Major change in responsibilities at work (e.g., promotion, demotion, lateral transfer)	29
23. Son or daughter leaving home (e.g., marriage, attending college, etc.)	29
24. In-law troubles	29
25. Outstanding personal achievement	28
26. Wife beginning or ceasing work outside the home	26
27. Beginning or ceasing formal schooling	26
28. Major change in living conditions (e.g., building a new home, remodeling, deterioration of home or neighborhood)	25
29. Revision of personal habits (dress, manners, associations, etc.)	24
30. Troubles with the boss	23
31. Major change in working hours	20

continues on page 612

TABLE 18-2, continued

Life Event	Mean Value
32. Change in residence	20
33. Changing to a new school	20
34. Major change in usual type and/or amount of recreation	19
35. Major change in church activities (e.g., a lot more or a lot less than usual)	19
36. Major change in social activities (e.g., clubs, dancing, movies, visiting, etc.)	18
37. Taking on a mortgage or loan less than $10,000 (e.g., purchasing a car, TV, freezer, etc.)	17
38. Major change in sleeping habits (a lot more or a lot less sleep, or change in part of day when asleep)	16
39. Major change in number of family get-togethers (e.g., a lot more or a lot less than usual)	15
40. Major change in eating habits (a lot more or a lot less food intake, or very different meal hours or surroundings)	15
41. Vacation	13
42. Christmas	12
43. Minor violations of the law (e.g., traffic tickets, jaywalking, disturbing the peace, etc.)	11

SOURCE: T. H. Holmes and R. H. Rahe, "The Social Readjustment Scale," *Journal of Psychosomatic Research*, vol. 2 (1967), p. 216.

Managing for High Performance and Low Stress

The ideal state is one in which performance is as high and stress as low as possible. To attain this, managers must learn to manage stress in themselves, as well as in subordinates. The following are a few suggestions for both.

Controlling Personal Stress at Work. People who are suffering from excessive stress at work should try the following techniques as appropriate:

1. Develop a priority system for your work. Rate your work into "must do today," "do later this week," and "do when I have time." This will enable you to deal with priority issues.
2. If you feel you honestly are at the point where you cannot take on any more work, learn to say no. Explain to your manager that you understand that the job is important. Then follow with a description of the specific priority jobs you are currently working on. If he or she insists it is essential to take on the new task, ask them what you should put aside until the new job is completed.
3. "Build an especially effective and supportive relationship with your boss. Understand his [or her] problems and help the boss to understand yours. Teach your boss to respect your priorities and your work load and to keep assignments reasonable."[59]

4. If you feel you are receiving contradictory requests (role conflict) from your manager or any two or more people, confront them. Explain how the discrepant requests are pulling you in opposite directions. Request a meeting with all the parties involved to clarify the matter. Don't have a blaming, defensive posture; merely explain how the discrepant requests are creating specific problems for you.
5. If you feel you are in a situation where expectations and/or how you will be evaluated are not clear (role ambiguity), communicate this to your manager or co-workers. Tell them you are somewhat uncertain about some specific job-related matters and you would like to have the opportunity to discuss these with them.
6. If you find your job is not challenging enough, discuss this with your manager. Once again, do not have a complaining attitude. Explain how you really enjoy challenging work and express that you would like the opportunity to get involved in other types of activities.
7. "Find time everyday for detachment and relaxation. Close your door for five minutes each morning and afternoon, put up your feet, relax deeply, and take your mind off the work. Use pleasant thoughts or images to refresh your mind . . . Get away from your office from time to time for a change of scene or a change of mind. Don't eat lunch there or hang around long after you should have gone home or gone out to enjoy other activities."[60]

In order to effectively manage others for high performance and low stress we suggest:

1. Assess your workers' abilities, needs, and aptitudes and try to match the quantity and type of work they do to these factors. As they demonstrate success in these tasks, increase the job challenge in complexity if they desire this. Delegate when appropriate.
2. Allow your workers to realistically say no to a request. If it is essential that they do it, explain why and prioritize their work so they will have the necessary time and resources to complete the additional job.
3. Effectively communicate specific areas of authority, responsibility, and work expectations. Use two-way communication and obtain feedback from your subordinates.
4. Use an appropriate leadership style for the demands of the situation.
5. Reward effective performance.
6. Play a coaching role with your subordinates by developing their abilities and discussing problem areas with them.

Other factors related to low stress are maintaining a proper diet, getting an adequate amount of exercise, and achieving an overall balance in one's life. Table 18-3 differentiates between a stressful and low-stress life style.

Table 18-3 High- Versus Low-Stress Life Styles

Stressful Life Style	Low-Stress Life Style
Individual experiences chronic, unrelieved stress	Individual accepts "creative" stress for distinct periods of challenging activity
Becomes trapped in one or more continuing stressful situations	Has "escape routes" allowing occasional detachment and relaxation
Struggles with stressful interpersonal relationships (family, spouse, lover, boss, co-workers, etc.)	Asserts own rights and needs; negotiates low-stress relationships of mutual respect; selects friends carefully and establishes relationships that are nourishing and nontoxic
Engages in distasteful, dull, toxic, or otherwise unpleasant and unrewarding work	Engages in challenging, satisfying, worthwhile work that offers intrinsic rewards for accomplishment
Experiences continual time stress; too much to be done in available time	Maintains a well-balanced and challenging workload; overloads and crises are balanced by "breather" periods
Worries about potentially unpleasant upcoming events	Balances threatening events with worthwhile goals and positive events to look forward to
Has poor health habits (e.g., eating, smoking, liquor, lack of exercise, poor level of physical fitness)	Maintains high level of physical fitness, eats well, uses alcohol and tobacco not at all or sparingly
Life activities are "lopsided" or unbalanced (e.g., preoccupied with one activity such as work, social activities, making money, solitude, or physical activities)	Life activities are balanced; individual invests energies in a variety of activities, which in the aggregate bring feelings of satisfaction (e.g., work, social activities, recreation, solitude, cultural pursuits, family, and close relationships)
Finds it difficult to just "have a good time," relax, and enjoy momentary activities	Finds pleasure in simple activities, without feeling a need to justify playful behavior
Experiences sexual activities as unpleasant, unrewarding, or socially "programmed" (e.g., by manipulation, "one-upping")	Enjoys a full and exuberant sex life, with honest expression of sexual appetite
Sees life as a serious, difficult situation; little sense of humor	Enjoys life on the whole; can laugh at him- or herself; has a well-developed and well-exercised sense of humor.
Conforms to imprisoning, punishing social roles	Lives a relatively role-free life; is able to express natural needs, desires, and feelings without apology
Accepts high-pressure or stressful situations passively; suffers in silence	Acts assertively to re-engineer pressure situations whenever possible; renegotiates impossible deadlines; avoids placing himself in unnecessary pressure situations; manages time effectively

SOURCE: Carl Albrecht, *Stress and the Manager* (Englewood Cliffs, NJ: Prentice-Hall, Inc., 1979), pp. 107–108. Reprinted by permission.

SUMMARY

The three stages of human resource planning are assessment of present supply, assessment of future needs, and development of a specific human resource program. Developing a program would require a specific timetable and the determination of actions required to attract, hire, train, and promote the people required to attain organization objectives.

Recruiting is the building of a pool of candidates for jobs either through external sources or, as often preferable, from within. The most common problem is creating unreasonable expectations.

The primary techniques for selection are testing, assessment centers, and interviews. Assessment centers use simulation techniques and have been proven effective, but are costly. Interviews are widely used but subject to problems. Structured interviews seem to improve accuracy.

Human resource development should begin as soon as the employee joins the organization, with formal orientation and socialization. Performance appraisal serves administrative, informational, and motivational functions. Studies show that criticism is not a useful way to communicate information about poor performance. The manager should create a nonthreatening climate and provide specific feedback. Appraisals should be relatively frequent, and performance and salary should not be discussed at the same time. McGregor advocates a strong focus on results and mutually set objectives. Most writers would agree that two-way communication is very helpful.

Training is teaching employees skills to improve performance at their present job. Development is preparing the person for a future position. For training to be effective, people must be motivated to learn, the climate must be conducive to learning, complex skills should be taught in sequential steps, and the trainee should receive feedback and reinforcement. Managers can be developed through courses, seminars, and job rotation.

Quality of work life can be improved by changing any variable affecting people. An appropriate combination of monetary rewards and fringe benefits, which can be successfully attained with a cafeteria compensation system, seems to improve satisfaction and reduce absenteeism and turnover. Work redesign involves increasing the intrinsic rewards of work, usually by enriching tasks to provide more autonomy, feedback, or challenge. Work redesign has been very successful, but is suitable only for certain people and in certain situations. It is particularly difficult to implement when technology is inflexible and may fail if management does not determine whether the work force actually has a positive attitude toward work redesign.

Excessive stress can be caused by having too much work, too little work, role conflict, role ambiguity, boredom, physical factors, and a variety of personal events.

REVIEW QUESTIONS

1. Identify and explain the stages in human resource planning.
2. What is job analysis and how is it used?
3. What makes a test useful in selection decision?
4. Describe an assessment center including techniques used.
5. What are some general guidelines that should be followed in developing an effective interview?
6. Define and describe the process of "organizational socialization."
7. Explain the three general purposes of performance appraisal.
8. What are the general requirements for an effective training program?
9. How do reward systems influence the quality of work life?
10. Compare and contrast job enrichment and job enlargement.

DISCUSSION QUESTIONS

11. What type of organization would be most likely to use an assessment center and why?
12. As a prospective employee, how would you prepare yourself for an interview?

13. What makes a performance appraisal system effective?
14. What changes in the social environment have emphasized the importance of career management?
15. Many companies today have developed in-house physical fitness programs. Why?

CASE INCIDENT

The Customer Accounting Department

Ivy National was a medium size, full service commercial bank with a burning desire for growth. It had emerged from the 1974–1975 recession in slightly better condition than many of its larger competitors, having written off a number of bad loans and been moderately successful in salvaging some marginal ones. In addition, Ivy National had recently reexamined the nature of its business, revised its strategy, restructured its organization, and with the help of an outside consulting firm instituted formal programs of MBO and performance evaluation. In short, Ivy was ready to get down to business and according to its president, William Gray, "mix it up with the best."

Of particular pride to Gray was the bank's new performance evaluation system. Computerized, it was designed to make certain that no one became lost in the shuffle and to ensure that each staff member's performance was properly recognized. Gray felt that people, the bank's employees, provided Ivy with its primary competitive edge. He believed that if employees are treated as individuals, then customers will be dealt with in similar fashion. It had been 14 months since Ivy had instituted its performance evaluation plan (PEP), and Gray, a person who believed that a bank president should be highly visible, decided to see how PEP was progressing.

Roger Wander was manager of the customer accounting department. While he loved his job, he thought the name change of his department from bookkeeping to customer accounting was just plain foolish. The change had been made when Ivy embarked on its new image and growth strategy. As far as Wander was concerned, it was bookkeeping when he came to Ivy 11 years ago and it should still be bookkeeping. "If they had asked me," Roger said, "I would have told them, but they didn't." Wander believed that his department was "behind the scenes and different and that his employees were more like production workers than bankers."

Wander was pleased when Gray stopped by but was not particularly happy to see him accompanied by Raymond Swift, Ivy's personnel director. Wander and Swift didn't always agree on management style. On more than one occasion Wander had suggested that Swift tend to his own affairs and "leave bookkeeping alone."

After complimenting Wander on his department's appearance, Gray said he was a bit concerned about how PEP was being implemented in customer accounting. Specifically, Gray wondered why everyone in customer accounting was rated average. Wander said, "I've already told Swift that for me to rate an employee average, I have a check list that takes 5 or 6 seconds to complete, but for me to rate one either superior or unsatisfactory, I have to justify it and this takes 5 or 6 pages. As far as I am concerned, they're all average."

Questions

1. Do you think that Wander's position is sound? Why?
2. If you were Gray, how would you respond to Wander?
3. If you were Raymond Swift, what might you say to Gray and Wander?

NOTES

1. William J. Pedicord, "Advanced Status Systems for Personnel Planning and Replacement," in *Computers and Automation* (Newtonville, MA: Berkeley Enterprises, 1966; T. I. Bradshaw, "Computerized Employee Search Program," *Data Processing Magazine*, November 1965, pp. 48–50; George Milkovich and T. Mahoney, "Human Resources Planning and PAIR Policy," in vol. 4, *PAIR Handbook*, Dale Yodder and Herbert Heneman, eds. (Berea, Ohio: American Society of Personnel Administrators, 1976); Robert Martin, "Skills Inventories," *Personnel Journal*, January 1967, pp. 28–30.
2. John B. Miner and M. G. Miner, *Personnel and Industrial Relations: A Managerial Approach*, 3rd. ed. (New York: Macmillan, 1977), pp. 154–155.
3. John P. Wanous, "Effects of a Realistic Job Preview on Job Acceptance, Job Attitudes, and Job Survival," *Journal of Applied Psychology*, vol. 58 (1973), pp. 327–332.
4. John P. Wanous, "Tell It Like It Is at Realistic Job Previews," in *Perspectives on Personnel/Human Resource Management*, eds. H. G. Heneman and D. P. Schwab (Homewood, IL: Irwin, 1978), p. 110–117.
5. George W. England, *Development and Use of Weighted Application Blanks, Bulletin 55* (Minneapolis: Industrial Relations Center, University of Minnesota, 1971); Clemm C. Kessler and George J. Gibbs, "Getting the Most from Application Blanks and References," *Personnel*, January-February 1975, pp. 53–62.
6. Alan Kraut, "Management Assessment in International Organizations," *Industrial Relations*, 1976, pp. 172–182; N. Howard, "An Assessment of Assessment Centers," *Academy of Management Journal*, vol. 17 (1974): no. 1, pp. 115–134; James Hock and D. Bray, "Management Assessment Center Evaluations and Subsequent Job Performance of White and Black Females," *Personnel Psychology*, vol. 29 (1976), pp. 13–30; G. N. Worboys, "Validation of Externally Developed Assessment Procedures for Identification of Supervisory Potential," *Personnel Psychology*, Spring 1975, pp. 77–91.
7. Eugene C. Mayfield, "The Selection Interview—A Reevaluation of Published Research," *Personnel Psychology*, vol. 17 (1964): no. 3, pp. 239–260; Edwin E. Ghiselli, "The Validity of a Personnel Interview," *Personnel Psychology*, vol. 19 (1966): no. 4, pp. 389–394; Orman R. Wright, Jr., "Summary of Research on the Selection Interview Since 1964," *Personnel Psychology*, vol. 22 (1969): no. 4, pp. 391–413.
8. R. E. Carlson, P. W. Thayer, E. C. Mayfield, and D. A. Peterson, "Improvements in the Selection Interview," *Personnel Journal*, vol. 50 (1971), pp. 268–275, 317; D. Schwab and H. G. Heneman, "Relationship Between Interview Structure and Interviewer Reliability in an Employment Situation," *Journal of Applied Psychology*, vol. 53 (1969), pp. 214–217; Benjamin Schneider, *Staffing Organizations* (Pacific Palisades, CA: Goodyear, 1976), chap. 4.
9. Miner and Miner, op. cit., p. 288.
10. Stephen J. Carroll and Henry L. Tosi: *Organizational Behavior* (Chicago: St. Clair Press, 1977), p. 97.
11. Edgar H. Schein, "Organizational Socialization and the Profession of Management," *Industrial Management Review*, vol. 9 (1968), pp. 1–16.

12. Marvin D. Dunnette, R. D. Arvey, and P. A. Banas, "Why Do They Leave?" *Personnel*, 1973, pp. 25–39.

13. David E. Berlow and D. T. Hall, "A Socialization of Managers," *Administrative Science Quarterly*, vol. 11 (1966), pp. 207–223.

14. Carroll and Tosi, op. cit., p. 97.

15. Bureau of National Affairs, Inc., "Management Performance Appraisal Programs," *Personnel Policies Forum Survey No. 104,* January 1974.

16. Alan Patz, "Performance Appraisal: Useful But Still Resisted," *Harvard Business Review*, May–June 1975.

17. H. H. Meyer, E. K. Kay, and J. R. P. French, "Split Roles in Performance Appraisal," *Harvard Business Review*, vol. 43 (1965), pp. 123–129.

18. David A. Nadler, J. R. Hackman, E. E. Lawler, *Managing Organizational Behavior* (Boston: Little, Brown, 1979), p. 59.

19. Douglas McGregor, "An Uneasy Look at Performance Appraisal," *Harvard Business Review*, vol. 35 (1957), pp. 89–94.

20. Nadler, Hackman, and Lawler, op. cit., p. 61.

21. F. G. Malm, "Analyzing Training Needs and Results," in Pidgors, Meyers, and Malm, *Management of Human Resources*, 3rd. ed. (New York: McGraw-Hill, 1973), p. 442.

22. Miner and Miner, op. cit., pp. 360–363.

23. John P. Kotter, L. A. Schlesinger, and V. Sathe, *Organizations* (Homewood, IL: Irwin, 1979), p. 20.

24. Leonard R. Sayles and G. Strauss, *Managing Human Resources,* 3rd. ed. (Englewood Cliffs, NJ: Prentice-Hall, 1977), p. 297.

25. William F. Glueck, "Career Management of Managerial, Professional and Technical Personnel," in *Perspectives on Personnel/Human Resource Management*, eds. H. G. Heneman and D. P. Schwab (Homewood, IL: Irwin, 1978), p. 156.

26. Ibid.

27. Ann Roe and R. Buruch, "Occupational Changes in Adult Years," *Personnel Administration,* vol. 30 (1967), pp. 26–32.

28. Oscar Grusky, "Career Mobility in Organizational Commitment," *Administrative Science Quarterly*, vol. 10 (1966), pp. 488–503; Andrall E. Pierson, "Sales Power Through Planned Careers," *Harvard Business Review,* vol. 44 (January-February 1966), pp. 105–116; Lawrence L. Ferguson, "Better Management of Managers' Careers," *Harvard Business Review,* vol. 44 (March 1966), pp. 139–152.

29. J. R. Hackman and J. Lloyd Suttle, *Improving Life at Work* (Santa Monica, CA: Goodyear, 1977), p. 4.

30. Ibid., p. 6.

31. Hackman and Suttle, ibid.; Lewis E. Davis and A. B. Cherns, eds., *The Quality of Working Life,* vols. 1 and 2 (New York: The Free Press, 1975).

32. Edward E. Lawler, *Pay and Organizational Effectiveness: A Psychological View* (New York: McGraw-Hill, 1971); Douglas T. Hall, *Career and Organizations* (Santa Monica, CA: Goodyear, 1976).

33. Lyman W. Porter and Richard R. N. Steers, "Organizational, Work, and Personal Factors in Employee Turnover and Absenteeism," *Psychological Bulletin,* 1966, pp. 94–118.

34. William Glueck, *Personnel* (Dallas: Business Publications, 1978), pp. 403–404.

35. Lawler, op. cit.

36. Glueck, *Personnel,* op. cit., p. 405.

37. Lawler, op. cit., p. 167.
38. J. B. Chapman and R. Ottemann, *Employee Preference for Various Compensation and Fringe Benefit Options* (Berea, Ohio: ASAP Foundation, 1979).
39. "Flexible Benefits: How One Company Does It," *Personnel Administrator*, vol. 10 (1974), p. 51.
40. J. R. Hackman and G. R. Oldham, "Motivation Through Design of Work: Test of a Theory," *Organizational Behavior and Human Performance*, vol. 16 (1976), pp. 250–259; A. P. Brief and R. J. Aldag, "Employer Reactions to Job Characteristics: A Constructive Replication," *Journal of Applied Psychology*, vol. 60 (1975), pp. 182–186.
41. Nadler, Hackman, and Lawler, op. cit., p. 89; Edward E. Lawler, "The New Plant Revolution," *Organizational Dynamics*, vol. 6 (1978), pp. 2–12.
42. William J. Hall, Jr., K. B. Robertson, and F. Herzberg, "Job Enrichment Pays Off," *Harvard Business Review*, March-April 1969, pp. 61–78.
43. N. Q. Harrick, "The Other Side of the Coin" (Paper delivered at the Twentieth Anniversary Invitational Seminar of the Profit Sharing Research Foundation, Evanston, IL, November, 1971).
44. F. J. Shotters, "Job Enrichment at Buick Products Engineering," GM Personal Development Bulletin, 22, June 4, 1973.
45. Frank Friedlander and L. D. Brown, "Organization Development," in Mark Rosenzeig and Lyman W. Porter, eds., *Annual Review of Psychology*, vol. 25 (1974), pp. 313–341.
46. S. A. Levitan and W. B. Johnston, "Job Redesign, Enrichment—Exploring the Limitations," *Monthly Labor Review*, July 1973, pp. 35–41.
47. W. Clay Hamner and D. W. Organ, *Organizational Behavior: An Applied Psychology Approach* (Dallas: BPI, 1978), p. 277.
48. Ibid.
49. John H. Morse, "A Contingency Look at Job Design," *California Management Review*, Fall 1973, p. 68.
50. Carl Albrecht, *Stress and the Manager* (Englewood Cliffs, NJ: Prentice-Hall, 1979), pp. 49–50.
51. Douglas B. Gasner, "The Creation of Stress," *MBA*, vol. 9, October 1975, p. 42.
52. Albrecht, op. cit., p. 42.
53. Ibid., p. 140.
54. Robert L. Kahn, B. N. Wolfe, R. P. Quinn, and J. D. Snoek, *Organizational Stress: Studies in Role Conflict and Ambiguity* (New York: Wiley, 1964).
55. Ibid.
56. "Stress and Boredom," *Behavior Today*, vol. 6 (August 1975).
57. Rolf E. Rogers, "Executive Stress," *Human Resource Management*, vol. 14 (Fall 1975), pp. 21–22.
58. Thomas H. Holmes and R. H. Rahe, "The Social Readjustment Rating Scale," *Journal of Psychosomatic Research*, vol. 11 (1967), p. 216.
59. Albrecht, op. cit., p. 253.
60. Albrecht, op. cit., p. 254.

CHAPTER 19

Making Organizational Design Effective

As we have pointed out so often, the many factors in organizational success are interrelated. Techniques for managing human resources, for example, will only increase the organization's ability to attain its objectives if they are both consistent with people's needs and supported by other management decisions. Among the most important of these decisions is the choice of organizational design. A structure that is not appropriate for the situation of the organization will probably severely impede management's ability to channel the efforts of its people, meet the needs of its customers, respond to its environment, and perform the control function. Therefore, in this chapter we return to the organizing process and elaborate on the situational factors management should consider when creating an organizational design. Our discussion will build on concepts presented in earlier chapters and strongly stress the interrelationships between organizational structure and other management variables and decisions.

After reading this chapter, you should understand the following important terms and concepts:

- internal variables that affect structure
- external variables that affect structure
- environmental volatility and structure
- span of management and effectiveness
- when decentralization is appropriate
- differentiation
- integration
- linking pin concept

Contingencies in Organizational Design

Organizing, as mentioned earlier, was the first aspect of managing to be studied formally. Henri Fayol, Mary Parker Follett, Frederick W. Taylor, Lyndall Urwick, James Mooney, A. C. Riley, and many who followed tried to delineate principles for structuring organizations. They wanted to come up with rules that, if followed, would invariably lead a manager to success. But, unfortunately, classical theorists often tended to concentrate on just one type of organization at just one point in its history. So, when managers working in different industries or places or times tried to apply these principles they often did not prove successful. The tendency, then, was to totally reject the principle and look for another that would, in fact, work in all situations.

Today, management theorists have come to recognize that there are no universal organizing principles. All logical systems of structure have both good points and drawbacks. A wide span of management, high degree of decentralization, and democratic leadership style may be effective for a scientific research firm but disastrous for a container factory that manufactures standardized products not significantly affected by technological and market changes. Bureaucratic structures may be effective for government and the auto industry but too rigid for developing a new engine that does not use fossil fuel. As Lawrence and Lorsch concluded from their study of ten organizations in three industries—plastics, standardized containers, consumer foods—operating in environments with different rates of change: ". . . the interfunctioning of organizations must be consistent with the demands of the organization task, technology, or external environment, and the needs of its members if the organization is to be effective."[1]

This finding supports those of Burns and Stalker, whose concept of organic structure was presented in Chapter 9, and that of Joan Woodward, whose work is described in Chapter 3. In summarized form, all these researchers concluded that the key to organizational success is to match the structural factor—decentralization, degree of specialization, span of management, etc.—to the specific situation of the organization. The best structure in a given situation is that which is best suited to the demands of the organization's tasks, technology, external environment, and characteristics of its employees. Since these variables differ for each organization, the best way to organize may also be different for different organizations and subunits.

At this point we will synthesize the findings of contemporary researchers into a simple contingency model of the organizing process. Following sections of the chapter will elaborate on this model.

A Contingency Model of the Organizational Design

As with every management function, the situational variables affecting organizing are too numerous and complex to analyze completely. Literally everything within the organization and much of the outside world has some impact on effectiveness. It therefore is necessary to narrow the variables down to those of major importance in determining the potential success of a given structure.

Writers on management have differing views on exactly which situational factors these are. William B. Wolf, for instance, identified 22 factors as critical in management and organizational design. His list includes ownership, labor force, history, leadership, size, physical facilities, existing formal structure, supervisors, job design, location, public image, technology, interpersonal interactions, competing organizations, and strategic plans.[2] Most management authorities would probably agree, however, that our much simpler model takes into account the major forces influencing structural decisions.

The model illustrated in Figure 19-1 shows that both internal and external variables affect organizational design. The internal variables, described earlier, are the organization's objectives and strategies, its size, tasks, the technology it uses, and people. These variables, as we know, are interrelated. They affect one another as well as organizational design, which is itself an internal variable that affects the others. Customers, competitors, sociocultural and legal factors, available technology (which the organization may or may not be using) are external variables affecting organization design. Volatility, the relative rate of change, is a contingency affecting all of these factors in different ways and of particular importance in designing an organization.

We have already noted some of the ways in which both external and internal factors may influence the effectiveness of organizational design. In Chapter 9, for example, we observed that when an organization's customers are dispersed over a wide geographical area, a territorial system of departmentation is often highly desirable. We also noted that the conglomerate business strategy of expanding through acquisition led to the use of free-form structures. Similarly, we have learned that social and cultural values affect people's attitudes toward authority and their needs. This, as we will elaborate on later, determines how people will probably respond to decentralization. Although not depicted in the model, we also know that the internal variables can sometimes affect the external variables. For example, if an organization changes its design and becomes more effective, it will meet customer needs better and probably take some customers from competitors.

Internal Variables and Organizational Design

Objectives and Strategies

The internal factors of primary importance in organizational design are the organization's objectives and strategies. These define what the organization is trying to accomplish, and structure must necessarily be based on them.

An organization, such as most businesses, whose objectives are primarily economic usually must use an organizational design that is highly

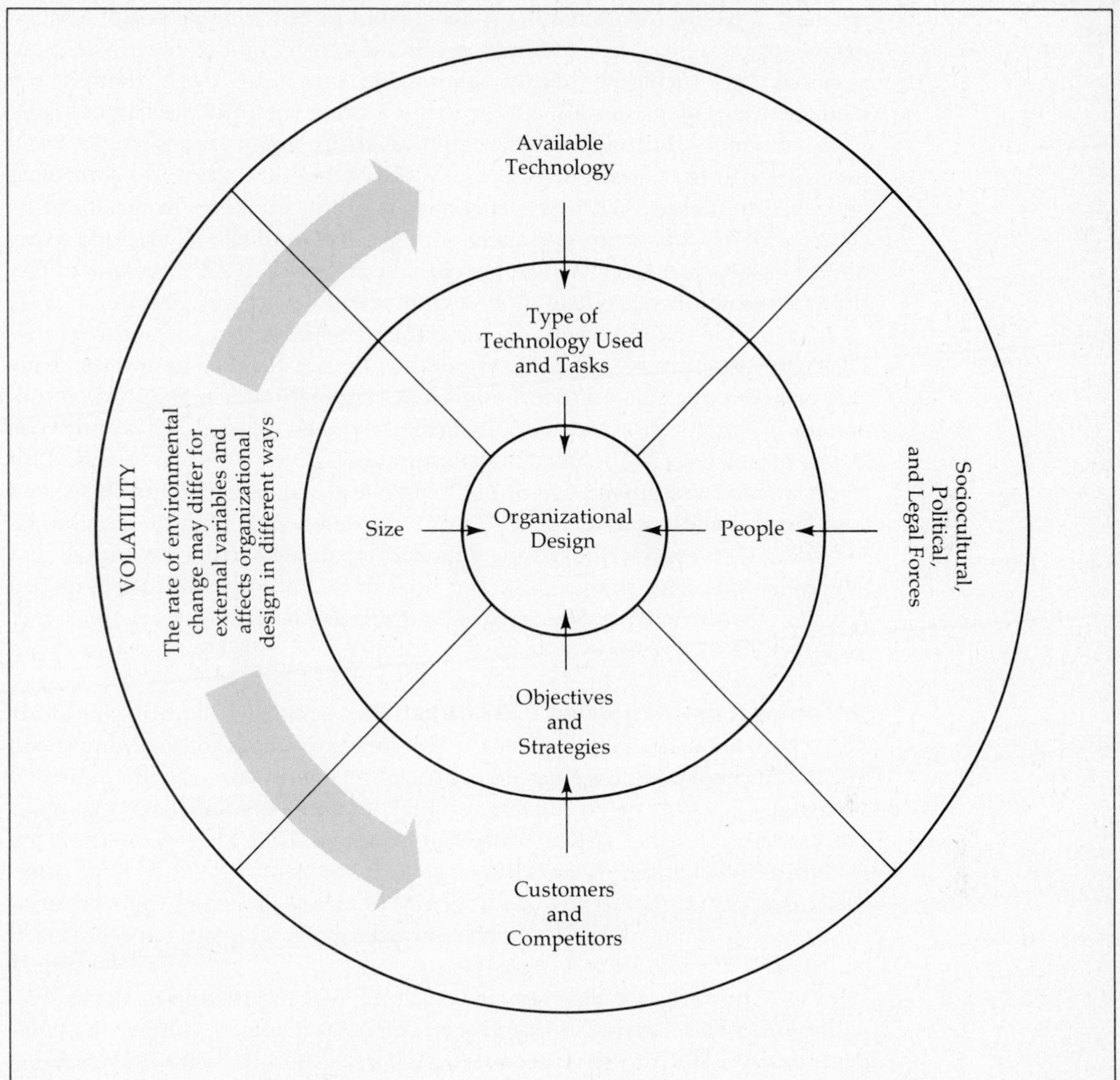

Figure 19-1 **Contingency Model of Organizational Design**
Arrows indicate the most significant interactions between the external variables in the outer ring, the internal variables in the inner ring, and organizational design. Actually, all of these factors are interrelated and factors in the external environment may directly affect which organizational design is most appropriate.

efficient. This often may require management to put aside its personal management preferences. For example, economic considerations may force management into using a highly centralized structure, even though top managers would genuinely prefer to give their subordinates almost complete autonomy. Failure to do so could result in serious economic loss and therefore failure to attain objectives. Excessive decentralization of control, as described in Chapter 11, was a major cause of the problems experienced by General Dynamics. Sears, a pioneer of high decentralization, decided to redesign its structure to centralize purchasing decisions in 1979 because of low growth and the need to take more advantage of economies of scale.

Governmental, educational, charitable, and other organizations whose objectives are primarily social and political do not need to base their structure on economic efficiency, although cost of operations is certainly a consideration in organizational design. Instead, they need a design consistent with their expressed social, political, and cultural objectives. This is one reason for the relatively widespread use of participative management, committees, and subunits to handle special interest groups in democratic governmental organizations. Universities, too, stress wide participation in management because it is consistent with their values and objectives. So do some businesses, especially in fields such as film making and television, where creativity is very important.

Structure Follows Strategy: Alfred Chandler. Strategic planning identifies the organization's broad objectives and its primary tactics for attaining them. The strong impact strategy has on organizational structure was first noted by Alfred D. Chandler, Jr. in his famous book, *Strategy and Structure.*[3] Chandler analyzed the histories of Du Pont, Sears, Standard Oil of New Jersey (now Exxon), and General Motors. All four of these successful organizations originally used centralized structures effectively. As the nature of their business environment changed, however, all four eventually adopted a decentralized structure.

Du Pont's original business, for example, was production of explosives. After World War I ended, demand for explosives declined, forcing the company to diversify into new products. This diversification into new markets with new suppliers involved an extensive range of tactical and strategic decisions that the original centralized structure could not cope with effectively. Sears began as a mail order firm. It needed to adopt a more decentralized structure after expanding into over-the-counter retailing. Decentralization proved more effective in coping with problems of coordination, supervision, and planning introduced by the new business. It also helped Sears cope effectively with changes in the external environment, such as increased urbanization and the widespread ownership of passenger cars, which helped retail stores thrive.

Standard Oil of New Jersey originally produced only kerosene. It adopted a decentralized structure to cope with the development of new products for the automobile, expansion into international markets, and its strategy of vertical integration. General Motors, similarly, changed to a decentralized structure because of the pressures on management created by producing many models of cars and trucks and internal production of certain parts and accessories.

As Chandler stated, "in these four enterprises, diversity created by the move into new lines of business and by continued expansion of technologically complex existing ones greatly increased the responsibilities of the top administrators."[4] In all four cases, the new decentralized structure freed top management from having to perform many routine tasks and gave it more time and information for long-range planning, policy formation, and coordination and evaluation of the company's divisions.

Although the underlying causes for these strategic decisions differed and so did the products, both Sears and Standard Oil came to use a very similar organization with excellent results. The new strategy of product diversification and geographic expansion required new structures. This led Chandler to coin the famous expression, "structure follows strategy." Although later studies have identified other factors of strong importance, an organization's strategy is indeed determinant of which organizational design it should use to attain its objectives effectively.

As Chandler states when discussing why the new decentralized structure succeeded, "The basic reason for its success was simply that it clearly removed the executives responsible for the destiny of the entire enterprise from the more routine operational activities and so gave them the time, information, and even psychological commitment for long-term planning and appraisal. Conversely, it placed the responsibility and the necessary authority for the operational administration in the hands of the general managers of the multi-function divisions."[5]

Chandler noted that in a number of industries, such as copper, nickel, and steel, centralized structures were most effective. As he states, "Because the copper companies are mining and processing enterprises producing a relatively few types of products to a well-defined market, they have been under less pressure to concern themselves with organizational matters. . . . Because of the simplicity of operations and the lack of technical and market changes, administrative decisions in the copper and nickel enterprises have been almost entirely operational ones."[6]

When Decentralization Is Appropriate. According to management writer Ernest Dale, a **decentralized organizational structure is most appropriate for the following conditions:**

1. When the environment is characterized by a changing product market, competition with diverse product lines, and rapid technological innovation
2. As organizations grow in size and complexity

As Chandler showed, when organizations grow in size and complexity, it becomes increasingly difficult for top management to be involved in day-to-day operating (tactical decisions) as well as long-range planning, policy formation, and the coordination and appraisal of plans.[7]

Tasks and Technology

A major aspect of an organization's strategy is the technology it uses. An organization in a competitive situation, as virtually all are, must use technology at least as efficient as its competitors, or it will not long survive. A company with similar labor costs that wishes to sell large numbers of automobiles in America, for example, must use manufacturing procedures at least as efficient as those of GM and Ford.

Woodward Studies. The landmark investigation of technology's effect on organizations was conducted by Joan Woodward, an English management researcher, between 1953 and 1961.[8] The original intent of the 100-firm study was to determine the relationship between a firm's organizational structure and application of management principles and its relative success. Success was measured by a composite of market share, rate of increase in market share, profitability, capital expansion, and less quantifiable indices such as employee attitudes and the firm's reputation. Surveys, case studies, and longitudinal and historical analyses were used to measure each firm's supervisory span of management, the number of levels in the hierarchy, relative use of oral and written communication, extent to which functions were divided among specialists, and the clarity and precision with which job duties and responsibilities were defined.

At first, the research group had little luck. Spans of management, varied from 10 to 90. The number of levels varied from 2 to 12. But no single organizational structure was uniformly associated with success. Nor was any relationship found between size, the number of employees, and success. The relationship between an organization's structure and its success only became apparent when Woodward's group reclassified the firms according to the basic technology they used.

All firms, they found, fit into one of three basic categories with respect to production technology. These were unit production, mass production, and process production. (You may wish to review the description of these technologies in Chapter 3.) Woodward found several definite relationships between structure and the type of technology used:

1. The number of management levels increased from unit to mass to process technology. The medians were 3, 4, and 6 levels, respectively.
2. The span of management of first-line supervisors also varied, but not in a direct way. Median spans were 15 in process production, 23 in unit, and 48 in mass production.

In all cases, the more successful firms in each technological category tended to have the *median* span and number of levels for that category. The "best"

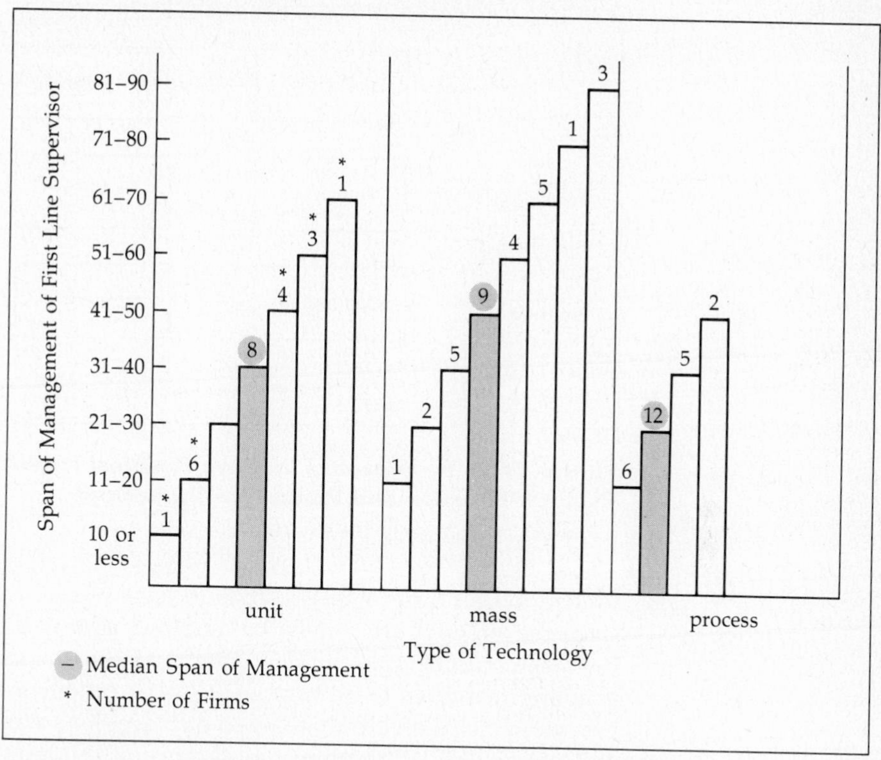

Figure 19-2 Relationship Between Span of Management of First-Line Supervisors and Type of Technology

span and length of chain of command, in other words, *varied with technology.*

Woodward's study also found that more successful unit and process production firms were structured more flexibly, organic, with job duties and responsibility less precisely defined. Successful mass-production firms tended to be more highly structured (mechanistic), with detailed statements of duties and responsibilities. Similarly, managerial functions in unit- and mass-production firms were less specialized than in mass-production firms. Also, the successful unit and process firms tended to use more oral than written communication. The reverse was true of mass production.

Business Functions and Technology. Woodward found a possible explanation for these findings by analyzing the sequence and relative importance of the critical functions of development, marketing, and production.

As Figure 19-3 shows, unit-production firms must first secure the order (market), then develop the product, then produce it. The firm must be able to adapt quickly to any changes in its market. Product development is a critical function because products must satisfy customer specifications and be acceptable to production personnel. Although the need for innovation is not

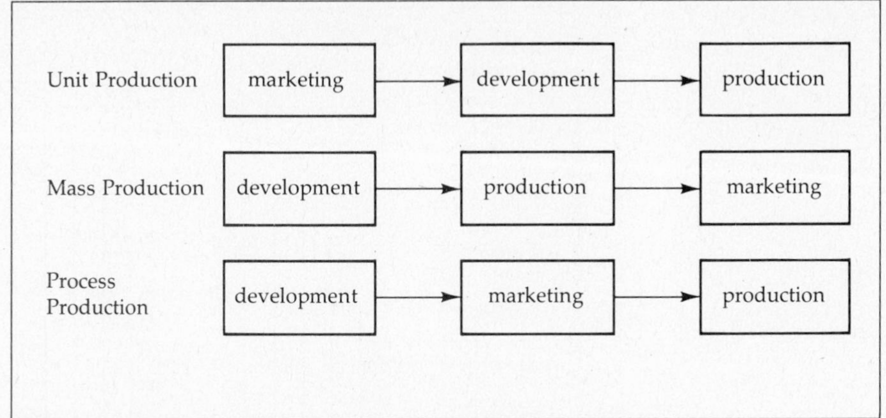

Figure 19-3 Relationship Between the Most Important Business Function and Production Technology

Arrow shows sequence of business functions.

limited to unit firms, a relatively high level of innovation is desirable. And, since the product often must be modified as it is being built, information exchange must be quick and accurate. As a result, a short chain of command enabling managers to be very close to the production function is desirable because it helps assure that day-to-day decisions will be made close to the scene of action and shortens the distance of communication. This facilitates the needed coordination among all three functions. Using oral instead of written communication further increases the speed and flexibility of information exchange. Small supervisory spans of management are desirable because the work is not repetitive and requires high levels of craftsmanship. Since products are being changed continuously, a flexible style, allowing considerable room for individual initiative, is conducive to attaining the firm's goal of innovation.

Process production begins with product development. However, marketing is the critical activity because the potential new product is feasible only if the firm can generate enough customers to offset the huge capital outlay associated with process technology. Pharmaceutical firms, for example, only produce a pilot sample of a new drug. Large-scale automated production does not commence until after the company's marketing department makes sure that many physicians consider the new drug desirable.

As with unit production, process firms are more successful when they use a flexible, organic structure. One reason is that the process firm also must exhibit high levels of innovation in product development and marketing. Another is that the automated technology of process production ensures that production will meet high standards of uniformity. Work is mostly done by small groups of highly skilled technicians. Since the work units are small, the spans of management also are very narrow in successful process firms.

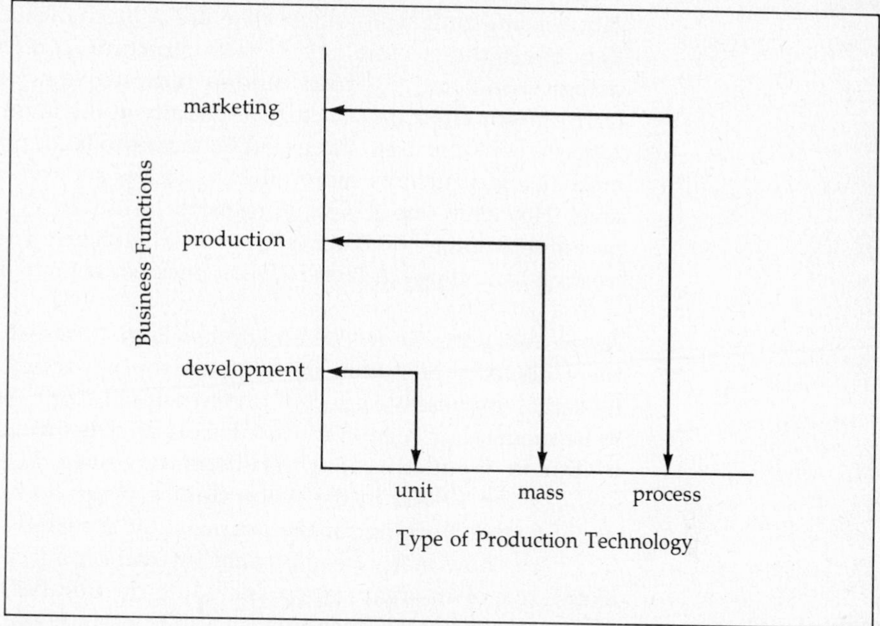

Figure 19-4 Most Important Business Functions and Technology

The hierarchy, however, is longer than in unit processing because the production process must be very carefully planned and implemented to prevent interruptions.

The success of mass-production firms is largely based on the ability to produce a product as inexpensively as possible. Maximum efficiency and standardization are needed to accomplish this. Therefore, work is broken into small units and carried on at a machine-set pace. It is highly repetitive; individual innovation at the production level is not at all desirable. In this situation, a mechanistic structure with relatively large spans of management seems most conducive to success, and written communication is often preferable to oral.

Control being more important than innovation, the rigid rules and procedures and precisely defined duties characteristic of mechanistic organizations are a big plus. Many of the drawbacks of a long chain of command do not materialize because the firm does not need to quickly communicate and implement changes in production. Even though a high degree of control is required at the production level, the work is so routine, well-defined, and paced by technology that a first-line supervisor has little need to interact with subordinates. Less interaction means that span of management can be much wider.

Size

Woodward's findings were, at first, interpreted as meaning that technology is the most important factor affecting organization design; that is, an organization using unit technology *must* use a mechanistic structure to succeed. This belief that technology dictates structure is referred to as the "technological imperative." Later studies indicated that technology often does have a major effect on structure, especially at the level or unit of the organization where it is used. For example, mass-production technology does make mechanistic structures more effective at the supervisory and assembly-line level. However, one review of research in this area concluded that "the impact of technology does *not* seem to be *all pervasive*. There is little support for treating technology as imperative; it does not seem to dictate structure."[9]

Aston Group Findings. When another English research group, a team from the University of Aston, investigated the impact of technology they also looked at the possible effect of organizational size.[10] They found technology to be moderately related to such factors as structuring of activities and concentration of authority. But "its effects were overwhelmed by the size of the organization."[11] *Size* in the Aston studies, it should be noted, was the number of people working for the organization at a single location. The relevant factor was how many people could interact on a face-to-face basis. The collective size of an organization, including the number of people it has and its geographic range of operation also may be important when making decisions on design.

The Aston findings do not wholly contradict Woodward's. The differences can be largely reconciled by the fact that most of the firms studied by Woodward were small. Because of their small size, the technology affected the structure of the entire organization. As the Aston group stated, "the smaller the organization, the wider the structural effects of technology."[12] Or, as other writers put it: "In larger organizations the authors speculate that managers are buffered from the effect of technology by the specialists, paperwork, and standard procedures that go with size. As a result the basic activities and structural framework of management is probably not affected much by the particular technology in which the organization is engaged."[13] Studies of industrial, hospital, and governmental organizations have supported the Aston findings.[14]

Impact of Size. The precise impact of size on organizing is difficult to assess. Size is an example of one facet affecting many other dimensions of structure. Increased size tends to result in a more complex structure: more managerial levels, more emphasis on formality (detailed procedures, rules, position descriptions), more sophisticated controls. Large organizations also tend to be more decentralized and more differentiated (see the following discussion of Lawrence and Lorsch). One often observes large firms adopting product departmentation in combination with federal decentralization.

We can conclude from these trends that large size seems to make a complex structure necessary. Although not all research supports this contention, it seems to be valid when large size is combined with sophisticated technology and multiple objectives and strategies.

FEATURE 19-1

International Harvester Reorganizes

Modernization of giant International Harvester Corporation began in earnest in 1971. But it was not until 1977 that large-scale corporate reorganization was undertaken. The old organization, as clearly seen from Figure 1, had grown unwieldy and confusing. The new organization, it is hoped, will help the company succeed in the fast-paced environment of the 1980s.

SOURCE: Harold Seneker, "Five International Harvesters in One," *Forbes*, April 15, 1977.

continues on page 632

People As we have discussed, research on organizational design indicates that variables such as technology and size make certain forms seem most appropriate at certain times. A mechanistic structure, for example, seems conducive to success at the production level of a firm engaged in mass production. However, management is not always free to organize in the way that is most technically desirable according to research. Managers always *must work within the limits of their resources.* It is easy for most managers to grasp that a small organization lacks the material resources of a giant like GM, IBM, or the U.S. government and therefore cannot tackle certain objectives. But managers sometimes forget that the most important resource in organizing is *people.* People are another major internal variable influencing organizational structure.

Two aspects of work-force characteristics strongly influence the choice of structure. These are the composition of the work force and its prevailing values, attitudes, and needs.

Composition of Work Force. By composition of the work force we mean the mix of college graduates, technical specialists, professionals, clerical workers, and blue-collar workers employed by the organization. Some organizations, notably those using assembly-line technology, are composed predominantly of relatively low-skilled, blue-collar workers. Many others require large numbers of people with special skills. Computer companies need many engineers and programmers. Insurance companies hire hundreds of actuaries. Pharmaceutical firms employ many chemists and medical researchers. The sales people of high technology industries are well-educated specialists. And, of course, even companies like Ford, whose workers are mostly blue collar at the production level, employ thousands of college-educated managers and staff specialists. Consequently, some subunits of an organization may have a work force with characteristics different from those prevailing in other subunits.

FEATURE 19-1, continued

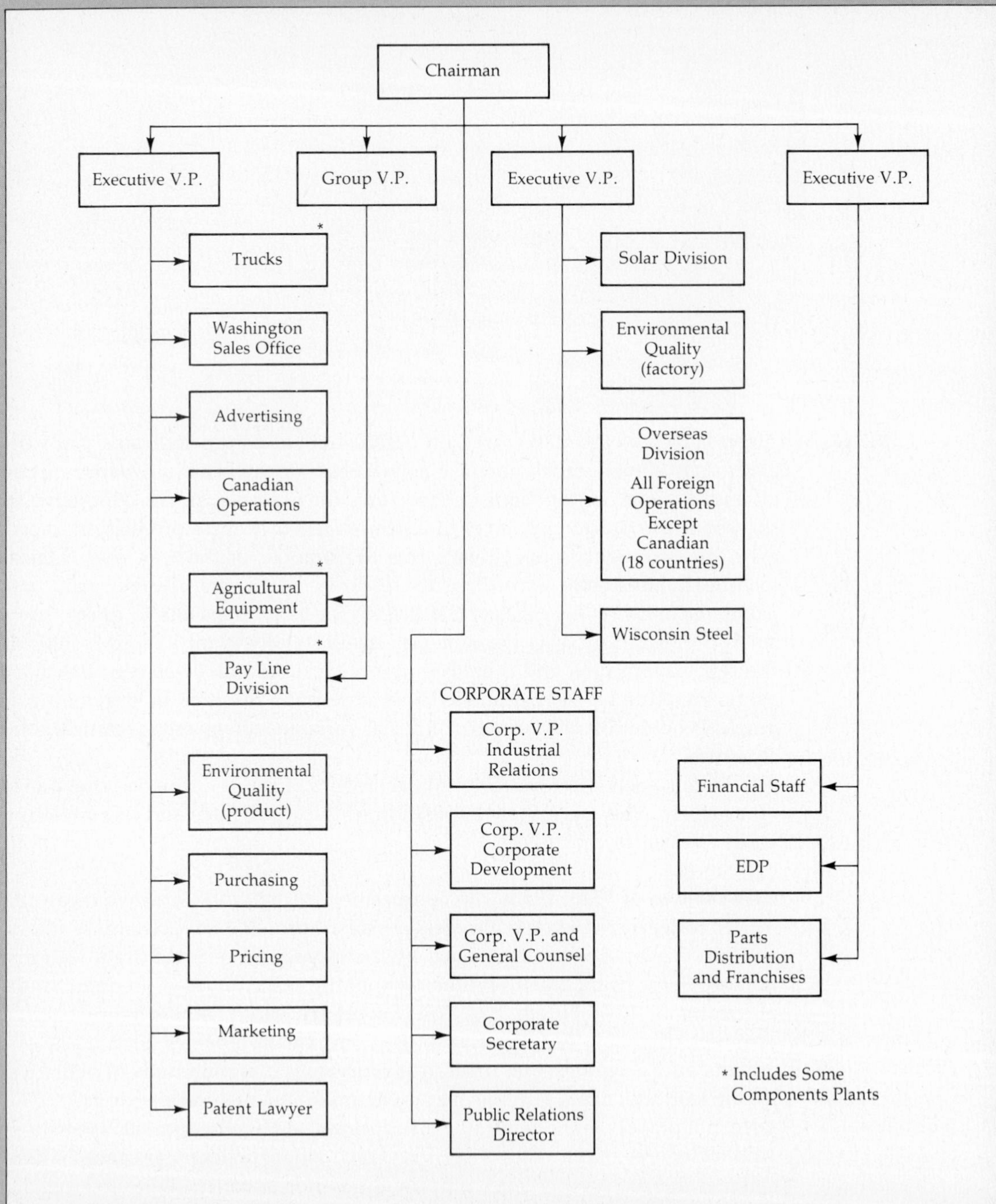

Figure 1

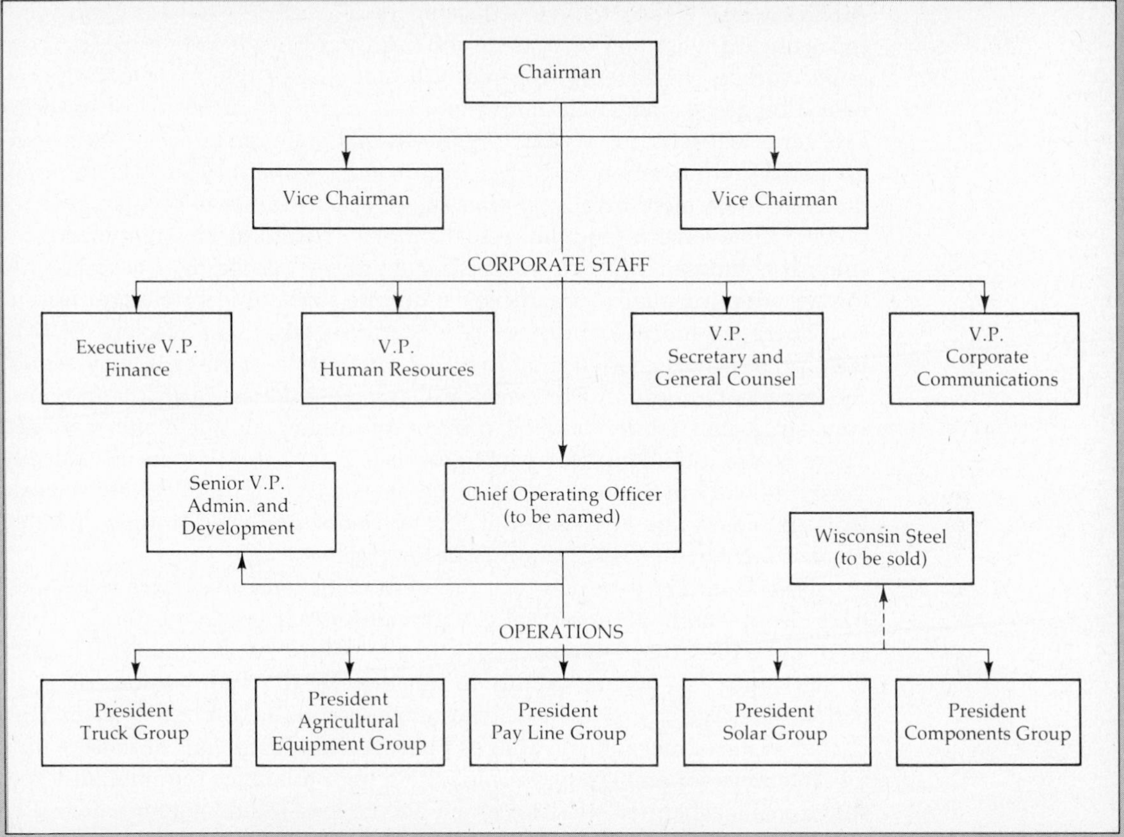

Figure 2

Figure 1 The Old Organization: A Minotaur's Delight

If you ask Brooks McCormick, Chairman of the Board, how the old structure evolved, his expression grows pained and he says, "Can I pass on that question?" Set up in 1943 as a fairly simple, divisional scheme, it was a success for many years. But as IH grew, making it continue to work became intolerably complex.

SOURCE: Harold Seneker, "Five International Harvesters in One," *Forbes*, April 15, 1977. Reproduced with permission.

Figure 2 The New International Harvester Organization After Combing Out the Nits

McCormick gives James J. Doyle, senior vice president administration and development, much of the credit for the new structure. Doyle, with consultants Booz Allen & Hamilton, Inc., found 40% of what IH manufactures crosses the old divisional lines on the way to market. Extracting a Components Group and dissolving the old overseas division simplifies managers' problems. Putting numerous staff functions under the new group presidents eliminates a good many more problems.

SOURCE: Harold Seneker, "Five International Harvesters in One," *Forbes*, April 15, 1977. Reproduced with permission.

Attitudes and Needs. College-educated people usually have different attitudes toward work and operate on different need levels than most less educated workers. In general, research indicates that people with more formal education desire greater autonomy and seek out more authority. They therefore tend to prefer an organic organizational style, one that leans toward greater decentralization and participative management.[15] Such a style will motivate them more because it offers more opportunities to satisfy needs for power, achievement, and self-actualization. Therefore, an organization or subunit composed primarily of highly educated people may be pressured toward adopting a more organic style, despite size and technological factors.

There are individual differences, of course. Also, other factors, particularly prior work experience and child-rearing style of parents, may reduce the impact of education. For example, a college graduate raised happily in a very structured family may be comfortable under an autocratic manager. There is also a tendency for people to place a higher value on intrinsically satisfying work in times of economic prosperity. When the economy is weak, workers seem to be more tolerant of unpleasant work conditions, probably because security needs temporarily become active.

It is important to realize that different management systems tend to attract people with different values and attitudes.[16] Mechanistic structures seem to be preferred by those with a low tolerance for ambiguity. Tolerance for ambiguity is a person's ability to function effectively in an uncertain situation. The high degree of structure and precise definition of responsibilities characteristic of mechanistic designs better satisfies the needs of those with a low tolerance for ambiguity. People with a high tolerance for ambiguity feel stifled in a mechanistic structure. Such people tend to prefer a high degree of autonomy. Contributing to this difference in values is that organic structures tend to attract individuals with more education and therefore more liberal values.[17]

For an organizational design to be effective, it clearly must correspond to the characteristics and attitudes of its work force. Attitudes of managers are particularly important, especially when the organization wishes to introduce a major change. An organization that has long used a conservative, mechanistic structure almost surely is heavily populated with managers comfortable with such a system. Many efforts at decentralization have been stymied by managers who could not or would not adapt their style and attitudes to the new system.

Satisfaction and Span of Management. We have already seen that size and technology are important determinants of which span of management is most appropriate in a given situation. Another consideration in the influence of span of management on employee satisfaction and performance. Considerable research has been done in this area.

One influential study was conducted at Sears.[18] In the experiment one group of stores was organized with a tall hierarchy and narrow spans of management. Another group was organized into a flat structure with wide spans of management. The performance of the stores with wide spans proved superior in all respects. This result was explained by the fact that narrow spans led to excessive red tape and communication problems. Managers tended to delegate less and supervise more closely. Subordinates working under wide spans with less supervisory control tended to exhibit more initiative and were more satisfied and productive.

Other studies do not conclusively support the finding that wide spans increase satisfaction and productivity. One, based on data from 75 percent of physiologists employed in the United States found no relationship between individual satisfaction and span of management.[19] Another, which surveyed 1900 U.S. managers, found that higher job satisfaction was associated with flatter structures in companies with under 5000 employees. In larger companies, tall structures with narrow spans led to higher satisfaction.[20] Similar results were found by a study of 2976 managers in 13 different countries.[21]

The wide variation in these findings and the inability to make a general conclusion about span of management and satisfaction demonstrates the interrelationship and complexity of the variables affecting organizing effectiveness. The indications are that there may be a cause-effect relationship between satisfaction and span of management but that size may be a more significant factor in determining what span is most appropriate. As management writers Filley, House, and Kerr state: "These findings imply that at some point in the growth of an organization it is necessary to formalize hierarchical relationships and establish limited spans of control."[22]

External Variables and Organizational Design

Organizations being open systems, variables external to the organization also may have a determining effect on which type of structure is most appropriate. To increase the probability of effectively setting, implementing, and attaining objectives, management should assess which factors in its direct action and indirect environment significantly influence the organization. Based on this diagnosis, management should choose the structure most appropriate for coping with these variables.

Environmental Volatility

We noted earlier that the environment of contemporary organizations seems to be changing at an increasing rate. *Environmental volatility* is the relative rate of change in an organization's external environment. The higher the rate of change, the more volatile the environment. As we will soon learn, environmental volatility differs from industry to industry, between organizations, and even between subunits of the same organization. Organizational environments can be characterized with respect to volatility as being stable, predictable, or turbulent.

Stable Environments. Although we often hear how fast the world is changing, it changes less quickly for some organizations than others. Even today, some organizations operate in a *stable environment*, one in which the rate of change is relatively slow. Brewing is an example of an industry in a stable environment. Although there are changes in products, such as the introduction of light beers, these changes have taken place at long intervals and do not require dramatic changes in the organization. Brewers have used the same basic technology and distribution channels for many decades. As Don Hellriegel and John Slocum state, "If there is a shift in demand, alterations in the production system would emerge slowly, because the final product is still beer. Schlitz or Carling, for example, would reduce the number of employees if beer sales dropped off rather than seek new products (e.g. making wine or 'hard' liquor). Changes in the production and distribution systems would be too costly."[23]

Stable environments are characterized not by total lack of change, for that is impossible, but by consistency and slowness of change. An organization in a stable environment will seldom change its goods or services. Technological advances will have little direct effect on it. Major competitors and customers will not change significantly for years, so growth will largely parallel population increases. A stable organizational situation also is free of radical labor difficulties, sharp shifts in regulation and taxation, and radical, swift shifts in political and social structure.

Relatively few businesses today operate in a stable environment. Some examples of relatively stable industries are candle making, meat packing, machine tools, and auto parts.

Turbulent Environment. At the end of the environmental volatility spectrum opposite the stable world of brewers and candle makers is the turbulent environment of contemporary high-technology industries. The characteristics of a turbulent environment include:

1. Continuous changes of competitors, with the entry and departure of major corporations
2. A swift series of technological innovations important enough to make old products or services obsolete virtually overnight
3. Government regulation strongly influenced by several different pressure groups, and therefore swift and unpredictable

An organization's environment would also be turbulent if a large percentage of the people who interact with it experience a sudden change of values and behavior.

The semiconductor industry is exemplary of environmental turbulence. In 1975 new technology drastically reduced the cost of semiconductors, the tiny chips used to store data and instructions. Several large companies, including Texas Instruments and National Semiconductor poured their resources into this industry which once had only a handful of competitors. Some, like Texas Instruments, branched out into new fields, such as the manufacturing and sale of wristwatches. Literally hundreds of new lines of calculators and digital watches were rushed to market during 1975 and 1976.

As the scale of production and the competition grew, the prices of memory chips and the devices using them plummeted. This caused disastrous losses for the firms that plunged into the business first and committed themselves to older (by a few months) technology. These companies found themselves holding enormous inventories of products made at a far higher cost than newer, more sophisticated ones. In the late 1970s, an even less expensive semiconductor and its close relative the microprocessor chip spread through the computer industry, which has always moved swiftly. The price and size of computers will almost surely nosedive during the 1980s. Inexpensive desk top computers already on the market are more sophisticated than the early Univacs that filled whole buildings and cost millions. And all industry eyes are on Tandy Corporation, which launched a $500 home and business computer through its Radio Shack stores in 1978.

Several other industries once relatively untroubled by rapid change are now battered by environmental turbulence. The automobile industry, for example, was badly shaken when the gasoline shortage of 1975 struck. People suddenly stopped buying large cars and craved gas-saving compacts. There also was a wave of new government regulations on auto efficiency and pollution control. By 1976, just when the big manufacturers had responded by beefing up small car production, gasoline prices stabilized. Customers began to again demand large, luxurious cars. But, the government did not pull back its mandate for improved overall mileage. The auto makers were able to adjust to these demands by designing, and convincing the public to buy, luxurious smaller cars. They doubtless will have to adjust many more times in the coming decade, which probably will see new engine technology introduced to the American industry for the first time since Ford built the V-8.

Another industry that is likely to become turbulent during the 1980s is television broadcasting and production. Technological innovations such as the video disc player, satellite transmission, and pay television are sure to severely disrupt the broadcasting industry and drastically change the distribution pattern of production. This change is described in Feature 19-2.

Of course, in today's world even though the historical pattern has been one of predictable change, volatility can increase suddenly. The impact of the gas crisis on automobile manufacturing and recreational vehicles is an example of this. Similarly, the introduction of videotape and video disc recorders may come to have as drastic an effect on manufacturing as on broadcasting and television advertising. Also, some industries are characterized by high volatility in their technology but less in their market, and vice versa. Therefore, subunits of the same organization may face very different rates of change and should be organized accordingly. We will now elaborate on this.

FEATURE 19-2

Television's Turbulent Future

Along with individualistic entrepreneurs who arrived on the TV scene only recently, numerous well-entrenched companies are scrambling to get in on the ground floor of a technology revolution that will change the face of the TV industry in the next decade. Many are turning their backs on areas that made them prosperous and are jumping wholeheartedly into new ventures. Others, uncertain which of a half-dozen technological innovations has the greatest potential, are hedging bets by moving gingerly in several new directions at the same time.

"It's as if the entire industry has come off the highway it has always known and onto a traffic circle with six or seven different exits," says an executive of American Broadcasting Co. "A few companies are circling, trying to decide which road to take to get farther ahead; others are driving down new roads—but they are watching in the rear-view mirror to see where the rest are heading, and they are wondering if they've done the right thing."

SOURCE: *Business Week*, December 17, 1979, p. 60.

An index of volatility was computed by Ramon Aldag and Ronald Storey.[24] They measured market volatility by determining variation in sales over ten years. Technological impact was measured by computing expenditures for research and development and capital expenditures. Figure 19-5 shows how different industries compare in technological and market volatility. Note that one must be careful to categorize an organization in the proper industry. Television broadcast networks, to give an obvious example, are in a very different business from television manufacturers.

Matching Structure to Environmental Volatility

A number of researchers have attempted to determine which structures are most appropriate in each rate of change situation. Two particularly important studies were those of Burns and Stalker and of Lawrence and Lorsch.

Burns and Stalker Studies. Sociologist Tom Burns and psychologist G. M. Stalker studied 20 firms in England and Scotland.[25] They investigated the rate of change of internal technologies and external markets. Classifying the firms' structures as being either mechanistic or organic (see Chapter 9 for definition), they tried to establish a relationship between structure and success. Scottish firms that had entered the electronics industry but failed were compared with successful English firms in the electronics industry.

	TECHNOLOGICAL VOLATILITY	MARKET VOLATILITY
High	Drugs—ethical Drugs—medical and hospital supply Chemicals and chemical preparation Office and business equipment Electronics Photographic	Chemicals—major Tire and rubber goods Flat glass Steel—minor Electrical and electrical leaders Aerospace
Low	Construction—special Plastic products—miscellaneous Machine tools Real estate Retail—variety stores Metal work—miscellaneous	Vegetable oil mills Machinery—specialty Auto parts and accessories Confectionery Food—meat packers Retail—department stores

Figure 19-5 **Technological and Market Volatility of Various Industries**

The Scottish firms entering the electronics industry had mechanistic structures. Originally in the textile machinery business, an industry with a stable environment, these firms had been successful. The English firms, in contrast, were already in the turbulent electronics industry. They used organic structures. This supported the general concept of a contingency approach to organizing. As Burns and Stalker noted:

> We have endeavored to stress the appropriateness of each system to its own specific set of conditions. Equally, we desire to avoid the suggestion that either system is superior under all circumstances to the other. In particular, nothing in our experience justified the assumption that mechanistic systems should be superseded by organic in conditions of stability. The beginning of administrative wisdom is the awareness that there is no one optimum type of management system.[26]

Discussing Burns and Stalker's findings, Ullrich and Wieland stated that: "one can infer that the more informal, organic structure suits organizations within dynamic industries while the more formal, mechanistic structure is appropriate for organizations within stable industries."[27]

Lawrence and Lorsch Studies. Professors Paul Lawrence and Jay Lorsch of Harvard also investigated the impact of environmental turbulence on structure.[28] They studied highly successful and less successful American firms in

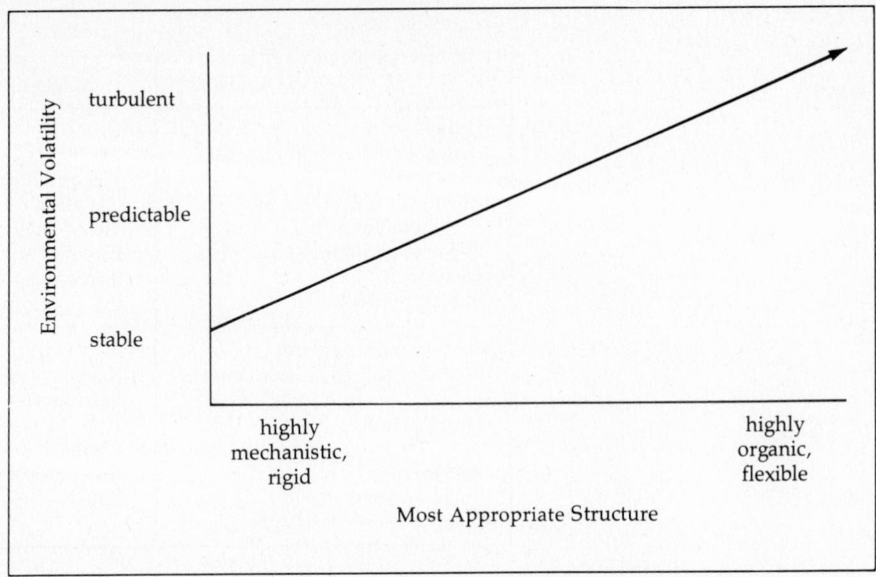

Figure 19-6 **Environmental Volatility and Structure**

the plastics, food, and container industry. These three industries were selected because of their different environments.

Lawrence and Lorsch recognized that different subunits of a firm may face different environments. Therefore, it may be desirable to structure subunits in different ways. Lawrence and Lorsch hypothesized that the more successful firms would, in fact, structure their subunits so that each was organized appropriately to meet the needs of its specific environment or subenvironment. The subenvironmental categories they used were customers, technoeconomic units and scientific units. These categories correspond respectively to the marketing, production, and research and development functions.

In some industries, such as standardized containers, the three subenvironments were found to be similar. They described such an environment as homogeneous. Thus, there should be little *differentiation* among marketing, production, and research subunits. Lawrence and Lorsch defined differentiation as "the differences in cognitive and emotional orientations among managers in different functional departments, and the differences in formal structure among these departments."[29] If, as was the case in the plastics industry, the subenvironments differed, the industry environment was considered diverse. Subunits in a diverse environment were found to be highly differentiated from each other in more successful firms.

Unsuccessful firms in each industry did not differentiate themselves enough to meet the demands of a heterogeneous environment. For example, the production departments of successful organizations having known, specific tasks were more formally structured and task oriented than the sales departments, whose tasks were more ambiguous and changing. Similarly, the research departments of effective organizations, as might be expected, had the least formal structures and tended to be managed democratically. This structure facilitated innovation, a primary objective of a research department.

Summarizing the Lawrence and Lorsch findings, Wieland and Ullrich state: "The researchers found that effective organizations were characterized by these interdepartmental differences, whereas less effective organizations tended to have people and department structures that were more or less homogeneous across the organization. This was especially true in dynamic environments requiring rather different technologies in the functional departments. To allow these needed differences is not an easy task."[30]

In addition to being able to differentiate subunit structures to meet demands of their respective environments, the most successful companies in the container, food, and plastics industries were better able to coordinate or integrate these subunits into a working overall structure. We will elaborate on the concept of integration in the last section of this chapter.

Customer, Market, and Competitive Variables

The rate of change of customers, markets, and competition, as just mentioned, is a factor contributing to environmental volatility. Volatility of these variables therefore partially determines whether mechanistic or organic structures are more appropriate for a specific organization or subunit. Customer, market, and competitive variables also strongly affect other critical organizing decisions. These decisions include which type of departmentation is most appropriate and what kinds of staff the organization needs.

Customers and Structure. When Theodore Vail defined AT&T's business as service, he was recognizing the importance of customers to the company's success. The same was true of Alfred Sloan's decision to reorganize General Motors along product lines, a concept radically different from Henry Ford's "The customer can have any color car he wants, so long as it is black." Product, customer, and territorial departmentation, described earlier, are all devices for helping an organization meet the needs of its customers better than competitors. Customer departmentation is the most obvious example. By dividing itself into units that specialize in a particular customer group—government, consumers, institutions, and so on—an organization can keep close tabs on what those customers want and provide them with goods and services specifically designed for them. Territorial departmentation is a way of putting the organization physically close to its major customers. This is why the sales function of almost every large company is organized geographically.

The more diverse its customers, the more differentiated an organization must be. Large conglomerates have moved to free-form structures with centralized financial control partly because they compete for customers in many very diverse areas. No one structure could meet all their needs.

Suppliers and Structure. Organizations do not just have customers. They are customers themselves. An organization's ability to secure personnel, raw materials, capital and energy of appropriate quality at a reasonable cost is crucial to success. This often requires the creation of subunits with specific responsibility for a particular input of production. Sometimes the supply market is so critical that the firm chooses to vertically integrate, manufacture its own major components. Such situations call for a division or department in that area. The electrical components group and mechanical components group of General Motors are examples. More often, responsibility for material resource procurement is delegated to a subunit created specifically for that purpose. The purchasing department of many companies is an example. The supply corps of the U.S. Army and the General Services Administration of the U.S. government are other examples of organizational divisions whose primary responsibility is dealing with supply markets.

Labor Market. The labor market is particularly important in organizing. In general, the tighter the labor market, the greater the degree to which labor is a constraint on organizational structure. For example, because the demand for skilled computer personnel is much greater than the supply, management must use an organizational design viewed favorably by these specialists to attract and hold them. When labor is very plentiful, employees are more likely to accept whatever practices related to structure the organization wishes to use. Fast-food firms such as McDonald's, for example, have little difficulty using a very highly mechanistic structure at the nonmanagerial level because the majority of employees are unskilled teenagers, a group characterized by chronic high unemployment. Having few employment alternatives, these people are likely to be more predisposed to accept a high degree of formalization of tasks and procedures and a high emphasis on hierarchy in communication and decision making.

Even though the number of people available may be large, a powerful labor union often imposes limits on management's choice of structure because it controls the organization's supply of certain types of labor and has a contract with the organization enforceable by law. Changes in structure usually involve changes in tasks, authority, and responsibility patterns that are formally specified in labor agreements. Because the contract with the union specifies what types of tasks each type of worker can be asked to perform, management probably is unable to change to a structure that gives workers more authority and autonomy. Labor contracts also often require promotion to be based solely on seniority. This may make it impossible for management to select for promotion to supervisor people with the ability to implement a more decentralized structure. A labor market controlled by a union is yet another example of the interrelatedness of external factors, people, tasks, objectives, and structure.

Sociopolitical Variables

Social and political factors are a pervasive, often subtle influence on organizational effectiveness. Changes in societal values, of course, are only the aggregate sentiments of the many individuals making up the society. Since almost everyone in our society works for an organization, these are the same people whose needs organizations must meet to attain their objectives. Thus, changes in societal values alter people's needs, expectations and attitudes.

When prevailing social values become more liberal, as they have in the last two decades, organizations must respond by creating structures that place less stress on authority and more on quality of working life. It was, for example, the widespread sentiment among young, blue-collar workers—a new generation with new social values—that necessitated and prompted job enlargement and enrichment programs described in Chapter 18. Changing needs of white-collar workers have recently also become a significant factor in organizing. Evidence suggests that college business graduates and MBAs seek jobs that will give them increased challenge, authority, autonomy, and decision-making ability.[31]

Political action often can have an immediate, direct impact on organizational structure. Laws regulating product safety, responsibility to consumers, and accounting practices require management to place more emphasis on control. This leads to a need for more staff specialists, perhaps enough for a distinct subunit, and may compel management to delegate functional authority to staff to ensure that government regulations will be met. Recent laws in the areas of environmental protection and equal employment opportunity have had a similar effect on larger organizations.

Integrating the Structure

Throughout this chapter we have stressed the need for a contigency approach to organizational design. The numerous examples and research cited all indicate that there is no *one* best way to structure an organization. As with all management processes, there is only a *most appropriate* design. The relative effectiveness of an organizational structure is determined by the external and internal factors which were discussed earlier in this chapter and are illustrated in Figure 19-1. Also, as noted, if subunits of an organization are characterized by a situation different from that of other subunits, their structure should differ accordingly. Another important factor in making organizational design effective is integration.

The Need for Integration

We pointed out in earlier chapters that contemporary organizations usually are divided into subunits on specialized lines. Such specialization in structure greatly increases the organization's *potential* productivity. However, for this potential to be realized, management must incorporate within its organizational design mechanisms that coordinate and integrate these segments. In the sense the term is used here, **integration** is defined by Lawrence and Lorsch as "The process of achieving unity of effort among the various sussystems (subunits) in the accomplishment of the organization's task."[32] Just as our bodies need well-coordinated muscular, respiratory, circulatory, and nervous systems to be healthy and effective, one requirement for organizational effectiveness is unity of purpose. An aspect of both the planning and organizing processes, creating unity of purpose helps ensure that the subunits do not pull the organization in different directions, and thereby diffuse its power and ability to attain overall objectives.

Effective Integration

Overall Impact on Objective Attainment. Top management, to effectively integrate the organization, must keep in mind the organization's overall objectives and communicate to members the need to focus on *overall* objectives. It is not enough that each of the organization's subunits and people perform efficiently. Managers should view the organization as an open system. Just as our brain cannot function effectively if our lungs do not effectively absorb oxygen, if one or more subunits of an organization are not effectively integrated with the rest of the organization, the health of the organization will decrease. Moreover, just as we can sometimes continue to perform with what we feel to be peak effectiveness for an extended time after one of our internal organs begins to fail, poor integration may not actually impair organizational effectiveness for six, twelve, or even eighteen months.

Consider, for example, a company manufacturing textiles in an environment characterized by high competition, frequent design changes to meet customer demands, and frequent changes of supply sources to meet changing fabric needs. The firm cannot just produce fabric of any kind as quickly as possible because changing fashions could cause it to be caught with a large inventory of undesirable output. Producing just a little of a specific fabric at a time would reduce the inventory risk, but would also cause a loss of economies of scale and, if the company cannot fill orders on demand, would lead to a loss of market share to competitors. Further complicating the problem of coordinating output to customer demand is that the lead time between production and actual sale is over six months. This means the company could easily commit its resources to production of a type of fabric that is unsaleable without realizing the mistake for over half a year. Thus, to effectively attain its overall profit and production objectives, the company needs effective communication and integrated decision making between its sales and manufacturing divisions. Unless its sales and manufacturing divisions are effectively integrated and working towards the objectives of the company rather than independently maximizing their individual effectiveness, the company may not be able to attain its true objectives, even though the sales department sells effectively and the manufacturing department is exceptionally efficient.

Techniques for Effective Integration. There are several techniques management can use to effectively integrate the organization. One, a technique advocated by writers of the administrative management school, is creating rules and procedures. However, according to management theorist James

APPROPRIATE INTEGRATION DEVICES	TYPES OF ENVIRONMENTS
Rules Procedures Schedules Management Hierarchy	Relatively stable and predictable environment characterized by slower changes in market, technological, and competitive variables. Organization or subunit usually characterized by mass production technology, repetitive tasks, and less formally educated workers.
Liaison Relationships Integrating Committees Cross-Functional Teams Inter-Departmental Meetings	More volatile environment characterized by rapid changes in market, technological, and competitive variables. Organization or subunit usually characterized by unit or process technology, more varied tasks, and workers with more formal education

Figure 19-7 **Integrating Techniques for Different Environments**

It should be noted that organizations or subunits in volatile environments also need to make use of rules, procedures, and hierarchy for integration. Similarly, interdepartmental meetings are useful in more stable environments. The difference is one of relative degree.

Thompson, this technique is only effective when the environment is relatively stable and predictable.[33] (Rules and procedures are essentially programmed decisions, which are best suited to repetitive situations. If the environment changes rapidly, situations tend not to repeat.) For organizations whose environment changes more rapidly, integration is achieved more effectively through individual liaison relationships, committees, and interdepartment meetings.

This technique is supported by the research of Lawrence and Lorsch, who found that the most successful companies in the container, food, and plastics industries were those that had achieved more effective integration of their manufacturing, marketing, and research and development subunits than the less successful companies.[34] The structural devices used to achieve integration were found to vary with the amount of differentiation in the organization. The highly differentiated plastics industry had a large network of integrating mechanisms: entire departments of integrating personnel, cross-functional teams, the design of the management hierarchy itself, and written plans and schedules. For firms in the less differentiated container

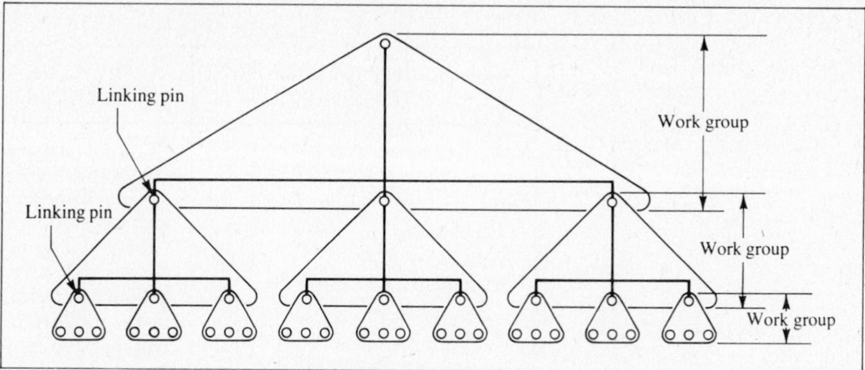

Figure 19-8 **The Linking Pin Concept**

industry, the management hierarchy and written plans and schedules were able to handle all integration.

Another important technique for integration highlighted by Lawrence and Lorsch is conflict management. It was found that the organizations that successfully achieved the balance of differentiation and integration required by the environment were those whose members effectively resolved conflict. In these effective organizations, managers openly discussed their differences and worked until a solution was found, rather than glossing over differences or denying their existence. The effective organizations also seemed to prevent or diminish the breeding of conflict by concentrating the real decision-making power in those subunits and managerial levels with the most knowledge and information about factors affecting the decision.

The **linking pin concept**, developed by Rensis Likert, is another structural technique to integrate the various subunits and groups that comprise the organization.[35] Since a manager is both in charge of his or her own group, as well as a member of a group managed by a higher level manager, Likert viewed the manager as a *linking pin* between these groups. By being a member of these overlapping groups, managers should be able to link the groups to the total organization. The linking pin concept is illustrated in Figure 19-8. Likert also felt that the group should be managed by face-to-face meetings with all subordinates present, rather than through various one-to-one interactions between the manager and each subordinate.

SUMMARY

There is no one best way to organize. Several situational variables must be considered in order to make organizing effective. Major internal contingencies are the organization's objectives and strategies, size, technology, and people. The most significant external variables are environmental volatility, customer and market factors, and sociopolitical factors. Often, these variables are interrelated and affect one another.

FEATURE 19-3

GE Organizes for the '80s

General Electric Company has long been famous as an innovator of management practice. It popularized decentralization in the 1950s and strategic planning in the early 1970s. In December of 1977, GE completed an innovative reorganization of top management designed to free its three-man executive office from internal concerns so that it could concentrate more effectively on external factors such as government regulation and taxation.

Called sector executives, the new layer of management reports to the executive office. Each of these five executives now heads a multi-billion dollar group of GE units with a clear, well-defined industry identity. The heads of major GE groups and the 49 strategic business units (SBUs) that are the foundation of GE's corporate planning system report to these sector executives instead of directly to the top office. Whereas the top office previously had to review each unit's plans, it now only has to read that of the sector executive, which includes a summary of each SBU plan.

"Our direct reports would have grown quite substantial if we had not made this change," explains chairman of the board Reginald Jones. "By 1980 we would have been faced with a really unmanageable situation. We saw the need to inject this new level called sector in order to reduce our span of control, enhance the manageability of the corporation, and still permit us to recognize the growth of the component areas of the company by elevating departments to divisions and divisions to groups. We can do this now and still not increase the span of control at the top."

Each sector executive, because he or she is effectively a chief executive in many respects, now represents GE in his or her particular industry. "We are trying to make each of these top management people spokespersons for an industry, insofar as GE's participation in it is concerned," states Jones. "It is a way to develop institutional leadership." The sector concept also plays an important role in management development. When the sector assignments were made, four of the five executives were assigned to units in which they had little or no experience.

"If you are going to understand the many markets we serve, you shouldn't have experience in just one," says Jones. "So don't be surprised if, in a couple of years, we shuffle again to give some of these operating people staff experience and vice versa."

Mr. Jones feels that it is imperative for a top manager to have staff experience and the ability to interact with staff:

> When you get to the top of this company, you find yourself making great demands on staff for counsel and guidance and for coordination of all

continues on page 648

FEATURE 19-3, continued

the varied operations of the company. The background I had in services has been inordinately helpful to me in this role, particularly in a time when externalities of the company have such an important impact on our earnings potential. Our future is being determined to an increasing degree by government. I'm spending a great deal of my time on tax reduction and reform.

He feels that this will be even more important in the 1980s:

We will have to be developing a cadre of managers who are extremely sensitive to externalities, who are able to function in an anticipatory mode, not a reactive one, who will be able to sense that this is what the public wants and should expect of the corporation in terms of what it feels the corporation should be doing.

SOURCE: "GE's New Billion Dollar Small Businesses," *Business Week*, December 19, 1979, pp. 78–79.

There is much truth in Alfred Chandler's saying, "structure follows strategy." Objectives and strategy determine the most fundamental organizing decisions. The use of unit, mass, or process technology is a strategic choice.

When Woodward studied the influence of technology she found that the number of management levels increased from unit to mass to process. Median spans of management were lowest in process, highest with mass-production technology. More successful firms tended to have the median number of levels and span for the type of technology used. More successful unit and process firms tended to have an organic structure and use oral communication more often. Successful mass-production firms were more mechanistically organized and used more written communication. Woodward explained these results by analyzing the sequence and relative importance of primary business functions of firms using each technology.

The findings of the Aston group indicated that the influence of size often overwhelmed that of technology. Large size often leads to more levels and formalization, more elaborate controls, and a greater tendency toward federal decentralization.

The composition of the work force and its attitudes and needs also strongly influence organizing decisions. More educated people tend to prefer more liberal systems. Mechanistic structures seem to be preferred by those with a low tolerance for ambiguity and vice versa. Since organizations tend to be populated with people attracted to its current system, reorganization often is difficult to implement.

The impact of span of management on individual satisfaction also should be considered. Some research indicates that satisfaction is higher with wider spans. Other studies hold this is true only in smaller organizations.

Recent research indicates that environmental volatility may be the most significant of the organizing contingencies. External environments can be characterized as stable, predictable, or turbulent. Generally, the more volatile the environment, the more appropriate a flexible, organic structure. Also, subunits of an organization may face different environments. Lawrence and Lorsch found that in such situations the more successful firms were those that differentiated their structure. Less successful firms facing a heterogeneous environment tended to impose one system of structure on all units, rather than allowing each to be structured in accordance with its particular needs.

The choice of a system of departmentation is strongly influenced by customer variables. The supply market may cause the firm to vertically integrate and create divisions to produce much of its production input. Often special staff must be created to deal with the supply market. The labor market often restricts management's structural options, especially if there is a strong union.

When social values change, the attitudes and needs of employees also change. Historically, the liberalization of society's values has moved organizations away from highly authoritarian patterns of organizing. Political action has led to an increased reliance on staff to meet government regulations.

Decentralization is usually desirable when the environment is characterized by changing markets, competition with diverse product lines, and volatile technology. It also becomes more desirable as organizations grow in size and complexity. When change is relatively slow or the organization is relatively small, a centralized structure may be preferable. The same would hold if people have a low need for autonomy.

Effective integration of the structure is essential to attain the benefits of specialization in design. Techniques for integration, too, are influenced by the situation. Organizations in stable environments using mass-production technology can appropriately use rules, procedures, and hierarchy for integration. Those organizations in more volatile environments, using unit or process technology often find integrating techniques such as liaison relationships, committees, and interdepartmental meetings more appropriate.

REVIEW QUESTIONS

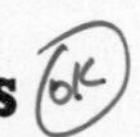

1. What are the major variables affecting organizational design?
2. What were the major findings of Woodward's studies?
3. What did the Aston group discover, and how did this affect the interpretation of Woodward's findings?
4. In what situations is decentralization more appropriate?
5. Give an example of objectives and strategy affecting structure.
6. Which integrating mechanisms are more appropriate for organizations operating in more volatile environments?
7. How have changes in sociopolitical factors affected organizational design in recent years?
8. What organizational design characteristics seem to be more appropriate for organizations using mass-production technology whose competition and customers do not change often?
9. What is the relationship between satisfaction and span of management?
10. What structural alternatives are more appropriate when the work force is composed of well-educated people?

DISCUSSION QUESTIONS

11. Describe an organizational design for a business, and show how it would differ from that of a nonprofit organization.
12. Many people predict a revolution in information technology during the 1980s. How is this likely to affect organizational structure?
13. Evaluate the organizational structure of your college in terms of its objectives, people, and environmental volatility.
14. Give four true examples that support Chandler's statement, "structure follows strategy."
15. Compare and contrast the Burns and Walker studies with those of Lawrence and Lorsch.

CASE INCIDENT

Mt. Paran College

We simply are not responsive enough, lamented Otis Smith, provost of Mt. Paran College. "We're using a 1950 organization design in the 1980s, and it doesn't work."

Mt. Paran, a small, private college with 827 undergraduates, was located in the suburbs of a medium-sized city. Over the years, it had built a reputation of academic excellence. The faculty was proud of the large percentage of students who went on to graduate study. The current president, Dr. Paul Miller, had held the post for 26 years. It was widely assumed that, even though he had only been provost a year, Dr. Smith would become president when Dr. Miller retired after the next academic year.

Dr. Miller was considered a good president, and had guided the college through some difficult times. Although the college was financially sound, it had experienced a 12 percent enrollment drop in the past two years. Further, indications were that with fewer high-school graduates and smaller families, additional decreases could be expected. It was this rather bleak prognosis that led Smith to conclude that Mt. Paran was not responsive enough to changing conditions.

Dr. Smith's views were not received favorably by the college's department heads. In particular, they objected to Smith's plan of action which included the following:

1. An aggressive advertising campaign
2. Evening classes to attract working students
3. The development of adult and continuing education programs
4. The utilization of the campus during the summer months for a sports camp
5. Changes in departments to meet the needs of these new types of students

Smith said, "not only do we have to reorganize, but we must give some serious consideration to what kind of business we're in." President Miller replied that Mt. Paran was an educational institution not a business and what worked well in the past should also work well in the future.

Questions

1. How do you think Dr. Smith should reply to President Miller?
2. How might organizational changes best be introduced?
3. Can we properly apply the organizing process often employed by profit-making organizations to educational institutions?

NOTES

1. Jay W. Lorsch and Paul R. Lawrence, *Studies in Organization Design* (Homewood, IL: Irwin, 1970), p. 1.
2. William B. Wolfe, *Management: Readings Toward a General Theory* (Belmont, CA: Wadsworth, 1964), p. 325.
3. Alfred D. Chandler, Jr., *Strategy and Structure* (Cambridge, MA: The M.I.T. Press, 1962).
4. Ibid., p. 302.
5. Ibid., p. 309.
6. Ibid., pp. 328–329.
7. Ernest Dale, *Organizations* (New York: AMA, 1967).
8. Joan Woodward, *Industrial Organization: Theory and Practice* (London: Oxford University Press, 1965).
9. J. H. Jackson and C. P. Morgan, *Organization Theory: A Macro Perspective for Management* (Englewood Cliffs, NJ: Prentice-Hall, 1978), p. 195.
10. D. J. Hickson, D. S. Pugh, and D. C. Pheysey, "Operations Technology and Organization Structure: An Empirical Reappraisal," *Administrative Sciences Quarterly*, vol. 14 (1969), pp. 378–398.
11. Jackson and Morgan, op. cit., pp. 181–182.
12. Hickson, et. al., op. cit., p. 395.
13. Jackson and Morgan, op. cit., p. 182.
14. Peter Blau and R. Schoenherr, *The Structure of Organizations* (New York: Basic Books, 1971); John Child, "Managerial and Organizational Factors Associated with Company Performance," *Journal of Management Studies*, vol. 11 (1974), pp. 175–189 and vol. 12 (1975), pp. 12–28; John Child and Roger Mansfield, "Technology, Size, and Organizational Structure," *Sociology*, vol. 6 (1972), pp. 369–393; Lawrence Hrebiniak and Joseph Alutto, "A Comparative Organizational Study of Performance and Size Correlates in Inpatient Psychiatric Departments" (Buffalo: State University of New York and Buffalo, 1970), monograph; Marshall Meyer, "Size and the Structure of Organizations: A Causal Analysis," *American Sociological Review*, vol. 37 (1972), pp. 434–441.
15. Joseph Alutto and James Belasco, "A Typology for Participation in Organizational Decision Making," *Administrative Science Quarterly*, vol. 17 (1972), pp. 117–125; Jay Lorsch and John Morse, *Organizations and Their Members* (New York: Harper & Row, 1974).
16. Lorsch and Morse, op. cit.
17. Lorsch and Morse, op. cit.
18. J. Worthy, "Organizational Structures and Employee Morale," *American Sociological Review*, no. 15 (1950), pp. 169–179.

19. Meltzer and Salter, "Organizational Structure and Performance and Job Satisfaction," *American Sociological Review*, no. 27 (1962), pp. 351–362.
20. L. W. Porter and E. E. Lawler, "The Effects of Tall Versus Flat Organization on Managerial Satisfaction" (Paper delivered to the American Psychological Association, Philadelphia, September, 1963).
21. L. W. Porter and J. Siegel, "Relationships of Tall and Flat Organization Structures to the Satisfaction of Foreign Managers," *Personnel Psychology*, no. 65 (1965), pp. 379–392.
22. A. C. Filley, R. J. House, and S. Kerr, *Managerial Process and Organizational Behavior*, 2nd ed. (Glencoe, IL: Scott, Foresman, 1976, p. 422.
23. Don Hellriegel and John W. Slocum, Jr., *Management: Contingency Approaches*, 2nd ed. (Reading, MA: Addison-Wesley, 1978), p. 146.
24. Ramon Aldag and Ronald Storey, "Environmental Uncertainty," *Proceedings, Academy of Management*, 1975.
25. Tom Burns and G. M. Stalker, *The Management of Innovation* (London: Tavistock Publications, 1961).
26. Ibid., p. 125.
27. George F. Wieland and Robert A. Ullrich, *Organizations: Behavior, Design, and Change* (Homewood, IL: Irwin, 1976), p. 78.
28. Paul R. Lawrence and Jay Lorsch, *Organizations and Environment: Managing Differentiation and Integration* (Boston: Harvard University Graduate School of Business Administration, 1967).
29. Jay W. Lorsch, "Introduction to the Structural Design of Organizations," in *Organizational Structure and Design*, G. W. Dalton, P. R. Lawrence, and J. W. Lorsch (Homewood, IL: Irwin, 1970), p. 5.
30. Wieland and Ullrich, op. cit., p. 82.
31. L. B. Ward and A. G. Athos, *Student Expectations of Corporate Life: Implications for Management Recruiting* (Boston: Graduate School of Business Administration, Harvard University, 1972); Patricia A. Renwick and Edward E. Lawler, "What Do You Really Want from Your Job?" *Psychology Today*, May 1978.
32. P. R. Lawrence and Jay W. Lorsch, "Differentiation and Integration in Complex Organizations," *Administrative Science Quarterly*, vol. 12 (June 1967), pp. 1–47.
33. James E. Thompson, *Organizations in Action* (New York: McGraw-Hill, 1967).
34. Lawrence and Lorsch, op. cit.
35. Rensis Likert, *New Patterns of Management* (New York: McGraw-Hill, 1961).

CHAPTER 20

Managing Conflict and Change

Early management writings tended to stress operating the organization smoothly. If only the correct formula could be found, it was thought, the organization would run like a well-oiled machine. Conflict within the organization was perceived as highly negative. Indeed, one of the primary aims of Weber's bureaucracy and the administrative school was to eliminate conflict. Management today recognizes that total lack of conflict within organizations is not only impossible but undesirable. Moreover, while a smooth integration of activities is needed, the organization cannot remain static and comfortable with the status quo. Rather, management must be proactive, creating change and responding appropriately to changes in the environment. Therefore, in this chapter we will broaden our understanding of modern management by learning more about the nature of conflict and change in organizations and the techniques for managing them effectively, including organization development.

After reading this chapter, you should understand the following important terms and concepts:

- conflict
- functional results of conflict
- dysfunctional conflict
- types of conflict
- causes of conflict
- interpersonal styles for conflict resolution
- approaches to organizational change
- organization development
- OD intervention

The Nature of Organizational Conflict

What Conflict Is

Like so many concepts in management, conflict has been defined and interpreted in many ways.[1] We define **conflict** as a disagreement between two or more parties, which may be individuals or groups. Each party attempts to gain acceptance of its view or objective and prevent the other party from doing the same. When the budget for the coming year is being prepared, for example, the presidents of CBS News and CBS Sports probably will each attempt to convince the CBS board of directors that they deserve a larger respective share of the company's resources. Or, two engineers at a meeting may try to get their different product specifications accepted.

Differing Views of Conflict. When people think of conflict, the images that most often come to mind are aggression, threats, arguments, hostility, war, and so forth. As a result, people often feel that conflict is always undesirable, should be avoided when possible, and should be immediately resolved when it does occur. This attitude is implicit in the writings of the scientific management school, the administrative school, and Weber's concept of bureaucracy.[2] These approaches to organizational effectiveness relied heavily on explicitly specifying tasks, procedures, rules, and authority relationships and developing a rational organizational structure. It was felt that such mechanisms would eliminate most conflict and could be used to correct problems when they did occur.

Writers of the human relations school also tended to believe that conflict is avoidable and should not occur. They acknowledged the possibility of conflict between individual and organizational objectives, between line and staff, between one's authority and abilities, and among different management groups.[3] However, the writers of the human relations school tended to interpret conflict as a sign of organizational ineffectiveness and managerial failure. Good human relations, they believed, could prevent conflict from occurring.

The contemporary view is that even in well-managed organizations some conflict is not only inevitable but actually may be desirable. Of course, conflict is not always positive. In some instances it can prevent both individual need satisfaction and attainment of organizational objectives. A person who argues for the sake of arguing during a committee meeting, for example, would possibly decrease other individuals' satisfaction of needs for belongingness and esteem and probably decrease the group's ability to make effective decisions. Group members might accept the arguer's viewpoint to avoid the stress of conflict, even though they do not feel it is, in fact, correct. But in many situations, conflict helps introduce differing points of view, provides additional information, helps identify additional alternatives or problems, and so forth. This makes group decision making more effective and also gives individuals an opportunity to express their thoughts and thereby satisfy personal needs for esteem and power.

Thus, conflict can be functional and can lead to increased organizational effectiveness. Or, it can be dysfunctional, a cause of decreased individual satisfaction and organizational performance. Which role conflict plays depends largely on how effectively *conflict is managed.* Before discussing how conflict can be managed, let us first describe the basic types of conflict, causes of conflict, and a model of the conflict process.

Types of Conflict

There are four basic **types of conflict:** conflict within an individual, conflict between individuals, conflict between individuals and a group, and conflict between groups.

Conflict Within an Individual. Conflict within an individual does not really meet our definition of conflict. However, its potential dysfunctional consequences are similar to other types of conflict. There are several forms of this. One of the most common is *role conflict,* which occurs when conflicting demands are made on an individual regarding job expectations. For example, a floor manager of a department store may tell a salesperson to always be available to give customers information and service. Later the manager may complain that this same salesperson is spending too much time with customers and not paying enough attention to keeping the stock orderly. To the salesperson, the do's and don'ts seem incompatible. A similar situation would occur if a production supervisor were instructed to step up output as much as possible by the production manager and instructed by the quality control manager to increase quality level by slowing down the output rate.

In both cases the individual is given contradictory tasks and job expectations. In the first, conflict is caused by the contradictory demands of a single person. In the second, the cause of conflict is violation of the principle of unity of command.

Conflict within an individual might also result when job demands conflict with personal demands or values. As we pointed out in our discussion of decision making, this is an increasingly common problem in contemporary organizations. For example, a manager may have planned for weeks to go away for a long weekend with her husband because working too hard had begun to affect their relationship adversely. But on Friday, her boss rushes in with a problem and insists it be resolved over the weekend. Or a sales representative may believe that bribery is highly unethical but may be given a strong hint by higher management to make the sale, no matter what it takes. Conflict within an individual could also be a response to work overload or underload. Research indicates that such inner conflict is associated with low job satisfaction, low confidence in one's self and the organization, and stress.[4]

Figure 20-1 Conflict Within an Individual

Conflict Between Individuals. Conflict between individuals is probably the most widely recognized form of conflict. It manifests itself in organizations in many ways. A common one is when two managers compete for limited capital, manpower, or equipment time. Each perceives that, because the resources are limited, he must convince top management to give them to him, not the other manager. Or two artists working on an advertising campaign develop different approaches. Each tries to convince the marketing manager that his is the one to use. Similar, but often more subtle and long lasting, is the conflict that may occur between two people being considered for the same promotion.

Conflict between individuals may also manifest as a personality clash. People with widely differing characteristics, attitudes, and values are likely to have views and aims that differ radically.

Conflict Between the Individual and the Group. As the Hawthorne experimenters discovered, work groups establish norms of behavior and output standards. In order to be accepted by the informal group and thereby satisfy social needs, an individual must adhere to these. However, if the group's

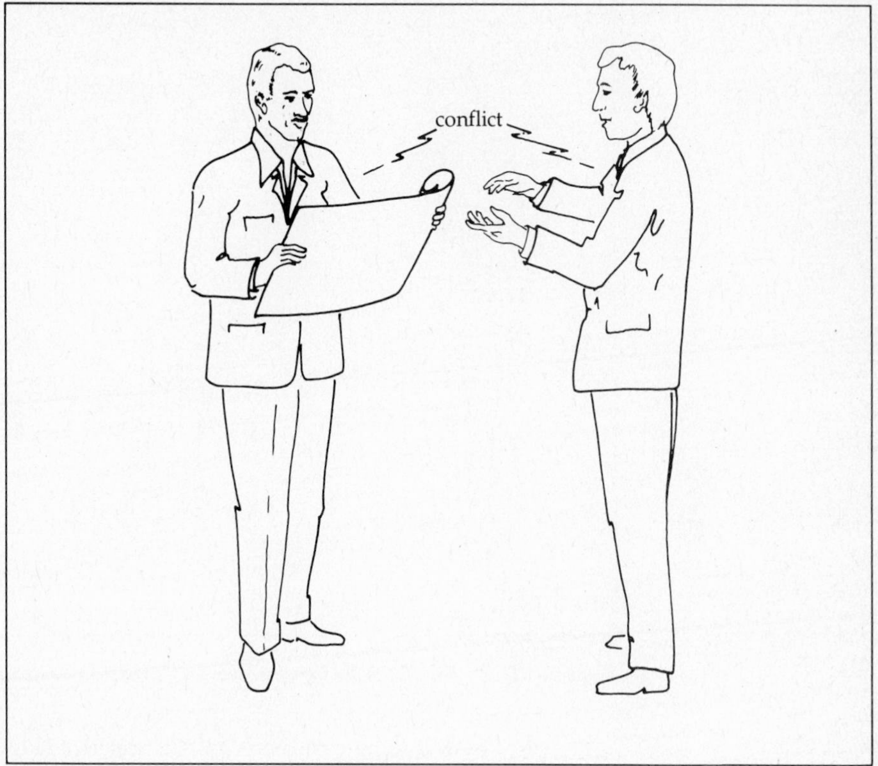

Figure 20-2 Conflict Between Individuals

expectations conflict with the individual's, a conflict may result. For example, a given individual may want to earn as much money as possible by working overtime or exceeding output quotas, but the group may consider working "too hard" as negative behavior.

Not dissimilar is the conflict that may arise from a manager's need for belongingness and to be accepted by subordinates. Like most people, managers usually want to be liked by the people with whom they work. However, part of the manager's job is ensuring that productivity remains at adequate levels and that the rules and procedures of the organization are followed. To accomplish this, the manager may be forced into taking disciplinary actions. These may be unpopular with the subordinate group and cause it to retaliate by treating the manager more coolly, being less committed to group objectives, and possibly decreasing productivity.

Conflict Between Groups. Organizations are composed of many groups, both formal and informal. Conflict between them is not uncommon in even the best-managed organizations. Informal organizations that feel management is treating them unfairly may become more cohesive and attempt to

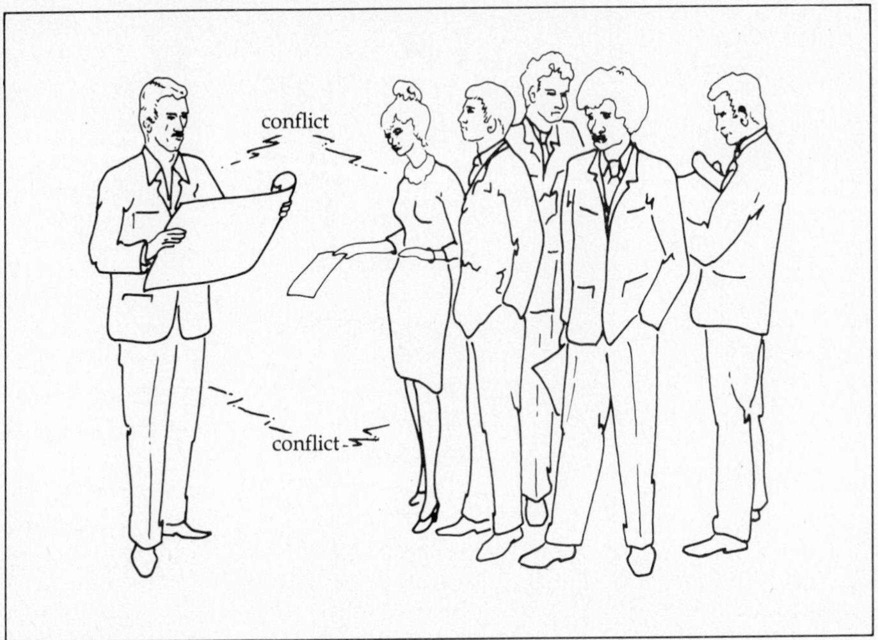

Figure 20-3 Conflict Between the Individual and the Group

"get even" by reducing productivity. During the Hawthorne studies, for example, it was discovered that workers actively banded together to produce below management standards. Active conflict between unions and management, of course, is another example of conflict between groups.

An unfortunately common example of conflict between groups is that between line and staff departments.[5] Staff personnel are generally younger and better educated than line managers, and tend to use technical jargon when communicating. These differences cause personality clashes and communication problems. The conflict may be exhibited by line managers rejecting staff recommendations and resenting their dependence on staff for information. In extreme situations, line management may deliberately implement a staff proposal in a way that guarantees failure to put staff "in its place." Staff, in turn, may resent their inability to directly implement decisions and cause conflict by keeping line managers highly dependent on them for information. These are clear examples of dysfunctional conflict.

Functional groups within the organization, because their specific objectives differ, often come into conflict with each other. A sales department, for example, is typically customer-oriented, whereas a production department is strongly concerned with cost effectiveness and economies of scale. Maintaining high inventories, as sales prefers in order to always be able to fill orders quickly, increases costs, which is perceived as negative by production. Another example of conflict between formal groups would be a day production shift blaming the night shift for maintenance problems and missing tools. In very large organizations, one division may attempt to increase its profitability by selling output to outside customers, rather than filling the needs of another division of the company at a lower price.

Causes of Conflict

The various types of conflict just described have several causes. The major **causes of conflict** are: shared resources, task-interdependence, different goals, differing perceptions and values, personality styles, and poor communication.[6]

Shared Resources. The resources of even the largest organization are limited. Management must decide how to allocate materials, people, money, etc., among various groups in order to attain the objectives of the organization as a whole most effectively. By necessity, allocating greater resources to a given manager, subordinate, or group means that others will receive a smaller share of the total. Whether the decision involves which of four secretaries is to get a new typewriter, which department of a university will be able to hire new faculty, or which manager will receive the funds to expand his or her division, people generally prefer to get more than less. Thus, the need to share resources is an almost inevitable source of conflict of all types.

Task Interdependence. A potential for conflict exists whenever an individual or group is dependent on other individuals or groups to perform their task. For example, a production manager may blame decreased productivity on the maintenance crew's failure to repair equipment quickly enough. The maintenance supervisor, in turn, may blame the personnel department for not hiring the new people she needed. Similarly, if one of six engineers working on a new product design does not perform his job properly, the others probably will feel their ability to perform their own jobs is impaired. This probably will result in conflict between the group and the engineer who is perceived responsible for poor performance. Since all organizations are systems composed of interdependent parts, if a subunit or individual's performance is below average, task interdependence may be a common cause of conflict.

Different Objectives. As noted in earlier chapters, task specialization and subunit differentiation is an important means of increasing organizational effectiveness. However, the potential for conflict increases as organizations become more differentiated and specific objectives are formulated.[7] This is because the specialized subunits may be more concerned with attaining their objectives, rather than those of the organization as a whole. For example, a sales department may press for as many different products and variations on products as possible because this gives them a competitive edge and increases sales volume. However, the production department's objectives of cost effectiveness are more easily met if there is less variation in the product line. Similarly, the purchasing department may wish to order large quan-

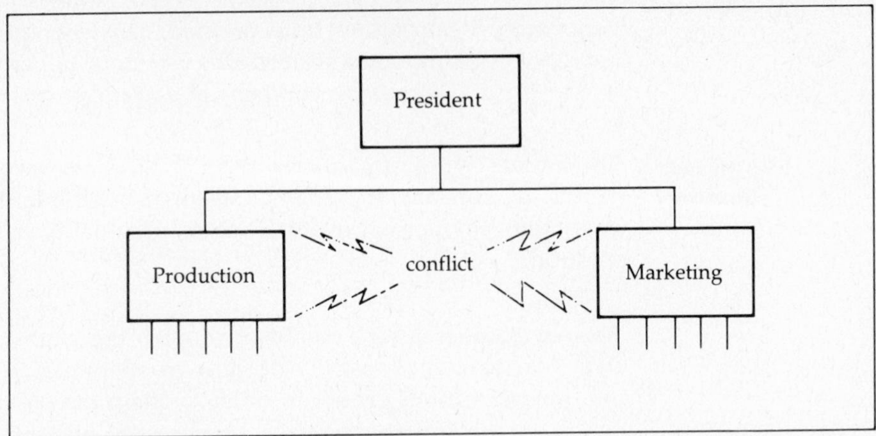

Figure 20-4 Conflict Between Groups

tities to lower the average cost per item. The finance department, on the other hand, may want to use the money purchasing intends for inventory to invest in order to increase overall return on investment.

Perceptions and Values. People's perception of a situation is affected by such factors as their desire to attain a given objective or what department they work for. Instead of evaluating a situation with an open mind, people may consider only those views, alternatives, and aspects of the situation they perceive as supporting their own group and personal needs. This tendency was illustrated by a study in which executives from sales, personnel, and public relations departments were asked to resolve a problem. Each felt the basic solution could be attained through his or her own functional area.[8]

Differences in values also are a common cause of conflict. Values are fundamental beliefs about what is right or wrong or relatively desirable. For example, a subordinate may believe that she should be able to assert herself at all times, whereas her manager may believe that subordinates should only speak when spoken to and do what they are told without question. Similarly, highly educated research and development personnel often highly value freedom and autonomy. If their supervisor believes in closely watching over the work of subordinates, the difference in values is likely to cause conflict.

Personal Style and Background. Differences in personal style and life background can also increase the potential for conflict. You doubtless have met people whose behavior is consistently aggressive, abrasive, or hostile, or who are predisposed to disagree on every issue. People with such abrasive personal styles are highly likely to induce conflict. Studies have shown that people with traits such as being highly authoritarian, highly dogmatic, and low in self-esteem are more likely to engage in conflict.[9] Other studies have shown that differences in background, values, education, length of service, age, and social patterns decrease the degree of interpersonal rapport and collaboration between unit representatives.[10]

Poor Communication. Poor communication is both a cause and result of conflict. Poor communication can catalyze conflict by preventing an individual or group from understanding the situation or the views of others. If management fails to communicate to subordinates that a new pay plan tied to productivity is meant to increase earnings and not "get too much" out of workers, the subordinates may behave in ways to slow down production. Other common communication problems that cause conflict are overly ambiguous job expectations, failure to fully and clearly define the duties and responsibilities of all individuals and subunits, and communicating expectations in a way that causes a subordinate to perceive that conflicting demands are being made upon him. These problems could be caused or aggravated by failure to develop and communicate clear job descriptions.

A Model of the Conflict Process

Figure 20-5 is a model of the conflict process. As the model shows, the existence of one or more of the sources of conflict just described increases the potential for a conflict situation to develop. However, even though the *potential* for conflict increases, the parties involved may choose not to respond in a way that further aggravates the situation. One group of researchers found that people often do not respond to conflict situations that involve low potential loss or that they perceive as minimally threatening.[11] In other words, at times people realize that the potential benefits of engaging in conflict are not worth the costs. Their basic response is, "I'll let him have his way this time."

In many situations, however, a person will respond in a way that involves actively blocking the other party's desired objectives. This true conflict is expressed often through an attempt to convince the other party or a neutral mediator that "This is why he is wrong and this is why my view is right." The individual may attempt to win acceptance of his view or block that of the other party through one of the primary influence means such as coersion, reward, legitimate power, expertise, or charisma.

The final stage of the conflict process is managing conflict. In the next section we will discuss several alternative ways of managing conflict. Depending on how effectively conflict is managed, its consequences will be functional or dysfunctional, which in turn will affect the potential for future conflict by eliminating or creating causes.

Functional Consequences of Conflict. As mentioned earlier, conflict is not necessarily dysfunctional and to be avoided. There are several functional consequences of conflict. One is that a problem can be resolved in a way that is acceptable to all parties involved. People should therefore be more committed to the solution as a result. This, in turn, should minimize or eliminate

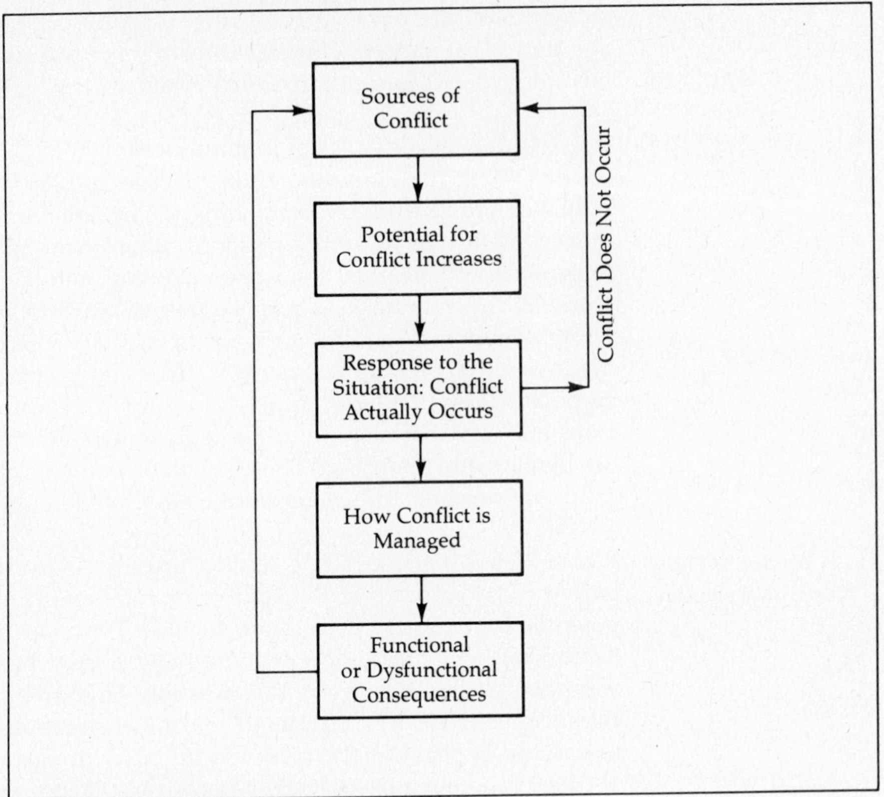

Figure 20-5 Model of the Conflict Process

problems in implementing the solution, such as feelings of hostility, unfair treatment, and being forced to do something against one's will. Another functional consequence of effectively managing conflict is that the parties will be more predisposed toward cooperation—as opposed to antagonism—in future situations with conflict potential.

Conflict also can help overcome the "yes man" syndrome in which subordinates do not present ideas they feel conflict with those of their managers, even though they realize the manager is incorrect. Similarly, conflict can decrease the potential for "groupthink," as described earlier. In these and other situations, conflict will benefit the organization to the extent that differing views increase the amount of relevant information related to a problem. This can improve the quality of decision making because additional diagnosis leads to better understanding of the situation, symptoms are differentiated from causes, and additional alternatives and criteria for evaluating them are developed. Also, through conflict potential problems in implementation can be worked out by group members before implementation takes place.

Dysfunctional Consequences of Conflict. If conflict is not managed effectively, the following dysfunctional consequences, all of which probably will cause decreased attainment of objectives, may occur:

1. Dissatisfaction, low morale, increased turnover, and decreased productivity.[12]
2. Less cooperation in the future.
3. More loyalty to one's own group and more unproductive competition between groups within the organization.
4. Perceiving the other party as an "enemy." By extension, perceiving one's own views and objectives as positive and those of the other party as negative.
5. Decreased interaction and communication between the conflicting parties.[13]

Managing Conflict

There are several ways of managing conflict effectively. These techniques and styles can be grouped within two categories: structural techniques and the use of alternative interpersonal styles.

Structural Techniques

Four structural techniques for managing conflict are: clarifying job expectations, the use of coordinating mechanisms and integrating techniques, the establishment of superordinate objectives, and use of the reward structure.

Clarifying Job Expectations. One of the best means of managing to prevent dysfunctional conflict is to clarify what each individual and subunit is expected to accomplish. This would include establishing performance levels, who is to provide and receive varying types of information, communicating authority-responsibility relationships, and establishing clear policies, procedures, and rules. Of course, it is not enough for the manager to clarify job expectations in his or her own mind. Two-way communication should be used to ensure that subordinates thoroughly understand what is expected of them in any given situation.

Coordinating Mechanisms and Integrating Techniques. Coordinating mechanisms are another means of managing conflict. The most widely used coordinating mechanism is the chain of command. As Weber and writers of the administrative school observed long ago, establishing a hierarchy of authority lends order to human interaction, decision making, and information flows within an organization. If two or more subordinates disagree on an issue, conflict can be avoided or minimized by their common superior making a decision. Adhering to the principle of unity of command facilitates use of the hierarchy to manage conflict, because a subordinate is absolutely certain whose orders are to be followed.

Integration devices such as the management hierarchy, the use of liaison personnel, committees and task forces, and Likert's linking pin concept, which we discussed in our chapter on making organizational design effective, are also useful in managing conflict. Research has shown that those organizations that achieve the amount of integration appropriate in their particular situation are more effective than those that do not.[14] For example, as one study reported, a company experiencing conflict between its interdependent sales and manufacturing departments resolved the problem by establishing a sales order liaison department. This department handled all communication between sales and manufacturing and resolved decisions on such matters as sales requirements, production capacity, pricing, and delivery schedules.[15]

Superordinate Objectives. The establishment of superordinate objectives is another effective structural technique for managing conflict.[16] These are objectives which require two or more individuals, groups, or departments to collaborate for the objective to be successfully attained. The underlying idea is to channel the efforts of all parties toward the same objective. For instance, if the three shifts of a production department are in a state of conflict, objectives should be set for the entire department, rather than each shift having separate objectives. Similarly, setting clear, overall objectives for the organization as a whole is a vehicle for getting divisional managers to make decisions benefiting the entire organization, not just their own functional area.

Reward Structure. Rewards can be used to manage conflict by influencing people to behave in ways that avoid dysfunctional consequences. Individuals who contribute to attaining superordinate objectives, aid other groups within the organization, and attempt to perceive all sides of an issue should be rewarded consistently with praise, pay, recognition, or promotion. Equally important, management must ensure that its reward system does not encourage an individual or group to channel behavior and performance in unproductive ways.

For example, rewarding store managers solely on the basis of increased sales volume may conflict with profitability objectives. Managers could increase volume by offering large discounts unnecessarily, thereby reducing the firm's average profit margin. Or conflict could occur between the sales and credit departments of the firm. In an effort to increase volume, sales may fail to adhere to credit guidelines. This would probably cause credit losses to increase, making the credit department look ineffective. In such a situation, the credit department may aggravate the conflict by withholding credit approval in any marginal situation, causing sales people to lose commissions.

In sum, systematic, coordinated use of the reward structure to encourage behavior conducive to the objectives of the organization *as a whole* helps people learn what management considers desirable behavior with respect to conflict.

Interpersonal Styles for Conflict Resolution

Five primary **interpersonal styles can be used to resolve conflict** when it occurs. They are avoidance, smoothing, forcing, compromising, and problem solving.[17]

Avoidance. An *avoidance style* is characterized by withdrawal from the conflict. As Robert Blake and Jane Mouton state when discussing avoidance, one way to deal with conflict "is to stay out of situations that provoke controversy, to turn away from topics that promote disagreement. Then one need not be stirred up even though the issue may need resolution."[18]

Smoothing. A smoothing style is characterized by behaving as though there is no need to get angry since "we are all one happy group and the boat shouldn't be rocked." The "smoother" attempts to cover up the expression of conflict or bitterness by appealing to the need for solidarity. Unfortunately, the underlying problem is never addressed. Discussing smoothing, Blake and Mouton state, "One might smooth the conflict emotions of another, saying, 'It's not too important. Think of the good things that happened today.' Peace, harmony, and warmth may result in this instance, but the problem persists. Emotions have no opportunity to manifest themselves. They seethe and build up. Common unrest is discovered and an eventual explosion is probable."[19]

Forcing. A *forcing style* is characterized by attempting to have one's own view accepted at any cost. The forcer shows no concern for the views of others. In general, the individual using a forcing style will behave aggressively and revert to coercive power to influence others. Discussing this style, Blake and Mouton state, "Conflict can be controlled by overpowering it, suppressing one's adversary, and extracting compliance on authority-obedience formula."[20] Forcing is potentially effective in situations in which the leader has considerable power over subordinates. The drawbacks of a forcing style is that it stifles initiative in subordinates, makes it extremely likely that all important factors are not being considered (because only one viewpoint is represented), and may cause resentment, especially with younger, better-educated personnel.

Compromise. A *compromise style* is characterized by acceding to the other party's views to some degree. Compromise is generally highly valued in management situations because it helps minimize ill feelings and often enables conflict to be resolved quickly to the satisfaction of both parties. How-

Table 20-1 Problem-Solving Techniques for Resolving Conflict

1. Identify the problem in terms of objectives rather than solutions.
2. After the problem has been identified, identify solutions that are mutually beneficial to all parties.
3. Focus attention on the problem, rather than personality issues or the other party.
4. Build trust by increasing mutuality of influence and sharing relevant information.
5. Establish positive feelings during communication by showing empathy and listening and minimizing the use of anger and threats.

ever, the use of a compromise style at an early stage of conflict over an important decision can lead to less diagnosis of the problem and shortening of the search for alternatives. As Blake and Mouton state, "It means agreeing so as to be agreeable, even though sacrificing sound action, settling for what you can get rather than working to what is sound in light of the best available facts and data."[21]

Problem Solving. A *problem-solving style* is characterized by openly acknowledging the differences of opinion and confronting them in order to understand the reasons for the conflict and find a view or plan of action that meets the needs of all parties. The person using a problem-solving style does not try to attain his or her objectives at the expense of others, but rather seeks the best solution to the conflict situation. Discussing this style, Blake and Mouton state, "disagreement is valued as an inevitable result of the fact that strong-minded people have convictions about what is right. . . . Emotions are confronted through discussion of them directly with the person involved in the disagreement. Insight and resolution are possible but involve maturity and real human skill. . . . Such problem-solving constructiveness in conflict situations promotes the candor among men [people] so essential for both personal and corporate success."[22]

Thus, in complex situations where a variety of opinions and accurate information are critical to making a sound decision, conflict should, in effect, be encouraged and managed though a problem-solving style. Other styles may effectively limit or prevent conflict but lead to a poorer decision because not all positions are thoroughly considered. Research has shown that high performing companies used a problem-solving style to deal with conflict to a greater degree than low performing companies.[23] Although more research is needed in this area, other studies also support the overall effectiveness of a problem-solving approach to conflict management.[24]

Table 20-1 contains some suggestions proposed by Alan Filley for using problem solving to resolve conflict.[25]

Figure 20-6 illustrates the relative suitability of the various styles of conflict resolution just described.

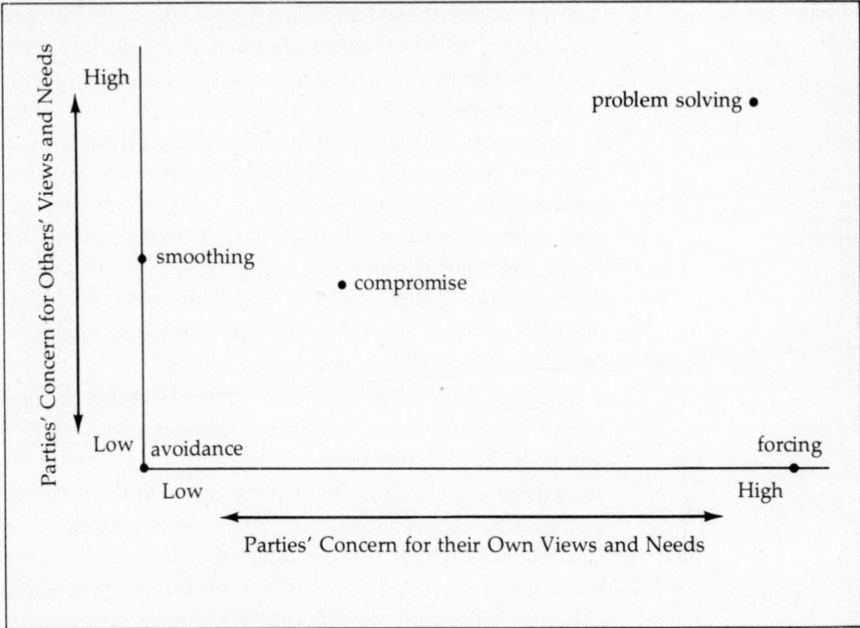

Figure 20-6 Problem-Solving Techniques for Resolving Conflict

The Nature of Organizational Change

When Bob Dylan wrote songs during the 1960s, the youth of America were acutely aware that change was blowing in the wind. Managers of large organizations, although maligned for their conservative economic and social views, were also keenly aware that a sink-or-swim situation had developed because the changing times would not wait for the bureaucrats. Now, a decade later, change is increasing at an even faster rate for many organizations, and astute managers of all organizations recognize the need to respond to it effectively.

Change is a relevant issue for all organizations. General Motors, the giant of the auto industry, in response to changes in fuel costs, retooled its plants in 1977 to produce a higher percentage of higher mileage cars. Its initial investment alone was $16 billion. The proliferation of very low-priced, efficient fast-food restaurants such as McDonald's and Burger King has forced many small, individually owned restaurants to lower their prices, change their menus, and consider more efficient technologies. After a cure for polio was found, the March of Dimes survived by changing its mission to fighting cerebral palsy. When the draft was abolished in 1973, the United States military began using television campaigns to change its image and appeal to individual needs for challenge and adventure. The military was also forced to relax some of its off-duty dress codes and alter training and work conditions in order to attract and hold contemporary young people.

However, as discussed in earlier chapters, organizations operating in volatile environments are usually more affected by change than those operating in more stable environments. In high technology industries such as data processing, major breakthroughs occur with stunning frequency and the need to manage change is a primary, continuous concern of management. Similarly, some subunits of an organization are more affected by change than others. Research and development departments, for example, actually attempt to create change, whereas production departments tend to operate in a relatively stable environment.

Finally, although managers on all levels must respond to change, the effect of change and the form of response varies with hierarchical level. For example, the actual decision to retool was made by General Motors's top management. Middle-level managers and technical staff participated by providing top management with information on what changes were required, cost-benefit trade-offs of various responses to change, and the technical alternatives for responding. First-line supervisors at GM were responsible for implementing the change at the task level and ensuring that new machinery and tools operated correctly, workers understood the new processes, and that quality standards were being maintained under the new technology.

Finally, change conjures up images of massive restructuring, major new products, and wholly different technologies. The need to cope with such changes effectively is obvious. Far less obvious is the necessity of coping with, in the words of Paul Lawrence, "the all-important 'little' changes that constantly take place—changes in work methods, in routine office procedures, and a location of a machine or a desk, and personnel assignments and job titles."[26] While such minor changes are insignificant to the organization, they can be extremely important to the individuals directly affected. Since it is ultimately individuals who attain the organization's objectives, management cannot afford to ignore their potential response to change.

Change and Internal Variables

In speaking of organizational change we really mean a managerial decision to alter one or more of the internal variables of the organization: objectives, structure, tasks, technology, and people. In making such change decisions, management's approach can be either proactive or reactive. A change to correct a problem caught by the control system would be a typical reactive response. A proactive approach would be to change an internal variable, even though no actual problem existed, in response to an opportunity in the environment.

When considering change in a given variable, the manager should keep in mind that the variables are all interrelated. Changing one variable necessarily will have some impact on others. Harold Levitt offers the following example of this: "The introduction of new technological tools—computers for example—may effect changes in structure (e.g., in the communication system or decision map of the organization), changes in people (their numbers, skills, attitudes, and activities), and changes in task performance or even task definition since some tasks may now be feasible of accomplishment for the first time."[27] In the following discussion of each variable, we will point out other examples of interrelatedness. Research has shown that change programs that focus on only one organization variable are not as effective as those that focus on more than one variable.[28]

Objectives. For the organization to survive, management must periodically evaluate and change its objectives in accordance with changes in the environment and changes within the organization. Modification of objectives is required for even the most successful organizations, if only because current objectives have been attained. The need for changing objectives is often discovered through the control system, which should inform management of the relative effectiveness of the overall organization and each subunit. A significant change in objectives often will affect every other variable. For example, when RCA Corporation decided to attain a major share of the market for video recorders, it had to form a division responsible for the new product, develop and implement the technology of production, train production personnel to perform the new tasks required, and hire and train large numbers of repair technicians.

Structure. Structural change, part of the organizing process, refers to changes in authority-responsibility relationships, coordinating and integrating mechanisms, departmentation, the management hierarchy, committees, and the degree of centralization. Structural change is one of the most common and visible forms of organization change. It is virtually mandatory when there has been a significant change in objectives or strategy. Whenever a large organization undertakes a new venture, it creates a subunit with primary responsibility for it and integrates the top management of the new activity with that of the organization.

Structural change has an obvious impact on the human variable, since new people may join the organization and reporting relationships are altered. (Fear that structural change will disrupt existing social and power relationships often causes resistance to it.) Less obvious is the effect on technology not directly related to the new structure. For example, the organization's management information system will have to be modified to provide information required by the new unit and permit control of its performance.

Technology and Tasks. Change in the closely related variables of technology and tasks refers to changes in the way work is processed and scheduled, introduction of new equipment or methods, changes in work standards, and job redesign. As with structural change, technological change often disrupts social patterns and must be managed carefully to avoid dysfunctional conflict. Generally an outgrowth of changes in planning, technological change may require modifications in structure and people. When newspapers began replacing the old typesetting method with computerized word processing systems, for example, they needed more electronics technicians and far fewer typesetters. At almost every paper, the announcement of change to the new technology was strongly resisted by unions fearing job loss.

People. Changing people refers to modifying the abilities, attitudes, or behavior of the organization's personnel. It may involve technical training, training in interpersonal and group communication, motivation, and leadership, performance appraisal, management development, team building, programs to increase satisfaction and morale, or actions to improve the quality of work life. People changes, because they so often arouse fear of need deprivation, can be particularly difficult to implement effectively. As pointed out in our discussion of motivation, the manager can never assume that an objectively favorable change will be perceived favorably by subordinates. Not everyone, for example, wants more responsibility or feels appreciative about additional training.

A change affecting people must be coordinated with other changes to be successful. To give an obvious example, sending a manager to a seminar on policy formulation creates expectations of increased responsibility. If this is not forthcoming, the money spent on training will be wasted and the manager will probably feel resentful. More subtle is the need for consistency and support when making people changes. For example, a landmark study at International Harvester found that supervisors trained in human relations skills could not use them on the job because their managers did not have similar training.[29]

Managing Change Effectively

As we have noted here and in other chapters, change is something management must respond to effectively for the organization to survive and succeed. Because of the complexities induced by the number of variables causing change and affected by it, the interrelationships among these variables, and the potential responses to change, managing change effectively is one of management's most difficult and challenging tasks.

We will now describe several approaches and concepts in managing change, beginning with the steps involved for successful organizational change.

Steps for Successful Organizational Change

Larry Greiner has developed a model of the process for managing organizational change successfully.[30] Illustrated in Figure 20-7, this model consists of six steps.

1. Pressure and Arousal. The first step is that management must realize the necessity of change. Top management, or other managers with the authority to make and implement decisions, must actively feel pressure to change and be aroused into doing so. This pressure can be exerted by external factors such as increased competition, economic changes, or new laws. Or it may be felt because of internal factors such as reduced productivity, excessive costs, high turnover, dysfunctional conflict, and excessive labor grievances.

2. Intervention and Reorientation. Although management may sense the need for change, it may not be able to accurately analyze its problems and thereby make the correct changes. As Greiner states, "Quite likely, top management, when under severe pressure, may be inclined to rationalize its problems by blaming them on a group other than itself, such as 'that lousy union' or 'that meddling government.' "[31] As a result, intervention by an outside consultant able to perceive the situation objectively may be necessary. Or, if they can be counted on to be impartial and express views not pleasing to top management, intervention can be accomplished through internal staff. In any event, for intervention to be effective, it must lead to reorientation. Responsible managers must come to understand the need for change and its true causes, which often involves accepting new viewpoints.

3. Diagnosis and Recognition. In this phase, management determines the true causes of problems requiring change by gathering information relevant to the issue. According to Greiner, "This process begins at the top, then moves gradually down the organization hierarchy."[32] However, if management attempts to diagnose the problem before receiving input from people lower in the hierarchy, it runs a strong risk of basing its decisions on inadequate or incorrect information.

4. Intervention and Commitment. After the problem is recognized and its causes diagnosed, management develops solutions, and changes to correct the situation. In most cases, it also must obtain commitment to the change from those responsible for implementing it. Commenting on this step, Greiner states, "The temptation is always here, especially for the power structure, to apply old solutions to new problems. Thus, a fourth phase—the intervention of new and unique solutions which have high commitment from the power structure—seems to be necessary."[33]

5. Experimentation and Search. An organization seldom risks making a major change in one fell swoop. Rather, it will test the planned change and

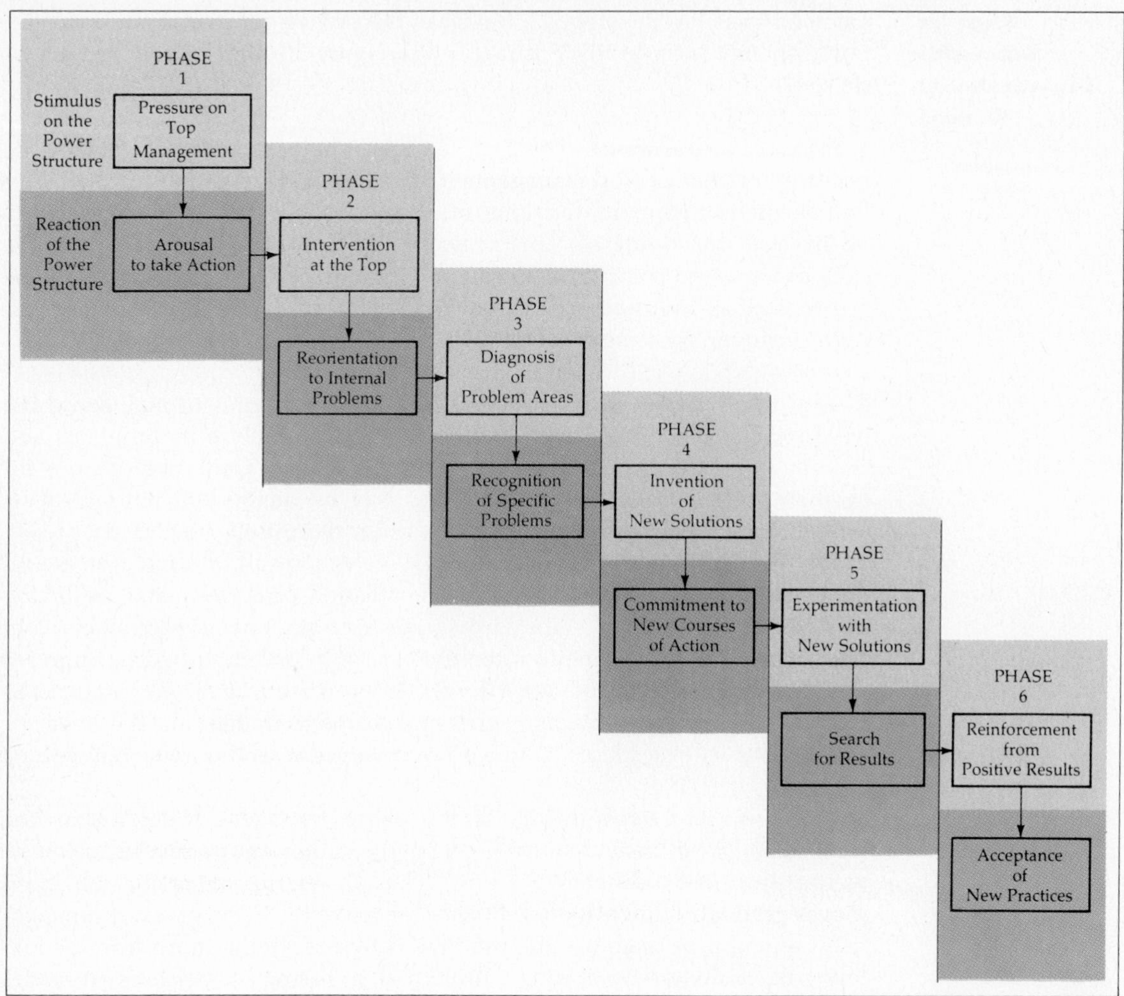

Figure 20-7 Model of Successful Organizational Change

SOURCE: Larry E. Greiner, "Patterns of Organization Change," *Harvard Business Review*, May-June 1967 in *Organization Change and Development*, eds., G. W. Dalton, P. R. Lawrence, and L. E. Greiner (Homewood, IL: Richard D. Irwin, Inc., 1970) p. 222. Reprinted by permission.

work the "bugs" out before introducing it on a large scale. Through control mechanisms, management determines to what degree the planned change is succeeding in remedying the problem, how well it is being received, and how implementation can be improved. Management may discover, for example, that some people need to be given additional authority or training, or that a committee should be created to oversee the program, or that one group is resisting the change strongly. Through experimentation and search for negative consequences, management hopefully will be able to take corrective action and modify its plans for change to make the plans more effective.

6. Reinforcement and Acceptance. The final step is motivating people to accept the change. This can be accomplished by convincing subordinates that the change is beneficial for both the organization and themselves personally and by consistently reinforcing behavior indicative of acceptance. As Greiner explains, when individuals are reinforced for making change successful, there "is probably a greater and permanent acceptance at all levels of the underlying methods used to bring about the change."[34] Possible techniques for reinforcing acceptance would include praise, recognition, promotion, and increased pay for improved performance.

The Use of Participation in Managing Change

Due to the influence of the human relations school, the use of participation is often highly recommended in change management. As Professor Paul Lawrence points out, there is a tendency for managers and staff personnel to view lower-level people or others affected by the change as having little to contribute to decisions. This is definitely not the case. The pragmatic know-how of those affected by the change, especially line supervisors, should not be overlooked when gathering information. Seeking participation when introducing change also helps overcome the tendency of some staff or managers to get so involved in technical aspects of the change that they become oblivious to human issues.[35]

But as we stressed in our chapters on groups and leadership, a high degree of participation is not appropriate in all situations. The three ways in which change can be managed, according to Greiner, are illustrated in Figure 20-8, each employs participation to a different degree.

Sharing of Power Approach. The sharing of power approach to change management is highly participative. Management and subordinates jointly define the needed change, develop alternatives for coping with it, and recommend actions to be taken. Or, in some situations, upper-level management might define the problem and lower-level personnel might participate in discussing what changes are needed in light of this problem. Sharing of power should be effective in situations similar to those favoring a highly participative leadership style, such as research and development, policy formulation, and the development of new marketing strategies.

Unilateral Action. The unilateral action approach involves the use of legitimate authority to implement change. As Greiner states, "The organization change is implemented through an emphasis on the authority of a man's [person's] hierarchical position in the company. Here, the definition and solution to the problem at hand tend to be specified by the upper echelons and

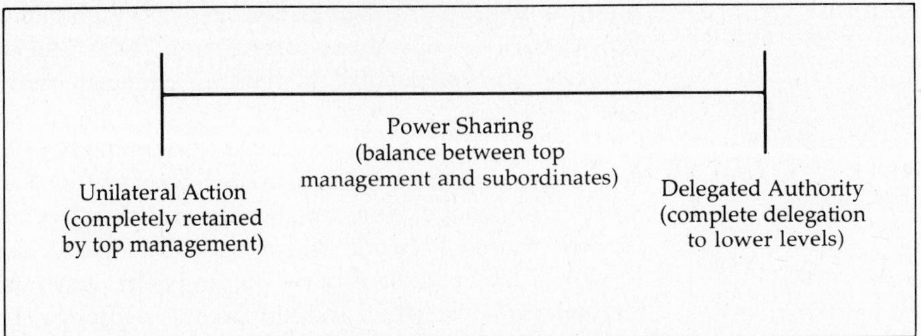

Figure 20-8 Power Distribution of Managing Change

directed downward through formal and impersonal control mechanisms."[36] This would probably be effective in situations where subordinates are basically receptive to legitimate authority, such as in military organizations, and when the need for diversity of opinion is minimal.

Delegated Authority Approach. The delegated authority approach to change management corresponds roughly to *laissez-faire* leadership. Upper management delegates authority for assessing and taking corrective action on needed changes to subordinates. For example, a manager may present information to the group of subordinates and let them discuss what changes are needed, how the changes should be implemented, and so on. The manager, according to Greiner, "encourages individual members to arrive at their own insights and that they are left to use them as they see fit. The implicit assumption here is that individuals, through the medium of discussion about concrete situations, will develop general problem solving skills to aid them in carrying out subsequent individual and organizational changes."[37] The advantage of this approach is that it eliminates most causes of future resistance to change and brings a wide range of opinion to bear on the problem. Offsetting this is that response may be slower, the decision could be affected by groupthink, and that subordinates may lack the experience needed to weigh all alternatives in terms of the organization's overall objectives.

Managing Resistance to Change

When a decision is made to change some aspect of the organization, people may resist it. Although not necessarily something to be avoided, after management has decided to introduce change, resistance must be overcome. That there will be resistance is extremely probable. According to one group of writers, any change in traditional methods creates resistance in all people, both managers and subordinates, affected.[38] Thus, resistance to change is a recurring problem that management must learn to cope with effectively. To do so, it is necessary to understand the reasons why people resist change.

Reasons for Resistance to Change. People resist change for three basic reasons: uncertainty, feelings of loss, and belief that the change will not be positive. The first of these, uncertainty, is easily understood. Because change means that things will be different, a person may grow anxious and apprehensive simply because he or she does not know what the impact will be. They may sense the change as a threat to satisfaction of security needs, which are among the most basic motivational drives. Because of this fear, the person consciously or unconsciously responds by expressing a negative attitude or behaving dysfunctionally during implementation.

Another possible cause of resistance is the person may feel the change will result in a personal loss, which results in decreased satisfaction of some need. For example, production line workers may believe that a change in technology such as increased automation will result in layoffs. This threatens their security needs. Often, people fear that change will disrupt their social relationships, thereby threatening loss of satisfaction of affiliation needs. As Lawrence observes, "Actually, what employees resist is usually not technical change but social change—the change in their human relationships that generally accompanies technical change."[39] Other things that people may feel will be diminished by change are decision-making authority, formal or informal power, accessibility to information, autonomy, and the inherent challenges of their task.

Lastly, people may resist change simply because they feel it is incorrect or undesirable for the organization. They may believe that the intended change will not resolve problems but increase them. For example, a manager may believe that a proposed computerized management information system will be too complex to use or generate the wrong kind of information. Similarly, and very commonly, a manager may feel that the problem lies not in his or her functional area, but another, and *that* department is the one that should be changed.

Overcoming Resistance. There is little doubt that the best time to overcome resistance to change is before it occurs; that is, management should recognize the high probability of resistance and take steps to forestall it. For example, as we just pointed out, a primary cause of resistance is fear that change will threaten existing social relationships. Therefore, as Lawrence states, management needs "a real understanding, in-depth and detail of the specific social arrangements that will be sustained or threatened by the change or by the way in which it is introduced."[40] This understanding usually means determining what the informal organizational network is and who the informal leaders are. By formally or informally reassuring the more powerful informal leaders that the proposed change will not affect them materially or even arranging the change around the informal organization's sentiments, resistance may be eliminated.

Participation prior to change is also a useful technique for overcoming resistance. Giving employees an opportunity to express their views on

FEATURE 20-1

Teaching Creativity to Managers

Creativity is a requisite for successful organization change and problem solving. As Professor Karl E. Weick observes, "Quantitative and analytical tools become dated. Eventually you can't plug them into every problem. Unless you have new ways of thinking, your ability to handle changing conditions can atrophy." Professor Gerald R. Salancik, agreeing, goes on to state, "Business schools teach terminology and techniques. What is needed is to teach uncertainty and to invent devices to force students to think."

This concept is not a new one. Professor Warren A. Schmidt started a course on creative problem solving at UCLA's management school in the early 1960s. Schmidt's approach is based on training students to use the right hemisphere of the brain, the half responsible for dreaming, abstract thought, and perceiving patterns. He also uses the technique of "imaging." This is visualizing a problem as already solved, and then working backward from the solution to determing how to reach it. Schmidt finds imaging particularly useful for planning because looking back facilitates seeing specific steps in greater detail than if one looks forward.

In his course on idea generation at Cornell, Professor Weick uses a similar technique, which he calls "future perfect thinking." To stimulate thinking, he combines reading assignments in conventional texts, poetry, and fiction with unusual exercises. One, for example, is "to compose a one-

change, potential problems, and modifications tends to decrease resistance and increase support and commitment. For example, in an early study workers in a clothing factory were asked to discuss how existing work methods could be improved and unnecessary operations eliminated. The result was increased productivity and decreased turnover.[41]

Effective two-way communication and using an appropriate leadership style are also means of overcoming resistance.

Organization Development

Our discussion of change management has focused on individuals and small groups. However, to make the organization genuinely responsive to change, management must build a capability for responsiveness into the overall organizational design and its managerial practices. Recognition of this led to

page graphic which you feel will summarize crucial issues associated with the concept of stress. Give the viewer novel access to the concept of stress by the images you choose and the way you arrange them." He also uses semantic variations that radically change the meaning of a statement.

Weick's objective is to jar people into thinking about problems in new ways. He wants to prime his students with numerous ideas and images, "to complicate" them, he says, so that the students find unexpected facets of situations.

Whether or not such courses will help students become more responsive to change and, as a result, better managers, is not yet proven. Such techniques have been used successfully, however, in practice. Executives of Winchell's Donut House, a division of Denny's Inc., attend seminars conducted by Professor Schmidt. One result of engaging in exercises in future perfect thinking at around the same time the annual plan was being developed, according to Winchell's President Ross E. Roeder, was "People no longer just looked at their little sphere but asked themselves, 'Do I have an idea that will help the whole company?'"

Another example is that of one of Professor Weick's students, who was working as a consultant to some local communities studying variations in service and rates of their local cable television company. "The student reread his class notes, toyed with some of the semantic techniques, and eventually determined that the problem was not primarily economic but political and legal—a realization that he says came to him because the course had opened his mind."

SOURCE: "B-School Buzzword: Creativity," *Business Week*, August 8, 1977, p. 66.

the concept of organization development, commonly referred to as OD. Organization development emerged in the mid-1960s. It has rapidly evolved to provide management with methods and techniques for systematically diagnosing, planning, implementing and sustaining change in order to increase the organization's effectiveness. The OD approach to change is broader and somewhat different from those we have described.

What Is OD?

Organization development is defined by Wendell French and Cecil Bell as, "a long-range effort to improve an organization's problem-solving and renewal processes, particularly through a more effective and collaborative management of organization culture—with special emphasis on the culture of formal work teams—with the assistance of a change agent or catalyst—and the use of theory and technology of applied behavioral science, including action research."[42]

Problem-solving processes are concerned with how the organization proceeds to assess and make decisions about the opportunities and threats to its environment. As French and Bell state, "Does it see its environment, and thus its mission, in terms of ten years ago, or is it continuously redefining its purpose and methods in terms of the present and the future?"[43]

Improving an organization's renewal processes is interrelated with the organization's problem-solving processes. Gordon Lippit describes organiational renewal as "the process of initiating, creating, and confronting needed changes so as to make it possible for organizations to become or remain viable, to adapt to new conditions, to solve problems, to learn from its experiences."[44] Other writers include the concern for avoiding organizational decay, and creating a management climate which is conducive to adaptability and innovation.[45]

Culture refers to the organization's social system; the prevailing norms, feelings, attitudes, and values of the people employed by the organization. In addition, the organization's technology is considered to be part of the culture. This is because the technical system affects the social system and vice versa.

Collaborative management of the culture implies some degree of participation in the management of the culture. Changes in the organizational culture are not the exclusive right of top management. Unilateral action by the hierarchy is eschewed in favor of giving subordinates some degree of power in issues related to diagnosis and making recommendations about changing the organization's culture.

Formal work teams are considered to be the key unit for OD activities. This includes the manager and his or her subordinates. As French and Bell state, "in most management development activities the focus is on the individual manager or supervisor—not on his or her work group. Traditionally the manager has participated in the learning experience in isolation from the dynamics of the work situation."[46] In contrast to this, there is an emphasis on the development of the entire work team.

A *change agent* or catalyst is used to get various people in the organization to objectively look at such issues as their feelings about various aspects of the organization and management, what things are getting in the way of getting work done, how things could be done more effectively, etc. The change agent can be an outside consultant or from the organization's OD or human resource department.

The use of theory and research findings from the behavioral sciences, for example, psychology, social psychology, sociology, and anthropology, is the primary knowledge base for OD activities. However, applications from the fields of economics, management, and industrial engineering are also used.

Action research is the basic intervention model that runs through most of these efforts. This research involves the following steps:

1. Diagnose the organization or subunit through the use of such data-gathering devices as interviews, questionnaires, observations, and company records.

2. Feedback of this data to various organizational members.
3. Decide on specific action plans to take in light of the data.
4. Implement these action plans.
5. Evaluate the action plans through the use of data-gathering devices, and continue through the cycle.

Underlying Assumptions and Values of OD

There are various assumptions and values inherent in OD. These are concerned with people as individuals, people as group members and leaders, and people as members of the organization.

People As Individuals. People are viewed as driven toward personal growth and satisfaction of higher order needs if the environment is supportive and challenging. As French and Bell state, "Most people want to become more of what they are capable of becoming."[47] A second assumption, related to the first, is that, "most people desire to make, and are capable of making, a high level of contribution to the attainment of organizational goals than most organizational environments will permit. A tremendous amount of constructive energy can be tapped if organizations recognize this; for example, by asking for and acting on suggestions. Frequently, however, organizational members learn what they perceive to be constructive efforts may be self-defeating in the sense that these efforts are not rewarding and may be penalized. For example, attempts at lateral communication between two departments to solve some problems may be throttled through adherence to some principle about the chain of command."[48]

People in Groups and Leadership. One assumption is that the work group and its prevailing social system, especially at the informal level strongly affects the satisfaction and competence of the members. If there are negative attitudes among the members of the work group and feelings are suppressed, it is assumed that this can be detrimental to problem solving, personal growth, and job satisfaction. It is also assumed, "that the level of interpersonal trust, support, and cooperation is much lower in most groups and organizations than is either necessary or desirable."[49] People are assumed to want to belong to and interact cooperatively with some type of group. Finally, it is believed that the group leader cannot perform all the tasks and maintenance functions we described in our discussion of group dynamics. As a result, group members must play some of these roles and assist each other with effective leadership and group behavior.

People and Organizations. The attitudes and behavior of people in an organization are assumed to be strongly influenced by the leadership style and climate of higher level management. As French and Bell state, "conditions of trust, support, openness and teamwork tend to influence the style of managers lower on the hierarchy and rub off onto their subordinates. Similarly, conditions of mistrust, political in-fighting, guardedness, and lack of cooperation tend to be transmitted both upward and downward and tend to influence attitudes and interactions at those levels."[50]

A second assumption is that conflict resolution by forcing, such that one party wins and the other party loses is not beneficial in the long run to the solution of organizational problems. Finally, in order to make changes in the culture and people, a long-term perspective is required. In addition, changes in performance "stemming from organization development efforts need to be sustained by appropriate changes in the appraisal, compensation, training, staffing, task, and communications subsystems—in short, in the total human resources system."[51]

An Overview of OD Interventions

The term **OD intervention** refers to the various planned activities that the organization, subunit, or work group participates in during the OD program. French and Bell state, "these activities are designed to improve the organization's functioning through enabling organizational members better to manage their team and organization cultures."[52] These activities can be planned with the aid of a consultant or initiated by members of the organization with some training or prior participation in OD programs. Some of the many OD interventions are:[53]

1. *Diagnostic activities.* Collecting information about the health of the organization of subunits through such data-collection methods as interviews, questionnaires, meetings, observations, and perusal of organizational records.
2. *Survey-feedback activities.* Communicating the information obtained from the diagnosis to the members and designing action plans based on this information.
3. *Education and training activities.* Designing activities to enhance and improve the skills, abilities, and knowledge of individuals. These activities may be concerned with technical and task-related issues, or interpersonal, social systems related issues.
4. *Technostructural or structural activities.* Activities designed to improve the organizational structure or procedures to perform tasks. Included here would be the design and implementation of a modification to the present organizational structure, work redesign, and management by objectives.
5. *Process consultation activities.* These activities are designed to help the organization members more accurately perceive and understand and act upon events within their organization or subunit. "Primary emphasis is on the processes such as communications, leader and member roles in groups, problem solving and decision making, group norms and group growth, leadership and authority, and intergroup cooperation and competition. Emphasis is also placed on learning how to diagnose and de-

velop the necessary skills to be effective in dealing with these processes."[54]

6. *Team building activities.* Activities designed to improve the effectiveness within the work groups. "They may relate to task issues, such as the way things are done, the needed skills to accomplish tasks, the resource allocations necessary for task accomplishments; where they may relate to the nature and quality of the relationships between the team members or between members and the leader."[55]
7. *Intergroup activities.* These are similar to the team-building activities but are designed to improve the effectiveness between interdependent work groups, such as sales and production, or hospital administrators and doctors.

Conditions for Success

In order for OD efforts to be successful a number of conditions are necessary.[56]

1. Key people in the organization should be part of the initial diagnostic activities. These people should also understand the relevance of the behavioral sciences in solving these problems.
2. Employing a behavioral science consultant to start the OD effort. This should be followed by the development of internal OD resources, such as managers and other organizational members, to eventually take over and sustain the OD effort.
3. The support and involvement of management of a higher level than the level of the OD intervention. For example, if sales personnel and the sales manager are the intervention level, the vice-president of marketing should be supportive of the intervention and to some degree involved in the OD effort.
4. Allowing the participants to acquire an understanding of what OD is about, how aspects of OD are similar to many prior management practices they may have experienced, and enable the participants to experience early success in the OD program.
5. The use of an action research model: diagnosing the organization or subunit, feeding back the information collected to the members, making action plans on the basis of the information, followed by future diagnosis.
6. The participation of work teams along with the manager of the team.
7. The involvement of personnel and industrial relations people, and changing any personnel policies and practices so as to support the OD effort. As French and Bell state, "What is done in the OD program needs to be compatible with what is done in selection, promotion, salary administration, appraisal, and other formal aspects of the human-social subsystems."[57]

8. The effective management of the OD process, maintaining the process, and measuring the results. Both the consultant and organizational members must work effectively together. In addition, results of the OD effort are data for planning future intervention activities.

SUMMARY

Conflict is a disagreement between two or more parties in which one party attempts to gain acceptance of its views and prevent the other party from doing the same. Inevitable even with good management, conflict may occur between individuals, between individuals and groups, and between groups within the organization. Primary causes are shared resources, task-interdependence, differences in objectives, differences of perception, values, personal style, or background, and poor communication. These increase the potential for conflict, but do not necessarily lead to it. People often do not respond to conflict situations involving minimal personal loss or threat.

Structural techniques for managing conflict are clarifying job expectations, the use of coordinating and integrating mechanisms, superordinate objectives, and the use of the reward structure.

There are five interpersonal styles for managing conflict. Avoidance is characterized by withdrawal from the conflict. Smoothing is behaving as though there is no need to get angry. Forcing is using legitimate power or coersion to impose one's view on the other party. Compromise, acceding to the other party's view to some degree, is effective but may lead to settling for a less than optimal solution. Problem solving, the style preferred in situations requiring diversity of opinion and information, is characterized by openly acknowledging differences of opinion and confronting them to find a solution acceptable to both parties.

Potential negative consequences of conflict are decreased productivity, dissatisfaction, low morale, increased turnover, decreased social interaction, worsening of communication, and increased loyalty to subgroups and informal organizations. However, if managed effectively, conflict can have positive consequences such as greater commitment to solutions, diversity of opinion in decision making, and improved cooperation in the future.

Change affects all organizations and all levels of management, but those operating in volatile environments are more strongly affected than others. Change can take place in and involve any of the internal variables. Since these variables are interrelated, management must consider the effect on others when considering change in any one.

The steps for making organizational change effective are: pressure and arousal, intervention and reorientation, diagnosis and recognition, intervention and commitment, experimentation and search, and reinforcement and acceptance.

Participation is often recommended, but may not be desirable in all change situations. At times, unilateral action may be preferable to the sharing of power and delegated authority approaches.

While not necessarily undesirable, resistance to change must eventually be overcome. The main reasons for resistance to change are a feeling it will result in personal loss, uncertainty about the outcome, and belief that the change intended is incorrect or undesirable.

Organization development is a long-range effort to improve the organization's ability to renew itself, solve problems, and respond to change. It strongly emphasizes more effective management of the organization's culture, especially that of formal work teams, behavioral science techniques, and the use of a change agent. OD interventions are activities designed to improve the organization's functioning. They include diagnostic activities, feedback, education and training, structural change, process consultation, team building, and intergroup activities. For an OD program to be successful, a number of important conditions must be met.

REVIEW QUESTIONS

1. Discuss briefly the four types of conflict discussed in the chapter.
2. What are some of the various types of conflict mentioned in the text?
3. Discuss the functional consequences of conflict.
4. Briefly describe the dysfunctional consequences of conflict.
5. Briefly describe the four structural techniques for managing conflict.
6. Describe five primary interpersonal styles that can be used to resolve conflict.
7. Compare and contrast several of the approaches and concepts in managing change that are mentioned in the chapter.
8. Briefly describe the three ways change can be managed.
9. What are the underlying assumptions and values of OD?
10. In what environment would a firm be more affected by change? Why?

DISCUSSION QUESTIONS

11. Why is participation often highly recommended in change management?
12. In your words describe organizational change and discuss its interface with organizational development.
13. How would one effectively manage conflict in the following organizations:
    Profit
    Not-for-profit
    New Venture
    Be sure to discuss the difference in the three types of organizations.
14. Compare and contrast various intervention techniques and sight examples of where each technique would be effective in organizations you are familiar with.
15. Why is the support of top management a prerequisite for an effective OD program?

CASE INCIDENT

Worldco-South

Marsha Denton was described as one of the "new breed" of industrial relations managers. Unlike her predecessor, who moved into industrial relations from production, Denton was college-trained in industrial relations and had received her master's degree in personnel and industrial relations. Additionally, she was the first woman to hold the top IR position at Worldco-South.

Worldco-South was one of The Worldco Company's older plants. For the most part, it had been a highly profitable operation. However, Sherman David, Worldco's corporate VP-Industrial Relations, was tremendously concerned about what he considered to be the deterioration of Worldco-South's working climate. It was David's feeling that there would probably never be an absence of some conflict between the company and the union, but that there had to be a better way of managing the conflict and minimizing its destructive aspects.

David shared these views with Denton and asked her to come up with some way of "diagnosing the problem, so that proper treatment might be administered."

Denton suggested that an independent study be made by an outside firm, acceptable to the company and the union, and that the study focus upon Worldco-South's internal climate and its impact upon grievances.

After interviews were held with several interested consulting firms, the contract was awarded to Source, Inc., a group which worked primarily in the area of organizational development and productivity.

The Source study lasted for months and today's meeting was called by Denton for the purpose of distributing the completed report to company and union representatives and to have Source discuss the study's summary and conclusions.

The following represents a partial listing of conclusions pertaining to Worldco-South's plant environment:

1. An antagonistic relationship exists between management and the workers as a constant state. Nevertheless, the operating system continues to function although we do not know at what level of efficiency compared to an environment where the antagonism did not exist.
2. High grievance rates for both supervisor- and worker-related cases exist in the Raw Materials Preparation Division.
3. High worker-related grievance rates exist in the Subassembly Products Division.
4. High supervisor-related grievance rates are associated with group/machine-paced technology.
5. High worker-related grievance rates are associated with solitary/person-paced technology.
6. Extremely low grievance rates are associated with mixed person/machine-paced technology.
7. Workers with one year or less experience in their present position are involved in 53 percent of all filed grievances.
8. Supervisors with two years or less experience in their present position are involved in 53 percent of all filed grievances.

Questions

1. How do you think the company would react to these conclusions? Why?
2. How do you think the union would react to these conclusions? Why?
3. How might company/union conflict be minimized at Worldco-South?
4. How can organizational change affect the various types of conflict described in the Source report?

NOTES

1. Stuart M. Schmidt and T. A. Kochan, "Conflict: Toward Conceptual Clarity," *Administrative Science Quarterly*, vol. 17 (1972), pp. 359–370; C. F. Fink, "Some Conceptual Difficulties in the Theory of Conflict Resolution," *Journal of Conflict Resolution*, vol. 12 (1968), pp. 413–458.
2. David L. Austin, "Conflict: A More Professional Approach," *Personnel Administrator*, vol. 21 (July 1976); Mary Parker Follet, *Dynamic Administration* (New York: Harper & Row, 1940). (It should be noted that the writings of Mary Parker Follet showed exceptional concern for conflict at an early point.)
3. William R. Scott, "Organization Theory: A Reappraisal," *Academy of Management Journal*, vol. 4 (1961), pp. 7–26.
4. R. L. Kahn, D. M. Wolfe, R. P. Quinn, J. D. Snoek, and R. A. Ros, *Organizational Stress: Studies in Conflict and Ambiguity* (New York: John Wiley, 1964).
5. Melville Dalton, "Conflicts Between Staff and Line Managerial Officers," *American Sociological Review*, vol. 15 (1950), pp. 342–351.
6. Schmidt and Kochan, op. cit.; Richard D. Walton and J. M. Dutton, "The Management of Inter-departmental Conflict: A Model and Review," *Administrative Science Quarterly*, vol. 14 (1969), pp. 73–84.
7. R. G. Corwin, "Patterns of Organizational Conflict," *Administrative Science Quarterly*, vol. 14 (1969): pp. 507–521; Paul Lawrence and J. J. Lorsch, *Managing Differentiation and Integration* (Boston: Harvard University Press, 1967).
8. D. C. Dearborn and H. A. Simon, "Selective Perception: A Note on the Departmental Identification of Executives," *Sociometry*, vol. 21 (1958), pp. 140–144.
9. Walton and Dutton, op. cit., p. 342.
10. Richard Walton and R. D. McKersie, *A Behavioral Theory of Labor Negotiations* (New York: McGraw-Hill, 1965).
11. Robert R. Blake, Jane S. Mouton, and H. A. Shepard, *Managing Inter-Group Conflict in Industry* (Houston: Gulf, 1964).
12. W. N. Evan, "Conflict and Performance in R&D Organizations," *Industrial Management Review*, vol. 7 (1965), pp. 37–45.
13. Blake, Mouton, and Shepard, op. cit.; M. Scherrif, O. J. Harvey, B. J. White, W. R. Hood, and C. W. Scherrif, *Intergroup Conflict and Cooperation: The Robbers Cave Experiment* (Tulsa: The University of Oklahoma Book Exchange, 1961).
14. Lawrence and Lorsch, op. cit.
15. A. J. M. Sykes and J. Bates, "A Study in Production-Sales Liaison," *Management International*, vol. 5–6 (1964), pp. 57–67.
16. Scherrif, et al., op. cit.
17. Robert R. Blake and Jane S. Mouton, *Building a Dynamic Corporation Through Grid Organization Development* (Reading, MA: Addison-Wesley, 1969), pp. 66–67.
18. Ibid., p. 66.
19. Ibid.
20. Ibid.
21. Ibid., p. 67.
22. Blake and Mouton, op. cit., pp. 67–68.
23. Lawrence and Lorsch, op. cit.
24. Allan C. Filley, R. J. House and Stephen Kerr, *Managerial Process and Organization Behavior*, 2nd. ed. (Glenview, IL: Scott Foresman, 1976), pp. 175–177.

25. Alan C. Filley, "Some Normative Issues in Conflict Management," *California Management Review*, vol. 21 (1978): no. 2, pp. 61–66.
26. Paul R. Lawrence, "How to Deal with Resistance to Change," in *Organization Change and Development*, G. W. Dalton, P. R. Lawrence, and L. E. Greiner, eds. (Homewood, IL: Irwin, 1970), p. 183.
27. Ibid., pp. 193–194.
28. Frank Friedlander and L. D. Brown, "Organization Development," *Annual Review of Psychology*, vol. 25 (1974), p. 314; John P. Campbell and M. D. Dunnette, "Effectiveness of T-Group Experiences in Managerial Training and Development," *Psychological Bulletin*, vol. 70 (August 1968), pp. 73–104.
29. E. A. Fleishman, E. F. Harris, and H. E. Burtt, *Leadership and Supervision in Industry* (Columbus: Bureau of Educational Research, Ohio State University, 1955).
30. Larry E. Greiner, "Patterns of Organization Change," *Harvard Business Review*, May–June 1967, in Dalton, et al., eds., op. cit., pp. 223–229.
31. Ibid., pp. 223.
32. Ibid., p. 224.
33. Ibid., p. 224–225.
34. Ibid., p. 226.
35. Lawrence, op. cit., pp. 186, 188.
36. Greiner, op. cit., pp. 215–216.
37. Ibid., p. 217.
38. Carl A. Bramlette, D. O. Jewell, and M. H. Mescon, "Designing for Organizational Effectiveness: How It Works," *Atlanta Economic Review*, vol. 27 (November-December 1977), p. 14.
39. Lawrence, op. cit., p. 182.
40. Ibid., p. 183.
41. L. Coch and J. R. P. French, "Overcoming Resistance to Change," *Human Relations*, vol. 1 (1948), pp. 512–533.
42. Wendall L. French and Cecil H. Bell, Jr., *Organizational Development*, 2nd. ed. (Englewood Cliff, NJ: Prentice-Hall, 1978), p. 14.
43. Ibid.
44. Gordon L. Lippit, *Organization Renewal* (Englewood Cliffs, NJ: Prentice-Hall, 1969), p. 1.
45. Chris Argyris, *Management and Organization Development: The Path from XA to YB* (New York: McGraw-Hill, 1971).
46. French and Bell, op. cit., p. 16.
47. Ibid., p. 30.
48. Ibid., p. 31.
49. Ibid., p. 32.
50. Ibid., p. 34.
51. Ibid., p. 34.
52. Ibid., p. 101.
53. Ibid., pp. 107–109.
54. Ibid., p. 108.
55. Ibid., p. 107.
56. Ibid., pp. 177–187.
57. Ibid., p. 183.

PART SIX CASE STUDY 1

Carlson Companies

SHEILA A. ADAMS

Department of Management, Arizona State University

A frequently quoted comment illustrates an important source of Carlson Companies' phenomenal growth "I could never run any of these businesses myself!" insists Curtis LeRoy Carlson, board chairman and president of Carlson Companies, Inc. He believes that sustained growth requires keen management and one of his criteria for acquisitions is that companies have capable executives willing to stay at their jobs. The strategy seems to work. With it, Carlson has parlayed a borrowed $50 investment into a $1 billion-a-year business and one of America's largest privately-held companies. The company has more than 70 subsidiaries and divisions employing more than 10,000 people in a wide variety of businesses. International operations, organized in ten groups, include: a hotel group, a restaurant group, a contract services group, a real estate group, a retail group, a financial group, a food group, a manufacturing group, and an acquisitions group.

While selling soap for Procter & Gamble Co. in 1937, Carlson observed a Minneapolis department store considerably increase its sales by offering trading stamps. Noticing that few grocery stores in the area offered such stamps, he perceived an opportunity to concentrate on an untapped market segment. With his $50 in borrowed capital, Carlson formed the Gold Bond Stamp Co. which, after a slow start during the shortage-plagued World War II years, brought its founder his first million dollars. As trading stamps lost favor with retailers and consumers worried about inflation in the early sixties, Carlson saw a need to diversify. Accordingly, he purchased the Radisson Hotel in Minneapolis, the first of a group which now numbers 20 with at least four more on the drawing boards.

Radisson Hotel's 7,500 guestrooms and $90 million in revenues for 1978 is small compared to such industry giants as Hyatt (25,250 rooms, 1978 revenues of $285 million) and Mariott (16,993 rooms, 1978 revenues of $373 million). Nevertheless, the hotel group received a 1979 Distinguished Award from *Sales and Marketing Management* for "its aggressive moves to become a major factor in the lodging industry." With units currently located in 11 states and the Caribbean and one proposed for Egypt the group ranks in the top 25 hotel corporations in the United States.

Carlson's strategy for the hotel group calls for seeking out faded old hotels and recycling them. Restoration of downtown properties is contingent upon the attitudes of a city. Carlson moves when, "people want to put their city back in order." He believes that major hotels are essential to keeping downtowns alive. Renovation of landmark hotels in Detroit and Kansas City indeed helped to stimulate local economies.

Recent market research indicates that people choose chain hotels for dependability but are increasingly turned off by sameness and predictability. Capitalizing on these seemingly contradictory factors Radisson initiated a forceful advertising campaign stressing the physical uniqueness of each Radisson unit. The campaign punchline invokes visions of expensive art, fine furniture or precious jewelry. "The Radisson Hotels—A Collection, Not A Chain."

A three-way growth strategy propelled Radisson into the upper ranks of the lodging industry. The strategy includes: (1) ownership of some properties, (2) renovation or building of some hotels as a joint venture with local business people, and (3) restoration and operation of some units via management contracts (with no ownership). Carlson forsees more management contracts and less ownership for the future. "It's better for us and for the city if the 'city fathers' have an interest," Carlson believes. Radisson management provides the necessary professional managerial skills to achieve success.

Advantages provided by the group include efficiency in referrals and reservations, advertising, a national sales effort, savings from volume purchasing and the opportunity to attract top management people.

An important factor in a number of the hotel restoration projects is the Contract Services Group which includes Contract Service Associates, Inc. (CSA). Ann Richardson, vice-president of administration for Carlson Companies and a top construction industry executive recently was named president of CSA, Carlson's construction and design firm. CSA directed the restoration of the Radisson Cadillac (downtown Detroit), the Radisson Muehlebach (Kansas City) and the Radisson Ferncroft (north of Boston in Danvers, Mass.). It also directs construction of new hotels and additions to existing structures as well as interior design and furnishings programs.

Carlson's restaurant group includes the 330-unit Country Kitchens International Inc. and the 15-unit TGI Friday's Inc. Friday's, usually located in suburban areas near office buildings or industrial parks, has a not-entirely-deserved reputation as a singles' restaurant. Its multimillion dollar sales volume testifies to its broad appeal. Customers fall into four groups: businesspeople at lunch, shoppers in the afternoon, young families in the early evening, and nightlife seekers, later. Friday's garish decor and central bar provide patrons a constant air of excitement.

Country Kitchens, in contrast, is the typical small-town family restaurant. While competing in the same market as Denny's and Sambo's it seeks to avoid head-on confrontations by locating where they aren't. The strategy is to fill a niche just above the fast-food operations—low prices but sit-down convenience and a substantial variety on the menu including a separate children's section for the under-12 set. At the end of 1978 only nine of the 330 stores were company-owned. A Carlson change in franchising strategy plans one-quarter of a projected 1,000 units to be company-operated by 1982.

Carlson's management style leans heavily on ambitious goal setting. As required by Carlson Companies' rapid expansion, he has turned to professional managers for such specialties as financial planning, acquisitions, and legal affairs. He has learned to delegate authority as needed but, he says, "I'll never delegate goal setting!" He believes one should never be content with reaching a goal but immediately set a new and more ambitious one. A chief executive must set higher goals for subordinates than they set for themselves. For example, when he acquired Country Kitchens, company executives were planning to maintain expansion at the rate of 60 new units a year. Carlson asked if the chain could open 60 units a year why not 100? After some prodding, the head of the chain agreed and is now more enthusiastic than ever.

It was in 1975 that Carlson set a target for his executives of $1 billion in sales by 1981, more than double the sales figure at the time. Despite the skeptics the company is well ahead of schedule, reaching the $1 billion mark in 1978, whereupon he immediately set a new goal for the executives—"Billions TWO in '82."

Carlson enjoys his promoter image saying a little flair and showmanship "is appropriate at a hotel opening." At a company meeting, he donned a yellow hard hat along with the other executives as he revealed plans to reward them with a round-the-world trip for reaching the $1 billion goal. He also gives each of his top 20 executives the use of a new luxury car. The cars are all the same model and color. One year it was maroon Cadillacs; another year he selected cinnamon-gold Lincoln Continentals.

Carlson prefers to keep his company privately owned. There are no stockholders to criticize management or demand dividends. As a private company, the objective is "not to build earnings and pay dividends but to build assets and hold earnings down to minimize taxes," he explains with reference to the hotel chain. There is a substantial tax shelter in hotels in accelerated depreciation.

Carlson's disciplined style, his personal work addiction, and his keen sense of putting the right people in top management positions make the "Billions TWO in '82" seem a very reachable goal.

Questions

1. By admitting "I could never run any of these businesses myself!," is Carlson defying the classical description of the entrepreneur? Explain your reasoning.
2. Explain the connection between corporate objectives and strategies as practiced at Carlson Companies.
3. Is Carlson's management style appropriate for a billion-dollar corporation?
4. What chances would you give Carlson Companies for achieving two billion dollars in revenues by 1982?

SOURCE: *Business Week*, June 25, 1979, pp. 91–96.

PART SIX CASE STUDY 2

The Dissatisfaction at AT&T

Through all the years when American Telephone & Telegraph Co. was good old Ma Bell, hovering maternally over her army of employees, she also had a tough side. The company could, and often did, exert an unusual control over workers through technical and administrative systems. In recent years, competitive pressures have pushed Bell toward increasing use of these controls, and now its work force, dominated by the independent-minded, better-educated "baby boom" generation, is rebelling—and not always in the quiet way Bell trains its employees to behave. AT&T says it recognizes the problem and has created a new management unit to respond to it.

AT&T is by no means alone in experiencing worker restiveness. Surveys show that American workers generally are demanding more freedom on the job and more involvement in making job-related decisions. Discontent of this kind has appeared in the steel, auto, and coal industries, among others, and it probably is surging through the entire society. The problem at Bell may be more pervasive and difficult to deal with than in other corporations, partly because AT&T—the nation's largest employer—has an enormous bureaucracy that defies easy change.

"We are people, not machines."

To publicize the unrest at Bell, the Communications Workers of America, which represents 484,000 of AT&T's 720,000 union-eligible employees, designated June 15 as "job pressures day." "We are people, not machines," the CWA advertised, as it staged demonstrations across the country. It hoped to generate enough support to convince Bell, which thrives on public approval, that it should take some steps to alleviate pressures that create dissatisfaction. These include stringent absentee- and lateness-control programs, "forced" and excessive overtime, the monitoring of worker performance through elaborate indexes and computer tracking programs, and general "oversupervision" by management at all levels.

Complaints about these and other pressures have been growing in recent years, causing an increase in grievances and arbitration cases throughout the Bell System. "These same problems exist in all working units, everywhere," says CWA President Glenn E. Watts. "There is a changing attitude in the work force. The modern or younger worker is much more interested in having a job that is satisfying than older workers like me, who were concerned with job security."

The CWA's decision to demonstrate for recognition of these problems, instead of taking a more militant action, betrays an uncertainty about how to deal with the nontraditional issues. In the past the union was concerned with other priorities—establishing nationwide bargaining in the Bell System and winning hefty wages and benefits—and has only touched on issues of working conditions. But it will raise such issues in 1980 negotiations at AT&T. "Job pressure demands have escalated to the foreground," says Dina G. Beaumont, vice-president of the CWA's Los Angeles-based Region 11. "The CWA is on point on this issue, and if we don't deal with the times, we won't be around tomorrow."

AT&T also concedes that there is reason for concern. Last January it created a "work relationships unit" under Rex R. Reed, labor relations vice-president, to assess the impact of societal changes on Bell's employee relations and propose any changes that are needed. AT&T decided to take this step, Reed says, because surveys of worker attitudes showed "some desire on the part of people to be more involved in the process, and that's true societally. It's another way of saying employees respond less well to authoritarianism than to feeling part of the system."

Reed and his new unit will exchange ideas with the CWA's entire 22-member executive board in an unusual meeting next month. But even if leaders on both sides develop some consensus on dealing with job pressures, a sharp division in union and management attitudes is likely to continue at the local and regional levels. And it appears that the most severe pressures are occurring along the fault line that divides low-level supervisors and workers in the field.

This division has intensified in the last 10 years, as the Bell monopoly began to meet growing competition at many levels of its business. AT&T's mammoth reorganization last fall, coupled with the continuing introduction of new technology in the highly automated Bell System, has put enormous downward pressure on supervisors and workers to increase productivity. "The vice-president sends the message to his managers that they missed their objective by 13%," says Paul Morton, president of a CWA local in Bremerton, Wash., "and the low-level supervisors get so involved in the daily effort to meet indexes and workloads that they lose sight of the pressures they're putting on the workers."

This was one of the main categories of complaints aired at a two-day conference of CWA members in early June in San Francisco. Managers pass down the "unrealistic expectations and evaluations to promote productivity" from above, creating a demand for "too much from too few people too soon," said Alice Colacino, a Los Angeles accounting clerk. There was much criticism of how the company measures workers by average workload—so many seconds per call in the case of operators—and by various indexes allotting average time to each element of an equipment installer's work.

"The minute you meet company averages, the next day they raise them out of sight," complained Shirley Allen, a service representative in Santa Cruz, Calif. The result is "dehumanization and a defeatist attitude," she added.

Indeed, Bell is able to monitor workers' performance in a more minute way than most other employers. Computers track each call handled by overseas, directory assistance, and other types of operators, and provide printouts breaking down the seconds required to deal with each element of every call daily—some 600 to 700 calls per worker. These figures are used to improve quality of service but also to rate the operator in performance appraisals that determine promotions—and there can be little arguing with the computer's findings.

Moreover, "service observers" are constantly "plugging in" to an operator's board to monitor the service. "The union has no problem with monitoring the quality of service," says John C. Carroll, a top CWA negotiator with Bell. "What we object to is when supervisors monitor individual operators, sometimes without their knowledge, and use this observation to rate the operator, or for harassment." The union wants to eliminate all monitoring except for quality of service.

"The operators are petrified about oversupervision," says Chester Macey, executive vice-president of CWA Local 1150, which represents overseas operators in Manhattan. "The supervisors will yell at you, 'Get that light.' When you have to go to the bathroom, you have to raise your hand, get put on a list, and then wait maybe 20 minutes." Adds Carroll: "We object to workers being considered an extension of the computer, as interchangeable parts."

Company officials reply that such charges exaggerate the operators' problems. An operator does, indeed, have to signal for relief—beyond the two 15-minute breaks and a 30-minute lunch period per day—but this is because someone has to fill in. As for harassment, "I don't buy it," says Robert B. Stecker, vice-president of AT&T's Long Lines Dept. in New York. "We have to monitor calls because our concern has to be with the 'tone' of the service."

Bell craftsmen, such as installers, repairmen, and maintenance workers, complain about working too much overtime, thus hurting their family life. This is a concern in many industries and one that is not easily addressed, because most workers want some overtime—though not too much—and the company has to balance work schedules and production needs.

Craftsmen also charge that managers are overzealous in administering absentee- and tardiness-control programs, often penalizing workers for absences they could not prevent. And they insist that the quality of service is being eroded by job speedup. "For years and years, it was most important to the company that we give excellent service," says Edward Dempsey, president of Local 1101 in New York. "But it's more important now to get it finished than to get it right, and the guy who considers himself a real craftsman can no longer be a craftsman."

It appears that the massive bureaucracy in the Bell System, the layer upon layer of mediocre supervision, and the pressure for conformity in many levels of management are at the root of worker discontent. Such a workplace bureaucracy will not easily relax its control over workers down the line, although that is the primary problem. "This authoritarian style of management has got to go," says the CWA's Beaumont. "Workers today have no tolerance for all of this big brother, big mother looking over their shoulder." Some of the Bell companies, such as Ohio Bell Telephone Co. and Pacific Northwest Bell Telephone Co., have tried to boost morale, give the worker more to say in how he does the job, and increase productivity by improving communications between workers and managers. This is done through various kinds of meetings, including in the case of Ohio Bell a two-day "live-in" at a Cleveland motel.

Larry Lemasters, a Bell executive who runs the project in Ohio, says that before it got started, "there was a general feeling of apathy. The Bell System is so big and keeps rolling along day to day, and it is questionable whether an individual can really influence it." But through what he calls "the new democratic approach," Lemasters says, productivity in some areas has improved and workers are happier. But for some workers, the change is only cosmetic. "I think Mr. Lemasters' program was nice for two days," says Donald F. O'Malley, president of CWA Local 4304 in Cleveland. "That was the two days we were in the motel, away from the job pressures."

Rex Reed and his work relationships unit are studying the experiments in Ohio and elsewhere, hoping to initiate other projects in the Bell System. "What we need to find out is, does the worker today respond to a little different style of management than we did?" Reed says. "I think there is a desire to have more freedom at the workplace, as opposed to a structured situation. It's a question of to what extent can you do that."

Questions

1. This article, judging from its title, deals with motivational problems at AT&T, a company with over 900,000 employees. But are the difficulties Bell is experiencing with worker dissatisfaction *really* caused by Bell management's failure to perform the motivating function effectively?
2. What other managerial functions seem to be involved?
3. Which external and internal variables seem to be influencing the situation?
4. Is the problem the "fault" of AT&T management, or was the company's management an innocent victim of social change?
5. If you were in charge of the new management unit AT&T created to deal with worker dissatisfaction, how would you go about solving the problems? Do you think the problem is capable of solution? Given what you know, what actions would you recommend AT&T take—keeping in mind the company needs to please both its shareholders and governmental rate regulators?

Epilogue

We have traveled far and quickly down the road to understanding organizations and management. Limitations of time and space sometimes may have forced us to move too quickly to fully appreciate the subtleties and complexities of the territory. Perhaps there were side roads or topics you would have enjoyed exploring in more detail. We hope so, for one of our aims was to generate enthusiasm for further study. Nevertheless, since the objective we set was to communicate only a basic understanding of management, we hope you will agree that we attained it.

One thing we learned is that management is an eclectic and evolving discipline. Management theory, research, and practice have drawn heavily from the work of social scientists, mathematicians, and even engineers. As these fields became more sophisticated, management also matured and became better able to understand and effectively cope with the complex web of interdependent factors affecting organizational success. This continuing process of evolution resulted in the formation of several schools, each with a unique perspective on attaining objectives through other people. Although later research often uncovered fallacies in some concepts of earlier approaches, the contributions of the scientific management, administrative, human relations, and behavioral writers have been lasting ones. Basing organizational structure on strategies and objectives, as administrative writers suggested decades ago, for example, is still considered exceptionally sound management practice.

The contemporary approaches on which we focused built upon the concepts of earlier schools that were proven through practice and verified through research. With each step, managers gained a more comprehensive understanding of the manager's job and the organization. The process approach gave us the concept of viewing management as an unending cycle of interrelated functions. Systems writers demonstrated the need to consider the organization as an open system, an entity composed of interdependent parts that interacts with its environment. Management science showed how quantitative methods could be applied to improve the manager's ability to make objective decisions. The latest stage in the evolution of management thought, the contingency approach, is based on the premise that there is no "best" way to manage. Contingency theory holds that the most appropriate technique is determined by the situation. The effective manager must take into account significant variables in both the internal and external environments when making an important decision. Contemporary management researchers are working toward identifying exactly what these relevant variables are and how they interact, a monumentally complex task still far from completion.

As you realize by now, although we drew from every school of thought, our presentation tended to stress the contingency approach. Because we feel there is no inherently "right" way to manage, we avoided setting forth specific methods for handling problems. Our not providing a set of pat techniques you could memorize and apply may have left you with a discomfortable feeling of uneasiness. Unpleasant as this may seem, a moderate feeling of uneasiness is not undesirable in a manager. Feeling absolutely secure out of certainty one has the solution implies one is certain what the problem is. The foolhardiness of so rigid and smug an attitude is proven all too often. Bankruptcy courts are jammed with managers who at one time *knew* they had *the* solution. Unemployment offices are filled with their former subordinates.

Because the organization is a dynamic entity whose success is dependent on effective interaction with a dynamic environment, the manager's problems and therefore appropriate solutions continuously change. Even the most brilliant solutions, decisions that lead an organization to the pinnacles of success, eventually tarnish and fail. Ford genuinely identified what at one time was the best way to produce an automobile. Certain he had the answer, Ford failed to realize that the public's needs had changed and Sloan of General Motors had found a better way of managing a car company. Similarly, because each manager faces a somewhat unique internal environment and is a unique individual, one manager's effective solution can easily be another's path to failure, or even his or her own in a different situational context. General Douglas McArthur's charisma and military expertise enabled him to inspire armies with extraordinary success. However, the tactics that worked with his soldiers only enraged his superior, Harry Truman, and led to McArthur being relieved of command.

So, to avoid giving you a false sense of security, we deliberately avoided presenting specific approaches for resolving common managerial problems. Although we did teach you a great deal *about* managing, we did not try to teach you *how* to manage. However much one learns of theory and practice from books, there is and always will be a critical body of knowledge that can only be gained by experience. There is no way one can become an effective manager without actually being a manager. Moreover, as the best managers realize, there is no point at which one can categorically state they have learned all there is to know on the subject. Like the management functions, learning to manage effectively is an unending process. Having attained the objective of acquiring a basic understanding of management, you must redefine and expand your objectives in order to perpetuate your success. For some of you this will involve further study, perhaps a graduate degree in management or a related subject. For others, due to differences in needs, interests, and abilities, the optimal choice will be to get a managerial job and learn to perform it successfully.

What we have tried to do in this book is to communicate a way of approaching managerial decisions that is applicable in *any* situational context. We concentrated on the contingency approach not only because it is the most current, but because the core of the contingency approach is that there are no "right" answers. We stressed the concept of the organization as an open system only partly because systems theory is considered a major contribution to management thought. We did so primarily because to make a decision that contributes to attainment of the organization's objectives, the manager must take interdependencies into account. Even a supervisor should recognize that a decision that improves one part of the organization to the detriment of all others is not a good one.

What we have tried to communicate, in simple terms, is the need to approach each important managerial decision with an open mind, not a preconceived notion of what the correct response is, and to look below the surface for the true causes of a problem.

We therefore are not going to conclude this book, as many authors do, with a discussion of management in the future. Our telling you what to expect would encourage you to form expectations, preconceptions about what techniques will be most appropriate when you are in a position of responsibility. Even if our every prediction proved correct, we could easily lead you astray. You are not going to be dealing with *the* future, but rather *your* future. It is possible that ten years from now 90 percent of the organizations in America will have computers. You might work for one in the minority. The trend toward a work force comprised predominantly of highly skilled and educated people may continue to the point where quality of work life issues are a major concern of every Western company. You, however, may find yourself running a plant in a Third World nation with a labor force that is 70 percent illiterate.

What we can state unequivocally about the future is that the challenges managers will confront will dwarf those of the past. The problems of modern society—energy shortages, overpopulation, rampant inflation, the possibility of worldwide food shortages, the potential for irreparable damage to the ecosystem—are massive ones. The only possible means of solving them is through the synergy generated by effectively coordinating the efforts of many people toward a well-chosen common objective, through organizations. The survival of our organizational society, thus, is literally dependent on the skill and vision of managers.

Ominous as they are, these problems should not be viewed as a threat, something to be feared. Rather, managers should consider them an exciting, unparalleled opportunity. The organizations that develop efficient electric automobiles, economical alternatives to petroleum-based energy, better ways of protecting the environment, cures for cancer, techniques for controlling crime without eliminating personal freedom, or methods that simultaneously increase productivity and facilitate meeting individual needs will enjoy a success equal to that of the IBM's, AT&T's, and General Electric's of today. The managers who participate in solving these problems will enjoy both financial rewards and the satisfaction that comes from setting a difficult objective and meeting it.

Chances are good that some of those reading these words will be among these richly rewarded managers of the future. Why not you?

The End

At Last

The Beginning

Name Index

Subject Index

82 83 84 9 8 7 6 5 4